Keynes, Pigou and Cambridge Keynesians

Keynes, Pigou and Cambridge Keynesians

Authenticity and Analytical Perspective in the Keynes–Classics Debate

Gerhard Michael Ambrosi

First published 2003 by
PALGRAVE MACMILLAN
Houndmills, Basingstoke, Hampshire RG21 6XS and
175 Fifth Avenue, New York, N. Y. 10010
Companies and representatives throughout the world

PALGRAVE MACMILLAN is the global academic imprint of the Palgrave Macmillan division of St. Martin's Press, LLC and of Palgrave Macmillan Ltd. Macmillan® is a registered trademark in the United States, United Kingdom and other countries. Palgrave is a registered trademark in the European Union and other countries.

ISBN 0–333–63390–3 hardback

This book is printed on paper suitable for recycling and made from fully managed and sustained forest sources.

A catalogue record for this book is available from the British Library.

Library of Congress Cataloging-in-Publication Data
Ambrosi, Gerhad Michael.
   Keynes, Pigou and Cambridge Keynesians: authenticity and analytical perpective in the Keynes-Classics debate / Gerhard Michael Ambrosi.
      p. cm
   Includes bibliographical references and index.
   ISBN 0–333–63390–0 (alk. paper)
      1. Keynes, John Maynard, 1883–1946. 2. Pigou, A.C. (Arthur Cecil), 1877–1959. 3. Keynesian economics. 4. Macroeconomics. 5. Neoclassical school of economics. I. Title.
HB99.7.A39 2003
330.15'3–dc21

2003050455

10   9   8   7   6   5   4   3   2   1
12   11   10   09   08   07   06   05   04   03
Printed and bound in Great Britain by
Antony Rowe Ltd, Chippenham and Eastbourne

Contents

List of Tables

List of Figures

Preface

This book is the outcome of many years of intermittent preoccupation with 'the economics of Keynes'. My interest in this topic goes back to the beginning of the 1970s when I spent a year as a research student at Cambridge University. At that time I became personally acquainted with some of the economists featuring on the following pages. Richard Kahn was still lecturing occasionally, although handicapped by his stroke. Joan Robinson still held her seminars with *grandezza*. Nicholas Kaldor was still productive, interested in matters of current economic policy and in old economic theory, and he was – under mild grumblings – quite approachable.

Appreciative of the *spiritus loci* of Keynes' Cambridge, I was nevertheless disturbed by an acute impression that important elements of Keynes' original impetus had evaporated in that very surrounding. It was amusing to hear Joan Robinson's invectives against 'besotted neoclassicists' – but was the essence of Keynes' theoretical drive *really* to be found in a particular way of *not* expressing economic ideas? I could not believe that Keynes' *general* theory[1] was an exclusive one – or that it needed a specific *generalisation* as was the belief cultivated in Cambridge for many years. In particular, I could not follow the methodological line that a book which abounds with the term 'marginal' could be *anti*-marginal in its economic analytical intentions. But what then was its revolutionary message?

Questions of this type led me in the subsequent years to try to re-create in my own mind the analytical steps which might have been taken by Keynes himself in reaching his results. The outcome of my endeavours during those years were a book on Keynes' employment function (Ambrosi, 1981b), a number of published articles on several other aspects of Keynes' theory (on his 'wage effect',[2] on the microfoundations of his consumption function[3]). There was also a considerable amount of 'grey literature' published as discussion papers at the University of Constance and at Berlin Free University. From all of this it emerged that the most fertile approach to Keynes was not so much to see him from the vantage point of the long-period 'extensions' propagated at Cambridge in the 1960s and 1970s. It seemed to be more illuminating to reread Keynes in the context of the original debates which he was engaged in around the time of writing the *General Theory* and this pointed towards understanding him as the propagator of short-period rather than of long-period analysis. In any case, the original debate between Keynes and Pigou became of paramount interest for me in the attempt of understanding what went on analytically in and around the *General Theory*.

The main theme of this book thus is 'Keynes *and* Pigou' and not predominantly 'Keynes *versus* Pigou'. Once this theme was set, the corollary suggested itself to inspect also the impact of this theme on those economists who considered themselves to be the executors of Keynes' analytical will at Cambridge. There are some interesting findings of cases of sluggish defence, of intended[4] and of factual[5] suppression of publication and of some surprising persistence of analytical allegiance with supposed opponents. But this book is not the outcome of a rush to dabble in history but the result of a lengthy attempt to come to terms with a largely evasive collective understanding of major developments in the field of economics in the twentieth century. This book therefore ends not on a historical note but on the theme of 'analytical perspective'.

In writing this book I have incurred a long list of indebtedness. I am very grateful to the British post-Keynesians for many instances of friendly interest in my work. Vicky Chick has done a heroic deed of friendship in reading and commenting on a previous version of this manuscript. Without implication I would like to express my gratitude for her time, her mind and her friendship. Geoff Harcourt also read an earlier version of the manuscript and magnanimously passed some encouraging comments although my criticisms of Cambridge Keynesians certainly will not be much to his liking. Tony Thirlwall and the Master of Keynes College at the University of Kent at Canterbury repeatedly invited me to the magnificent Keynes conferences they used to organise. Those were great events of bringing together personalities, memories and finest scholarship in honour of the namesake of Keynes College.

As far as American post-Keynesianism is concerned – and the literature makes much distinction in orientation, spelling and significance concerning the different brands of post-Keynesianism but those differences are not of much interest in the present context – I am much obliged to Sidney Weintraub. I hope my grateful mentioning of him reaches the proverbial 'eternal hunting grounds' where his soul might now reside. He lavishly praised and editorially polished a little contribution of mine on 'Keynes and the 45° cross' (Ambrosi, 1981a). This piece later found not unfriendly mentioning in a number of related publications.[6] That experience contributed to my perseverance in 'Keynesiology' and to my presentation of the results of my enquiries.

The beginnings of this particular manuscript go back to the 1980s when I was doing postdoctoral work at the Berlin Free University. I would like to thank my past colleagues and especially my academic supervisor Professor Klaus Jaeger for friendly support for a project of which I have the suspicion that some of them were – and maybe still are – not at all convinced.

My last expression of gratitude goes to my family, my wife and my daughter who put up with much inconvenience during the years I was pursuing the project of writing this book.

Micheal Ambrosi
Trier, June 2003

Part I
The Spent Revolutions: Lost Directions in Economic Debates

1
The Volatility in Macroeconomic Paradigms

It is sometimes said that economics as a scientific discipline has never witnessed a 'scientific revolution' of the kind the natural sciences have experienced.[1] In seeming contradiction to such a position, 'new' and 'revolution' are epithets combined with almost any contribution to economics over the last decades. Referring to macroeconomics in general, John B. Taylor (1989, p. 185) once diagnosed 'at least one revolution or counter-revolution per decade'.

The recent and then quickly disillusioned fascination with the 'New Economy' is the last of a long row of episodes which demonstrate how quickly old paradigms of economics appear to be obsolete and in doubt – and that there might be little substance behind the fascination with the seeming novelties.[2] Before the episode of the 'new paradigm' at the end of the 1990s, there were also several new economic paradigms about to change the world at the end of the 1980s. Some reviewers at that time sensed the victory of a '*new Keynesian* counter-revolution' while others preferred to see a '*real business cycles* revolution'. None of these supposedly budding or even seemingly manifest revolutions made great changes to the way economics is taught in most universities after the turn of the millennium.

The supposedly dramatic turns in academic economics of recent times had earlier precursors which entered the profession with no less dramatic claims. They were the '*rational expectations* revolution' of the 1970s and the '*monetarist* counter-revolution' of the 1960s, the revolution of the 1970s supposedly heralding an age of *New Classical Economics*. Before these revolutions and counter-revolutions we had, of course, the old *Keynesian* revolution – which, however, never was the type of revolution Keynes 'really' intended, according to several authors, Leijonhufvud (1968) having maybe been the most noticed of them. In his much debated monograph *On Keynesian Economics and the Economics of Keynes* he claimed that during all the time that the old Keynesian revolution had its sway, Keynes' 'true' analytical intentions were not correctly received. So Keynes' *real* revolution is

3

an unfinished analytical programme according to that reasoning. Could it be that we had not too many revolutions but that we are still missing one? The present answer to this question, basic for the reasoning of this book, is: we should stop thinking in this type of terminology and classifications. Over decades, it did not bring progress in analysis but disillusionment with the intellectual integrity of professional economics. What is needed in economic discourse is not another rupture in reasoning – that is, after all, the meaning of economic 'revolution' – but the systematic development and re-creation of a dialogical exchange of arguments.

Before embarking upon this line of argument we should briefly stay with the debate as it *did* unfold in the past, however, in order to fathom its frustrating lack of direction. Let us remember that quite often it was asked – and it is still being asked today – whether the Keynesian revolution was not a chimera in the first place no matter in which guise it is presented. This, after all, is easily the conviction of those who subscribed to the paradigms of the new classical revolution and who denied the relevance of effective demand analysis in the context of business cycles or even the existence of such cycles unless they are provoked by mischievous economic political 'do-gooders'. This is not only the stance of provocative academic startups. It is a fashionable line of argument for the New York journal *The New Criterion* where, reviewing Skidelsky (1992), David Frum (1994) could tell the world:

> Keynes was one of the most influential thinkers of our [20th, GMA] century, and his influence has been almost entirely bad . . . Keynes's fertile and subtle mind manufactured a huge armory of clever defenses of bad public policy.[3]

Keynes still has his adherents, though. Robert B. Reich (2000), US Secretary of Labor from 1993 to 1997, sees his influence quite differently. His contribution about 'John Maynard Keynes' to the *Time Magazine* series about the 100 most influential scientists and thinkers of the twentieth century is subtitled 'His radical idea that governments should spend money they don't have may have saved capitalism'. He points out that the wartime effort of the USA between 1939 and 1945 led to almost a doubling of national income and to a drop of the unemployment rate from more than 17 percent to just over 1 percent, relating this to Keynes' theory and commenting: 'Never before had an economic theory been so dramatically tested . . . it seemed to work exactly as Keynes predicted.' This is, of course, not a very rigorous test of a theory. But when we compare what is said here about Keynesian economics to evaluations of the achievements of the rival schools, then we do notice a remarkable difference. With regard to the New Classics' mental influence and factual relevance we may note the following.

On the basis of citation counts and of a review of conference activities, Robert J. Gordon (1989, p. 181) provides evidence that 'the inventors of new-classical macroeconomics created much less of a revolution than is generally recognised.' In his version of events, the supposedly dramatic reorientations of research programmes in economics may be seen to have failed the test of really shaping dramatically and persistently 'the minds of the young' – whereas the original Keynesian revolution of 1936 was indeed a considerable success if judged by this – admittedly debatable – standard (Gordon, *ibid.*). Thus, with hindsight, the Keynesian 'revolution' – although its true character might still be in doubt – might be considered to have been the more relevant revolution – at least the one with more academic impact.

The conclusion of the last paragraph is not without irony. It should be remembered that on the occasion of the centenary celebrations for John Maynard Keynes in 1983, such a knowledgeable commentator of macroeconomics as Axel Leijonhufvud (1983, p. 180) once diagnosed the belonging of the once-victorious Keynesian economics – 'all of it, not just Keynes himself' – to the history of economic thought.

Only a few years later, the scene had changed completely. Oblivion was not what fate had in store for Keynes, after all. Soon after the gloomy predictions, outside observers of the academic scene in economics like Robert Shapiro (1988, pp. 43f) detected a 'current Keynesian retroboom'. After earlier suppositions of a landslide victory of monetarism, Robert Hall of Stanford University was now quoted as noting: 'There are no more young monetarists.' A new Keynesian mainstream seemed to be emerging into which 'almost everybody in policy economics is buying' (*ibid.*).

But this development is not limited to 'policy economics'. One of the paragons of the seemingly utterly a-Keynesian general equilibrium theory, Nobel Laureate Kenneth Arrow (1987, p. 227) emphasised the paramount significance of Keynesian economics in the following passage:

Feiwel: Would you care to classify by order of importance the most significant contributions to economics in the last 50 years?

Arrow: I would still put the development of Keynesian economics at the top of the list; the vision if not the theory contained therein.

The nature of this assessment maybe becomes clearer when confronted with the parallel answer given two years later by the same Kenneth Arrow (1989, p. 168) when asked about the supposed analytical rival of Keynesianism, the 'new classical macroeconomics':

Feiwel: Can we return to the question of 'new classical macroeconomics'? How do you feel about it?

Arrow: I think it is wrong . . . what is wrong is not rational expectations exactly . . . but just the assumption that in the future markets will clear .

. . The fundamental question is one of market clearing. I believe there is no market clearing and for the short-run fluctuations of the economy it is a very important fact.

We have here the re-emphasis of non-market clearing problems for macroeconomics, in particular of the old Keynesian problem of excess supply on the labour market. This is seen by Arrow in connection with the problem of insufficient intertemporal co-ordination due to deficient futures markets, as would become even more clear from inspecting the wider context of these remarks. Such a statement implies the reinstigation of analytical paradigms which for several years and for a considerable number of academic economists seemed to be utterly defunct – and not only as a challenge for practical politicians but also for a 'hard' theorist like Kenneth Arrow and whoever wants to side with his just quoted paradigmatic statements.[4]

The most astonishing aspect of this development is perhaps not so much the surprising revival of the supposedly defunct Keynesianism. Even more surprising might well be the volatility in the public acceptance of paradigms which present themselves as worlds apart and which generally are seen as mutually exclusive.

A surprising volatility of views about the appropriate economic paradigm might be found even with some contributors to these debates themselves. John Hicks is a case in point. For decades, he had no objection to seeing countless macroeconomics textbooks being based on his 1937 article on 'Mr Keynes and the Classics: a Suggested Interpretation'. But after Leijonhufvud (1968) supplied a scathing criticism of 'Hicks–Hansen' type 'orthodox Keynesianism', Hicks (1974, pp. 6f.) himself renounced the plausibility of his own former interpretation of the Keynes–Classics issue.

But we might also take the case of the revolutionary Axel Leijonhufvud himself in order to make our point about the paradigmatic fickleness to be found in the Keynes–Classics debate. While Leijonhufvud (1968, p. 52) originally believed:

In the Keynesian macrosystem the Marshallian ranking of price- and quantity-adjustment speeds is reversed . . . The 'revolutionary' element in the *General Theory* can perhaps not be stated in simpler terms[5]

he soon was to abandon this supposedly central idea about the Keynesian revolution. In fact, a few years later Leijonhufvud (1974, p. 169) emphatically declared:

it is *not* correct to attribute to Keynes a general reversal of the Marshallian ranking of relative price and quantity adjustment velocities. (emphasis in the original, GMA)

This was a clear disclaimer, all right, but what was the 'Keynesian revolution' all about in this case? The reader of Leijonhufvud is left in doubt and the question of the relevance of differing speeds of adjustment of price vs. quantities is a recurring theme of investigation in Keynes-oriented writings.[6]

But in spite of the quoted disclaimer concerning the relevance of relatively sluggish price adjustments in a Keynesian context, a whole new school of 'Fix-price Keynesianism' has developed taking Leijonhufvud as their intellectual godfather and Edmond Malinvaud (1977) with *The Theory of Unemployment Reconsidered* as their direct ancestor. We find here a taxonomy of Keynesian and classical cases of unemployment which – at least on the European continent – has inspired much research.

But the 'Fix-price' approach cannot put much claim to being a proper interpretation of Keynes' intended economics. Even in his seminal publication about 'Keynesian' and 'classical' unemployment, Malinvaud (1977, p. 32, n. 26) declared unequivocally:

> The name 'Keynesian unemployment', which I shall be using here, should . . . be understood to refer to the views of post-war Keynesians rather than to those of Keynes himself.

This confession certainly is strange when seen in context with Leijonhufvud (1968). That book had as its programme to overcome the post-war 'Keynesian' distortions and to bring 'authentic Keynes' to the fore. In this passage, however, the supposedly aberrant post-war Keynsians are the name-givers for 'Keynesian unemployment'. The discerning reader of Malinvaud (1977) is left in bewilderment concerning the original ideas which Keynes' theory was supposed to convey.

In the last paragraphs we mentioned three prominent authors who attempted an interpretation of the Keynes–Classics issue. Each of them – and each of them progressively faster than the previous interpreter – withdrew their interpretation in one way or the other. Thus, it turned out in the 1970s that whether a newcomer to economic research turned to Hicks, to Leijonhufvud, or to Malinvaud, in no case could he be confident that he was presented by a consistent and authentic version of Keynes' economics. It is perhaps small wonder if the volatility in the minds of these interpreters spilled over into a disorientation of a larger section of the economics profession.

This development coincided with a new emergence in several stages of a Keynes-critical monetarism, culminating in the 'New Classical Economics' as exemplified in the writings of authors such as Thomas Sargent, Robert Lucas and Robert Barro. This latter development has been reviewed in a number of articles, among them by Alan Blinder (1988), Robert Gordon (1989), and John Taylor (1989). It would be beyond the scope of this chapter to cover that entire debate anew. Most commentators seem to agree that there was a certain element of ideology involved in this development, or, as Blinder (1988, p. 286) put it:

The secret of the success of the new classical economics was that it managed to be at once *ideologically backward* looking and *technologically forward* looking. Given the temper of the times, that was a winning formula.

Or, rather, it was a winning formula in academia . . . [But] the empirical implications of new classical theory were wide off the mark . . . [and] the theory that swept academia made hardly a ripple in the world of policy. (emphasis added, GMA)

One may add, after reading Krugman's assessment of the management of the Asian and Latin American economic crises of the 1990s (Krugman, 1999): where the 'new' classical thinking *did* make a ripple – in particular among the economists of the International Monetary Fund – there the mental ripple caused havoc in the real economies which had to succumb to that type of academic advice. There is indeed very little on the empirical side to commend the New Classical Economics. Or, as Clower and Howitt (1998, p. 173) put it in attributing some academic success to this school:

As many observers have remarked, the victory of New Classical Economics over Keynesianism was accomplished without the benefit of empirical refutation. Keynesian economics was not out-performed in its prediction but in its ability to offer an intellectually satisfying story.

We might describe this diagnosis as relating a case of 'victory of scholasticism over reality' – a good recipe for scientific decline. Its root cause is not so much a scientific victory of the New Classicals but a lack of well-argued defence put up by the Keynesians (Leijonhufvud, 1983). But insofar as public disillusionment with the New Classicals has set in, again the Keynesian tradition was not actively defended but returned into the limelight because of pragmatic economic political requirements.

Thus, both in its decline and in its revival, modern Keynesianism appears as a driftwood of external influences. Its acceptance by the wider public seems to depend more on the vagaries of the business cycle and other economic and social realisations and not on a consistent argumentation on the side of the Keynesians.

Just recently, this pattern of events has been repeated in connection with the terrorist attacks of 11 September 2001. Addressing a meeting organised by the Central Bank of Venezuela, the celebrated biographer of Keynes, Lord Robert Skidelsky (2001), declared:

Monetarism and rational expectations have not replaced Keynesianism but they have had a profound influence on how economists think and talk, especially about public policy. As I write at the end of the third volume of my biography of Keynes: 'Keynes's ideas will live so long as the world has need of them.'[7] That depends on whether our new global economy has enough natural stability to be politically acceptable. Only events will give us the answer.'

That answer might come sooner than we think.

Robert Skidelsky, 8 September 2001

That answer did indeed come sooner than anybody might have thought: three days later the twin towers of the World Trade Center, the erstwhile pride of New York's skyline, came down in destruction. More than a year after that event, the world still holds its breath in apprehension that economic stability might come down likewise.

Ever since those events of the by now proverbial date '9/11' (2001), we have had a flow of articles about the revival of Keynes' ideas about stabilising the economy. A month after that date Baker and Crooks (2001) of the *Financial Times* depicted a portrait of Keynes side by side with George W. Bush, the acting president of the United States. Under the title 'Keynes revisited . . .' they quote Fred Bergsten of the Washington-based Institute for International Economics as praising the governments of the developed economies for their co-ordinated 'general response to the terrorist attacks'. He is reported as proclaiming: 'Now is the appropriate time for the G7 countries to mount a co-ordinated fiscal stimulus.' In this connection they report that 'Mr Bush presented his credentials as the newest and most important member of the Keynesian club'.

A number of articles could be cited which are similar in orientation. This is not to say that controversies about Keynes have entirely ceased after '9/11'. But it is remarkable how quickly seemingly forgotten old economic political paradigms are eagerly brought up again soon after – sometimes simultaneously with – their sonorously proclaimed passing away. This seems to reveal a principal problem, the impression of a will-o'-the-wisp-led economic debate. This impression cannot just be rebuked. It should be explicitly addressed.

Long before the recent summersault of public views about the guiding ideas for economic policy, there seemed to have been an emerging awareness that such a pattern of argumentation does not further the progress of economic knowledge. Thus, in his already quoted review of 'The Evolution of Ideas in Macroeconomics', John B. Taylor (1989, p. 189) remarked:

> It is frequently said the swings in political sentiments influence the flow of new ideas in macroeconomics . . . But, in my view, such political influence on research can be counterproductive even in the more technical areas.

As Taylor elaborates, the 'baby' of sensible analyses and methods embodied in each of the competing schools might be thrown out along with its temporarily supporting political 'bath water'.

But obviously that exhortation to stop an unsatisfactory type of academic discourse was not particularly effective. It appears that it could be repeated every few years all over again with no significant consequence. What is eventually needed is a firm professional commitment about a code of conduct. As there are rules of discourse in all walks of life, there should be one in economics; as there is 'netiquette' for net-based communication, maybe there should be an 'economi-quette' for how to argue about economic ideas. Its first commandment should be: 'Thou shalt not use the term "revolution".' This term seems to have found its limit of applicability in economics. It is time to question the economic profession's practised belief that knowledge progresses through a repetitive series of 'revolutionary' summersaults. There are indications that a more appropriate model for the accumulation of economic knowledge is one of patient gathering and diligent arrangement of arguments and evidence. Let us remind ourselves in this context of the motto of Alfred Marshall's *Principles*:

Natura non fecit saltum – Nature does not leap.

But how can one deny the fact that economics *did* experience the just described sequel of jumps and 'revolutions' between and among a variety of Keynesian and Classical camps?

This question leads to a further one which is somewhat intractable, however, namely the question of the 'reality' of things we talk about. In order to appreciate the sense of this questioning we might remind ourselves of an episode in Lewis Caroll's *Alice in the Wonderland*, namely the left-over grin of the Cheshire Cat. There once really *was* that cat. But how real could the talked-about grin be, once the cat had vanished? Similarly, one may concede that there *was* a debate between Keynes and economists named 'Classics'. But how real could that debate be considered to be nowadays in the just contemplated sense, if Keynes *and* his 'Classics' have evaporated long ago from anything under discussion in the recent stages of the Keynes–Classics debate? As Alice was left with a grin without cat, we might turn out to be left with a Keynes–Classics debate with *neither* Keynes nor Classics – nor even a 'real' debate, for that matter. That seems to me to be a rather disturbing point of the often-heard complaints about directionless re- and re-re-revolutions in economics.

Eventually it will not be complaints and accusations that cure the dissatisfaction with economic discourse but rather it will be reflection and topical discipline. One advisable reflection might address the professional perception of the road to the present state of the debate. It must be granted that much was and is made of repeated revolutionary changes in the discipline of economics. But one must discern the *consequence* of a change from the *genesis* of that change. Thus, if it is granted that after the *General Theory* economists argued and researched differently than before, this does not mean that the author of that book really thought so radically different than it appears if regarded with hindsight. The problem of present economic debate might then well be – at least that is the 'vision' of this book – that with a wrong hindsight the economic community might have cultivated a wrong perception of its own intellectual basis and about the agenda to be built on that basis. But with a wrong intellectual basis, economics might well follow a faulty path into the future.

With this reflection in mind, we might address a further question, namely: What could be an 'alternative hindsight' for economics which could change our perception and then maybe also our cultivation of 'appropriate' present academic discourse? In pursuit of an answer, one should first of all turn to the beginning of the unsatisfactory rigmarole of revolutions, namely to the *real* 'Keynes–Classics debate' as it was initially conducted between real actors.

The main issue in this context is not so much whether the mainstream of present economics has the right or the wrong perception of the namesakes of the Keynes–Classics debate. Although that question might have some interesting aspects, as will be argued in the next two chapters, the more intriguing question is whether we have an authentic perception of the issues which were in fact actually *debated*. Answering this latter question means, of course, that we must inspect a concrete historical debate and we will propose below (ch. 4) to take the original debate between Keynes and Pigou as the main focus of attention.

In economics it is a cherished topic – but in hard sciences probably a rather rare one – to investigate who wronged whom, in particular who was unfair to whom in the Keynes–Classics debate. It might be helpful to get this meta-analytic matter out of the way by looking for some authentic pieces of evidence in this particular context (see below, ch. 5). But such emotion-laden and polemical investigations should not distract economists from the really important issue: what was *really* under discussion with regard to economic analysis?

With this basic question in mind, it will emerge that we must take the relevant writings of A. C. Pigou as the 'node' of the debate. This is the theme of the next part of this book. With this starting point, we should appeal to all those economists who regretted – rightfully – the disregard of Pigou in the context of the development of macroeconomics. Our focus is centred on those issues, however, which are of relevance for the debate just stated. For the further discussion of the matters of outline we refer the reader to chapter 6 below.

2
The Problem of Authenticity in Keynesian Economics

In the last chapter we saw that the very economists who proclaimed that they, at long last, can give the authoritative account of economics in the tradition of Keynes, eventually – sometimes even simultaneously – admitted that what they presented is 'not correct' (see above, p. 6 for Leijonhufvud's (1974, p. 169) retraction) or that it just is not authentic (see above, p. 7 for Malinvaud's disclaimer).

In the case of Leijonhufvud (1974) such an admission must have appeared as rather embarrassing – after all, it was he himself (1968) who proclaimed the importance of turning from Keynesian economics to the economics of Keynes. But such disclaimers have become quite fashionable amongst newer writers on Keynesian economics. One example is given by David Colander (1999, p. 365) who declared:

> Although I argue that Keynesian economics should be saved ... Quite honestly, I do not care what Keynes said when; I do not care whether what I call Keynesianism is what Keynes really meant, and I do not think students care either. I am not even sure that Keynes really knew what he meant.

In a similar vein, Mankiw (1992, p. 560), writing about 'The Reincarnation of Keynesian Economics: Keynesian Economics Today', implicitly *warns against* reading Keynes:

> Since Keynesian economics is derived, by definition, from the work of John Maynard Keynes, one might suppose that reading Keynes is an important part of Keynesian theorizing. In fact, quite the opposite is the case. Few young economists – Keynesian or otherwise – concern themselves with question of what 'Keynes really meant'. New Keynesians view their work as following in the broad tradition that evolved from Keynes, but their goal is to explain the world, not to clarify the views of one particular man. If new Keynesian economics is not a true representation of Keynes's views, then so much the worse for Keynes.

In an abstract way, such a position is quite understandable. In itself, authenticity often is no particularly interesting criterion for economic theorising, of course. If a body of theories is operationally successful there will hardly be much merit in putting substantial effort into debating the question whether it is possible to trace their formulation to particular utterances of particular authors. But when a science lacks a clear sense of direction as the noted paradigmatic volatility in contemporary macroeconomics suggests, then one of the sensible reactions to such a condition could well be a systematic reconsideration of the origins of the research programmes of that science. Then the folklore about 'Keynes, the unwitting author' which is perpetuated in a long list of various variants of Keynesianism, could well be a *hindrance* for further progress, not a liberation.

It was with this type of motivation that similar disregard for authenticity was met with a comparison from the world of paganism when Leijonhufvud (1968, p. 35) attacked the earlier Keynesians:

> The impression of Keynes that one gains from such comments is that of a Delphic oracle, half hidden in billowing fumes, mouthing earth-shattering profundities whilst in a senseless trance – an oracle revered for his powers, to be sure, but not worthy of the same respect as that accorded the High Priests whose function it is to interpret the revelations.

At that time, Leijonhufvud (*ibid.*) exclaimed in exasperation: 'If this is how Economics develops – where will it all end?' – a comment which has not lost its relevance today, especially since Leijonhufvud himself soon had to retract his own attempt at giving a more authentic version of Keynes-oriented theory.

But by now one should be philosophical about such exasperations: although Leijonhufvud's exclamation still might be considered as being topical, it must be noted that his lament had no consequence then and it probably will have not much consequence now. The search for authenticity in Keynesian economics seems to be too frustrating a pursuit to warrant any further attempt.

Shall one leave things at that? One may at least wonder what makes the scientists – supposedly ruthless investigators in their pursuit of knowledge – so timid when it comes to knowing what is documentable about *Keynes*-ian economics. It cannot be a lack of relevant material. With the publication of Keynes' *Collected Writings*,[1] with the publication of a number of lecture notes of some of his important lectures,[2] with at least four well-researched biographies about Keynes,[3] there should be enough material around for at least attempting to authenticate whatever is claimed about Keynes.

A disclaimer made by Alan Coddington (1983, p. 1), similar in substance to the more recent ones just quoted, might give an indication about the reasons behind them. His still much-referred-to study about *Keynesian Economics: the Search for First Principles* is introduced with the proclamation:

> I am not at all concerned with questions of authenticity: neither with what Keynes actually said, nor with what he really meant when he said it, nor even what, according to various guardians of the purity of his thought, he was really trying to say and is only now succeeding in saying through them. (Wide-ranging though Keynes's talents were, I do not believe they extended to posthumous ventriloquism.) ...
>
> I would not bother to make these merely negative points except that a great deal of work in this area has consisted of a – as it appears to me – pointless attempt to excavate and uphold a profound but elusive 'Economics of Keynes' (himself) in contrast with a shallow and vulgar 'Keynesian Economies' (of the textbooks and the public domain).

We gather from this passage that one of the reasons for the rejection of any attempt to authenticate what is said about Keynesian economics is that it might require arguing against 'posthumous ventriloquism' – and this indeed would be hopeless for fruitful academic discourse.

The position which corresponds to this characterisation Coddington (1983, pp. 93–100) later discusses under the heading of 'Fundamentalism'. In a footnote Coddington (1983, p. 113, n. 1) elaborates that the adherents of this school of Keynesianism use the original text 'in a highly selective manner, and, in effect, make them the springboard of what are in reality their own ideas'. Since he foreswore the ambition of authenticity, he is relieved of proving this claim. Instead, he just gives a number of fairly self-explanatory quotes, among them a remark by Joan Robinson (1973d, p. 3), who was one of Keynes' important discussion partners during the preparation and defence of the *General Theory*. According to her testimony: 'we had some trouble in getting Maynard to see what the point of his revolution really was, but when he came to sum it up *after* the book was published he got it into focus.'[4]

The tenor of this passage is quite similar to the one of the two statements quoted at the beginning of this chapter. This one states that Keynes, when writing the *General Theory*, did not know what the point of his revolution 'really was'. It had to be shown to him by Joan Robinson and her colleagues with 'some trouble'.[5] After having written the book, Keynes proved to be an understanding pupil of those who *did* know this point. There is not a great difference between such a statement and Colander's 'I am not even sure that Keynes really knew what he meant.' But while Colander combines with this statement a renunciation of any claim to authenticity, Joan Robinson seems to have wanted to state that she and her fellows were the guardians of a – in some sense – *fundamental* authenticity which goes beyond what is written in Keynes' *General Theory*. Indeed, in Joan Robinson's judgement, in the closing passages of the *General Theory*, Keynes totally messed up what *should* have been his message and he himself laid the foundation of an illegitimate 'bastard' Keynesianism.[6] If that is so, then the basis for *genuine* Keynesian thought should definitely *not* be sought in these misconceived passages of the *General Theory*.

It seems to have been this type of statement which Coddington (1983, p. 1) felt to be unrewarding to debate. Joan Robinson had the authority of having had personal contact and intensive intellectual exchange with Keynes. How is an outsider to argue against her claim of representing Keynes' 'true' position?

An answer to this question might not be required, however. It speaks for itself that apart from the 'fundamentalist' position of the type just discussed, there are a number of other ones, also claiming to be in the tradition of the writings of Keynes. Coddington (1983) lists and discusses 'hydraulicism' (circular flow analysis) and 'reconstructed reductionism' (neoclassical microfoundations) as such alternative positions. What really counts with regard to these alternatives is not primarily their 'authenticity' but their analytical appeal to economists. Their merits should not be evaluated by quotes but by results.

Such considerations might make it understandable why, in spite of protracted debates about Keynesian economics, so very little of non-controversial substance is available as far as authenticity is concerned. Yet, it is not a satisfactory intellectual solution to refuse to investigate a topic which is of demonstrable interest to a considerable number of economists.[7] A solution to this problem might lie in shifting attention from the search for the 'authentic Keynes' – which is too much laden with 'ventriloquism' and 'post-mortems' etc. – to some other form of authenticity, namely the authenticity of documentable intellectual exchange. That might relieve us not only of the problems we related when trying to retrace Alan Coddington's argumentation. After the next chapter it will appear that such a perspective will also relieve us of the similarly frustrating engagement with the equally intractable question of the authenticity of the opposing 'classical' position.

3
The Problem of Authenticity in 'Classical' Economics

Keynes' *General Theory* features several polemics against 'classical' economics in general and against some economists in particular whom Keynes
considered as representing such 'classical' views. The term 'classical' was
subsequently bitterly fought over. A main issue was that Keynes used the
term in an unauthentic way in the sense that nobody ever did hold those
views which Keynes deemed to be 'classical'. A number of Keynes' contemporaries considered themselves or others to be treated in a particularly
unfair way by Keynes' use of terminology. Thus issues of 'fair' treatment
also became associated with this term, but that discussion really should be
kept separate from the question of authenticity and so we return to the
question of 'fairness' in a separate chapter below.

In more recent times the proponents of the 'New Classical' revolution in
economics once more took up the issue of 'classical' economics. They
defiantly accepted this controversial epithet. They, too, like the generations
of economists before them, did not do much to clarify the substance of
authentic 'classical' economics, however. But their appearance led to a new
interest in the substance of 'classical' economics as it might sensibly be associated with modern macroeconomics (Ahiakpor (1998a); Kates (1998)). In
this context the doctrine of 'Say's Law' regained considerable prominence,
this being also an element of economics the authenticity and substance of
which is under notorious dispute.

An interesting characterisation of these issues was recently given by Mark
Blaug (1997, p. 231). His opinion is particularly noteworthy since it comes
from an eminent historian of economic thought. He summarised the
debates about the matter just mentioned in the following way:

> It was Keynes who planted the idea that all economists before him
> subscribed to Say's Law of Markets – that was indeed his definition of a
> 'classical economist' – and by Say's Law of Markets he meant the
> doctrine that the economic system is always, or nearly always, operating
> at its full employment ceiling, since 'supply creates its own demand',

recessions and depressions are necessarily short lived and self correcting. He agreed that Say's Law as such had long been abandoned by most economists but he insisted that they had never ceased to believe in the working assumption of full employment and full capacity production.

I think that Keynes was quite right thus to characterize Keynesian economics, but to label this as a belief in something called 'Say's Law of Markets' – a term that had long disappeared from the economic literature – and then to hang it on a catch-all definition of classical economics was to invite hopeless confusion about the history of economic thought. John Hicks added mayhem to mischief with the title of his famous IS–LM paper, 'Mr Keynes and the Classics: a Suggested Interpretation'. And who were Hicks' classics? Adam Smith, Ricardo and John Stuart Mill and/or Marshall and Pigou.

Thus we have here a considerable conundrum of issues involving authenticity: Keynes' own use of the term 'classical economics' seems to be an unauthentic 'catch-all', it is associated with 'Say's Law' which is of dubious authenticity as far as Jean-Baptiste Say is concerned after whom it is named, and which Keynes associated with people who never did proclaim the validity of such a 'law'. This complex of issues was then propagated for further economic debate by Hicks (1937). The problem lies here in the fact that this article turned out to become a central piece of old orthodox Keynesianism, but that it also was extremely doubtful with regard to its authenticity, as we saw in the last chapter. Thus the 'classics' became twice removed from authenticity in economic debates: first by Keynes, then by Hicks. All together, this gives a brew of rather indigestible problems.

Again, as in the case of the 'authentic Keynes' debate we looked at in the last chapter, one might ask whether it is really worth the effort to enter such a debate. There are a number of economists who strongly argue in the affirmative. Thus Kates (1997a, p. 201) recently pleaded urgently that economists reconsider Say's Law and that they recognise the distortions which Keynes brought into the whole issue:

Economists due to the enormous influence of the *General Theory*, have been in the theoretical wilderness for the past sixty years. They have lost the guiding influence of one of the most important economic principles ever developed ... A return to an economic theory guided by Say's Law would mean a return to theory which denied the possibility of demand failure and accounted for recession and unemployment by other means.

There is by now a feeling that the economic community had been misled outright by Keynes himself – and this more or less intentionally. As Ahiakpor (1998b, p. 4) recently stated: Keynes' treatment of Say's Law was 'bordering on the fraudulent' (see below, p. 389). He thereby perpetuated an old theme of Keynes' '(probably intentional) fraud' (Clower, 1994, p. 381).[1]

But why should such accusations involving long defunct economists agitate readers today, in the twenty-first century? Behind such charges there seems to be a more or less explicit conviction that Keynes pursued a destructive programme which still exerts its influence. Even nowadays, so a belief seems to go, Keynes' sophistry could endanger our economic sanity. This might be the reason why there are still serious writers who are eager to convince the public anew that (a) Keynes is not only physically but also intellectually dead and (b) Keynes is (almost) a fraud, at least as far as his dealings with the Classics are concerned.

The remarkable fears and triumphs of the wider public which are associated with the Keynes–Classics debate are described by Ross McKibbin (2001, p. 13) in a review of Robert Skidelsky's (2000) third volume of Keynes' biography. Addressing the readership of the *London Review of Books*, that reviewer on the one hand stressed the towering intellectual stature which Keynes did have and still does seem to have for many, but on the other he points out that Keynes has this stature in a strangely unaccepted way:

> He [Keynes, GMA], Adam Smith and Marx are the holy trinity of Western political economy ... [But] Keynes is the most marginalised of the three. Certainly, it is on his grave that the free-marketeers dance most triumphantly. Why is this?

McKibbin (*ibid.*) then proceeds to give as reason for this marginalisation of Keynes his much debated – and for a wide readership unacceptable – attacks on 'classical' economics:

> The real problem was who and what Keynes attacked. He said he was trying to overthrow 'classical' economics. But Keynes's classical economist, as has often been noted, was a straw man: it is hard to find any economist who actually held all the views he attributed to classical economists – certainly not poor Pigou who was singled out in *The General Theory*.
>
> Like Marx, what Keynes was trying to demolish, at least in the interwar years, was that whole edifice of commonsense economics – 'wise sayings' as he called it – by which most of us, not just bankers, conduct our lives. He was thus arguing a case which affronted, and affronts, a view of the world most of us think entirely reasonable.
>
> It is this which gave Keynesian economics its subversive and dissident character; and because it undermines the reasonable many hold it responsible for the economic misfortunes of the 1970s. The victory of Mrs Thatcher in 1979 re-enthroned the commonsense economics that has dominated the thinking of our political elites ever since.[2]

We find here a concise summary of an apparently well-established perception of Keynes' attack on the 'classics' and of its meaning for the general public. It seems to be clear, according to this quote, that Keynes attacked normal citizens' 'commonsense economics' dressed up (or rather: dressed down) by him as a 'straw man', that 'poor Pigou' was just a substitute for that straw man; that Keynes, in his attacks on established economics was in a sense 'like Marx'. That 'normal' citizen can well be understood if they 'marginalise' Keynes – more so even than Karl Marx.

According to this characterisation the public perception of Keynes hinges on the question of 'who and what Keynes attacked', as the beginning of this quote states. Thus it is indeed of great importance to have a clear perception of the nature of the 'Keynes–Classics debate' and if it can be shown that there are misconceptions in this regard, they should be addressed in the interest of enlightened public debate.

One might object to this argumentation that the addressees of the passages just quoted are not necessarily experts in economics. Since all sorts of unqualified opinions can be found in all walks of life, one should not make too much of such views. Contrary to such a dismissal, it must be noted that the quoted views are not limited to the uninformed. Quite to the contrary: a number of serious scholars support and even suggest them. A number of examples were given above already. Others may easily be added. Take for example the case of 'poor Pigou' – seemingly Keynes' straw man standing for a whole army of 'classical' straw men.

It is among serious scholars that the belief still has adherents that the 'Classics' – even the Pigou of the *General Theory* – are 'Keynes' invention', as was recently put by Leeson (1998a, p. 2) (similarly by Leeson 1998b, p. 125 and p. 127):

> In *The General Theory* Keynes accused Pigou of fathering the modern 'classical' version of the wage cutting argument. This chapter [in: 'The Economic Consequences of the Klassical Caricature', GMA] examines the consequences for economics and economists of this potent and enduring macroeconomic creation myth. The term 'Klassical' (with a K, after Keynes) is used to indicate that the caricature under attack was, to a large extent, Keynes' invention.

But it is not only the particular question of classical 'wage cutting' that is allegedly treated in an inaccurate way by Keynes. The author (*ibid.*)[3] extends such accusations against Keynes' quotes from Pigou *in general*:

> the *General Theory* contains a few quotes culled from Pigou (ripped all bloody from their context) ... But Pigou's (1933) ultra-theoretical analysis of wage flexibility was not adequately or fairly represented by the macroeconomic creation myth ... it appears that Keynes's caricature of Pigou is inaccurate.

Such passages perpetuate a line of literature which by now is decades old – down to the 'K'lassical spelling – as we learn when turning to Hutchison (1978, p. 123):

> The adjective 'classical' as applied to macroeconomic 'models' has come to possess little or no historical significance ... Insofar as we are actually quoting from or commenting on Keynes we can hardly avoid using his term 'classical' (though we shall spell it 'Klassical', when using it in Keynes's sense.)

What then *is* an authentic, context-sensitive rendering of a classical position? In search of the Classics, Hutchison (1978) goes deep into the history of economic thought. But he does not seem to have settled the matter satisfactorily, judging from the reoccurrence of the same old questions in the secondary literature to Keynes. Indeed, formulating a conclusion from a recent symposium on Say's Law (in relation to Keynes' criticism of the Classics) Steven Kates (1997b, pp. 238–9) remarked: 'As Baumol [(1997), GMA] has shown, the meaning and validity of Say's Law has been a focus for discussion for more than two centuries. There is likely to be no last chapter in this ongoing debate.' With this quote we have an indication of the perpetuity of this type of debates and their openendedness. But in that setting it seems to be rather unrewarding to search for 'the' authentic version – be it now of Say's Law or of Classical economics.

We must discern, however, the rather hopeless search for supposedly 'authentic' elements of generic classical economics on the one hand from the similarly interminable issue on the other hand about what in fact went on in a specific historic debate. In the latter context it might be not quite as intractable as it is in the former one to ask for authentic statements. Thus, when the question is, as stated above, 'who and what Keynes attacked', then it might indeed be the case, as McKibbin (2001) wrote in the quote given earlier, that the feeling of the 'you and I' of public opinion is that in attacking the Classics, Keynes in fact wanted to destroy 'the whole edifice of commonsense economics'. But should well-informed scholarly opinion concur with such popular perception? As a description of Keynes' intended *debate* with the Classics it seems to be quite beside the point. Keynes did not in fact want to fight common sense but he appealed to '*good* common sense' with the help of a critical discourse about 'bad' theory. It should not be forgotten that in the eyes of some readers Keynes did achieve this aim. If the general public did not perceive this, then that might be due to some unfinished academic debates.

In order to substantiate the last paragraph we may turn to Allin Cottrell (1994, p. 691) who, on the basis of a 'reader's guide' to the appendix to chapter 19 of the *General Theory* in which Keynes offers a detailed discussion of Pigou's (1933) model, proclaims: Keynes (*General Theory*, p. 277) was 'dead on target' when he claimed that Pigou's 'good common sense ceases to overbear his bad theory'. In other words: in that reader's judgement Keynes was correct in making the said distinction between 'good common sense' and bad theory which cannot support *good* common sense. Some of the grudging 'triumphalism' noted by McKibbin (2001) might then be related to the proverbial enmity of the good and the not so good as applied to varieties of common sense and of economic models.

One may, of course, question the soundness of a judgment like Cottrell's. But such questioning should be done on the basis of economic arguments as they were actually put forward. In any case, Cottrell's contribution shows that what is needed in the context of receiving the Keynes–Classics debate is not so much the sweep of witty polemics or the probing into the substance of Say's eight or seven laws.[4] What still seems to be needed most is the detailed work of a 'reader's guide'. For a balanced judgement it is important to turn to the details of the arguments on *both* sides as they were in fact put forward in that debate. This then involves the quest not for the 'true' Classics but for the authentic Keynes–Classics *debate*.

What commends such an approach? First of all there is the fact that the issue of 'Keynes and the Classics' still is highly topical, as we might have gathered from the quotes just given. The general public and a sizeable number of academic economists seem still to be puzzled by this topic and they seem still to be eager to debate what stand should be taken. That being so, the best reason for a scrutinising approach to the contested positions is that there is no intellectually satisfactory alternative. In academic debate there is no alternative to demonstrating that when it is claimed that something has never been said, to show that in fact it *was* said and *vice versa* for affirmative statements. For example: in the earlier reception of Keynes' critique of classical economics, Hutchison (1978, p. 190, n. 17) commented that when Keynes complained about lack of consistency between policy advice and published model in Pigou and other 'classical' authors 'no attempt is made to explain just what this alleged "inconsistency" amounted to in, for example, the writings of Pigou'. This is simply wrong, as Cottrell (1994, p. 691) demonstrated: Keynes (*General Theory*, p. 277) expressly addresses Pigou's (1933, p. 75) rejection of the multiplier relation.

In closing this chapter, let us make two observations: first of all, it should be noted that in a specific context of the debate with Pigou, Keynes claimed to side with 'good common sense' against inconsistent logic. Ironically, nowadays Keynes seems to be the object of disdain because he appears as having *undermined* 'our' generally accepted 'common sense' according to McKibbin (2001). The addressees of the quoted assessment were not necessarily economic experts. But it is mirrored by other comparable statements about Keynes' 'bad' influence as we saw in chapter 1. There are also a number of academic authors who, in the context of discussing the Keynes–Classics debate, accuse Keynes of more or less intentional misrepresentation with the effect of clouding the economic political issues. Thus there is a spectrum of opinions ranging from, say, McKibbin (2001) to, say, Kates (1997a) who accuse Keynes of using his misconstrued views of the 'Klassics' to disorient his readership and the public.

Secondly, the above passages do supply what Hutchison (1978, p. 190, n. 17) claimed was missing, namely, a reference to the writings of Pigou 'with chapter and verse' where the claim is substantiated that Pigou is inconsistent in his rejection of certain policy measures. Thus, it appears that important parts of what was still said in the year 2001 against Keynes concerning the Keynes–Classics debate is not maintainable once that authentic debate is actually taken note of.

We conclude from the discussion of this chapter: it should be widely accepted by now that when asking for the 'Classics' in the context of assessing the *General Theory*, the answer clearly must first of all consider Pigou (1933) because this is, after all, the starting point of Keynes' original discussion – or distortion, depending on the working hypothesis of the enquiry – of the macroeconomic issues at stake. But whatever the preconceived starting point, a full enactment of such a programme must focus Pigou's original treatment in its original context. Much of the hitherto quoted literature is lacking in this particular respect.[5]

Leeson (1998a, b) himself does not go into expository details, referring to a future book where he will supply the hitherto missing substantiations. The author does refer to a large selection of other literature where we might find relevant information. Among the many authors quoted in that context, the contribution by Aslanbeigui (1992) seems to be the one which addresses the issue of Pigou's (1933) reception in Keynes' *General Theory* most directly. But her hints at Keynesian 'misconceptions' have been inspected and by and large explicitly rejected by Cottrell (1994). Aslanbeigui (1998, p. 97, n. 1) acknowledges his counter-arguments without in the least responding to them. Instead she (*ibid.*, p. 85) repeats sweeping complaints about Keynes' and the Keynesians' 'erroneous assessment of Pigou's work'. Her argument is duly rejected by Marcuzzo (1998, p. 101) as far as the claim is concerned that 'Keynes misrepresented Pigou'. But one may predict that this repeated rejection will be met as before, by acknowledgment of the rejection without consequence for the argumentation.

What does the academic community say as arbiter in this particular debate? Is it significant for a new academic consensus in this field that in his authoritative account on *Fabricating the Keynesian Revolution*, Laidler (1999) does cite Cottrell (1994) who criticises Aslanbeigui (1992), but Laidler does not even *mention* the latter author? Is Keynes vindicated as *correctly* rendering Pigou? In fact, Laidler (1999, p. 281, n. 4) trusts that his readers will sense in some way the exact *opposite*, namely that he himself sides with Leeson – who in turn refers to Aslanbeigui (1992) – and that he considers him to have made a 'strong case':

> Robert Leeson (1996) has made a strong case that a careful reading of Pigou's work will show that he had at one time or another anticipated all the important elements of the *General Theory*. As will be apparent to the reader, I believe that there is something to be said for that view.

Unfortunately, the quoted work by Leeson (1996) seems to exist only as 'grey literature' of Murdoch University, Perth, Australia. Surely Laidler cannot trust that his views are 'apparent' to his readers with regard to *this* particular literary reference, since it just is not widely available. Maybe the already quoted work by Leeson (1998a, b) is also indicative for the type of opinion which Laidler wanted to second. But the gist of this opinion is that Keynes grossly misrepresented Pigou. Implicitly Laidler seems also to suggest that Keynes gave us a rather unauthentic rendering of Pigou, since, according to Leeson (see above) Keynes' quotes were 'ripped all bloody from their context'.

This ongoing debate suggests to any serious commentators on the Keynes-and-the-Classics issue that they will have to make up their own minds on this issue, cutting through the tangle of suggestions and appearances by going back to the original context of the debates.

4
Reconsidering Pigou as Keynes' Authentic Classic

During the era of orthodox Keynesianism, a number of comments about the *General Theory* expressed the view that it was the *absence* of an identifiable classical counterpart to Keynes which posed a particular problem for a proper understanding of his original argumentation. Subsequently that problem should have disappeared in so far as it became clear that such an absence was spurious. Keynes' classic was not a chimera – it had its concrete existence in Pigou (1933).

But then a new problem was perceived. The very fact that Keynes – in the first chapters of the *General Theory* – was preoccupied with A. C. Pigou made that book 'confusing', as we may learn from Kohn (1986, p. 1202, n. 15) who claims:

[The introduction which Keynes (1936)] finally adopted – 'The Postulates of Classical Economics' and the awkward equilibrium analysis of chap. 3, 'The Principle of Effective Demand' – seems also to have resulted from Keynes's preoccupation with Pigou's [(1933)] book.[1] One may speculate that the *General Theory* would have been less confusing a book had Keynes ignored Pigou's work on unemployment entirely and stuck to what he himself had had to say.

In the first part of this quote, the author thus first confirms the view that in the *General Theory* Keynes was partly preoccupied with Pigou's *Theory of Unemployment*, namely in those chapters where Keynes set the theme of attacking the 'classical' view. But then the author sees herein a particular problem for understanding Keynes' book.

This theme meanders now for years through the comments on Keynesian analysis. Mizen and Presley (1998, p. 2, n. 2) take it up again in writing:

Part of the difficulty in evaluating Keynes's *General Theory* was due to Keynes's taking Pigou as his representative classical economist. Few could handle the complexity of Pigou's *Theory of Employment* [*sic*,[2] GMA]

(1933). Hicks's contribution [1937] in many ways was to make the comparison less arduous by simplifying the classical position.

It might well be the case that there are merits to the Hicks–oriented approach (1937) to the Keynes–Classics debate. But there seems to be agreement that it has little to do with the *authentic* positions – neither with Pigou (1933) nor with Keynes let alone with the issues which were in fact discussed between the two. The result is that subsequently neither the 'complexity' of Pigou (1933) was made better understood nor did the *General Theory* become 'less confusing a book'.

To this very day the general readership has not faced the problem: if indeed a significant extent of the confusion surrounding the modern reception of the *General Theory* stemmed from its partial preoccupation with Pigou's *Theory of Unemployment*, then – Keynes' book having been written the way it was – the most fruitful approach to it might well be via a detailed analysis of its Pigovian starting point. But in spite of countless endeavours to elucidate the contents of the *General Theory*, this still is not the generally accepted approach. There is no fully fledged discussion of the Pigovian model under the perspective of its relevance for the *General Theory*.

Paradoxically, the neglect of the contributions of Pigou in the Keynes–Classics debate could find some explanation by the fact that during the years of orthodox Keynesianism there was so little belief in Keynes' own analytical aptitude.[3] Whatever there was in the way of microfoundations of Keynesian macroeconomics, therefore, was received by many economists as a posterior development *after* the writing of the *General Theory*,[4] not as a survival of previous analytical elements inherited, say, from – and together with – A. C. Pigou.

Thus, with the successful propagation in the postwar era of a type of Keynesian economics viewed as a theoretical development emanating from 'billowing fumes' as Leijonhufvud (see above p. 13) put it, the appreciation of a possible – albeit antithetical – analytical lineage to Pigou was broken. Together with the belief that macroeconomics as a subject was virtually reinvented by Keynes,[5] this meant that in the Keynesian era Pigovian analysis was dormant as far as mainstream economics is concerned, so that nowadays there appears to be little to fall back on in a new Pigou-oriented approach to Keynes. Even modern macroeconomic analysis of the 'new classical' brand seems curiously remote from the writings of this classical ancestor, as Solow (1980, p. 7) once remarked.[6]

Solow made his plea for giving more attention to A. C. Pigou's 'classical' economics in the course of a presidential address to the American Economic Association. Due to its wording and due to its context this may well be interpreted as a proposal of an agenda for future research. Its programmatic nature becomes even more apparent when related to an associated remark which Solow (1980, p. 3) made on that occasion: 'It might be interesting to have a history of the evolution of economic ideas about unemployment, and their relation ... to the internal logic of the subject.' It is suggested in the quote that such a study should not content itself with just reconsidering the history of the development of some economic ideas about unemployment. It should also reflect the 'internal logic' of the subject which – given the common Marshallian background of Keynes and Pigou, must be related to be the specifically *economic* logic of a microfoundation of the doctrines in question.[7]

It should be evident that in such a history the authentic original exchanges between Keynes and Pigou should be of considerable interest. But it seems that no history of evolving *models* of – and not just utterances on – unemployment has come forth so far which takes thorough account of what Keynes *and* Pigou have actually written and *discussed* with each other in their relevant context, as is witnessed, for example, by the just quoted remark from Mizen and Presley (1998).

That is not to say that since the time of Solow's (1980) presidential address there has not been considerable progress in Pigou-oriented scholarship. But much of it is still controversial and some of it is of a polemical nature generating 'more heat than light'. In our judgement, some of Leeson's already quoted utterances fall into the latter category. Take a passage like the following from Leeson (1998a, b, p. 2, p. 126 resp.):

> Without wishing to suggest that the macroeconomic 'Old Testament' [*General Theory*, GMA] had been plagiarised from the 'classical devil' [Pigou], it appears that Keynes's caricature of Pigou is inaccurate.

After Leijonhufvud's 'Delphic oracle', the stage of the Keynes–Classics debate has now the addition of a 'classical devil', of an 'Old Testament', and of a lingering – but rejected – suspicion of plagiarism. All very amusing – but where is there some solid economic analysis? Who has appeared in the literature to comment and dissect the seemingly forbidding 'complexity' of Pigou (1933) which has kept readers and quoters of the *General Theory* from entering Keynes' train of thought from the Pigovian 'end' – or rather from its Pigovian beginnings according to the judgements just quoted?

Laidler (1999) does give the modern reader some valuable guidance to the authentic Keynes–Classics debate, *including* a critical assessment of budding but deficient general equilibrium aspects of Pigou (1933). In the end, Laidler considers it as being 'apparent to the reader' that he sides with Leeson's assessment of this debate as we saw at the end of the last chapter. But as we stated there already, on the basis of the evidence available to us, we consider Leeson's assessment as being not at all convincing.

There have been so many quick and seemingly obvious conclusions in this debate which just miss the central points that one should be wary to perpetuate that type of argumentation. Take, for example the fairly recent assessment offered by Jörg Niehans (1990, p. 355) who also believes that there was not much of a Keynesian revolution if his model is seen in proper context with that of Pigou: [Keynes' (1936)] 'model was not entirely novel. Its outlines could clearly be discerned in pre-Keynesian literature (as, for example, in Pigou).' According to Niehans (1990, p. 354) not only was Keynes' model about the same as that of Pigou – the *results* of the two authors were about identical in an essential way:

> What Keynes [*sic*] was able to demonstrate was ... that money wages, held rigid above their equilibrium level, result in unemployment. This proposition was neither new nor startling. In fact it was in the main-stream of the traditional theory of unemployment. This is well illustrated by Pigou's *Theory of Unemployment* (1933).

If it was all that clear to everybody that the whole ground had been fully covered by Pigou (1933) already, why then did Pigou (1937, 1938) himself return twice to the topics of 'Real Wages and Money Wages' in the course of the unfolding Keynes–Classics debate? The issue cannot have been so banal and obvious as Niehans and some newer commentators of this debate made it appear. The particular case of the relation of real wages and money wages to each other and to employment was a contentious one from one of the first reviews of Pigou (1933) on[8] and, of course, in the *General Theory* itself.

We do *not* want to rebuke here any idea about a close similarity in some of the analytical approaches of Keynes and Pigou. Quite the contrary. We think that there should be no doubt that these two authors are products of the same analytical school and tradition, that they had so many common concerns and interactions that it would be most implausible to start from the working hypothesis that they were by and large unrelated to each other as economists. Exactly *because* they are so strongly related might it be par-ticularly interesting to have a close look at the break in paradigms if there ever was one. It is immaterial whether we call such a break a 'revolution' or a 'change in model building' or something else still. But before we have at least tried to established the mere fact of an analytical relation and of its precise nature by our own and independent investigation, we can neither deny nor confirm nor judge it. The prerequisite for all further evaluation is therefore a close look at the authentic debate. But the centrepiece for that debate is Pigou (1933).

5
The Question of Fairness in the Keynes–Pigou Debate

Arguments about fairness play an astonishingly large part in the Keynes–Pigou debate. Thus, Pigou (1936) charged Keynes that in the *General Theory* he dealt unfairly with the 'Classics'. Keynes (JMK, XIV, p. 79) charged Hicks (1937) to have been 'scarcely fair to the classical view'. Pigou claimed that he did not discuss Keynes' 'stuff' because 'he thought it unfair to bother a sick man'.[1] Corry (1978) charged Keynes to have been 'grossly unfair' in his treatment of Pigou. Pigou (1933, pp. 74–5) 'was to ridicule employment-multiplier analysis' of the type set out by Kahn (1931) according to Laidler (1999, p. 175). Thereby 'Pigou was ... being unfair' (Laidler, *ibid.*). A special twist in this type of comment is to remark on authors *not* commenting on Keynes' unfairness against Pigou (1933).[2]

In scientific discourse lamentations about lacking fairness tend to have an emotional touch which could border on the comical in an otherwise supposedly dispassionate 'scientific' context. But they do appear not too rarely in the course of the Keynes–Classics debate as is indicated by the quotes just given. Such 'unscientific' lamentations are probably particularly likely to appear in debates about paradigms. Since the selection of a specific paradigm *determines* and influences 'normal science', the argumentative level of such debates is situated *beyond* the conduct of 'normal science' itself. Discussions about paradigms are metascientific discourses in which it is not just logical consistency which counts but 'reasonable vision' as well. If that is felt lacking, then attacks quite unrelated to scientific method might be provoked.

If seen in this light, Pigou's (1936, p. 115) tirades against the Keynes of the *General Theory* – à la 'Albert Einstein actually did for Physics what Mr. Keynes believes himself to have done for Economics'[3] – just show that Pigou was very much aware of at least the *claim* that paradigm changes are involved and he succumbed to the type of discourse one can easily expect in such a situation.

For all those commentators who do not believe that any significant analytical change can be made out between Keynes and Pigou, the paradigm-oriented explanation of the agitated style of the Keynes–Classics debate is rather unconvincing, of course. Thus Hoover (2001, pp. 541–2) reports, not without sympathy:

> Laidler [1999] conveys a sense of his having a mission to right an intellectual injustice ... The worst injustice was perhaps Keynes's treatment of Pigou – the *bête noire* of Chapter 19 of *The General Theory*.

But why should Keynes commit such very bad injustice? For some commentators a plausible explanation seems to be Keynes' attempt at literary salesmanship: 'Keynes' three most successful books ... successfully employed the rhetorical device of a whipping boy', according to Leeson (1988a, b, p. 1, p. 125 resp.), and in the *General Theory* this had to be Pigou. But why Pigou (1933)? There is no convincing reason why Keynes singled out just this book by this author for his mischievous treatment.

The problem with the above description of the sources of the Keynes–Pigou debate is that it lacks some important historical detail which we do find in Clarke (1988, p. 273), however. Arguing from a predominantly historical point of view Clarke characterised the development towards formulating the *General Theory* in the following way:

> [Pigou considered] that economists who had concentrated on monetary explanations of depression had tended 'to overstress somewhat the role that money plays in more normal times'. (Keynes's lectures for two years had been called 'The Monetary Theory of Production'.) Pigou called his own study *The Theory of Unemployment* and began his preface: 'This book is addressed to students of economics.' By December 1933 Keynes had upstaged him by changing the title of his forthcoming study to *The General Theory of Employment* and was to begin his preface: 'This book is chiefly addressed to my fellow economists.'[4] Keynes's choice of Pigou as his prime target of criticism has often occasioned surprise throughout the world of economics; in its own parochial setting it is readily comprehensible. (*ibid.*)

The quote gives a glimpse at an academic scene where there was considerable theoretical 'teasing' and sublime provocation going on between Keynes and Pigou, both of them being sometimes either the active part who communicates something the other is supposed not to stomach easily, or the passive part who reacts to such academic provocations. In this setting, an interesting bone of contention was Pigou's *Theory of Unemployment*. By its approach and by its foreword it challenged all those who entered this topic from the 'monetary end'. Not only Keynes could have felt this to be a challenge.[5] How was Keynes to react in the face of this prominent challenge to his past approach? It would have been rather

pointless to stick to his own approach to unemployment problems cultivated over the previous years. Clarke's narrative suggests that Pigou *meant*
to provoke Keynes who, after all, was the exponent of the monetary school
at Cambridge. The final orientation of the *General Theory* may easily be
understood to be the result of Keynes' chewing at and digesting that very
bone of contention which was placed between him and Pigou by none
other than by Pigou himself.

But the preface of Pigou's *Theory of Unemployment* went further than just
teasing Keynes intellectually. It could well be understood to be a rather
conceited posturing of 'The Prof', parading his supposed intellectual superi-
ority in front of his junior King's College fellow. As Clarke (1988, p. 273)
remarked in the context just quoted:

> [Pigou] was, after all, the Professor of Political Economy at Cambridge,
> and not inclined to submit to the intellectual hegemony of [Keynes,] a
> junior colleague, returned like a prodigal son from the flesh-pots of
> Whitehall.

But Pigou's sentences which could be understood in this way were not just
a reassertion of intellectual leadership, *vis-à-vis* Keynes, they were in fact a
demeaning comment on many years of Keynes' life dedicated to public
affairs.

Keynes had spent years of his life as masterful economic political
commentator – his global best-seller *The Economic Consequences of the Peace*
(1919) being the starting point of many years of further activities along
such lines, much of which were republished in 1930 under the title of
Essays in Persuasion. Such activities were shunned by Pigou (1933, p. v) as
menial and as undignified for a 'real' economist like himself:

> While it is natural and right in the present deplorable state of the world's
> affairs that many economists should seek to play a part in guiding
> conduct, that is not their primary business. They are ... engineers, not
> engine drivers.

In other words: a person like Keynes who publishes *Essays in Persuasion* in
the hope of 'guiding conduct' should be seen as an 'engine driver'. In terms
of the contemporary cultural life such a dictum could well make Keynes
appear to be not so much the Cambridge don he was but rather a character
like Eugene O'Neill's *Yank*, the coal-shovelling 'Hairy Ape' (1922) in the
theatre play of that name. This play was bound to find heightened public
attention as soon as it was published since O'Neill won the Pulitzer Prize
for Drama in that year. The play physically reached Cambridge in the
1928/29 season when it was performed by the company of the Cambridge
Festival Theatre. Thus, only a short time before Pigou warned academic

economists against being 'engine drivers', Cambridge academia was confronted with passages like:

> *Paddy* [a co-worker]: Is it a flesh and blood wheel of the engines you'd be?
> *Yank*: [who has been listening with a contemptuous sneer, barks out the answer] Sure ting! Dat's me! ... I'm de end! I'm de start! I start somep'n and de woild moves! It – dat's me! – de new dat's moiderin' de old! I'm de ting in coal dat makes it boin; I'm steam and oil for de engines.

With Yank's (Yenks) name, one almost has an anagram of Keyn(e)s. In any case, equating the two names gives a vivid idea of what Pigou could have been understood to insinuate to witty intellectuals of his time and surroundings when he warned economists against posing as 'engine drivers'. But it is not just the quoted words which make this reference so topical. In addition, the engine driver *Yank* repeatedly poses like Auguste Rodin's famous sculpture of 'The Thinker', as O'Neill's play directions say. Thus, one can take it to be a hilarious joke about Keynes and those who pose as economic 'thinkers' eager to 'guide conduct' when Pigou likens such persons to engine drivers. A shocking specimen of an engine driver was just seen on stage, preposterously believing to be moving 'de woild'.[6]

Public opinion about Keynes indeed seemed to go somewhat into that direction, as Elisabeth Johnson (1978a, p. 17) reports for the time around 1931: 'Keynes, a swinging weather vane of a man, was the most unscientific of individuals – a cartoonist's dream.' Pigou therefore could well be taken to appeal to this cliché of Keynes, the 'most unscientific of individuals', if in 1933 he prefaced his new book on the *Theory of Unemployment* with a reminder to busybodying pseudo-colleagues that their 'true' vocation was *not* to be 'engine drivers'. For full measure Pigou (1933, p.v) extends his rebuke also to service in public council chambers: 'The main part of such contribution as they [the economists, GMA] may hope to make must be indirect; in the study, not ... even in the council chamber', it being well known that in 1929 Keynes was appointed to the Macmillan Committee on Finance and Industry in which function he questioned A. C. Pigou on unemployment in 1930. In the beginning of that year Keynes was also appointed to serve as chairman of Prime Minister Ramsay MacDonald's Economic Advisory Council, the task of which was to 'advise His Majesty's Government in economic matters' (Skidelsky, 1992, p. 344). Keynes himself had proposed that Pigou was to be included on this 'Committee of Economists' (Moggridge, 1992, p. 497) and he did serve on that committee. In the passage just quoted Pigou thus belittled a function which he himself received a few years before that statement through none other than Keynes and which he filled under the chairmanship of Keynes.[7]

It is thus not the case that Keynes disassociated himself in an unfair and incomprehensible way from his 'poor' colleague A. C. Pigou in 1936. Quite the contrary – the preface of Pigou (1933) can be understood to be Pigou's outspoken disassociation from much that Keynes stood for in the years before that date. If Pigou had no objections to Keynesian positions as far as economic political substance was concerned – a point which later commentators often stressed in the defence of Pigou against Keynes' supposedly 'unfair' onslaught – then Pigou's just quoted passages appear as a provocation.

Maybe Pigou was indeed unaware that by comparing his *Theory of Unemployment* to contemporary economists' attempts to master unemployment, he grossly belittled their effort to use economic insights for the purpose of public service. But no matter what Pigou's factual or professed intentions were, if read by somebody like Keynes, his fellow collegiate in Cambridge and his erstwhile fellow committee member and chairman, then Pigou's just-quoted utterances could easily be understood as an august academic comment on the merits of what Keynes hitherto had done. In any case, Keynes could well regard Pigou's published views as – at least – challenges to his intellectual status, if not even negations of it. Accepting such a challenge certainly should involve responding to it. Thus it was not Keynes wilfully picking a quarrel with 'poor Pigou' if he went through the analysis of Pigou (1933). He reacted to the pompous and belittling claims which, in the preface of that very book, were directed at people just like Keynes – and since there were not many people like him, most likely they were directed at nobody else.

Thus we tend to agree with Clarke (1988) that if Keynes is seen in his historical setting, it appears very plausible and justified that he should consider himself challenged by Pigou – both, in his position as an academic economist and Fellow of King's College Cambridge and as an expert who wanted to give well-argued advice to his community in a situation of crisis.

One could now argue that the above interpretation of Pigou's preface was an over-interpretation, that Pigou was far too kind a person to mean what we read out of those passages. We certainly should grant him the benefit of the doubt. But that there was a tendency in Pigou at that time to belittle Keynes occasionally can hardly be the object of reasonable doubt if we read that Pigou (1936, p. 119), in his ill-humoured review of the *General Theory*, elaborately tried to question Keynes' ability to express himself scientifically:

That there should be this difficulty about Mr. Keynes' scientific writings about economics – it was present also in less degree in the more theoretical parts of his *Treatise on Money* – is very curious. How is it that an author, whose powers of exposition enabled him to write on the philosophy of Probability in a way that amateurs could follow – not to say one whose vividness of phrase has made him a valued contributor to the *Daily Mail*,[8] when he comes to the subject to which he has devoted most attention, is barely intelligible to many – for I am not alone in this – of his own professional colleagues?

From Pigou's footnote to this passage calling it a 'poisoned dart' (see n. 8 to this chapter) we infer that he himself felt that he overdid it with the bit about Keynes writing for the *Daily Mail* – but then, being 'The Prof', one has to stand manfully not only to one's virtues but also to one's 'poisoned dart'.

This was not a rash and immediately regretted quip. It became a stereotype, a stock reaction of Pigou's when – as his only reaction to Keynes (1937b) – he bluntly declared in a footnote (Pigou, 1938, p. 134, n. 1): 'I have not been able to follow the reasoning of Mr. Keynes' short note.' For the normal reader, especially the one who studied Pigou (1936, p. 119) – and our passage just quoted from that article – before, this might well read as: 'As before, Mr. Keynes is incomprehensible for me as The Cambridge Professor of Political Economy.'[9] If this passage was written with motives different from the ones we just read into it, then they seem not to have been particularly convincing to Keynes. In a prior correspondence Keynes (JMK, XIV, p. 266) noted that Pigou brought health matters into this context (both Keynes and Pigou had heart problems at that time), and that Pigou wrote:

> I [Pigou, GMA] have said nothing about your note [Keynes 1937b, GMA] because, to tell you the truth, I do not understand it, and also I am sure that you ought not to be dragged into economic discussions while you are unfit. (Letter of Pigou to Keynes, quoted in: JMK, XIV, p. 266)

To this seemingly caring statement Keynes answered in a letter dated 3 January 1938 (JMK, XIV, p. 267), questioning its reasoning in the following way: 'I am sorry you could not follow my short note. As far as I can see, you now accept all my contentions. And to be told that would have done my health no harm!' But Pigou seems to have been resistant to Keynes' attempted bluff-calling when he later did publish his 'courteous' footnote mentioning Keynes (1937b) as being incomprehensible, full stop.

All in all, if we follow Clarke (1988), we see that there is more to the 'whipping boy' story than meets the eye which is just fixed on the *General Theory* and on Pigou's subsequent laments about it. If we look at Pigou's *Theory of Unemployment* and its preface as well, then we may gather that the spanking also went the other way round. But although these are colourful biographical and historical details, there is more to the Keynes–Classics debate than the question 'who started being unfair'. It is important to look at the details of model building that went into this debate.

6
An Abstract of the Arguments

The repetitive 'revolutions' and 'counter-revolutions' in the Keynes–Classics debate have left the field of macroeconomics in considerable disarray. Part of the explanation for the persistence of inconclusive turmoil might be found in a diagnosis of 'more heat than light': between the opposing economic camps there was in fact little productive interaction on basic scientific issues in spite of much antagonistic rhetoric. This lack of clear substance extends even to the conflicting camps themselves. There is much debate and insecurity about the substantive analytic content of either 'Keynesian' or 'classical' economics itself. For the case of Keynesian economics such inconclusive debate was documented above by referring to Leijonhufvud's monograph *On Keynesian Economics and the Economics of Keynes* and to the ensuing disclaimers concerning the correctness of their own positions from both, the attacked inspirer of orthodox Keynesianism, John Hicks, and from the attacker Axel Leijonhufvud.

One of the long-serving interpreters of Keynesian economics, Robert Clower, recently resigned in frustration from earlier attempts at interpreting the *General Theory*, co-authoring the following diagnosis (Clower and Howitt, 1998, p. 163):

> earlier interpreters who sought a rational basis for the 'Keynesian Revolution' in the *General Theory* were over-optimistic; the *General Theory*, like the Copernican classic that dethroned Earth as 'Center of the Universe,' though 'revolution making' (Kuhn, 1953 [our reference: Kuhn (1970), GMA]) was not revolutionary in its *analysis*.

We consider this passage to be not quite so negative as it might seem. If Keynes was *not* revolutionary in the same way as Copernicus was not revolutionary, then Keynes certainly is in good company. Such a finding liberates us for a new attempt at making sense of Keynes, namely for trying to find contrast where formerly there seemed to be only antagonism. Indeed, as Copernicus' shift in paradigm might be better understood by seeing his analysis in the context of the not so different *analysis* of his contemporary scientists, so it might well be with Keynes: if we fail to understand him better by searching for a new economic logic, then it might well be that we can make good sense of what he wrote by looking at him in the light of the traditional analysis which was the explicit backdrop for his writings.

Recent years have seen reconsideration of several aspects of the situation just outlined; the emergence of yet another revolution, the 'new Keynesian counter-revolution', has brought home some of the repetitive aspects of the contemporary macroeconomic debate, and thus it might have stimulated some reflection about a more desirable type of debate in economics. This could lead the contemporary commentator of past developments in the field of macroeconomics to a stronger stress on evolutionary developments and to look less for a pattern of a succession of revolutions.

This in turn could lead to having more concern for past theoretic developments than was customary in more 'revolution-minded' eras. In addition, the earlier interest in a 'new classical economics' left some commentators wondering about its relation to the old classical economics as exemplified by A. C. Pigou and this, too, might have been conductive for new reflections on the evolution of subject matters and methods in economic analysis. Finally, from Leijonhufvud's stress on authenticity in the Keynes–Classics debate, there could possibly be a lasting influence on the style of such reflections.

In the light of these developments we diagnose the desirability of a fresh look at the authentic starting point of these somewhat strange revolutions and counter-revolutions. In particular, we propose to reinspect the original debates between Keynes as the founder of Keynesianism and at Pigou as the exponent of the type of classical economics against which Keynes intended to argue. In doing so we propose to stress more the evolutionary aspect of that initial debate than its abrupt confrontational aspects. This will mean trying to reconstruct an exchange of arguments which in many cases was indeed not quite as smooth and as explicit as an evolutionary-minded commentator might like to have it.

The following enquiry has three main parts:

- Keynes' critical reception of Pigou on a Marshallian basis of economic argumentation (Part II).
- Pigou's reaction to the Keynesian challenge and the subsequent reformulation of the Keynesian challenge on a Pigovian argumentative basis (Part III).
- The intended taking up of the Keynesian challenge in a Pigovian context by Joan Robinson (Part IV).

The normal expectation one could associate with such an outline is that the first of these parts formulates Keynes' challenge against Pigou, the second part presents Pigou's rejoinder to Keynes, and the last part gives an example of the first round of reactions to this exchange in which the debate is carried further by one of the Young Keynesians. If matters could be structured in such a simple way, however, there would probably be no need for such an enquiry at this late stage of the debate.

The problem associated with the first of these parts is that basically Keynes does not really challenge Pigou as being false in a specific way but as having an incomplete model of the type of phenomenon which Pigou may be seen to have claimed to have modelled when, in the face of the Great Depression, he presented to the public a *Theory of Unemployment* in 1933. To bring this out therefore requires first a reconstruction of the Pigovian model along appropriate lines, then a discussion of Keynes' critique of classical analysis as exemplified by that model, and finally a closing of that classical model along the lines proposed by Keynes.

We therefore structure the subject matter of part II of our inquiry into three main aspects:

(i)   a reconstruction of the basic Pigovian model of employment, the analytical guidelines for such a reconstruction being taken from Marshallian economics;
(ii)   a presentation of Keynes' internal critique dealing with the formulation problems posed by the specific model proposed by Pigou; and
(iii)   an external critique dealing with closing the allegedly incomplete model taken over from Pigou by Keynes.

In part III we will be able to present a fresh look at the classical beginnings of macroeconomics and at the question of which role classical analysis played for Keynes' own presentation of analysis in the *General Theory*.

The problem with a review of Pigou's rejoinder to Keynes which might be expected to be falling under the heading of our subsequent part III is that initially Pigou claimed that he did not intend to maintain a discussion with Keynes, professing concern about Keynes' bad health. Thus, the tradition of talking at cross-purposes and avoiding argumentative interaction may be seen as having been established at the latest at this early stage of the Keynes–Classics debate. In actual fact, in discussing 'Real and Money Wage Rates in Relation to Unemployment', Pigou (1937) does come to address a central topic of Keynesian economics, namely the question whether money wage changes could have any effect on employment unless they also induce interest rates to change. In this sense then, we may proceed by understanding that there was in fact a Keynes–Pigou debate, after all, and that it did comply with normal patterns of scientific discourse.

But there is indeed a sense in which this stage of the debate misses Keynes' original discussion and thus contains an element of talking at cross-purposes: the conception of short-period analysis is basically different between Keynes and Pigou. For Pigou, short-period analysis is to be conducted as a discussion of a deviation from long-period stationary state equilibrium. For Keynes, short-period analysis implies shifting temporary – or as we call them further down, occasionally: 'momentous' – equilibria where the longer run perspective is by no means necessarily a stationary one.

Keynes was prepared to concede that in Pigovian conditions of long-period equilibrium it is formally correct to postulate the validity of the time-preference theory of interest. In fact, he treated this result as a special case of his own analysis and in a separate excursus we try to re-create this part of his reasoning, thereby covering critically some ground anew which was covered by Leijonhufvud (1968) in interpreting Keynes and by Barro (1990) in interpreting the Keynesian consumption function.

But even if generating formally correct results, the Pigovian approach of assuming as an analytical starting point the existence of a 'frozen land' economy (as Keynes apostrophised his stationary state assumption) was factual nonsense in his eyes.[1] In his critical discussion with Pigou, Keynes intended to bring this into clearer relief but his supposed followers failed to co-operate. We consider this to be one of the remarkable aspects of the Keynes–Classics debate, as will be pointed out in more detail in part III below.

The published outcome of this stage of the debate was that Nicholas Kaldor – then still an outsider as far as Keynesian authors were concerned – was the only person besides Keynes who systematically challenged Pigou's defence of the classical view on money wage changes. But the resulting 'Kaldorian synthesis' between Keynes and Pigou was based on the Pigovian stationary state conception of short-period analysis. Kaldor claimed that there was no significant difference between the two conceptions of short-period analysis. Although Keynes strongly disagreed on this point, he unfortunately committed his divergent view only to a letter to Pigou and not to his own publications so that this potential theme for the Keynes–Classics debate just faded without any clarification.

It is of some irony that this 'defence of the Keynesian view' led to one of the first applications of the much-maligned Hicksian *IS–LM* scheme by Kaldor who later was to be regarded as one of the exponents of the younger generation of Keynesians. This fact gives us occasion to briefly review some of the issues posed by the interpretation of the *General Theory* along these lines. The main analytical results of this part will be, however, that besides the already mentioned clarifications about Keynes' intertemporal analysis, there will be a detailed exposition of Pigou's 'simplified model' and of the model of the 'Kaldorian synthesis'.

But these analytical results should not distract from two major remarkable non-results of this debate:

(i) the already mentioned lack of clarification of the method of short-period analysis in Keynesian and in Pigovian analysis; and

(ii) the lack of discussion of the money supply process in a macroeconomic context.

Both these topics were proposed by Keynes as weak points in Pigou's defence of the classical view. But the discussion of both was actively opposed by Keynes' students: the time period issue was given up under the influence of R. F. Kahn, the monetary issue under that of Joan Robinson. This is remarkable because a later Keynes-oriented critic of the post-Keynesian Cambridge tradition, Jan Kregel, noted these very defects with the newer Cambridge School: a demonetisation of Keynesian economics and a lack of disassociation from long-run analysis.

There is the question, however, to what extent Joan Robinson could have been expected to come up with a systematic critique of Pigou's stationary state model. Such a criticism would have involved disassociating oneself from the very methodology employed by Pigou. But in her *Essays in the Theory of Employment* Joan Robinson (1937a) was just proposing to 'extend' Keynes' analysis into this strange analytical realm. It is this aspect which is scrutinised in the third complex of questions in part IV. It will then be seen in more detail that in the hands of Joan Robinson (1937a) the supposedly 'Keynesian extension' turned out to be in fact an extension to those realms which were defined as the analytical terrain of Pigou's classical rejoinder.

A closer scrutiny of the Robinsonian essay may be justified with reference to the strategic importance which later writers, in particular Jan Kregel (1983) and other post Keynesians, attributed to this piece of Keynesian exercise for many later debates inspired by Cambridge Keynesians. It is doubtful, however, whether these debates were in fact able to establish the classics-critical paradigm which they intended to create. It will be therefore a major task of part IV to find out in which relation the Robinsonian essay stands to Keynes' original analytical intentions. Although our evaluation of her analytical approach will lead to a sceptical reception, an assessment which we will find to be in accordance with Joan Robinson's own position in her later years, we want to stress the indeed positive aspect of her approach, namely the beginning of a systematic treatment of the problem of depreciation in a macroeconomic context – a problem left by Keynes as unfinished business. It is particularly in this regard that we consider a re-creation of the microfoundations of Joan Robinson's early employment-theoretical essay as a rewarding exercise.

Having established a new perception of the authentic analytical issues in the early Keynes–Classics debate, there is the obvious question of the new directions which this exercise opens up for modern-day macroeconomics. We consider the main results to be in the fields of reconsidering the microfoundations of macroeconomics and in the establishment of the Keynesian concept of equilibrium. In essence, we will plead for a synthesis of Pigovian marginal analysis of the supply decisions under conditions of imperfect competition, Keynesian liquidity preference in a short period context, and Robinsonian analysis of depreciation.

Part II
The Pigovian Node of the Keynes–Classics Debate

7
Questions and Methods

After a long and distinguished career as historian of economic thought Mark Blaug (2001, p. 152) remarked:

> I have come to the conclusion that the only approach to the history of economic thought that respects the unique nature of the subject material, rather than just turning it into grist for the use of modern analytical techniques, is to labor at *historical* reconstructions, however difficult they are. *Rational* reconstruction makes past thinkers appear to be a bit more like us than they were; *historical* reconstructions make them out to be a little less like us than they were. (emphasis added, GMA)

But he adds (*ibid.*) that many practitioners in this field make an attempt at 'having your cake and eating it too' – and he does not exclude himself from having occasionally succumbed to committing the sin of mixing the two approaches in the history of economic thought.

Their differences may be stated in the following way: rational reconstruction uses modern analytical techniques and relates past economic thought in an ahistorical context. On the other hand, *historical* reconstructions, according to Blaug (2001, p. 151),

> involve accounting for the ideas of past thinkers in terms that these thinkers and their contemporary followers would have accepted as correct description of what they intended to say ... They require careful reading not only of the texts of the economists that one is studying, but also of the previous generation of thinkers in order to understand the context in which the economists in question were writing.

This latter approach is the one envisaged in the following enquiry. It attempts to reconstruct the analytical issues brought up by Keynes in the *General Theory* not in the usual ahistorical way but in the analytical context set by one of his most prominent contemporaries.

41

A realistic assessment of the methods applied in the following must admit, however, that a totally pure isolation of the two aforementioned approaches will not be feasible. To a certain extent this essay might have to admit to a similar 'sin' as the one Blaug (2001) admitted to. A safeguard against a potential mingling of ahistorical modelling and historical argumentation is our stress on 'authenticity'. In respecting this criterion, we hope to lean more to the side of the *historical* reconstruction, thereby following the method favoured by Mark Blaug in the quote just given. But in any case, a present *re*construction is a *current* activity. As such, it will always be prone to meet the accusation of being ahistorical. We can attempt, however, to apply *authentic* methods of reconstruction. Therefore, some of the following investigation will also be directed at inspecting technical questions of model building such as the acceptability of a general equilibrium perspective, and the role of partial elasticities of production or of utility etc. as historically acceptable building blocks in the construction of economic models, and to *apply* these building blocks in a way which is by and large covered by the criterion of authenticity.

In the following chapters of part II we will start out by inspecting Pigou's *Theory of Unemployment* under the perspective that it is to be regarded as the authentic beginning of the Keynes–Classics debate. But as such it was a model *reconstructed* by Keynes, and one aspect of the current debates in this context is that it was considered to be a 'wrong', 'unfounded', 'unfair', 'trivial', 'irrelevant', 'almost plagiaristic', 'partly mistaken', but also as an 'essentially correct' reconstruction. The spectrum of accusations and praise directed against Keynes in this context was inspected above in part I. In the light of this long list of contradictory assessments of Keynes' approach to Pigou it is not advisable to address this debate directly. The approach chosen here is rather to isolate first an *independent* 'reduction' of the Pigovian model, to lay bare its building blocks and to ask for the explicit micro-foundations of the main structural relations stressed by Pigou. Thus we do not intend a 'readers' guide' to certain passages of the *General Theory* – as might be found in Cottrell (1994) – nor do we want to 'review' certain elements in Pigou and Keynes – as might be found in the excellent treatment by Laidler (1999).

The specific approach followed here is that we orient ourselves towards the – sometimes in the original not entirely explicit – analytical groundwork of the author in question and reconstruct his argument as if from its atoms upward. Thus, for example, we do not restrict ourselves to relating to the reader with Laidler (1999, p. 163) that 'as a practical matter, Pigou thought that the demand for labour was highly elastic with respect to the real wage'. We rather demonstrate that with constant partial elasticities of production, and Pigou's assumption that the said elasticity was numerically at least -3, he must have assumed that labour's share in the wage-good industries was at least 2/3 and that the elasticity was numerically higher the higher this share.[1]

For many purposes it might be of no great interest how Pigou arrived at this result and for those contexts it might suffice just to tell the reader what Pigou wrote. In view of the unending debates about the proper understanding – and manipulation of the implications – of the model found in Pigou (1933), we think that there is a place for the different approach chosen for the following enquiry.

Going back to the analytical 'atoms' of Pigou (1933) and building the 'molecules' of his structural equations on that basis does not pose great problems as far as labour demand in his model economy is concerned. But two further steps are taken in the following and those might be considered to be more controversial. The one rather speculative step taken below is concerned with Pigou's labour supply doctrine. There was some denial concerning the importance of the disutility of labour concept of labour supply in Pigou (1933) in private correspondence between Keynes and Hawtrey immediately after publication of the *General Theory*.[2] More recently, Aslanbeigui (1992, p. 418) claimed in that vein that 'Pigou's theory was based on a non-neoclassical aggregate labor-supply function'. If that was indeed the case, this certainly should be a major challenge for a historian of economic thought, since before and after the *Theory of Unemployment*, Pigou did adhere to the conventional labour supply theory and he never renounced neo-'classical' labour supply doctrine on any systematic ground. We will endeavour to speculate on the background of this peculiar debate, trying to regain the neoclassical position in the context of *historical* reconstruction.

The second challenge before us concerning the method of historical reconstruction relates to the 'equation counting' with which Keynes attacked Pigou (1933) in the *General Theory*. The issue is of utmost historical importance, because, as Leeson (1998a) tells us, Milton Friedman originally wanted to make this very problem the centrepiece of his self-presentation, since he planned one of his most important articles to run under this very heading. What then was the *historical* context of Keynes' 'equation counting'? Later in this book it will be argued that it was a clear conception of general equilibrium modelling which Keynes inherited from Alfred Marshall and with which he confronted Pigou. Again we must be wary of the charge of arguing ahistorically and out of context. Therefore we will expressly address the opinion that questions concerning the working of the 'economic system as a whole' were remote from Alfred Marshall (see below, p. 73). If that view can be rejected, it will appear less implausible that his two disciples Pigou and Keynes took this very framework of reference as being relevant for their own theorising. In fact, a general equilibrium approach to Pigou (1933) should find easy acceptance nowadays if one agrees with Laidler (1999, p. 165) that 'Pigou was aware of what we would now call the general-equilibrium nature of that issue', namely of this elasticity of labour demand with respect to changes in the real wage.

At the outset of this enquiry it should also be stressed what it is *not* concerned with: it does not debate economic political positions – and who held which view in which context.

It is our contention that a proper assessment of this aspect of 'Keynesiology' requires an inspection of some general equilibrium aspects of macroeconomic modelling. This might appear as totally ahistorical to some readers. But in fact, general equilibrium thinking was deeply entrenched in economic thinking

Some of the reasons for such an endeavour were discussed in the introductory chapters of this book: it was stated above that there seems to be an increasing general awareness that Pigou's monograph on unemployment received particular attention by Keynes, both in the conception and in the exposition of the *General Theory*. As Keynes (1936, p. 7) was to write in the introductory pages of the *General Theory*, this book was 'the only detailed account of the classical theory of employment which exists'.

Understanding Pigou's model therefore may be considered as being important for an understanding of the type of model which Keynes had in the back of his mind when he criticised the 'classics' and possibly also when he devised some of his own doctrines. The debate about such 'exegetical' questions still continues among a considerable number of economists and could be seen as a sign of a continuing search for 'first principles' in macroeconomic analysis.

We would like to emphasize, however, that 'Keynesiology' is not the only reason for studying Pigou. Now, in a time which just saw the rise – and according to some commentators also the subsequent decline – of a New Classical Economics, there is some curiosity among economists to see in which way this new classical research programme was related to its old namesake. That curiosity cannot be sufficiently satisfied from the existing literature, however, and this is one of the additional reasons why in the following we intend to reformulate this once influential employment theoretic model inherited from pre-Keynesian times.

The particular questions to be worked through in the following chapters of this part of our enquiry may be listed under the following headings:

1. What exactly was the employment theoretic model which was put forward by Pigou? (chs 8 and 9)
2. In what way was this model received critically in Keynes' *General Theory*? (ch. 10)
3. Which analytical steps did Keynes take in going *beyond* 'classical analysis'? (ch. 11)
4. What significance does the present investigation have for a deeper understanding of classical and Keynesian economics? (chs 12 and 13)

Before addressing these questions in the following chapters, a brief statement concerning our method of approaching them might be helpful, however, in order to steer the direction of the reader's expectations about the future course of our argumentation.

It was stated above (ch. 4) that basically we intend to follow Solow's call for a history of economic thought on unemployment which is combined with a study of the 'inner logic of the subject'. In our view, realising the Solovian programme means that a combination of doctrine historical investigation and analytical microfoundation is called for. It should be pointed out that such a combination prestructures the following argumentation to a considerable extent.

Part of the debates between Keynes on the one side and 'Classics' like A. C. Pigou on the other originated from Keynes' conviction that many of the reasonable things which they said about practical economic matters had no consistent theoretical foundation.[3] But if one is to insist on a combined discussion of doctrine and theoretical foundation, then many such 'reasonable' utterances could be of only very minor interest for the present exposition.

Thus, when in the *Theory of Unemployment* Pigou discusses separately two types of 'elasticities of demand for labour as a whole' namely one 'in terms of wage-goods' (pp. 88ff.) and one 'in terms of money' (pp. 100ff.), then we will concentrate on the first of these, implicitly using the justification just mentioned. There is then an implicit claim by us that it is possible to construct a congenial theoretical foundation for the former elasticity, but none for the latter. Such selection might be open to doubt in some cases.[4] But it saves us from an encyclopaedic listing of employment-theoretical utterances with sometimes little theoretic relevance.

Besides the 'Solow programme' just outlined and which is directed at establishing an analytically well-founded doctrinal history, we intend to subscribe to a further approach which, in obvious reference to important prior work in this field, might be subsumed as a 'Leijonhufvud programme'. This latter type of approach would be directed at authenticity as one of the main criteria for the inclusion of a specific piece of analysis.

These two types of research programmes could come into conflict with each other when intricate theoretical foundations are discussed for which there is no obvious textual justification. This problem might be solved pragmatically by submitting the implications of results derived in the context of a supposedly congenial theoretical reconstruction to certain authenticity tests. More specifically, in order to justify the claim to authenticity in the present context of a discussion of Keynes and Pigou, we propose two tests, one for each author:

- The first test, to be discussed in ch. 9 below, will concern the validity of our intended reconstruction of the central concept of the Pigovian theory of employment, namely his 'real demand for labour'. This test will consist in a detailed discussion of the workings of an analytical reconstruction of the Pigovian model to be undertaken in the next chapter under the original Pigovian perspective of the postulated existence of a well-defined 'Elasticity of the Real Demand for Labour'.

• The second test in connection with the present reconstruction will be concerned with Keynes' reception of the Pigovian analysis. It consists in the attempt, to be undertaken in ch. 10, to generate exactly those employment-theoretical measures which Keynes (1936, p. 7) claimed to be the substance of the Pigovian classical theory. We are not aware that any such reconstruction of the analytical basis of this seemingly incoherent list of measures has yet been supplied in the Keynes–Classics literature so far.[5] But only if it can be established that the classical model presented here is really in essence the one which Keynes had in mind when referring to the classical theory of employment does it seem sensible to proceed to a more detailed inspection of Keynes' critique of the Classics which will be the object of ch. 11.[6]

The purpose of such an inquiry will be reflected upon in ch. 12. It may be seen to lie in gaining insight into the general style of analysis prevalent in the 'Cambridge mind' at the time of the publication of the *General Theory* and into the *differentia specifica* of the Keynesian analysis.

8
Pigou's 'Real Demand for Labour'

Turning now to the reconstruction of the employment-theoretical model in Pigou (1933), it has to be noted that there is little in economic literature which addresses this particular problem. The most important contributions mentioning Pigou's *Theory of Unemployment* are by Collard (1981), Solow (1980) and by Corry (1978). Of these authors it is only Solow (1980) who attempted a presentation of Pigou's model. Only he went into any detail of its components. It will emerge below, however, that Solow's presentation could not stand as it is without further elaborations because it omitted some of the more important contributions of Pigou (1933). Among these was the disaggregated approach to macroeconomics which Pigou propagated in the *Theory of Unemployment*.

8.1 Sectoral disaggregation and the Pigovian approach

Solow (1980) concentrated on those aspects of Pigou's theory which could be easily represented with the help of a neoclassical macroeconomic production function. What seems to have generally been lost in the modern reception of Pigou's Theory of Unemployment – if it is noted at all – is the particular way in which his work dealt with and reflected the problem of a disaggregated microfoundation of macroeconomic labour demand theory.

It seems to have generally gone unnoticed in economic literature so far that Pigou (1933) is one of the founding fathers of neoclassical two-sector analysis. The significance of this fact is that as such Pigou must be represented as having been well aware that neoclassical principles holding on a comparatively low resolution level of an 'industry' or of a sector of an economy cannot necessarily be transferred to a discussion of the economy as a whole. The dichotomy between 'the theory of the individual industry or firm' on the one hand, and 'the theory of output and employment as a whole' on the other hand, as advocated later by Keynes (1936, p. 293) thus already appears in Pigou's *Theory of Unemployment*.

The essentially disaggregated approach in Pigou (1933) cannot be over-looked by any reader of his, of course. In part II of that book Pigou discusses at considerable length the particular problems resulting from the existence of several 'different centres of production'. But his modern readers seem to have difficulties in assessing the significance of these passages. Solow (1980, p. 4) does note this discussion but he refers it to labour market segmentation in the sense 'that "labor" is not a well-defined homogeneous factor of production'.

Pigou's main concern in this context is different, however. It deals with the problem of inferring changes of macroeconomic labour demand from changes of industry specific real wages. But industrial differences need not rely on a lack of homogeneity of qualifications of workers. They could result simply from technological differences. If such differences exist, then the demand for even a homogeneous workforce could not – in principle – be seen as depending on some representative real wage since changes in labour demand in one sector might be counterbalanced by offsetting changes in another sector. We find here a theme which was later discussed in considerable detail by some younger Cambridge authors.[1]

In the face of the difficulties resulting from the complexities of disaggregated analysis the main concern of Pigou (1933, p. 71) was not labour market segmentation. Instead, a substantial part of his book is devised to reach just the negative result that 'the concept of a number of independent demand functions for labour ... cannot be used as an instrument for analyzing the factors that determine aggregate labour demand'. It is in this context that Pigou states that he is clearly aware of the fundamental differences between aggregate analysis on the one hand and an analysis conducted on a different resolution level on the other hand, the latter analysis having not an entire economy as its object of enquiry, but specific sectors of production.

A reconstruction of Pigou's theory of employment must, in our judgement, take explicit account of this awareness of the micro–macro dichotomy in Pigovian analysis.

8.2 The basic assumptions of the Pigovian employment model

8.2.1 The Pigovian programme of a model-oriented theory of employment

Pigou's main intention is, of course, not the negative result just stated. It is rather the investigation of a 'simplified model' as Pigou (1933, p. vi) announces in his preface:[2]

> What I have studied is a simplified model of the economic world rather than that world itself in its full completeness.

In that context he elaborates that, faced with the choice between starting his theory from a non-monetary 'real end' or from a 'monetary end' he preferred the former:

> I have chosen to write my book from the real end, and to bring in the monetary factor only at a fairly late stage.

In addition, Pigou (1933, p. v) expressly announces his book as being addressed to economists. This meant for him, as he further elaborates, to have the liberty to discard the 'cotton-wool' of verbal restatements of 'mathematical ideas', and to state his arguments in 'a direct manner' involving explicit utilisation of elementary calculus.

The reader of Pigou (1933) is thus led to expect the study of a formal model economy which relies mainly on non-monetary 'real' concepts and which will, as the title suggests, generate situations of unemployment. A well-specified model of this type will be sought in vain, however. The model which in fact is employed in Pigovian analysis must be reconstructed by the reader himself, following the hints which Pigou reveals here and in other passages of his book.

8.2.2 The textual basis

Pigou (1933, pp. 89f) proceeds from the negative result concerning aggregate labour market analysis just discussed to a presentation of the positive aspects of his theory in explicating a number of 'basic' assumptions:[3]

> The position from which we start may be set out broadly as follows
> [i] There are engaged in making wage-goods ... x men.
> [ii] The output in value of wage-goods of these men we call $F(x)$: and
> [iii] the general rate of wage is $F'(x)$.
> [iv] There are also engaged in other industries y further wage-earners, the wage payments to whom amounts, of course, to $yF'(x)$.
> [v] There is thus a total wage payment $(x + y)F'(x)$: and there is left over, as so to speak, a trading surplus to non-wage-earners in the wage-good ... industries, $F(x) - (x + y)F'(x)$ value of wage-goods ...
> [vi] Given the surrounding conditions, we are entitled to write $(x + y) = \phi(x)$.

With this list we are indeed supplied with an outline of a 'real', i.e. a non-monetary model economy. Its exact structure is not easily intelligible from these statements, however, because they are not all of the same order of complexity. Partially they just state that there are – two – different sectors of the economy with associated – presumably 'neoclassical' – production functions and with labour inputs x and y. But the last three 'assumptions' describe three aspects of interactions between these x and y which are not necessarily self-evident and which incorporate a substantial amount of economic deduction. In the next section we will try to sort out these different levels of complexity by a 'reductionist' approach to the Pigovian model, i.e. by reducing this list to the underlying canonical neoclassical assumptions.

At the apex of complexity of Pigou's construction stands his 'assumption' of sectoral interdependence of employment stated under [vi] in this list. Here, Pigou postulates the existence of a reliable functional relationship $\phi(x)$ between total employment $(x + y)$ as dependent variable on the one hand and sectoral employment on the other. This formulation enables him to break up the analysis of labour demand into two resolution levels, namely

(a)   a $F'(x)$-theory of sectoral labour demand and
(b)   a $\phi(x)$-theory of aggregate labour demand.

Thus we find in this construction the positive consequence which Pigou drew from his negative statement concerning the impossibility of using *independent* labour demand functions in the discussion of *aggregate* labour demand. But why and under which conditions are we indeed 'entitled' to formulate such a function like the one which Pigou proclaimed in the quote just reproduced?

There are some who believe that Pigou just was inconsistent in his belief to this 'entitlement'. Thus Rotheim (1992, p. 46) believed:

> Why Pigou permitted himself to use aggregate relationships which were based on micro-entities even though it was impossible to map the latter onto the former is simply a curiosity. Perhaps he suffered from a sort of Ricardian Vice in formulating theory which prevented him from recognizing the illogical nature of the theory that he was espousing. Such a vice did not plague the likes of Sraffa and Dobb.

The following discussion is supposed to find an answer to this question.

It is indeed remarkable that Pigou quickly proceeds from the statement of the existence of a $\phi(x)$-function to a detailed discussion of the characteristics of his newly invented concept without giving hints for its theoretical generation. He seems to regard its existence as virtually self-explanatory within the argumentative context which he presupposes. This argumentative context is, of course, that of the marginal analytical English School as developed in the writings of Jevons up to Alfred Marshall. When the attempt is made to explicate the analytical foundations of the Pigovian $\phi(x)$-function then this concept should therefore be referred to the canonical assumptions of the English School. We will restate these assumptions in the next sections. First of all, it seems important, however, to realise that the model used by Pigou is virtually the same as the one which we encounter still today in elementary presentations of the pure theory of foreign trade. This will be demonstrated presently. After restating the analytical basis of the Pigovian model graphically and verbally, we will then proceed to a reformulation of the Pigovian $\phi(x)$-function, recreating the analytical steps which are implicit in its conception and stating the characteristic parameters which may be used for a further discussion of the implications of Pigou's novel macroeconomic tool.

8.2.3 The two-sectoral background

The model which Pigou (1933) outlines in the passages just quoted is about the same as the 'specific factors model' which beginning students of the theory of foreign trade still have to deal with today in the relevant textbooks.[4] For easy reference it is reproduced below together with references to the individually numbered Pigovian passages [i] to [vi].

Figure 8.1 on p. 52 shows that clause [i] on p. 49 identifies labour input, clause [ii] gives the corresponding output in the 'x'-sector. Its quantity (not denoted as such by Pigou) is given as Q_x on the northern part of the perpendicular axis. Clause [iii] refers to the tangent to the $F(x)$-curve expressing, as $F'(x)$, the sectoral real wage, its value being depicted in figure 8.1 as tan α. Clause [iv] states the existence of a second sector 'y'. Neither the corresponding sectoral production function nor the corresponding output is expressly mentioned by Pigou and must be inferred. They are represented by grey lines and by grey letters if additional symbols are required. Sectoral employment x and y may be added up to give total employment $n = x + y$ along the 45°-line in the south-western quadrant. Given total employment, the north-eastern quadrant shows the corresponding production possibility curve of standard literature.

We save our comments on clause [v] for later and just finish by noting that the ominous ϕ-function of clause [vi] appears as a corresponding curve in the south-western quadrant of Figure 8.1.

It follows from this scheme that with a determined real wage rate $F'(x) =$ tan $\angle \alpha$ we have determined values of x and y, and of the corresponding output quantities Q_x and Q_y on the production possibility curve in the north-eastern quadrant. Supply and demand in that context determine the relative price p_y/p_x. Only the black parts of Figure 8.1 are really spelled out by Pigou. The rest has to be 'appropriately' inferred on the basis of 'common – Cantabridgian – knowledge'.

8.2.4 A reductionist approach to the Pigovian model

We will now first attempt to disentangle the various levels of complexity in Pigou's list of 'basic' assumptions by reformulating that list. In doing so we will orient ourselves by that original list, but we will relate it as far as possi-

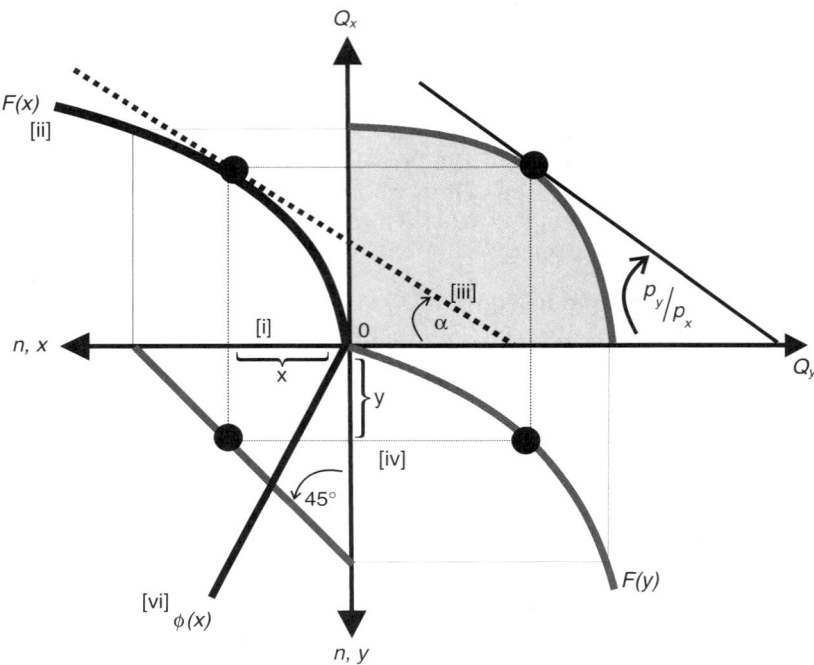

Figure 8.1 Pigou's two-sectoral background

ble to the standard assumptions of the English School. In order to min-
imise doctrine historical discussion in this context, we will relegate
justifications for the inclusion of specific items to the footnotes. As stated
in the introduction of this chapter, the ultimate test of the correctness of
the present reformulation will consist in the investigation whether the
Pigovian model and the further discussion of it in Keynes' *General Theory*
may indeed be related to the present reconstruction of the Pigovian model.

A reformulated set of assumptions which may be seen as standing behind
Pigou's model economy as just quoted on p. 49 above then reads:

A.1 There are two sectors of production with sectoral employments being
given by the variables x and y,[5] and labour being the only variable
factor of production.[6]

A.2 The production functions are 'normal' in the sense of the marginal
analytical theory of production.[7]

A.3 Labour is remunerated by its marginal product.[8] Markets and competition are perfect and entrepreneurs maximise their profits.

A.4 Workers' households have a utility function in which wage goods create
positive utility (pleasure) but working creates negative utility (pain).[9] As

far as they are concerned, the real wage reflects the marginal calculus resulting from utility maximisation in this choice theoretic framework.[10]

A.5 Workers' income is spent entirely on wage goods. Non-workers have a choice between wage goods and non-wage goods. Typically the latter class demand both types of goods.[11]

A.6 The demand for goods by households other than workers' households follows the equimarginal rule.[12]

The main difference between this list and the original list lies in the treatment of the $\phi(x)$-function. Here it is missing. It is replaced by a number of choice theoretic postulates which may be seen to be part of the standard stock of conventional economics of the English School. Thus the present list is more 'primitive' than the former one in refraining from utilising Pigou's novel analytical tool.

The eventual task ahead in this discussion of the Pigovian model is to inspect whether this reduction of a model economy to its underlying choice theoretic assumptions may indeed be linked to exactly that theory which Pigou did in fact advance. In particular, if it is possible to rebuild his $\phi(x)$-function from these 'primitive' elements derived from Pigou's analytical background, then we may conclude that this was indeed the implicit procedure which Pigou presupposed when he proclaimed that we are 'entitled' to use this function for an analysis of aggregate employment. But in order to bridge the gap between these verbal restatements and the Pigovian $\phi(x)$-function we must first arrive at the statement of a number of 'primitive' functional relationships based on these reformulations. This will be the object of the next section.

8.3 The microfoundations of the Pigovian model

In this section we complete the intended reconstruction of the groundworks of the Pigovian employment-theoretical model by supplying the functional relationships which the present reformulation suggests to be holding in that model. The approach of this section is comparable to much of the 'microfoundations' literature developed in the Keynesian literature[13] but virtually non-existent in the case of Pigovian economics.

Model constructions similar to the present one have been proposed previously in the extensive 'two sector' growth model literature.[14] The main difference of the present construction with regard to the growth model literature is that the latter utilises the concept of a consumption function and the idea of economic growth through capital accumulation. Both of these elements are not in order in the present context, however, since the concept of a consumption function postdates Pigou (1933) and capital accumulation is expressly assumed to be out of consideration as stated in connection with A.1 of the previous section.

The modelling of production in the present context is straightforward. On the basis of A.1 and A.2 we may state sectoral production functions. In the case of wage goods we may resort to Pigou's original formulation stating the existence of a function

$$Q_x = F(x); Q_x = \text{wage goods} \tag{8.1}$$

For non-wage goods we have correspondingly

$$Q_y = G(y); Q_y = \text{non-wage goods} \tag{8.2}$$

The 'first classical postulate' as mentioned in connection with A.3 gives the real wage in the wage goods sector as

$$\frac{w}{p_x} = F'(x) \tag{8.3}$$

where w = nominal wage, p_x = price of wage goods, and $F'(x)$ is the marginal product of labour in the wage goods sector.

The relative price of goods reflects the relative marginal cost which in the present context is given by relative real wages since labour is the only variable input. Thus we have:

$$\frac{p_y}{p_x} = \frac{F'(x)}{G'(y)} \tag{8.4}$$

where p_y = price of non-wage goods and $G'(y)$ stands for the marginal product of labour in the non-wage goods sector, representing the real wage w/p_y in terms of the output of that sector.

Turning now to the utility of the workers as mentioned in A.4, denote their 'wage goods' by Q_{xw} and the negative utility argument by the term $(\bar{t} - n)$ where $\bar{t}$ represents workers' time constraint and n their working time. If

$$U^w = U^w(Q_{xw}, \bar{t} - n)$$

is the utility function of workers, representing the choice theoretic set-up mentioned under A.4 above, then the equimarginal rule for utility maximisation requires

$$\frac{\partial U^w}{\partial Q_{xw}} / p_x = -\frac{\partial U^w}{\partial n} / w \tag{8.5}$$

to hold whence one obtains an algebraic formulation for the 'second classical postulate' as expressed by the second sentence of A.4 as

$$\frac{w}{p_x} = \frac{-U_n^w}{U_{Q_{xw}}^w} \quad \text{with} \quad U_n^w \equiv \frac{\partial U^w}{\partial n} \quad etc. \tag{8.6}$$

where U^w_{Qxw} represents the marginal utility of workers from consuming the wage goods and where $-U^w_n$ is the marginal disutility of labour with $-U^w_n = U^w_{\bar{t}-n}$; *i.e.* the marginal disutility of labour is just the negative value of the marginal utility of leisure. For convenience's sake we will denote these derivatives also by the equivalent expressions

$$U^w_{Q_{xw}} \equiv \frac{\partial U^w}{\partial Q_{xw}} \equiv U^w_1; \ U^w_{\bar{t}-n} \equiv \frac{\partial U^w}{\partial (\bar{t} - n)} \equiv U^w_2. \tag{8.7}$$

and later on we will return to this simplified notation (see Table 9.1, on p. 62 below and the related discussion).

The wage goods in this set-up are divided up between workers and non-workers. If the consumption of wage goods allocated to workers has the index xw and that of wage-goods allocated to non-workers has the index xk we have to write

$$Q_x = Q_{xw} + Q_{xk} \tag{8.8}$$

But in this expression, the quantity of consumption of wage goods by non-labourers is required to satisfy the equation

$$Q_{xk} = Q_x - \frac{w}{p_x} n \tag{8.9}$$

according to Pigou's concept of a 'trading surplus' as quoted under [v] on p. 49 above. The magnitude n in this expression stands for total employment so that we may write

$$n = x + y. \tag{8.10}$$

Finally, the choice of non-workers between wage goods and non-wage goods postulated in A.5 suggests the existence of a utility function $U^k = U^k(Q_{xk}, Q_y)$ containing these two goods. The equimarginal rule invoked under A.6 above then gives

$$\frac{U^k_{Q_{xk}}}{p_x} = \frac{U^k_{Q_y}}{p_y} \tag{8.11}$$

where $U^k_{Q_{xk}}$ is the marginal utility from consuming Q_x goods by non-workers (who have the index k) and where $U^k_{Q_y}$ is the marginal utility from consuming Q_y goods which are only consumed by non-workers.

What has now been gained by these reformulations? Given the customary assumptions about well-behaved production and utility functions, it is possible to determine simultaneously from this system of nine equations the nine endogenous variables Q_x, x, y, n, Q_{xw}, Q_{xk}, Q_y, w/p_x and p_y/p_x. Thus we have a rough check that the model under discussion is indeed 'complete' in the sense of meeting the basic requirements of consistent model building. We may then discuss the simultaneous changes of the endogenous variables in the well-known comparative static way and we might thus arrive, among other results, at a theory of the behaviour of employment n.

But it should be remembered that the object of this exercise is not just classics-inspired model building. It is to reconstruct Pigou's original procedure in the formulation of a theory of employment and his approach was not just a discussion of a simultaneous equation system. He employed the detour of formulating a $\phi(x)$-function relating sectoral employment x to total employment n. It is this analytical 'detour' and its relation to the model economy reconstructed so far which has to concern us next.

9
The Workings of the Basic Pigovian Model

In this chapter we test the 'reductionist reconstruction' of the last chapter by submitting it to the 'authenticity test' outlined in ch. 7. In particular, we will test whether the reconstruction of ch. 8 is indeed capable to generate those workings of a model economy which were originally stressed as being important by Pigou (1933).

In the following section 9.1 it will emerge that the concept of the 'elasticity of the real demand for labour' is of central importance for Pigou's model-oriented theory of employment. Section 9.2 below will then offer several variants of formulating this elasticity on the basis of the model proposed in the last chapter. In a final section 9.3 we will check the present interpretation against a former one supplied by Solow (1980).

9.1 The elasticity of the real demand for labour as the centrepiece of the Pigovian model

9.1.1 The definition

The basic approach of the Pigovian theory of employment was characterised above as being one which aims at establishing a functional relationship between macroeconomic employment on the one hand and a sectoral or microeconomic real wage on the other hand without resorting to the type of analogical theorising which may be found in much of more modern macroeconomic model building.[1]

The analytical procedure of Pigou (1933, p. 90) is now to advance from listing a number of 'basic assumptions' which were discussed above in sect. 8.2 (see p. 48) to postulating the existence of an elasticity

$$E_r = \frac{\phi'(x)}{\phi(x)} : \frac{F''(x)}{F'(x)} \qquad (9.1)$$

This expression is meant to represent the behaviour of total employment *via* his novel concept of a $\phi(x)$-function.

57

The reconstruction of this function is the object of our present reformulation. Intuitively, one may gather from just regarding this expression that it relates the real wage in the $x-$ sector $w/p_x = F'(x)$ to total employment $n = \phi(x)$. But how exactly does the author arrive at the postulated elasticity E_r?

It might be helpful to restate this elasticity: it obviously is supposed to represent the reaction of the total demand for labour in response to changes in the worker's real wage rate. It follows then from the mere definition of elasticities, that the identity relation in equ. (9.2) must hold.

$$E_r \equiv \frac{dn}{d\left(\dfrac{w}{p_x}\right)} \cdot \frac{\left(\dfrac{w}{p_x}\right)}{n} = \frac{dn}{d\left(\dfrac{w}{p_x}\right)} \cdot \frac{F'(x)}{\phi(x)}. \tag{9.2}$$

Replacing now w/p_x and n in the identity relation by the corresponding functions gives the last expression in equ. (9.2) in terms of the basic economic variables resp. functions just discussed, namely the real wage function $w/p_x = F'(x)$ and the total employment function $n = \phi(x)$.

Furthermore, since $dn = \phi'(x)dx$ and $d(\frac{w}{p_x}) = F''(x)dx$, it emerges that in equ. 9.2, we may make the further replacement:

$$\frac{dn}{d\left(\dfrac{w}{p_x}\right)} = \frac{\phi'(x)}{F''(x)}. \tag{9.3}$$

After some elementary manipulation, we will then arrive again at the expression for E_r given in equ. (9.1). Thus, the alternative formulation is consistent with the original one but it might make it more transparent what reasoning lies behind the definitions.

9.1.2 *Intra-* and *inter*sectoral aspects

With equ. (9.2) we have established how the 'elasticity of the real demand for labour' of equ. (9.1) depends *formally* on more conventional statements of economic relations and their derivatives. But this does not yet solve the question concerning the *economic rationale* lying behind equ. (9.1). Obviously there is some sort of general economic equilibrium concept behind it, because it relates the particular real wage, w/p_x to total employment n. Since the economic rationale lies in this very transition from the sectoral to the total level, a satisfactory explanation of equ. (9.1) can only be given by re-creating the underlying chain of reasoning which, in the case of Pigou, must be based on partial economic equilibria. It is in this sense that some sort of a 'general' equilibrium context must *a priori* be considered as being the analytical aim of any endeavour to understand Pigou (1933). This will be the object of the following section 9.2.

To round off the definitional discussion in this section, let us point out that alternatively to the reformulation given in equ. (9.2) we could also have started from the elasticity equ. (9.1) and re-write it as

$$E_r \equiv \mathrm{E}_{F'(x)}^{\phi(x)} = \mathrm{E}_x^{\phi(x)} : \mathrm{E}_x^{F'(x)} \qquad (9.4)$$

where E stands for the elasticity operator with the upper index being the dependent variable and the lower index being the independent variable. Equation (9.4) is, of course, just a tautological manipulation of equ. (9.1), obtained by enlarging with dx/x.

This decomposition of E_r into two component elasticities, although tautological, might nevertheless be helpful insofar as it again shows that E_r depends on *two* quite different relationships: an *intrasectoral* relationship relating sectoral employment x and sectoral marginal product $F'(x)$ on the one hand and an *intersectoral* relationship $\phi(x) = x + y$ on the other hand, relating *total* employment $x + y$ to *sectoral* employment x. This latter, intersectoral, relationship stresses an inherent necessity in Pigou's model to argue this case in some sort of a general equilibrium context, showing how the sectoral and the total economic outcomes interact.

9.1.3 The significance for the Keynes–Pigou debate

Labouring over one single algebraic term, namely Pigou's E_r, might easily appear to be too tedious to warrant further effort. But let us note that the discussion of the 'Elasticity of the Real Demand for Labour' takes up considerable space in Pigou's exposition of his theory of employment so that its detailed reconstruction may seem to be justified under a purely historical perspective. But our aim is not just to cover history but to understand argumentative interaction. It is therefore important to note that this term connects Keynes and Pigou in quite a substantial way because it is also a main 'quaesitum' in Keynes' (1936; pp. 272ff.) critical discussion of the Pigovian model. Understanding this concept and its debate is therefore important specifically under the aspect of our intended revisiting of the original Keynes–Pigou debate. It is particularly significant since Keynes proclaimed that 'there is no significant difference between this and my own modes of expression'.

We may briefly enlarge on this latter point, quoting Keynes further. From this statement he proceeded (*ibid.*) to conclude that:

> Professor Pigou's 'elasticity of the real demand for labour in the aggregate' is a concoction similar to some of my own, depending partly on the physical and technical conditions in industry (as given by his function F) and partly on the propensity to consume wage-goods (as given by his function ϕ).

Thus, if Keynes' characterisation is correct, a thorough discussion of this concept is warranted and is even required–not only in order to elucidate Pigou's original theoretical position and its reception by Keynes, but also to understand better Keynes' own position since he regarded this concept as similar to some of his own 'concoctions'. In this context it is particularly remarkable that Keynes specifically related elements of his own theory to Pigou's *F*- and *ϕ*-functions. This observation suggests that from reconstructing the relation of these functions to each other and to the elasticity of the real demand for labour we may also gain some further knowledge about the general analytical method which was acceptable to Keynes for the purpose of macroeconomic model building.

Formal similarity does not preclude paradigmatic difference, of course. Such difference may then find its expression in a choice of definitions. One issue where this becomes apparent in the present context is the question of dependent and independent variables. Thus, in equ. (9.4), we may make the reformulations:

$$E_x^{F'(x)} \equiv \frac{dF'(x)}{F'(x)} : \frac{dx}{x} = \frac{1}{\eta} \tag{9.5}$$

where

$$\eta \equiv E_{w/p_x}^x = \frac{dx}{x} : \frac{dF'(x)}{F'(x)} = \frac{F'(x)}{xF''(x)} \tag{9.6}$$

is Pigou's elasticity of labour demand in the wage goods sector.

Formally, equs. (9.5) and (9.6) are, of course, just inverses of each other if well-defined functions do exist as required – a point which was readily conceded by Keynes. Paradigmatically, the two formulations are very different, however: equ. (9.5) expresses that changes in employment *x* 'cause' in a functional way the real wage *F'(x)* to assume a specific new value. This is the economic substance which Keynes conceded to the Classics by accepting their model assumptions. Pigou's elasticity (9.6) says that the causative chain is just the other way round. This is the paradigm which Pigou insisted upon by choosing this formulation rather than an alternative one. Thus, when Pigou (1933, pp. 91f.) allots considerable space to contrasting his 'narrower elasticity *η* to the wider elasticity *E_r*', he conveys two messages, namely:

(i.) sectoral employment and total employment follow *different* functional forms because they have their specific elasticity expressions;
(ii.) sectoral employment and total employment follow the *same* mechanism in that they have as independent variable the sectoral real wage.

These messages are, of course, important issues between Keynes and Pigou. But the important interpretational question is where the *strategic* issues are located.

The important differences between Keynes and Pigou being on the paradigmatic level, they should not be blurred by constructing analytical differences which have little to do with the paradigmatic ones – like assumptions about technology or about the level of competition.

It is in order to have a clearer view on the paradigmatic differences that we try first to reconstruct the common analytical ground which does exist between the two in spite of all the much debated differences.

9.2 Quasi-general equilibrium formulations of the Pigovian 'elasticity of the real demand for labour'

9.2.1 Formulating the demand and technology interaction

The essential hint for a more explicit formulation of the Pigovian 'elasticity of the real demand for labour' concept may be seen in Keynes' just quoted claim that it involves a 'concoction' of technical conditions and the propensity to consume. But since the latter concept is one of Keynes' inventions, it is not possible to follow Keynes literally in a Pigovian context.

Since Pigou refrained from explicitly formulating consumption functions, we must now go back to the conventional Marshallian formulation of demand as given by the 'equimarginal rule' invoked above under A.6 and reformulated as equ. (8.11) on p. 55. This expression may be rearranged to represent relative price p_y/p_x as a ratio of relative marginal utilities. But since relative price is also given by relative marginal cost of production as stated by equ. (8.4) on p. 54, combining these two equations then gives an equilibrium relationship between demand conditions and technology in the reconstructed Pigovian model as

$$\frac{p_y}{p_x} = \frac{U^k_{Q_y}}{U^k_{Q_{xk}}} = \frac{F'(x)}{G'(y)}. \tag{9.7}$$

This expression is just a partial equilibrium one, of course, since it is only in terms of the non-workers' demand for goods. But its analytical scope can be easily extended: non-workers' consumption of wage-goods was related to total consumption of these goods via equ. (8.9) on p. 55. Using the production function equ. (8.1) of the last chapter and assuming equilibrium we thus get a connection to total production of this sector. Furthermore, equ. (8.2) identified non-wage goods production and the associated employment $y,$ *etc.* In short, using the basic assumptions and the basic structure of the Pigovian model discussed in the last chapter, we may restate the reconstructed Pigovian model of labour demand as depicted in Table 9.1, using simplified notation along the line defined on p. 54 after equ. (8.6).

The equations in Table 9.1 have been discussed in detail above and should not require further comment. The five equations (a) to (e) describe a system which may be solved simultaneously for the three employment variables n, x and y, and for the two demand variables Q_{xk} and Q_y which are contained in the V-function. This system is *more* than a partial equilibrium one, since it depicts sectoral interdependence. It is *less* than a general equilibrium system, however, since it does not take account of the U^w-function which is supposed to represent workers' preferences. Thus, we consider this system to be a 'quasi-general' equilibrium one.

In this system the real wage w/p_x may be treated as an exogenous variable so that we may ask for the effect of a change in this magnitude on the one hand and total employment n on the other, the answer requiring the context of a reduced form of the differentials of the system of equations just described.

9.2.2 Labour demand in a reduced form context

This, then, is in essence the employment-theoretical approach which is embodied in Pigou's postulate of the existence of a well-defined 'Elasticity of the Real Demand for Labour'. Arriving at this concept involves the comparative-static discussion of total labour demand in a reduced form of the model just outlined. The differentials of the relevant variables are given by equ. (9.8),

$$\begin{bmatrix} \Omega_1 & \Omega_2 & -\Omega_x & -\Omega_y & 0 \\ 1 & 0 & -F' & 0 & \frac{w}{p_x} \\ 0 & 1 & 0 & -G' & 0 \\ 0 & 0 & -F'' & 0 & 0 \\ 0 & 0 & -1 & -1 & 1 \end{bmatrix} \begin{bmatrix} dQ_{xk} \\ dQ_y \\ dx \\ dy \\ dn \end{bmatrix} = \begin{bmatrix} 0 \\ -n \\ 0 \\ -1 \\ 0 \end{bmatrix} d\left(\frac{w}{p_x}\right) \qquad (9.8)$$

where the Ωs stand for derivatives of equation(a) in Table 9.1 in the following way:

$$(a)\ \Omega_1 \equiv \frac{U_1^k U_{21}^k - U_2^k U_{11}^k}{(U_1^k)^2} > 0;\ (b)\ \Omega_2 \equiv \frac{U_1^k U_{22}^k - U_2^k U_{12}^k}{(U_1^k)^2} < 0 \qquad (9.9)$$

Table 9.1 The reconstructed Pigovian model

(a)	$\dfrac{U_2^k}{U_1^k} = \dfrac{F'(x)}{G'(y)}$
(b)	$Q_{xk} = F(x) - n\dfrac{w}{p_x}$
(c)	$Q_y = G(y)$
(d)	$\dfrac{w}{p_x} = F'(x)$
(e)	$n = x + y$

and

$$\text{(a) } \Omega_x \equiv \frac{F''}{G''} < 0; \quad \text{(b) } \Omega_y \equiv -\frac{F'G''}{(G')^2} > 0. \tag{9.10}$$

The sign values of these expression follow because marginal utilities U_1^k resp. U_2^k are assumed to be positive but falling so that $U_{11}^k < 0$ and $U_{22}^k < 0$ holds but cross derivatives are positive. Likewise it is assumed that marginal productivities F' and G' are positive but falling so that $F'' < 0$ and $G'' < 0$ holds.

On the basis of the definitions discussed above and on the basis of system (9.8) we now obtain the crucial derivative

$$\frac{dn}{d\left(\dfrac{w}{p_x}\right)} = \frac{\phi'(x)}{F''(x)} = \frac{\left|D_{\left(\frac{w}{p_x}\right)}\right|}{|D|} < 0 \tag{9.11}$$

where $|D|$ is the characteristic determinant of system (9.8), namely

$$|D| = -F''(\underset{+}{\Omega_1} \frac{w}{p_x} - \underset{-}{\Omega_2 G'} + \underset{+}{\Omega_y}) > 0 \tag{9.12}$$
$$\quad +$$

and where

$$\left|D_{\left(\frac{w}{p_x}\right)}\right| = \underset{+}{\Omega_1}(nF'' - F') + \underset{-}{\Omega_2 G'} - \underset{+}{\Omega_y} < 0 \tag{9.13}$$

is the determinant which is obtained when the right-hand column in equ. (9.8) replaces the last column in the left-hand matrix of (9.8).

The important outcome of this somewhat involved exercise is that it shows that equ. (9.11) has a determined negative value if standard neoclassical assumptions are made. This is remarkable because it shows that Pigou (1933) is quite correct in insisting on the existence of a negative relationship between sectoral, *microeconomic*, workers' real wages on the one hand and total employment on the other. This follows from rather general 'classical' choice theoretic assumptions as was shown in our 'reconstruction' of the Pigovian model.

This detailed demonstration is necessary as long as we have an accusation against Pigou of adhering to a 'Ricardian Vice' of not recognising the 'illogical nature' of his theory because it is allegedly 'impossible to map' microeconomic relationships on the aggregate level, as quoted above on p. 50. This claim is not warranted. One does not understand the thinking of Pigou if one does not understand the reasoning behind equ. (9.11).

From this expression it follows also that – under Pigovian assumptions – there is a well-defined $\phi'(x)$-function, since multiplying equ. (9.11) with F'' gives

$$\phi'(x) = \frac{\Omega_1(nF'' - F') + \Omega_2 G' - \Omega_y}{-(\Omega_1 \frac{w}{Px} - \Omega_2 G' + \Omega_y)} > 0 \qquad (9.14)$$

where the Ωs have the above defined values.

Thus the essential analytical parts of Pigou (1933) fall here into place. It was demonstrated here that the functional relations which are central for the employment theoretic argumentation in Pigou (1933) must be seen as being based on quite a complex model as summarised in Table 9.1. As stated by Keynes already in the slightly different context discussed above, this Pigovian analysis is based indeed on a conglomerate of technological conditions as expressed through the shape of the *F*- and *G*-functions and of preferences as expressed through the utility function $U^k(.)$.

But under standard neoclassical assumptions it can be shown that in this extended analytical context, too, the partial analytical result holds, that labour demand is a determinate negative function of the real wage which has to be paid to workers.

9.2.3 Some simplifications – a constant elasticities approach

The above reconstruction of the Pigovian model does indeed generate the central relations and conclusions discussed by Pigou (1933). But the expressions (9.8) to (9.14) on the preceding pages which do demonstrate the general validity of his claims are so involved and cumbersome that they ask for simplification. Such simplifications always require more or less 'heroic' assumptions. Pigou (1933) himself went to the extreme of postulating numerical values for the macroeconomic elasticities under discussion. The consequence was that many of his readers were at a loss about the implicit analysis. Some of his simplifications exposed him to ridicule for allegedly returning to a pre-Marshallian wage fund theory.[2] Less drastic simplifications could concern the structure of the model by transforming it into a single-sector model.[3] But Pigou's main point was to stress that such an argumentation is not warranted, that care must be taken not to simply equate sectoral and total functional relations in an economy. Therefore the single-sector approach is not appropriate.

The *desideratum* for a simplified reconstruction of the Pigou (1933)-model is that it preserves enough of the neoclassics which obviously is at the basis of this model and that it also preserves some of the two-sectoral complexity which is the main concern of its author. The solution for these requirements is to assume constant algebraic values for the strategic elasticities on the microeconomic sectoral level. The total analytical relations may then be demonstrated to contain these sectoral parametric expressions in a specific way, permitting simple comparative static discussions of the total model.

Under this approach we define the elasticities of production

$$\alpha_x \equiv \frac{xF'(x)}{F(x)}; \alpha_y \equiv \frac{yG'(y)}{G(y)} \qquad (9.15)$$

and the elasticities of utility

$$\gamma_x \equiv \frac{Q_{xk}U^k_{Qxk}}{U^k(Q_{xk},Q_y)}; \; \gamma_y \equiv \frac{Q_yU^k_{Q_y}}{U^k(Q_{xk},Q_y)} \qquad (9.16)$$

These elasticity expression may now be rearranged in order to substitute the respective marginal productivities and marginal utilities in equ. (9.7) on p. 61. Those equations may then be rewritten as

$$\left(\gamma_x\frac{U^k(\cdot)}{Q_y}\right):\left(\gamma_x\frac{U^k(\cdot)}{Q_{xk}}\right)=\left(\alpha_x\frac{F(x)}{x}\right):\left(\alpha_y\frac{G(y)}{y}\right) \qquad (9.17)$$

Replacing $F(x)$ resp. $G(y)$ by Q_x resp. Q_y, then dividing out the Q_y-s and the U^k-s and finally rearranging gives equ. (9.18) while equ. (8.9) gives equ. (9.19):

$$\frac{Q_{xk}}{Q_1} = \frac{\gamma_x}{\gamma_y}\frac{\alpha_x}{\alpha_y}\frac{y}{x} \qquad (9.18)$$

$$\frac{Q'_{xk}}{Q_1} = 1-n\frac{F'(x)}{F(x)} = 1-\frac{n}{x}\alpha_x \qquad (9.19)$$

Equating now (9.18) and (9.19) and eliminating y in (9.18) via (8.10) on p. 55 gives, after some further elementary manipulation, a relationship between n and x reading

$$n = \frac{\alpha_x\gamma_x + \alpha_y\gamma_y}{\alpha_x\gamma_x + \alpha_x\alpha_y\gamma_y}x = \phi(x); \text{ with } E^{\phi(x)}_x = 1 \qquad (9.20)$$

as a version of the Pigovian $\phi(x)$-function. Equation (9.20) is the sought simplification of the Pigovian model as given by Table 9.1 on p. 62 resp. by system (9.8). The fraction in equ. (9.20) is a simplification of the corresponding one given in the more general terms of equ. (9.14).

The $\phi(x)$-function of equ. (9.20) gives a straight line from the origin, since its coefficient has only constant values. Thus it has unit elasticity throughout, as stated right beside that function. If we now substitute this unit value for $E^{\phi(x)}_x$ in equ. (9.4) and if we further substitute there the value for $E^{F'(x)}_x$ by $1/\eta$ as given by equ. (9.5), we see immediately that

$$E_r|_{\text{Cobb-Douglas}} = \eta = \frac{-1}{1-\alpha_x}, \qquad (9.21)$$

i.e. that in this simplified case of generalised Cobb–Douglas type constant elasticities the *total* elasticity of the real demand for labour is the same as the *sectoral* one as given by η, respectively by α_x where this last result follows immediately from the definition of such production functions.[4] This result holds although the sectoral elasticity of production α_y in the non-wage goods sector might be quite different from that in the wage good sector. Thus this formulation does heed Pigou's concern that sectoral differences must be taken account of – a point which entered in particular the formulation of equ. (9.20).

With the present version of the Pigovian $\phi(x)$-function we thus are led to believe that we have found a satisfactory compromise between authenticity and simplicity and we will make it the basis of the further discussion of Pigou's classical theory of employment. For convenience's sake we briefly state its main comparative static characteristics as given by

$$n = \phi(x; \underset{+}{\alpha_x}, \underset{-}{\alpha_y}, \underset{+}{\frac{\gamma_y}{\gamma_x}}) \qquad (9.22)$$

where signs under a variable denote the sign value of its respective partial derivative. Put verbally, the present version of this function states that the following relationships hold:

- Total labour demand n is a monotonously increasing function of sectoral employment x.
- A change in technology in the wage goods sector due to an increase in the elasticity of production α_x leads to decreased total labour demand.
- A change in technology in the non-wage goods sector due to an increase in the elasticity of production α_y leads to increased total labour demand.
- A change in preferences so that non-wage goods become more attractive to their users due to an increase in the elasticity of utility of non-wage goods relative to the one for wage goods as expressed by the ratio γ_y/γ_x leads to an increase in total labour demand.

In a comparatively simple framework which we built up from a microeconomic reduction of the Pigovian model we have thus reconstructed a function which may be considered as being an essential element of Pigou (1933) and hence of his contemporary academic macroeconomic theory of employment, namely of his 'Elasticity of the Real Demand for Labour'.

9.2.4 A graphical representation of Pigovian labour demand

A graphical rendering of the discussion covered so far is given in Figure 9.1. It depicts the sectoral production function $F(x)$. The input of $\bar{x}$ workers in this sector is determined through the real wage $F'(x) = \tan \angle \alpha$, i.e. through the tangency point I. on $F(x)$. Total employment $n = x + y$, depicted on the horizontal axis. Then the stretch to the north of point T must be the total

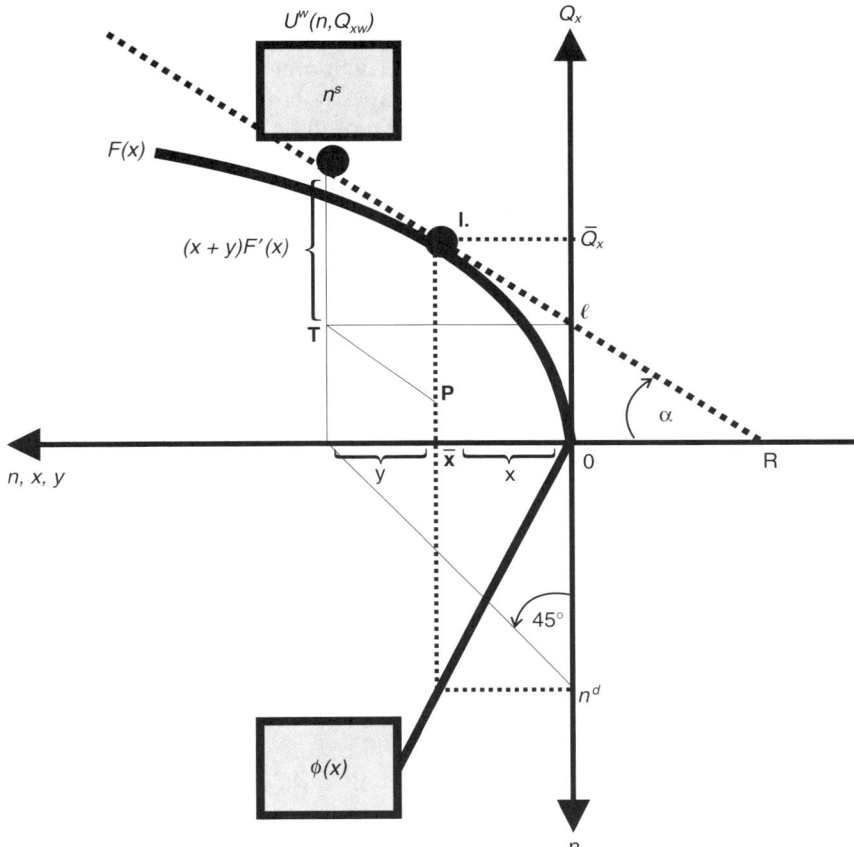

Figure 9.1 The Pigovian labour demand model

real wage bill. Because if tan $\angle$ **TℓI.** = tan $\angle\alpha$ = $F'(x)$, then the said stretch must be $(x + y) F'(x)$ so that this side over **Tℓ** = $x + y$ gives tan α = $F'(x)$. This total wages bill must at least be covered by the production of the wages good sector. In this case the amount of production which goes to workers is **I.P**, the 'wage-fund, as we may call it' in Pigou's unfelicitous words.[5] The rest of wage goods production, **P$\bar{\mathrm{x}}$**, is the 'trading surplus' of non-workers in Pigou's words.[6]

On top of this fairly straightforwardly neoclassical system are two 'black boxes': the $\phi(x)$-curve, relating sectoral employment x to $x + y = n^d$ in the lower quadrant and the 'labour supply' box n^s in the upper quadrant. We attempted to elucidate the $\phi(x)$-curve in the present chapter. We will deal with the labour supply doctrine in the next chapter, indicated here already with $U^w(n, Q_{xw})$ that this must have something to do with neoclassical utility analysis.

If we accept this figure as it stands for the moment – i.e. without filling the 'black boxes' – then the implications are straightforward: the $\phi(x)$-curve shows that any increase in employment n requires also an increase in x. But such an increase requires that the 'real wage point' I. on $F(x)$ moves away from the origin. This in turn requires lower α-values, i.e. lower real wages. In short: no higher employment without lower real wages – unless, of course, the functions themselves are altered, but this will be a matter to be dealt with later.

9.3 The reception of the Pigovian theory of employment

With the result just stated we have passed the first of the authenticity tests announced in ch. 7 above. Before we turn to the second one concerning Keynes' reception of this model, we want to add a few further reflections on our particular reconstruction of the Pigovian model.

9.3.1 The comprehensiveness of the reconstructed Pigovian model

First of all, there might be the feeling that this model cannot be all that there was to Pigou's lengthy monograph on unemployment. To which further uses did he put this model and what alternative to or elaboration of this model did he advance? To this question we want to respond briefly in stating that the primary concern in the present discussion is to re-create the most important theoretical elements in the debate between Pigou and Keynes. And it was indeed one of the main contentions of Keynes that this was essentially all that there was to Pigou's (1933) 'classical' theory of employment.[7]

As already mentioned, in part III below we will see that Pigou (1937) later sanctioned this view to a certain extent, so we will not now discuss the justification of it at greater length.

9.3.2 Intertemporal analysis and the characteristics of Pigovian non-wage goods

The particular problems which Pigou's exposition poses might be illustrated with reference to the intertemporal aspects of his model. In our reconstruction, we have abstained from the modelling of any intertemporal aspect of his theory, treating implicitly his non-wage goods as a luxury item and the economy as a whole as a stationary one with unchanging capital stock. In doing so we tacitly anticipated the analytical setup which Pigou (1935) did in fact use in his *The Economics of Stationary States*. A further case in point will be discussed below in part III. Pigou (1933, e.g. p. 249) does occasionally refer to investment in capital goods so that one could doubt the appropriateness of our procedure. But when Pigou (1933,

p. 83) discusses 'the representative non-wage-earner who invests in hiring labor', he simplifies matters by postulating that he 'expects to have the same income and the same tastes in the future that he has now' – and Pigou never clarifies how he reconciles this postulate with the assumption of positive investment. Actually, Pigou (1933, p. 145) was convinced that from the standpoint of his theory of employment it did not matter whether non-wage goods were luxury goods or investment goods, stating:

> Just as there is no net addition to the aggregate demand for labour, and so to employment, if wage-goods are shifted to road-making from machine-making, so also there is no net addition if they are shifted to it from the making of luxury motor cars or silk dressing-gowns.

Therefore we feel justified in simplifying matters in treating his non-wage goods *in toto* just as luxury goods.[8]

9.3.3 Solow's single-sector interpretation of the Pigovian model

But there is one possible simplification in the reception of Pigou (1933) against which we would like to warn as unacceptable. In commenting on him in his address 'On Theories of Employment', Solow (1980, p. 6) tried to relate him to the presently common practice of discussing macroeconomic employment problems with reference to a single macroeconomic production function:

> Let me remind you that in the old standby, two factor Cobb–Douglas case, the elasticity of demand for labor with respect to the real wage is the reciprocal of the share of capital. Every body's back-of-the-envelope puts the capital share at $\frac{1}{4}$ and the elasticity of demand for labor at 4. This is not exactly the way Pigou proceeds, but he reaches the same conclusion. (emphasis added, GMA.)

The argumentation in this quote is that in the Cobb–Douglas case mentioned, macroeconomic output is given by

$$Q = AN^\alpha K^{1-\alpha} \quad \text{with} \quad F_N \equiv \frac{dQ}{dN} = \alpha AN^{\alpha-1} K^{1-\alpha} \qquad (9.23)$$

where A = efficiency parameter, N = aggregate employment, K = capital input and where α resp. $1 - \alpha$ are the elasticities of production of these two factors. It is well known that under the assumption of perfect competition these parameters represent the share in total output going to the respective factors so that the share of capital is given by $1 - \alpha$. But then the real wage $w/p = F_N$ has the elasticity

$$E_N^{F_N} = \alpha - 1 \qquad (9.24)$$

or rather its inverse has the value

$$(E_N^{F_N})^{-1} = E_{(w/p)}^{N} = \frac{-1}{1-\alpha} \qquad (9.25)$$

The denominator in this expression is just the share of capital in output as Solow pointed out in the quote.

Since it was shown above (see equ. (9.21) on p. 65) that in Pigou's analytical set-up one might also reduce his 'Elasticity of the Real Demand for Labour' to an inverse of an elasticity of the marginal productivity of labour, Solow might seem to be justified to see a correspondence between his argumentation leading to expression (9.25) and the one in Pigou (1933). But the last sentence in this quote seems to indicate that Solow is conscious that this is not quite an authentic representation. It is based on casual empiricism and not on analytical argumentation.

It is true that Pigou (1933, pp. 92ff.) does get involved in a lengthy discussion of the realistic values of his elasticity and in this regard there might indeed be seen a correspondence between him and Solow. But one of Pigou's important points is that total and sectoral analysis is *not* identical. Even in the simplified case of equ. (9.21) it emerged that it is the *sectoral* elasticity of production α_x which is of relevance. A macroeconomic analogue was never proposed by Pigou, at least not in this context. In an authentic reproduction of his analysis this difference must be insisted upon.

9.3.4 The wage fund interpretation

There is a long tradition of associating Pigou's labour demand theory with a 'variation of the wage-fund doctrine' as stated by Aslanbeigui (1992, p. 420). This tradition can be traced way back to Harrod (1934, p. 21) who ridiculed Pigou for his 'Wage-Goods Fund theory':

> This revival [of the 'old Wage Fund theory', GMA] is a welcome one. 'Popular writers' have been in the habit of stating that the old classical theories of this type have been long since disproved and superseded by the marginal productivity theory.[9] Such statements are both erroneous and harmful. These old theories are firmly founded on tautology, and may well prove, as is evidenced by Professor Pigou's book, to be most useful analytical tools.

There can be hardly a more facetious compliment paid to Pigou (1933) than to praise this book for its good use of 'old theories' based on tautology.[10] If our 'Marshallian reconstruction' is correct, then it appears to be quite ridiculous to bring Pigou (1933) into opposition to the marginal productivity theory. But it must be admitted that to a certain extent Pigou (1933, pp. 143f.) has to blame himself for being thus ridiculed, because he claimed:

When the real rate of wage stipulated for is given, the quantity of labour demanded in the aggregate of all industries varies, and can only vary, in precise proportion to the quantity of wage-goods available for, and devoted to the payment of, wages.

Pigou himself (*ibid.*) defines this quantity as 'the wage-fund, as we may call it'. But what goes on analytically behind this terminology? In order to answer this question, let us return to the employment function based on constant elasticities, i.e. to equ. (9.20) on p. 65. We rewrite it as

$$n = \frac{x}{\alpha_x} \cdot const. = \frac{F(x)}{F'(x)} \cdot const. \tag{9.26}$$

where $\alpha_x \cdot const.$ is equal to the fraction in equ. (9.20) and where x/α_x in the first equation is replaced according to the definition given in equ. (9.15) on p. 65 giving the second of these equations.

On this basis, two alternative formulations are possible, using the marginal productivity theory in the form $F'(x) = w/p_x$, namely

$$n \frac{w}{p_x} = const. \cdot Q_x \quad \text{or} \quad \text{alternatively} \quad n = const. \frac{p_x Q_x}{w} \tag{9.27}$$

where $Q_x = F(x)$.

The first of these variants shows now the correctness of Pigou's passage just quoted: if the real wage rate relevant for workers (w/p_x) is given, then total employment n can vary if and only if Q_x, the amount of wage-goods varies. All this follows clearly from an analysis based on *neoclassical* elasticities of production and of utilities given by the α-s and by the γ-s entering the constant value of proportionality. It is therefore *not* warranted to accuse Pigou of returning to pre-neoclassical analysis in the context of his 'wage-fund' doctrine. The most plausible explanation of this passage is that it is based on a model which makes liberal use of parametrically given partial elasticities of utility and of production.

It is therefore not the case that Pigou returned to pre-marginalistic 'tautology'. Quite the contrary, he 'de-tautologised' logical possibilities by implying assumptions like equ (9.26). They are ultimately based not on tautology but on behavioural assumptions and on reality. In some passages Harrod affirms the qualifications just stated. Nevertheless, his 'praise' does not seem to have endeared his later writings to Pigou, as emerges from interesting passages in Young (1989, pp 61f.) and from the correspondence betwen Keynes and Pigou in the wake of Harrod (1939).[11]

10
Keynes' Internal Critique of Pigou and the Classics

The last chapter offered the Pigou-oriented 'authenticity test' for our reconstruction of the Pigovian model of ch. 8. The present chapter will see the corresponding Keynes-oriented test. The working hypothesis in this attempt is that Keynes had a perception of the classical view of the workings of an economy very similar to the one embodied in the model set out above in ch. 8.

Since the model of ch. 8 was built on Marshallian analytical foundations there is, of course, the question whether the Keynes of the *General Theory* may indeed be seen as being sufficiently linked to the Marshallian tradition in order to justify such an approach. It might be argued that this is not a controversial question anymore ever since Leijonhufvud (1968, p. 50) observed that 'Keynes was very Marshallian'. But what does such a *dictum* mean – and how far is it accepted in the relevant literature?

The answer to such questions may be sought on interpretational lines which are either predominantly text-oriented or on more analytical lines. Both lines will be followed below. Section 10.1 will deal with the question whether it is sensible to construct a link between Keynes and Marshall if *Marshall* was never interested in the type of macroeconomic problems which Keynes tried to address. This Marshallian lack of interest is occasionally claimed in the literature, as we will document below, but it will emerge that such a concern is not warranted. After this is established, section 10.2 then shifts the perspective and asks whether *Keynes* did in fact *apply* the Marshallian analytical approach when he discussed the 'classics', i.e. when he criticised Pigou.

Sections 10.1 and 10.2 are meant to give 'chapter and verse' for justifying the analysis which then follows. In section 10.4 it will be argued that one aspect of Keynes' criticism of Pigou – his 'internal' critique – was that he claimed that the *Theory of Unemployment* was lacking in Marshallian general equilibrium perspective and that the Pigovian model had to be completed along specific analytical lines to be discussed in the following.

The resulting model generates a number of comparative-static results concerning employment. The discussion in section 10.5 then constitutes the here intended 'Keynes-oriented authenticity test' of our classical reconstruction.

Section 10.6 will finally restate the basic pattern of this 'internal' Keynesian criticism of classical economics.

10.1 Keynes, Pigou and the Marshallian conception of general equilibrium

The insight that Keynes is acknowledged as having been a competent Marshallian economist does not carry us very far so long as it is not also made clear what exactly Marshallian analysis is. Marshall's *Principles of Economics* is a masterpiece in partial analytical economics. But what does this tradition imply for the type of macroeconomic problems to which Keynes addressed himself in the *General Theory*?

It seems that among those economists who reflect about the Marshallian tradition, some might subscribe to the view articulated by Robert Clower (1975, p. 4) that '[Marshall] never felt the need to model the workings of the economic system as a whole.'

In this section we want to argue against such a view, however, because it might lead to the unwarranted impression that Keynes and Pigou, insofar as they stood in the Marshallian tradition, could not be related to the concept of a general equilibrium representation of an economic system.

A view quite different from the one just quoted is to be found in Schumpeter's *History of Economic Analysis* where Schumpeter (1954, p. 836) refers to a passage from Alfred Marshall's *Memorials* in which Marshall (1925, p. 417) emphatically communicated to his famous American colleague J. B. Clark: 'My whole life has been given and will be given to presenting in realistic form as much as I can of my Note "XXI".' This 'Note XXI' is in the appendix to Marshall's *Principles* and it is remarkable that Marshall could state that it contains his life's ambition in economics. A casual reader or normal student of the *Principles* could not grasp the enormous significance which Marshall seems to attribute to it. This note has a rather technical appearance. It is concerned with the determinateness of a system of interdependent demand and supply equations. Marshall concludes there that because of an equality of equations and endogenous variables 'the problem' is always 'determinate'.

The argumentation in that note has essential elements of a general equilibrium theory so that Schumpeter (1954, p. 920, n. 1) could comment about this note:

> the contents of 'note xxi' ... constitute the core of Marshall's theoretical analysis. This note blocks out a system of general equilibrium.

According to Schumpeter, the general equilibrium perspective certainly was deeply entrenched in Marshall's own mind.

Thus, contrary to what Clower (1975, p. 4) claimed, there is strong evidence that Marshall worked out the formal prerequisite for a general equilibrium theory and that he considered his life's aim to be giving a realistic rendering of that formalism. There seems to be little room for doubt that Schumpeter (1954, p. 836) is right when he concludes:

> It seems fair, therefore, to list Marshall also among the builders of the general-equilibrium system.

The analytical substance generally subsumed under the notion of 'general equilibrium' thus seems to be an important element of the Marshallian tradition.

But even if it can be substantiated beyond reasonable doubt that Marshall himself was strongly committed to the idea of general equilibrium, there remains the question whether this Marshallian commitment had any relevance for his disciples Keynes and Pigou. In this connection it is now important to note that it was not Marshall himself but his disciple A. C. Pigou, who – as editor of Marshall (1925) – published Marshall's confession of being a devotee of the idea of general equilibrium as expressed in 'Note XXI'. Furthermore, the preface of that publication reveals that these papers were chosen in close collaboration with none other than John Maynard Keynes. Thus there are indications that Keynes and Pigou – insofar as they considered themselves as standing in the Marshallian tradition – must have been aware that in that tradition the ultimate analytical reference for their theories – if they were to be of relevance for an economy as a whole – must be a system of general 'determinate' equilibrium.

A close reading of Pigou (1933, pp. 296f.) will show indeed that he was more or less consciously aware of the general equilibrium nature of his model. In the passages just specified he discusses the connection between real wages and money wages and insists that 'one point should be added that is of significance analytically', namely

> the monetary factor ... affects the whole complex of balancing forces, and thereby brings it about that the real rate of wage stipulated for [on the one hand, GMA] and the quantity of labour demanded [on the other hand, GMA] are *both* modified. These movements, though bound together in a rigid nexus, are not successive links in a causal change, but joint effects of a process that stands behind them. (Pigou's emphasis)

The stress on the 'analytical significance' of a 'not-causal' but 'rigid' nexus relating to the 'real rate of wage' must appear as a flowery incantation of an atemporal comparative static model in the tradition of Marshallian general equilibrium analysis. In a section on Marshall's 'famous Note XXI' and his associated general equilibrium analysis, Niehans (1990, p. 241) points out:

> He [Marshall, GMA] never tired of emphasizing that economics is a field not of unidirectional causal chains but of mutual interdependence.

The passage from Pigou (1933) just inspected must appear as an echo of this very position, in particular in a book which its author presents as studying 'a simplified model of the economic world rather than that world itself' (Pigou, 1933, p. vi).

It might well be that 'Pigou did not, however, fully appreciate the analytic importance of that way of viewing matters' as Laidler (1999, p. 167) commented after a quote from the same context which is here under discussion. But in so viewing matters, Pigou invited to be evaluated along the general equilibrium lines the 'analytical significance' of which he stressed himself. We therefore conclude that it is not a violation of the spirit of 'historical reconstruction' if the debate between Keynes and Pigou is also seen in a general equilibrium context, especially when it comes to appreciate the criticism Keynes uttered against the model to be found in Pigou (1933).

10.2 Keynes' perspective on general equilibrium

It seems to be part of the exegetical folklore surrounding the *General Theory* that its critique of Pigou was formulated in a rather superficial manner, not doing sufficient justice to its analytical complexity. Thus, one commentator states (Aslanbeigui (1992, pp. 417f.)):

> Perhaps the reason why the *Theory of Unemployment* has been misinterpreted by Keynes and others is the fact that it is extremely 'tough and laborious' to read (Harrod, 1934, p. 19).

But if Harrod (1934) is quoted here as an authority as far as judgements about the *Theory of Unemployment* are concerned, then it must be noted that he gave ample comments on proofs of the *General Theory*. He certainly could have ironed out grave misconceptions about Pigou – if there were any. (See JMK, XIII, *passim*)

In fact, the charge that Keynes dealt superficially with Pigou's *Theory of Unemployment* is quite unfounded. In a letter to D. H. Robertson, Keynes claimed (see JMK, XIV, p. 87) that he 'took great care' in the *General Theory* when he criticised Pigou in the 'Appendix on Prof. Pigou's *Theory of Unemployment*'. Certainly Robertson must be considered as being an appropriate person to complain to if Keynes' criticism of Pigou (1933) is dismissed as being superficial, since, dating as far back as 3 September 1933, there is a voluminous correspondence about this book between him and

Keynes. The discussion went into considerable formal detail. (See JMK, XIII, *passim*)

From the publication of that correspondence we know by now that Keynes' initial critical reaction to Pigou (1933) may be seen as an application of the main theme of Marshall's 'Note XXI'. In Marshall's own words (Marshall (1920, p. 704)), this note was written 'with the object of making sure that our abstract theory has just as many equations as it has unknowns, neither more nor less'. It came to the conclusion that 'the problem', namely the solution for prices and quantities in the Marshallian model, was indeed 'determinate' because this condition was 'always' fulfilled. This was the way in which Marshall checked not only his own work but also that of others as was stressed by Niehans (1990, p. 241) in relating that

> Marshall 'described how he began his study of economics by expressing Ricardo and Mill in the form of equations and checking if he had enough equations to determine the unknowns'.

If Keynes read Pigou (1933) before such a Marshallian analytical background, the question quite likely to be raised could have been whether Pigou's model economy was really 'Marshallian' in this sense. In order to fulfil the Marshallian analytical requirements, Pigou's model must give a determinate solution in the context of a Marshallian analysis of supply and demand. The 'forces' of supply and demand may be seen either at work in a single household as outlined in A.4 of ch. 8 on p. 52 above or, more generally, in the general equilibrium framework of the maximisation of utility and profits in the interaction of economic agents.

In any case it was seen above in our Marshallian reconstruction of the Pigovian model that from that modelling of consumption and production decisions as expressed by equs. (8.1) to (8.11) (see pp. 54f. above) there resulted indeed a model with partial analytic microfoundations which was 'determinate' in the Marshallian sense in generating the same number of equations as endogenous variables. Among the endogenous variables were real wages (w/p_x) and employment (n), of course. Without a change in the parameters of the functions describing the economic model or some other exogenous shock no change would be possible in such a determinate model.

It seems now that in his initial reaction to Pigou (1933), Keynes approached that model indeed with the Marshallian understanding that if it is a complete economic model, real wages and employment must be treated as *endogenous*. How then could the real wage be thought to be *set* exogenously through wages policy? The following quote documents that Keynes assumed that the Pigovian model under discussion was indeed such a determinate 'Marshallian' model like the one which was outlined in ch. 8

above. But then a manipulation of employment through real wage changes could not be regarded as a sensible employment political measure, as he (JMK, XIII, p. 312) was to note in a letter to D. H. Robertson:

He [Pigou (1933)] arbitrarily takes two items, namely employment and real wages, out of a complex, but presumably determinate, system and then [– by formulating the elasticity E_r –] treats them, without proof or enquiry, as being analytic functions of one another. But they are not independent variables. If everything is given except real wages and employment, then neither real wages nor employment are capable of more than one value.

The strong Marshallian orientation of Keynes in his critique against Pigou (1933) and the importance which Keynes gave to the forces of demand and supply determining relative prices – and, in particular, real wages – might be appreciated further if we briefly inspect his critical exchange concerning labour supply which Keynes had with R. G. Hawtrey *after* the publication of the *General Theory*.

Hawtrey's defence of Pigou against some of the criticism in the *General Theory* resorted to questioning the concept of 'marginal disutility of labour' on principal grounds:

the marginal disutility of labour plays a very restricted part in the works of the great economists ... Has anyone ever brought it into relation with unemployment? Pigou does not mention it in that connection. (JMK, XIV, p. 18)

To this Keynes (JMK, XIV, p. 25) replied:

When ... you tell me that 'the marginal disutility of labour plays a very restricted part in the works of great economists' I am again simply staggered. The whole of Pigou's *Theory of (Un)Employment* ... is based on the level of employment being the resultant of what he calls the real demand for labour given by the schedule of the different quantities of labour, the marginal disutility of which is balanced by differing amounts of wage goods. Moreover, the whole of Marshall's theory is based on this and, above all, the whole of Jevon's theory. In fact, there is no other theory that I am acquainted with.

This Marshall–Jevons tradition of labour supply analysis was invoked above in the formulation of the 'reconstructed' Pigovian assumption A.4 (see p. 52 above). But this particular part of Keynes' understanding of Pigou – and of our reconstruction of his analytical elements – has repeatedly come under severe criticism which shall be taken account of in the following subsection.

Thus there seems to be further evidence that Keynes saw the classical theory in the context of Pigou (1933) as a theory of 'general equilibrium' very much along the lines of the Pigovian reconstruction of ch. 8 above.[1]

10.3 'Historical reconstructions' of Pigovian labour supply

10.3.1 Pigovian labour supply as focus for controversy

Hawtrey's claim that Keynes misrepresented Pigou in attributing to him labour supply considerations was recently revived. Echoing that old debate, Aslanbeigui (1992, p. 418) voiced the opinion that the

> first and crucial Keynesian misconception [concerning Pigou (1933)] surrounded the concept of labor-supply behavior ... Keynes had written *The General Theory* assuming Pigou's labor supply to be an increasing function of real wage rates.

As evidence for her judgement the author reproduces a depiction of a reverse L-shaped labour supply curve which Pigou sent to Keynes in May 1937 as a consequence of the Keynes–Hawtrey exchange just mentioned. Pigou proclaimed this to be *the* 'supply schedule of labour' which he assumed as being the relevant one for his *Theory of Unemployment* (letter published in JMK, XIV, p. 54).

One subsequent reader thought that Aslanbeigui (1992) was right in attributing a 'misconception' of Pigou (1933) to Keynes and that Keynes was indeed in error – but that this error was not 'crucial' (Cottrell, 1994, p. 686). Another reader (Brady, 1994, pp. 698, 699) thought that an examination of Pigou (1933) 'reveals Keynes's criticisms to be dead on target' and that 'Pigou's labor supply function must be ... the standard one.' Subsequently there have been a number of newer contributions to the history of economic thought, covering the time period relevant for the present enquiry, but none of them seems to have given a 'canonical' view of the relevant labour market model.

The exegetical debate of labour market analysis in Pigou (1933) and in the *General Theory* is likely to remain contentious because the original exposition in Pigou (1933) was not very clear, to say the least. Even Hawtrey, who was strongly in favour of defending the analytical position of Pigou against Keynes' criticisms, had to admit that Pigou's 'clarification' using the reverse L-shaped figure of labour supply was not very helpful. It did not follow from anything that was in fact written in Pigou (1933):

> how is any reader of the *Theory of Unemployment* to guess what Pigou has in mind, seeing that there is not a single word about it from the beginning of the book to the end? (Hawtrey in a letter published in JMK, XIV, p. 55)

In view of this situation an attempt at a 'historical reconstruction' is called for in the above sense of a context-sensitive re-creation of the economic doctrine which would fit into this particular phase of the historical development of economic thought.

Concerning labour supply doctrine at the time of Pigou's writing the *Theory of Unemployment*, it seems not unreasonable to invoke Robbins (1930, p. 123), who, in an article addressing expressly Frank Knight and A. C. Pigou, set out by stating:

> It is a generally accepted proposition of theoretical economics that the effects of a change in the terms on which incomes from work can be obtained depend upon the elasticity of demand for income in terms of effort.

In this context Robbins derives a labour supply curve as an 'offer curve' of workers who demand real income in the form of goods produced. He insists that labour supply is a corollary of such a demand curve and demonstrates that 'normal' goods demand – i.e. one which obeys the 'law of demand' – may go together with labour supply which either rises or falls when real wages rise in a comparative static context.

He then criticises (*ibid.* pp. 126, 128) Frank Knight and A. C. Pigou (*Economics of Welfare*, p. 593) for implicitly assuming *falling* supply curves for labour without giving sufficient evidence for such an assumption. Robbins (1930, p. 129) then reiterates:

> any attempt to predict the effect of a change in the terms on which income is earned must proceed by inductive investigation of elasticities. The attempt to narrow the limit of possible elasticities by *a priori* reasoning must be held to have broken down.

Robbins' contribution is interesting in the historical context for two reasons. On the one hand, it demonstrates that at least by 1930 Pigou was directly confronted with the consideration that if one contemplates demand for 'wage goods' it should be self-evident that the other side of the budget must contain wage income and hence labour supplied. On the other hand, Robbins' contribution stresses that the old Marshallian apparatus of demand and supply elasticities must be applied to labour supply as a general concept and that Pigou was not very circumspect in taking heed of this consideration.

There are no published reactions by Pigou. Thus we can only speculate what his immediate reaction might have been. Was Robbins (1930) the reason that soon after that article Pigou (1933, p. 6) went through all sorts of pseudo-empirical musings, such as about workers' wives being forced to go to work at low real wages and then returning to the domestic hearth when real wages rise? One might further wonder whether this article was the reason why Pigou (1933) was extremely hesitant to make any definitive statement about labour supply at all, thus avoiding a repetition of the charge that he made rash *a priori* statements about labour supply. In any case, it is Pigou's temporary reticence to make *any* outspoken statement about labour supply which could lead Hawtrey to believe that: 'the assumption [in Pigou (1933), GMA] is that there is no "supply function" at all' (Hawtrey in JMK, XIV, p. 39).

In view of the recent revival of interest in the Keynes–Hawtrey exchange about this matter it is important to stress that this belief is untenable for reasons of economic consistency (see Robbins (1930) and for reasons of historic authenticity. In fact Pigou *did* assume the existence of a labour supply curve, namely a reversed L-shaped one, as was just seen.

This observation should settle doubts about Keynes' fairness in attributing labour supply considerations to Pigou (1933): it was quite correct to do so. Indeed, it would have been rather unfair *not* to give Pigou the benefit of the doubt in conceding to him an implicit theory of labour supply if he wrote an entire monograph about the *Theory of Unemployment*. But the question is still open concerning the reasoning behind Pigou's reverse L-shaped version of labour supply. Did he propagate this particular labour supply curve because it kept the middle ground between the falling curve which Robbins (1930, p. 128) detected in Pigou on the one hand and the rising curve which Pigou (1935) later did assume? Was Pigou aware that in his book of the year 1935 he made just that assumption about labour supply which Keynes attributed to him when he wrote about Pigovian labour supply one year later in the *General Theory*?

These questions are largely intractable since there was no published reaction from Pigou to Robbins' criticism. The lack of guidance given by Pigou (1933) himself flabbergasted even his faithful defendant Hawtrey, as was seen above. In this situation it seems to be quite correct that Keynes invoked the canonical teachings on labour supply of 'great economists' (see above, p. 77). In his view they were the basis for understanding the essential but sometimes only implicitly stated assumptions in Pigou (1933). In the following subsection 10.3.2 we suggest looking somewhat closer at the canonical teachings on household behaviour in the light of what has been just stated about 'reverse L-shaped' labour supply.

If we check the results of the present restatement by invoking the reception of the canonical teachings in Joan Robinson's (1937a) contemporary contribution about the theory of employment, we see a solid family resemblance (see below, subsection 10.3.3). Although the style of argumentation is admittedly somewhat different – Joan Robinson does not go back to the choice theoretic foundations of the model in great detail – we nevertheless can register by and large consistent assumptions about the labour supply curve.

There are some modifying considerations concerning the 'floor' of labour supply which are suggested by some earlier statements made by Pigou (1927) concerning the role of trade unions. These considerations may also be incorporated into the model here under discussion as will be seen in subsection 10.3.4. But they are at odds with the concept of 'involuntary unemployment in the strict sense'. The canonical model here under discussion gives the opportunity to look closer at this concept which was originally coined by none other than Pigou himself.

All these considerations suggest that Keynes was quite correct when he pointed out that aspects of labour supply – and its frustration in conditions of involuntary unemployment – should have found more explicit formulations than the ones given by Pigou (1933) originally. The consequence of this conclusion leads then to a logical extension of the Pigovian system which will be further discussed in section 10.4, p. 92 below.

10.3.2 The canonical pleasure–pain model of labour supply

As Keynes pointed out in his exchange with Hawtrey quoted above, with regard to labour supply 'there is no other theory' but the utility–disutility model – pleasure–pain model for short – which was cultivated over decades by such authors as Jevons, Marshall and by Pigou as well. Modern textbooks refer in this context more to a model involving the choice between two positive experiences, namely the enjoyment of leisure and the consumption of products.[2] It is the latter type of model which nowadays may be considered to be the 'canonical' one. But formally the two types of household models are quite similar and the distinction need not occupy us here.[3]

Jevons' model had an additive utility function with labour as 'bad' giving disutility or negative utility and with real income as 'good' the consumption of which giving positive utility. Individual labour supply is then conceived as the outcome of optimising behaviour in this framework.

Figure 10.1 represents a variant of that type of model in the upper part and an ensuing labour supply curve in the lower part.[4] The indifference curve marked $\bar{U}$ in the upper part is typical for a choice involving pain (labour, N) and pleasure (wage goods, Q_x).

Given a real wage $w/p_x = \tan \angle \alpha$, the attainable set for the household is represented by the grey triangle in the upper part. Its lower bound is defined by a 'starvation level' of consumption Q_x^-. Labour can only be supplied up to the 'exhaustion level' $L-$.

The household's equilibrium point is given by E^* on the indifference curve $\bar{U}$. If the elasticity of substitution between N and Q_x has the value of unity ($\sigma = 1$), then the *locus* of equilibria is a straight line when the real wage rate changes. It goes through points E and E^*. It translates into a straight labour supply curve $N^s E'$ in the lower quadrant. This black line turns into a grey one when real wages drop very low. The reason is that

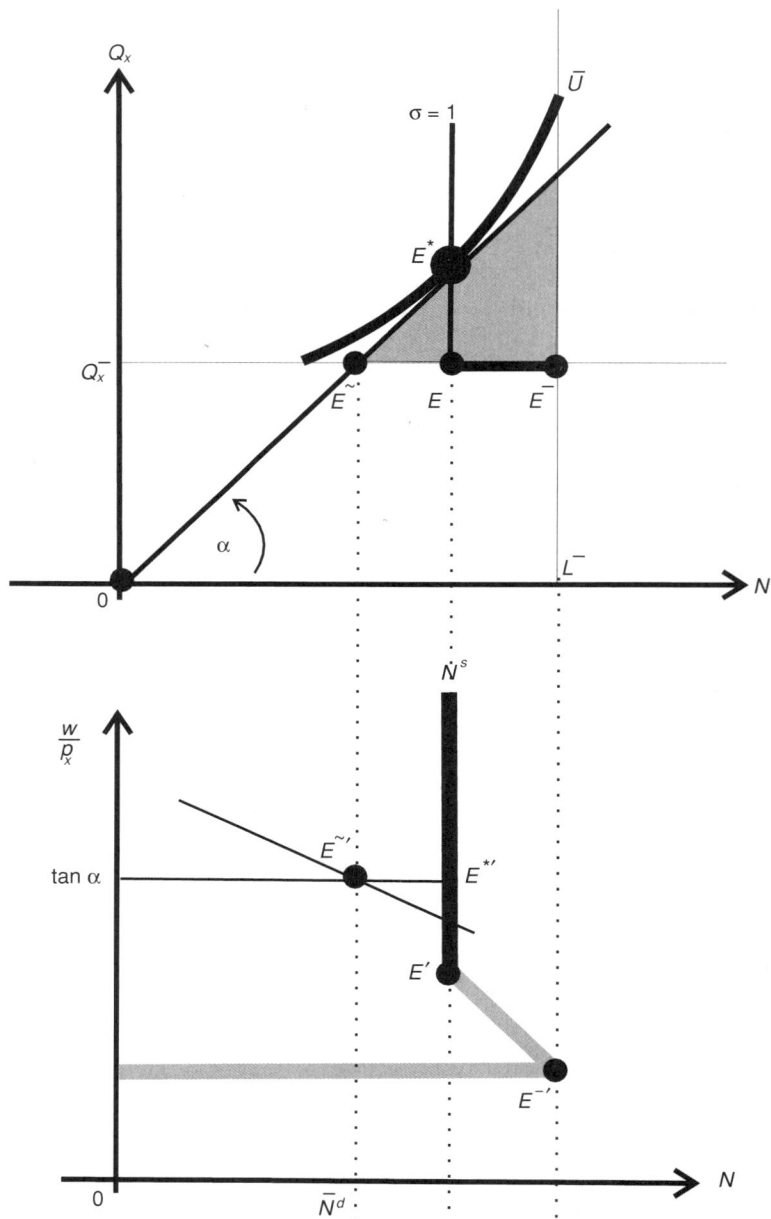

Figure 10.1 Preferences and Pigovian labour supply

here the constraint is different because household choices are eventually limited by the 'starvation level' of food and by the 'exhaustion level' of work $(L-)$ – considerations which are not relevant in the former case. The food-constrained equilibria are given by the *locus E* to E^- in the upper figure, translating into a *falling* labour supply curve where workers labour for mere survival, sending wives and maybe even children to work because of dire need.[5] This type of labour supply might be the one Marx had occasion to describe in *Capital* ('Marxian drudgery': stretch E' to $E^-{}'$). Clearly in such circumstances marginalistic labour supply conditions are obsolete because labour supply is not preference-determined but physiologically determined. If real wages drop even further, workers are totally exhausted and die or emigrate or become criminal ('Irish famine case': horizontal line through $E^-{}'$) – in any case, they leave the labour market. According to the letter of Pigou to Keynes containing the reverse L-shaped labour supply curve, Pigou's unemployment may be interpreted to occur on the horizontal 'starvation/exhaustion wage' stretch.[6]

There are some – somewhat abstract – points one could make about unemployment in this analytical context: if there was unemployment in the sense that workers want to work but do not find employment for real wages higher than the ones associated with point E resp. E' and if competition among workers were really great and if they could really influence the real wage, there is a tendency that the employed workers must content themselves with the starvation / exhaustion wage. The rest *do* starve in the long run (and solve the unemployment problem by *exitus* from the labour market). This seems to be the old 'iron law of wages', according to which workers cannot rise above the subsistence wage. This observation gives a somewhat cynical view on the phenomenon of unemployment in the just stated sense: if such a situation does exist and if real wages are not rigid, then there must be a tendency towards the starvation wage floor. If even at that low level of real wages there is unemployment in this sense, then it can only be a short-period phenomenon, because those prospective workers who do not find employment at that level will obtain no food and hence 'leave' the labour market in some way or another. Thus, if this model is thought to its market analytical end, it seems to be able to say: either unemployment is only a temporary problem in the above sense or it is an adjustment problem in the sense that falling real wages cannot do their equilibrating (or exterminating) job.

As we will see presently, this type of argumentation played a certain role when Joan Robinson (1937a, p. 119) presented the received labour supply theory. She referred to it as the 'Malthusian view'. But one may ask whether this variant of the labour supply model really does meet the *spirit* of the situation to which Pigou (1933) intended to refer. Unemployment in Great Britain of the 1930s was not comparable to the situation at the time of the Great Irish Famine of the 1840s or to the situation of the working of the 'iron law of wages'. Thus it does not seem to be 'mistaken' if Keynes did not think along 'iron law of wages' lines in reading Pigou (1933), particularly since there is not a word about this particular conception of unemployment in the entire book, as Hawtrey testified.

10.3.3 Joan Robinson's rendering of received labour supply doctrine

Although of doubtful actuality, the 'iron law of wages' argument for a horizontal stretch of the labour supply curve did have proponents in the British labour supply theory of the 1930s and Joan Robinson (1937a, p. 119, n. 1), in a section on 'The Supply Curve of Labour' relates, among others, these views and also alternative ones:

> In the simple Malthusian view the supply of workers is perfectly elastic at a certain wage, representing the minimum standard of life ... Professor Pigou (*Stationary States*, p. 167) restates the Malthusian argument in terms not of a physical minimum but of a customary standard of life ...
>
> It is sometimes argued that in the Western world the Malthusian law is reversed (cf. Robertson, *Economic Fragments*, p. 16) and that a community which has become accustomed to an improved standard of life will experience a decline in the birth rate.

Joan Robinson (*ibid.*) rejects, however, both the 'Malthusian law' which could explain a lower floor to labour supply and the 'reverse Malthusian law' which could explain a back bending of labour supply due to diminished population because she regards population as independent of real wages. Nevertheless, after some further discussions, some of them on the basis of labour–leisure choice considerations as just mentioned, she does propose the labour supply curve of Fig. 10.2. The horizontal stretch in the lower part of our Fig. 10.1 is here a slightly rising one, the pointed 'nose' of our stretch $E^{-\prime}$ E' is smoothed out and rounded and our vertical stretch is now a backward bending one. This shape corresponds to the labour supply curve as drawn by Robbins (1930) in the already mentioned context as an offer curve in terms of effort supplied and real income demanded. This type of curve then seems to express a generally held view about labour supply at that time.

Joan Robinson (1937a, p. 122) stresses, however, that this is only the *locus* for full employment points. It is possible that:

> either Trade Union policy or spontaneous feeling dictate a minimum level of real wages, such that workers will *prefer* to face the hardship of unemployment rather than accept it'. (emphasis added, GMA)

In that case a highly elastic lower part of such a curve will then express not full employment *loci* but minimum wage ones which could entail unemployment in the just stated sense.[7]

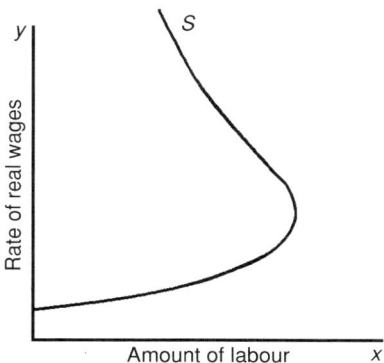

Figure 10.2 Joan Robinson's view of the labour supply curve

There are some indications that it is in the latter sense that Pigou wanted to see his labour supply curve to be understood.

10.3.4 Pigovian unemployment and horizontal labour supply

Kaldor (1983a, p. 12, n. 20) characterised the type of unemployment envisaged by Pigou (1933) in the following way:

> unemployment was caused by the downward rigidity of money wages resulting from trade unions and collective bargaining, but which did not indicate (or not necessarily) that real wages correspond to the real supply price (or marginal disutility) of labour.

We have here a variant of the just quoted view: trade unions might set a comparatively high 'floor' to real wages. Such a floor could mean that employers' labour demand hits the 'real wage floor' at an employment level which is lower than the individually intended labour supply at that real wage. As Joan Robinson worded that case in the previous statement, it might involve individual preferences. This suggests referring such a case to preference considerations as depicted in Fig. 10.1.

This market situation is given in Fig. 10.1 via point $E^{\sim\prime}$ in the lower part. The horizontal line going through that point at the real wage corresponding to the value of $\tan \angle \alpha$ is the real wage floor. The falling curve going through $E^{\sim\prime}$ is the relevant labour demand curve. Unemployment is then equal to the horizontal distance between $E^{\sim\prime}$ and $E^{*\prime}$, i.e., the distance between $\bar{N}^d$ and N^s.

The corresponding choice situation is depicted in the upper part of the figure as represented by point $E^{\sim}$. This is not an equilibrium point in the sense that if an indifference curve were drawn through this point, the marginal rate of substitution in that particular point would be such that it showed that workers would be willing to work at a lower real wage. But with a lower real wage, more labour would be demanded and a market equilibrium might be reached where the labour demand curve intersects the supply curve as shown in the lower quadrant. If, however, trade unions successfully prevent the higher level of real wages from falling, then there will be *ceteris paribus* enduring unemployment.

Although conventional marginal calculus shows that for a small decrease of real wages more labour will be offered, the unemployment point E^- might indeed be preferred to the 'full employment' one as given by point E: in the latter case workers work more but still have just the survival level of goods Q^-_x. Obviously an indifference curve through the latter point should have a lower index value than one through the former point. Workers behave rationally if they do not accept that type of full employment.

One may now ask: is *this* the explanation for the Pigovian 'floor' of labour supply – and what would this entail for economic policy? Although this question was not discussed in the *Theory of Unemployment*, some 'reservation wage floor' related considerations were indeed addressed earlier by Pigou (1927) who contemplated at least two 'floors': one which was set by unemployment benefits, and one which was set by a comparatively high real wage in an economically advanced sector of the economy. If the rest of the economy is less advanced but workers insisted on having the same real wage, then it might well be that at the comparatively high real wage of the former sector the latter sector's labour market cannot clear and unemployment might result in the latter sector. It can be shown, however, that such a situation does not necessarily entail lasting unemployment if the real wage does not drop in the backward sector. A subsidy to employers in the less advanced sector could raise their demand for labour such that higher real wages can be paid. Then the formerly unemployed workers would be willing to work since the seeming discrimination against the workers in the backward sector is halted and the resulting higher profits and lower unemployment benefits might well lead to an overall increase in welfare.

A more recent discussion of this model can be found in Casson (1983). We refrain here from pursuing this discussion much further because, as Casson (1983, p. 132) points out, Pigou (1927) himself does not think that this is a fertile approach to unemployment policy, the reason being fear of strategic lobbying by special-interest groups. This fear is not unreasonable, since it involves state intervention in order to assure the realisation of higher real wages.

Indeed, it might be questioned why supporting economic political intervention should be called for in situations where trade unions can successfully organise their members for the defense of real wages which are higher than the 'normal' market clearing ones – unless, of course, there are social-political considerations to lighten the lot of the 'working poor'. It is in this spirit that Pigou (1927, p. 366) proclaims:

> I conclude, therefore, that insistence by wage-earners upon maintaining uneconomically high wage-rates must involve large unemployment and associated social evils, and that, in a democracy such as ours, these evils cannot be effectively cancelled. The inference is that it is against the interest of the community as a whole for wage-earners to insist upon uneconomically high wage-rates. That interest requires the restoration, at not too distant a date, of an equilibrium between wage-rates and demand and supply conditions.

We are here back at Kaldor's characterisation of Pigovian unemployment given at the beginning of this subsection: unemployment *results* from 'uneconomically high wage-rates'. The involved social *evils* have to do with the fact that wage-earners *insist* on such high wages. But demand and supply for labour cannot be brought together at those wage rates. Pigou states here expressly that unemployment in this sense is an excess supply condition. In this sense Pigou adheres here to his earlier definition of involuntary unemployment (Pigou, 1914, p. 16):

> The amount of unemployment ... which exists in any industry, is measured by the number of hours' work ... by which the employment of the persons 'attached to' or 'occupied in' that industry fall short of the number of hours work that these persons would have been willing to provide at the current rate of wages under current conditions of employment.

But one may doubt whether such workers as hitherto discussed are really *involuntarily* unemployed. Unemployment in the above cases is either the result of a refusal of workers to be reduced to 'drudgery' as was just suggested above in the context of our choice theoretic model when contemplating the transition from the (superior) unemployment point E^- to the (choice theoretically inferior!) full employment point E. Alternatively, if it results from an insistence on 'uneconomically high wage-rates', it is an attempted 'investment' into higher real wages through collective action. But Keynes (*General Theory*, p. 8) stated expressly that he would *not* consider such collective action of workers as falling under the heading of 'involuntary' unemployment in the strict sense.

In a sense we have so far a consensus between Keynes and Pigou: the latter would recommend none of his tentatively discussed policy actions[8] while Keynes states that he does not want to consider this type of economic situation as falling under his type of investigation. The difference between the two approaches towards unemployment still has to be pinned down in more detail.

10.3.5 Keynes' 'involuntary unemployment in the strict sense'

In an economist's context 'involuntary' unemployment cannot mean any-thing else but excess supply of labour if the labour supply curve is the *locus* of the voluntary choices of the households. In this respect we have little reason to be surprised when we read that

> the term 'involuntary unemployment' was in use well before Keynes brought it to the fore. (Corry, 1997, p. 222)

Corry substantiated this finding with, among other references, the quote just given from Pigou (1914). But it was never claimed by Keynes that Pigou had a different definition of involuntary unemployment. The issue was that Pigou did not *address* this problem. In fact, Keynes himself (*GT*, p. 5, n. 1) *quotes* that Pigou (*Ec. of Welfare*, p. 127) [1920] writes that 'some resources are generally unemployed against the will of their owners'. The *analytical* issue associated with such a statement is whether, *when* it applies, the situation requires a specific theory which can address the situation recognised to exist when such a statement is made. Keynes (*ibid.*), points out that in the context of that quote Pigou gives a negative answer and continues:

> Prof. Pigou, in a book which is specifically directed to the problem of the national dividend, maintains that the same theory holds good when there is some involuntary unemployment as in the case of full employment.

Thus, the issue is not whether one has the same definition for involuntary unemployment but whether one has the same subsequent theory of the economy once it is admitted that situations of involuntary unemployment do exist.[9] In Keynes' eyes the *raison d'être* for the *General Theory* is that, con-trary to Pigou (1933), it supplies that theory of employment which also applies to involuntary unemployment.

It is, of course, important to define one's topic of discourse. Therefore questions of definition are of considerable interest also in the present context. The statement that 'involuntary unemployment' means 'excess supply of labour' contains a number of semantic and analytic problems: one is that supply functions are a theoretical construction of economic analysts. Labour market statistics cannot identify supply pure and simple but only market outcomes. The statistical 'identification problem' exists for the labour market as it does for any other market.

A further problem is that 'voluntary' choices *on* a labour supply curve are not unconstrained choices. Their modelling assumes that households have accepted a number of constraints – of time, health, wealth, information, expectation, to name but a few. If households believe foolishly that times are good when in fact they are bad, they have a wrong perception of the constraints under which they operate and thus they have 'wrong' supply curves. Thus they have to blame not others but themselves when they are 'off' the supply curve 'appropriate' for full employment. In the extreme, one might extend such a view to believing that *all* unemployment is not a problem of a malfunctioning of the economic system but of misperception by workers. They themselves just did not identify the 'correct' supply function.

It is in the face of such rather intractable identification problems that Keynes (*GT*, p. 15) attempted to define 'involuntary unemployment in the strict sense' by stating:

> Men are involuntarily unemployed if, in the event of a small rise in the price of wage-goods relatively to the money-wage, both the aggregate supply of labour willing to work for the current money-wage and the aggregate demand for it at that wage would be greater than the existing volume of employment. (original emphasis omitted, GMA)

To this very day economists muse about the sense or nonsense of this passage.[10] What does it state exactly and how does it differ from the conception of involuntary unemployment in the sense of Pigou? Strictly speaking, this sentence is not a definition of terms but a thought experiment involving an economy's labour market outcomes. Such an approach to identifying 'involuntary unemployment' seems to be reasonable in view of the identification problems just mentioned.

For a better understanding we might decompose this sentence into the following elements:

1. Regard a drop of the real wage which comes about through an increase in the price level of wage goods (through raising p_x in the household model of Fig. 10.1).
2. The decrease in the real wage ought to be small.
3. The consideration refers to market outcomes involving an increase in employment offered by firms.
4. The drop in the real wage ought to go together with an increase in labour supplied.

This rather involved scenario is meant to deal with the following analytical problems.

ad 1. If money wages are claimed to be insisted upon at too high a level as was done by Pigou (1927) in the quote just given, then the real wage might nevertheless drop, namely if the price of wage goods increased. One must be clear that money wage rigidity is not synonymous with real wage rigidity.

ad 2. If the drop in real wages is large, the associated choice for households might involve 'starvation wages' at full employment (see the choice between point E^- and point E in Fig. 10.1). In such a case it might indeed be economically rational to stay 'off' the full employment supply curve. This type of problem is excluded by the design of the thought experiment.

ad 3. Higher employment at lower real wages and constant production must involve changed technology (in the sense of a reduced average and marginal productivity of labour). But since technology is taken to be constant in the short run, this case must involve more production at *constant* technology. Since, however, in the short run not only technology is given but preferences and the degree of competition as well, therefore we have a determined general equilibrium situation and neither output nor employment can change under the set of assumptions. We thus have a contradiction. If we *do* observe the said changes, then some economic units cannot have been in a general equilibrium situation before. Since it is plausible that firms do employ more workers at lower real wages, the disequilibrium needs not to be seen as lying in their sphere.

This item is an *indication* for the existence of a disequilibrium employment situation in some sense, but not a proof nor a causal explanation.

ad 4. If in this setup we do observe more labour being supplied at less real wages, we cannot possibly have a movement on the lower leg of Pigou's reverse L. Because if that is the bottom floor, then workers are *off* the labour market if the real wage drops any further (through an increase in p_x, see item 1). Employment would drop because supply dried out. If instead *more* work is supplied (and employed – see item 3), then the analytical situation must be of a different nature than the one discussed by Pigou. The *General Theory* is to refer to situations of this type insofar as it refers to unemployment in the sense of Keynes.

If we evaluate this scenario in the context of the argumentation of this chapter, then we may point out that Keynes' situation is one where in the canonical model of fig. 10.1 we are in the situation described by point E^- in the upper diagram resp. by point $E^{-\prime}$ in the lower one. Its co-ordinates there are the real wage tan α and the employment level $\bar{N}^d$. Workers are quantity constrained in this case by that labour demand. If that constraint were removed at unchanged real wages, they would immediately go to labour supply N^s. Even if the real wage has to drop slightly, workers would supply far more labour than before if they were not under the said quantity constraint. The difference between Keynes' and Pigou's views on unemployment can be put now quite simply by saying that Keynes' unemployment is determined by the vertical $\bar{N}^d$-line while Pigou's unemployment is determined by the horizontal tan α-line. The market situation is identical in both cases but their implications are quite different. Whereas the involuntariness of unemployment might be doubted in the case of Pigou, in the case of Keynes there is no choice theoretic reason for such doubts.

It should be noted that in commenting on item 3 we had to bring in some general equilibrium considerations. We are not yet prepared analytically to discuss this aspect but we stressed its importance already at the beginning of this chapter. It seems that some of the critics of Keynes' 'definition' of unemployment lost sight of this aspect. This applies also to Joan Robinson (1937a, p. 127, n. 1) who soon claimed that there are weak points in this definition:

> Mr. Keynes' definition is appropriate only to short-period conditions, when [*i*] a fall in real wages is a symptom of an increase in effective demand, and [*ii*] it is formally correct only for cases in which the elasticity of supply of labour in terms of real wages is zero or positive. (numbering added, GMA)

In view of the longlasting debate about the appropriateness of Keynes' definition, a brief comment might be called for at this point.

Since Keynes intended the whole *General Theory* to refer to the short period, one cannot say that he made false claims in this regard if his definition referred to such an analytical situation. That his definition refers only to the short period is, of course, not a criticism if his entire investigation refers just to the short period. In addition, insofar as it refers to Pigou (1933), it is clear that his analysis also is a short-period one. There cannot be any fault in this aspect of Keynes' 'definition'.

If now in this short-period context Joan Robinson's case [*i*] were violated so that *in*creasing marginal returns were relevant, employers themselves could offer higher real wages while employment increased and thus it would appear as if workers were motivated to work more only because of such higher wages, not because they were involuntarily unemployed before. Keynes' thought experiment would go astray in this case. But Keynes presumed that decreasing returns in the short run belong to the few 'incontrovertible propositions' of economics.[11] Indeed to this very day many textbooks of economics make this very assumption. There is no specificity in this aspect of Keynes' definition. Again, the reader who is aware of the Pigovian context of this presumption cannot find fault with this aspect.

If Joan Robinson's above case [*ii*] were violated, a movement along the *locus* of equilibrium labour supply would show that workers work more for lower real wages. This would wrongly suggest involuntary unemployment in the sense of Keynes' definition whereas in fact workers would move *on* their equilibrium *locus* and thus they would *not* be involuntarily unemployed although they complied to the results of Keynes' thought experiment.

Here now the essentially general equilibrium character of Keynes' analysis must be remembered. Such criticism appears to be a valid one in a *partial* analytical context. It was just seen that 'back-ward bending' of labour supply was an assumption quite common at the time of his writing the *General Theory*. Thus, although Keynes guarded himself against a violation of case [*i*] by insisting that he always accepted the conventional assumption of real wages decreasing with higher employment as far as labour demand was concerned, he seems to have failed do devise a similar 'insurance' with regard to labour supply. It is therefore maybe not surprising, that when Jacob Viner (1936) made a criticism similar to the one which Joan Robinson implied with the just discussed case [*ii*], Keynes (1937a, p. 110) readily conceded that 'In regard to his [Professor Viner's, GMA] criticisms of my definition and treatment of involuntary unemployment, I am ready to agree that this part of my book is particularly open to criticism.' He continued (*ibid.*) that he felt 'in a position to make improvements' and that there was not 'anything fundamental between us here'.[12] But Keynes' envisaged 'improvements' were never published. It is therefore small wonder that these passages remained controversial. One possible line of defence could have been for Keynes to point out that Robinson and Viner refer to cases of partial analysis in which a multitude of real wages is imaginable. Along a labour supply curve real wages are undetermined. Keynes' thought experiment refers to a total analytic framework in which real wages *are* determined and can change only if (a) preferences change; (b) technology changes; (c) degrees of competition change; (d) effective demand changes. Since in the explicitly stated short-period context (a) to (c) do *not* vary (and tax rate changes are not under consideration), the partial analytical results – though not unreasonable if viewed in isolation – are clearly irrelevant in the argumentative context of the *General Theory*. Keynes was quoted above already (see p. 77) as saying: 'If everything is given except real wages and employment, then neither real wages nor employment are capable of more than one value' – except, of course, that we have the just mentioned case (d) 'effective demand changes'. Thus, involuntary unemployment in the strict Keynesian sense and deficient effective demand become virtually synonymous.[13]

This conclusion does not follow from Keynes' *definition* of unemployment, of course, but from some analytical considerations relating to the Pigovian *Theory of Unemployment* which will now be inspected.

10.4 Keynes' extension of the Pigovian model of the 'real demand for labour'

10.4.1 An outline of Keynes' criticisms of Pigou

As was just seen on p. 77, in his initial reaction to Pigou's *Theory of Unemployment*, Keynes' criticism was that this model was underdetermined from the standpoint of general equilibrium analysis. If that was not so, Pigou's model could not have had the degree of freedom for an exogenous variation of the real wage which Pigou assumed to be feasible. On this level of argumentation a critical stance could be: Pigou's type of employment theory required first of all to be completed to become a *full* model of an economy. Only *then* could its implications be evaluated – be it now affirmatively or critically. The rest of this chapter will concentrate on this type of critical approach. This line of argumentation will be referred to as '*internal* critique' since it takes as standard of reference the classical technique of building general equilibrium models and in the discussion of this model it argues from *inside* that standard approach.

In addition to this type of critical approach Keynes also came up with an entirely different criticism, namely that Pigou's *Theory of Unemployment* as a theory of involuntary unemployment was not *over*determined. Since shortly before he made the statement amounting to this type of criticism, Keynes (1936, p. 275) claimed that the Pigovian theory is a full employment theory, he implicitly characterised a theory of unemployment as one which – from the standpoint of full employment general equilibrium theory – *must* be overdetermined. In Keynes' view, a theory of unemployment must therefore go *beyond* a full employment general equilibrium model. But this means that it first must have as its analytical basis that what it *leaves* analytically.

Maybe it was this procedure which, once understood, appears as having solid economic reasoning behind it, which made reading the *General Theory* so difficult for some readers. Some readers expected to be enlightened by Keynes just on effective demand and/or unemployment but did not want to be bothered with Pigovian stuff which – for them – made the *General Theory* so 'confusing a book'[14] because of its seemingly unmotivated 'preoccupation' with Pigou (1933). Contrary to this view, Keynes obviously thought that when one wants to construct a model of frustrated wishes for employment ('involuntary unemployment in the strict sense'), one must first of all have some idea about a model of unfrustrated wishes for employment. Thus we must first have a full employment model and then there must be some analytical element generating an additional equation giving a constraint on employment other than labour supply. Since this type of criticism necessarily comes from outside of standard relative price theory, we will refer to it as '*external* critique'. This type will be the subject matter of chapter 11.

It is in this latter context that Keynes (1936, p. 276) came to proclaim that in the Pigovian system, 'We are, as I have said, one equation short.' In the process of the development of this argument Keynes then set the theme of 'equation counting'. As such, it was by no means invented by him as was just seen. In the Cambridge School it seems to have originated with Alfred Marshall. But Keynes gave this theme an entirely new connotation in not only demanding for determinate equilibria but also for over-determined ones.

Although hardly appreciated in the latter connotation, ever since Keynes, questions relating to equation counting became a repeatedly debated problem in macroeconomic model building from Pigou (1941) up to Friedman (1970) who liberally quotes Keynes in that connection. Basically, all of them used an approach of critical evaluation cultivated by Alfred Marshall.[15]

Summarising, we may note: Keynes' criticism of Pigou has two aspects: an 'internal' and an 'external' one. The 'internal' criticism is concerned with bringing home the general-equilibrium-full-employment nature of the Pigovian model. The 'external' criticism is concerned with developing further the idea of the 'missing equation' for an employment constraint. In this chapter we will explicate Keynes' internal criticism, turning to the external one in the next chapter.

10.4.2 Keynes' extension of Pigovian labour demand analysis

In his detailed review of Pigou's *Theory of Unemployment* in the appendix to his chapter 19, Keynes (1936, p. 274) reached the following conclusion concerning the Pigovian model:

> Thus, cleared of all complication, Professor Pigou's analysis amounts to an attempt to discover the volume of actual employment from the equations
>
> $$x + y = \phi(x)$$
> $$\text{and} \quad n = \chi(x).$$
>
> But there are three unknowns and only two equations. It seems clear that he gets round this difficulty by taking $n = x + y$. This amounts, of course, to assuming that there is no involuntary unemployment in the strict sense, i.e. that all labour available at the existing real wage is in fact employed. In this case x has the value which satisfies the equation
>
> $$\phi(x) = \chi(x). \tag{10.1}$$

In this quote the symbols of the variables have in general the same meaning as in our discussion so far except that n stands in Keynes usage at first just for labour supply and $\chi(x)$ is now a new function which Keynes claims to be implicit in Pigou's analysis. The quote ends by claiming that when remembering the existence of this latter function, the Pigovian model must be treated as one not of unemployment, as Pigou's title suggests, but as one of *full* employment.

On the basis of our reconstruction of the Pigovian model in ch. 8, Keynes' claim that the $\phi(x)$-function does not give the entire information contained in Pigou's model does not seem to be unreasonable. After all, when we put that model to use in chapter 9 in investigating the analytical steps which lead to Pigou's concept of the Real Demand for Labour, we utilised only a part of the original model, reducing the system of nine equations of (8.1) to (8.9) to a system of five equations as given by (a) to (e) (Table 9.1, p. 62) when reproducing the Pigovian $\phi(x)$-function. What should be done with the rest of the information contained in the model of ch. 8?

Keynes' review of Pigou's model amounts to proposing that those elements of that model which did not enter into the formulation of Pigou's $\phi(x)$-function should be worked into a $\chi(x)$-function analogous to the function explicitly stated by Pigou.

10.4.3 Labour supply in a reduced form context

10.4.3.1 Household equilibrium

Keynes' proposal of formulating a $\chi(x)$-function centres on the labour supply theory as mentioned in A.4 and formulated in equ. (8.6), p. 54, and further discussed in sect. 10. 3 on p. 78. Together with the accounting equations for wage goods as given by equs. (8.8) and (8.9) on p. 55, these parts of the model give a sub-system of the model economy. Formulating that sub-system explicitly, we restate worker households' equilibrium condition equ. (8.6) as

$$\frac{w}{p_x} = \frac{-U_n^w}{U_{Q_{xw}}^w} \tag{10.2}$$

Their budget constraint is given by

$$Q_{xw} = \frac{w}{p_x} n \tag{10.3}$$

For exogenous real wages w/p_x this system of two equations may now be solved for two endogenous variables: goods demanded by workers Q_{xw} and labour supply n^s. For changes in real wages a *locus* of household equilibria describes the labour supply curve discussed between Keynes and Hawtrey in the quote given on p. 77 above and as further elaborated in sect. 10.3. It is well known that this curve may be 'backward bending', a straight line or a rising curve, depending on the elasticity of substitution of the utility function.

10.4.3.2 Constant labour supply

As already mentioned, Pigou wanted to see this curve – at least in 1937 – to be a straight line. Algebraically expressed, this means that he assumed the supply model to rest on a utility function

$$U^w = Q_{xw}^{\delta_x} \cdot (\bar{t} - n)^{\delta_t} \tag{10.4}$$

where δ_x is workers' (partial) elasticity of utility from consuming wage goods and δ_l is the corresponding elasticity of consuming leisure. The marginal utilities are then given by

$$-U_n^w = \delta_\ell \frac{U^w}{\bar{t}-n}; \quad U_{Q_x}^w = \delta_x \frac{U^w}{Q_{xw}} \tag{10.5}$$

Substituting now equs. 10.5 into equ. 10.2 and then equ. 10.3 into the equation thus obtained, will show after some minor re-arrangements that the *locus* of household equilibria is given by

$$n = \bar{t} \frac{\delta_x}{\delta_x + \delta_\ell} = const. \tag{10.6}$$

– just as Pigou would have liked it to be above the lower floor of real wages, as was seen above.

10.4.3.3 Increasing labour supply

With a labour supply curve like equ. 10.6 – which certainly would have been a rather special one – Keynes' postulate of the existence of a $\chi(x)$-curve would not have been wrong – the curve would have been just a straight line, perpendicular to the n, x, y-axis of fig. 10.1 on page 82.

But Keynes could not count on such an assumption to be held – neither by Pigou nor by other 'Classics'. It was seen above (p. 79) that Robbins (1930) criticised Pigou for an implicit assumption of a falling labour supply curve and in a newer publication, Pigou (1935, p. 168) came to the conclusion that labour supply in the aggregate should definitely – albeit 'moderately' – be rising with real wages:

> on the evidence available, the maintenance curve for labour power at work is ... forward-rising in a moderate degree.

If that were so, then Keynes' appropriate assumption about 'classical' labour supply would indeed have been that it rises when households perceive that exogenously given real wages have risen.

10.4.3.4 Endogenous real wages

The transition to the characteristics of Keynes' $\chi(x)$-function follow now from the observation that real wages are only exogenous from the standpoint of the household sub-model. For the model economy as a whole, as soon as sectoral employment is determined, real wages are endogenous in the sense of being given by the marginal productivity in the wages goods sector. The model thus generates the two derivatives

$$\frac{dn^s}{d\left(\frac{w}{p_x}\right)} \quad \text{and} \quad \frac{d\left(\frac{w}{p_x}\right)}{dx}. \tag{10.7}$$

The first of these represents the characteristics of the household model (10.2) and (10.3). Its sign value is not determined but was proclaimed to be positive by Pigou (1935), as was just seen.

The second derivative in 10.7 represents the characteristics of the $F'(x)$ function as discussed above. Its sign value is definitively negative. Through multiplication, these derivatives may then be combined to give the derivative of Keynes' $\chi(x)$-function as

$$\chi'(x) = \frac{dn^s}{d\left(\frac{w}{p_x}\right)} \frac{d\left(\frac{w}{p_x}\right)}{dx} \gtrless 0 \tag{10.8}$$

This derivative has no unique sign value because labour supply does not increase reliably with real wages as was just pointed out. If, however, we take Pigou (1935) seriously, we should assume the first of these derivatives to be positive, making the final value of expression (10.8) negative.

For an assessment of the working of the Pigovian model thus extended, it is important to know which parameters and which considerations affect the shape of this – until now – only loosely conceived addition to his model.

10.4.4 Keynes' 'Pigovian' $\chi(x)$-function

10.4.4.1 The analytical procedure

We have established so far that the $\chi(x)$-function postulated by Keynes as being implied by the Pigou (1933) model

1. is based on an increasing labour supply curve
2. is a reduced form of sub-model contained in Pigou (1933). That sub-model combines labour demand conditions as expressed by the physical marginal product of labour in the wage goods industry.

Following the procedure just outlined with reference to equ. 10.8, the construction of this curve is straightforward:

1. construct an increasing labour supply curve
2. combine the labour supply curve with the technologically (and price theoretically) determined real wage of the system.

10.4.4.2 The algebra of increasing labour supply

Robbins (1930) stressed the crucial importance of choosing the 'appropriate' elasticity in labour supply analysis. Without now going into attempts to prove in detail whether Keynes and Pigou did read and react to this article, we presume that it is not likely to be a violation of the spirit of *historical* reconstruction, if this knowledge is presupposed in the attempt to reach clear-cut comparative static results concerning the characteristics of the $\chi(x)$-function.

A utility function with the elasticity of substitution $\sigma = (1 + \beta)^{-1}$ parametrically given could read

$$(U^w)^{-\beta} = aQ_{xw}^{-\beta} + b(\bar{t} - n^s)^{-\beta} \quad \text{with} \quad 0 > \beta > -1 \qquad (10.9)$$

where the order condition for β assures that we always have $\sigma > 1$ and where a and b are parameters determining the marginal rate of substitution between goods and leisure as follows:

$$\left. \frac{dQ_{xw}}{d(\bar{t} - n^s)} \right|_{U^w = const.} = \frac{-U_n^w}{U_{Q_{xw}}^w} = \frac{b}{a} \left(\frac{Q_{xw}}{\bar{t} - n^s} \right)^{1+\beta}. \qquad (10.10)$$

Thus, an increase in the *(b/a)*-ratio means that the marginal rate of substitution along an indifference curve increases in such a way that the absolute value of the marginal disutility of labour as measured by U_n^w is raised.

Since in equilibrium this marginal rate of substitution must be equal to the real wage, as we know from (10.2), and since Q_{xw} in (10.10) may be substituted via the budget equation (10.3), this expression may be changed into the labour supply function

$$\left(\frac{w}{p_x} \right)^{-\beta} = \frac{b}{a} \left(\frac{n^s}{\bar{t} - n^s} \right)^{1+\beta} \qquad (10.11)$$

whence – with this specific type of a utility function and this particular constellation of parameters – a positive elasticity of labour supply may be derived as given by

$$E_{\left(\frac{w}{p_x} \right)}^{n^s} = \frac{-\beta}{1+\beta} \frac{\bar{t} - n^s}{\bar{t}} > 0 \quad \text{for} \quad -1 < \beta < 0, \quad \text{i.e. for } \sigma > 1 \qquad (10.12)$$

10.4.4.3 The $\chi(x)$-function

A constant-elasticity-of-production function as discussed in the previous chapter and which may be restated here as

$$F(x) = A_x x^{\alpha_x}, \qquad (10.13)$$

gives the real wage

$$\frac{w}{p_x} = \alpha_x A_x x^{\alpha_x - 1}. \qquad (10.14)$$

Replacing the real wage in the labour supply function equ. (10.11) by equ. (10.14) gives an expression in sectoral employment x and total labour supply n^s – and thus an implicit form of the $\chi(x)$-function. It can easily be verified that this function has the following comparative static characteristics:

$$n^s = \chi(x; \underset{-}{\alpha_x}, \underset{+}{A_x}, \underset{+}{\frac{b}{a}}) \tag{10.15}$$

for $x > 1$. It has the property that for $x \to 0$ we have $n \to \bar{t}$ i.e. if x is so low that the real wage would go towards infinity, then total available time $\bar{t}$ would be devoted to labour. But labour supply is continuously decreasing from this maximal level when the real wage is lowered.

In short, if we assume 'normal' neoclassical conditions to hold in this narrow sense of 'appropriate' order conditions concerning the utility function describing labour supply decisions, then it can be shown that a well-defined (falling) $\chi(x)$-function is implied by the completed Pigovian model. This was Keynes' contention in the above quote (see p. 94) which, with the just discussed clarifications, must be considered as quite justified.

10.4.5 Graphical presentations

10.4.5.1 Keynes' conception of Pigovian general equilibrium

We are now in a position to visualise the nature of Keynes' perception and extension of the Pigovian classical model. If we return to the graphical presentation of the Pigou (1933)-model given by fig. 9.1 on page 67, we note the following changes in fig. 10.3

1. The Pigovian $\phi(x)$-function is now identified as a n^d-curve. It is matched by an $n^s = \chi(x)$-curve in the lower quadrant of fig. 10.3
2. The n^s-'black' box in the upper quadrant of fig. 9.1 on page 67 is now replaced by an indifference curve $U(n, Q_x)$ with a tangent point marked **2nd**.

The reasons for these changes should be mostly transparent from the discussion so far. In particular, the nature of the $\chi(x)$-function has been just elaborated above in considerable detail. The points **1st** and **2nd** relate to Keynes' characterisation of classical economics with reference to its 'two fundamental postulates' (*General Theory*, p. 5).

The 'first classical postulate' says that the (real) wage is equal to the marginal product of labour. This is, of course, what Pigou always maintained. The corresponding point in fig. 9.1 on page 67 was marked as **I.** and had the same significance there as point **1st** has it here. Keynes maintained that the analytical significance of this postulate is not contested by him and that he is in complete agreement with the Classics concerning this particular analytical element.

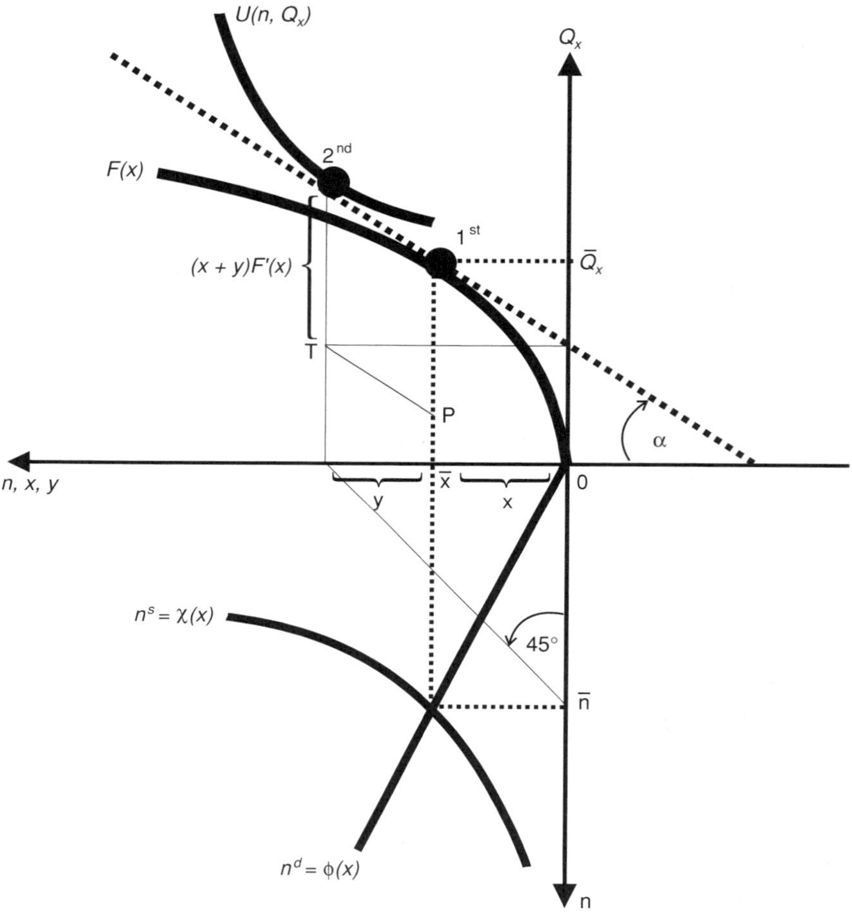

Figure 10.3 The Pigou (1933) model as seen by Keynes (1936)

The 'second classical postulate' says that at the same time the real wage also expresses the preference of workers concerning the disutility of work resp. the utility of leisure on the one hand and the utility of consuming goods on the other hand, namely in a way which is manifested in their respective marginal utilities. It is, of course, to this very day the standard stance concerning the blessings of the market system that this system is able to make equal the subjective valuations of households with the market valuations. It is an essential part of modern price theory that household equilibrium requires

$$\frac{w}{p_x} = \frac{-U_n^w}{U_{Q_{xw}}^w} = \frac{dQ_x}{dn}\bigg|_{U^w = const.} \tag{10.16}$$

to hold,[16] if there is a utility function with the corresponding arguments Q_x and n. But in equ (10.16) the first element represents the real wage as given exogenously by the market system – and as is expressed by tan $\angle\alpha$ in fig. 10.3 – while the last element gives the subjective valuation of goods required for sacrificing one more unit of effort along an indifference curve. This is exactly what point **2nd** expresses and this is indeed a quintessential part of the sub-jective 'value theory' as cultivated in the Marshallian school and found proba-bly in every modern textbook on macroeconomics. As such, the flat denial of the validity of this postulate would violate the entire understanding of the modern theory of relative prices. Keynes *did* deny the validity of this postulate and made himself appear as the iconoclast of modern economics. It is not the place here to evaluate this particular iconoclasm of Keynes'.[17] Rather, the question one may ask in the present context is: was Keynes correct in *attribut-ing* this particular postulate to Pigou (1933)? It will be remembered that we quoted Hawtrey on p. 80 above as claiming that in Pigou (1933) 'there is no "supply function" [for labour, GMA] at all'. If that were true then the present representation of his model would be incorrect. We addressed this issue in sect. 10.3 on p. 78 in view of some recent authors commenting in the 1990s on Keynes, taking recourse to the position which Hawtrey took in 1937. It was our conclusion in the above that Pigou did admit to the relevance for his the-orising of this type of labour supply analysis. He also subscribed to what Keynes called the 'second classical postulate' and thus far we consider this figure to be indeed a correct representation of Pigou (1933). But irrespective of this conclusion, fig. 10.3 on p. 100 is a representation of Keynes' perception of the Pigou (1933) model. It represents a general equilibrium model.

In this *type* of model of the interplay of technological possibilities, factor supplies and preferences, the price system as expressed by tan $\angle\alpha$ is *deter-mined*. This was the important point of Marshall's equation counting in his 'famous' note xxi. There should be only *one* determinate value for the real wage if the model meets Marshall's standards. This is the rationale behind the remark Keynes made to Robertson and which was quoted above on p. 77 concerning the single permissible value of the real wage.

In the *General Theory*, it seems that the position is somewhat changed. There, Keynes accepted that the apparatus expressed – by us – graphically in the upper quadrant of fig. 10.3 may be translated to the *n, x, y*- and *n*-plane in the lower quadrant of our visualisation. But if Pigou devises his $\phi(x)$-func-tion for this plane, he should also make explicit his equally – albeit in his original presentation only implicitly – present $\chi(x)$-function. If that is done, the intersection of the corresponding two curves again gives one single determinate value and then we are there where Marshall wanted economic modelling to be and where Keynes said that Pigou's model in fact *is*.

The two curves in question could perhaps have weird shapes. The $\chi(x)$-curve could be a straight line, as was seen above. But if there is a determinate price system, there is only one single intersection point. Real wages and employment can change only then and so far as the whole economic system changes and hence the positions of these two curves change. Therefore employment political debate cannot concentrate on the movement *along* only one of these curves. In particular, the paradigm of moving along the $\phi(x)$-curve for alternative real wages is not correct. If there are changes in the system, at least one *curve* in the lower quadrant must change. Therefore, in this framework, the shift parameters for the underlying curves would have to be evaluated – a topic which will occupy us on the subsequent pages.

10.4.5.2 Excursus: *alternative conceptions of general equilibrium*

(a) *The Koopmans diagram of general equilibrium.* The Pigovian general equilibrium model just discussed seems to be rather confusing and pedestrian if compared to more 'modern' renderings, as may be found, e.g., in Koopmans (1957). They are based on concepts which, at the time of Pigou (1933), were quite unfamiliar in the context of wider economic discourse, like 'convex supply sets' or 'no-worse-than-x sets' or 'bounding planes'. In this context the existence and the Pareto efficiency of competitive equilibria are then analysed in a very general framework.

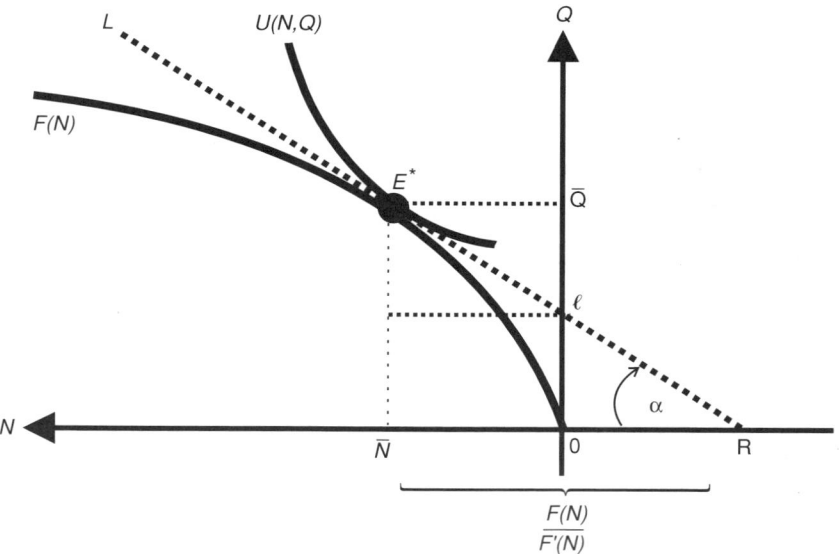

Figure 10.4 A 'Koopmans diagram' of general equilibrium

In spite of all this analytical generality, when it comes to visualising these analytic concepts, as is the intention of Koopmans (1957), the 'convex sets' reappear in the economically relevant realms with boundaries which have an appearance very much like the production curves and indifference curves of the above 'pedestrian' analysis. The general equilibrium problem is then illustrated by Koopmans (1957) by taking recourse to Robinson Crusoe (*ibid.* p. 20) with certain characteristics:

Robinson [Crusoe, GMA] can separate his supply and consumption decision by the following procedure. He uses the slope of the separating line L to define two prices, not both zero, one of labour (the wage rate) and one of food etc.

The author goes on to describe how, given the price system, Robinson then maximises the value of his profit, measured as $\overline{O\ell}$. He then hands over this profit to himself as 'Robinson the consumer-worker' who, starting from this income, now trades labour for food. Given the price line $L\ell$ he then finds a constrained utility maximum. If the price system is right, the optimal production point and the optimal consumption point coincide. This two-dimensional analysis is seen as an illustration of the solution to an economic co-ordination system of a competitive model economy with many agents and goods. With the help of alternative utility functions, it is then shown (*ibid.* p. 36) that there could be an 'energetic Robinson' working a lot (his fig. 1.19a), or a 'lazy Robinson', working (and producing) little (his fig. 1.19b). Similar exercises can be done in the Pigovian system by changing the parameters of the workers' utility function.

(b) *Keynes and classical employment in the Koopmans diagram.* What significance has this model for the present discussion? First of all, it illustrates Keynes' dictum, quoted above on p. 77 that if everything is given except real wages and employment, then these magnitudes can assume only a single value. Thus if U(·) and F(·) is given and the degree of competition, then E* and all the rest is determined. If the associated relative prices (real wages) and quantities (employment) are to change, then the position of E* has to change but this requires that 'our' Robinson must become either more 'energetic' or more 'lazy'. In any case the basic functions must change. This means that 'classical employment policy' in this type of model necessarily must identify and address these parameters determining supply and demand in the entire economy and then must manipulate their values in a way which will be illustrated in more detail below (see Table 10.2 on p. 111).

(c) *Accounting units in the Koopmans diagram.* Furthermore, it is significant that in this model, output and income can be depicted in a variety of ways, among other in Keynes' wage units. If, e.g., NE^* is total output in a one-product world, then this output accrues to non-workers as $\overline{Ol}$ and to workers as $\overline{lQ}$ if the accounting is done in terms of output. Alternatively, accounting could be done in terms of Keynes' wage units. Then wage incomes in terms of wage units is nothing else but employment $\overline{ON}$. Profits, which in terms of goods were $\overline{Ol}$, in terms of wage units are the projection of this amount upon the N-axis, given by $\overline{OR}$. Thus total income in terms of wage units is $\overline{NR}$. Alternatively, we may start out from determinate output $F(N)$ and arrive at the value of total output in terms of wage units in the following way. If it is accepted that $\tan \angle\alpha = w/p$, we obviously have

$$\tan \angle\alpha = \frac{\overline{NE^*}}{\overline{NR}} = \frac{F(\overline{N})}{\overline{NR}} = \frac{\overline{Q}}{\overline{NR}} = \frac{w}{p} = F'(\overline{N}) \qquad (10.17)$$

hence

$$\overline{NR} = \frac{F(\overline{N})}{F'(\overline{N})} = \frac{\overline{Q}}{\frac{w}{p}} = \frac{p\overline{Q}}{w}. \qquad (10.18)$$

Thus the stretch marked $F(N)/F'(N)$ measures the money value of output pQ in terms of the wage rate w. Put differently, it measures output in terms of the wage unit – which, of course, is identical with the corresponding income as just discussed.

(d) *The analytical and temporal scope of the Koopmans diagram.* The Robinsoniad here under discussion offers only a very dim view of the questions of economic allocation. The main problem in this context is that just one schizophrenia (worker *vs* non-worker) will not do for 'our' Robinson. We should also have dealings between a thrifty and a spendthrift Robinson and between an interest income oriented rentier on the one hand and an entrepreneurial investor on the other. What would happen if the thrifty Robinson would like to abstain from consumption in order to have more of it at a later date? Under which conditions will Robinson the rentier have equilibrium transactions with Robinson the investor?

The issues behind these questions are, of course, the ones which are also behind those associated with Keynes' 'effective demand' analysis and it will be a major concern in the following to relate 'effective demand' to the Koopmans diagram and to general equilibrium concepts like 'Walras' Law'. But why don't the questions concerning effective demand come up in the original context as set out by Koopmans (1957)? The answer can be that implicit assumptions assure that they are not of relevance. These assumptions can be of two types: either (a) 'collapsing' ones or (b) 'expanding' ones. Thus, with regard to (a), it could be argued that all the present and future market transactions are collapsed into a single transaction covering all conceivable markets including future markets in such a way that unspecific savings just do not occur. With regard to (b) it can be assumed that savings do not occur because net investments do not occur because we have a stationary state which repeats itself indefinitely without ever requiring the troublesome market co-ordinations just mentioned which involve saving and investment.

(e) *The 'modern' conception of general equilibrium.* Variant (a) represents the 'modern' conception of general equilibrium according to Arrow (1989, p. 147):

> The Walrasian system in its modern form is not actually very interested in the idea of the steady state or long-run equilibria ... In the neoclassical framework equilibrium really means market clearing. It has nothing to do with stationarity over time in and of itself. The full modernized Walrasian general equilibrium system, as set forth, for example, in Debreu's *Theory of Value* (or in our joint paper five years before that), involves equilibrium over time. That does not mean stationary state. It means that at any moment of time we have a set of prices for the present and for the future and that there are demands and supplies of products for the present and for the future. So, at time 0, say today, we have planned demand for and supply of each product for each future period. If you find a set of prices such that all markets clear, that is an equilibrium.

This really means that time disappears as an economic problem. But the basic problem with such a conception of general equilibrium is that it *assumes* markets to exist which in fact are just not there.

(f) *The 'customary' conception of general equilibrium.* Variant (b) represents the conception of general equilibrium as we know it from the typical models of the theory of foreign trade and from a multitude of two-sector models of equilibrium allocation, as perhaps best represented by Krauss and Johnson (1974). The authors offer a general equilibrium model with two sectors of production, two consumers and two factors of production (belonging to the households of the model). The model is static. The factors of production live eternally. Krauss and Johnson (1974, p. 51) stress, among other assumptions, that 'both goods are consumption goods: there is no investment and saving'. This is a Pigovian 'frozen land' economy *par excellence*. Again, time has disappeared. But in this context it disappeared differently: in the 'modern' general equilibrium theory of the last paragraph time is collapsed into a single market transaction. Here it is extended into a never-ending repetitiveness without accumulation, depreciation, needs for liquidity etc.

In spite of its lack of a reasonable intertemporal structure, this type of model is used by Krauss and Johnson (1974) in order to explain virtually any economic problem: production, distribution, international trade, public goods, economic growth(!), the rate of savings finally appearing in a model in which it has been expressly assumed away (see the last quote). The problem with this 'type(b)' variant of general equilibrium models, although still essential for much of what is taught about the 'pure theory of foreign trade' and other macroeconomic topics, is on the one hand its blatant lack of realism due to the stationarity assumption (or quasi-stationarity assumption in the case of growth theory). But it is not only way off the mark of reality. It just is not 'modern' if we may believe Arrow's quoted statement.

Thus, by the standards of Kenneth Arrow, one of the most knowledgeable representatives of modern general equilibrium theory, neither the above 'type(a)' nor the 'type(b)' variant of general equilibrium theory is satisfactory: the former assumes markets to exist that are not there, the latter makes unacceptable assumptions about perpetuity and about lacking intertemporal provisions through savings and accumulation. The latter set of economic decisions problems are typically assumed away – or restricted to comply to externally posited equilibrium requirements in the case of growth theory.

(g) *A 'momentous' interpretation of general equilibrium.* There is a third conceivable variant of viewing general equilibrium. One could name it the 'momentous' conception. It is based on the question: could one not(c) consider the Koopmans diagram as an *interpretation* of (in principle) observable market transactions which do exist in that momentous time period of the economy when they are *really* happening – or at least when they are conceivable as happening in a realistic model? With this conception one avoids any statement concerning non-observable future market transactions or concerning stationarity. This type of general equilibrium concept could then just refer, as Koopman's above quoted presentation of this model in terms of a plausible story suggested, to an interpretation of what actually *did* happen, of what Robinson the worker and Robinson the non-worker *did* do in a specific time period, namely to work, consume and to engage in productive activity under conditions of constrained maximisation. This variant(c) would require additional modelling of those market transactions not covered by the figure just given but which are constituent parts of modern life, namely saving and investment.

Such a 'momentous' conception of general equilibrium would avoid the conceptual difficulties arising from accepting either assumptions concerning atemporal economies (variant(a)) or eternal economies (variant(b)).

These considerations might be better discussed, however, once we have covered more extensively Keynes' criticism of Pigou. We will return to these issues below in chapter 26, in particular in connection with discussing fig. 26.1 on page 385 where we supply the graphical extensions of the Koopmans model just mentioned as suggesting themselves under our 'momentous' interpretation.

10.5 The workings of the extended Pigovian model

10.5.1 Employment policies in Keynes' view of the Pigovian model

So far, the following picture emerges concerning Keynes' reception of the classical theory: Keynes takes up in considerable detail the original analysis of Pigou (1933) and confronts it with the Marshallian perspective of general equilibrium. In the light of this perspective he then extends the Pigovian model with the statement of a $\chi(x)$-function, stressing by this means its general equilibrium features.

But the main aim of the critical reconstruction of the Pigovian model in the *General Theory* is not just to show that it is a general equilibrium model. Keynes rather intends its *reductio ad absurdum* by going further and discussing the rather limited nature of employment political measures which can logically follow from the Pigovian model. Thus, after restating and extending the Pigovian model, the next step of Keynes' handling of the Pigovian model is then to explicate the type of employment political measures which this analytical framework permits. In this section we turn to this step of his discussion of 'classical' analysis.

It might well be that Keynes' two-step procedure in the dealings with the classical model was not entirely transparent in the way he presented it in the *General Theory*. He relegated the first step of the reconstruction of the Pigovian model to the appendix of his ch. 19 – perhaps because it involved some technicalities like equation counting and shuffling of algebraic symbols. Far more readable than the discussion in the appendix to ch. 19 – albeit hardly understandable by itself – is the list of partly strange classical employment political measures which Keynes gave in his introductory chapter 2 claiming that it is 'to the best of my understanding ... the substance of Professor Pigou's *Theory of Unemployment*'. Although Keynes (1936, p. 7, n. 1) expressly refers to the necessary first step in that context, namely his detailed discussion of the Pigovian model after ch. 19, the reader is confronted with the last step first by him. In the present development of the argument we reversed that procedure and we intend now to investigate the second step in some detail.

Keynes (1936, p. 7) claimed that in Pigou's classical theory of employment 'there are *only* four possible means of increasing employment' (emphasis added, GMA). We restate them in an abbreviated way as:

(a) diminishing 'frictional' unemployment
(b) diminishing the marginal disutility of labour
(c) increasing the marginal productivity of labour in the *wage goods* industries

(d) shifting non-wage earners' demand from wage goods to non-wage goods.

After stating this list without any further elaboration, Keynes (*ibid.*) proceeds to reiterate that these classical employment political 'categories' are 'comprehensive'. But this must seem to be a queer claim to make after such a seemingly incoherent list.

10.5.2 The question of authenticity of Keynes' 'classical' list

Such a list is nowhere stated in quite this way in Pigou (1933). But then, the Pigovian model itself was seen to have been presented by its author in a not very systematic manner. It had to be pieced together by his readers from a number of analytical presuppositions and scattered hints. So the reader may feel justified to go by himself through that model, asking for the employment political measures which it suggests.

Actually, Pigou does mention a number of these measures. Thus, concerning (a) 'frictional unemployment', Pigou (1933, p. 290) discusses and quotes the Webbs' investigation of employment effects of Employment Exchanges.[18] Concerning (b), the 'marginal disutility of labour', little may be found in Pigou (1933) but quite a bit in his *Economics of Stationary States*, published shortly afterwards.[19] Concerning (c), Pigou (1933, p. 160) does regard favourably 'improvements in productivity' in the 'wage-good industries regarded as a unity'. And the last measure (d) is also discussed tentatively by Pigou (1933, pp. 158f.), albeit with unclear final conclusion (see his note 1, p. 159).

With our reconstructed Pigovian model at hand, we have a framework to which we may refer critically the Keynesian contentions. In the following we intend to go through this list, referring it to the discussion of the Pigovian model in the last chapters.

10.5.3 Classical employment measures in graphical representation

Turning first to the graphical presentation just discussed, the following comments concerning this list suggest themselves:
ad (a) diminishing 'frictional' unemployment:

> This measure involves an off-curve analysis not strictly the domain of traditional Marshallian analysis, although a number of authors like Hutt (1939) and Phelps (1970) have shown in later years that the traditional principles of economic analysis may very well be applied in a discussion of certain economic aspects of 'frictions' caused by search and by time-consuming acquisition of knowledge. In the rather different Pigovian context here under discussion, Keynes' point concerning frictions may be illustrated with reference to the above fig. 10.1 by saying that the equilibrium point E in that representation is not really the relevant one.

Instead, point F with the associated relatively low employment level n is claimed as characterising the economic situation due to frictions in the economy which prohibit the enactment of the frictionless plans as represented by the $\phi(x)$- and $\chi(x)$-curves. Employment policy could then aim at reducing frictions, thereby shifting the broken lines determining a comparatively low level of employment in such a way as to come nearer to the frictionless point E with its higher level of employment. This measure is represented in fig. 10.1 by the arrow towards E marked (a). A practical case in point is the proposal for Employment Exchanges mentioned in the previous section.

ad (b) diminishing the marginal disutility of labour:
This alternative item refers to reducing 'voluntary' unemployment by making workers prepared to supply more work for a given real wage as determined by a given level of sectoral employment x. This measure amounts to an outward shift of the $\chi(x)$-curve – and thus of equilibrium point E in fig. 10.1 – so that a new equilibrium is feasible at an employment level higher than the original one (see arrow (b)).

ad (c) increasing the marginal productivity of labour in the *wage goods* industries:
With this item, Keynes shifts the focus of attention from the marginal utility of workers to their marginal productivity. But why does he mention just the wage goods sector? It is plausible that with an increased marginal productivity in the wage goods sector, for any level of x there is a higher real wage and hence under 'normal' labour supply conditions there must also be a higher n forthcoming along the $\chi(x)$-curve which thus is seen to have shifted away from the origin similarly as in the previous case (b). But why should comparable technological improvements in the non-wage sector be not worth mentioning in this context? We will return to this question presently. (For a graphical representation of this measure, see arrow (c) in fig. 10.1.)

ad (d) shifting non-wage earners' demand from wage goods to non-wage goods:
In this item it is claimed that a relative price increase in non-wage goods has beneficial employment effects in classical analysis. Again the reader could easily be left wondering just why that should be the case. Alluding to plausibility again, one could say that if non-workers consumed less wage-goods, then this will lead, *ceteris paribus*, to less employment of x-workers, their marginal product thus increasing. But this would mean that the real wage for workers in general has increased. With 'normal' labour supply, this would lead to labour supply increasing with higher real wages.

In terms of fig. 10.1, what is happening in this case is a shift in the $\phi(x)$-curve towards the n-axis so that a new intersection with the $\chi(x)$-curve could be realised, employment having increased beyond the original level. (See arrow (d).)

Thus, with this list Keynes seems in essence to confirm the tentative conclusion of the graphical discussion of sect. 4(a) above: since the completed Pigovian model consists of two intersecting curves, apart from simultaneous movements of both curves there are only two 'categories' of alternative employment measures available – either the one curve moves or the other. An off-curve analysis might also be attempted although there was little available in this regard at Keynes' time beyond the mere statement that there might be some further economic influences not covered by conventional Marshallian considerations and which might be subsumable under the name of 'frictions'.

But these results are principally true in a two-curve analysis. Thus, our graphical discussion is only able to supply a rough structure to Keynes' discussion of classical employment measures. For a more detailed look at these measures we have to turn to the algebraic formulation of the curves underlying this analysis.

10.5.4 The comparative statics of Keynes' classical employment measures

If we adopt the characterisation of the Pigovian system as quoted on p. 94 above from Keynes (1936, p. 274), namely as a three-equation set-up, then we may reproduce it as in Table 10.1.

Its entire comparative static characteristics are then given by

$$
\begin{bmatrix} 0 & 1-\phi' & 0 \\ 1 & -x' & 0 \\ 1 & -1 & -1 \end{bmatrix} \begin{bmatrix} dn \\ dx \\ dy \end{bmatrix} = \begin{bmatrix} \phi_2 & 0 & 0 & \phi_3 & \phi_4 \\ 0 & x_2 & x_3 & x_4 & 0 \\ 0 & 0 & 0 & 0 & 0 \end{bmatrix} \begin{bmatrix} d\left(\frac{\gamma_y}{\gamma_x}\right) \\ d\left(\frac{b}{a}\right) \\ dA_x \\ d\alpha_x \\ d\alpha_y \end{bmatrix} \tag{10.19}
$$

where indices $i = 1, 2, 3$, or 4 indicate partial derivatives of the respective functions with regard to the argument standing in second, third etc. posi-

Table 10.1 Keynes' model of Pigou (1933)

(9.22)	p. 66	$x + y = \phi\,(x; \alpha_x, \alpha_y, \frac{\gamma_y}{\gamma_x})$
(10.15)	p. 99	$n = \chi(x; \alpha_x, A_x, \frac{b}{a})$
(8.10)	p. 55	$n = x + y$

tion of that function, their respective sign values having been discussed above already when these functions were presented in chs 9 and 10. Table 10.2 then contains all the influences on total employment n which are imaginable in this system together with their respective sign values, * denoting an indeterminate sign value. The last line in this table gives Keynes' classical employment political measures as denoted above on p. 107, the first item (a) of that list not being included here since it pertained to an off-curve analysis which is beyond the comparative statics of the Pigovian system. It is then seen that Keynes' item '(b)' amounts to decreasing the marginal rate of substitution of goods against leisure along the workers' indifference curve as given by (b/a) in equ. (10.10) on p. 98 above. His item '(d)' also refers to a marginal rate of substitution along an indifference curve, namely to that of wage goods against non-wage goods as given by equ. (9.7) (p.61). The A_x-column in Table 10.2 denotes changes in the marginal productivity of labour in the wage goods sector as discussed above in connection with Keynes' item '(c)'.

The lingering doubts in the previous discussion that Keynes' 'comprehensive' list of classical employment measures could not be quite complete seem to be confirmed by Table 10.2, since his items (b), (c) and (d) obviously do not cover all the comparative static possibilities which the Pigovian model as reconstructed by us could offer. But if we turn to the α_x-column depicting increases in the elasticity of production of workers in the wage goods sector, then it appears that this potential measure offers no clear-cut results, the reason being that it has two opposing influences on the ϕ- and the χ-curves. As shown in equ. (9.22), the former curve is tilted downwards, thus leading *cetersis paribus* to less employment whereas the latter curve, according to equ. (10.15), is shifted outwards and hence *ceteris paribus* towards more employment, the net outcome of the two effects being indeterminate.

Thus the only determinate effect not covered by Keynes in his discussion of the Pigovian model is the one listed in the α_y-column of Table 10.2. In the following excursus we will permit ourselves to speculate about the reasons for this seeming deficiency. It will appear that it was not Keynes

Table 10.2 Influences on employment in the Pigovian model

| | preferences | | technology | | |
| | non-workers | workers | | | |
	$\dfrac{\gamma_y}{\gamma_x}$	$\dfrac{b}{a}$	A_x	α_x	α_y
n	+	−	+	*	+
policy	(d)	(b)	(c)		

but Pigou who excluded this potential comparative static effect through his assumption of 'normal technical improvement'.

Anticipating the results of the following discussion we note that after the considerations of the following excursus we may conclude that Keynes' list of classical means of increasing employment is indeed complete and comprehensive.

10.5.5 Excursus: the comparative statics of technological parameters and Pigou's concept of 'normal improvement in productivity'

Dismissing plain oversight as too simple an explanation for Keynes' omission of α_y-variations, one could presume that Keynes believed such changes as not being covered by Pigou's short-period analysis in which even capital equipment was assumed to be unchanging as was noted in connection with A.1 of ch. 8. But then Keynes' discussion of changes in the marginal physical productivity of labour in the wage goods sector, identified here as A_x-changes, would have been an inappropriate overextension of the Pigovian analytical set-up. A more satisfactory explanation could be given within the present reconstruction of the Pigovian model, if it could be demonstrated that Pigou did permit the latter type of change but not the former one.

In fact, in the *Theory of Unemployment* there are various instances of discussions of changes in technology. But after Pigou (1933, pp. 113ff.) pointed out that 'improvements in the productivity of labour' might have all sorts of effects, he later (*ibid.*, p. 159) declared that he 'shall leave aside complex types of improvements and consider only ... the normal type'. Now this 'normal type of improvement' is defined in such a way that it leaves unaffected the ratio of the marginal product of labour to the level of output[20] so that for non-wage goods one could write in this case

$$\left(\frac{G'(y)}{G(y)} \right)^{-} = \left(\frac{G'(y)}{G(y)} \right)^{+} \quad \text{or} \quad \left(\frac{\alpha_y}{y} \right)^{-} = \left(\frac{\alpha_y}{y} \right)^{+} \tag{10.20}$$

where '−' denotes the situation before improvement and '+' denotes the situation after it and where the values of the first brackets are transformed into those of the second ones by utilising the definitions of equ. (9.15) (p. 65).

From the last of these two equations it now follows that under Pigovian 'normal type of improvement' the elasticity of production is necessarily assumed to be unchanging. Because if we compared the two situations for identical employment levels y, any change in α-s would violate the equality and thus Pigou's assumption of 'normality' as stated in equ. (10.20).

An efficiency parameter like A_x in equ. (10.13) could very well change, however, since this parameter cancels out in the type of constancy condition Pigou assumed to be holding under 'normal' improvement. This might be illustrated, for example, with reference to equ. (10.13) by pointing out that Pigou's normality assumption requires that for A_x-variations

$$\left(\frac{\alpha_x A_x^- x^{\alpha_x - 1}}{A_x^- x^{\alpha_x}} \right)^- = \left(\frac{\alpha_x A_x^+ x^{\alpha_x - 1}}{A_x^+ x^{\alpha_x}} \right)^+ \tag{10.21}$$

must hold – a condition which would always be fulfilled if technological change were limited just to the technological parameter A.

Thus our search for a reason for Keynes' exclusion of changes in α_y in his discussion of the classical measures for employment comes to the conclusion that this omission is in accordance with Pigou's preference for a discussion of technological change only as 'normal improvement'. In this case such variations are not permitted. On the other hand, efficiency changes as discussed under Keynes' item '(c)' are not an overextension of the Pigovian set-up.[21]

We conclude that Keynes' list of classical employment measures is indeed 'comprehensive' in the reconstructed Pigovian model of the last chapters.

10.6 A restatement of Keynes' internal critique of classical employment theory

At the beginning of this chapter we set ourselves the task of testing the present reconstruction of the Pigovian employment-theoretical model with regard to its capacity to reproduce the essential elements of Keynes' 'internal' critique of the classical approach. This test demands that a classical model in the sense of Keynes is able to generate exactly those classical measures for increasing employment which Keynes claimed in ch. 2 of the *General Theory* to have derived from that model. This test was passed by our candidate, as just noted.

But what, one may now ask, is so critical about this list? Keynes does not discuss this question in the context of stating it but quickly passes on to questions of involuntary unemployment proper in the sense of the 'second classical postulate' not being fulfilled. In the process he seems entirely to step out of the analytical framework discussed by him until then and he enters a realm of 'external' critique of the 'classics' in which he develops quite a different system of argumentation.

In assessing the critique which Keynes intended to articulate in connection with his statement of the 'classical means of increasing employment' we must note once again that the argumentation in ch. 2 of the *General Theory* was not supposed to be self-contained. It was supposed to be seen in connection with his detailed later review of Pigou (1933). Again we might see a two-step argumentation at work. In the first instance of argumentation Keynes presented this list as if it were so banal and unrealistic in the then pressing context of mass unemployment that he refrained from stating the obvious in ch. 2 of the *General Theory*. But in a second round of a more formal systematic criticism of Pigou (1933) he returned to this theme and Keynes (1936, p. 278) was quite explicit in his charge that Pigou was 'forgetful how narrow a thing' his real demand function for labour was.

For a final assessment of Keynes' internal critique of Pigou it might be interesting to inspect this charge in its wider context which reads:

> Finally, when Pigou comes to the 'Causation of Unemployment' he speaks, it is true, of fluctuations in the state of demand, much as I do. But he identifies the state of demand with the Real Demand Function for Labour, forgetful how narrow a thing the latter is on his definition ... Yet in Part V of his *Theory of Unemployment* fluctuations in the state of 'the real demand for labour' are given a position of importance ... To the reader [of the *General Theory*] all this seems, at first, reasonable and familiar ... But if we go back to the definition of the 'real demand for labour', all this loses its plausibility. For we shall find that there is nothing in the world which is less likely to be subject to sharp short-period swings than this factor. (italics added, GMA)

These passages from the last two pages of Keynes' review of Pigou (1933) contain a restatement of the method followed in the present chapters, namely to 'go back to Pigou's definitions' and to work out the analytical scope offered by his model. Thus Keynes himself advocates a type of reductionist approach to Pigou which involves criticising him not just from without but from within a detailed reconstruction of his definitions and analytical concepts.

Keynes' criticism of Pigou concentrates here on his extended discussion of the real demand function for labour for an explanation of the level of (un)employment. But this criticism leads also to the list of 'classical means' discussed above. With reference to this function there are just two logically possible explanations for changes in the level of employment if we exclude an off-curve analysis: movements on its curve and movements of its curve, the latter being given much prominence by Pigou as was noted by Keynes. Its elasticity was shown to be

$$E_r \equiv E^{\phi(x)}_{F'(x)} = E^{\phi(x)}_x : E^{F'(x)}_x \qquad (10.22)$$

and a microfoundation of this expression showed that it will indeed be likely to be a very stable magnitude because it consists of parameters characterising production functions and utility functions which generally are assumed not likely to change very much during short-period analysis.

In the Pigovian set-up, a movement on the real demand for labour curve requires – according to Keynes – a change in labour supply as characterised by Pigou's implicit $\chi(x)$-function. But a microfoundation of this function showed that it also is characterised by parameters which generally are assumed to be comparatively stable.

In an explicit reconstruction of the Pigovian model, both types of movements can be shown to reduce to just three 'classical means of increasing employment' apart from dealing with problems of market 'frictions'. These measures are quite obviously outside the realm of responsible public employment political discussion even of Keynes' and Pigou's times. To make explicit the very limited nature of these measures makes it understandable why Pigou (1933, p. v) prefaced his monograph on unemployment with the remark:

> I offer no apology ... for publishing, in a period when the tragedy of unemployment is of unexampeled magnitude, a book on that subject strictly academic in tone and content.

Thus, Pigou himself was very well aware of the 'academic' nature of what he had to offer in his book. But this is not just a question of argumentative style. It is important to realise that in all their employment political banality the 'classical means of increasing employment' are indeed comprehensive for a systematically reconstructed Pigovian model. To point this out is as far as Keynes could go in the context of an internal critique of classical employment theory.

Leading over to the external critique of the classics, the gist of Keynes' argument as analysed so far may be restated more specifically, using Keynes' own terminology, by stating: Pigou did discuss the composition of demand and employment with the help of a 'concoction' similar to some to be found in Keynes' own analysis. But this does not determine the absolute level of economic activity yet. What Pigou left undiscussed was 'effective demand' as determining the volume of demand and employment. This latter viewpoint is what Keynes thought to be new in his own theory and thus to be the centrepiece of his external critique of the classical theory of employment.

11
Keynes' External Critique of Pigou and the Classics

This chapter addresses the third of the questions listed at the beginning of Part II, on p. 44. It is concerned with the analytical steps which were taken by Keynes in going beyond the type of 'classical' Pigovian models just discussed.

In terms of our distinction between Keynes' 'internal' and 'external' critique of the classics, we now deal with the latter. In the last chapter we saw that his 'internal' critique focused on the general equilibrium character of the classical models and on the very limited employment political prescriptions they could offer in such an analytical context. In the following it must now be shown in which way the classical general equilibrium was seen by Keynes to be overdetermined so as to generate involuntary unemployment in the sense of an excess supply of labour.[1]

In terms of the argument of the *General Theory*, this chapter is concerned with the transition from chapter 2 on 'The Postulates of the Classical Economics' to chapter three on 'The Principle of Effective Demand' – two chapters which seem 'to have resulted from Keynes' preoccupation with Pigou's [(1933)] book.[2]

The subject matter of the latter of those two chapters, the effective demand doctrine, 'is the real starting point of everything' as Keynes wrote to Richard Kahn while he was still struggling to give the contents of the *General Theory* their final shape.[3] After publication, he again insisted on the paramount importance of this concept, observing its absence in the draft version of Harrod (1937a) (review of the *General Theory*).[4] In addition, Keynes commented to Harrod on that occasion: 'You do not show how in conditions of full employment ... my theory merges with the orthodox theory.' This comment would, of course, have been strange if Keynes himself did not see his effective-demand theory of employment in relation to the orthodox one. And the Pigovian *Theory of Unemployment* was – for Keynes (1936, p. 7) at least – 'the only detailed account of the classical theory which exists', as we had occasion to observe already above on p. 44.

Thus, if Keynes' theory does in fact merge under conditions of full employment into the orthodox one, it should also be possible and in the present context the logical next step to show explicitly how his theory departed from the Pigovian reconstruction which was under discussion so far. This will be the subject matter of the following pages.

11.1 Analytical foundations for the Keynesian transition to an external critique of the classical theory of employment

11.1.1 The absence of a case for employment political action in the Pigovian model

There are two important employment theoretic implications which originate from the general equilibrium nature of the classical approach:

(α) The classical approach as a theory of general equilibrium has to assume the fulfilment of all the plans of all economic agents in the economy. In such a model economy one might have extensive comparative static discussions of changes in economic plans and theoretical realisations when there are changes in preferences or technology, as was done in the last chapter. But there is really no clear-cut choice theoretic case for specific policies directed at higher employment if – under the given conditions – everybody maximises utility and profits in the eyes of the analysing economists anyhow.[5]

(β) The analytical presupposition of general equilibrium poses a problem from an empirical side if an economist decided to face the obvious fact of drastic changes in employment levels and if he, as a concession to public demands on his expertise, sets himself to devising employment policies. Since in the economic model at hand it is individual economic agents and the invisible hand of competition which determine economic outcomes, and since in this context it is clear that under perfect conditions there will always be full employment, for given tastes and technology the classical economic theory as such has no specific economic handle to offer by which to move the economy towards outcomes which the public tells the economist to be socially preferable – except that classical economics suggests the advice to do away with imperfections.

In a situation of mass unemployment there is thus a considerable gulf between reality demanding for action and the contentions following from the equilibrium concepts of conventional economic theory.

Pigou (1933, p. v) *articulated* this gulf rather than bridged it when he stated in the preface to his *Theory of Unemployment* that 'economists ... are physiologists, not clinical practitioners; engineers, not engine-drivers'. The implication of these statements was that, according to Pigou, the theoretical lingo of the economic 'engineers' permitted no participation in guiding the conduct of the economic political 'engine-driver'. But this must have been an unsatisfactory conclusion even for Pigou himself who is well known to have attempted to supply the public with economic political advice which was at times not very different from later 'Keynesian' prescriptions.

11.1.2 Reason and means for employment political action in the Keynesian departure from classical analysis

Originally, the above contentions concerning the limitations of classical economics in the face of dramatic levels of unemployment were not made by Keynes in quite the way just stated. But a negative version of the first of them was given explicitly by Keynes (1936, ch. 2) and it was declared to be 'our point of departure from the classical system'. Restating this negation of classical equilibrium and elaborating somewhat we may note:

(α) *Negation of the Second Classical Postulate*: Economists must give a choice theoretic reason for devising a separate economic theory of unemployment. Unemployment is a clear economic problem if it represents a disequilibrium of households in the sense of their marginal conditions not being fulfilled with regard to labour supply. An economic theory of unemployment may therefore be based, not on the supposition of general equilibrium, but on the explicit supposition of household disequilibrium.

  The particular equilibrium postulate to be negated is thus the one concerning labour supply, Keynes' (1936, p. 5) 'second postulate of classical economics'. Starting from the working hypothesis that this postulate is not fulfilled makes economic policy justifiable as an attempt to bring the economy to its full employment general equilibrium solution.[6]

This negation of the factual existence of equilibrium would give a reason for a specialised economic theory of employment and unemployment. There remains to find an economic theoretical means for employment political action directed at full employment. It is supplied by Keynes' theoretical 'starting point' of a doctrine of effective demand. The proposal of this doctrine may be seen as a negation of the classical 'imperfections' approach to unemployment:

(β) *The effective demand doctrine as negation of the imperfections approach to employment*: If, under conditions of unchanged tastes and technology, labour supply and demand do not meet in a situation of unemployment, this situation is not to be treated exclusively as the outcome of some meta-theoretical 'imperfection' of real life vis-à-vis pure economic theory. Rather, there must be a clear economic theoretical reason given if economic agents are constrained not to reach the full-employment general equilibrium solution theoretically attainable if such a constraint were not present. This constraint may be given by the problem of co-ordinating the real turnover plans of an economy on an aggregate level, generating a specific level of 'effective demand'. Economic policy directed at higher employment could then be addressed at influencing the workings of this constraint.

The exact contents of Keynes' effective demand doctrine has been the subject of incessant debates and we will investigate below how the present reconsideration of the Pigovian classical model could throw some light on this particular issue. Here, we are concerned with the mere groundworks of Keynes' departure from the classical analysis and it is remarkable that Keynes, although not sparing polemics against the Classics in other contexts, repeatedly stressed the limited nature of his departure from the established analytical postulates.

11.1.3 The limited extent of Keynes' departure from classical analysis

In principle, it was just the assumption of unemployment which distinguished his theory from the orthodox one since, according to Keynes own judgment, it should be possible to show that the two theories merge into one under conditions of full employment. And it was just the 'second classical postulate' which Keynes wanted to be seen as disposed of under his conditions of unemployment, and not the 'first classical postulate' of marginal productivity (*modulo* market conditions) determining real wages. Keynes (1936, p. 17) proclaimed his maintaining the first classical postulate as an 'important point of agreement' with the classical system.

From these observations it follows that

- Keynes clearly did not intend the construction of a fix-price theory of *dis*equilibrium under unemployment, as, e.g., attempted by Barro and Grossman (1971) and by Malinvaud (1977).
- Keynes also did not intend the overthrow of classical analysis *in toto*. Even the classical 'disutility' theory of labour supply was not rejected by him as analytically unsound in principle. All he wanted to point out in his rejection of the 'second classical postulate' was that labour supply was no binding constraint for the economic system under conditions of involuntary unemployment.[7]
- Since Keynes wanted to see just the second classical postulate rejected, he implicitly *maintained* those parts of the Pigovian analysis which did not rely on this postulate. In particular, he had no grounds to reject his ϕ-function analysis as analytically incorrect.[8]

For some readers, there might be a confusing aspect in Keynes' arguing at first in favour of general equilibrium modelling, then against equilibrium. Scrutinising the genesis of the *General Theory*, Dimand (2002) sees a historical transition from an early general equilibrium orientation of Keynes around late 1933 to an abondonment of that approach by 1936. Our distinction of general equilibrium oriented '*internal* critique' against Pigou (1933) *versus* an over-determination and hence *dis*-equilibrium oriented '*external* critique' offers an alternative, methodologically based, explanation for an approach which might seem to be lacking in consistency for some readers.

11.2 Keynes' doctrine of 'effective demand' and the reconstructed Pigovian model

11.2.1 Keynes' problematic presentation of the concept of 'effective demand'

In seeming contradiction to the above characterisation of Keynes' departure from the classical analysis as being of rather limited nature, in developing his concept of 'effective demand', Keynes appeared to break entirely with the main tools of classical economics.

Although in the second chapter of the *General Theory* Keynes went out of his way to stress his acceptance of the first classical postulate, a few pages later, in the third chapter, he seemed to be in an entirely different analytical world. Real wages and marginal products seem to fall into oblivion.[9] Instead of these concepts, Keynes suddenly discusses an 'aggregate supply price' (Z) which is some 'expectation of proceeds' but which, Keynes (*GT*, p. 24, n. 1) warns, should not be confused 'with the supply price of a unit of output in the ordinary sense of this term'. Pretty soon this sort of 'expectation of proceeds' is then equated to some other magnitude of 'expected proceeds' (D). The outcome of this equation is then called 'effective demand'. This concept is postulated to be related to the macroeconomic level of employment and Keynes (*GT*, p. 25) concludes that 'this is the substance of the *General Theory* of Employment'.

In this brief summary we intentionally related the crucial passages about the 'substance of the *General Theory*' in a way which might make understandable that Keynes' presentation of 'effective demand' is often considered as being extremely infelicitous, if not erroneous. His modern editors expressly note that they did not correct his 'more substantial errors such as the unsatisfactory presentation of aggregate supply and demand'.[10] But the belief that 'substantial error' should be involved in the presentation of an idea so central for his entire theory and which he had worked at for a considerable time before publication is so sensational that it could not be accepted lightheartedly – at least not by someone interested in giving an authentic rendering of Keynes' economics.

Unfortunately, the editors just mentioned did not elaborate which particular error in Keynes' presentation required correction. Particular dissatisfaction with his reasoning might well be directed against his concept of 'aggregate supply'. In the next section we will therefore turn our attention to this concept, discussing it in relation to the Pigovian analysis reviewed so far.

But why should the Keynesian concept of aggregate supply be regarded as the first candidate for further clarification? In principle, there are three elements involved in Keynes' doctrine of 'effective demand'. In a summing up of his effective demand theory Keynes (1936, pp. 28f.) reduces it to the following constituent elements, namely[11]

- an aggregate supply function $\Phi(N)$
- a consumption function $\Xi(N)$
- a volume of investment D_2

claiming that, according to his theory, employment N is given as a solution to the equation

$$\Phi(N) - \Xi(N) = D_2 \qquad (11.1)$$

But the latter two of these three elements, constituting the components of aggregate demand, are discussed by Keynes at great length in books III and IV of the *General Theory*, addressed specifically to consumption resp. to investment.

Thus, we are led to believe that dissatisfaction with his presentation of his theory could be expected to be mainly concerned with his concept of aggregate supply as represented by his $\Phi(N)$ – function which later on in his book finds no more direct clarification.

11.2.2 Keynes' Pigovian conception of aggregate supply

The seemingly incomprehensible abruptness in Keynes' transition from an exposition of the analytical principles of the classics to the statement of his own theory of effective demand in chs. 2 and 3 of the *General Theory* offers room for extended exegetical speculations. We limit ourselves to the proposal that Keynes argued under the understanding of a common analytical basis which, in Keynes' own mind, was uncontroversial and therefore taken by him as being generally accepted as part of common knowledge in economics and thus not requiring his detailed restatement.

In this line of approach we can refer in particular to a passage in Keynes (1936, p. 89) where he stated explicitly that it was mainly the aggregate demand function 'which has been overlooked', but noting in this context:

The aggregate supply function, however, which depends in the main on the physical conditions of supply, involves few considerations which are not already familiar. The form may be unfamiliar but the underlying factors are not new.

But if the aggregate supply function may be regarded as conventional economics in just an alternative garb, it seems understandable that Keynes refrained from giving an extended treatment to this part of his theoretical argument.

Our interpretational proposal that Keynes departed only in a very limited way from classical analysis finds some further textual support in a number of statements of Keynes' in which he professes his agreement with Pigou concerning specific analytical elements. A case in point is found in the context of Pigou's ϕ-function analysis discussed above. In that context Keynes (1936, p. 273) declared in particular:

In so far as we can identify Professor Pigou's wage-goods with my consumption-goods, ... his $F(x)/F'(x)$, being the value of the output of the wage-goods industries in terms of the wage-unit, *is the same* as my C_w. (emphasis added, GMA)

But such a statement might appear as being somewhat strange and inconsistent with other related passages in the *General Theory*. Thus, the reader might remember that in an earlier passage of the *General Theory* Keynes (1936, p. 90) gave his consumption function as $C_w = \varXi(Y_w)$ where Y_w is national income in terms of wage units. Therefore, in *that* context, Keynes obviously argues that C_w is a function of *national income*. But now, in the quote just given, Keynes relates C_w to *sectoral employment x*. Does he have a new theory of consumption here in relating himself to Pigou? The answer to such a question is that we must discern here as in all questions of *effective* demand between 'abstract' demand on the one hand and 'concretely materialised' demand on the other. Although the interaction of demand and supply leaves just one specific value of effective demand, it is here as in other economic contexts the *interaction* which must be seen behind an economic materialisation.

The relevance of this observation for the quote just given is that it refers to the *alternative* aspect of the interaction related to consumption, namely to the supply side as manifested in an employment function for a particular industry which Keynes (1936, p. 280), shortly after the quote under discussion, gave as[12]

$$N_r = \mathcal{F}_r(D_{wr}) \qquad (11.2)$$

where D_{wr} is 'an amount of effective demand, measured in terms of wage units, directed to the r-th firm or industry' which 'calls forth an amount of employment N_r in that firm or industry'. If we now remember further that Keynes (1936, p. 44) defined industry production functions as

$$O_r = \Psi_r(N_r), \qquad (11.3)$$

then we have all the ingredients for the following stepwise translation of the Pigovian $F(x)/F'(x)$ of the above quote into Keynesian concepts relevant for our attempt at elucidating his aggregate supply function.

For this purpose, let us denote Keynes' consumption goods sector by index 1. On the basis of the correspondence given in the quote we may then write

$$\frac{F(x)}{F'(x)} \Leftrightarrow \frac{\Psi_1(N_1)}{\Psi_1'(N_1)} = \frac{O_1}{\frac{w}{p_1}} = \frac{p_1 O_1}{w} = \frac{C}{w} \equiv C_w \qquad (11.4)$$

That is, if, as Keynes states in the quote under discussion, we may let Pigou's wage goods correspond to Keynes' consumption goods, then the Pigovian $F(x)$-function corresponds to a Keynesian Ψ_1- function. The rest of equ. (11.4) then follows from the respective definition of variables. We may therefore proceed from the conceptual correspondence just stated to noting that the 'first classical postulate' is assumed to hold in Keynesian economics according to ch. 2 of the *General Theory*. But then the numerator in the Pigovian ratio corresponds to the output (O_1) in Keynes' consumption goods sector and the denominator corresponds to the real wage (w/p_1) in that sector as stated in the next step of equ. (11.4).

In the further transformations given in equ. (11.4) it is then simply stated that in this case this ratio is nothing else but the money value of the production of consumption goods (C) divided by the money wage w, that is, it is nothing else but the value of consumption in terms of wage units.[13] *This* is the chain of reasoning which Keynes alluded to when stating that his C_w is the same as the Pigovian ratio given in the above quote. Its significance for the concept of an aggregate supply function is that is supplies a relationship between the value of production (C_w) on the one hand and sectoral employment N_1 on the other. Some such relationship was given by the employment function of equ. (11.2) where, for $r = 1$, we have $D_w 1 = C_w$ and $N_r = N_1$. We may then invert the function of (11.2) obtaining

$$C_w = \mathcal{F}_1^{-1}(N_1) = \frac{\Psi_1(N_1)}{\Psi_1'(N_1)}. \tag{11.5}$$

The significance of this manipulation will become apparent when we note that according to Keynes (1936, p. 280) the employment function 'only differs from the aggregate supply function in that is is, in effect, its inverse function and is defined in terms of the wage-unit'. But if that is the case, the inverse of the sectoral employment function (F_1) as given in (11.5) should be nothing else but the aggregate supply function of the consumption goods sector (Φ_1) when its output is measured in terms of the wage unit.

On the basis of this discussion we therefore believe that we are able to confirm the proposal that insofar as Keynes was prepared to see his C_w as being the *same* magnitude as the Pigovian $F(x)/F'(x)$, he did not think in terms of a consumption function but in terms of a 'aggregate supply function' for the consumption sector. But then the characteristics of the aggregate supply function follow immediately from this ratio or from the Keynesian equivalent as stated in (11.4).

We thus reach on the basis of this discussion a 'Pigovian' conception of the Keynesian aggregate supply function. If formulated for the industry (or 'sector') and if the value of aggregate supply is measured in terms of Keynes' wage units it may be given as[14]

$$Z_{wr} = \Phi_r(N_r) = \frac{\Psi_r(N_r)}{\Psi_r'(N_r)} \qquad (11.6)$$

where $\Psi_r(\cdot)$ is a conventional (neoclassical) production function.[15]
The questions ahead concern now the characteristics of these sectoral 'aggregate supply' functions and their relation to the global aggregate supply function for an economy as a whole as introduced by Keynes in ch. 3 of the *General Theory*.

11.2.3 Keynesian aggregate supply and demand further considered

11.2.3.1 Keynesian expectations and 'classical' supply and demand analysis

It seems to be a special trait of Keynes' economics that it pays particular homage to the role of expectations in determining economic outcomes. A whole chapter (ch. 5) is devoted to this topic and also in the definitions of aggregate supply and demand functions in ch. 3 of the *General Theory* expectations are mentioned in each case. It might be instructive to reproduce the relevant passages from pp. 24f. of the *General Theory*:

> the aggregate supply price of the output of a given amount of employment is the expectation of proceeds which will just make it worth the while of the entrepreneurs to give that employment ... Let Z be the aggregate supply price of the output from employing N men, the relationship between Z and N being written Z = *φ(N)*, which can be called the *aggregate supply function*.
>
> Similarly, let D be the proceeds which entrepreneurs expect to receive from the employment of N men, the relationship between D and N being written D = *f(N)*, which can be called the *aggregate demand function*. (emphasis and paragraphing added, GMA)

The remarkable aspect of these definitions of aggregate supply *and* demand is that both supply *and* demand are defined on the basis of expected proceeds of the *entrepreneurs*, that is of just *one* set of economic agents. Yet, these expectations formed by the entrepreneurs as one single group are supposed to be divisible into two separate functional relationships, the co-ordination of which should, in the ensuing analysis, determine employment.

But then, if each entrepreneur in a free enterprise society forms his own expectations, can these separate expectations be expected to converge in every analytical moment to a consistent macroeconomic 'aggregate demand'?

Keynes was confronted by these types of doubt in an extended debate with R. G. Hawtrey and it is remarkable that in this context he believed in doing nothing else but articulating explicitly what he considered to be implicit conventional wisdom:

The demand which determines the decision as to how much plant to employ must necessarily concern itself with expectations. And I am in this respect simply trying to put more precisely what is implicit in most contemporary economics.[16]

Keynes even went so far as to sketch a deterministic and a stochastic version of rational expectations, continuing:

I am saying that in so far as employers have correct foresight, they will curtail the amount of employment they offer in accordance with the principle I state. But ... it would all come to exactly the same thing if one were to suppose that the decisions of employers were not brought about by any rational attempt to foresee on the lines I indicate, but merely functioned by modifications at short intervals solely based on the method of trial and error. For the method of trial and error would lead to exactly the same results.

From this explanation we must conclude that the demand functions of Keynesian economics are considered by Keynes to be some sort of 'rational' expectations of entrepreneurs about the behaviour of the economy.

It seems that, according to these and related passages, Keynes attributed to the workings of 'trial and error' some mechanism which in other price theoretic works was attributed to the activity of a Walrasian auctioneer.

But to clarify this question satisfactorily would involve us in speculations leading too far from the present topic. In the present attempt at clarifying the Keynes–Classics issue it must suffice to conclude that there is no reason to believe that in this particular regard expectations were devised by Keynes to play a novel analytical role – at least not according to his own judgment.

11.2.3.2 Imperfect competition and effective demand

There are readers of Keynes' doctrine of effective demand who believe that it should – or implicitly does – imply imperfect competition in a significant way. Thus, B. Ohlin commented on the *General Theory* in this regard.[17]

When reading his book one sometimes wonders whether he [Keynes] never discussed imperfect competition with Mrs Robinson.

This gave Keynes the opportunity to reply:

The reference to imperfect competition is very perplexing. I cannot see how on earth it comes in. Mrs Robinson, I may mention, read my proofs without discovering any connection.

From this comment it seems that Keynes had in mind a formulation of effective demand which was valid under any assumption concerning the state of competition.

It should be remembered that Keynes (1936, p. 17) accepted the first classical postulate of real wages being equal to the marginal product of labour subject 'to the same qualifications as in the classical theory' and that a qualification expressly mentioned by Keynes (1936, p. 5) was 'that the equality may be disturbed, in accordance with certain principles, if competition and markets are imperfect'.

The essential assumption in this context is that the disturbances possibly – or rather, very likely – arising from imperfect competition are subsumed under the 'givens' of the economy under consideration, as stated in detail by Keynes (1936, p. 245) when restating the *General Theory* in his ch. 18:

> We take as given
> [1] the existing skill and quantity of available labour,
> [2] the existing quality and quantity of available equipment,
> [3] the existing technique,
> [4] the *degree of competition*,
> [5] the tastes and habits of the consumer,
> [6] the disutility of different intensities of labour ...[18]

The first three of these 'givens' determine the shape of the production functions and the marginal productivity functions as represented in, e.g., equ. (11.6) above and the last three determine the extent of the disturbance from the marginal productivity real wage just mentioned.[19] These disturbances could be easily included as separate parameters in a 'Pigovian' restatement of the aggregate supply functions. Under conditions of imperfect competition one would thus have for the real wage in the sector or industry when the produced good and and labour are homogeneous

$$\frac{w_r}{p_r} = \frac{1 + \epsilon_r}{1 + \xi_r} \Psi_r'(N_r) \tag{11.7}$$

with ϵ_r (where $-1 < \epsilon_r < 0$) describing how marginal returns are affected through price changes when there are variations in output O_r, and $\xi_r \geq 0$ describing how marginal labour cost in nominal terms are affected through wage changes when there are variations in labour input N_r.[20]

Under changed conditions of competition the parameters in the expression for aggregate supply would, of course, also change. With the help of equ. (11.7) it could be shown in which way that change should be represented. For a uniform wage unit $w = w_r$ one would thus have for aggregate supply not the expression as given in equ. (11.6) which holds for the case of perfect competition only but an extended one which would read

$$Z_{wr}^{\text{imp}} = \frac{p_r O_r}{w} = \frac{1+\xi_r}{1+\epsilon_r} \frac{\Psi_r(N_r)}{\Psi_r'(N_r)}. \tag{11.8}$$

But such changes in formulation, at least in Keynes' judgement, did not involve a matter of principle concerning effective demand analysis and he tugged them away in the array of 'givens' as seen above. In so far as the classics were prepared to set $\xi_\tau = 0$ and $\varepsilon_r = 0$ as Pigou (1933) obviously was in much of his theory,[21] Keynes saw no point in quarrelling about this assumption.

11.2.3.3 Technological assumptions

In view of later critical comments by Cambridge Keynesians like Joan Robinson about the acceptability of the conventional concept of a production function, there might be the supposition that Keynes was also critical of this analytical tool. This is clearly not the case, however. It was seen above already that he had no problem in formulating such functions and that he accepted diminishing returns to labour as an 'incontrovertible' proposition.

Under conditions of perfect competition the average value of aggregate supply permits a direct conclusion concerning technology because in this case we have in any profit maximising industry

$$\frac{Z_{wr}}{N_r} = \frac{p_r O_r}{w N_r} = \frac{\Psi_r(N_r)}{\Psi_r'(N_r)N_r} = \frac{1}{\alpha_r} \tag{11.9}$$

where α_r is the elasticity of production of labour.

Rearranging this expression permits the formulation of the aggregate supply function of a profit maximising industry as

$$Z_{wr} = \frac{1}{\alpha_r} N_r \tag{11.10}$$

where α_r contains all the relevant technical information.

In principle, this elasticity could be formulated as a functional relationship

$$\alpha = \alpha_r(N_r, K_r) \tag{11.11}$$

where K_r stands for the stock of capital 'equipment' which was assumed by Keynes to be one of the 'givens' of his analysis. Even if capital equipment does change, under Pigovian conditions of 'normal improvement' we have unchanging conditions in the sense of $\alpha_r^- = \alpha_r^+$ as seen above. We conclude therefore that insofar as Keynes accepted the Pigovian production theoretic framework,

$$\frac{d\alpha_r}{dK_r} = 0 \tag{11.12}$$

must hold because of the assumption of Pigovian 'normal improvement'. Similarly, it seems that concerning labour Keynes assumed likewise that

$$\frac{d\alpha_r}{dN_r} = 0 \tag{11.13}$$

holds. This can be deduced from the fact that in his analysis the aggregate supply curve was permitted to be a straight line from the origin. In this case the aggregate supply function of equ. (11.10) should give a constant α_r.

For completeness' sake it might be noted that in the case of imperfect competition an argumentation similar to the one leading to (11.10) would, on the basis of the modified marginal productivity equation (11.10), give

$$\hat{Z}_{wr} = \frac{1}{\alpha_r} \frac{1+\xi_r}{1+\epsilon_r} N_r \tag{11.14}$$

For exogenously given ϵ-s and ξ-s, a straight-line sectoral aggregate supply curve would again result for constant α_r.

11.2.3.4 Problems of Pigovian 'processing' and of Keynesian 'user cost'

The production model just discussed is the one employed by Pigou (1933, pp. 88ff.) in developing his concept of the 'real demand for labour' in a two-sector model of an entire economy and we tried to document and to discuss in detail that Keynes was prepared to link his own theory to this Pigovian approach. But it should be mentioned that both Keynes and Pigou deviated from this production theoretic model at times.

When discussing 'the short-period elasticity of demand for labour in particular occupations', Pigou (1933, pp. 41ff.) introduced the concept of 'processing' in such a way that the production process involved the collaboration of not just labour and fixed capital equipment, but the utilisation of raw material as well. It is then clear that the marginal real cost of such 'processing' is not just the respective real wage but involves the marginal real cost of raw material as well. This type of modified marginal calculus did not enter the 'starting position' for the Pigovian $\phi(x)$-function as discussed above, however.

Thus when, in the *General Theory*, Keynes (1936, pp. 23ff.) introduced the concept of 'user cost' as, among other items, being that part of a particular entrepreneur's cost 'which he pays out to other entrepreneurs for what he has to purchase from them', he did not introduce entirely new considerations in comparison with Pigou. He rather extended in that context the type of analysis of 'raw material cost' contained in the particular Pigovian conception of 'processing'. But the same inconsistencies present in Pigou (1933) were also to be found in the *General Theory*.

In fact, after the publication of the *General Theory*, the modelling of 'user cost' turned out to be one of the weakest analytical aspects of Keynes' book.[22]

11.2.4 Pigovian 'real demand for labour' and Keynesian effective demand

It was seen above that the Pigovian 'real demand for labour function' was a specific way of stating certain sectoral equilibrium conditions in the context of a sub-model of an economy. It contained in particular the proposition that marginal conditions for product demand by non-workers' households may be assumed to match those for product supply (see equ. (9.7) on p. 61 and equ. (9.17) on p. 65).

Furthermore, it was seen above that Keynes (1936, p. 273) accepted the Pigovian $\phi(x)$-function which was shown to follow from those equilibrium conditions as a 'concoction similar to some of my own'.

One may now ask about the precise nature of the analytical correspondence between Keynes and Pigou in this regard, that is: how do the Pigovian equilibrium conditions translate into Keynesian concepts and which parts of Keynes' analysis link up with the Pigovian concept of a $\phi(x)$-function?

In order to answer this question in an exemplary way, we turn to the equilibrium condition of equ. (9.17), the starting point of the reconstruction of the Pigovian $\phi(x)$-function of equ. (9.20).

11.2.4.1 An algebraic correspondence

Restating equ. (9.17) in Keynesian notation and rearranging gives

$$\frac{p_2}{p_1} = \frac{\gamma_y / O_2^d}{\gamma_x / O_{1k}^d} = \frac{\alpha_1 \Psi_1(N_1)}{N_1} \cdot \frac{N_2}{\alpha_2 \Psi_2(N_2)} = \left(\frac{N_2}{\alpha_2} / O_2^s \right) : \left(\frac{N_1}{\alpha_1} / O_1^s \right) \quad (11.15)$$

where, as before, the small Greek letters represent elasticities of utility (γ_r) resp. of production (α_r) whereas the capital Greek expression Ψ_r stands for Keynes' denotion of a production function as given by equ. (11.3) above, where we always have $r = 1, 2$. Output demanded is represented by O^d, with index ik denoting consumption goods (or the Pigovian wage goods) demanded by capitalists, while index 2 stands for the Pigovian non-wage goods which Keynes cautiously likened to his investment goods. Finally, index s in equ. (11.15) stands for goods supplied.

The right-hand side of (11.15) states the equilibrium conditions for goods supply as did the corresponding part of (9.17) from which the present version was derived.

This expression of entrepreneurial equilibrium may be transformed into

$$\frac{p_2 O_2^s}{w} \frac{w}{p_1 O_1^s} \equiv \frac{Z_{w2}}{Z_{w1}} = \left(\frac{N_2}{\alpha_2}\right) : \left(\frac{N_1}{\alpha_1}\right) \tag{11.16}$$

In this version it is then seen to just restate the Keynesian equilibrium condition (11.10) relating profit maximising aggregate supply and employment via the α_r.

The left-hand side of (11.15) may be transformed into

$$\frac{p_1 O_{1k}^d}{w} \equiv D_{w1k} = \frac{\gamma_x}{\gamma_y} D_{w2} \tag{11.17}$$

stating that the equilibrium value of wage goods demand by non-workers will be in a specific relation to the demand for non-wage goods. But in Keynesian notation the Pigovian accounting equation for the 'trading surplus' of non-workers with regard to wage goods as given by equ. (8.9) (p. 55) may be written as

$$\frac{p_1 O_{1k}^d}{w} \equiv D_{w1k} = D_w - N. \tag{11.18}$$

Equating (11.17) and (11.18) and rearranging thus gives from the demand side of Pigovian equilibrium in Keynesian notation an expression linking total employment N and sectoral demand via

$$N = D_{w1} - \frac{\gamma_x}{\gamma_y} D_{w2} \tag{11.19}$$

whereas the supply side equilibrium as expressed in (11.16) or (11.10) gives a relationship between total employment and sectoral aggregate supplies reading

$$N = \alpha_1 Z_{w1} + \alpha_2 Z_{w2} \tag{11.20}$$

since total employment is $N = N_1 + N_2$ and the sectoral employments N_1 and N_2 may be replaced through the stated equilibrium relationships linking them to the values of sectoral supply.

11.2.4.2 A graphical representation

The two expressions (11.19) and (11.20) represent separately the information given by the right-hand side and the left-hand side of (11.15). They are shown graphically in the north-eastern quadrant of fig. 11.1 on p. 131. The Z_w-curve there corresponds to equ. (11.20) and represents the profit maximal production possibility set *in terms of wage units* for a specific level of total employment. The characteristics of this Z_w-curve follow from those of the sectoral Z_{wr}-curves given in the north-western and in the south-eastern quadrants. Thus, for a specific level of total employment $\bar{N}$, the maximum attainable value of $C_w = Z_w1$ follows from allotting all of that employment to the corresponding sector as depicted in the north-western sector by means of the Z_w1-curve.

It should be noted that the Z_{wr}-curves lie above (or below) the ones of the corresponding production functions (here: ψ_1 (N_1) resp. $F(x)$ if the reciprocal real wage is larger than unity (or is less than unity) since we have, e.g.,

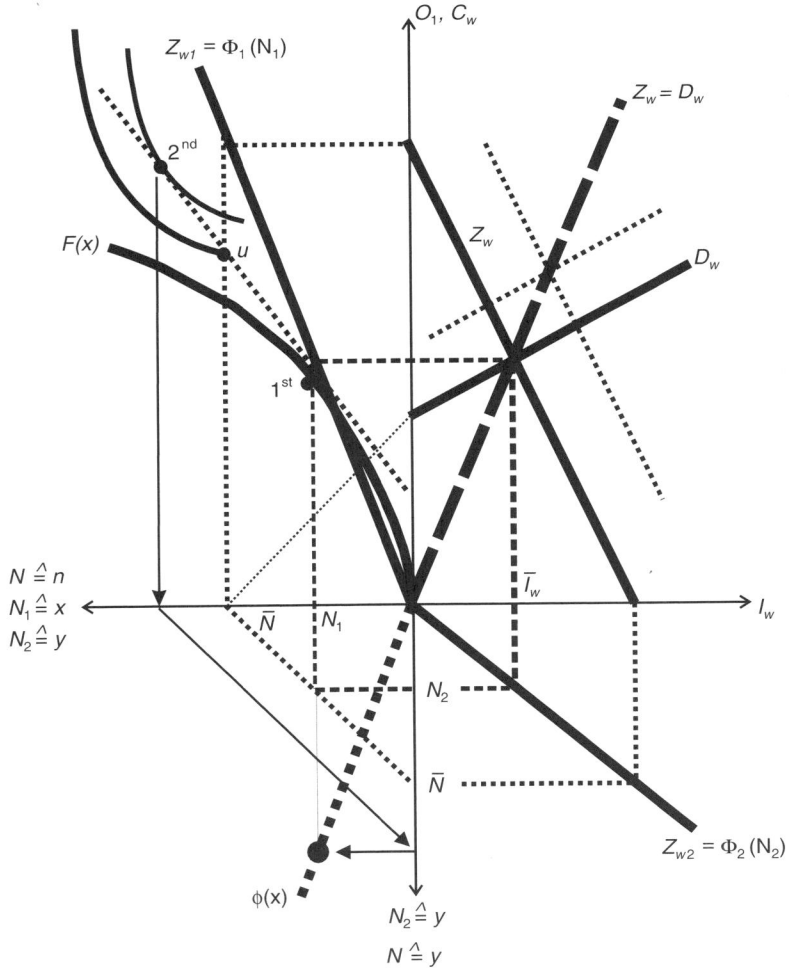

Figure 11.1 Keynes' 'effective demand' and the Pigovian approach

$$Z_{w1} = \frac{p_1}{w} O_1 = \frac{p_1}{w} F(x). \tag{11.21}$$

The two curves cut each other if the real wage is unity. Such a case of equality is assumed to hold in the present case just right of the point marked I.

The second of these expressions, equ. (11.19), is represented in fig. 11.1 by the curve marked D_w. When $C_w = D_{w1}$ and $I_w = D_{w2}$, we may re-write (11.19) as

$$C_w = N + \frac{\gamma_x}{\gamma_y} I_w, \tag{11.22}$$

thus obtaining an algebraic expression for the D_w-curve as drawn in fig. 11.1. In the present case – which is only a first approximation to Keynes' original analysis, however, as we will note presently – the intercept of that curve is given by $\bar{N}$.

With increased employment, the Z_w curve and the D_w curve shift parallel upwards as shown by the corresponding broken lines. Their intersection then describes a *locus* marked $Z_w = D_w$ in fig. 11.1. This *locus* represents 'effective demand' in the sense of Keynes.

Keynesian 'effective demand' is defined as that demand which can become effective because it meets a corresponding supply. In terms of the present model this gives the equations

$$D_{w1} = Z_{w1} = C_w \tag{11.23}$$

$$D_{w2} = Z_{w2} = I_w \tag{11.24}$$

and for alternative values of N the system (11.19) to (11.24) generates a *locus* of alternative realisations of effective demand values as expressed in fig. 11.1 where the values are given as those of consumption goods (C_w) in terms of the wage unit and as corresponding values of investment goods (I_w). Each of the latter two was treated as either a demand magnitude or a supply magnitude by Keynes. Its algebraic expression is given by

$$C_w = \frac{\alpha_2 + \frac{\gamma_x}{\gamma_y}}{1 - \alpha_1} I_w. \tag{11.25}$$

For alternative employment levels N there are alternative realisations of effective demand levels in the north-eastern quadrant of fig. 11.1 along the $Z_w = D_w$ line depicted there. But this line is the *locus* of equality of alternative D_w- and Z_w-curves which in turn just represent alternative equilibria as expressed by the right-hand side and the left-hand side of (11.15) resp. (9.17) as was seen above.

Thus, the $Z_w = D_w$ line contains the same information and equilibrium postulates which were used in the construction of the Pigovian 'real demand for labour' curve. It follows that the Pigovian $\phi(x)$-curve is just an alternative presentation of a Keynesian effective demand curve in a two-sectoral setting.

We are now back at the old observation of a close correspondence between Keynesian and Pigovian concepts of which Keynes himself was well aware when reviewing the Pigovian concept of a $\phi(x)$-function. Yet, the concept of effective demand here under discussion is supposed to be the crucial analytical point where Keynes parted company with the 'classics'. How do these two seemingly contradictory statements fit together?

The answer to this question has two aspects: firstly, it must be stressed that although formally related to Pigou's real demand for labour function, Keynes' original development of the concept of effective demand was based on quite different demand theoretic considerations as will emerge from the discussion of the next section.

Secondly, the basic employment theoretic problem is *not* whether there is a *locus* of alternative entrepreneurial equilibria, but to determine *which* of these equilibria is the relevant one. It is here where the fundamental difference lies between Keynes and Pigou as will emerge from the last section of this chapter.

11.3 Reconsidering the concept of effective demand under Keynesian perspective

11.3.1 Reconsidering the characteristics of Pigovian demand

In ch. 9 above it was stated that from Pigou's own point of view a clarification of the exact characteristics of the non-wage goods was immaterial. As far as he was concerned, they could well be treated as luxury motor cars or silken dressing gowns (see p. 65). Keynes' position was sharply different from this one when he equated the Pigovian wage goods with his own consumption goods and the Pigovian non-wage goods with his investment goods.

In the Keynesian analysis the principal choice facing a consumer before demanding an additional consumption good is, by the generic significance of the term, not between consuming an item typically demanded by workers or one typically not demanded by this type of household. The choice is rather between additional consumption or abstention from additional consumption in the present period, the act of non-consumption being *saving* – and saving being not *uno actu* a demand for a specific non-wage good.

Savings, in the Keynesian view, are typically not in kind. They consist rather to a considerable extent in acquisitions of financial assets or of additional holdings of idle balances of money. The financial assets demanded by the savers are supplied by other economic agents who seek finances for their expenditures for goods and services. These considerations then lead to the following Keynesian characterisation of the demand for non-wage goods: from the standpoint of consumers they are no specific demand in the current period at all – or, as Keynes (1936, p. 210) put it:

> An act of individual saving means – so to speak – a decision not to have dinner to-day. But it does *not* necessitate a decision to have dinner or to buy a pair of boots a week hence or a year hence or to consume any specific thing at any specific date.

Only insofar as that part of current income not used up by consumption is then taken up by economic agents for other types of expenditure – typically this would be investment expenditure – only to this extent will non-consumption then result in factual demand for goods. But exactly this analytical step, namely a thorough discussion of investment demand, was omitted by Pigou (1933) according to Keynes (1936, p. 279):

> Professor Pigou has altogether omitted from his analysis the unstable factor, namely fluctuations in the scale of investment, which is most often at the bottom of the phenomenon of fluctuations in employment.

It seems that Pigou would not necessarily disagree with what Keynes had to say with regard to savings and investment and in his *Employment and Equilibrium* he later followed very closely the Keynesian terminology. His first reaction to the *General Theory*, to be investigated in greater detail below in part III, was, however, to claim that one could very well formulate economic models in which consumption goods are indeed the only produced goods in an economy. But if it is postulated that there is no net investment going on in the model economy under consideration then an explicit analysis of the demand for investment goods might be regarded as superfluous – or even as downright contradictory.

But no matter how Pigou justified in later writings his omission of an analysis of investment demand, the Keynesian position vis-à-vis the Pigovian model in this particular regard must now be brought in better relief.

11.3.2 The microfoundation of Pigovian demand and the Keynesian consumption function

In this sub-section we want to investigate whether the reconsiderations just discussed introduce some analytical inconsistency into Keynes linking up with Pigovian analysis. Put differently, we may pause to ask whether it is still possible to reach a representation of a model economy as just given in fig. 11.1 of the last section. A positive answer will be given in sub-section(c) below.

11.3.2.1 The intertemporal character of the Keynesian consumption function

In the context of developing the economic model as represented in fig. 11.1, the crucial step was to adapt the Marshallian microfoundation of Pigovian demand to Keynesian terminology through the formulation of equ. (11.17). It was stated there that in equilibrium

$$D_{w1k} = \frac{\gamma_x}{\gamma_y} D_{w2} \qquad (11.26)$$

must hold. This formulation does not correspond to the considerations just discussed since, via the elasticities of utility γ_x and γ_y it postulates a purely preference determined relation between D_{w1k} and D_{w2}. In this sub-section we want now to state in more detail how such an equilibrium condition is affected by the reconsiderations of the last section. The main modification brought about by Keynes' insistence that non-consumption is foremost a non-demand for goods and services in the present period, may be represented by formulating an intertemporal budget equation

$$D_{w1k} + \frac{D_{w1k}^f}{\delta} = Y_{wk} + \frac{Y_{wk}^f}{\delta} \qquad (11.27)$$

where δ is a discount factor for a future value of consumption demand D_{w1k}^f or of an expectation of future income Y_{wk}^f.[23]
   Suppose now that analogous to equ. (11.17) there is a certain equilibrium ratio between present demand and the present value of future demand[24] so that

$$\frac{D_{w1k}^f}{\delta} = \frac{\iota^f}{\iota} D_{w1k} \qquad (11.28)$$

holds where ι and ι^f are again elasticities of utility, namely of present resp. of future consumption. Substituting (11.28) into (11.27) and rearranging would then give

$$D_{w1k} = \frac{1}{\iota + \iota^f} (\iota Y_{wk} + \frac{\iota Y_{wk}^f}{\delta}) \qquad (11.29)$$

linking the value (in terms of the wage-unit) of the present demand by non-workers for type 1-goods, i.e. of consumption goods, to their present income Y_{wk} and to the (expected) present value of their future income. Thus equ. (11.29) represents a type of Keynesian consumption function.

11.3.2.2 The goods demand ratio in the Keynesian setting

Since the demand for type 2-goods, being investment goods in Keynesian analysis, must be met by savings (S_w), and since the non-workers are assumed to be the only savers in the economy, it follows that the invest-ment-savings equation

$$D_{w2} = Y_{wk} - D_{w1k} = \frac{1}{\iota + \iota^f}(\iota^f Y_{wk} - \frac{\iota Y_{wk}^f}{\delta})$$ (11.30)

must hold when D_{w2} represents investment demand. Dividing now (11.29) through (11.30) and rearranging gives then

$$D_{w1k} = \frac{\iota Y_{wk} + \frac{\iota Y_{wk}^f}{\delta}}{\iota^f Y_{wk} - \frac{\iota Y_{wk}^f}{\delta}} - D_{w2}$$ (11.31)

as an analogous expression in place of the goods demand ratio of (11.26) which was stated in the beginning of this section. Equation (11.31) permits now an answer to the question posed at the beginning of this section con-cerning the significance of Keynes' theory of consumption for his formal linking up with classical analysis as discussed in the previous chapters.

If expectations of future income are discarded, as they appear to have been in the case of the Pigovian model, then the ratio in (11.31) reduces to ι/ι^f and the analogy between the Keynesian expression as formulated via (11.31) and the adapted Pigovian expression of (11.26) is straightforward.

If the intertemporal assumptions are more realistic and do take future income and expenditure into account along an intertemporal budget equa-tion like (11.27) and an associated choice theoretic model, then the Keynesian expression of (11.31) does not reduce so nicely. But for given expectations concerning the present and future income constraints, investment demand D_{w2} is, via (11.31), still linked to non-workers' consumption in the Keynesian case in a similar, although not identical, way as in the Pigovian case. The minor changes concerning the representation of effective demand which follow from these 'Keynesian' reconsiderations will be briefly treated below.

11.3.3 The reconsidered model of effective demand

11.3.3.1 The limited formal extent of the Keynesian reconsideration confirmed

In section two of this chapter the Keynesian concept of effective demand was developed in the Pigovian setting by relating the goods demand ratio of equ. (11.17) to total employment via equ. (11.19). Goods supply was related to total employment via equ. (11.20). The effective demand *locus* $Z_w = D_w$ of fig. 11.1 followed then after assuming that sectoral demand may become effective only when it meets a corresponding supply as stated in equs. (11.23) and (11.24).

An analysis identical to the one just described could now be repeated with the sole difference that the Keynesian goods demand ratio (11.31) takes the place of the Pigovian one of equ. (11.17), since Keynes accepted the Pigovian theory of supply without any material change as documented in section 2b) above.

We conclude therefore that the type of analysis leading up to the construction of the north-eastern quadrant of fig. 11.1 is indeed possible whether we base our analysis on a reformulation of the Pigovian model as demonstrated above or whether we base our construction on Keynesian consumption demand considerations as in the present section. In both cases we may construct similar effective demand *loci* as given by the $Z_w = D_w$-line or the corresponding ϕ-curve of the third quadrant of fig. 11.1.

We may confirm therefore Keynes' own contention concerning a close formal correspondence between his and the Pigovian model. Even when entering in greater detail into the Keynesian theory of consumption than we did initially in the previous section by merely adapting the reconstructed Pigovian model of goods demand to Keynesian terminology, the basic structure of the adapted Pigovian model may be treated as unaffected. The formal correspondence between Pigovian and Keynesian analytical elements discussed so far may be maintained.

But this finding leaves us in continued search for the *substantive* differences between these authors.

11.3.3.2 The Keynesian version of effective demand in the two-sector model

In order to clarify further the relation between Keynesian and Pigovian analysis, it might be instructive to give an algebraic representation of the consequences of the reconsiderations discussed so far.

In developing such a representation, the investment-savings equation (11.30) may be taken as the analytical starting point. When current non-wage income in terms of the wage-unit (Y_{wk}) in that expression is given as the value of total expected proceeds after the deduction of total wages (also in terms of the wage unit), we have

$$Y_{wk} = Z_{w1} + Z_{w2} - N \qquad (11.32)$$

But since the sectoral employment N_τ is related to the sectoral supply values Z_{wr} via the α_τ as already discussed in detail above (see equ. (11.20)), N in this expression may be replaced by

$$N = N_1 + N_2 = \alpha_1 Z_{w1} + \alpha_2 Z_{w2}, \qquad (11.33)$$

giving[25]

$$Y_{wk} = (1 - \alpha_1) Z_{w1} + (1 - \alpha_2) Z_{w2}. \qquad (11.34)$$

Substituting this expression and the effective demand conditions of equs. (11.23) and (11.24) into (11.30) and rearranging gives then the Keynesian effective demand *locus* in the present context as

$$C_w = a + bI_w \qquad (11.35)$$

where

$$a \equiv \frac{1}{1 - \alpha_1} \left(\frac{\iota}{\iota^f} \right) \frac{Y_w^f}{\delta} \quad \text{and} \quad b \equiv \frac{1}{1 - \alpha_1} \left(\frac{\iota}{\iota^f} + \alpha_2 \right) \qquad (11.36)$$

are exogenously given through preferences and expectations about the future. The alternative $Z_w = D_w$ locus described by equ. (11.35) is the main difference which has to be contemplated in fig. 11.1 when basing the demand theory of that model on genuinely Keynesian foundations.

From a formal point of view this difference is indeed minute when we compare it with the corresponding algebraic formulation of the $Z_w = D_w$ *locus* as given by equ. (11.25). It is just that the 'genuinely Keynesian' effective demand *locus* has an intercept on the C_w-axis, whereas the 'pseudo-Pigovian' *locus* has none. But as already stated, this formal correspondence is not really the decisive matter. It is rather the supposed mechanism of determining a specific position on the effective demand *locus* – whichever way that *locus* is derived.

The Keynesian position in this latter regard is also represented in fig. 11.1. It is that if a specific value of investment demand $\bar{I}_w = D_w 2$ is given, a specific point on the $Z_w = D_w$ *locus* is determined. Via the $Z_w 1$- and $Z_w 2$-lines in the north-western resp. the south-eastern quadrant, the effective demand values are translated into sectoral employment levels, their sum giving total employment $\bar{N}$ as shown in the south-western quadrant.

This analysis is in conflict with the classical one which regards employment as determined through the real wage as given through the slope of the tangent to the $F(x)$-curve in point I (see the broken line in the north-western quadrant of fig. 11.1) as discussed in the last chapter. According to that analysis the Keynesian proposition of an employment level of $\bar{N}$ is faulty because the maximal isoquant reachable in that case is lower than the utility maximal one going through point II.

But this is exactly the problem in a situation of involuntary unemployment, according to Keynes: the relative price and income incentives are such that more labour would be forthcoming *if* it could find employment. The classical reaction to such a position would, however, be that the relative prices are wrong and should be permitted to adjust. But according to Keynes they cannot do this unless effective demand changes.

We thus have reached a crucial point of disagreement between the two camps.

11.4 The Keynesian concept of effective demand as an instrument of critique

Apart from the speculations discussed in the last few paragraphs, the search for the Keynesian analytical *differentia specifica* might seem to have been without dramatic result so far. In Keynes as well as in Pigou's macroeconomic model there is an essential assumption of equilibrium of supply and demand of the value of goods produced.

It could therefore be said that the central concepts in both type of theories are misnamed: Pigou's 'real demand for labour' is *not* just a labour demand relationship but it relies on an assumption of goods market equilibrium as well. Similarly, Keynes' 'effective demand' concept does not describe demand characteristics alone but a conglomerate of these together with equilibrium considerations of goods supply and labour demand. Concerning this aspect of his model, Keynes was well aware that there is a strong correspondence of his theory with that of Pigou as was documented in section 11.2 on p. 119 above, in particular in connection with the discussion of the quote in which Keynes linked his own 'algebra' to that of Pigou (see p. 121 above).

Our subsequent consumption theoretic reconsiderations discussed in section 11.3 on p. 133 above seem not to have established fundamentally new analytical structures apart from minor changes in the formulation of the Keynesian effective demand *locus*. Yet, they seem to us to be important for stressing the new Keynesian paradigm that non-consumption is not necessarily an *alternative demand* for goods. It might rather be perceived to be just a *non-demand* for goods in the current period.

This consideration brings in a new equilibrium concept not discussed by Pigou, namely the matching of those funds released by non-consumption with those funds required for the financing of investment projects. The analytical consequence of this new equilibrium concept is that its workings determine a specific point on the effective demand *locus*, thereby also determining a specific level of employment. The claim that this mechanism was implicitly assumed away by the classical school is the central critical point of Keynes' 'effective demand' doctrine.

The particular way in which Keynes formulated this criticism in the context of his chapter on the 'Principle of Effective Demand' was to attribute to the classical doctrine the categorical statement that 'Supply creates its own Demand' i.e. he attributed to the Classics the assumption of the validity of 'Say's Law' as Keynes (1936, p. 26) named this doctrine after elaborating:

> 'Supply creates its own Demand' must mean ... that when there is an increase in $Z(= \phi(N))$ corresponding to an increase in N, $D(= f(N))$ necessarily increases by the same amount as Z. The classical theory assumes

... that, whatever the value of N may be, the proceeds D assume a value equal to the aggregate supply price Z which corresponds to N. That is to say, effective demand, instead of having a unique equilibrium value, is an infinite range of values all equally admissible.

In this quote Keynes first describes verbally the construction of the $Z_w = D_w$ line of fig. 11.1 which was the *locus* of intersections of a Z_w locus with a D_w locus described algebraically by equs. (11.19 resp. 11.20) and generated for alternative values of employment N in these equations. It is now Keynes' contention that the difference between himself and the classics is that the latter argue with reference to this entire $Z_w = D_w$ locus whereas he argued that only a single point on this *locus* is of employment theoretic relevance.

From this quote it becomes now clear why the search for the Pigovian and the Keynesian effective demand *loci* did not establish the significant Keynesian *differentia specifica*: if it was Keynes' essential point that implicitly the classics argued with reference to such a *locus* whereas he himself argued with regard to a specific *point* on an effective demand *locus*, then neither the establishment of a classical effective demand line nor of an alternative Keynesian one could catch Keynes' essential point that it was not so much the effective demand *line* itself but a singular *point* on it which determined employment.

In order to elaborate on this *differentia specifica*, a simple juxtaposition of the Pigovian theory of employment and of a Keynesian alternative may now be given along the lines shown in Table 11.1: both systems of five equations, the Pigovian and the Keynesian one, determine the five endogenous variables: employment N and the demand and supply variables D_{w1}, D_{w2} resp. Z_{w1}, Z_{w2}. Equations (a) to (d) in Table 11.1 describe the $Z_w = D_w$ lines just discussed.[26] Employment in the Pigovian system is then determined by the real wage w/p_1 of row (e) in Table 11.1 which the suppliers of labour services are prepared to accept, the rest of the system accommodating to this value. In the Keynesian system it is investment demand $\bar{I}_w$ which fixes the demand for type 2-goods so that the rest of the economic system including employment accommodates to this magnitude. In Keynes' set-up it is the investors who, so to speak, determine aggregate employment. In the Pigovian system it is the suppliers of labour services who decide on the real wage for which they are prepared to work and hence determine the level of their employment.

Thus, in essence it is only the last row in Table 11.1 which is different in these two representations. There are minor differences between Pigovian and Keynesian employment-demand functions as given here in row (a) by the functions $N^P(\cdot)$ and $N^K(\cdot)$ which stand for the above equs. (11.19) resp. (11.31). But it was seen above that these differences are not very important as far as the basic structure of the model is concerned. The strategic difference between Keynes and the classics is, as Keynes himself pointed out,

Table 11.1 Employment: Pigou vs. Keynes

	Pigovian employment	Keynes' alternative
(a)	$N = N^P(D_{w1}, D_{w2})$	$N = N^K(D_{w1}, D_{w2})$
(b)	$N = \alpha_1 Z_{w1} + \alpha_2 Z_{w2}$	$N = \alpha_1 Z_{w1} + \alpha_2 Z_{w2}$
(c)	$D_{w1} = Z_{w1}$	$D_{w1} = Z_{w1}$
(d)	$D_{w2} = Z_{w2}$	$D_{w2} = Z_{w2}$
(e)	$N = N^s(\frac{w}{p1})$	$D_{w2} = \bar{I}_w$

that in the Pigovian set-up it is the real wage of the suppliers of labour ser-vices which limits employment whereas in his own theory it is the level – and not the mere existence – of effective demand.

In this connection it should be emphasised that Keynes' rejection of Say's Law does not imply the rejection of a

similar-looking proposition which is *indubitable*, namely that the income derived in the aggregate by all elements in the community con-cerned in a productive activity *necessarily* has a value exactly equal to the *value* of the output.[27]

Thus Keynes obviously accepted the identity between total income accru-ing in a specific period of production on the one hand with the value of total production on the other.[28] This observation seems important in the light of some Keynesian interpretations exemplified by Malinvaud (1977) in which the value of production on the one side and income on the other may differ from each other. The quote just referred to gives an important indication that macroeconomic reconsiderations along such analytical lines are not in accordance with the original Keynesian approach.

12
Assessing the Classical Reconstruction

In this chapter we intend to finish off the reconstruction of the classical analysis as received by Keynes by attempting an answer to the last of the questions listed in chapter 7, namely the one concerning the significance of such a reconstruction for a proper understanding of classical economics in the context of the Keynes–Classics controversy.

12.1 Reconstructions and perceptions of 'Cambridge' macroeconomics

The present reconstruction of the classical macroeconomic model as received by Keynes might have some significance not only for an understanding of Keynesian economics in particular but also for a proper assessment of the general workings of the economic 'Cambridge mind'.

Modern economists harbour two popular ideas about orthodox Cambridge economics. Insofar as it is Marshallian, it seems to be predominantly partial analytic. But insofar as it is addressed to macroeconomics, the orthodox Cambridge mind seems to have moved in the confines of a model with a single aggregate production function. Quotes in point from Clower (1975) and Solow (1980) were given and discussed above.

The seemingly consistent conclusion from these two ideas would then be that in the Cambridge tradition macroeconomic results were generally derived – if they were considered to be of interest at all – by merely transposing partial analytic results in a simple analogy to the workings of an entire economic system. In accordance with such views H. G. Johnson (1978b, p. 149) declared: 'The Cambridge mind ... never stretched to the two-sector model until they began working on the line of proving that capitalism could not work.' There have been lengthy investigations purporting to convey that Keynes' macroeconomic model in particular must have been of a single-sector structure (Froyen (1976)).

In the preceding chapters we demonstrated that such a reception of the Cambridge tradition in economics is not supported by the writings of its main contributors, Marshall, Pigou and Keynes. The general equilibrium perspective was emphasised strongly by Alfred Marshall, the founding father of Cambridge economics. He considered his 'whole life' to be dedicated to presenting in 'realistic form' the formal outlines of the general equilibrium system contained in his mathematical 'note XXI' of the *Principles*. Pigou's *Theory of Unemployment* clearly stands not only in Marshall's partial analytic tradition but also stressed the differences between partial analytic labour demand and total analytic labour demand in a multi-industry setting. Finally, Keynes was clearly aware of the general equilibrium perspective contained in Pigou's theory and he considered the classical model as a limiting case of his own analysis. Both Keynes and Pigou resorted repeatedly to two-sectoral macroeconomic analysis and this fact could not have escaped such a knowledgeable economist as H. G. Johnson. His remarks about the limited analytical scope of the 'Cambridge mind' – although not unrepresentative for a popular perception of the Cambridge tradition – therefore seem somewhat surprising.

If the quoted comments about the analytical scope of the Cambridge economists cannot be justified as being based on an authentic perception of the writings of the most renowned representatives of this school, there is the question of which other reason could be seen as standing behind it. In the case of Johnson (1978b, p. 149) there seem to be reasons of analytical differences because he combined his derogatory characterisation with the statement:

In a two-sector model there are two ... industries using labour and capital in different proportions. A shift of production towards the labour-intensive industry increases the demand for labour.

Thus, in Johnson's perception of a two-sector model there would seem to be an obvious employment political action never explicitly contemplated by the classical Cambridge School, namely to shift product demand from less labour intensive parts of the economy to those parts which are more labour intensive. In terms of the reconstructed classical model the labour intensity is measured by the α_τ so that Johnson's prescription suggests a shift of product demand from the sector with a low α_τ to that sector which has a high one and that, *vice versa*, employment would decrease if demand shifted from high-α_τ products to low-α_τ ones.[1]

But the reason why the traditional 'Cambridge mind' never explicitly stated this type of employment political action was not that it had no grasp of a simple two-sector model of the economy. It was rather that it employed a two-sector model different from the one alluded to by Johnson. The latter seems to have had in mind a particular model in which capital is not only 'malleable' – a condition which gives sectoral production functions with variable input combinations of capital and labour so that 'well behaved' production functions in the neoclassical sense may be generated. This condition was implicitly accepted by Pigou and Keynes as was seen above. For Johnson's thought experiment to work if effective demand is not explicitly assumed to be constant as in the Keynesian analysis of the preceding footnote, capital must in addition be 'shiftable' from one sector to the other. Otherwise the increased production in any sector will decrease the real wage – and hence the equilibrium full employment – due to decreasing returns to labour. This shiftability condition was not accepted by Pigou (1933) who based his two-sectoral model on the assumption of sectorally fixed capital. But this does not mean that Pigou did not resort to two-sector model building at all.

It seems that Johnson based his judgement about the limitations of the 'Cambridge mind' upon a two-sector model which was itself rather limited in the sense that it just did not cover the two-sectoral case assumed to be relevant by Pigou (1933) and accepted by Keynes (1936). Thus we conclude that there are not only no authentic grounds to question that the Cambridge school stretched its economic mind to the two-sector model of an economy before it contemplated that capitalism could not work. In addition, the analytical discussion given by Johnson (1978b) in this connection also carries no conviction. The present reconstruction of the Cambridge classical model of the economy therefore might be able to aid in reassessing the general analytical perspective of that school.

It follows from the present reconstruction of the classical model and of its reception by Keynes, that contrary to the quoted popular beliefs, the 'Cambridge' model of Pigou and Keynes was built on the paradigm of a two-sectorally disaggregated economy, both authors accepting the concepts of

(i) well behaved sectoral production functions, and
(ii) profit maximising firms under externally given market conditions.

12.2 Problems of functional aggregation

The persisting popularity of single-sector macroeconomics stems, in part at least, from the considerable problems of aggregation which must be encountered in the analytical transition from lower to higher resolution levels of economic phenomena. In particular, except for trivial cases of sectoral identity, it is well known to be impossible to take neoclassical production functions which depict production and marginal productivities on different sectoral levels and to aggregate them so that the selfsame functional relationship is then generated on the resolution level of the economy as a whole.[2] Since this Gordian knot cannot be unravelled, modern economists tend to do away with it by 'heroic assumptions', i.e. by *postulating* the existence of the macroeconomic functions which cannot be deduced from a disaggregated analysis.

It was seen above that Pigou (1933) was not unaware of this type of problem. He dealt with it by relating sectoral phenomena – in particular the sectoral employment x and the associated real wage $F'(x)$ – to macroeconomic employment (as given by $x + y$ in Pigou's context) via a specific new function of considerable conceptual complexity and of an entirely different analytical content than the conventional macroeconomic production function. In the above discussion, this novel $\phi(x)$-function turned out to be the centrepiece of the present classical reconstruction and we should pause here to point out that its interest is by no means purely derived from its doctrine historical significance. Its analytically interesting feature is the fact that the dimensionality of the dependent and the independent variables is identical, since it relates sectoral employment x to total employment $x + y$.

This aspect of Pigou's construction survived in the *General Theory* in the guise of the 'employment multiplier' k' as Keynes (1936, p. 273) pointed out in some detail when he discussed the Pigovian $\phi(x)$-function. But he did not only accept this function with its implicit consistent dimensionality. Keynes (1936, p. 41) carried the dimensionality aspect even further when, in discussing his choice of units, he proposed to conduct his entire theory of employment in terms of just 'two fundamental units of quantity, namely, quantities of money-value and quantities of employment'. Since money values of, say, aggregate supply Z may be easily transformed into units with the dimensionality of employment simply by dividing with the Keynesian 'wage unit' giving, say, Z_w in terms of wage units, this proposal amounted to intending to explain Keynesian employment N with reference to magnitudes of the self-same dimensions.[3]

With these remarks we are in the middle of Keynes' wage-units analysis, a topic sometimes considered to be one of the trickiest of the *General Theory*. Actually, the analytical concepts following from this type of approach are rather simple. It was seen above that the wage-units approach to sectoral and to aggregate economic magnitudes had the advantage of permitting to combine marginal analysis, sectoral disaggregation, well behaved production functions, and yet to end up with rather simple sectoral input-output structures as given by the Keynesian 'aggregate' supply functions of, e.g., equ. (11.10).

But we cannot hope to develop in the present context the topic of Keynesian wage-units analysis much beyond the unravelling of its classical aspects. Bringing this debate to a close, we emphasise that no matter which difficulties post-Keynesian readers may have with his wage-units, it should be realised that the underlying analytical idiosyncrasies are not really very novel. They may be traced back at least to Pigou's attempt to circumvent problems of sectoral disaggregation in macroeconomic model building without resorting to partial analytical analogies.[4]

12.3 'Classical' entrepreneurs and Keynesian 'aggregate supply'

Since Keynes repeatedly related his own theory to the classical one, the present reconstruction of the classical model as received by Keynes is, of course, also of considerable interest for a clarification of the Keynesian approach itself. The above discussion established that Keynes accepted the classical theory of supply and production and that he considered his own theory of 'aggregate supply' to be just a reformulation of the classical theory.

Since the classical theory of supply by profit maximizing entrepreneurs was – and still is – considered by many economists as being comparatively well founded, it might come somewhat as a surprise to read that Patinkin (1982, p. 150) once commented

> that the obscurity with which the aggregate supply curve is presented in the *General Theory* is a sign not of profundity, but of obscurity: not, as some would have us believe, of a deep underlying analytical framework in which everything falls into place.

This view was intended to refer just to Keynes and not to the theory of supply as such. But as a rendering of Keynesian theory this view of Patinkin's and previous similar ones to which the quoted statement was supposed to refer carries very little conviction as was argued in detail by Roberts (1978) and by Casarosa (1982). Referring to their rejection of Patinkin's interpretation of Keynes, we see no need to reopen that debate in the present context.

It might be noteworthy, however, that none of the critics of Patinkin's Keynesian interpretations made any reference to Keynes' reception of Pigovian analysis. Arguing from a reconstruction of the Pigovian position would have been particularly relevant in this context, however, since it was none other but Patinkin (1978, p. 593) who stated in a related context:

> a clarification of this issue depends first and foremost on a proper perspective on the nature of the history of ideas in general, and of the history of the development of Keynes ideas in particular.

But if this is indeed the method which Patinkin saw as appropriate, then he clearly should have investigated the Pigovian element in the development of Keynes' ideas. Having failed to do this, his conclusions must, by his own standards, appear as not well founded.

If it is realised that the Keynesian theory – in particular insofar as it refers to sectoral and to aggregate supply – incorporates to a considerable extent a number of Pigovian analytical elements, then a generalising charge of 'obscurity' leaves open whether the unclear elements in the Keynesian framework are really attributable to this author or whether they are not rather part of the common theoretical heritage which Keynes shared with Pigou and other 'classics'.

It could very well be argued that the conventional theory of supply is full of obscurities if analysed in a macroeconomic context. What is the 'Walrasian auctioneer' and how indispensable is he for the determination of supply and demand in a model economy? How are atomistic entrepreneurs imagined to form expectations if they are assumed to believe to be facing horizontal demand curves for their products? What consequence does it have for employment if profit rates are not uniform along the equilibrium supply curves of the entrepreneurs? Many more such questions could be thought up which relate to central problems of the consistent formulation of a theory of the determination of prices and quantities in an entrepreneurial economy. They cannot all be considered to have been clarified to every theorist's satisfaction. They certainly play an important role in the Keynesian context but such questions are not less important in a Pigovian or a modern 'neoclassical' context.

Keynes himself believed that in his theory of supply he did nothing else but to incorporate the conventional wisdom about supply curves and profit maximising firms. The connection between his own and the classical approach were discussed in some detail in the preceding chapters. If economists should one day widely accept the approach proposed by Patinkin (1976, p. 93), namely that 'those words should simply be deleted from the *General Theory*' which state that for a particular value of effective demand 'entrepreneurs' expectation of profits will be maximised', then corresponding re-editions and textual changes should also be suggested to all those authors whom Keynes incorporated in developing this doctrine. This would mean a rewriting of Pigovian and other classical economics. But such a far-reaching change of economic theory has not been seriously suggested by a significant number of economists so far.

It seems therefore safe to conclude that insofar as the Pigovian theory of the determination of prices and quantities of goods produced in the short-period context of a capitalist economy may be attributed to the profit maximising behaviour of entrepreneurs operating under given market conditions, the analogous determination in the Keynesian context may also be attributed to the same analytical setup.

12.4 The Keynesian model emerging from the classical reconstruction

In an assessment of the theoretical significance of the present classical reconstruction one of the questions suggesting themselves concerns the significance of this model for the emergence of the Keynesian alternative to this model. Put differently, one may ask in this context: what would the

Keynesian model look like if it were constructed with the minimal departure from the reconstructed classical model? To a certain extent this question was already answered at the end of the last chapter. But the main focus there was still on the Pigovian model and on the associated sectoral disaggregation. The Keynesian model is in terms of total, not sectoral production and income. In the present section we will now attempt to elaborate and restate those considerations with the intention to bringing them nearer to the way Keynes presented his model in ch. 3 of the *General Theory*.

The model to be constructed in this context is a very rudimentary one, of course. It is just the one which could be seen as emerging from the first three chapters of the *General Theory*. Those chapters have not yet dealt with monetary matters nor with the question of the determination of investment. The consumption function is just stated and not yet discussed in its more subtle complexities. Questions of intertemporal allocation are left implicit. All these theoretical elements must, of course, find detailed treatment in a full reconstruction of the Keynesian theory. But this is not the aim in the present assessment of the classical model. The question is rather: what could Keynes have got out of his perception of the classical model if he restricted himself to an imaginative reuse of the classical theoretical elements which he had discussed in ch. 2 of the *General Theory*? After all, Keynes (1936, p. 25) himself attempted such an argumentation when he endeavoured to give an overview of 'the substance of the *General Theory of Employment*' immediately after his critical review of the postulates of the classical economics. In this sense we consider this step of our discussion also to be covered by the criterion of authenticity.

In relating the Keynesian model to the reconstructed classical one, it seems important to re-emphasise that Keynes (1936, p. 20) based his own approach on a

> proposition which is indubitable, namely that the income derived in the aggregate by all the elements in the community concerned in a productive activity necessarily has a value exactly equal to the value of the output.

Thus, if Y_w is the Keynesian income in the aggregate in terms of the wage unit, and if Z_{wr} are the corresponding values of sectoral production, it is clear that for $r = 1, 2$ we must have

$$Y_w = Z_{w1} + Z_{w2} \qquad (12.1)$$

Since income in the present context accrues either to labour (index ℓ) or to non-labour (index k), we have also

$$Y_w = Y_{w\ell} + Y_{wk} = N + Y_{wk} \qquad (12.2)$$

because nominal labour income $Y_\ell = wN$ in terms of the wage unit w is obviously $Y_\ell/w = Y_{w\ell} = N$.

The characteristics of sectoral aggregate supply functions were discussed in detail in the previous chapter. It was seen there that they may be formulated either exclusive of distortions due to imperfect competition (see equ. (11.10)) or inclusive of such distortions (see equ. (11.14)). A general formulation of those functions may be given as

$$Z_{wr} = \frac{\mu_r}{\alpha_r} N_r; \frac{\mu_r}{\alpha_r} > 1 \qquad (12.3)$$

where μ represents the market conditions as considered appropriate. If competition is perfect they take on a value of unity. If it is less than perfect they rise above this value, thus *ceteris paribus* 'crowding out' employment. Since the α_τ are less than unity, the total ratio of these two magnitudes is definitely larger than unity as stated in equ. (12.3).

It was mentioned above that the α_τ do not necessarily have to be treated as fixed parameters but that they may be considered as representing functional relationships (see equ. (11.11)). Similarly, more elaborate versions of the aggregate supply functions may depict the μ_τ as functions. But since we have little authentic debate concerning the influences on these magnitudes which, if taken account of at all, were normally taken as the 'givens' of the economic system under consideration, a scrutiny of the arguments and of the exact shape of such imagineable functions cannot concern us here.

Total consumption demand (C_w) may be seen as being composed of workers' demand $D_{w1\ell}$ which, in accordance with Pigou, may be assumed to be equal to the wage payments N plus non-workers' consumption as given by equ. (11.29) so that we have

$$C_w = N + D_{w1\ell} = (1-\theta)N + \theta Y_w + \theta \frac{Y_w^f}{\delta} \qquad (12.4)$$

where the positive magnitude $\theta \equiv \iota/(\iota + \iota^f) < 1$ represents the ratio of elasticities of utility which were mentioned in connection with the formulation of equ. (11.29) and where $Y_{wk} = Y_w - N$ in that equation was replaced via equ. (12.1) so that equ. (12.4) follows after some elementary reformulations.

Total employment is, as in the preceding chapters,

$$N = N_1 + N_2 \qquad (12.5)$$

and demand is considered as effective demand which is met by supply so that

$$C_w = Z_{w1}; \bar{I}_w = Z_{w2} \qquad (12.6)$$

holds where $\bar{I}_w$ is investment demand which – at this stage of the development of the Keynesian argument – is considered to be exogenously given. Replacing the Z_{wr} in equs. (12.1 and 12.3) via equ. (12.6) permits us now to write the Keynesian system emerging out of this discussion as a system of linear equations which may be given in matrix notation as

$$\begin{bmatrix} 1 & -1 & 0 & 0 & 0 \\ \theta & -1 & 1-\theta & 0 & 0 \\ 0 & -1 & 0 & \frac{\mu_1}{\alpha_1} & 0 \\ 0 & 0 & 0 & 0 & \frac{\mu_2}{\alpha_1} \\ 0 & 0 & 1 & -1 & -1 \end{bmatrix} \begin{bmatrix} Y_w \\ C_w \\ N \\ N_1 \\ N_2 \end{bmatrix} = \begin{bmatrix} 1 & 0 \\ 0 & -1 \\ 0 & 0 \\ 1 & 0 \\ 0 & 0 \end{bmatrix} \begin{bmatrix} \bar{I}_w \\ \frac{\theta Y_{wk}^f}{\delta} \end{bmatrix} \qquad (12.7)$$

assuming the parameters of the matrix of coefficients in (12.7) to be constant.

Formally, it is now quite easy to solve for the endogenous variables on the left-hand side and to generate a 'reduced form' as given schematically by the system (12.8) below where $|D|$ and where the D_{ij} are comparatively involved expressions which later will be discussed in some more detail.[5]

Expression (12.8) represents the macroeconomic outcomes of the system under discussion. The independent, explanatory, variables are given by the right-hand column. The last element therein identifies the long-term expectations Y_{wk}^f and how these communicate themselves to the present time-period through the preferences as expressed by θ and through the market rate of discount δ. These long-term expectations Keynes (1936, ch. 5) assumed as given, as was noted in the previous chapter, and as not liable to sudden change. In his view, the short-run fluctuations in income and employment are not to be explained along this line, however.

$$\begin{bmatrix} Y_w \\ C_w \\ N \\ N_1 \\ N_2 \end{bmatrix} = \frac{1}{|D|} \begin{bmatrix} D_{11} & D_{12} \\ D_{21} & D_{22} \\ D_{31} & D_{32} \\ D_{41} & D_{42} \\ D_{51} & D_{52} \end{bmatrix} \begin{bmatrix} \bar{I}_w \\ \frac{\theta Y_{wk}^f}{\delta} \end{bmatrix} \qquad (12.8)$$

The other explanatory variable for the outcomes of system (12.8) is investment demand $\bar{I}_w$ and it is this magnitude to which Keynes gave prime importance for determining the short-run macroeconomic outcomes which he wanted to analyse. This is not immediately obvious from the present formulation, of course, since here $\bar{I}_w$ is just another exogenous variable. But it should be noted that it was only in the introductory and rudimentary exposition of his principle of effective demand at the beginning of the *General Theory* that Keynes assumed investment demand to be given. Later on in the *General Theory*, in Book IV on the 'Inducement to Invest' he discussed the determinants of investment at considerable length.

For the present purpose it must suffice, however, to point out verbally that the approach just outlined does capture this important aspect of Keynes' theory, namely that the current realisation of investment demand is the strategic short-term variable for the determination of the macroeconomic outcomes. There is now a considerable 'authenticity problem' in this context since Keynes obviously did not introduce his effective demand doctrine in the context of a simultaneous equation system as just outlined with reference to (12.7). From a certain point of view this might be regretted because such a simultaneous equation formulation would have satisfied all those later critics of the *General Theory* who read it now as an inappropriately isolated representation of various aspects of an economic system through an additive discussion of a number of single equations.[6] That such a view is not quite correct was shown above already when we discussed his 'internal critique' of Pigou (see ch. 10). There the general equilibrium tradition present in the writings of Pigou *and* Keynes was emphasised.

It certainly would have been strange if Keynes had been able to complete the Pigovian model in the Marshallian spirit of 'note XXI' as a simultaneous system of equations and to forget all about such economic modelling when he had to expound his own theory. If Keynes did not make this explicit himself, we assume that the most likely reason for his different approach was that writing out the simultaneous equation system just outlined did not meet the expositorial requirements faced by Keynes. Instead, he fell back on the precedent of Pigou's, namely to boil down a comparatively complex model economy to a few 'semi-reduced' relationships like the Pigovian $\phi(x)$-function which occupied us so much above.

Let us therefore remind the reader that that function incorporated a number of quite diverse structural characteristics[7] and thereby attempted to accentuate in a simplified way a central macroeconomic relationship. It is in this Pigovian spirit as exemplified by that $\phi(x)$-function that we must interpret the theorising presented by Keynes in his juxtaposition of his own theory with that of the Classics in ch. 3 of the *General Theory*.

Thus we may conclude that it is not an over-interpretation if we attribute to Keynes the awareness of the appropriateness of a simultaneous equation presentation of his departure from the classical theory – just as done here with the help of (12.7) and (12.8). But how could he then content himself to use just these three magnitudes: a $\Phi(N)$-function, a $\Xi(N)$-function, and the volume of investment as was seen in ch. 11 above?

In an attempt to answer this question let us return to the reduced form of (12.8). It is clear from that model that for alternative levels of investment we may represent macroeconomic changes in income (dY_w), in consumption (dC_w) and in employment (dN). Relating now these endogenous macroeconomic variables among each other in a similar way as Pigou when he related his n and x *via* his $\phi(x)$-function, we may proceed to constructing the following derivatives

$$\frac{dZ_w}{dN} = \Phi'(N) = \frac{a_{11}}{a_{31}} = 1 + a \quad \text{and} \quad \frac{dC_w}{dN} = \Xi'(N) = \frac{a_{21}}{a_{31}} = 1 + \theta_a \quad (12.9)$$

where θ is the same magnitude as the one defined in connection with equ. (12.4) and where a is a rather involved combination of the structural parameters which entered the matrix of coefficients in (12.7). It is given by the expression

$$a \equiv \frac{\theta \frac{\mu_2}{\alpha_2}(\frac{\mu_1}{\alpha_1} - 1)}{\theta \frac{\mu_2}{\alpha_2} + (1 - \theta)\frac{\mu_1}{\alpha_1}} \quad (12.10)$$

For an evaluation of the characteristics of the newly formulated derivatives, the important thing about the magnitude a is that it is positive. Since in addition we know from equ. (12.4) that $\theta < 1$, it follows immediately from (12.9) that

$$\frac{dZ_w}{dN} > \frac{dC_w}{dN} \quad (12.11)$$

must hold.

Thus we have re-established the well-known pattern of aggregate supply and demand analysis of the old Sidney Weintraub tradition (see Davidson and Smolensky (1964)) that 'aggregate supply' as expressed by Z_w always rises faster than 'aggregate demand' as expressed by C_w.

We may now summarise our perception of the Keynesian model of ch. 3 of the *General Theory* as follows:

- The $Z_w = \Phi(N)$-function of aggregate supply is a function the slope of which is determined by the *supply parameters* α_r, by the *market conditions* as expressed by μ_r and by the intertemporal demand parameter θ.
- The $C_w = \Xi(N)$-function of effective consumption demand incorporates the *same* type of demand and supply parameters as entered the $\Phi(N)$-function.
- Neither of these functions can be regarded as a mere partial analytical generalisation transposed to macroeconomic analysis. Rather, each one is a genuinely macroeconomic relationship in the sense of being based on supply and demand *interaction*.
- The greater the level of employment N, the greater is *ceteris paribus* both aggregate supply Z_w and consumption demand C_w. But since the curve for the latter magnitude rises less than the one for the former one, there is a widening gap which must be filled by increasing investment demand I_w.

Neither of these results is novel, of course. Since it was our intention to reproduce the Keynesian effective demand analysis they were in fact not at all intended to be original in the first place. Nevertheless they might be considered as helpful for an understanding of the way in which Keynes may be seen as building on the classical analytical foundations in his departure from that theory.

12.5 Was Keynes a 'reconstructed Classic?'

The comparative ease with which Keynes effective demand analysis could be related to the Pigovian model once that model was reconstructed from the marginal analytic microfoundations of the Marshallian School might suggest that the outcome of our analysis is devised to lead to the conclusion that this type of theorising was intended by Keynes to be seen behind his aggregate analysis. In the present section we will guard against such a conclusion, however.

In fact, soon after the publication of the *General Theory* Keynes disassociated himself emphatically from 'the old associations of my mind' (see JMK, XXIX, p. 246). Since this seems to be a proclamation of considerable importance for the characterisation of Keynes' post-*General Theory* analytical programme, it merits a more detailed inspection. In a fuller quotation that statement may be seen to have two interesting aspects:

> [i] I have got bogged in an attempt to bring my own terms into rather closer conformity with the algebra of others than the case really permits ... It amounts to very little, contributes nothing to the understanding of the argument and is simply encouraging the reader to waste his time in a rather futile sort of way.
> [ii] I am conscious that this, like a good deal else in the book, is largely the product of the old associations of my mind, the result of always trying to see the new theory in its relation to the old and to discover more affinities than really exist. (paragraphing added, GMA)

This passage is of particular interest for the present approach of trying to relate the new Keynesian theory to Keynes' old associations with Marshall and Pigou. We have here, in part [ii] of this quote, an authentic statement that this was exactly what Keynes was 'always' trying to do himself. So if one intends to understand the mental genesis of Keynes' analytical argument against the 'Classics', then this approach certainly is covered by the criterion of authenticity.[8]

But it is – at least in Keynes' view in part [i] of this quote – quite a different matter how a reader newly introduced to Keynesian economics should approach that subject matter. In that context he believed that 'the algebra of others' – supposedly that of Pigou – 'amounts to very little'. The regretful and self-accusatorial tone of that statement suggests, however, a question as to what exactly triggered off these laments about an excessive association with the 'algebra of others'.

The wider context of Keynes' second thoughts about his style of argument in the *General Theory* was a correspondence with H. Townshend, a former student and extremely diligent reader of Keynes who spotted a number of definitorial inconsistencies in Keynes' treatment of user cost in chs 4 and 20 of the *General Theory* (see JMK, XXIX, pp. 239–47). It was seen above in connection with discussing the characteristics of aggregate supply functions that there were indeed some grave analytical problems in that regard which seem to have escaped Keynes until his attention was drawn to them by Townshend. In his replies to him, Keynes made some tentative reformulations of his original algebraic formulations but soon confessed his frustration, the quoted passage being a documentation of them.

To take full account of Townshend's critical questions concerning the treatment of user cost in the *General Theory* would have required a rather involved modelling of production, taking particular account of the fact that typically it is not done just by means of capital and labour, but that there is also a considerable extent of 'production of commodities by means of commodities' which are used up in the process. This latter characterisation of 'typical' production is, of course, a paraphrase of the title of Sraffa (1960) and it is remarkable that – although he was not on particularly cordial terms with Keynes – Sraffa was one of the young Cambridge economists supported by Keynes and in constant discussion with the 'inner circle' of Keynesian disciples. Indeed, Sraffa was a member of the Cambridge 'circus' itself. It is therefore perhaps not just an intellectual or personal whim that there was later considerable affinity between a number of them on the one side and Sraffa on the other. But Sraffa (1960) intended a revival of Ricardian economics, to go back to the *antecedents* of Alfred Marshall and not to enlarge on the paradigms of the *followers* of Marshallian economics. In the eyes of adherents of the Sraffian approach there is a dramatic break with Marshallian marginal analytic microfoundations. Thus *his* approach was analytically not at all in the stream of arguments inspected so far in this book.

Although this must remain a mere speculation for the moment, it seems doubtful that Keynes himself would have accepted the Sraffian approach as the appropriate analytical framework for his own ideas. He never declared this to be the case. Even after his disillusionment with the 'algebra of others' Keynes never showed enthusiasm for Sraffa (1960)-type exercises. There seems to be, of course, a good physical reason for this: Sraffa (1960) was published much more than a decade after Keynes had died in 1946. But in view of the long gestation period of that book, described by Sraffa (1960), it is somewhat strange that during decades of life as an economist at Cambridge, his mind never did meet in great unison with that of Keynes if there was indeed a strong affinity of paradigms.

In addition, it must be noted that the Sraffian approach pertains not so much to the Keynesian short-term analytical set-up but rather to a long-term analysis. This seems to be a plausible reason why the two approaches do not appear to be compatible with each other.

One approach which seems to have found relatively little attention in recent Keynesian reconsiderations will be inspected in some detail below in part IV. It is the attempt at a 'Keynesian extension' of the theory of employment to the long-period setting proposed by Joan Robinson (1937a). Since it still relies heavily on the old Marshallian marginal analytical concepts, this essay constitutes a sort of 'half-way post' in the departure from the short-period analysis of the *General Theory* towards the Sraffian approach. As such it will later on in this book permit us to reconsider the turning points in the post-Keynesian debates.

13
Summary and Conclusion of Part II

The present part II of our enquiry dealt with the protohistory of the *General Theory* and with the question of how the specific beginning of that argumentative strand might be seen to have led to Keynes' own argumentation. This line of thought addressed the fact that Keynes was very specific in his criticism of the 'Classics' – of the economic school of thought against which he directed his argument. For Keynes, the paradigmatic statement of the theory of employment of that school was supplied by Pigou (1933). But to this very day there is much academic dispute whether Keynes did in fact take up Pigou (1933), whether he did this correctly and fairly etc. In such a dispute the *ratio ultima* must be the authentic text. But, of course, the report about a text often reveals not only what *was* in the book, but also what was *put* into that book by later readers. Thus, if reading Pigou (1933) with Koopmans (1957) in the back of one's mind (see fig. 10.4 on p. 102), is one then not *bound* to receive him ahistorically and in that regard out of context? This type of question was recently addressed by Blaug (2001) in rather general terms. It is in his methodological sense that we intended to return to the Keynes-and-Pigou debate.

But this required facing the Pigovian beginnings of the Keynesian argument in the *General Theory* and the use to which that analysis was put by Keynes in that particular argumentative frame-work. The method of enquiry was that of 'historical reconstruction' in the sense of Blaug (2001) (see above, p. 41). Such an enquiry seems to be of wider interest for economics and for economists for several reasons:

(i) From the standpoint of contemporary economics, the recent revival of classical economic paradigms in the form of the New Classical Economics poses a number of questions which this enquiry might help to answer in bringing into better focus the methods and contents of *historical* classical analysis.

(ii) From the standpoint of the history of economic ideas, there is the remarkable phenomenon that A. C. Pigou, who once, as successor of

Alfred Marshal to the Chair for Political Economics was *the* academic authority in British economics, has virtually disappeared from the view of the scientific community apart from minor issues like the Pigou tax. There should occasionally be a contemplation about the justification of such a development. Reshaping Pigou's macroeconomic argumentation in the framework of a 'historical reconstruction' might open the mind again for a fresh look at Pigovian economics.

(iii) There seems to be increasing awareness that much of Keynesian economics was developed with explicit reference to Pigou.

(iv) There are persistent doubts in the literature whether Keynes dealt fairly with the economic theories of this his main classical antagonist.

Pigou (1933) offers considerable difficulties to the modern reader. His exposition is marred by a frequent change of notation and of analytical perspective. Since there is only a little secondary literature available on which to fall back, we therefore considered it to be our most urgent task to supply a detailed reconstruction of the Pigovian model. This was the main subject matter of ch. 8 above where, starting from the authentic textual evidence, a consistent model was built up from a Marshallian microfoundation. From this exercise emerged a two-sector model similar to the ones of modern neo-classical growth theory but different in the sense that it was a short-period model with non-shiftable capital between the two sectors of production.

The central concept of Pigou's *Theory of Unemployment* was that of a real demand for labour function and its elasticity. This concept had to be discussed in particular detail (ch. 9). In a very general formulation, this function was seen to contain a highly original but somewhat bewildering combination of demand and supply characteristics (see equ. (9.11)). The simplification of the Pigovian approach proposed by Solow (1980) was discussed under the perspective of preserving these Pigovian idiosyncrasies. An alternative simplification was presented and justified (see equ. (9.20)). This simplified two-sectoral version of the Pigovian model formed the basis for the rest of the discussion in part II.

In ch. 10 above, we turned to an inspection of one aspect of Keynes' critique of Pigou, namely to – what we called here – his 'internal critique'. That type of criticism was seen to consist in completing the Pigovian model in the spirit of the Marshallian 'equation counting' of 'note XXI' of the *Principles*. The general equilibrium perspective of that note was stressed and its importance for an assessment of the Marshallian tradition was discussed. The workings of the completed Pigovian model were seen to generate exactly those employment political measures which Keynes attributed to the classical school in ch. 2 of the *General Theory*. We considered this result as the successful passing of a test whether the present approach to Keynes' reception of the Classics was covered by the criterion of authenticity which was discussed and accepted in the introductory part I.

In ch. 11 above, Keynes' 'external critique' of the classics was discussed with reference to his 'principle of effective demand'. This discussion necessitated a clarification of the Pigovian concept of demand for goods, leading to a preliminary consideration of the Keynesian consumption function and of the associated intertemporal budget constraint. By itself, this aspect of Keynes' theory was seen not to be particularly critical concerning the conclusions of the classical model. The essential difference to Keynes was rather that the classical model implied a continuum of effective demand realisations whereas Keynes' approach stressed the realisation of just one single point of effective demand determined by the level of investment.

In ch. 13, an assessment of the present classical reconstruction has led eventually to the question of its significance for the way Keynes wanted to see his own theory received. In the face of criticism concerning the representation of intra-firm turnover in the framework of his adaptation of the classical model, he voiced considerable frustration about his attempt to relate his own theory 'to the algebra of others' which he than came to denounce as overdone and unhelpful for an understanding of his own argument. But although Keynes came eventually to denounce his approach of relating his own theory to the 'algebra of others', that statement confirms that that was indeed the approach followed by Keynes in the exposition of the *General Theory*. If we intend to get a clearer understanding of the development and of the substance of the Keynesian theory, then a sensible starting point for recreating the argumentation on which that theory was based cannot fall back on Keynes' later denouncement of his own approach. Rather, it seems necessary to make more explicit just why Keynes became so disillusioned with his earlier approach. This conclusion suggests itself particularly since in modern post-Keynesian debates it remains quite unclear so far which analytical alternative is appropriate if Keynesian theory is to be put on an alternative theoretical footing.

Part III

The Fledgling Debate: Pigou's Classical Rejoinders and the Problematic Reformulation of the Keynesian Challenge

14
The Problematic Unfolding of the Keynes–Pigou Debate

Part II above was concerned with the Keynes–Pigou debate as initiated by Keynes himself in the *General Theory*. Part III will reconstruct and interpret the ensuing discussion of Keynesian and Pigovian positions in the wake of the publication of Keynes' challenge. The execution of this attempt is encumbered by the peculiarities of the unfolding of this debate, however. These peculiarities will now be briefly commented upon before entering the more substantive issues of the debate in the next chapters.

One somewhat astonishing aspect of the Keynes–Pigou debate is the seeming paucity of actual exchanges of views of the main actors concerned. From Keynes' point of view it was Pigou who was responsible for this lack of communication. Later commentators blame Keynes for not supplying substantive arguments against Pigou. It will appear in the following, however, that ironically it was predominantly the Young Keynesians who, after all, considered themselves as the guardians of Keynes' real intentions who refrained from a systematic working through the issues raised by Keynes and Pigou.

Immediately after its publication the *General Theory* was reviewed at considerable length by Pigou (1936). Thus it might seem that Pigou did indeed quickly take up Keynes' challenge. But Keynes (JMK, XIV, p. 87) complained to D. H. Robertson that Pigou was lacking in substance: 'indeed I thought the Prof's review profoundly frivolous in substance'. And Keynes (*ibid.*) continued: 'It was characteristic that he made no allusion to the appendix [to ch. 19, *General Theory*] about which I took great care, which is solely devoted to his argument.'

It seems that in pursuing the pattern of argumentation as set out in the previous part II, Keynes had hoped to initiate not just a personal attack against Pigou but rather a substantive public exchange of views with him. When that was not forthcoming,[1] he was not prepared to accept passively Pigou's evasive moves in this matter.

Keynes complained not only to Pigou's intellectual supporter D. H. Robertson about this lack of interchange but somewhat later also to Pigou himself, writing to him insistingly.[2]

> I wish very much that you would now, in the light of the more recent discussion, read over again chapter 19 of my book together with the Appendix. This is the source of the theory that the effect of changes in money wages on employment in a closed system is through the rate of interest.

This 'more recent discussion' to which Keynes is here referring was initiated by an article by Pigou (1937) which will be the subject matter of much of part III. In this source at last we find a more substantive classical reaction to the Keynesian theory of employment although it is marred by a continuing reluctance of Pigou to address Keynes directly.

Pigou persistently tried to avoid the impression that he did argue against Keynes, but Keynes – although severely ill at that time – did not abstain from a critical discussion of the new 'simplified model of employment' offered by Pigou (1937). Keynes (1937b, p. 264) even welcomed this piece in a certain sense:

> His 'simplified model' has the great advantage that it enables the root of the differences between us to be clearly exposed.

Posterity did not follow him in this judgement, however, and in the standard renderings of the Keynes–Classics debate there is hardly a trace to be found of this model. Thus a major effort of part III will be directed at its reconstruction.

Part III should also throw some additional light on the reciprocal charge of intentional or unintentional lack of intellectual appreciation of the opponent's arguments made against Keynes and his school themselves. Thus, a historian of economic thought Aslanbeigui (1992, p. 1)) recently claimed:

> Careful analysis of Pigou's theory of unemployment proves that he had an unemployment model that Keynes failed (refused?) to understand.

In that attempted proof, Pigovian publications are then quoted ranging from his 1914 booklet on 'Unemployment' up to his 'Lapses From Full Employment' of 1945, but the really strategic article of Pigou (1937) is left out of account.

In this article Pigou (1937, p. 405) himself states that 'until recently' a negative relationship between money wages on the one hand and employment on the other was generally simply taken for granted and that Pigou now wanted to supply the hitherto missing 'classical' model of this relationship. But if this is the case, Keynes' preceding claim that exactly this point was insufficiently argued in the classical school cannot be considered as being based on either a failure or a refusal on his part to understand the Pigovian model of employment. Thus we may take Pigou himself as witness for the appropriateness of the view that at the time of Keynes' writing there just was no complete model of the classical nexus between money wages and employment.

In the context of commenting on pecularities of the unfolding of the Keynes–Classics debate we may also note the remark made by T. W. Hutchison (1978, p. 180) that 'neither Keynes nor his followers have ever spelt out, with relevant texts, just what Pigou's logical failure amounted to'.

It will emerge presently that it is only in a very limited sense that this statement can be accepted. As far as Keynes himself is concerned, we hope to have demonstrated already in sufficient detail that Hutchison's verdict is not justified as a general statement. There are many instances of discussions of Pigovian 'relevant texts' by Keynes in which he attempted to document the exact nature of his divergence from Pigou. It was exactly because Keynes thought it important to spell out the logical failure of Pigou's theory of (un)employment that he welcomed Pigou's presentation of his 'simplified model' as a 'relevant text' and entered into a discussion of it.

But among Keynes' followers astonishing patterns of discussion may indeed be documented which do warrant some comment: when Pigou (1937) did get around to his more detailed defence of the classical belief in wage cutting against 'recent questioning' of this doctrine, there seems to have been considerable verbal debate over this piece among them but no systematic reformulation of the Keynesian position was published by any member of the 'inner circle' of Keynesians. This was particularly astonishing because it was thought that Pigou addressed himself primarily against one of them.[3]

It was left to Keynes (1937b) himself to publish a brief reply to Pigou. In addition, there was a critical comment by Nicholas Kaldor (1937) who then was still considered as an outsider as far as the Keynesian camp was concerned. Although there was a further rejoinder by Pigou (1938), there still did not emerge any direct contributions to this debate from Keynes' disciples themselves.

The Young Keynesians' reluctance to write up any direct criticism of Pigou is particularly surprising when it is noted that their former 'Messenger Angel' R. F. Kahn[4] (unsuccessfully) pleaded to Keynes not to favour the outsider Kaldor by publishing his comment, Kahn's argument being that an abundance of comparable articles could be written by them if Keynes so wished:

> After all we could all of us write replies to Pigou if you wanted them and I do not see why Kaldor should be thus favoured.

But Keynes (JMK, XIV, p. 262) pointed out that in fact no one else besides Kaldor had sent him any comment on Pigou (1937). Keynes (*ibid.*) announced that from then on he wanted to abstain from any further comments on Pigou. He combined this announcement with an invitation to the complainant to take the initiative in writing the replies for the second round of debates which was opened by Pigou (1938). But again there was absolutely no such reaction – in spite of R. F. Kahn's just quoted offer on behalf of 'all of us' to write replies to Pigou, supposedly involving at least himself, Gerald Shove, Piero Sraffa and Joan Robinson. This really must be fully realised: Kahn offered Keynes the chance to present replies to Pigou by 'all of us' if Keynes wanted them. Keynes did want them. Absolutely nothing came from Kahn and 'his' people.

Thus, after extensive published and unpublished debate the situation emerged in which Keynes did indeed intend to refrain from any further comment on Pigou's 'relevant texts' while Keynes' followers continued to abstain from a substantive debate with Pigou. It is in this limited sense that Hutchison's above quoted characterisation of the Keynes–Pigou debate may be accepted. But who was the beneficiary of this 'breakdown in communication'?

It is a major contention of this book that it was predominantly the Keynesian perspective which suffered as a consequence of this peculiar unfolding of the debate. But this contention cannot be elaborated until a more substantive discussion of the basic and more specific issues of this debate have been worked through.

15
Basic Issues and Pigou's Rejoinders

15.1 Money wages and employment

We just saw that in Keynes' opinion ch. 19 of his *General Theory* together with its appendix could have been a possible starting point for a substantive debate with Pigou. On reflection, such an expectation does not appear to be totally unreasonable. After all, in the appendix to that chapter Pigou was indeed addressed directly and with extensive reference to a specific model, namely that of Pigou's 'real demand for labour'.

But the subject matter of ch. 19 goes beyond the specific model discussed in its appendix. That chapter deals with the nexus between money wages and employment. Thus it aims beyond the limited scope of the model of Pigou's 'real demand for labour' and at the heart of the *Theory of Unemployment* in general since in Pigou (1933) the transition from the real analysis to a supposedly 'realistic' monetary analysis happens via the concept of the 'elasticity of demand in terms of money for labour as a whole', 'E_m', this magnitude denoting the percentage change in total employment associated with a corresponding change in the general level of the money wage rate. This relationship is nothing else but the wider subject matter of ch. 19, *General Theory*. Hence here in particular the thematic framework was set by Keynes in such a way that if the minds of the two discussants would not meet in good, at least they could have had a common battleground, both on the 'real' and on the 'monetary' front.

Elaborating on these observations we may note that Pigou (1933, p. 100) was, of course, well aware of the fact that it is unrealistic to postulate real wages as being the decisive economic political lever:

> It is money rates, and not real rates, that are the subject matter of wage bargains. Therefore it is of practical moment to know what changes in real wages are implied by given changes in money rates.

Thus the 'practical' discussion in the *Theory of Unemployment* turns from debating the magnitude E_r as discussed in part II above to investigating the magnitude E_m as just defined verbally.[1]

With regard to the 'practical' question of the relationship of changes in real wages to changes in money wages Pigou is well aware of one particular view of the money wage and employment nexus which later was to become quite important for Keynes' seemingly impertinent characterisation of the view which the classical school 'ought' to have adhered to. It might therefore be of some interest to quote the relevant passage from Pigou (1933, pp. 100f.):

> It is possible to imagine ... that the price level, alike of wage-goods and of anything else, is altered in the same proportion as the money wage-rate, that the real wage-rate remains what it was before, and that everything goes on exactly as it used to do ... Meditation along these lines has suggested to some persons the view that in actual life reductions in the money rate of wages would simply be reflected in a proportionate fall in prices; so that no effect whatever either on the real rate of wages or on the volume of labour demanded would be produced. This suggestion ... deserves investigation.

This view amounts to the assumption that E_m as just defined necessarily is equal to zero. If that were indeed the case, there would not have been much point in entering a discussion of this concept in the first instance, however. It is clear then that Pigou had to reject the quoted view. He does so on the grounds that it is based on the fallacious presupposition that the quantity of employment remained unaltered (*ibid.*).

Such a presupposition would indeed be unsatisfactory for Pigou, since the volume of employment is exactly the magnitude under investigation. But in the macroeconomic context chosen by Pigou it would be a fallacy of the same nature to assume at the outset of the analysis that a change in money wages would change only this category of incomes. Thus, when Pigou (1933, p. 102) starts his alternative discussion of changes in the money wage-rate with the assumption that '[a]t the outset nothing has happened to non-wage-earners' money income', and under this presupposition claims that as a result of a drop in money wage-rates '[a]dditional labour must be employed', then it is not surprising that Keynes (1936, p. 276) insisted that 'the same mistake' which Pigou just criticised was then made by Pigou himself. When Pigou (1933, p. 103) proceeds from the initial assumption of constant non-wage income as just discussed to the assumption of constant aggregate nominal income in an algebraic discussion of his new magnitude E_m, then again one must ask for the rationale of such an assumption and likewise when he defines a function $\psi(n)$ which is supposed to relate aggregate employment to aggregate nominal income.[2]

The way in which these assumptions are presented in that context makes them appear as being mere postulates and it is not apparent on which grounds they should be theoretically better founded than the postulates which lead to the conclusion that E_m may be zero.

The mere postulation of Pigou's alternative assumptions cannot be taken as a satisfactory disproof of the view just quoted, namely that a change in money wages might leave real wages virtually unchanged. If then Keynes (1936, p. 12) states:

> Thus if money-wages change, one would have expected the classical school to argue that prices would change in almost the same proportion, leaving the real wage and the level of unemployment practically the same as before,

then he does not really attribute an argumentation to the 'Classics' which they 'ought' to have made but never did make. Rather, he echoes a suggestion which none other than Pigou considered as *deserving investigation*,[3] which Pigou then *attempted* to show to be irrelevant, but with far too clumsy a method to bring home his point.

The crucial point here is that his discussion, via E_m, of the effect of money wage changes on total employment reveals 'Pigou's intuitive grasp of the general-equilibrium nature of the problem of unemployment' as Laidler (1999, p. 165) put it. He continues (*ibid.*):

> It [Pigou's intuitive grasp, GMA] is even clearer from his observation that in order to know just how much extra employment would be involved, information about the nature of the monetary system would be required.

These remarks are noteworthy because in the context of Laidler's diligent investigation they reinforce the impression that, on the one hand, the crucial aspect of Pigou (1933) is indeed its *implicit* discussion of a monetary general equilibrium model but that Pigou had only an *intuitive* grasp of the nature of his own analysis, on the other hand.

These remarks seem to mark *the* pivotal point for the interpretational carousels marring the Keynes–Pigou debate to this very day: if Keynes (1936), with his combination of debating monetary matters and employment problems, just took up elements already laid out by Pigou before him, then is it not true that what Keynes 'was able to demonstrate' was 'modest', was 'neither new nor startling' and was 'well illustrated' by Pigou (1933) before him, as Niehans (1990) claimed in the quote above on p. 00? Was the *General Theory* then 'plagiarised' by Keynes from Pigou in essential aspects? One could well think so. Although this must be denied (Leeson, 1998a, p. 2), 'Keynes' caricature of Pigou is inaccurate' according to a persistent school of interpreters, also quoted above on p. 26. Even Laidler (1999), who wavers between the pro-Keynes and pro-Pigou camps, expressly refers to Robert Leeson's view that Pigou in one way or another did anticipate the essential arguments of the *General Theory* (Laidler, 1999, p. 261, n. 4) and trusts that it 'will be apparent to the reader [that] I believe that there is something to be said for that point of view'. But what is that 'something'? What *exactly* can be said for that point of view? It is the present author's conviction that such claims can only be evaluated in a detailed reconstruction of the argumentation in question. Such an endeavour must go into investigating the relevant passages at considerable detail – not in the way of just relating quotes but in the way of relating the relevant, fully spelt-out models. This is, in any case, the rationale of the present enquiry.

When one turns to the passages in Pigou (1933, pt. II, ch. x) to which Laidler drew attention in the context just quoted in the last two paragraphs, then it must be kept in mind that Pigou's remarks which revealed his intuition for the money wage and money supply nexus were not really intended to lead to a systematic discussion of the money market.[4] They were rather cursory remarks for introducing the concept of a $\psi(n)$-function relating employment to nominal income which was mentioned on p. 167 already. And it was stated there that his discussion of this function amounted just to *postulating* its existence and to attributing specific values to its derivative. If he did have a consistent view of the workings of the money market he did not reveal it.

It is true that in this context Pigou (1933, p. 104) does even mention such monetary theoretic subtleties as interest effects on the demand for money, stating that with decreased money wages there might be an *increase* in the real rate of interest and that

this tempts people to shift money out of passive into active balances, thus augmenting the volume of money income per unit of time, even though the stock of money is unchanged.

The view expressed here that rising interest rates might release idle money holdings to be activated for transaction purposes sounds quite similar to the liquidity preference theory of interest if one has the *General Theory* in the back of one's mind.[5] But in fact the Pigovian analysis of the interdependence of wage rates and interest rates is diametrically opposed to the later one of Keynes as Pigou himself was quite well aware.[6]

In short, as far as the monetary analysis in Pigou (1933) is concerned, we have a number of tantalising suggestions for interesting themes of analysis but no systematic discussion of the relevant macroeconomic interconnections. In fact, as far as the theory of interest is concerned, it was later pointed out by Pigou (1937) that he firmly stood by the side of the classical time preference theory of interest in the analysis of macroeconomic effects of money wage changes. He had no intention of presenting himself as a precursor of the Keynesian theory of liquidity preference.

The fact that Pigou (1937, p. 406) later did return to the complex of questions associated with Keynes' analysis of the relationship between money wages and real wages, proclaiming now that it is indispensable to have a relevant model:

> To attack effectively the problem ... it is necessary to set up a simplified model. For no advance in this field can be made without one

might be seen as an – at least implicit – admission that he did not have a *consistent* model before and that indeed Keynes was quite right in having said so. Such an impression might also have been a reason for Pigou's continuing reluctance really to admit to entering into a direct substantive debate with Keynes about this matter – a fact which was discussed in the previous chapter.

An alternative reason given by Pigou for his reticence as far as Keynes was concerned, namely that he did not want to bother him in his – then acute – state of bad health,[7] was repeatedly rejected as implausible by Keynes himself.[8] In short, eventually Keynes' expectation concerning ch. 19, *General Theory* as a catalyst for a substantial debate with Pigou proved to have been justified: Pigou (1937) did take up the theme set by Keynes in that context and he did discuss in some detail and in the context of a specific model the role of the rate of interest in connection with the money wage and employment nexus. In spite of disclaimers from Pigou and others, what Pigou (1937) wrote in this context must be regarded as a rejoinder to Keynes' criticism articulated in the *General Theory*. The specific traits and the exact nature of this discussion will be investigated in a separate chapter below.

15.2 Capital and time

Parallel with the money wages issue just discussed there appeared a further one in the Pigovian rejoinders to the criticisms of the *General Theory*: the question of the treatment of capital in short-period analysis. The significance of this issue for the unfolding – or rather for the lack of it – of the Keynes–Pigou debate seems to have been underrated by most investigators of that debate to this very day.[9]

It will be remembered from part II that for Pigou (1933, p. 88) the analytical time period was defined by the behaviour of capital, the short period being one in which capital equipment may be taken as constant 'in the sense that slow-working reactions from changes in fixed capital are left out of account'. Pigou made it clear in that context that his whole book is based on this assumption and – although he never stated this corollary explicitly in that context – from this assumption he seems to have inferred that then investment necessarily must always be zero because if investment were going on, capital could not be treated as constant since investment, by definition, is a change in the stock of capital. In accordance with this view, it was suggested in section 9.3.2 on p. 69 above that Pigou's 'non-wage goods' should be interpreted not as investment goods but as luxury goods.

If Keynes (1936, p. 275) criticised Pigou (1933) for not taking sufficient account of changes in investment activity, stating that he considered it as being

> strange that Professor Pigou should have supposed that he could furnish a theory of unemployment which involves no reference at all to changes in the rate of investment

then this criticism must have appeared to Pigou as being extremely ill-conceived. In fact, it must have suggested to him that Keynes was rather muddled concerning the appropriate analytical time period.

This then was indeed a major criticism which Pigou (1936, p. 122) articulated against the *General Theory*. He pointed out that Keynes (1936, e.g. p. 245) assumed 'the existing quality and quantity of equipment' as 'given' but that nevertheless Keynes supposed that new investment was undertaken in every year. From this Pigou concluded: 'He [Keynes] is assuming in fact a stationary state and at the same time a moving one.' From this supposed fact Pigou then proceeds to infer wide-ranging conclusions about the extent of Keynes' analytical confusion.

It is astonishing that this criticism did not provoke immediate reaction from Keynes. Not even when D. H. Robertson repeated this charge in private correspondence with Keynes do we find any reaction.[10] But when Pigou (1937) presented a more substantive rejoinder in the form of a 'short-period' model of the money wage and employment nexus, then Keynes (1937b) did react. In drafting that rejoinder Keynes wrote (JMK, XIV, p. 238) – but did not publish – the express criticism that in the model proposed by Pigou (1937) income and employment are unchanging. Keynes continued as follows:

> There also seems to be a confusion between a 'short period' during which finished capital equipment is assumed to be constant, and a 'short period' during which no new capital goods are allowed to be in course of production. The former 'short period' merges into the long period and the changes of the real world; but the latter relates to a frozen land remote in its characteristics from all experience.

The background for this remark is an assumption concerning short-period analysis quite similar to but more detailed than that of the *Theory of*

Unemployment. According to Pigou (1937, p. 406) his simplified model operated under the assumptions that

> land and fixed capital (i) last for ever ... and (ii) consist of things of which it is impossible to make any more. [And] of the things it is possible to make i.e. consumption goods, each sort has exactly the same period of production; which period cannot be altered ...
> This model is designed for the investigation of the short-period consequences of all-round cuts in wage rates.

Thus we have here an economy without production of investment goods and with an eternally unchanging stock of capital – in short, we have here a model of 'Simple Reproduction' of an existing capital-using society, as it would be named by Marxists. Such an analytical setup might be considered as 'interesting' insofar as it is immune both against Keynes' criticism of Pigou (1933) and against Pigou's criticism of the *General Theory*: since net investment is absent by express assumption, the model cannot be asked to represent changes in investment and thus Keynes' criticism that Pigou does not deal with investment at any length is taken account of. In addition, since 'Simple Reproduction' represents a stationary state plain and simple, there is no question of inconsistent analytical time periods and thus criticism *à la* Pigou (1936) is avoided. Maybe it was such considerations which made the analysis of 'Simple Reproduction' an attractive proposition for Richard Kahn as well, even years before Pigou (1937). According to the testimony of Joan Robinson (1973e, p. 253), Richard Kahn – Keynes' 'Messenger Angel' for the participants of the 'Cambridge circus' of 1930 to 1931 (see p. 443, n. 4) – took 'infinite pains' to explain to his surroundings 'what Keynes was doing' by propagating a reinvented model of 'Simple Reproduction' ever since controversy set in around Keynes' *Treatise*.[11]

Let us point out one important, and for Joan Robinson's later reflections about 'appropriate' model building, crucial, analytical aspect of the 'Simple Reproduction' approach: changes in such a framework can just be of a 'comparative dynamic', or rather, 'comparative stationary' nature. It is – and it was – clear to anybody who thought through these models that a disturbance of the stationary state would generate economic reactions which could not be modelled within the same models and that the ensuing 'historic' adaptation processes could possibly take a long time before a new stationary state was reached again – if it ever existed and ever would be attained. There is then indeed the question of the realism of a discussion of such alternative 'frozen-land' economies as Keynes nicknamed this set-up. A debate of economic political action concerning money wage rates in a modern society might well seem to be devoid of any meaning in this context and one could have only wished that Keynes or one of his adherents brought out more clearly the problematic nature of Pigou's supposedly 'short-period' set-up. Table 15.1 tries to give a brief synopsis of these issues. They relate to fundamental differences between Keynes, Pigou and – in some sense – 'Cambridge Keynesians' and therefore they deserve special attention. We will see below (p. 247) that Joan Robinson places this discussion in a wider context spanning the whole decade – from Richard Kahn's unpublished reception of Keynes (1930) up to Roy Harrod's (1939) celebrated attempt at growth theory. Therefore, these contributions are also included in this context. Richard Kahn's contributions to this debate were 'in oral discussion, not published' at that time, however, as Joan Robinson (1973e, p. 253) stressed and as is marked accordingly in Table 15.1. His views in these matters must therefore be inferred from his correspondence with Keynes, published much later, and from Joan Robinson's already mentioned later account. But there is good evidence that we have to place Kahn into the 'stationary state' column of Table 15.1 where we identify whether the analysis of the respective author rests on the assumption of a pre-specified stationary (or quasi-stationary) situation of the economy.

The next column relates to the characteristics of the determination of income in a single economic period. The last column should show whether the long-period view of the respective author may be seen as a limiting case of a wider range of possible, not necessarily stationary, income patterns.

The 'Keynes'-row in Table 15.1 shows that the latter view is the distinctive feature of the *General Theory*. Its method is to start out from the determination of the economy in a single time period and then to ask what will happen subsequently, given some special assumption. One of many imaginable special assumptions about the path of income is to *assume* a stream

Table 15.1 Stationary and 'moving' states

	Stationary state postulated		Short period income determination	Long period of specified income patterns
Keynes (1936)	"frozen land"		$\approx \bar{K}; I = S > 0$	$Y_0 = \ldots = Y_t = \ldots = Y_n$ $n \to \infty; r = \rho$
Kahn c. 1931	$(r \neq \rho)$	$\bar{K};$	(unpublished)	
Pigou (1933)	$(r = \rho)$	$\approx \bar{K};$		
Robinson (1936)	$r \overset{!}{\neq} \rho$	$\bar{K};$	$(I = S = 0)$	
Pigou (1937)	$r = \rho$	$\bar{K};$	$I = S = 0$	
Kaldor (1937)	$r = \rho(\underline{n})$	$\bar{K};$	$I = S = 0$	
Pigou (1938)	$r = \rho(\underset{-,+}{n})$	$\bar{K};$	$I = S = 0$	
Harrod (1939)	$\hat{K} \overset{!}{=} g_n = g_w = g_a$			$g_w \gtrless g_a$

of constant income at zero net investment and then to show that Keynes' economy ends up in a state where time preference rules the rate of interest. This is the way in which Keynes himself interpreted and saw Pigou (1937), as we will see presently (below, p. 177). In addition, this row restates that aspect of Keynes' theory of income determination which Pigou (1936) thought to be so contradictory: the assumption of (virtually) constant capital ($\approx \bar{K}$) while investment (and saving) are supposed to be positive.

Joan Robinson would later call this analytical set-up an 'anomaly'[12] and Table 15.1 is so drawn to make this visually clear. It is therefore not without irony to note here that this very idea could be thought of as having been inspired by none other than Pigou (1933, p. 88) himself. As was seen (p. 436, n. 6) it was *him* who made there a number of – seemingly clear and explicit – assumptions which were meant to hold good 'throughout' his book. For further discussion, they may now be expanded in the following way:

1. The analysis relates to the 'short period'.
2. Changes in fixed capital are admitted to exist; [$\Delta K (= I?) \neq 0$].
3. Changes in fixed capital cause reactions in the economic system; some of these are fast, some of them are slow.
4. The slow reactions – although well known to exist – should be 'left out of account' in short-period analysis.

How do these assumptions affect the modelling of an economy? Keynes, in the *General Theory*, was totally explicit that the changes mentioned under item 2 in such a list must be considered to be attributable to net investment and that they have multiplier effects in the short period. But Pigou (1933) himself left open what caused the changes in fixed capital which he *did* mention. The natural idea in this context is, of course, to consider such changes as happening through net investment. This is the position taken by Keynes and he could well have believed himself to be following the lead given by none other than Pigou, although when it comes to the detailed working of his model, Pigou's discussions of changes in net investment were deficient in Keynes' eyes in any case, as just seen.

Pigou's (1936) just quoted criticism of Keynes' alleged 'inconsistency' now makes it possible to discern more clearly the specific analytical set-up characterising Keynes and Pigou (1933). Although Pigou (1936) is just a review and does not itself offer an elaborate model, nevertheless, what he states there does give important information about the type of analysis he can or cannot accept. We can now be sure that capital cannot change in Pigou's set-up through positive net investment, because if such changes of capital stock were permitted, Pigou could not very well consider himself to be consistent in *criticising* Keynes for such an 'inconsistency'. Therefore we can *now* conclude that there just is no net investment production in Pigou

(1933). With the benefit of the hindsight after Pigou's criticism of the *General Theory*, it now appears that in this regard the similarity between the *Theory of Unemployment* and the *General Theory* can only be an apparent one.

This finding supports a previous statement of ours concerning the character of Pigou's non-wage goods, namely our claim that they can be only 'luxury goods' and nothing else (see p. 437, n. 8). In the previous context such a claim might have seemed as being a mere speculation. Now that speculation is confirmed. It emerges now that that must indeed have been *the* authentic Pigovian assumption. But since this finding can only be *inferred*, we omit investment and saving in the Pigou (1933) line of Table 15.1, thus preserving some of the flavour of unfolding clarification in the course of the debate.

In the year following his review of the *General Theory*, Pigou (1937) clarified this issue considerably. This will be discussed below in the next chapter (pp. 200ff.) where we will substantiate that this model started out from a stationary state and that interest rates were time-preference determined, as represented in the 'Pigou (1937)'-line of Table. 15.1. But there is one rather strange aspect of his new contribution: he is reported as having claimed that this article was not really directed against Keynes but rather against Joan Robinson.[13] This necessitates a thorough assessment of her contributions in this debate and that will be done below in part IV. Let it suffice here to say that here contribution must be seen in the context of her intensive connection with Richard Kahn's economic mindset. Kahn was convinced that with regard to Pigou the issue definitely was 'not one of schools of thought'[14] but just one of erroneously assuming time-preference determined interest rates.

Joan Robinson, like Richard Kahn in the quoted correspondence with Keynes, believed that she could deny the relevance of time preference under conditions of stationariness, whereas Kaldor and Keynes realised that stationariness was the essence of the classical theory of the rate of interest. If assumed as an analytical basis for a model economy, this stationary state *implies* $r = \rho$ even for Keynes' analytical system. The main difference between the subsequent Kaldor row and the Robinson rows thus is the treatment of the rate of time-preference, as depicted in the respective rows of Table 15.1. The Kaldor (1937) row shows that his significant contribution is to make time-preference depend on employment n in a negative way and to postulate this as being the essence of Keynes' approach. The next line then represents the fact that Pigon (1937) by and large accepted Kaldor's approach but took exception to his specification of the $\rho(n)$-function. Pigou claimed to have generalised the Keynesian approach thus restated by Kaldor by postulating that the $\rho(n)$-function might also be rising.

Thus the main mark of distinction between Joan Robinson – and Richard Kahn – on the one side and Pigou on the other is this very issue of the determination of the rate of interest, as shown in the Kahn and Robinson rows of Table 15.1 on the one side and in the Pigou (1937) and Kaldor (1937) rows on the other side. But this was by no means a strategic point for Keynes himself and it remains to be seen whether there was a solid analytical basis for his belief.

It is rather strange that, as far as Joan Robinson and Kahn were concerned, the debate between Pigou (1937) and Keynes (1937b) was left in a by and large uncommented on state – at least as far as published or otherwise systematic comments were concerned.

Some of the issues debated were put on a new plane by Harrod (1939) by extending a (quasi) stationary model into a dynamic context in which some of Keynes' problems of effective demand appeared which then could lead to dramatic dynamical instabilities. We include this contribution in Table 15.1 for completeness' sake. But it must be observed in this context that the model did not really address the authentic Keynes-and-Pigou debate. Indeed, there was a certain agreement between these two that Harrod's contribution was in the end unsatisfactory and in any case not directly related to their issues.[15]

Certainly if time-preference was such a fundamental issue between Keynes and Pigou as Kahn proclaimed, one could have expected that Keynes' followers would thrash that out once the first round of exchanges was over in which the 'big shots' had their go. This was indeed the expectation which Keynes himself did have. Particular hopes in this direction could have rested with Keynes' 'Messenger Angel' Richard Kahn. Not only was he intimately acquainted with Keynes' thinking for many years by 1937.[16] Kahn himself must also be included among those whom Keynes professed to be in a position to write a critical note about Pigou if only Keynes invited them to do so – and Keynes did do this as was just seen. And finally Kahn could have been considered as being particularly well equipped for a critical assessment of the Pigovian concept of short-period analysis since Kahn's fellowship dissertation was about this very subject.[17]

It is, however, quite ironic that Richard Kahn not only did not fulfil the hopes which could have been placed in him in this context. He even successfully urged Keynes to abstain from publishing the little Keynes *had* written about Pigou's problematic conception of economic politically relevant analysis.

Keynes' above-quoted criticism of the stationary state of Pigou's 'simplified model' may indeed be rejected in arguing that Pigou's model does not preclude a 'comparative stationary' analysis of changes in income and employment in the context of comparisons between alternative 'frozen land economies'. Such an argument would not invalidate Keynes' quoted criticism concerning the remoteness from reality of such a set-up. But such a retort would have permitted Pigou to maintain that his model does indeed admit changes in income and employment – albeit not really in 'historical time' but at least in 'logical time', as Joan Robinson would have called it late in her life.

In this limited sense Pigou could have defended the claim he reportedly made to Richard Kahn concerning the changeability of income in his set-up. The arguments which Pigou did use at that time are not known apart from the statements made by Richard Kahn. In any case, Kahn proved to have been sufficiently convinced by this type of Pigovian arguments to urge Keynes to suppress the entire paragraph, including the important 'frozen land' analogy just quoted:

> As I expected, Pigou has seized on your last paragraph (which I am still opposed to your printing) and declared triumphantly that you have misunderstood him. Why not concentrate on what is important by agreeing to omit the final paragraph? (JMK, XIV, p. 260)

Under protestations, Keynes gave in and did not publish that very important 'frozen land' passage:

> Since Pigou disclaims the idea that he is assuming constancy of income, I am now deleting my last paragraph ... But I still believe that it represents something at the bottom of his head. (JMK, XIV, p. 261)

Thus an important part of Keynes' criticism against Pigou's classical method was cut out, *against* Keynes' own conviction, and with Richard Kahn playing no minor role in this development.

This episode must appear as a riddle if one thinks in terms of Keynes 'the master' and 'Cambridge Keynesians' as his disciples. But such a perception would be quite wrong as is documented in several passages of this book. The interesting question is now: in which direction must we revise such a perception? More specifically: was the role of pupil and master just *reversed* between Keynes and the Cambridge Keynesians?[18] Or was it rather that the Cambridge Keynesians had their own agenda which had really rather little to do with Keynes' just stated analytical intentions? There is considerable evidence for an affirmative answer to the latter question.

We noted in part I already that Joan Robinson reported that she and her associates felt that they had considerable trouble telling Keynes 'what the point of his revolution really was'. Her account seems to speak more in favour of the 'role reversal' view of Keynes and his putative disciples. But we will see later (see below, p. 247), that Joan Robinson also reported that as soon as controversy had set in around Keynes (1930), the precursor of the *General Theory*, Richard Kahn, put great effort into telling and teaching his surroundings that Keynes had to be interpreted in terms of a model which, in Marxian parlance, is one of 'simple reproduction', in other words: a model of a stationary state. Since he did not publish anything along this line of interpreting Keynes, there is no documentary evidence for Kahn's endeavours except Joan Robinson's statements to that effect. But there is indirect evidence confirming her reports. For easy reference we also put that evidence down in Table 15.1. It is contained in the lines bearing the names of Richard Kahn and that of Joan Robinson. It appears that we put Richard Kahn himself into a mental camp quite near to the 'frozen land' conditions which Keynes intended to attack. As already stated, his contribution was only indirect, through his teaching others, of whom Joan Robinson must be taken to have been a particularly receptive partner for several academic and biographic reasons to be discussed later in more detail. It is quite clear that Joan Robinson (1936), very soon after the publication of the *General Theory*, put up an 'extension' of Keynes' theory into a long period setting which, apart from the rejection of the time-preference theory of interest, was very much in the mould of Pigou. The quick appearance of this publication and the rather critical view of the *General Theory* it offers suggests that it must have some other roots than the *General Theory* itself. We suggest that use see these roots in the proximity to Richard Kahn. Her published article and the way she relates herself to Kahn thus leads us to place these two entries more in the vicinity of Pigou than of Keynes in Table 15.1.

15.3 Time preference and the rate of interest

In the last section it was argued that the non-publication of Keynes' 'frozen-land' criticism could well be considered as a major loss for the subsequent development of post-Keynesian analysis. It was pointed out that Kahn did not consider this issue as an important one, however, and that he urged Keynes to drop it. For him the issue of time preference or rather 'the rate of discount of the future' had to be 'forcibly' *negated*, not analytically discussed. Since Pigou (1937) based the determination of the rate of interest on this concept, Kahn wrote to Keynes (JMK, XIV, p. 260):

> It is clear that D. H. R[obertson], Kaldor, and Pigou still all fail to see the fundamental fallacy – which is the determination of the rate of interest by the rate of discounting the future ... I am not sure whether your own reply [to Pigou (1937)] brings out the grossness of this error sufficiently forcibly.

In view of Keynes' previous attacks against the classical theory of interest it might indeed appear an astonishing oversight if he permitted Pigou (1937) to bring back into the discussion that old classical idea of the rate of discounting the future determining the rate of interest.

Subsequently it turned out, however, that Keynes intentionally spared Pigou (1937) criticism concerning his time preference theory of interest, answering Kahn that he was 'not so clear about this'. The reason which (*nota bene*) Keynes *himself* (JMK, XIV, p. 261) gave for his reluctance to accept Kahn's verdict concerning Pigou's 'fundamental fallacy' was:

> On the assumptions of the simplified model, where saving is assumed to be zero, the rate of interest has to be such that the inducement to save is exactly zero. Does this not mean, leaving out complications, that it will have to be just equal to the rate of discount of the future?

But although the wording of this passage seems to be clear, its meaning might appear less so. For a stout Keynesian this passage might even be downright unintelligible. Did not Keynes (1936, e.g. p. 93) go out of his way to argue that there is no clear-cut influence of the rate of interest on consumer *spending*? How is it then that in the quoted passage he now concedes to Pigou that there is indeed such an influence of the rate of interest on *saving*?

Two answers suggest themselves with regard to this puzzle. A short one would be that this is one of the instances where Keynes revealed that he just did not know what he had written. The wording of Kahn's just quoted letter about the 'grossness' of Pigou's error and about Keynes' supposedly deficient reply in this regard suggests that this episode might appear as a case in point for Joan Robinson's remark that 'we had some trouble in getting Maynard to see what the point of his revolution really was' (see above p. 14).[19]

An alternative answer which, unfortunately, will involve considerable expositorial effort, would start from the presupposition that Keynes knew very well what he wrote. In this case it must then be demonstrated that Keynes based his seemingly contradictory statements on an analytical framework which could generate each of them under specific conditions. Under the specific 'frozen land' assumptions of Pigou's 'simplified model' it must be shown that Keynes' analysis did indeed generate the quoted results whereas under the assumptions underlying the *General Theory*, the alternative statements would have to be shown to hold. This is what the entry in last column of Table 15.1 on p. 172 tried to convey and this position must now be made clearer on the following pages.

If it can be shown that Keynes could well have been aware that important Keynesian and Pigovian interest theoretic results depended on alternative assumptions within a basically similar analytical framework, then it would indeed have been impossible for Keynes to criticise Pigou for his conclusions, unless he criticised the assumptions on which they rested. But since the 'frozen land' assumptions went uncriticised, it would follow that Keynes' critical hands were bound with regard to the Pigovian interest theoretic conclusions.

This argument must appear as purely speculative as long as the analytical framework to which it is referring has not been actually presented. This will be the object of the following excursus.

15.4 Excursus on time preference

15.4.1 The Keynesian use of time preference analysis

One of the exegetical legends surrounding the *General Theory* is that its consumption theoretic parts are based primarily on more or less well taken *ad hoc*-ery,[20] but not on systematic time preference analysis. If that were indeed the case, our intention to associate Keynes' own thinking on these matters with time preference must appear as anachronistic and purely speculative.[21] In order to avoid such a charge and because of the considerable importance of this point for a proper understanding of Keynes, we intend first to establish that in the development of his theory of consumption, Keynes did refer to time preference analysis and that he was acquainted with its subtleties.

In the *General Theory* (on p. 166) Keynes stated only very briefly that what 'I have called the propensity to consume' is just an 'aspect' of the 'psychological time-preferences of an individual'. From the brevity of this reference to time preference it might be inferred that he was not particularly interested in the potential theoretical foundation of his theory of consumption via this route. An alternative interpretation would be that he did not want to elaborate the technicalities of a theory which he considered to be well known by then.

In accordance with the latter interpretation we find in the now published drafts leading up to the published version of the *General Theory* that Keynes originally did indeed go into greater length concerning the time-preference theoretic foundations of his theory of consumption but that at that time already he considered the whole analysis as 'fairly clear' and limited himself only to a brief recollection of it. Nevertheless, this passage is important because it states clearly what Keynes considered as the 'givens' in this context (see JMK, XIII, p. 400):

> For a single individual the notion of time preference is fairly clear. Given all the relevant attendant circumstances which are fixed for me by the actions of others including my income [Y], actual and prospective, and the prices, actual and prospective, of debts, assets and consumables [Q_c], it is my state of time preference which determines what part of my income I spend on consumables and what part I reserve.

Keynes then elaborates why he considered this analysis only 'fairly' clear. The reason he gave was that the individual actions might, to a very limited extent, have repercussions for the self-same individual on the magnitudes which were just listed among the 'givens'. Assuming constancy of the 'givens' in the thought experiment relating to an individual consumer therefore generates only an approximate result, which Keynes was prepared to accept as sufficient in that context, however.[22]

For the further elaboration of the Keynesian approach to the micro-founda-tions of the theory of consumption it might be helpful to translate this quote into algebraic terms. Apart from the acceptance of the concept of time prefer-ence it is obviously based on the conception of budget equations which for the simple two-period case may be written in the simplest version as

$$Y_0 = p_{c0}Q_{c0} + S \tag{15.1}$$

$$Y_f + (1+r)S = p_{cf}Q_{cf} \tag{15.2}$$

where Y is income and indices 0 resp. f represent present resp. future 'prospective' magnitudes. Keynes' distinction of debts and other assets has been collapsed into one single variable S, for savings. They fetch an interest rate r. Consumption in the sense of the Keynesian theory is given by $P_{c0}Q_{c0} \equiv C$ where p_c is the price and Q_c is the quantity of the 'consumables' of the quotation. The demand for these is the decision variable which, under the acceptance of the concept of time preference, must be derived from a pref-erence ordering given by *e.g.* a utility function

$$U = U(Q_{c0}, Q_{cf}) \tag{15.3}$$

We take this algebraic rendering as being clearly covered by the quotes from Keynes just given. We will show below in more detail how they relate to Keynes' theory of consumption and postpone a more detailed debate on the 'authenticity' of these formulations.

Let us emphasise, however, that these formulations are more likely to err on the side of oversimplification rather than overextension. Keynes was well aware of the then existing literature on time preference. In the *General Theory* he expressly refers to G. Cassel (1903), *Nature and Necessity of Interest* (*GT*, p. 182) and to Irving Fisher (1930), *Theory of Interest* (*GT*, p. 140) both of which contain extensive expositions of the concept and the analysis of time preference. In addition, Keynes himself is documented in the litera-ture as a major inspirer in this field, since Frank Ramsey (1928, p. 545) reported that 'Mr. Keynes has shown me that the rule governing the amount to be saved can be determined' from considerations involving intertemporal consumption and production.

We conclude: Keynes expressly related his theory of consumption to time preference analysis. When writing the *General Theory* he was acquainted with the major contemporary contributions on this field as exemplified by the writings of Cassel, Fisher, and Ramsey. The latter acknowledged consid-erable inspiration for specific mathematical formulations of his theory from Keynes. In reconstructing Keynes' major tenets concerning the propensity to consume it is the most plausible approach to start from this type of time-preference analysis.

15.4.2 The concept of time preference

Neither Keynes nor Pigou was particularly clear about what exactly they meant by time preference or by 'the rate of discounting of the future'. In order to clarify these concepts, we propose considering two variants of intertemporal utility formulations.

On the one hand, it may be assumed that reference to time-preference theory may be taken simply to mean that there are utility functions of the type just specified under 15.3 above with particular characteristics. In particular, it may be assumed that depending on the time period of consumption there are different elasticities of utility

$$\frac{\partial U}{\partial Q_{co}} \frac{Q_{co}}{U} = \gamma_0 \qquad \frac{\partial U}{\partial Q_{cf}} \frac{Q_{cf}}{U} = \gamma_f \tau_f \qquad (15.4)$$

where γ_i = goods elasticity of utility of consumption, $i = 0$ for present time period, $i = f$ for future time period, and where τ_f = time elasticity of utility of consumption – the former elasticities pertaining to utility in the conventional atemporal sense, the latter denoting an elasticity of utility which depicts the particular significance of the fact that a good is available for consumption only on a future date. It is these latter elasticities which then express the concept of time preference in the narrower sense. If there are several future time periods, it is normally thought to be appropriate to assume

$$1 > \tau_1 > \tau_2 > \ldots > \tau_f > \ldots > \tau_n \geq 0. \qquad (15.5)$$

This formulation expresses the idea that ceteris paribus comparatively early consumption is considered by an individual to create higher utility.

Such an intertemporal utility function would then read, in logarithmic notation

$$\ln U = \gamma_0 \ln Q_{co} + \gamma_1 \tau_1 \ln Q_{c1} + \ldots + \gamma_f \tau_f \ln Q_{cf} + \ldots + \gamma_n \tau_n \ln Q_{cn} \quad (15.6)$$

Alteratively, using the concept of the rate of discounting of the future, it may be assumed that there are n future utility functions, each of the future utilities being mentally discounted by a factor $(1 + \rho)$, giving total utility by[23]

$$U = U_0(Q_{co}) + \frac{1}{1+\rho} U_1(Q_{c1}) + \ldots + \left(\frac{1}{1+\rho}\right)^f U_f(Q_{cf}) + \ldots + \left(\frac{1}{1+\rho}\right)^n U_n(Q_{cn})$$
$$(15.7)$$

The idea of higher individual valuations of comparatively early consumption here is expressed by the assumption that $\rho > 0$ holds so that later utilities of consumption will have a progressively lower weight as the exponent f increases in equ. (15.7).

There is now the question of which formulation of intertemporal utility is the more general one. Some readers might consider this problem as a rather esoteric one. It is, however, of some interest because Keynes claimed to have used a formulation of economic theory which contains the classical theory as a special case.

If we accept this claim as a working hypothesis, then we may propose to use the formulation of equation (15.6) as a basis of the Keynesian approach because it presupposes less about the pattern of temporal utilities, since the postulate of the existence of the 'time elasticities of utility of consumption', τ_f, is less restrictive than to assume that they have to be represented by a geometric row.

But it might be added that the formulation of equation (15.7) could easily be generalised by assuming non-constant ρ-s such that for any consecutive time periods f, g, there exists a specific magnitude ρ_{fg} defined by the associated ratio of marginal utilities U'_f and U'_g such that

$$\frac{U'_f}{U'_g} = 1 + \rho_{fg}, \quad f < g \tag{15.8}$$

holds.[24] The problem with this formulation, however, is that it does not measure just the time preference proper since the marginal utilities in each time period normally have to be considered as being a function of the quantities Q_{cf} resp. Q_{cg} so that this definition then incorporates an additional effect, namely a time-period effect and a quantity effect. In order to isolate a pure time-period effect, additional assumptions are then necessary concerning the time pattern of consumption. In Pigovian analysis such an assumption is supplied by the postulate of a stationary state.

Apart from these considerations, the two formulations of intertemporal utility patterns here discussed are equivalent in the sense that

(i) both are additive separable, and
(ii) the concept of the existence of an elasticity of utility is a general one which holds for any differentiable utility function.

It remains to show the relationship between the parameters of the two formulations under the classical conditions assumed by Pigou. Those conditions are characterised by:

(i) a stationary state in the sense that period specific preferences and quantities are identical over time, and
(ii) an infinite time horizon.

These assumptions permit us now to write in the case of the formulation of equ. (15.6) the simplified expression

$$\ln U = \gamma \ln Q_c (1 + \Sigma \tau_f) \text{ where} \tag{15.9}$$

$$\gamma = \gamma_0 = \gamma_1 = \dots = \gamma_n \; ; \; Q_c = Q_{c0} = Q_{c1} = \dots = Q_{cn} \; ; \; f = 1,2,\dots,n \; ; \; n \to \infty. \tag{15.10}$$

Alternatively, using the concept of the rate of discounting the future, these assumptions permit us now to simplify equ. (15.7) to

$$\ln U = \gamma \ln Q_c \left(1 + \Sigma \left(\frac{1}{1 + \rho} \right)^f \right) \text{ where } \Sigma \left(\frac{1}{1 + \rho} \right)^f = \frac{1}{\rho} \tag{15.11}$$

Setting these two expressions equal to each other and simplifying gives

$$\rho = \frac{1}{\Sigma \tau_f} \; ; \; f = 1,2,\dots,n \; ; \; n \to \infty. \tag{15.12}$$

This result shows that if $\rho > 0$ holds, then the condition given in expression (15.5) *must* hold so that the sum in this denominator converges.[25] The significance of this result will become apparent when we will attempt to relate the Keynesian theory of consumption to the Pigovian theory of interest at the end of this excursus.

15.4.3 The Keynesian consumption function and time preference

We have established so far that Keynes personally – and not just later interpreters of his theory – related his theory of consumption to time-preference analysis. In section (a) of this excursus it was seen that Keynes verbally described the relevant intertemporal budget constraints where the 'givens' were: present and prospective incomes and the corresponding prices of goods and assets. Generalizing the two budget equations given there to n periods, we therefore have

$$Y_0 + \left(\frac{1}{1 + r} \right) Y_1 + \dots + \left(\frac{1}{1 + r} \right)^f Y_f + \dots + \left(\frac{1}{1 + r} \right)^n Y_n = \tag{15.13}$$

$$= \rho_{c0} Q_{c0} + \left(\frac{1}{1 + r} \right) \rho_{c1} Q_{c1} + \dots + \left(\frac{1}{1 + r} \right)^f \rho_{cf} Q_{cf} + \dots + \left(\frac{1}{1 + r} \right)^n \rho_{cn} Q_{cn}$$

when the rate of interest is assumed to be constant.[26]

Household equilibrium then requires the maximisation of the time-preference function (15.6) subject to the budget constraint (15.13).[27] The resulting first order conditions may then be written as

$$\frac{\partial U}{\partial Q_{c0}}\frac{Q_{c0}}{U} : \frac{\partial U}{\partial Q_{cf}}\frac{Q_{cf}}{U} = \frac{\gamma_0}{\gamma_f \tau_f} = P_{c0}Q_{c0} : \left(\frac{1}{1+r}\right)^f P_{cf}Q_{cf} \ . \qquad (15.14)$$

From these expressions it will then appear that present consumption $C_0 \equiv p_{c0}Q_{c0}$ may be related to any future consumption $C_f \equiv p_{cf}Q_{cf}$ via

$$\left(\frac{1}{1+r}\right)^f P_{cf}Q_{cf} = \frac{\gamma_f \tau_f}{\gamma_0} C_0 \ . \qquad (15.15)$$

Substituting all the future consumptions in the budget equation (15.13) accordingly, gives an expression relating present and future incomes to present consumption. Rearranging gives then an expression explaining present consumption by the given prospective and present levels of income, namely

$$C_0 = \underbrace{\frac{\gamma_0}{\gamma_0 + \Sigma \gamma_f \tau_f} \Sigma \left(\frac{1}{1+r}\right)^f Y_f}_{a} + \underbrace{\frac{\gamma_0}{\gamma_0 + \Sigma \gamma_f \tau_f} . Y_0}_{b} ; \ f = 1, 2, \dots, n \ (15.16)$$

which obviously complies to the standard Keynesian form of the consumption function

$$C_0 = a + bY_0 \quad \text{with} \quad 0 < b < 1 \qquad (15.17)$$

where b is the marginal propensity to consume.

It should be noted that this value of the marginal propensity to consume is a *general* result which does not depend on special assumptions concerning the elasticities of utility – if it may be presumed that they exist as positive values.

It is our contention that equation (15.16) and the microeconomic analysis leading up to it were by and large the authentic basis of the theory of consumption which Keynes used in writing the consumption theoretic parts of the *General Theory*. We will substantiate this claim in the following section.

But before entering that discussion, a point concerning the Keynesian consumption function should be briefly touched upon which is to be found in the recent textbook literature about this subject. According to the textbook by Barro (1990, p. 505) it may be argued that the income variable enters that function because some consumers find themselves to be 'liquidity constrained' in the sense that they cannot obtain a loan 'at a "reasonable" interest rate'. This argument is then refuted on empirical grounds (*op. cit.*, p. 512).

It should therefore be pointed out that this is *not* the argument used here and there are no indications whatsoever that Keynes used the argument later stated by Barro. That the debt variable S of equations (15.1 and 15.2) disappeared in the later treatment of the household model is a mere consequence of the fact that – barring bankruptcy – debts have to be repaid on maturity and therefore may be eliminated on the lines stated in note 26 on p. 445. In fact, households are free in this model to hold any positive or negative volume of debts in accordance with their equilibrium conditions.

The reason why the income variables enter into the Keynesian consumption function is rather that with regard to future incomes households are assumed to have given expectations. With regard to present incomes it is assumed that they treat income as depending on the interaction with (and of) other agents and that they make their own expenditure plans depending on the net outcome of such interactions on the macroeconomic resolution level.

15.4.4 The question of authenticity of the micro-founded Keynesian consumption function

Our contention concerning the authenticity of equation (15.16) is based on the fact that almost all the important tenets which Keynes held concerning individual consumption may be generated from this equation. This certainly would be a strange coincidence if it was based purely on accident – especially so in view of the already documented fact that Keynes himself related his theory of consumption to time preference.

Six important correspondences between the present micro-foundation on the one hand and the verbal exposition of the consumption function in the *General Theory* may be stated:[28]

(i)   Since b is equal to the marginal propensity to consume dC_0/dY_0 and since it was established above already that under quite general conditions $0 < b < 1$ always holds, equation (15.16) expresses Keynes' (1936, p. 96)

> fundamental psychological law ... that men are disposed ... to increase their consumption as their income increases, but not by as much as the increase in their income.

(ii) As long as the present value of future receipts – and thus term a in equation (15.16) – is positive, the average propensity to consume is given by

$$\frac{C_0}{Y_0} = \frac{a}{Y_0} + b \quad \text{with} \quad \frac{d}{dY_0}\left(\frac{C_0}{Y_0}\right) < 0 \qquad (15.18)$$

and thus the proportion of consumption declines with increasing current income. Correspondingly, the proportion of savings must then increase. Thus equation (15.16) illustrates algebraically Keynes' (1936, p. 97) statement about 'a greater proportion of income being saved as real income increases'.

(iii) Since the marginal propensity to consume b is independent of the rate of interest, equation (15.16) is in accordance with the discussion in the *General Theory* where the marginal propensity to consume is always mentioned without any reference to the rate of interest.

(iv) But although the marginal propensity to consume is independent of the rate of interest, the absolute level of consumption clearly is not, since differentiating equation (15.16) with respect to the rate of interest shows that $dC/dr < 0$ always holds for positive present values of future receipts. With this result our equation generates what Leijonhufvud (1968, p. 190) labelled Keynes' 'second psychological law of consumption'. This negative interest effect on consumption depends on interest changes generating a revaluation of a given stream of future receipts in terms of their present value. This 'indirect' revaluation effect of higher interest rates and its negative influence on present consumption is indeed considered as important by Keynes (1936, pp. 93f.).

(v) But Keynes (*ibid.*) discerns the 'indirect' effect just mentioned from a 'direct' effect which negates a significant direct influence of the rate of interest on consumption, stating:

> Apart from this [indirect effect] ... the short-period [direct] influence of the rate of interest on individual spending out of given income is secondary and relatively unimportant.

In abstracting from the 'indirect effect', Keynes contemplates the possibility of holding wealth in such a form that it is invariant to changes in the rate of interest. The holding of non-interest bearing money would be a case in point. Denote this type of wealth by M and replace in term b of equation (15.16) the component $\Sigma(1 + r)^{-f}Y^f$ by M. After such a replacement it will be immediately apparent that *now* $dC_0/dr = 0$ must hold.[29]

(vi) Since equ. (15.16) contains *two* types of income, namely present income Y_0 and future income Y_f, the consumption function might have particular characteristics due to a particular relationship between these magnitudes. This possibility is mentioned explicitly by Keynes (1936, p. 95) 'for the sake of formal completeness'. He rejects a significant influence of this factor. One of the reasons given is that 'it is a matter about which there is, as a rule, too much uncertainty for it to exert much influence' (*ibid.*).

Thus equation (15.16) supplies a consistent framework to reproduce two 'psychological laws' and some other statements to be found in the context of discussions of the Keynesian theory of consumption. It therefore seems to us that it would be a very strange coincidence if Keynes was totally unaware of the existence of such an analysis but stated its conclusions in detailed exposition. The most plausible conclusion seems to us therefore to be that this is indeed the authentic analytical framework which was used by Keynes himself.

15.4.5 Keynes' consumption function and modern intertemporal analysis[30]

In his discussion of *The Economics of Keynes*, Leijonhufvud (1968, p. 198) rightly drew attention to the fact that intertemporal questions such as the ones discussed in this excursus 'have been almost completely ignored by Keynesian interpreters'. His own interpretation of the choice theoretic foundations of the Keynesian consumption function is highly problematic, however, since it leads him to postulate the existence of a special 'Cassel–Keynes world' where individuals have rectangular intertemporal indifference curves.

Basically, the problems of Leijonhufvud's approach stem from his attempt to interpret Keynes' 'direct' and 'indirect' consumption effects in terms of Hicksian 'substitution' and 'income' effects on consumer demand. In order to clarify this matter, we reproduce such choice theoretic decompositions in equations (15.24), (15.25) and in (15.31) below and contrast them to the original decomposition made by Keynes.

15.4.5.1 A two-period model

The discussion of this section will be based on the simple two-period version of intertemporal analysis outlined in equations (15.1 to 15.3) above. Using those equations, we formulate the Lagrangian

$$L = U(Q_{c0}, Q_{c1}) + \lambda \left(W - \rho_{c0} Q_{c0} - \frac{1}{1+r} \rho_{c1} Q_{c1} \right) \tag{15.19}$$

where λ is a Lagrange multiplier and W is 'wealth' in the sense of the present value of a given stream of income (see (15.22) below). The first-order conditions for household equilibrium are given by

$$U_0' - \lambda \rho_{c0} = 0 \tag{15.20}$$

$$U_1' - \frac{\lambda}{1+r} \rho_{c1} = 0 \tag{15.21}$$

$$W \equiv Y_0 + \frac{1}{1+r} Y_1 = \rho_{c0} Q_{c0} + \frac{1}{1+r} P_{c1} Q_{c1} \tag{15.22}$$

where U_0' represents marginal utility from present consumption and U_1' represents marginal utility from future consumption.

Assuming the second-order conditions to be fulfilled, the 'substitution', 'income' and 'wealth' effects of conventional microeconomic literature and the 'direct' and 'indirect' effects of Keynes' analysis may then be generated from the functional

$$
\begin{bmatrix} U_0'' & 0 & -\rho_{c0} \\ 0 & U_1'' & \frac{-\rho_{c1}}{1+r} \\ -\rho_{c0} & \frac{-\rho_{c1}}{1+r} & 0 \end{bmatrix} \begin{bmatrix} dQ_{c0} \\ dQ_{c1} \\ d\lambda \end{bmatrix} = \begin{bmatrix} \lambda & 0 & 0 & 0 \\ 0 & \frac{\lambda}{1+r} & \frac{-\lambda \rho_{c1}}{(1+r)^2} & 0 \\ Q_{c0} & \frac{Q_{c1}}{1+r} & \frac{-\rho_{c1}Q_{c1}+Y_1}{(1+r)^2} & -1 \end{bmatrix} \begin{bmatrix} dp_{c0} \\ dp_{c1} \\ dr \\ dW \end{bmatrix}
$$

$$(15.23)$$

where the second derivatives U_0'' and U_1'' are negative because of decreasing marginal utility and where the cross derivatives of U are zero because it is assumed that the intertemporal utility function has an additive separable structure (see sect. (b) of this excursus).

The central question in this context is now: how does present consumption in terms of quantities Q_{c0} react when the exogenous magnitudes listed in the right-hand vector of (15.23) are changed?

15.4.5.2 The price effects

The answers of conventional microeconomic modelling with regard to 'direct' and 'cross' price changes are reproduced in the following two equations[31]

$$
\text{'direct'} \quad \frac{\partial Q_{c0}}{\partial p_{c0}} = \underbrace{\lambda \frac{D_{11}}{D}}_{\text{substitution effect}} + \underbrace{Q_{c0} \frac{D_{31}}{D}}_{\text{income effect}} < 0 \quad (15.24)
$$

$$
\text{'cross'} \quad \frac{\partial Q_{c0}}{\partial p_{c1}} = \overbrace{\frac{\lambda}{1+r} \frac{D_{21}}{D}} + \overbrace{\frac{Q_{c1}}{1+r} \frac{D_{31}}{D}} \lessgtr 0 \quad (15.25)
$$

where

$$
D = -U_1''(p_{c0})^2 - U_0'' \left(\frac{p_{c1}}{1+r} \right)^2 > 0 \quad (15.26)
$$

is the determinant of the Jacobian given by the first matrix in (15.23) and where D_{ij} is the cofactor of the element in the *i*th row and in the *j*th column of the Jacobian matrix.

The decomposition of the 'direct' and 'cross' price effects into substitution and income effects as stated in these two equations follows the customary textbook procedure and need not be commented on extensively in the present context.

(a) *Direct price effects.* It can easily be verified, however, that with the type of additive separable intertemporal utility functions normally proposed, the direct price effect on the *quantity* of present consumption – but not necessarily on its *value* in the sense of a price-quantity scalar product – is always negative as stated by the 'less than zero'-term after the first of these equations. This is so because the substitution effect and the income effect of rising present prices on present consumption are both negative as will be apparent when the coefficients given in the functional (15.23) are used to calculate the sign values

$$D_{11} = -\left(\frac{p_{c1}}{1+r}\right)^2 < 0 \ \text{and} \ \frac{D_{31}}{D} = -\left(\frac{\partial Q_{c0}}{\partial W}\right)_{r, p_{c0}, p_{c1} = const.} = p_{p_{c0}} U_1'' < 0$$

$$(15.27)$$

(b) *Cross price effects.* We turn now to a discussion of the sign value of the cross price effect as given by equation (15.25). This must be a bit more involved than that of the direct price effects because in the case of rising future prices there are opposing sign values of the component effects on present consumption.

Consider first the substitution effect as given by (15.28). That it has a positive value may be demonstrated by going through the stated calculations:[32]

$$\left(\frac{\partial Q_{c0}}{\partial p_{c1}}\right)_{U = const.} = \frac{\lambda}{1+r} \frac{D_{21}}{D} = \frac{U_1'}{p_{c1}} \frac{p_{c0} p_{c1}}{1+r} \frac{1}{D} > 0 \qquad (15.28)$$

This result is of immediate significance for the present discussion of alternative interpretations of Keynesian economics because it contradicts Leijonhufvud (1968, p. 196) who believed that in Keynes' original framework 'intertemporal substitution effects are to be ruled out'. But since a positive value of the substitution effect of a cross-price change is generally considered as being the criterion for substitutability (see Henderson and Quandt (1958, p. 29), and since this effect is positive for any separable additive intertemporal utility function, Leijonhufvud must attribute rather strange types of utility functions to Keynes for which he cannot supply any evidence. We will give additional reasons below why we consider his interpretation as unacceptable.

To complete the discussion of the total cross-price effect on present consumption we must still inspect the income effect as given by the second overbraced term in (15.25). As in the case of direct price changes it is again negative and now reads

$$\frac{Q_{c1}}{1+r} \frac{D_{31}}{D} = \frac{Q_{c1}}{1+r} p_{c0} U_1'' \frac{1}{D} < 0. \qquad (15.29)$$

We have now definite sign values for the two component effects and we may now state a condition for the cross-price effect to be zero. This is clearly the case when the absolute value of (15.28) and (15.29) is equal so that

$$\frac{U_1'}{1+r}\,p_{c0} = -\frac{Q_{c1}}{1+r}\,p_{c0}U_1'' \quad i.e \quad \frac{U_1'}{Q_{c1}} = -U_1'' \tag{15.30}$$

holds. But it can be easily shown that this condition is always fulfilled for the type of additive logarithmical intertemporal utility functions here assumed to be the appropriate ones for interpreting Keynes.[33] Furthermore, if the quantity Q_{c0} is unaffected by p_{c1}-changes, so is, of course, the value $C \equiv p_{c0}Q_{c0}$ of consumption.

A similar analysis for the cross-price effect of changes in present price p_{c0} for *future* consumption Q_{c1} would show that this effect is also zero. Thus, a present price change results in an equiproportional reduction of present consumption so that the net outcome is again a zero change of $C \equiv p_{c0}Q_{c0}$ in *value* terms.

The result that for what we propose to be regarded as 'Keynes' authentic intertemporal utility function' the cross-price effects is necessarily zero is of immediate significance for the discussion of Keynes' consumption function. It gives a *choice theoretic reason* for the statement that in spite of intertemporal substitutability of consumption, both present and future prices leave unaffected the value of present consumption.

It is thus not necessarily a *negation* but could well be a Keynes-oriented *application* of modern microeconomic analysis when it is said that intertemporal price changes for consumers' goods are to be neglected in discussing the Keynesian consumption function $C = a + bY$.

15.4.5.3 *The interest rate effects in conventional analysis*

Finally, the reaction of present consumption with respect to changes in the rate of interest is given by a collection of three terms as stated by the following equation

$$\frac{\partial Q_{c0}}{\partial r} = \overbrace{\underbrace{\frac{-\lambda p_{c1}}{(1+r)^2}\frac{D_{21}}{D}}_{\text{Keyne's direct effect}}}^{\text{substitution effect}} \quad \overbrace{\underbrace{-\frac{p_{c1}Q_{c1}}{(1+r)^2}\frac{D^{31}}{D} + \underbrace{\frac{Y_1}{(1+r)^2}\frac{D_{31}}{D}}_{\text{Keynes' indirect effect}<0}}_{}}^{\text{wealth effect}\lessgtr 0}$$

$$\tag{15.31}$$

In some modern textbook discussion it is customary to interpret these terms in seeming[34] analogy to the price effects on consumption as just stated (see Henderson and Quandt (1958, p. 239) and Barro 1990). The conventional interpretation collects the last two of these terms and considers them as a 'wealth effect' as denoted by the overbraces in (15.31). The remaining term then gives a substitution effect which may be related to the one previously discussed under the heading of cross-price effects. It will then be seen that using equation (15.28) the first term on the right-hand side of (15.31) may be expressed as

$$\left(\frac{\partial Q_{c0}}{\partial r}\right)_{U=const.} = \frac{-p_{c1}}{1+r}\left(\frac{\partial Q_{c0}}{\partial p_{c1}}\right)_{U=const.} < 0 \qquad (15.32)$$

and therefore it must have a negative sign value.

The problem with the conventional approach is, however, that it generates an a priori indeterminate result concerning the 'wealth effect' because in collecting the last two terms we get the expression

$$\frac{Y_1 - p_{c1}Q_{c1}}{(1+r)^2}\frac{D_{31}}{D} = \frac{-S}{1+r}\frac{D_{31}}{D} = \frac{S}{1+r}\left(\frac{\partial Q_{c0}}{\partial W}\right)_{r, p_{ci}=const.} \gtreqless 0 \; for \; S \gtreqless 0$$

$$(15.33)$$

as will be apparent when we reconsider equation (15.2) where the relation between present savings S and future income (here: Y_1) and future consumption (here: $p_{c1}Q_{c1}$) was explicitly stated.[35]

In eliminating S from those early formulations of sequential budget equations when proceeding to the formulation of a household model it was left open whether the household in question had positive or negative savings in the current period. But now it is essential to know the sign value of S: when it is positive, the 'wealth effect' on current consumption of an increase in the rate of interest will be *positive*, but when S is negative, the 'wealth effect' will also assume the opposite sign value.

There are two problems with this use of the concept of a 'wealth effect': the one is what to do about this indeterminacy. The solution proposed by Barrow (1990, p. 89) is to assume it away:

So for the purposes of aggregate analysis, we shall find it satisfactory to neglect wealth effects from changes in the interest rate. This result is very important. It says that for aggregate purposes, the important effects from changes in the interest rate are the intertemporal-substitution effects.

This amounts to a zero savings condition in the old Pigovian 'classical' sense.[36] It means that in an aggregate analysis of a 'wealth effect' – in the sense of equation (15.33) – savings are *assumed* to be zero. But if what Barro (*ibid.*) calls 'the average person' is *postulated* to have zero savings, because 'the aggregate stock of bonds is always zero', then that person should have zero savings not only due to the wealth effect but also due to the substitution effect named by Barro in this quote. But that effect definitely is negative. We have thus a contradiction which is solved in the model of a 'stationary state' economy by having not the interest rate as exogenous variable of the model but the time preference. Although the two are equal, it is only the latter which could meaningfully change such that the zero savings condition is fulfilled in alternative stationary states. But such a set of assumptions, although consistent in an abstract intertemporal model, has little to do with macroeconomic problems.

In addition, the assumption of zero savings is certainly a far cry from the situation in many actual economies. In the Federal Republic of Germany savings amount to about 14 per cent of GNP. Similar figures hold for most industrialised countries. The USA might be an exception but not because of an *absence* of wealth effects but rather because of positive wealth windfall effects due to increasing asset prices.

Once it is admitted that in fact we *are* in a world with positive savings, the interest effect on present consumption is – in principle – indeterminate: equation (15.32) shows that the substitution effect is negative but equation (15.33) shows that the 'wealth effect' is positive for $S > 0$. Therefore nothing definite can be said about the combined influence of these two effects on present consumption.

From a Keynesian position, this result of conventional discussion of time-preference analysis may seem to be quite welcome: since the total effect of interest rate changes on present consumption is indeterminate, the same is true for their effect on current savings. Therefore even conventional analysis casts well-founded doubts on the classical contention that the rate of interest could reliably co-ordinate savings decisions with interest-dependent investment decisions. But there is the unsatisfactory element in this whole discussion that we need a definite statement about the magnitude S – whether it is positive or negative – in order to derive even an indeterminate result concerning the comparative statics of this very magnitude with respect to changes in the rate of interest. In addition, there is the 'paradigmatic' problem that in a real-life context where S is positive, the 'wealth effect' of higher interest rates appears to be positive. But surely, with a given stream of positive future incomes the present value effect on perceived wealth should be negative since future incomes are valued less the higher the rate of interest at which they have to be discounted.

This brings us to a second set of problems concerning the very concept of a 'wealth effect' in this context. If wealth represents the present value of a stream of receipts as stated in (15.22) above – and this, *modulo* asset endowments, is the generally accepted definition of wealth – then savings are quite immaterial for this magnitude. Although savings do generate higher future income due to the interest payments which they fetch, for the assessment of their present value they have to be discounted with the selfsame interest rate which they will earn so that their present value will stay constant. Why then should the sign value of savings be so important for the workings of the 'wealth effect'?

The answer to this question is to be found in an implicit alteration of the wealth concept which in this type of analysis is believed to be in terms of 'overall utility'. The relevant argument may be rendered in the following way: if a household plans to have positive savings S^0 in this period in order to spend an amount $S^0 (1 + r^-)$ in the next period, his attainable set for future consumption will clearly increase if the rate of interest increased from r^- to r^+. Even if we disregard substitution effects and hold S^0 constant, it follows that the larger attainable set for the future enables the house-hold to reach an equilibrium on an intertemporal indifference curve with a higher index value than previously. Thus we may conclude, according to Barro (1990, p. 89, n. 12), 'This perspective makes it clear that overall utility – and hence, wealth – must increase' (emphasis added, GMA). Thus, in terms of 'overall utility' this type of 'wealth' may be considered as having increased whereas in terms of a discounted stream of future receipts, an alternative type of wealth could at best have stayed constant if future non-interest receipts were zero or otherwise would have declined if the household counted on other exogenously given future receipts as well. We do not consider this to be a particularly felicitous use of terms.

In closing this section, it should be noted that the problem of double wealth concepts is not so relevant when we limit ourselves to a discussion of price changes as discussed in the previous section. Since in that case the rate of interest is in fact constant, so is the present value of wealth. It is then clear that any change in 'income' or, correspondingly, in 'wealth' in that context is just a hypothetical one from the standpoint of the present time period. Thus, the analogy between the price effects of equation (15.24), (15.25) (p. 188) exists only between the cross price effects of (15.25) and the first two terms in (15.31). The latter are easily seen to be just the $-p_{c1}/(1 + r)$-fold of the former. But the last term in (15.31) is really a totally new effect with no direct analogy to the former discussion of price effects resp. of wealth effects.

It is now interesting to note that Keynes' decomposition of interest effects makes a distinction exactly on this dividing line between warranted analogies.

15.4.5.4 *The interest rate effects in Keynes' analysis*

We have used considerable space for an exposition of the problematic elements of conventional discussions of interest rate effects on present consumption in order to be able to demonstrate that Keynes' structuring of these effects is not just a *possible* alternative but one which structures the different aspects of those effects in a more meaningful way. Before summarising this case in the following section 15.4.5.5, we will first restate his distinction of 'direct' and 'indirect' interest effects. We will then discuss the problem of authenticity posed by this restatement. Finally, we will turn to the intended evaluation.

(a) *A translation of Keynes' 'direct' and 'indirect' interest effects.* Keynes' alternative collection of the terms of equation (15.31) on p. 150 due to his distinction of 'direct' and 'indirect' interest effects on present consumption is represented there by an underbrace marking his 'indirect' interest effect. The preceding two terms of that equation signified his 'direct' interest effect. An interesting aspect of such a 'direct' interest effect in the sense of Keynes was just noted at the very end of the preceding subsection 15.4.5.3. There it was seen that those first two terms on the right-hand side of (15.31) which signify Keynes' 'direct' interest effect may be compared with the cross-price effect of equation (15.25). On the basis of that comparison it is clear that Keynes 'direct' interest effect on consumption may be stated as a 'cross price effect' as shown below in the first of the two underbraced terms of (15.34). This cross price effect was assumed to be zero by Keynes – a choice theoretically unproblematic assumption since there is no choice theoretic reason to attribute to cross price effects positive or negative sign values a prior.

Keynes' remaining 'indirect' interest effect on consumption may be seen as being composed of a 'pure' wealth effect in the sense that $-D_{31}/D$ in (15.31) measures just that effect which we would get from (15.23) if we enquired about the change in Q_{c0} which would be generated by changing W, holding p_{c0}, p_{c1} and r constant. And the then remaining expression $-Y_1/(1 + r)^2$ in (15.31) is nothing else but the present value effect on wealth as defined in (15.22) which would be generated by a change in the rate of interest.

Thus, the Keynesian structuring of the combined interest effects on present consumption may also be represented by

$$\frac{\partial Q_{c0}}{\partial r} = \underbrace{\frac{-p_{c1}}{1+r}\left(\frac{\partial Q_{c1}}{\partial p_{c1}}\right)_{r=const.}}_{\text{cross price effect} = 0} + \underbrace{\left(\frac{\partial Q_{c0}}{\partial W}\right)_{r,\, p_{ci}=const.} \times \left(\frac{\partial W}{\partial r}\right)}_{\text{present value effect} < 0} \qquad (15.34)$$

(b) *The question of authenticity further considered.* The stated sign values of these effects follow from the previous discussion and might not require further extensive comments concerning the algebra involved. But there might be some questions remaining concerning the authenticity of this new interpretation. We therefore pick up the thread of arguments inspected above further down on p. 185 (section 15.4.4 of this excursus).

The distinction between Keynes' 'indirect' resp. 'direct' interest effects was documented there under points (iv) resp. (v) of that section and it was seen there already that Keynes' dividing line between the two effects followed indeed the criterion whether a present value effect of interest changes is conceivable or not. Let us reiterate that Keynes (1936, pp. 92f.) was very outspoken about the importance of these effects, stating in particular:

> The consumption of the wealth-owning class may be *extremely susceptible to unforeseen changes in the money-value of its wealth.* (emphasis added, GMA)

A few lines later Keynes then elaborates that it is predominantly changes in the interest rate which he has in mind in this context:

> Perhaps the most important influence, operating through changes in the rate of interest, on the readiness to spend out of a given income, depends on the effect of these changes on the appreciation or deprecia-tion in the price of securities and other assets. For if a man is enjoying *a windfall increment in the value of his capital*, it is natural that his motives towards current spending should be strengthened, even *though in terms of income his capital is worth no more than before.* (emphasis added, GMA)

We thus have here a verbal description of a consumer with a constant stream of income $Y_1, Y_2, \ldots$ who experiences a rise in the present capital value of this unchanged stream due to lower interest rates.[37] This was also the analytical basis of the present discussion which so far seems to be in accordance with the quoted statements.

It is furthermore stated by Keynes in the context of these quotes that from the present value considerations there follows a considerable (nega-tive) influence of changes in the rate of interest on present consumption. These verbal arguments are the ones represented by the 'present value effect' and its associated sign value in equ. (15.34). We therefore consider this part of our interpretation to be an authentic rendering of Keynes' state-ments in this context.

Turning now to the 'cross price effect' in equ. (15.34) we remind the reader that it was mentioned above already that if Keynes' intertemporal utility function was of the logarithmic additive separable type given by equation (15.6) on page 181 then the condition for a zero cross-price effect as given above by (15.30) is always fulfilled. Was he aware of this fact? We suggest two indications for an affirmative answer. One relevant quote was given in section 15.4.4 of this excursus already (see page 185), where it was seen that Keynes (1936, p. 94) stated that apart from the 'indirect' present value effect, the 'direct' interest effect on present consumption is 'relatively unimportant'. This may then be taken as an indication that in terms of equation (15.34) Keynes assumed the cross-price effect to be virtually zero.

A further argumentation by Keynes (1936, p. 93) in this context points in the same direction. Before turning to a discussion of consumption effects due to changes in the rate of interest, he states that a fuller analysis of the relevant magnitude in this context must consider changes 'in the rate of time-discounting, i.e. in the ratio of exchange between present goods and future goods' (italics omitted, GMA) and he elaborates:

> This is not quite the same thing as the rate of interest, since it allows for future changes in the purchasing power of money in so far as they are foreseen ... As an approximation, however, we can identify this with the rate of interest.

From the fact that Keynes first did mention the potential influence of changes of future prices on present consumption and then, in the last sentence, dismissed this influence, we conclude in the following paragraph that here, too, he assumed the cross-price effect on present consumption to be zero. We therefore take this passage as a further indication that Keynes thought in terms of the present model and in terms of a zero cross-price effect on present consumption.

In order to substantiate this claim we turn to the equilibrium conditions (15.20)–(15.22) from which the present discussion of price and interest effects was derived. We note that from the first two of them it follows that the 'rate of time-discounting' in the quoted sense is given by

$$-\frac{dQ_{c1}}{dQ_{c0}} = \frac{U_0'}{U_1'} = (1+r)\frac{p_{c0}}{p_{c1}} \tag{15.35}$$

where changes in p_{c1} would signify the 'future changes in the purchasing power of money' of the quote. If now Keynes decided to disregard the influence of p_{c1}-changes as he was just quoted to have done, then this may well be interpreted to mean that he considered that changes in p_{c1} have no significant influence on present consumption Q_{c0}. But this is then just another way of saying that the cross-price effect on present consumption is zero.

We conclude that Keynes' presentation of his theory of consumption was based on repeated statements amounting to the assumption of a cross-price effect on present consumption of zero. Therefore the interpretation expressed in equation (15.34) above may be taken as an authentic rendering of his views.

15.4.5.5 Summary and evaluation of alternative discussions of interest rate effects

We may now summarise the arguments set out in our discussion of the relation of the Keynesian consumption function to modern intertemporal analysis.

Keynes' view of interest rate effects on present consumption was seen to have been based on a distinction of a 'direct' interest rate effect – which we related to an intertemporal cross-price effect – and and an 'indirect' discounting effect of interest rate changes.

The price effect of interest rate changes is comparable to a 'cross-price' effect of conventional analysis because, abstracting from the discounting effect, a rise in the rate of interest makes present consumption 'dearer' not by reducing the maximum possible present consumption but by *increasing* the maximum of the future consumption out of present savings. The resulting increase in the attainable set of intertemporal consumption possibilities may well be used for increasing *present* consumption – although the relative price of present consumption goods has increased. Thus, the 'direct' effect of changing the rate of interest has the same ambiguities in principle as any other cross-price effect.

On the basis of conventional time-preference analysis it is possible to reduce this ambiguity and to assign a zero value to the 'direct' interest effect on present consumption. This is so because intertemporal utility functions are generally assumed to be of the 'additive separable' type. If such a utility function may be represented (or approximated) by a weighted sum of the logarithms of the quantities consumed in the different time periods, then the zero value of the 'direct' interest effect follows on formal grounds. Keynes assumes this case to be a generally accepted approximation. Therefore, there is no 'direct' interest effect on present consumption.

Nevertheless, there might indeed be a significant *negative* effect of higher interest rates on present consumption. This must then be based theoretically on their 'indirect' effect on present values. If individuals count on a given stream of incomes, their present value and hence the present wealth *must* decrease when the rate of interest rises. It is intuitively clear that if a householder has to decide whether to consume more or less under conditions of decreased present-value wealth, he will take the latter option. This result may, of course, also be brought out from a choice theoretic model. But this effect depends on the structure of wealth. If the present value of wealth is invariant to changes in the rate of interest, then this 'indirect' effect on present consumption will disappear.

The conventional analysis of interest effects on present consumption uses the same basic model but structures the components of the interest effects differently. It therefore must make different assumptions in order to reach determinate results. More specifically, it uses a wealth concept which mixes together the concept of imputed 'wealth' measuring utility indices of indifference curves and the concept of wealth measuring the present value of a given future income. The influence of this conglomerate wealth effect on present consumption is assumed to be zero in the aggregate in the New Classical approach of Barro (1990). It was seen above that this amounts to assuming that total savings are zero. This assumption is the same as that of Pigou's strange construction of a stationary-state 'short run'.

Keynes' approach avoids the conventional discussion of 'substitution effects' of hypothetical movements along a particular indifference curve. Hence it does not get involved in that awkward double concept of 'wealth' of conventional analysis of interest rate effects for present consumption. And hence it does not have to rely on the counterfactual assumption of zero savings in the aggregate.

Thus we have again reason to consider Keynes to be a 'better' user of micro-economic analysis than his classical counterparts. But we have no reason to conclude that he was a 'negator' of the basic approach underlying the conventional discussion of interest rate and price effects on present consumption.

15.4.6 The classical time-preference theory of interest as a special case of the Keynesian consumption function

Suppose now that Keynes did in fact derive his theory of consumption in the way which we claimed to be the authentic one. Suppose further that Keynes, in reacting to Pigou's (1937) rejoinder, had two options:

(i) Either he criticised the underlying assumptions of stationariness etc. under the heading of 'frozen-land economy',
(ii) or he forgot about (i) and discussed Pigou (1937) given the assumptions of the 'simplified model'.

Since Kahn successfully beseeched Keynes not to pursue option (i), only the latter approach seemed logically open to him. But given the Pigovian assumptions there is the obvious question as to which of his original theoretical elements Keynes could validly place against the statements made by Pigou.

We ask now in particular: What happens to Keynes' consumption function if we accept the Pigovian assumptions? As already stated, the assumptions of Pigou's 'simplified model' were:

(a) There is a stationary state so that there is just one value of income Y to be considered over all the time periods.
(b) Savings are zero so that $Y = C$ always holds.
(c) Preferences are unchanging so that the elasticity of utility of consumption is identical for all time periods.
(d) The time horizon is infinite.

Using assumptions (a) and (c) we turn now to our reconstruction of 'Keynes' authentic consumption function' (15.16), p. 184 and rewrite it as

$$C = \left(\Sigma \left(\frac{1}{1+r} \right)^f + 1 \right) \frac{\gamma}{\gamma + \gamma \Sigma \tau_f} . Y \ ; \ f = 1, 2, ..., n \ ; \ n \to \infty. \quad (15.36)$$

But because of assumption (b) the magnitudes C and Y cancel. The γ-s also cancel. Because of assumption (d) the geometric row of discount factors in the parentheses has the value $1/r$. And from equ. (15.12) we know already that under Pigovian stationary conditions

$$\rho = \frac{1}{\sum \tau_f} \; ; \; f = 1, 2, \dots, n \; ; \; n \to \infty \qquad (15.37)$$

must hold where ρ is the rate of discounting the future.

After these manipulations and substitutions and after minor further rearrangements the Keynesian consumption function (15.16) resp. (15.36) finally reduces to the statement that

$$r = \rho. \qquad (15.38)$$

Thus we obtain the result that the rate of interest is equal to the rate of discounting the future.

This is no startling result in itself. Indeed, this is the assumption underlying Pigou's simplified model. But it should be noted how this result was derived: we started out from a consumption function for which we claimed and documented that it is the authentic Keynesian one because it was derived from an explicit time-preference analysis and we claimed that it was in a similar way how Keynes himself arrived at his theory of consumption. Our claim concerning authenticity was then substantiated by demonstrating that at least five important consumption theoretic proposals actually made by Keynes could be generated from our reconstructed consumption function. In the present section we then introduced Pigou's special assumptions into the *Keynesian* consumption function which then collapsed into the *classical* theory of interest.

Let us embark upon one final speculation and let us assume somebody came up to Keynes with the criticism that Pigou was wrong in assuming the time preference theory of interest in the context of his simplified model. Keynes then could have pointed to the options discussed above under (i) and (ii). If it was then decided by the critic to opt for (ii), and if Keynes was aware of the rest of the argumentation of this section, then he could only tell the critic that Pigou was not wrong as far as Keynes could see because the time-preference theory of interest would also follow from Keynes' own theory of consumption under Pigou's special conditions.

But the episode proposed as a speculation in the preceding paragraph was in fact a streamlined account of the interactions between Keynes and Kahn concerning the appropriate reaction to Pigou (1937). Since Keynes did in effect give that answer to Kahn which we suggested that he would arrive at in our hypothetical scenario, we conclude that this scenario was not so hypothetical, after all.

Keynes maintained repeatedly that the classical theory is a special case of his own and it would have been only in the interest of his argumentation to come to the result that the classical theory of time-preference determined interest rates is a case in point.

16
Pigou's 'Simplified Model' as a Rejoinder to the Model of the 'Keynes Effect'

Before we enter into a discussion of specific issues raised by the Pigovian 'simplified model', let us briefly summarise the more general results established so far.

In the last chapter it emerged that out of the several candidates for basic issues to be raised in the debate between Keynes and Pigou, it was only the modelling of the money wage and employment nexus which survived. One of the alternative candidates, the methodological question of an appropriate short-period analysis, was seen to have been regarded by R. F. Kahn as not 'important' in this context. Reluctantly, Keynes followed Kahn's advice to drop this issue from publication.

Instead, Kahn proposed considering the time-preference theory of interest to be the 'fundamental fallacy' in Pigou (1937) and in related discussions. But Keynes did not accept his proposal on analytical grounds, as was seen above in a relevant quote on p. 177. In the last chapter together with its excursus we saw why that was the case: Keynes accepted the idea of the time-preference theory of interest as a special case of his own theory, given the particular equilibrium conditions which Pigou assumed to hold in his analysis.

The question to be asked in the present chapter is now: given the Pigovian concept of equilibrium, was his new modelling of the money wage and employment nexus indeed a consistent construction and in which way did it confirm a classical position in the face of the Keynesian challenge?

In answering this question, we suggest first reformulating the Keynesian challenge to which Pigou (1937) may be seen to have responded (sect. 16.1). We then investigate whether Pigou (1937) was indeed 'so far gone' as Joan Robinson and others suggested (sect. 16.3.2). Finally, we reconsider the potential of critical arguments which emerged for the Keynesians in this particular context.

16.1 The model of the 'Keynes effect'

We saw already that if we took the *Theory of Unemployment* in its entirety, it was not so much the critical discussion of the 'real demand for labour' concept of that book which posed Keynes' major challenge to Pigou, but the proposal of the macroeconomic working of a money wage mechanism which later became to be known as the 'Keynes effect'.

The challenge posed by this effect was predominantly a programmatic one. This was so because of the peculiar analytical nature of the Pigovian E_m-theory against which it was set: whereas Pigou's 'real demand for labour' concept was based in principle on the well-established Marshallian analytical approach, the explication of its microfoundations having been the subject matter of part II above, his concept of 'demand in terms of money for labour as a whole' was not similarly to be explicated. So much was simply taken for granted by classical argumentation in the latter context, as Pigou (1937) was just seen to have eventually admitted, that any critical assessment of that argumentation necessarily had a strong element of constructing implicit arguments which indeed 'nobody before Keynes ever actually used', as many later critics of Keynes remarked. The main critical impetus coming from Keynes in this context was not the imputation of hypothetical argumentations, however, but the establishing of the necessity to construct a specific macroeconomic model for the discussion of the workings of money wage restraint.

The general idea of the 'Keynes effect' is well known by now and might require only cursory restatement. It relies on the idea that changes in the money wage rate imply changes of the real quantity of money and these in turn result in changes of the rate of interest which then lead to changes in effective demand – and hence employment. But newer presentations of this effect do not clearly link up either with what Keynes actually wrote in this context nor with Pigou's alternative construction. In particular, neither Keynes' analysis in terms of 'wage-units' nor his original conception of 'liquidity preference' can be said to have entered standard textbook presentations of the 'Keynes effect'. A particular problem in this context is the customary bastard-Keynesian approach of thinking in terms of the standard *IS–LM* model which starts from the paradigm of a given money supply. It will be seen below that a central element of the Pigovian approach was to regard the money supply as being not constant, but to be interest-dependent. This could be one reason standing behind the hitherto lack of reception of this part of the Keynes–Classics debate. Before turning to Pigou's 'simplified model' we will therefore briefly restate the 'Keynes effect' along lines which are nearer to the original presentation.

The presentation of real effective demand in terms of wage units should pose no basic conceptual problem – in particular not to the reader who went through part II above. It was seen there to consist simply of a division of nominal values through the currently relevant wage unit w. Thus, presenting the consumption function (15.16) in that form generates the expression

$$C_w = c_a - bY_w \tag{16.1}$$

where $C_w \equiv C_0/w$, $Y_w \equiv Y_0/w$ and $C_a \equiv a/w$.[1] It follows then that savings $S_w \equiv Y_w - C_w$ are given by the right-hand side of (16.2) below, where c_a is represented as interest dependent due to the considerations just discussed in note 1 (p. 446).

The left-hand side of (16.2) represents investment in terms of wage-units with $I'_w < 0$. For positive investment the total expression gives a negatively sloping IS-curve in the Y_w and r plane as shown in fig. (16.1), similarly as in standard macro-economic analysis:[2]

$$I_w(r) = -c_a(r) + (1-b)Y_w. \qquad (16.2)$$

If, however, Pigovian conditions of stationariness prevail, then investment is zero and the IS-curve degenerates to a straight line at $r = \rho$ in the income and interest plane as was demonstrated algebraically in the excursus of the last chapter (see equ. (15.38), p. 199).

In Keynes' analysis the rate of interest is now determined in conjunction with the money market. According to Keynes (1936, p. 199) the latter may be represented by

$$M = M_1 + M_2 = L_1(Y) + L_2(r) \qquad (16.3)$$

where the L_1-function stands for the transactions and precautionary motive for money demand and the L_2-function represents the speculative motive. If income is measured in wage units, however, the L_1-function must be changed accordingly so that the money market equation then reads

$$M = L_1(w.Y_w) + L_2(r) \quad \text{with} \quad L'_1 > 0; \ L'2 < 0 \qquad (16.4)$$

where w is the wage unit as before.

Standard macroeconomics now takes this expression and, assuming a given money supply $\bar{M}$, constructs an LM-curve in the r and Y resp. Y_w-plane combining rates of interest and income levels under the assumption that this money supply may be considered as the market equilibrium value for all alternative levels of interest and income along that LM-curve. But in fact it is only a single combination of r and Y_w which does generate money market equilibrium, namely that value which represents the intersection of the LM-curve with the IS curve of equ. (16.2) above. If, for example, the interest rate is higher than that value, effective demand as depicted on the IS-curve is relatively low and this means, of course, that transactions demand for money as identified by the L_1-component of liquidity preference resp. by Keynes' M_1 also is relatively *low*.

In contrast to this statement, the LM curve analysis must postulate that for relatively high interest rates the transactions demand for money is relatively *high.* This follows from the fact that for high interest rates the M_2 component of money demand as given by the L_2-component of liquidity preference is relatively low so that it seems that the M_1 component *must* increase in order to make up for the decline in M_2 if the total quantity of money M is given. But there is just no economic reason for this assumption to be justified: in such a case the economy would have to be outside its attainable set as given by the effective demand conditions of the *IS*-curve. But it was seen in part II above that such an assumption was alien to the real model standing behind the *IS*-curve analysis.

Therefore, if the rate of interest is relatively high, the money market is clearly in excess supply. Analogous reasoning for comparatively low rates of interest shows that for a given amount of money the money market then is in excess demand. Thus, given the behavioural assumptions as expressed by the L_1 and L_2 curves of equ. (16.2), a point on the *LM* curve is always a point of money market disequilibrium – unless it is the point of intersection with the *IS*-curve.

It is for the peculiar implicit disequilibrium assumption that it seems important to stress that the *LM*-curve analysis has absolutely no authentic basis in the *General Theory*. Instead, Keynes (1936, pp. 200f.) clearly expounds a theory of the money market which simultaneously contemplates

(i)   changes in M_1 as given by the L_1-curve,
(ii) changes in M_2 as given by the L_2 curve *and*
(iii) changes in Y resp. Y_w as given by the *IS*-curve.

It is the latter item which the standard *LM*-curve analysis omits when modelling the money market.

An algebraic model of Keynes' analysis of money demand could easily be generated by simply replacing Y_w in the money market equation (16.4) by the value of Y_w as given by the *IS*-equation of (16.2). The resulting relationship

$$'LIS' \quad M = L_1(w\frac{I_w(r) + C_a(r)}{1-b}) + L_2(r) \tag{16.5}$$

describes then a '*LIS*'-curve in the money and interest rate plane incorporating the *IS*-curve. For given M and w the rate of interest r is then determined on the money-demand *locus LIS*.

But with a rate of interest determined in this way, the corresponding effective demand Y_w – and hence employment – follow directly from the *IS*-relationship (16.2).[3]

The discussion of the 'Keynes effect' then consists simply in pointing out that changes in M as depicted on the left-hand side of (16.5) are analogous to changes in w as depicted on the right-hand side. In the former case there

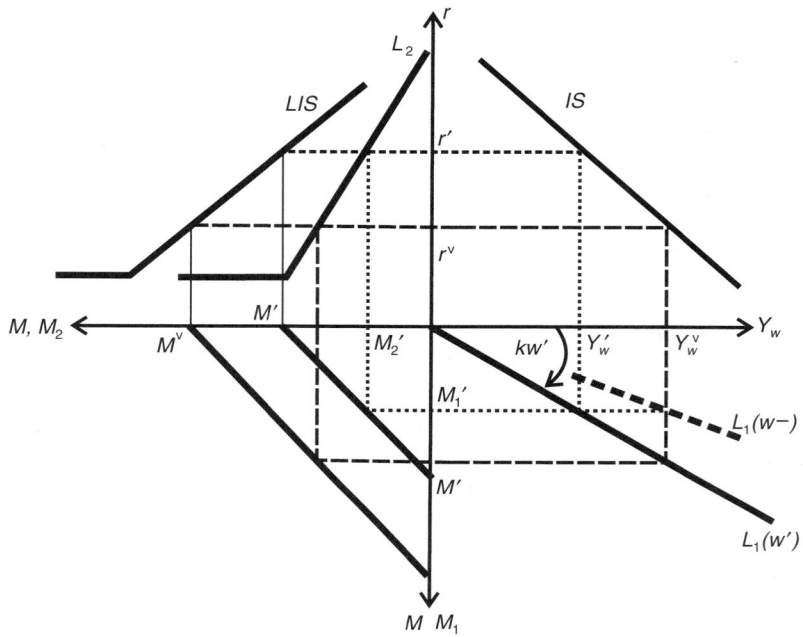

Figure 16.1 Liquidity preference and the Keynes effect

is then a supply effect on the rate of interest via M. In the latter case there would be a demand effect on the L_1-component of liquidity preference via w. This statement might be illustrated graphically as in fig. 16.1.[4]

In fig. 16.1 the north-east quadrant depicts an *IS*-curve, the south-east quadrant depicts the transactions component of liquidity preference as $L_1 = kwY_w$, and the north-west quadrant represents the L_2 component of money demand via the L_2-curve drawn there. It follows then from the *IS*-curve that for a given rate of interest, say r', effective demand Y_w will be such that with a wage unit w the requirement of money for transactions purposes will be M_1' as shown in the south-east quadrant. For the same rate of interest r', the north-west quadrant shows that the requirement of money for speculative purposes is M_2'. Total requirement for money is $M' = M_1' + M_2'$ as shown in the south-west quadrant where the drawn-out lines are 45° lines. Thus, r' and M' in the north-west quadrant give the co-ordinates for a point on the total liquidity preference curve *LIS*.

An analogous procedure for a lower rate of interest r^v and an unchanged wage unit w' shows the required volume of money to be M^v, these magnitudes generating a further point on the *LIS*-curve. Thus, with M^v of money available, the lower rate of interest r^v will release a higher effective demand Y_w^v and hence a higher level of employment and a lower real wage as was shown in the real analysis of part II.

The essential point of the 'Keynes effect' is now that a comparable increase in effective demand could be brought about with an unchanged volume of money M' but a decrease in liquidity preference due to a decrease in the wage unit. In graphical terms, this follows from the transactions balances analysis of the south-east quadrant: for a lower rate of wages w^-, the former $L_1(w')$-curve is changed to a new position $L_1(w^-)$ towards the Y_w-axis, thereby reducing requirements for transactions balances for any level of effective demand Y_w. Such a change in the wage unit will have consequences for total liquidity preference as it was just analysed in the north-west quadrant of fig. 16.1. It follows in that context that for any level of interest rates, total liquidity preference will decrease from $LIS_{w'}$ to LIS_w- as is depicted in figure 16. 2.

Thus, with a given amount of money M', the consequence of a decreased money wage could well be that the rate of interest will drop, e.g., to a level of $r-$ and this will then lead to an increase in effective demand and employment analogous to the one just mentioned in the case of monetary expansion. Given the accepted Pigovian real wage theory, the increased employment will lead to a lower real wage and in this rather circumvental way, money wage cuts result in real wage cuts at higher employment.

With this result, Keynes seems to reach a conclusion concerning the efficacy of money wage cuts for employment political purposes which is the same as the one the Classics believed in all along – albeit one should admit that they did not have the same macroeconomic modelling of money demand as the one just looked at.

But the critical momentum in this analysis derives not from a bickering about the appropriate modelling of the successful working of money wage cuts. Rather, this analysis opens the door for questioning the proposal for nominal wage policy altogether: if the money wage policy works only via the money market, it is the latter which should really be the main target for employment political action.

If, however, the economic political authorities should claim that the monetary situation was such that there was no employment political point in taking action on the monetary front, then it follows from this analysis that money wage cuts would be equally fruitless for raising employment, as Keynes (1936, p. 266) insisted:

> wage reductions, as a method for securing full employment, are also subject to the same limitations as the method of increasing the quantity of money. The same reasons ... which limit the efficacy of increasing the quantity of money as a means of increasing investment to the optimum figure, apply mutatis mutandis to wage reductions.

The crucial point in Keynes' money wage analysis is whether the rate of interest drops. If it does drop in response to money wage cuts it could be lowered with far less social strain by monetary expansion. If the latter does not bring about a change in the rate of interest, then wage cuts won't work either.

Such a problematic case is depicted in fig. 16.2 for a situation where money supply is not M' but M^-. In this case the economy is in a 'liquidity trap' at the rate of interest r^- due to the speculative demand for money L_2 becoming 'absolute', i.e. perfectly interest elastic. If the associated effective demand Y^-_w were too low for full employment, then an increase in money, leading to leftward movements along $LIS_{w'}$ would be inconsequential for the rate of interest and hence for effective demand and employment. But likewise, a drop of liquidity preference due to a drop of money wages from w' to $w-$ would equally leave unaffected the rate of interest, the effective demand and the level of employment in this case. The position of the $LIS(w')$-curve would then be shifted to that of the LIS_w-curve drawn as a broken line. Although outside the liquidity trap this decrease would indeed release money holdings from the transactions balances to bring down the rate of interest, since the drop in the wage rate would reduce the transactions requirements. But if employment does not change, real wages also stay constant. Thus, although the money wage was cut, the real wage was unaffected.

With this observation we have linked up again with the discussion of the 'simplified model' because Pigou (1937, p. 406) introduced it in referring to 'recent' contentions to this effect in which

it is argued that, even in conditions where a cut in the real wage would necessarily lead to an increase in the quantity of employment, a cut in

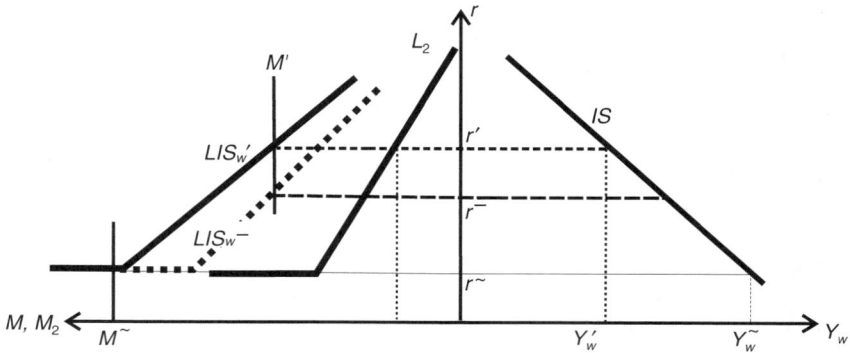

Figure 16.2 The liquidity trap and the Keynes effect

the money rate of wages need not improve employment, because it need not ... entail a cut in the rate of real wages.

Pigou (*ibid.*) continues that the purpose of his model is to 'attack effectively the problem which these contentions raise'.

But since 'these contentions' clearly are the main critical substance of the 'Keynes effect', as was just seen, there should be little doubt that this model must be seen primarily as a rejoinder against Keynes' *General Theory*.[5]

16.2 Pigou's perception of the 'Keynes effect'

If we want to attribute to Pigou (1937) the intention to react to the Keynes effect, then we work under the supposition that this effect was indeed *perceived* by Pigou. Laidler (1999, p. 280) casts doubt on such a view, stating:

> Pigou thus erroneously attributed to Keynes a belief that money wages affected employment through a chain of events in which the real wage played a critical causative role.

Laidler (1999, p. 280) comes to this conclusion after quoting a passage from Pigou (1936, pp. 127–8; original publication) in which Pigou writes that in the end Keynes *does not* deny that 'by a process of repercussion' money wage cuts 'can bring about a reduction in real wages'. The wording in the quoted passage from Pigou does not suggest that Pigou does indeed attribute to Keynes the belief in a 'causative role' of real wages. If one looks at the wider context of this quote, one finds that Pigou (1936, p. 128) indeed is fully aware of crucial differences between himself and Keynes in this context:

> though, if I am right, the results which Mr. Keynes and I forecast are the same, the processes by which we respectively look for them to be brought about are entirely different. He has failed, I think, to see that the consequences for employment of a given reduction in money wage rates, like the consequences of a given act of individual hoarding, are indeterminate until the character of the banking policy that is being pursued is known.

Thus Pigou seems to be very much aware that the said 'process of repercussion' of money wage cuts works via the money *market*. This is for Pigou – as it is for Keynes – the essential 'causative' element. But the market has demand ('hoarding', 'liquidity preference') *and* supply ('banking policy'). Obviously Pigou, in this passage, brings into memory those parts in his *Theory of Unemployment* where he discusses 'banking policy' in order to come to an estimate of the magnitude of his E_m (see above, sect. 15.1, p. 165). We mentioned in the last chapter already (n. 4 on p. 167) that Pigou (1933, pp. 104–6) engaged in money-value accounting and in money market analysis out of an intuitive belief that his real wage analysis must be embedded in a monetary general equilibrium context.

Keeping this in mind, we are not convinced that Pigou (1936, pp. 127–8) attributed to Keynes a money wage mechanism in which the essential *causa causans* was the real wage. Instead, it seems quite clear that in the quoted passages the transmission mechanism of money wage changes involved first of all the money market. Whatever happened *there* was essential for what later happened with the real wage and employment in the models under discussion – and not the other way round, that the real wage in some causative way by itself affected the money market.

From these considerations we conclude that Pigou (1936) knew quite well already that Keynes' money wage analysis involved first of all the money market and that Pigou (1937) was a conscious reply to this analysis.

16.3 Pigou's 'simplified model' of employment, interest and money

16.3.1 The Pigovian argument: an overview

If the 'Keynes effect' view of money wage changes is correct, there cannot be an increase in employment unless the rate of interest changes. Thus, in arguing against this 'recent' analysis, Pigou's main aim had to be to find an analytical counter-example to this particular aspect of the 'Keynes effect'.

This purpose could be served by the time preference theory of interest. As already mentioned, if this theory holds, then the Keynesian *IS*-curve (see equ. (16.2) on p. 202) may be considered as degenerating to a straight line in the interest rate and income field. In this case the same mechanism which Keynes invoked for his 'Keynes effect' would work quite differently than originally envisaged: consider the stock of money as given, as before, and contemplate once more a lowering of the money wage rate. As in the Keynesian case discussed in the last section, the transactions balances will again be reduced for any given amount of real income and employment due to the decreased wage cost. But since the rate of interest is now constant as long as the time preference does not change, the money released from transactions balances cannot spill over into an increased speculative demand for money. People will find themselves with excess money holdings which, when spent, will drive up the real demand for goods and hence for labour. Due to decreasing marginal productivity, the higher demand for goods and for labour will be met at a lower real wage but at a constant rate of interest.

Basically, this chain of reasoning would suffice – if it could be established as being plausible – in order to discredit the 'Keynes effect' view of the relationship between money wages and employment. But Pigou (1937) wanted to go further than that. He wanted to reverse Keynes' statement that employment can increase only when the rate of interest drops.

It will emerge from the rest of this section that some of the peculiarities of the 'simplified model' result from this Pigovian intention.

16.3.2 The Pigovian application of the time-preference theory of interest

The entire Pigovian argumentation hinges on the question of the applicability of the time-preference theory of interest.

The problem with this theory is, however, that even in a rather simple comparative-static context of a discussion of employment policies it involves some rather delicate balancing between potentially mutually exclusive assumptions. On the one hand, it requires particular constancy assumptions concerning capital, income, preferences, etc. Without these the rate of interest cannot be reliably assumed to represent the rate of discounting future satisfactions as was pointed out in the excursus of the preceding chapter. On the other hand, the comparative statics of employment require exactly that event to take place which just was supposed to be absent, namely changes in the level of employment, real income, etc.

As mentioned in section 15.2, in particular on p. 171, discussions of 'changes' as may be conceived in the context of such models pertain to a special branch of comparative dynamics, namely comparative stationary states. The customary pedagogical way to present such discussions is therefore in the context of 'island parables' where the changes under discussion are associated with atemporal comparisons between alternative isolated economies in long-period equilibrium.

Pigou refrained from any such pedagogical device. But instead of referring to other authors' fuller expositions of the time-preference theory of interest, he entered into a half-hearted discussion of underlying assumptions. As it turned out, however, his discussion of the 'simplified model' did not keep the balance between the potentially contradictory assumptions in a very convincing way. Indeed, he confounded his readers (see the last part of his §7) by first describing at considerable length that with expectations of rising prices and/or of rising real income the rate of interest r will not be equal to the rate of discounting future satisfactions p. He then renounces these considerations by continuing that 'these things do not matter ... so long as employment and real income are unaltered'. But the whole point of his analysis is how to bring about just those changes the relevance of which he is denying in this passage.

It is not apparent how Pigou believed himself to be able to combine the mutually exclusive assumptions just discussed and thus his 'simplified model' model could be criticised on the account that it did not supply a convincing justification for the time-preference theory of interest which it relied upon. This was Kahn's suggestion of a critical approach to Pigou which was rejected by Keynes, however, as was stressed above. Such a criticism could possibly have been understood as touching mainly the pedagogy and not necessarily the analysis of Pigou's article, since it is well known, of course, that there are appropriate assumptions under which such a theory would hold.

In a critical reception of Pigou's 'simplified model' one could, however, follow the approach taken by Kaldor (1937, p. 747) who, in a later discussion of this model, invoked the exposition of the time-preference theory of interest as it is to be found in Ramsey (1928). This seems even more appropriate when considering that Pigou (1941, p. 111) himself later explicated his time-preference theoretic beliefs along these very lines, stating that

> our man will save nothing and dissave nothing if his rate of time preference is exactly equal to the rate of interest. This is a well-known proposition. Anyone to whom it is not apparent is referred to Frank Ramsey's [(1928)] article.

But if we are authorised by Pigou to turn to Ramsey's analysis as a guide to his own 'zero savings case' we may also point out that it is clear from Ramsey's article (*ibid.* p. 543) that this is an equilibrium condition in a very restrictive setup of assumptions:

> we have to suppose that our community goes on for ever without changing either in numbers or in its capacity for enjoyment or in its aversion to labour; that enjoyments and sacrifices at different times can be calculated independently and added.

In addition, in this type of equilibrium, the marginal product of capital must also be equal to the rate of discounting future utilities ρ – unless we have conditions of 'bliss' (maximum utility) or 'subsistence'. If, however, the marginal product of capital is higher than ρ, then there will be an incentive to sacrifice present consumption for investment – or, as Ramsey (1928, p. 556) put it:

> Then there will be not equilibrium, but saving, and since a great deal cannot be saved in a short time, it may be centuries before equilibrium is reached, or *it may never be reached.* (italics added, GMA)

Such then is the analytical scope for the application of the time preference theory of interest and it is indeed astonishing that Keynes gave in to

Kahn's suggestion not to criticise Pigou's claim that it is possible to conduct 'short-period' analysis in this type of analytical set-up.

16.3.3 The microfoundations of production in the 'simplified model'

One of the peculiarities of Pigou's 'simplified model' is to be found in its representation of production. Contrary to the two-sectoral approach chosen in his earlier discussion of the 'real demand for labour' investigated in part II above, he now uses a 'representative' production function. In this framework he then formulates the marginal value product of labour as being not equal to the money wage but as fulfilling the equation

$$w(1 + r) = p\psi'(n) \qquad (16.6)$$

where, as before, w = money wage rate, r = rate of interest, and p = price of goods, and where n is (representative) employment. Setting the number of representative firms equal to unity permits us to regard n as standing also for total employment.[6]

Pigou does not clarify how exactly the rate of interest enters his expression for the marginal value product. We reconstruct expression (16.6) from the consideration that if it is the outcome of a profit maximal solution, then the underlying expression for profits (II) could have read:

$$\Pi = pQ - wn - rwn \qquad (16.7)$$

where Q, the quantity of goods produced, is given by the production function

$$Q = \psi(n) \quad \text{with} \quad \psi' > 0 \quad \text{and} \quad \psi'' < 0. \qquad (16.8)$$

It may then be easily verified that differentiating (16.7) with respect to n and assuming an extreme value for profits gives, after minor rearrangements, the marginal value product expression (16.6).

We gather from this result that the production theory contained in the Pigovian 'simplified model' has certain elements of later capital-theoretic models where cost of production consist of 'direct labour cost' (wn) and of 'indirect labour cost' (rwn). Alternatively, the production process may be described as one involving 'circulating capital' of the volume of wn which, after one time period, has to be repaid together with the interest accrued at a rate of r.

The circulating capital just mentioned cannot be the only capital involved in the model, however, as will be apparent from the following considerations: with $\psi''(n) < 0$ Pigou assumes decreasing returns to n. Therefore the production function (16.8) cannot be linear homogenous with regard to n. Hence the remuneration by its marginal product $\psi'(n)n$ cannot exhaust total product and therefore the profit equation (16.6) must, in profit maximising equilibrium, represent positive profits. But insofar as Pigou assumes perfect competition, extra profits must be nil. Hence we conclude that Π represents factor income for capital stock which in equilibrium may be given by

$$\Pi = rp\,\bar{K} \qquad (16.9)$$

where $\bar{K}$ is total capital.

In this model income in terms of wage units is given by

$$Y_w \equiv \frac{pQ}{w} = (1+r)\frac{\psi(n)}{\psi'(n)}. \qquad (16.10)$$

This expression relates value of output to employment n. We thus have here a concept very similar to the one discussed in part II under the heading of 'Keynes' Pigovian concept of aggregate supply'. The only difference to the type of aggregate supply functions formulated there is that now the rate of interest comes into play.

As before, the significance of the aggregate supply function is that under normal productive conditions it permits us to use the real value of production and employment interchangeably because there is a monotonous relation between the two, given by

$$\frac{dY_w}{dn} = (1+r)\left(1 - \frac{\psi(n)\psi''(n)}{\psi'(n)^2}\right) > 1 \qquad (16.11)$$

so that any increase in aggregate supply is tantamount to an increase in employment.

Pigou's introduction of the rate of interest into the formulation of the marginal product of labour has an interesting consequence for the theory of functional distribution of income. As is well known, labour's share in income normally is given by its partial elasticity of production α_x if competition is perfect. In the present context this magnitude is defined as

$$\alpha \equiv n\frac{\psi'(n)}{\psi(n)} \quad \text{whence we have} \quad \frac{\psi(n)}{\psi'(n)} = \frac{n}{\alpha}. \qquad (16.12)$$

A simple algebraic expression for labour's share in this model (λ^p) may then be formulated by assuming α to be constant and by substituting $\psi(n)/\psi'(n)$ in equ. (16.10) via the expression given in (16.11). It follows then after minor rearrangements of the resulting expression that

$$\lambda^p \equiv \frac{wn}{pQ} = \frac{n}{Y_w} = \frac{\alpha}{1+r} \qquad (16.13)$$

must hold. Thus there emerges a 'λ^p and r' relationship expressing the statement that functional distribution under conditions of perfect competition is determined by (i) technology as expressed by α, *and* (ii) by the rate of interest r in such a way that with increasing interest rates labour's share must decrease.

This is quite an interesting distribution theoretical result because it will be seen later on that Joan Robinson believed that the fact that in her set-up labour's share depended on the rate of interest constituted a major challenge against the established classical theory. As it just turned out, her particular distribution theoretic result is not an anti-Pigovian one, however. What are the analytical reasons for this similarity between Joan Robinson and Pigou?

Anticipating results which will only later be developed systematically (see below, p. 283), we may note that Joan Robinson's corresponding $\lambda^r - r$ relation depends on the fact that her model contains capital goods production for the purpose of reinvestment. At first sight, this observation seems not to help very much in answering the question just posed. With regard to depreciation, the 'simplified model' seemingly is of quite a different nature than the one of Joan Robinson, since Pigou (1937, p. 406) assumes that in his model 'no element of depreciation enters into prime cost'. He justifies this statement with the observation that his model is based on the assumption that fixed capital lasts for ever. But Pigou's just quoted statement is somewhat misleading: although it is true that in the profit equation (16.7) there is indeed no obvious element of depreciation, it must be noted that his particular formulation of the cost of labour amounts to an implicit introduction of just such a cost element. Since labour cost is given by $(1 + r)wn$, this cost element is really comparable to a capital outlay of wn which, after one period, causes interest cost at a rate of r and which after one time period must be written off at a rate of 100 per cent. Contrary to Pigou's denial of the existence of depreciation in his model, we thus have in fact a rate of depreciation of 100 per cent and it is this characteristic of his model which generates the similarity with that of Joan Robinson.

16.3.4 The macroeconomic markets in the 'simplified model'

The Keynesian model is often represented as one of three interacting macroeconomic markets, namely one for labour, one for goods and one for money. Since the 'simplified model' may be seen as a response to the Keynesian one, a parallel presentation suggests itself here.

16.3.4.1 The labour market

The Pigovian labour market is comparable to the Keynesian one in the sense that in both conceptions labour supply is no constraint for an expansion of output and employment. Thus Pigou, like Keynes, implicitly assumes labour to be in excess supply.

One of the idiosyncrasies of Keynes' labour market analysis is his 'employment function' which relates effective demand in terms of the wage unit to total employment. A similar relationship may also be formulated for the Pigovian approach. Indeed, equ. (16.10) above was just such a relationship.

A formulation of value in terms of wage units is somewhat unsatisfactory in this context, however, because it splits up the marginal cost which is $w(1 + r)$ in the present case and allots the wages-component to the left-hand side and the interest-component to the right-hand side of the aggregate supply function resp. of the employment function. If the rationale of counting value aggregates like effective demand in terms of a 'cost unit' is to separate conceptually such value aggregates from underlying assumptions concerning production and competition, then a slightly different approach seems to be called for. It consists in defining a (marginal) cost unit

$$z \equiv w(1+r) \tag{16.14}$$

and to normalise money values with this unit instead of the wage unit, giving value aggregates in 'cost units' as

$$Y_z = \frac{pQ}{w(1+r)} = \frac{\psi(n)}{\psi(n)} \quad \text{with} \quad \frac{dY_z}{dn} > 1 \tag{16.15}$$

where the stated value of the derivative may be inferred from referring back to equ. (16.11).

Expression (16.15) relates a 'real value' in terms of the cost unit to technological assumptions as expressed by the production function $\psi(n)$ and to assumptions concerning competitive remuneration as expressed by the marginal productivity function $\psi'(n)$ in exactly the same way as the Keynesian aggregate supply function resp. his employment function did – with the only difference that now the cost unit includes the interest rate.[7]

16.3.4.2 *The goods market*

The Keynesian *IS*-curve is generally seen as the *locus* of equilibria on the goods market.[8] This curve survives in the Pigovian 'simplified model' in the shape of a straight line at $r = \rho$ as was seen above already (see the considerations in connection with equ. (16.2) above).

Whereas in the Keynesian system it was the task of the goods market to determine effective demand for any given level of interest rates, this role could not be played by the modified goods market *locus* of the 'simplified model'. The consequence of the Pigovian modification of this construction is namely that with a given equilibrium rate of interest the associated effective demand is indeterminate and cannot be derived from the 'goods market' proper. Instead, the volume of effective demand must be determined via the money market.

16.3.4.3 The money market

In his monetary analysis Pigou (1937, p. 409) starts out in seeming accordance with Keynes' view that

(i) the income velocity of the total amount of money depends positively on the rate of interest.
(ii) But he adds that the distribution of income might also play a role in determining money demand.
(iii) Eventually Pigou ends up denying a significant influence of the rate of interest on money demand.

This argumentation might best be described in terms of some algebraic notation. Starting out from the money demand equation

$$M^d = \frac{1}{V^T} Y \tag{16.16}$$

where M^d is money demand and V^r is the income velocity of money. Pigou (1937, p. 410) postulates a functional relation of the following type

$$V^T = V^T(r, \lambda^P) \quad \text{with partial derivatives} \quad V_r^T > 0, \ V_{\lambda^P}^T > 0 \tag{16.17}$$

The first argument of this V^T-function represents the idea traditionally associated with Keynes, that with higher rates of interest the opportunity cost of holding money increases and that this induces people to hold less of it, thereby increasing the velocity of circulation of the money in existence. The inclusion of the second argument in (16.17) is plausible if monetary transactions increase with a relative increase in wage income. The reason given by Pigou (1937, p. 409) for this assumption is that wage earners receive their money at comparatively short intervals and that therefore the velocity of circulation increases if the share of wages in income increases. With this formulation of the V^r-function we thus have restated stages (i) and (ii) of the above outline of Pigou's monetary argumentation.

Stage (iii) of the monetary theoretic argumentation of the 'simplified model' follows from the following consideration: due to the $\lambda^P - r$ relation discussed in connection with equation (16.13), the second argument in the V^T-function is in turn a function of the rate of interest. The derivative of V^T is therefore given by

$$\frac{dV^T}{dr} = \frac{\partial V^T}{\partial r} - \frac{\partial V^T}{\partial \lambda^P}\frac{\alpha}{(1+r)^2} \gtrless 0,$$ (16.18)

an expression with an indeterminate sign value. Thus, in the Pigovian view nothing definite can be said about the interest effect on the income velocity of money. In this framework it might just as well be taken as being constant – an assumption which was made explicit only in a further rejoinder (Pigou, 1938).

In the final result, Pigou's discussion of money demand, although seemingly conciliatory to Keynesian ideas, in fact turns out to be opposed to them.

Concerning money supply, Pigou (1937) also deviates considerably from Keynes in postulating that money supply is an increasing function of the rate of interest. Modern terminology would attribute such a supply function to 'inside money' offered by the commercial banking system. Total money supply may then be interpreted to be given by

$$M^s = M_0 + M(r) \quad \text{with} \quad M_r^s > 0$$ (16.19)

in the Pigovian view, where M_0 is the 'outside money' component supplied by the monetary authorities and where subindex r again signifies a partial derivative.

Using this equation and the transactions demand for money equation (16.16), equilibrium in the money market of the 'simplified model' may then be represented by

$$M^s = M^d = M_0 + M(r) = \frac{z}{V^T}Y_z$$ (16.20)

where the formulation of $zY_z \equiv Y$ utilises the definition of the 'cost unit' as given by equ. (16.14). It follows then from monetary equilibrium in this sense that for a rate of interest given as $r = \rho$, total money supply is given. But from the last term in (16.20) it follows further that in this case z and Y_z, and hence employment, are also given.

Thus we may conclude that Pigou's 'simplified model' produces the view that the money market has a central position in determining macroeconomic outcomes. In this regard it is quite similar to the argumentation in the *General Theory*. But it reaches this result in quite a different way and with quite different employment political suggestions, as will be shown in more detail in the following section.

16.3.4.4   *The Pigovian view of employment policy in the 'simplified model'*

If now the money wage drops, employment is seen in a very simple way to rise via the workings of the money market: it follows from (16.14) that in this case the cost unit z must also drop. But since the product $zY_z \equiv Y$ was just seen as being given for any given ρ, any drop in z must raise real output Y_z – and hence a drop in wages *must* raise employment as long as standard assumptions concerning production are justified. There is no room for Keynesian agnosticism concerning the employment political efficacy of money wage cuts in this model.

But one of the important aspects of the 'simplified model' seems to have been for Pigou not only to demonstrate that money wage cuts do indeed have a reliable effect on employment. He also wants to show that is not the rate of interest which is the linchpin of the working of the labour market. It is therefore important for Pigou (1937, p. 411) to point out:

> It is not true ... that, if the same temporary cut in that rate [i.e. the interest rate, GMA] were made and money wage was not reduced, employment would be affected to the same extent and for the same period as it is under a money wage cut.

But after some tentative discussion of disequilibria Pigou left it to the reader to search his 'simplified model' for an illustration of this statement.

An attempt to justify this judgement in the context of the 'simplified model' seems to require the answer to two questions:

(i) In which context could that unjustified impression have come up which was criticised by Pigou?
(ii) What exactly is Pigou's view of an important difference between the two employment political measures?

Concerning question (i) the answer suggesting itself is that *both*, changes in w and changes in r, affect the cost unit z in quite a similar way. If a drop in the money wage rate ww is so beneficial for employment because it reduces $z = w(1 + r)$, why does not the same hold true for the other cost factor, the rate of interest, r?

This question then leads to the second one, concerning the employment political peculiarities of interest rate changes in the context of the 'simplified model'. They lie in the money market equation (16.20): from inspecting that equation it appears that lowering the rate of interest does not only lower the cost unit z, thereby enabling real output in cost units Y_z to increase. It also lowers the $M(r)$-component of money supply, and, with a constant income velocity of circulation V^T, this leads to a decreased $Y \equiv zY_z$. Thus there appears here a contractionary influence on Y_z and hence on employment which does not appear in the case of money wage changes.

Comparing interest rate reductions and money wage reductions one may thus note that in the 'simplified model' 'the two processes are entirely different' (Pigou, 1937, p. 411). Money wage reductions appear as being the more reliable employment political instrument in this context.

This is, of course, not the full story of employment determination in the Pigovian model. A number of other policy measures could be discussed, 'among which a manipulation of banking policy is one' (*ibid.*). One such measure could be changes in the M_0-component of money supply. But Pigou (*ibid.*) is not interested in such a discussion:

> It is enough for my purpose to show that a money wage cut is not simply a piece of ritual that enables the real cause of employment expansion – a fall in the rate of money interest – to take effect.

16.3.4.5 A graphical representation of the 'simplified model'

Figure 16.3 represents graphically the way in which employment resp. the value of real output is determined by the three macroeconomic markets described in the last section.

As was mentioned above, under Pigovian conditions the Keynesian *IS*-curve deteriorates to a $r = \rho$-line according to which the rate of interest r is determined by ρ, the rate of discounting future utility (see the north-easterly quadrant).

Total money supply is then determined in the north-western quadrant along the M^s-curve which rises with increasing interest rates and the position of which might depend on the supply of outside money M_0.[9] If monetary

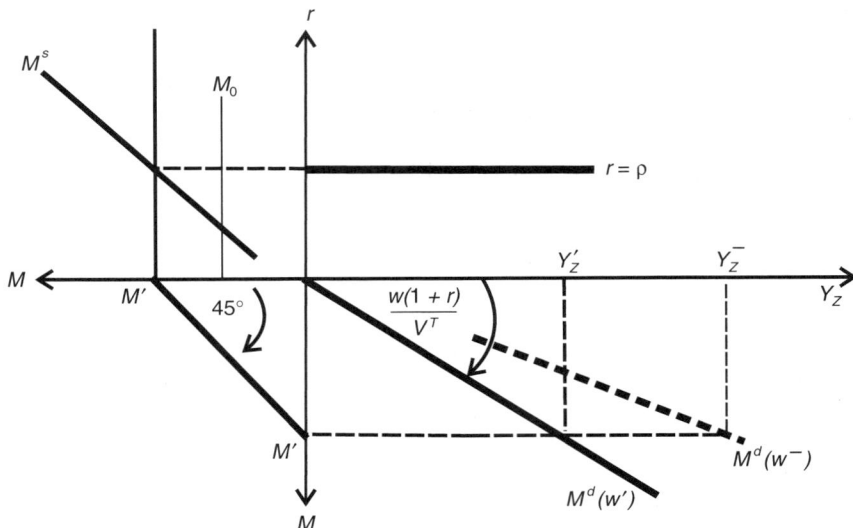

Figure 16.3 Pigou's 'simplified model' of employment

equilibrium prevails, total money supply M' – via a 45° construction in the south-western quadrant – meets a corresponding money demand determined by the transactions requirements as represented by the curve $M^d(w')$ in the south-easterly quadrant.

The value of real output is then determined as Y'_z. Since real output and employment are monotonously related with each other through a Pigovian employment function as discussed in the previous section, employment is determined as well.

Employment resp. the value of real output may now be manipulated by lowering the money wage rate, say to a value of w^-. The resulting change in money demand is represented by the corresponding broken curve in the south-easterly quadrant. Since money supply is unchanged at M', monetary equilibrium now requires an increase in the value of real output and employment.

Lowering the rate of interest r would affect money demand in a similar way as lowering the money wage rate. But in addition to this effect it would lead to a decrease of money supply by inducing a lower position on the M^s-curve in the north-western quadrant. The net effect of lowering the rate of interest could then be not an expansion of real output and employment as Keynesian analysis would have it, but a contraction of employment.

16.4 Problems and perspectives of a Keynesian assessment of the 'simplified model'

16.4.1 A vindication of the classical view?

In assessing the 'simplified model' as a contribution to the Keynes–Classics debate, one of the first questions arising might be directed at its fulfilment of the task which Pigou set for it: how convincing is this model as a vindication of the classical view of the economics of wage cutting?

It will be remembered that in ch. 15 (section 15.1) we noted that in the context of wage-cutting analysis Pigou (1933) just postulated the validity of those analytical elements which he needed for the generation of his positive employment political evaluation of such a measure. Cases in point were the assumptions that nominal income was constant or that it was an increasing function of employment when the nominal wage changes. It was argued in that context that such a procedure was the basis for Keynes' (1936, p. 276) criticism that Pigou just assumed those elements of his classical theory of employment to exist which really should follow from a systematic economic analysis.

Such criticism seems to be met by the 'simplified model' insofar as it now offers a systematic discussion of the determination of the volume of money and its relation to money income. In this context the discussion of the income velocity of money as expressed by the V^T (r, λ^p)-function (16.17) played an important role. Although it was seen that in the end Pigou assumed V^T to be constant and money income to be also constant as long as the rate of discounting ρ was constant, nevertheless we do have here the attempt at a fulfillment of a *desideratum* noted in the context of earlier criticism of the classical theory of employment.

The weakest, yet crucial point in this seeming vindication of the classical view is, of course, the application of the time-preference theory of interest in the context of a stationary economy. There are two aspects of reacting critically to this point:

(i) There is the possibility of a rejection of the way in which that theory is applied, and
(ii) the fact that this theory is employed could also meet criticism irrespective of the particular version of the theory.

Both observations are of relevance as far as Keynes' personal reactions are concerned.

Concerning point (i), Keynes (JMK, XIV, p. 264) insisted in the published version of his note about Pigou (1937) that:

> Professor Pigou implicitly assumes that ... a man's time preference is a psychological propensity which is irrespective of whether he is rich or poor, so that at a given rate of interest his real savings will be the same irrespective of the amount of his real income.

This follows from the fact that $r = \rho$ is assumed to hold in his set-up irrespective of the level of real income. It is clear from Keynes' restatement of this implicit assumption that he thought it rather unlikely to be plausible and he relates it critically to his own 'fundamental assumption that the amount of real saving is, in part, a function of real income' (*ibid.*).

Concerning point (ii), it may be insisted that the Pigovian assumption of an economy in a stationary state equilibrium as the benchmark for analysing contemporary employment policies is so outlandish that it could hardly be defended without a detailed demonstration in which regard its applicability is indeed warranted. But although Keynes made some critical attempts along such lines in his first draft of a note about Pigou (JMK, XIV, pp. 237f.), we saw above that he was successfully diverted from this endeavour.

But then, one might ask: is it really firmly established that Pigou intended his vindication of the classical view to take place in the context of a stationary economy?

16.4.2 The methodological ambiguity

Reviewing the doctrines concerning the 'economics of wage cutting' at the time of Keynes, Blaug (1968, pp. 660f.) took account of Pigou's *Theory of Unemployment* remarking:

The argument is difficult to summarize because it does not seem to hang together on comparative static grounds and appears to depend on quasi-dynamic considerations introduced *ad hoc* in an otherwise static context.

This judgement is even more appropriate about Pigou's 'simplified model' because it seems to have *two* levels of argumentation, each being able to convey the points which Pigou seems to have intended to make: on the one hand, there are the 'quasi-dynamical' arguments noted by Blaug in the quote just given. These are, of course, hardly capable of being systematically evaluated. On the other hand, there are the structural relations of the 'simplified model'. In this context it is quite possible to derive the intended Pigovian results.

Elaborating on these points, let us remember that in sect. 16.2 above it was seen that the 'simplified model' is so devised as to prove in a static and stationary context that lower money wages *must* be associated with higher employment and that interest rate changes only *might* have a comparable result. These are the main conclusions which verbally Pigou proposed to be drawn from his discussion and they are indeed easily reproduceable formally from a comparative stationary analysis of his model. Finally, it should be noted that for an interested reader of Pigou (1937) it must appear as quite plausible to make such an inference from a Pigovian standpoint since they contradict Keynes' claim that it is only via interest rate changes that money wage changes can affect employment.

A closer reading of his literal argumentation shows, however, that Pigou (1937, p. 410) lets the conclusion concerning the importance of wage cutting which was just quoted at the end of section (e) be preceded by the statement that 'what will happen to the rate of interest ... cannot be discussed here'. Presumably the 'here' of this quote means the context of his 'simplified model'. But if that is the case, on which scientific basis does he build in making the statements about the relative importance of changes in money wage rates and interest rates which he did make?

We must now note that for the discussion of the money wage and interest rate nexus Pigou abandons the equilibrium framework of the 'simplified model'. He rather invokes a disequilibrium situation instead in which bankers drive down the rate of interest below the rate of discounting future utility ρ. But in such a case the initial zero savings equilibrium of the 'simplified model' is disturbed and there will be an incentive towards dissaving. At the same time there must be an incentive for new investment if the increased employment increases the marginal productivity of capital as Pigou (1937, p. 421) argues in his article in a separate section on long-period effects of wage cuts. In such a disequilibrium, brought about by a wage cut, there will then be a strongly increased demand for borrowing but no additional supply of funds. How is the economic system supposed to react in the face of such a possibility?

There is no answer to this question given by Pigou. Neither in this context nor in any later publication did he supply a systematic version of the type of suggestive period analysis which he likes to allude to. The reader in search of a systematic treatment of these phenomena is likely to resort then to a comparative static discussion of the original 'simplified model', not knowing, however, whether Pigou would not disassociate himself from any criticism against conclusions derived in such a procedure.

It is perhaps in this sense that Joan Robinson's dictum may be understood that one had to rationalise Pigou in order to find a coherent error (above, ch. 14, n. 3). In any case it certainly had to be considered as a major achievement if a clarification of these methodological muddles could be brought about.

This is what in fact was done in Kaldor's contribution to this debate which will be inspected at more detail in the following chapter 17. Before leaving the present chapter, however, one further aspect of the 'simplified model' should be briefly looked at.

16.4.3 The monetary perspective of the 'simplified model'

One aspect of the 'simplified model' which warrants particular attention is the theory of money supply which it implies. With its (implicit) distinction of interest-dependent 'inside' money created by banks and exogenously given 'outside' money brought into existence by the monetary authorities, it seems to bring into the analysis an interesting – but totally anti-Keynesian – monetary world.

Even more than four decades after the publication of the 'simplified model' we find repercussions of its monetary elements in an address given by Nicholas Kaldor (1983a, p. 20) which, ironically enough, was supposed to celebrate Keynes and *not* Pigou:

> The extraordinary feature of all the monetary writing in this century ... has been that the exogenous character of the money supply was almost never questioned, despite the fact that most money assets originate in bank credit – through borrowing either by the public sector or the non-bank private sector.

Thus, Kaldor is seen here as claiming that modern literature failed to see that there is a sizeable component of inside money in contemporary money supply. But from the above discussion of the money market of the 'simplified model' it should be clear that Pigou's (1937) article constituted a notable exception to this characterisation. This cannot have escaped Kaldor as will become apparent from the discussion in the next chapter.

It is perhaps particularly interesting that Kaldor proceeded from the observation just quoted, to detect a major flaw in Keynes' argumentation which amounted to criticising him that he did not follow the argumentative line suggested by the 'simplified model'. After having observed that in the *General Theory* we have a money market equation of the type $M = L(Y, r)$ with money treated as *exogenous* (*op. cit.*, p. 18), Kaldor (1983a, p. 22) remarked:

> Most of the stir created by Friedman's activities might have been avoided if Keynes had explicitly recognised that the quantity of money *M* is also an *endogenous* variable ... writing $M(r) = L(Y, r)$.

With its $M(r)$-function depicting interest elastic money supply, this algebraic expression for the money market is nothing but a variant of the money market equation (16.20) which characterised the 'simplified model'. Thus, although this passage was not explicitly intended by Kaldor to be read in this way, in an assessment of the 'simplified model' we may nevertheless interpret it to convey the message: if Keynes (1936) had written on money supply like Pigou (1937) later did in his critique of Keynes, then Milton Friedman could not have had such an impact as he did have in the 1960s and 1970s.

One could think that the extension of Kaldor's just quoted remark to the Keynes–Pigou controversy is an *over*extension. Was not Kaldor one of the most prominent Cambridge Keynesians? We will look in more detail at the relation between these three economists in the next chapter. But it may be noted here already that Kaldor (1937) was an expert on the Pigovian model to which we just related *Kaldor's* criticism of Keynes. It is inconceivable that in such an explicit criticism of Keynes as the one just quoted, he could not remember that that was the very point with which he had to deal in his *grande entrée* to Cambridge economic debate – because Kaldor (1937) was just that, as will appear presently.

Here, we just note that in the particular respect just quoted, Kaldor's (1937) discussion of Pigou's 'simplified model' appears to have had a lasting impression on his idea about an appropriate modelling of macro-economic money supply. It is also remarkable that Keynes' position in this very matter was a very conscious one. It was not just oversight or stubbornness if Keynes failed to anticipate Kaldor's appreciation of Pigovian monetary views. Rather, he believed that they were deficient because they were 'a result of confusing bank loans with bank balances' (JMK, XIV, p. 237).

It seems that Keynes' idea in this context was that the volume of activity of commercial banks was determined by a number of non-identical interests:

(i)   by those of the depositors 'who desire to spend less than their liquid resources' (*ibid.*),

(ii) by those of the debtors 'who desire to spend more than their liquid resources' (*ibid.*),

(iii) by the bank managers who have to decide upon the optimal length of the balance sheet of their banking firm.

In effect, Keynes asks here for the microeconomic foundations of the Pigovian money supply function – which, however, have not come forth, so far. None of these aspects of the activities of banking firms and their relevant partners is particularly clear – neither in Pigou, nor in Kaldor, for that matter. Again, the young Keynesians did not produce a noteworthy drive to clear up these matters. Joan Robinson (JMK, XIV, p. 240) advised Keynes not to press for a clarification:

> I think it rather dangerous however to refer to the confusion between bank loans and bank balances, as you are on the edge of the abyss – better leave it alone altogether.

Keynes did heed her advice and refrained from publishing his criticism. Thus a further potential for a critical assessment of Pigou was left idle.

16.4.4 Assessing the Keynesian assessment of the 'simplified model'

Taking a general view of the critical reaction against Pigou (1937) by Keynes and his disciples, it is astonishing how little the latter seem to have felt involved. This manifests itself not only in the fact that none of them offered any systematic and published critical assessment of Pigou (1937). Their reluctance to participate in this debate shows up in a number of – by now published – personal communications with Keynes as well.

It is *Keynes* who comes up with a whole array of suggestions for critical clarification like:

• the methodology of short-period analysis
• the appropriateness of stationary-state economics for economic political discussions
• the microfoundations of the Pigovian money supply assumptions.

But concerning short-period methodology, the Cambridge 'expert' on short-period analysis R. F. Kahn not only did not feel 'turned on' by Keynes' remarks at all himself, he also *actively persuaded* Keynes 'to concentrate on what is important' and to cut out any reference to that topic from his own publication, as was mentioned earlier in ch. 15.

Similarly, the Cambridge expert on the theory of the firm (as Joan Robinson could be considered after her publication of *The Economics of Imperfect Competition* (1933)) *actively persuaded* Keynes not to enter into any reference to Pigou's shaky microeconomic foundations of a discussion of the banking firm and better to 'leave it alone altogether'.

It was noted above that one possible reason for the reluctance of the Young Keynesians to participate in a critical debate of Pigou (1937) could be seen in his methodological ambiguity. But after this question was cleared by Kaldor (1937) and by Pigou (1938) accepting the Kaldorian interpretation, this reason could not have been valid any more. Yet, although *expressly invited* by Keynes to take over in a second round of debates, his supposed supporters kept silent.

We think that this silence should find more attention in Keynesian literature than it has done until now and we will return to this subject below.

17
The Kaldorian Synthesis of Keynes and Pigou

17.1 The significance of Kaldor's reception of the 'simplified model'

The methodical ambiguity of Pigou's argumentation in the context of his discussion of the 'simplified model' made it desirable to have a methodically more consistent rendering of the workings of this model. This is what Kaldor's (1937) note offered, and in view of Pigou's (1938) later acceptance of much of the Kaldorian interpretation the methodical clarification which this implied must be regarded as being of major significance for the Keynes–Pigou debate.[1]

In addition, Kaldor (1937) is noteworthy because he attempted to find a synthesis between the particular stationary equilibrium world of Pigou and the non-stationary temporary equilibrium world of Keynes. Since this attempt was received favourably by Pigou (1938) and since Keynes then claimed that this showed that Pigou accepted virtually all the essential points of Keynesian analysis, this note also could assume considerable significance for an understanding of Keynes' analysis and of the analytical context in which it might be put.

It is along such lines that Kaldor himself wanted to see the significance of his note and it might be instructive to reproduce in some detail a quote from Young (1987, p. 109) in which Kaldor gives a personal assessment of his note:

> If you read my little 1937 paper in answer to Pigou, it is notable because Pigou admitted that he was wrong and Keynes was right after that … I showed that as an equation system his [Pigou's] method shows that you can get the Keynesian results from a classical-orthodox approach just as easily. And then much to everybody's surprise – chiefly Robbins's – Pigou replied to me very nicely and said that he now accepts my main point – which is really accepting Keynes's general position – and he withdraws what he said.

Finally, Kaldor's interpretation merits particular attention because it contains one of the first propagations of the – by now orthodox – Hicksian *IS–LM* diagram.

In short, the particular significance of Kaldor's note derives from the fact that it stands at the decisive crossroads of divergent interpretational developments in the Keynes–Classics debate, involving the time-preference theoretic interpretation of Pigou (1937), the alleged Pigovian acceptance of Keynes' *General Theory*, and the Hicksian *IS–LM* scheme as an instrument for the interpretation of 'Keynes and the Classics'.

17.2 Kaldor's restatement of the Pigovian case for money wage policy

17.2.1 An outline of the argument

In his note about Pigou's 'simplified model', Kaldor (1937) sets out by recreating that model more or less along the lines followed in the previous chapter and represented graphically in fig. 16.3. This is reassuring in view of the methodological doubts discussed in the preceding chapter, particularly since Pigou (1938) himself later sanctioned Kaldor's interpretation and extension of his argument.[2]

At first, Kaldor accepts the Pigovian $r = \rho$ doctrine as just set out by us. He then modifies that model in successive stages, first introducing a dependence of savings on employment. In the context of our graphical representation, this modification leads to a downward sloping $r = \rho$ line since employment is a monotonous function of the real value of output. Thus we have again a downward sloping equilibrium *locus* in the (real) income and interest rate plane – just as in the case of the old Keynesian *IS*-curve. But it will be remembered that the construction of the Keynesian *IS*-curve was based on the assumption of positive savings and investment. Here we are in a stationary Pigovian world in which the zero savings assumption holds. Nevertheless, with Kaldor's modification we are back at Keynes' doctrine that employment can only increase if the rate of interest were lowered – with the only difference that whereas in the case of Keynes we had to move along an *IS-locus*, in the case of Pigou we had to move on an $r = \rho$*-locus*.

In arguing his criticism of Pigou, Kaldor finally refers the reader to the *IS–LM* apparatus of Hicks (1937), demonstrating that the Hicksian *LM*-curve will shift to the right when the wage rate is lowered – presumably for a given quantity of money. The intersection with the (unchanged) *IS*-curve will then equally shift to the right, and real output and employment will increase. This is nothing else than the monetary effect of wage reductions which Keynes himself analysed in the *General Theory*, as Kaldor (1937, p. 752, n. 2) duly points out.

But according to Pigou (1937) the quantity of money is not given. It is a function of the rate of interest. In an ingenious twisting of Pigou's argumentation, Kaldor now suggests that pathological money supply might have a similar significance for economic policy as pathological money demand could have had in the 'older' scheme: if the money supply function $M^s(r)$ is strongly interest elastic, then a decrease in the money wage rate might hardly be effective – although under the conditions of the last paragraph it would *ceteris paribus* have led to a decrease of the rate of interest which in turn would have triggered off the increase of employment as discussed above. But taking account of interest elastic money supply changes the analytical situation in such a way that now it is seen that the impact effect of a decrease in the rate of interest could lead to such a strong decrease in the quantity of (inside) money that the eventual decrease in the rate of interest and hence in the increase in employment is severely limited.

Although Kaldor sticks firmly to the Pigovian assumption of a stationary economy, he nevertheless is able to arrive quite elegantly at the important Keynesian conclusion that contrary to Pigou's contention the fall in the money rate of interest must always be the root cause for employment expansion. Insofar as such a fall is forestalled, money wage reduction must be futile for employment expansion.

17.2.2 An algebraic formulation

Expressed algebraically, Kaldor's restatement of the 'simplified model' takes the $r = \rho$ condition of that model in the modified form of equ. (17.1) below. He combines this stationary state analogue of the *IS*-curve with the Pigovian money market condition of equ. (16.20) which is stated in a slightly more general formulation as equ.(17.2) below:

$$r = \rho(n) \qquad \text{with} \quad \rho'(n) < 0 \qquad\qquad (17.1)$$

$$M^s(r) = L(zY_z(n),r) \quad \text{with} \quad L_1' > 0, \quad L_2' < 0 \qquad (17.2)$$

where in (17.1) L_1' is the partial derivative of $L(\cdot)$ with respect to the first argument and L_2' L is the corresponding derivative with respect to the second argument. It will be remembered that z was defined above (see p. 214) as the cost unit $z = w(1 + r)$.

The comparative statics of exogenous changes in the wage rate w in the system (17.1) and (17.2) with employment n and the rate of interest r as endogenous variables then follow from

$$\begin{bmatrix} \rho'(n) & -1 \\ -L_1'zY_z' & m \end{bmatrix} \begin{bmatrix} dn \\ dr \end{bmatrix} = \begin{bmatrix} 0 \\ L_1'(1+r)Y_z dw \end{bmatrix} \qquad (17.3)$$

where

$$m \equiv \frac{d}{dr}(M^s - L) = M^{s\prime} - L_1'wY_z - L_2' \overset{!}{>} 0 \qquad (17.4)$$

expresses the assumption that for static stability considerations excess supply of money ($M^s - L$) should decrease when the rate of interest decreases. The two strategic questions to be put to this model are then:

(i) How do exogenous changes in the money wage rate affect the endogenous level of employment? This question leads below to the formulation of the derivative (a) in (17.5).

(ii) How do such changes in the money wage rate relate to changes in the rate of interest as an endogenous variable of this system? This leads to the formulation of the derivative (b) in (17.5).

$$\text{(a)} \quad \frac{dn}{dw} = \frac{L_1'(1+r)Y_z}{J} < 0 \qquad \text{(b)} \quad \frac{dr}{dw} = \rho(n)\frac{L_1'(1+r)Y_z}{J} > 0 \qquad (17.5)$$

where

$$J \equiv \rho^1(n)m - L_1 z Y_z < 0$$

Thus it may be seen that (a): high wages must mean low employment and *vice versa*, just as classical employment theory says. But (b): this does not mean that the rate of interest stays constant as Pigou would have argued in the context of the 'simplified model'. Rather, interest rates move in the same direction as the money wage rate.

There are limiting cases in which r does not change. Such cases are in particular imaginable if in (17.5) we have $J \rightarrow -\infty$. That could happen if the parameters characterising the money market as expressed by m took on some pathological value. From the definition of m as given by equ. (17.4) it follows that one possibility for such a case is given by the condition $-L_2' \rightarrow \infty$. This condition expresses the old 'liquidity trap' case of liquidity preference becoming 'absolute'. But it follows from (17.4) also that an alternative 'trap' could be opened, namely by letting $M^{s'}$ take the value $M^{s'} \rightarrow \infty$. This latter condition would be a new trap, the 'Kaldor trap', limiting changes in the interest rate due to money supply factors.

We thus have a Keynesian money demand oriented liquidity trap *and* a Kaldorian money supply oriented liquidity trap. In the end, the distinction is immaterial. In *both* of these cases we have $|J| \rightarrow \infty$ and hence it follows from (a) in (17.5) that there will be (virtually) no reaction of employment to changes in the money wage rate, since in this case we have $(dn/dw) \rightarrow 0$.

In this sense one may conclude with Kaldor that once it is admitted that in the 'simplified model' ρ must be substituted by $\rho(n)$ with $\rho' < 0$ then the conditions for a constant rate of interest are sufficient for a constant level of employment and hence also for a constant level of the real wage – irrespective of the level of money wages.[3] The position of Keynes as set out in the context of the exposition of the 'Keynes effect' may thus be vindicated even in the alternative world of Pigou's 'simplified model'.

17.2.3 A graphical representation

Figure 17.1 depicts graphically some of the algebraic considerations of the last section. The significant modifications of the Pigovian model of fig. 16.3 on p. 218 are to be found in the two northern quadrants. The north-eastern quadrant represents the $\rho(n)$-function discussed above. The north-western quadrant represents, as before, the money supply curve M but with two modifications: the upper part represents what we called the 'Kaldor supply trap'; the lower part offers an alternative representation of the conventional 'liquidity demand trap'. The workings of the 'Kaldor supply trap' are as follows: consider a level of interest rates r^+. This corresponds to a level of employment n^+ and this corresponds in turn to a level of real production Y_z^+, the latter being depicted in the north-eastern quadrant. With a given income velocity of circulation of money V^T and a given rate of money wages w^+, money demand will be M^+ as depicted along the $M^d(w^+)$-curve in the south-eastern quadrant. The 45° construction in the south-western quadrant matches money demand with money supply, which will be duly forthcoming due to perfectly elastic supply conditions at r^+, as depicted in the north-western quadrant.

If now the wage rate were reduced from w^+ to w', money demand would drop to M' but this demand would be satisfied at the old rate of interest r^+

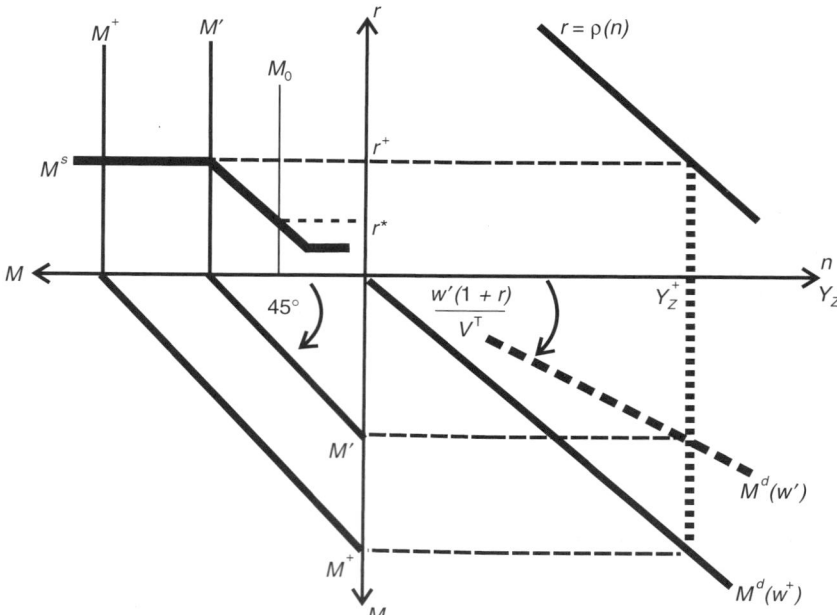

Figure 17.1 The Kaldorian synthesis

and no increase in real output and employment would materialise. Wage cutting would have been futile for employment augmenting purposes.

If, for some reason, the rate of interest dropped from r^+ to a level of r^*, money supply would be exactly equal to outside money M_0. After that, any further drop in the interest rate must lead to a negative 'stock supply' of money, i.e. to a stock *demand* of money. That demand could be met by economising on transactions balances. This could be done by lowering money wages – and hence lowering the cost unit. In this case it is indeed essential that the money wages give in, if increases in employment are to be brought about. But as in the case of Keynes, it is not the labour market which is essential for this result, but the money market and its deficient supply. Furthermore, when the rate of interest dropped to the level corresponding to the lower horizontal stretch of the M^s-curve, no further drop in the rate of interest is possible and again wage cutting would be futile for employment political purposes.

Thus, fig. 17.1 is capable of representing the two problematic cases of the last section, namely $M^{\prime s} \to \infty$ and $|L_2^{\prime}| \to \infty$, in one single framework, interpreting the latter case as a variant of the former.

17.3 The Hicksian and the Kaldorian syntheses

17.3.1 Kaldor (1937) and/vs Hicks (1937)?

In accepting as a starting point for an analysis of money wage cuts the extreme classical position expressed in Pigou (1937) and then gradually changing that position so that it is able to generate Keynesian results, Kaldor achieves an interesting synthesis of Keynes and Pigou. But such a synthesis naturally suggests the question of the relationship of *his* interpretation of these two authors to the 'neoclassical synthesis' of Keynes and the Classics proposed by Hicks (1937).

This question is of heightened interest in view of the fact that an important final step in Kaldor's argumentation was seen above to have been taken with express reference to the interpretation of the *General Theory* given by Hicks (1937). Thus it may be observed with Young (1987, p. 107) that:

Kaldor – who was shown the [*IS–LM*, GMA] diagram by Hicks – was among the earliest, if not the first, to apply the *IS–LM* approach and Hicks's diagram in practice.

But as was noted in ch. 1 above, the *IS–LM* approach was eventually discredited by Hicks (1974) himself. In view of this it is therefore desirable to find out in more detail to what extent Kaldor did in fact embrace the Hicksian interpretation.

When asked directly about his matter in the middle of the 1980s, Kaldor is reported by Young (1987, p. 114) to have considered the *IS–LM* scheme as 'a clever exposition' and as 'a useful bit of geometry to simplify Keynes'. And in this context Kaldor is quoted (*op. cit.* p. 113) as confessing to have hardly known what all the fuss concerning *IS–LM* was about:

> Honestly, all these years I didn't realize what all this about *IS–LM* being a misrepresentation of Keynes was about ... I see now that in Keynes's theory an important part was played by sudden variations in the MEC [marginal efficiency of capital] which are not explained ... by current events.

But certainly such 'sudden variations in the MEC' as mentioned in this quote could hardly justify a wholesale rejection of the *IS–LM* scheme – especially not on the grounds that it is a misrepresentation of Keynes, since he himself firmly believed in an *IS*-type functional relationship between the rate of interest and income as will be documented in the context of the next footnote.

Thus, if the variability of the MEC were the only reason for rejecting the *IS–LM* scheme, it would be not surprising if Kaldor was reluctant to do so. Indeed, when confronted with R. F. Kahn's (1984) condemnation of *IS–LM*, Kaldor (*op. cit.* p. 115) proclaimed the charges against this scheme as unsubstantiated and frankly disassociated himself from Kahn's position.

It is rather astonishing, however, that Kaldor is so lenient with the *IS–LM* scheme. After all, it was seen above that Kaldor (1983a) considered one of the major faults of Keynes to be his failure to introduce a money supply function $M(r)$ into his monetary analysis. Why should this objection not hold *a fortiori* for the *LM*-curve which is constructed under the very assumption of a given money supply? Why should the *LM*-curve with its dubious concept of 'money market equilibria beyond the attainable set of the economy' be so well equipped to represent Keynes who never had such an idea?

Even Kaldor's own contributions seem to get too little credit in his assessment. Thus, we find no mentioning of the 'supply trap' idea just praised as an interesting invention of Kaldor's note of 1937. Also, there is no discussion by the elder Kaldor of the alternative equilibrium concepts involving positive resp. zero volumes of investment which could be seen behind the *IS*-curve and which the younger Kaldor *did* discuss.

But that Kaldor in his later years kept silent on the latter set of problems is perhaps significant in itself because his construction of a Pigovian $\rho(n)$-curve as an analogue to Keynes' *IS*-curve is indeed a rather problematic step. Keynes (1936, p. 178) himself seemed to have suggested such a step, however, in stating:[4]

If the classical school merely inferred … that … the level of income and the rate of interest must be uniquely correlated, there would be nothing to quarrel with.

Kaldor's $\rho(n)$-curve together with the Pigovian aggregate supply curve appears to supply that very *locus* of agreement between Keynes and the Classics which Keynes invokes in this quote.

The problem with Kaldor's approach is, however, that it stays within the Pigovian stationary state in which the very restrictive conditions are met for the time-preference theory of interest to hold. Contrary to others – and in particular contrary to Robertson[5] – Kaldor clearly believed that there would be not much difference whether one argued in a Pigovian or in a Keynesian equilibrium context, writing to Robertson in the letter already quoted (23 Oct. 1937 as quoted by Young, 1987, p. 111):

I really do not think it makes much difference to the argument, with which of the short-run models one works, and I think my argument holds just as much for the Keynesian short-run … as for the original Pigou model. This, however, is not easy to show.

Kaldor hereby implicitly supports a position taken by Joan Robinson (1937a). We return to that issue in more detail below in part IV. In the present context we will see that Kaldor's argumentation left an argumentative loophole for Pigou's (1938) rejoinder. In essence – though just in principle and not in reality – Pigou was able to question the entire Keynesian concept of a *downward* sloping *IS*-curve as we will see presently.

Finally, it must be pointed out in this context that as an interpretation of Keynes, Kaldor's (1937) application of the *IS–LM* scheme is not identical with that of Hicks (1937). In one respect, it offered a significant improvement over Hicks' original.

It will be remembered that, apart from the alleged misrepresentation of the Classics, one of Keynes's criticisms of the Hicksian scheme was that he made 'saving a function of money income' (JMK, XIV, p. 80). Keynes points out in that context that this is only 'all right so long as you assume wages constant'. Thus, when it comes to a discussion of money wage changes, Hicks' scheme is not applicable as it stood. Kaldor's improvement over Hicks lies in the fact that he expresses the values like income, investment and savings in real terms.[6] Only after this change is he able to state quite simply the different impact effects which a change in money wages has for the *IS*-curve on the one hand and for the *LM*-curve on the other. Since the former curve now expresses equilibria of real savings and investment, a change in money wages will have no direct effect on the position of the *IS*-curve. But the *LM*-curve is different in identifying nominal magnitudes. A change in the wage unit must then immediately affect the nominal amount of transactions which a specific quantity of money could maintain – unless there are simultaneous changes in the marginal productivity of labour or in what Keynes named the 'propensity to hoard'. Thus, only after this analytical change is it possible to embark upon the type of analysis of the 'Keynes effect' which was discussed in the last chapter.

With such a presentation Kaldor (1937) became the first author to state a 'Keynes effect' of money wage changes in the context of a modified *IS–LM* analysis.[7]

We conclude that:

(i)   Kaldor's acceptance of the *IS–LM* scheme is not based on quite the same version as the one presented by Hicks (1937).
(ii)   Hicks failed to incorporate into the *IS–LM* scheme Kaldor's cherished idea of the 'endogeneity of the quantity of money'.
(iii) Kaldor's remarks about the volatility of the MEC did not lead him to a rejection of *IS–LM* analysis altogether. He disassociated himself from summary rejections of it by his later Cambridge colleagues Joan Robinson and Richard Kahn.

17.3.2 The Kaldorian synthesis in a wider context

Kaldor's 'Keynesian synthesis' is just one of several attempts at coming to grips with the diffuse macroeconomic alternatives offered by Keynes and the Classics. Over the last decades an extensive literature has built up trying to systematise such attempts.

In the context of a history of the *IS–LM* scheme, Young (1987) points out that Hicks' famous interpretation of the Keynes–Classics issue must be regarded not so much as an original and new piece of analysis but as a synthesis of earlier interpretational attempts by Harrod (1937a) and Meade (1937). Young's (1987, p. 29) synopsis of the 'equational structure of *IS–LM* papers and the *General Theory*' does not include the later papers of Pigou (1937) and Kaldor (1937) which could also be included in that context, as was seen above.[8] In addition, that presentation is based on the somewhat unfortunate idea that the distinctive feature of the *General Theory* was that consumption must be treated exclusively as a function of income – whereas Keynes in fact went out of his way to stress the importance of interest rate changes for the propensity to consume, though 'indirect' in their working, as was seen in the excursus on time preference (see sect. 15.3, p. 177). We therefore believe that the history of the Keynes–Classics literature could well do with a further synoptical attempt.

In Table 17.1 we take up the idea of giving a synopsis of *IS–LM* type developments although we structure the subject matter differently to Young (1987), accepting, however, his idea that Hicks (1937) may be taken to stand also for his inspirers Harrod and Meade.

Table 17.1 A synopsis of Keynes, the 'Classics' and Kaldor

Author	$\dfrac{dw}{dN}$	$\dfrac{dM^3}{dr}$	$\dfrac{dL_2}{dr}$	$\left.\dfrac{dr}{dY_w}\right|_{IS}$	
Keynes (1936)	$0, +\infty$	0	< 0	< 0	
Hicks (1937)	0	0	$0, -\infty$	< 0	
Pigou (1937)	0	> 0	$\geqq 0$	$[\geqq]0$	tp
Kaldor (1937)	0	$0, +\infty$	< 0	< 0	tp

tp: assumption of time preference determined interest rates

In the last column of Table 17.1 we give a synopsis of the views of the respective authors on the existence and the characteristics of an *IS*-curve. There can be little doubt that Keynes and Hicks were in agreement in this regard. Although Pigou was seen above to have initially negated this concept in the context of his application of time-preference analysis, the Kaldorian synthesis seems to have caught up with the other authors. In accepting this reinterpretation, Pigou (1938) follows suit. But as will be seen in more detail below, he insists that the Keynesian case of a falling *IS*-curve is really a special case – although a very plausible one. Nevertheless, it must be pointed out that for Pigou (1938) the *IS*-curve remains quite a different analytical tool than what it was for Keynes and Hicks, since he insisted that in principle its derivative might be either positive or negative as shown in Table 17.1. Even after the Kaldorian synthesis, the main difference remains that in Kaldor's and Pigou's application of the *IS*-curve the Pigovian concept of stationary equilibrium is the analytical base whereas in Keynes and Hicks it is not.

The most salient differences between Keynes and his interpreters and critics must be sought in the realm of monetary analysis. Unfortunately, the secondary literature to the *General Theory* generally overlooks that, for Keynes, 'liquidity preference' refers to the total demand for money, including the transactions demand.[9]

It is therefore really for reasons of liquidity preference that effective demand cannot expand when an economy reaches full employment: in that condition any intended expansion of output and employment must meet immediate reactions in the cost unit resp. the wage unit which then thwart the initial expansionary intention through upward pressure on the interest rate.

In this context we consider as the crucial analytical element which distinguishes Keynes' approach from that of his interpreters to be a 'wage function' given by equ. (17.6) below. This function is an integral part of Keynes' analysis and insofar as this function is relevant, changes in the wage unit do have a high significance for Keynes. The wage function states that the wage unit, far from being constant when employment changes, will be affected by employment itself. This is, so to speak, a reversal of the perspective of wage rate induced changes in employment proposed in the discussion of Pigou's 'simplified model'.

But one should discern between endogenous and exogenous wage changes – i.e. changes in the wage rate which might be seen as following from the structural equation (17.6) proper and those changes which result from a change of a shift parameter (here: ω). The endogenous changes are accepted as a fact of life by Keynes. His issue with the Classics concerns the question whether it is sensible to conduct employment policy by manipulating the shift parameter of the wages function – here denoted by ω:

$$w = w(N, p, \ldots; \omega). \qquad (17.6)$$

Unfortunately, there is little that can be said about this wage function under the heading of authenticity. It is perhaps one of the more serious faults of the exposition of the *General Theory* that such a function is repeatedly alluded to but never stated explicitly. There is a brief definition of a magnitude e_w (*General Theory*, p. 285), an 'elasticity of money wages in response to changes in effective demand in terms of money'. Later Keynes (*op. cit.* pp. 295f) relates the money wage to employment instead, making first the simplifying assumption that under conditions of unemployment it is constant but finally ending up with the statement that 'The wage-unit will tend to rise, before full employment has been reached.' It was only *after* the publication of the *General Theory* that Keynes (JMK, XXIX, p. 284) made it absolutely clear that he intended 'to argue that money wages were as a rule a function of activity ... tending to rise and to fall with the level of employment'. This very argumentation is the one expressed algebraically by equ. (17.6). This function naturally comes into play once the real value of the volume of money is related to the value of the wage unit as is the case in Kaldor's application of the *IS–LM* analysis. It is a distinctive feature of Keynes' analysis, however, to take account of such a function – if not explicitly, at least in the side remarks just discussed.

The first entry in Table 17.1 takes account of this wage function. The limiting case of $+\infty$ stated there is the full employment case in which any attempt to increase employment (through increases in effective demand) must lead to an absorption of such attempted expansion through increases in the wage unit so that employment – and real effective demand – stay constant.

The rest of the entries in Table 17.1 are largely self explanatory after the discussions of figures 16.3 (p. 218) and 17.1 (p. 230): as far as the M^s-column is concerned, recall that it was seen in that context already that the interest dependent money supply function was one of the distinctive features of Pigou (1937) and in Kaldor (1937) – and that Keynes had grave doubts about such an assumption. Nevertheless, this approach is interesting for the 'supply trap' which Kaldor (1937) was seen to have wielded from it and which is denoted in Table 17.1 by the case that $+\infty$ was relevant as a derivative of M^s.

The L_2 column in Table 17.1 denotes the different ideas about interest-dependent money demand. Keynes was perhaps less outspoken concerning the possibility of a liquidity trap than Hicks, so that we attribute the liquidity trap case of a value of the relevant derivative of $-\infty$ to the latter author – although there cannot be a fundamental difference between the two about this matter. Pigou (1937) was seen to be a rather problematic case, however, in trying again to state that everything is possible as far as derivatives are concerned and that Keynesian economics is based on special assumptions.

Summarising the discussion of Table 17.1, it is noteworthy that it produces three alternative liquidity traps:

(i)   There is the well-known L_2-trap stated in the third column, after Hicks (1937) generally known as the hallmark of Keynesian analysis.
(ii) There is the other pathological case in the first column which was seen above to be a 'transactions balances demand trap'. In this case any intended increase in effective demand will result only in increased interest rates and prices. In Hicks (1937) it is the 'classical case'. But it appeared here to be a limited case contemplated in the *General Theory*.
(iii) Finally, there is Kaldor's invention of a M^s-trap as shown in the second column of Table 17.1.

The distinctive features of the 'Kaldorian synthesis' are the acceptance of the time-preference theory of interest and the postulate of interest elastic money supply. Analytically, these two elements are more akin to the approach of Pigou than to that of Keynes. But this question might be studied in more detail with reference to the reactions of the two authors concerned. Before turning to these in sections 17.4 (p. 240) and 17.5 (p. 242) below, we will briefly put together some critical considerations offering themselves under a Keynesian perspective.

17.3.3 Criticising the Kaldorian synthesis under Keynesian perspective

Since the Kaldorian synthesis is built on Pigovian foundations, whatever critical argument was brought forth against the latter must also be suspected of being of relevance for an assessment of the Kaldorian synthesis. This observation directs our attention back to the end of the last chapter where a critical assessment of the 'simplified model' under a Keynesian perspective was discussed. It turned out there that such an assessment was not feasible from the standpoint of a 'Keynesian consensus': apart from Keynes himself, there was just no active participant in this debate – if we abstract from Kahn's unsustainable belief that one could criticise Pigou for his time preference theory of interest but leave his concept of equilibrium untouched.

In the context of the last chapter we saw also that a particular problem for a critical assessment of the Pigovian approach was posed by its ambiguous methodology. This problem does not carry over to a discussion of the Kaldorian synthesis, however, since it is firmly based on the comparative statics of alternative stationary states. This methodological clarification enables the critic to reinspect those elements of Keynes' criticism of the 'simplified model' which might have appeared as having been dismissed on the grounds that they overinterpret the original analytical intentions. Cases in point are Keynes' 'frozen land' criticism of Pigou's stationary economy and his related dismissal of the Pigovian concept of short-run analysis.

It would not have been surprising if there had been a new flurry of critical debate concerning these points after Kaldor (1937, p. 746, n. 2) had claimed that:

> propositions obtained under the [Pigovian 'short-run'] assumption of zero-investment can be applied to cases where investment is assumed to be constant and positive, and *vice versa*

continuing later (*op. cit.* p. 751):

> So far we have assumed, in accordance with Professor Pigou's model, that investments are actually zero in short-period equilibrium. But it is easily shown that the argument is equally applicable to the more general case where investment is assumed to be constant and positive. In that case the critical rate of interest, for any given level of output, will be the one which secures a volume of savings equal to the volume of investments. The rest of the argument follows automatically.

Thus Kaldor here claims that there was nothing peculiar about the Pigovian 'short run' in comparison to Keynes' conception of this analysis – at least as far as comparative statics are concerned.

There was in fact some critical reaction to such ideas along argumentative lines which one could have expected from Keynesian quarters – astonishingly enough from Pigou's economic confidant D. H. Robertson whose critical remarks were quoted in n. 5 on p. 449. But there was no clarification of this point by the Young Keynesians although this really could well be considered as their appropriate concern. Again R. F. Kahn comes to mind as potential actor in view of his criticism of Kaldor's acceptance of the time-preference theory of interest and in view of his suggestion to Keynes not to publish Kaldor's note – and, of course, also in view of his expertise about short-period analysis. But, as noted in ch. 15, although Keynes expressly invited Kahn and his colleagues to participate in the debate after Pigou's (1938) rejoinder to Kaldor (1937), no such debate materialised.

As far as the substance of Kaldor's claim of the virtual equivalence of Keynes' and Pigou's concept of the short run are concerned, it is difficult to accept Kaldor's judgment as long as no exact exposition of these ideas is given – and that never occurred. It seems that as a 'Keynesian short run' he had in mind an analytical situation in which future income is given and does not change but where fixed positive investment goes on. Since $I = S$, the volume of savings is fixed by these investments as well. If now savings are an increasing function of the rate of interest and also an increasing function of income, then there necessarily must be a trade-off between interest rates and income if a fixed level of $I = S$ is to be maintained. Such a trade-off would then give a negative relationship between interest and income – and this is, after all, what the *IS*-curve shows. For this argumentation it would be really immaterial whether it was assumed that investment was fixed at some amount $I > 0$ or at $I = 0$. The former case could be described as the Keynesian one, the latter as the Pigovian one.

In this argumentation the big 'if' is whether savings out of given income really will increase if the rate of interest increases. This would require consumption out of given income reliably to decrease with increased rates of interest. In the excursus to ch. 15 it was seen that this was no problem when $S = 0$ held and present and future consumption were substitutable. In this case – which is the case of the Pigovian equilibrium – the 'wealth effect' of interest rate changes as given by equ. (15.33), p. 191, was zero and the substitution effect dominated so that the desired negative relationship between interest rates and consumption materialised.

But when savings were positive – as is the case in the Keynesian short run – then $S > 0$ generated a positive wealth effect which, in conjunction with a negative substitution effect, led to an uncertain reaction of present consumption on interest rate changes (see equ. (15.31)). Thus we have here a case where the Pigovian case of $S = 0$ generated a determinate result whereas the Keynesian case of $S > 0$ would not do so. Therefore, the two 'short runs' do not seem to be as equivalent as Kaldor believed.

Another theme taken over from Pigou (1937) in the Kaldorian synthesis is the question of interest-dependent money supply. Although the doctrine of a potential 'money supply trap' was used by Kaldor as an instrument of critique against Pigou's argumentation, Keynes' question about its microfoundations is not less relevant. There is a grave problem of plausibility implied in this assumption: it is quite plausible that commercial banks would be delighted to supply facilities for an expansion of current accounts as inside money since this implies gains in seigniorage. But it is *not* plausible that the customers of the commercial banks should have an infinite demand elasticity for credit facilities through which such newly created inside money could come into their hands.

17.4   Keynes' reception of the Kaldorian synthesis

At first sight, Kaldor's (1937) note on Pigou (1937) seems to be just an extension and elaboration of the one by Keynes (1937b): a major complaint of Keynes' was that Pigou failed to make the time preference of the representative individual depend on its real income. What Kaldor (1937) did now in constructing the crucial downward sloping $r = \rho$ *locus* was to make this very assumption. In this, he could be quite confident that this was entirely in the sense of Keynes.

There are personal communications between Keynes and Kaldor in which the two agreed that it was the implication of a horizontal *IS*-curve which constituted the essence of anti-Keynesianism in classical analysis (see JMK, XIV, p. 242). Thus, on the basis of his note about Pigou (1937), Kaldor ventured to propose the following view to Keynes:

> It really is the assumption that savings vary with real income which constitutes the main difference between the classical economics and the Keynesian.

And Keynes was quick to endorse that view (*ibid.*) – seemingly:

> I agree with you that the assumption of saving varying with real income is one of the most essential differences between my system and the classical.

This passage endorses Kaldor's *statement* but it does not endorse his article as a *synthesis*. That becomes clear if the reasoning behind it is inspected. For the classical time preference theory to be assured to hold in the sense of $r = \rho$ – a condition accepted by Pigou *and* by Kaldor – savings must be zero, irrespective of the level of income the stationary state happens to have.[10] This statement holds, of course, also if we have $\rho = \rho(n)$. Thus the *locus* of Kaldor's 'synthesis' is in fact a purely classical affair.[11] The construction of this *locus* constitutes an *internal* criticism of Pigou (1937), not really one which represents Keynes' analytical condition where the rate of savings always is positive. Keynes' just quoted answer should be quite clear for anybody who understood the analytical condition for the time preference analysis.[12] In the quoted correspondence, Keynes obviously had no inclination to go into these subtleties which should be clear to the well-initiated anyhow. To others this reply might seem banal or sibylic. For Kaldor it seemed to be a confirmation that by introducing his $\rho(n)$-function into the original Pigovian scheme he successfully changed a classical model into a Keynesian one. But that clearly is not the case.

A further element of the Kaldorian note was the illustration of a 'Keynes effect' in the framework of an appropriately reinterpreted Hicksian *IS–LM* scheme. In this regard, there was absolutely no difference of opinion between Keynes and Kaldor. In fact, Keynes was somewhat amused to find out later on that

[Pigou was of the] conviction that the theory of the relation between money wages and employment, via the rate of interest, was invented by Kaldor

as he wrote to R.F. Kahn (JMK, XIV, p. 267). He therefore let Pigou know (*ibid.*):

Kaldor is mainly a restatement of my *General Theory* with reference to your special assumptions. These special assumptions make it possible, of course, to reduce it to a simpler form without losing anything. On the other hand, it is really the general case one has to consider, and that it seems to me would be very difficult to treat along those lines.

The first sentence in the latter quote confirms the impression already formulated above, that Keynes accepted the Kaldorian synthesis as a restatement of *Pigou's* analysis. He declared it to be a presentation of the central ideas of the *General Theory* under *Pigovian* assumptions and in the last sentence he cautiously disassociated himself from such a procedure.

As already noted, the *exact* reasons for this disassociation are not explicitly stated in the surviving correspondence. But they may be reconstructed from the wider analytical and literary background. What exactly were then Pigou's 'special assumptions' which Keynes confronted in this quote with 'the general case one has to consider'? The answer to this question must seem to be speculative since Keynes did not elaborate them in this context. On the preceding pages they should have become sufficiently explicit, however. We briefly restate: it is well known that the validity of the $r = \rho$ doctrine – whether ρ is constant or not – depends on very special assumptions indeed. Since the Kaldorian synthesis is based on this doctrine, the old Pigovian assumptions must be invoked for his presentation as well, *vide* stationary states, infinite time horizons, zero savings, constant capital stocks, etc. In view of Keynes' initially intended critique of the Pigovian 'frozen land' assumptions his disassociation from the Kaldorian synthesis must be seen to refer to these underlying assumptions. The problem with these was, however, that Keynes, not having published his intended critique, now had to refer to them in vague and unsubstantiated terms.

Nevertheless, Keynes' evaluation of the Kaldorian synthesis must be seen under the perspective that the crucial critique against the Pigovian analysis would meet Kaldor's synthesis in exactly the same way.

17.5 Pigou and the Kaldorian synthesis

In his rejoinder to Kaldor (1937), Pigou (1938) expressly declared that he accepted 'Mr. Kaldor's main contention'. What exactly was that in Pigou's eyes?

On the basis of the last section one is easily led to believe that with such remarks Pigou wanted to credit Kaldor for the view that money wages and employment are related through a 'Keynes effect type' mechanism. But that was not quite the case.

According to Pigou (1938, p. 134), the 'fundamental matter' in this connection pertained predominantly to time preference:

> The fundamental matter is the relation between aggregate real income and the rate of time preference of the representative man, i.e. the man who, when our model is in equilibrium, desires neither to save or to dis-save.

It was Kaldor's treatment of *this* matter which delighted Pigou. Although Kaldor negated the $r = \rho$ doctrine for time-preference $= const.$, he nevertheless confirmed the relevance of time-preference in a Keynesian context as soon as ρ was presented as a function of real income resp. of employment.

Answering to this type of criticism was comparatively pleasant for Pigou, because that enabled him to muse at length about the 'realistic' characteristics of time preference (*op. cit.* p. 135):

> I can see no reason for thinking that an increase in real income will *raise* any man's rate of time preference ... It follows that, in a mixed community containing men of varying degrees of wealth, a rise in employment, and so in the general level of real income, is likely to be associated with *some* fall in the representative man's rate of time preference, and so in the rate of interest.

If, in the course of such considerations, he conceded that employment and the rate of interest were related to each other, then this was, of course, a major change in comparison to his previous argumentation where he took considerable pains to negate such a relationship.

But there were two positive aspects of this turn of the debate as far as Pigou was concerned:

(i) To be conciliatory on the account of the exact character of time preference enabled him to stick to the analytical principle of time-preference determined interest rates; it saved his analytical approach of 'frozen-land economics', as Keynes intended to apostrophise it, as an accepted tool of economic political analysis.

(ii) To make the character of time preference a question of empirical considerations meant that, in principle, this matter was undecided. In principle, anything may happen with the rate of time preference and hence with the rate of interest when employment and real income change as Pigou (1938, p. 138, §7) was eager to point out in detail.

Thus the Kaldorian synthesis permitted Pigou to claim that the shape of a relationship like the one depicted by the Keynesian *IS*-curve in the real income and interest rate plane is purely a matter of special assumptions about time preference.

18
The Unresolved Conflict

18.1 The premature end of the Keynes–Pigou debate

18.1.1 The seeming success of Keynes

We may now return to the theme set at the beginning of the present part III when, in ch. 14, the problematic unfolding of the Keynes–Pigou debate was mentioned.

Superficially regarded, the results of the debate inspected so far might appear as being not all that unsatisfactory from the Keynesian standpoint. In the crucial question concerning the nexus between the rate of interest and employment, Pigou did give in to Keynes. It was seen that in his rejoinder to Kaldor, Pigou (1938) finally admitted that under normal conditions a decrease in the rate of interest is a *sine qua non* of any positive employment effect of money wage cuts. This was very much contrary to his prior contention concerning the workings of money wage cuts. But this is a result which is very similar to what Keynes tried to establish. Indeed, it emerged in that debate that Pigou came to be regarded as not having intended an attack against Keynes after all.[1]

But if there were no fundamental differences between Keynes and Pigou what then was this debate all about? Richard Kahn tried to persuade Keynes to present his exchange with Pigou as being concerned with 'most *crashing* and *stupid* errors of statement' and not in the least as being one about analytical principles of different schools of thought (italics in the original):

> It is of *highest* importance to make it abundantly clear, so that the casual reader will recognise, that as far as Pigou is concerned the issue is not one of schools of thought but of the most crashing and stupid errors of statement and of reasoning, such as nobody would deny once his eyes were opened.[2]

In this context Kahn (*ibid.*) complained in particular about Pigou's theory of time preference determined rates of interest and wondered whether

Keynes' (1937b) 'own reply brings out the grossness of this error sufficiently forcibly'.

Keynes himself, however, did not consider Pigou's time preference theory of interest as erroneous at all, as was seen above. He rather saw it as a limiting case of his own theory of consumption. In Keynes' own view Pigou's theory was quite correct, once his 'frozen land assumptions' about stationary equilibrium were accepted as appropriate analytical paradigm.

It thus emerges that for Keynes himself the debate was structured quite differently than for R. F. Kahn: in the last resort, it was not concerned with Pigou's 'stupid errors' but with his fundamental methodological approach. But none of Keynes' disciples seconded him in this view. In particular, they were not prepared to see a paradigmatic dividing line between Keynesian and Pigovian short-period analysis. Kaldor, as a then 'extra-mural' Keynesian, was seen to believe that the argument in his note about Pigou (1937) 'holds just as much for the Keynesian short-run ... as for the original Pigou model' (above, p. 233). R. F. Kahn was seen to advise Keynes 'to concentrate on what is important' and to omit those passages which contained his reference to Pigou's 'frozen land' assumption (above, p. 176).

It is predominantly from this perspective that we propose considering the outcome of this debate as unsatisfactory – in spite of its seeming success. In crucial aspects of analytical method, Keynes was in fact unable to influence and to redirect the outlook of his own followers, let alone the outlook of his adversary.

From the standpoint of patterns of scientific debate, the Keynes–Pigou exchange was also rather unsatisfactory, being based in part on hearsay which reached Keynes via Kahn and others, with Pigou himself keeping silent concerning the more substantial matters. As was seen above, Pigou justified his silence concerning Keynes with being considerate for Keynes' ill health.

Another line of justifying avoidance of a direct debate with Keynes was that Pigou claimed that he was unable to mentally grasp what Keynes had written.[3]

Keynes (JMK,XIV, p. 267) seems to have believed in neither of these professed reasons and tried to bring this strange debate to a head by bluntly writing to Pigou:

I am sorry you could not follow my short note. As far as I can see, you now accept all my contentions. And to be told that would have done my health no harm.

Likewise, he wrote to Kahn (*op. cit.* p. 266):

He [Pigou] goes almost out of his way, apart from lack of any reference to me, in the candour and completeness of this retraction.

But again it is important to distinguish between Pigou's comparative statics on the one hand and his analytical framework on the other. It is in the former context that Pigou made his 'retraction'. But if only he had accepted Keynes' position in the latter context, too, the victory of the Keynesian position in this debate would have indeed been a significant one.

There is little reason to believe that Keynes himself believed in a victory in the latter sense. We saw already in ch. 15 that – although retracting his criticism of the Pigovian 'frozen land' assumption – Keynes proclaimed that he continued to believe 'that it represents something at the bottom of his [Pigou's] head' (JMK, XIV, p. 261).[4] And when Keynes (JMK, XIV, p. 267), in a personal letter, responded to Pigou's (1938) acceptance of Kaldor (1937) by pointing out that 'Kaldor is mainly a restatement of my General Theory', he cannot have been under the illusion that with such a statement he could convince Pigou to accept the analysis contained in the *General Theory* as well. In fact, Keynes immediately added that Kaldor's restatement was with reference to Pigou's special assumptions, continuing:

> On the other hand, it is really the general case one has to consider, and that it seems to me would be very difficult to treat along these lines.

This was the agenda which Keynes envisaged for the future rounds of debate with the 'Classics' in general and with Pigou in particular: to consider in a next round of debate *his* 'general case', i.e. to represent the relationship between money wages, interest rates and employment in a *non-stationary* short-period context which may or may not subsequently be shown to merge into a (*quasi*) stationary state under special conditions.[5] He could well expect his Cambridge confidants to follow his much debated agenda with the main focus on short-period income determination. After all, could not his closest collaborators Richard Kahn and Joan Robinson be considered as being at the 'origin of short-period analysis' as Maria Cristina Marcuzzo (1996) was later to argue? But it turned out that such an expectation was based on vain hopes.

18.1.2 Keynes' unfulfilled desiderata

The *General Theory* was seen by Keynes himself not so much as a rigid textbook-type analysis but rather as presenting an agenda for future research and discussion, as Keynes (1937a, p. 111) put it:

> I am more attached to the comparatively simple fundamental ideas which underlie my theory than to particular forms in which I have embodied them ... If the simple basic ideas can become familiar and acceptable, time and experience and *the collaboration of a number of minds will discover the best way of expressing them*. (italics added, GMA)

He could have been quite confident that such future debates and 'collaboration of minds' would in fact materialise. He spent much time and effort in debating economic theoretical questions with young and promising economists of whom he might have expected that they would subsequently also participate in such debates along the lines he believed he had cultivated with them.[6] From his disciples he had Richard Kahn's proclamation of his and others' preparedness to contribute to published debates of 'classical' ideas as expressed by Pigou (1937) 'if you wanted them' – and this Keynes clearly did, suggesting to Kahn that published criticism of Pigou's (1938) rejoinder to Kaldor would be an appropriate opportunity for an outlet of such preparedness.[7] The agenda for such future contributions was suggested by Keynes in the passage just discussed at the end of the last sub-section and, given the close contacts in this matter, its substance if not its wording certainly was known to Richard Kahn.

The fact is, however, that from the 'inner circle' of Keynes' putative disciples at Cambridge virtually nothing was published of which it could be said that it contributed towards optimising the expression of Keynes' original ideas.

There certainly was no shortage of topics for further discussion: it was seen above that there was considerable need for clarifying the microeconomics of the supply of 'inside money' which played a large role in Pigou (1937) and in Kaldor (1937). Furthermore, there was the eminently important but unresolved question of the equivalence of short-period analysis *à la* Keynes and *à la* Pigou. This latter theme was initially brought to paramount attention by Pigou (1936) when he criticised Keynes' supposed muddling of short-period and long-period analysis. It was taken up again by Keynes' with his drafted criticism of Pigou's (1937) 'frozen land' assumption. Especially in view of Richard Kahn's opposition to Keynes on this question one could have expected a clarifying piece of analysis from him. The same set of questions came up again in Kaldor's (1937) article and Keynes asked Kahn directly whether he did not agree that in a Pigovian stationary state Kaldor was correct. Keynes' (1937b) comment was certainly far too short for the general public but editorial prudence asked for utmost brevity. Especially in this case Keynes' erstwhile 'supervisor' could well have been expected to explain in how far this piece 'clearly exposed' the 'root of the differences' between Keynes and Pigou (see above, p. 162) – or whether it failed to do so. Particularly if Kahn felt so strongly that Keynes failed to bring out 'the grossness of this [Pigou's] error sufficiently forcibly' (see above, p. 177), then a reaction might have been expected to be forthcoming from Kahn but it strangely did not do so.

It is interesting how Joan Robinson (1973e, p. 252) – in a publication distributed since 1953 by the 'Students' Bookshop' at Cambridge and later published by her in her *Collected Economic Papers* – wanted to remember that fledgling debate which went on at and around Cambridge in 1936 and 1937:

Keynes starts out in a Marshallian short period. *It certainly does seem rather odd*, at first glance, *to assume zero accumulation when* the very things you are going to talk about – saving and investment – are two aspects of accumulation. A number of smart Alecs have noticed this *anomaly*. (italics added, GMA)

By referring to Keynes' analytical setup as an *'anomaly'* she seems to confirm the plausibility of such criticism, the lineage of which one may well trace to Pigou (1936).[8] But this wording is not so startling as her account of the factual debate at that time (*ibid.*, pp. 252ff.):

Keynes *was* a snob. If you had not been to a good school he cut you ... So he never explained himself, and left the smart Alecs to enjoy their triumph to their heart's content.

Professor Kahn is not a snob. He takes infinite pains to explain a point to you, whatever school you come from. So when the first controversy broke out over the *Treatise on Money* [Keynes, 1930] he reinvented Marx's schema for Simple Reproduction in an endeavour to explain what Keynes was doing. (This was in oral discussion, not published.) (emphasis in the original, GMA)

This seems to be a most remarkable mixture of fact and fiction with regard to the debate it refers to and which is here under consideration. The three volumes (XIII, XIV, XXIX) of Keynes' *Collected Economic Writings* dealing with the background of the *General Theory* bear witness that it cannot be quite true that Keynes 'never explained himself'. But this question and whether 'Keynes *was* a snob' might be left to expert biographers.[9] We also note without further comment that contrary to the above characterisation, it seems that Richard Kahn did *not* go out of his way to explain the grossness of Pigou's error – at least not in writing.

A few things should be registered in this context, however. Firstly: in connection with his *'anomaly'* concerning the stationary state, Keynes *did* try his best to debate the fact that he differed with regard to this particular point. That was the purpose of his rejoinder to Pigou (1937).[10] The irony of Joan Robinson's account is, in this regard, that it was *Keynes* who wanted to bring in a paragraph in which he elaborated why he was against Pigou's 'normal' steady state, and that it was *Kahn* who urged Keynes to cut that out.[11] In her account it seems as if Keynes' preparedness to elaborate was deficient due to his snobbishness. If ever that was a motive for his preparedness to re-explain his point, it certainly was not an issue when the point was to argue publicly against a 'smart Alec' named A. C. Pigou. If erroneously a different impression emerged for Joan Robinson, who, by the way, was most intimately acquainted with Richard Kahn's argumentation, then that might well be connected with a difference in perception due to a basically different research agenda or due to a plain lack of understanding.

Secondly, Keynes' appeal for a 'collaboration of minds' instead of repetitive lecturing and explanatory indoctrination does not appear to us as snobbery but as an expression of an egalitarian academic disposition.

Finally, and this should be registered in particular with regard to what was said under 'firstly' and what will appear in the following part iv: we learn from these passages that after the publication of Keynes (1930), Richard Kahn worked at and orally discussed – supposedly with the above mentioned 'infinite pains' – a translation of Keynes' ideas into what amounted to a Marxian model of 'Simple Reproduction', in other words a model of a stationary state with replacement of the wear and tear of capital.

If we may accept this latter part of Joan Robinson's narrative, the information given by her might be helpful in explaining some phenomena which would appear as being rather strange without knowledge of the background just set out by her. First of all, this passage might make clearer why it was so difficult for Joan Robinson and her colleagues to engage in a 'collaboration of minds' on equal paradigmatic terms with Keynes and why one could think in this camp of Keynes as being a 'snob'. It appears from this passage that the 'normal' context in which they discussed among themselves – if they were not confronted by Keynes with his *anomaly* – was quite a different analytical world than the one he propagated. This obviously did not mean that they were not sympathetic to Keynes' iconoclastic fervour and that they did not feel the fascination which so many other gifted people felt under his influence – at least as long as they were confidants in the gestation process of the *General Theory*. But when the *General Theory* appeared, they had spent the time since controversy set in around Keynes (1930) in translating Keynesian economics into a stationary state world. From this vantage point they seemed to be defenceless against the 'smart Alec' A. C. Pigou (1936) who for years had inhabited quite a similar analytical world of 'stationary states'.

An awareness of the quote just given and its characterisation of Richard Kahn's interpretations of and his own teachings about Keynes (1930) might also help to explain why Joan Robinson (1936) could present her stationary state 'generalisation' of the *General Theory* with such phenomenal speed, having her article published only months after the *General Theory* appeared. If it is true what she said about Kahn's influence on his surroundings, she must have discussed what she thought to be Keynesian ideas in a long period setting years before the *General Theory* appeared. If she was told since the early 1930s and if she thought herself that what Richard Kahn, with 'infinite pain', tried to bring across in terms of a reinvention of Marx's scheme of Simple Reproduction were Keynes' 'true' messages, then that would explain why, in the end, Keynes' analytical desiderata remained unfulfilled among his immediate local surroundings – and why Joan Robinson had such great problems to tell Keynes 'what the point of his revolution really was'.

18.1.3 The Cambridge Keynesians' post-Keynesian agenda

Joan Robinson's just related account of the reception of Keynes' ideas by R. F. Kahn and his associates at Cambridge might be somewhat idiosyncratic and one may well consider them as not quite reliable. But the facts of later publications do speak a similar language as far as analysed problems were concerned. The Cambridge Young Keynesians seem to have been in a particular analytical disposition which aimed at a half-way post between Keynes and Pigou. This disposition became most visible in the work of Joan Robinson (1936, 1937a) herself. We will inspect it in more detail in part IV. After that we will be in a better position to substantiate some of our further speculations about that disposition. But we may briefly go through some of the implications which such an agenda could have had for the unfolding of the Keynes–Pigou debate.

The motivation for the Cambridge Young Keynesians to embark upon a search for an analytical terrain between Keynes and Pigou could have been the conviction that each of these authors was lacking in theoretical elements which the other could offer: Keynes seemed to be blatantly deficient in long-period analysis.[12] But the long period was the analytical homeland of Pigou.[13] On the other hand, Keynes had an interesting theory of the rate of interest which seemed to be superior to Pigou's doctrine of time-preference determined interest rates. Why not combine what is good in both authors?

The problem with such an agenda is, however, that it might involve the actors in inconsistent plots. Thus, if Pigou's classical theory was indeed a special case of the *General Theory*, as Keynes claimed it was, then combining the two theories to some new construction should prove to be a rather difficult task. The task might be facilitated, however, if the two types of theories could be seen as separate entities. It would have been particularly convenient if the link between the Pigovian time-preference theory of interest and the Keynesian consumption function could be severed, or rather, if the existence of such a link could be denied.

In this context, it would therefore have been most convenient if one could believe that Keynes' consumption function had nothing to do with time preference or at least that Pigou's theory of interest was a 'gross error'. The latter belief was documented above to have been held by Richard Kahn, and it also was held by Joan Robinson as will become apparent presently.

This is not to say that Pigovian ideas about time-preference were not discussed at all in post-*General Theory* Cambridge. Indeed, Piero Sraffa who is reported as having agreed with Kahn that the 'fundamental fallacy' of Pigou (1937) was the determination of the rate of interest by the rate of discount of the future (see JMK, XIV, p. 260) seems to have changed his mind at least temporarily – he permitted himself to flirt with the Pigovian theory of interest as we learn from Joan Robinson (1979d, p. xxii):

For Pigou, the interest that rentiers demand governs the rate of profit. This concept is unnatural (though *Sraffa himself flirted with it*). (emphasis added, GMA)

We are not told how long this flirt lasted which Sraffa was believed to have had with the Pigovian theory nor are we told why he rejected it again – if he did so.

We are not even told why exactly Pigou's theory of the rate of profit is to be considered as 'unnatural'. The reader is supposedly expected to remember a relevant passage from the famous article on 'The Production Function and the Theory of Capital' where Joan Robinson (1953/54, p. 121) refers to Pigou's (1935) *magnum opus* on *The Economics of Stationary States* as the source of 'the idea of an ultimate through-going stationary state, in which the rate of profit is equal to the "supply price of waiting".' Against this idea she objects with the following argument (*ibid.*):

There is no a priori presumption in favour of a positive rate. Thus, the rate of interest cannot be accounted for as the 'cost of waiting'.

This form of rejecting the Pigovian theory is now significant for two reasons: First: it does not object to Pigou's idea of a stationary state as such. Secondly: it takes up an argument which was formulated in a comparable way by none other than Pigou (1935, p. 55) himself since it does not in the least touch the logic of this approach:

So far as *a priori* considerations go, it [the rate of discounting future satisfaction] may be anything whatever, 50 per cent per annum or even *minus* 50 per cent per annum. (emphasis in the original)

Indeed, if Joan Robinson's objection were right, and the 'cost of waiting' as expressed by the rate of discounting future satisfaction were negative, then the desire to consume in the present time period would be so strong that the marginal propensity to consume could easily be greater than unity – and not less than unity, as Keynes claimed it was.[14]

Surely the negation of positive rates of discounting future utilities cannot be considered as a very convincing Keynesian argument against Pigou – unless one starts out from the above described conviction that Keynes' consumption function has nothing to do with time preference.

There is the alternative procedure of criticising Pigou's time-preference theory of the rate of interest, namely to attack the Pigovian 'frozen land' assumption of a stationary state which was underlying that analysis. But this approach was not on the agenda of the Cambridge Young Keynesians, as we have had repeated occasion to observe. There seems to be considerable plausibility in the contention that a significant part of their later analysis was a 'pseudo' version of the Pigovian approach.[15]

We conclude that Joan Robinson's remarks concerning Pigou reveal pre-dominanantly that she strongly dislikes the whole idea of Pigou's theory of interest but they do not show where we may find a systematic critique of it. It is no substitute for such a critique just to call that theory 'unnatural'. It is 'natural' for theories to abstract from some aspects of reality and to impute new relationships not obviously apparent in real life. Of course the whole idea is 'unnatural' that the time preferences of rentiers determine the rate of interest and that this rate in turn should be equal to the rate of profit on capital. It is derived as a theoretical proposition in the context of long-period equilibrium and everybody agrees that that is an extremely unlikely state of affairs. Even in his monograph devoted just to this type of equilib-rium, in his *Economics of Stationary States*, Pigou (1935, p. 264) himself admitted: 'Transition rules always; stationariness never; the long run never comes.' But he immediately continued: 'The building is much more than the foundation. But, none the less, to take pains over the foundations is not to waste time.'

Thus, the concept of stationary long-period equilibrium is readily admit-ted to be just a thought-clearing device. The same is claimed for the quasi-stationariness of equilibrium growth as to be found in neoclassical growth theory or in Harrod's 'warranted rate of growth' – and in Joan Robinson's (1956) *Accumulation of Capital*.[16]

This methodological position lies also at the base of the famous 'Cambridge controversies in the theory of capital' – and it is Joan Robinson who must be considered as the 'founding mother' of this debate.[17] It is true that eventually Joan Robinson (1973d, p. 6) referred to this debate as being a 'tiresome controversy' which 'has to do with abolishing time'. When she goes on to mention:

> For a world that is always in equilibrium there is no difference between the future and the past, there is no history and there is no need for Keynes

then her views appear to be a late echo of Keynes' frozen and analogy of the Pigovian economy. But it is a very late echo indeed. In the following part IV of our enquiry we will see that originally Joan Robinson (1937a) was prepared to go to Pigou's extreme to set net investment equal to zero when she attempted a long-period extension of the *General Theory*.

18.1.4 Conclusions and speculations

It seems that the younger generation of Cambridge economists – although supposedly Keynesian in their theoretical orientation – for quite a long time accepted the methodological outlook set out in Pigou's (1935) *Economics of Stationary States*. This type of economics supplied the paradigm on which Pigou's (1937) 'simplified model' of employment was based. The young Cambridge economists R. F. Kahn and D. Champernowne were implicated in this position by more or less critical assistance to Pigou with this particular work as we learn from his grateful acknowledgement of their contributions to Pigou (1935, p.v). We will see in more detail below in which way Joan Robinson (1937a) is to be related to Pigou's methodological position. But insofar as there is an implicit methodological agreement between them, there emerges some sense from Kahn's above quoted communication to Keynes, to the extent that Pigou believed that his 'simplified model' was more a contribution to a controversy with Joan Robinson than with Keynes.

We conclude from the above discussion that the superficial impression is unfounded that the debate initiated by Pigou (1937) resulted in a vindication of Keynes' analysis. If Keynes himself made such statements to Pigou and to Kahn, they clearly must be taken with a pinch of salt. They may be understood as a provocation for further substantial debate. Such a debate did not materialise, however. Why that was so must appear as rather mysterious. After all, Kahn and Joan Robinson knew about the substantial complaints which Keynes had against Pigou's 'simplified model' but which he refrained from publishing – on their very advice. They knew also that after they had kept silent in the first round of comments to Pigou (1937), Keynes expected them to come forth with comments to Pigou (1938) – which they did not.

Any explanation for this peculiar course of the post-*General Theory* debate must be speculative since the non-participants did not explain their abstention but rather – in the case of R. F. Kahn – gave the impression of a general eagerness to participate. There is an admittedly kaleidoscopic character to our attempt to substantiate the claim that there was a Pigovian undercurrent in the approach of the Young Keynesians. In the case of Joan Robinson (1937a) an affinity to Pigovian concepts of equilibrium may be clearly documented, however, since the basic structure of her model was largely similar to that of Pigou (1937) as remains to be seen in part IV.

In the case of Kahn and Champernowne the material published until now permits only a rather indirect argumentation concerning analytical links with Pigou. There emerges some implication with the Pigovian position from their assistance in the writing of his *Economics of Stationary States* (Pigou, 1935). A further implication in the Pigovian view of economic analysis might be constructed from the fact that Kahn never found a reason to contemplate the difference between Keynesian and Pigovian conceptions of short-period analysis although – due to the topic of his fellowship dissertation – he has to be considered as the short-period expert among the Cambridge economists. He certainly did not side with Keynes in this field of debate.

As far as the later Young Keynesian N. Kaldor was concerned, we have seen that he strongly believed in the basic equivalence of Pigovian and Keynesian conceptions of short-period analysis. Certainly he should not be expected to be particularly likely to come up with proving the contrary.

Part of Keynes' agenda for the critique of Pigovian 'frozen land' economics reappeared eventually among the once-Young Keynesians. But this happened only in the last years of Joan Robinson's life when she insisted on the distinction between the concepts of 'logical time' as it is to be found in the capital-theoretic debates on the one hand and 'historical time' which supposedly may be found in the *General Theory*. But this was just a reformulation of an old agenda and not yet its enactment.

It is not necessary to be excessively speculative in interpreting the past debates, however, in order to come to the conclusion that one of the important themes which Keynes intended to set in his original comment to Pigou (1937), namely the question of the appropriate analytical formulation of the short period, was never taken up systematically by the Cambridge Keynesians.

18.2 The Pigovian diminuendo

Pigou repeatedly returned to questions of classical economics and related concepts of equilibrium, uncontested in his utterances by Keynes who stuck to his intention to leave these matters to his supposed followers but also persistently uncontested by the latter.[18]

Pigou's (1941) *Employment and Equilibrium* is particularly noteworthy in this context. This book is a thorough restatement of his theory of employment and as such it replaces the *Theory of Unemployment* which Pigou (1941, p. vii) felt to be 'still ... defective in many ways'. It is quite apparent that in the meantime Pigou benefited considerably from the controversy with Keynes,[19] and in the preface he gives due acknowledgement for this to his adversary. It would go beyond the scope of this inquiry, however, to scrutinise now the exact changes to be found in Pigou's employment theoretic views. Instead, we will concentrate on drawing our conclusion from an issue already discussed above, namely the concept of short period equilibrium employed in Keynesian resp. Pigovian analysis.

It was seen above that in the initial phase of his reaction to Keynesianism, i.e. in the presentation of his 'simplified model', Pigou tried to avoid the impression that he intended to discuss Keynes' analytical 'stuff'. This has now changed and he ventures (p. 43) an explicit suggestion for the 'sort of equilibrium [which] is the subject matter of Keynes' General Theory'. According to Pigou (1941, p. 43) this type of equilibrium is a 'short-period flow equilibrium' which he characterises in the following way:

> short-period flow equilibrium ... can never exist unless there is also the
> long-period flow equilibrium of a stationary state ... In using the
> concept, what we do in effect is to postulate all the conditions implicit
> in long-period flow equilibrium, save only that, instead of taking the

rate of investment to be nil, we take it to be positive and constant; and we then ignore the reactions which the existence of this positive rate of investment evokes in the other parts of the economic system.

The meaning of the terms in this quote are straightforward: 'long-period flow equilibrium' requires constancy of all economic flows and 'this condition cannot be satisfied except in the classical stationary state' (*op. cit.* p. 42). The term 'short-period flow equilibrium' then signifies a 'pseudo or hypothetical flow equilibrium' (*ibid.*) which differs from the former in the way described in the quote, namely by an ephemeral inclusion of investment in an analytical set-up characterised by the exclusion of this particular economic flow.

Thus, Pigou reiterates here the concept of 'short period' analysis as developed in the context of his 'simplified model' and attributes this concept to the *General Theory*. This is remarkable because Pigou could be expected to have known – and stated – that this was not at all the view taken by Keynes. The methodological position which is described in this quote is really the one of Kaldorian synthesis – and we know that Keynes communicated to Pigou that he considered Kaldor (1937) to be a rendering of the *General Theory* under Pigovian conditions but not under the ones intended by Keynes himself.

But there is really not much point in bickering over whether Pigou knowingly misrepresented Keynes or not. This episode in the Keynes–Classics debate turned out to be rather inconsequential for the understanding of the differences between Keynes and Pigou. For the general public, the Keynes–Classics issue seemed already to be settled by the – by then – well-established conventional interpretation along Hicksian lines. At least from across the Atlantic, this issue seemed to be predominantly one of modes of expression, not one of substance. As Samuelson (1941, p. 552) put it in his review of Pigou (1941):

> Professor Pigou's book ... reveals with remarkable force the extent to which the Keynesians all along have been speaking classical prose, at the same time that 'classicists' have thought in Keynesian poetry.

It seems that the subtleties of the differences of short-period analysis *à la* Keynes and *à la* Pigou were never taken up by the economic community – be it now Keynesians like Richard Kahn, Nicholas Kaldor or Joan Robinson or be it neoclassicists like Paul Samuelson.

Pigou (1943) returned to the issue of clarifying the characteristics of the 'classical stationary state' in response to some prompts to be found in Alvin Hansen's (1941) *Fiscal Policy and Business Cycles*. The central issue was again concerned with the efficacy of nominal wage policy as a means for securing full employment in a stationary economy which is in long-period equilibrium. Similarly, as before, Pigou defines such an economy as one where investment is zero. But, taking a 'long-run' view, capital is now variable and endogenous – *nota bene* at zero net investment. We are here in an anti-world to the Keynesian one where investment is variable and endogenous, but capital is constant due to an absence of capacity effects in the short run.

In this strangely constructed world, Pigou (1943) discusses once more the old topic inherited from his previous discussion of the 'simplified model' and supposedly settled when Pigou (1938) sided with the Kaldorian synthesis, namely whether money wage reductions may increase employment when the rate of interest does not change. Apart from the endogeneity of capital, the new argument now advanced by Pigou (1943) is that the propensity to consume might depend on the real money holdings of individuals. Thus, although the rate of interest might be in some trap or other on the money market, nevertheless, effective demand might change so as to lead to an increase in employment due to a decrease in the level of money wages, and hence in the price level – and hence an increase in the real value of a given volume of outside money.

We have here a type of argument well known in later macroeconomic literature: Collard (1981, p. 119) sees this analysis as the *locus classicus* for the 'Pigou effect'. But the Pigou effect of standard macroeconomics refers to a Keynesian world with positive investment going on and the stock of capital being exogenously given. In Pigou (1943) we do not have this world at all as was just pointed out.

18.3   The loss of the Pigovian perspective

Pigou must be credited with having stated quite clearly that insofar as he made definite statements about employment political relationships, he was referring to a stationary economy. A case in point is his original exposition of the 'Pigou effect'. As just seen, he expressly derived the relevance of this effect only in stationary and long-period conditions. When the question of the existence of a 'Pigou effect' is discussed in the context of 'Lord Keynes's alternative story', Pigou (1945, p. 24) thought it to be 'important to realize that for practice the issue is not a very important one'.

This clarity was not maintained in the subsequent reception of the 'Pigou effect' in the course of the Keynes–Classics debate. If we take the presentation of this matter in Leijonhufvud (1968) as indicative for the orthodox outcome of this debate, then we must consider it as quite significant that here all distinctions of analytical time periods between the 'Keynes effect' and the 'Pigou effect' have disappeared.[20] This unawareness of the particular temporal construction associated with the Pigou effect survived up to the present. Thus, Professor Knoester (1988, p. 92) writes that:

In 1943 Pigou launched his famous counterattack on Keynes ... Although Pigou himself did not elaborate this point, the policy implications of his effect were far-reaching. It provided a rationale for governments not to intervene in a depressed economy but to rely on 'automatic' recovery.

This characterisation of what is believed to be the essence of Pigou's effect is interesting because it reveals a number of misconceptions:

(i)   The discussion of the Pigou effect was stated by its author not to be a counterattack against Keynes, but to be a correction of the supposedly erroneous perception of the 'Classics' presented in Hansen (1941).

(ii) Pigou expressly stated that for 'practice' the issue raised by him was not a very important one, as was just quoted above.

(iii) The question dealt with, according to Pigou (1943, p. 344) was whether a classical 'full-employment *stationary state* is possible and, *if an appropriate wage policy is adopted*, will be secured' (italics added, GMA). Thus, it is not about real life 'depressions and recoveries' as was believed in the above quote. It is about the 'classical stationary state' – as Pigou's (1943) very title appropriately states. And it is not about 'automatic' changes in employment but about such changes in employment as might be induced by money wage *policy*.

Even during Pigou's lifetime there seems to have occurred a general loss of awareness for the original Pigovian analytical framework. This seems to have gone so far that Pigou himself eventually was unable to recognise theories that passed under his name. Anecdote has it that Pigou himself once asked Kahn, at dinner, to explain to him the workings of the 'Pigou effect'.[21]

This anecdote might, of course, alternatively be understood as illustrating not so much the loss of an authentic Pigovian analytical perspective by academic economists in general. It might just show the tragic loss of Pigou's mental ability. We do not think that this is a relevant consideration in the present context, however. The analytical approaches cultivated by Keynes and Pigou – sometimes by skilfully writing at cross purposes – were indeed so little received in modern macroeconomic discussion that one could well believe that the old combatants eventually had to ask the younger participants for their view of the current scenario because the older ones felt deprived of the battlegrounds they intended to stand upon.

This development was far more consequential for the analytical aspirations of Keynes who intended to lay the foundation for a new paradigm than it was for those of Pigou who offered a refinement of an old one.[22] It lead to the virtual abandonment of Keynes' original research programme, as we will argue in the following chapter.

19
The Evaporation of Keynes' Analytical Aspiration

The main conclusion to be drawn from our inspection of the unfolding of the Keynes–Pigou debate is that in spite of some statements to the contrary made by Keynes and Pigou,[1] Keynes' analytical approach did not replace the old Pigovian one – neither as far as the work by Pigou himself was concerned nor as far as the work by Keynes' followers was concerned. Instead, Keynes' analytical program disintegrated in the hands of its supposed guardians.

At the later stages of the Keynes–Classics debate, this conclusion might not have been particularly controversial with prominent members of Keynes' former entourage themselves. But insofar as they published their opinions about the unsatisfactory reception of Keynes' analysis in their later years, they tended to put the blame for the stagnation of Keynesian economics on the long-established 'neoclassical synthesis' of Keynes and the Classics, a combination of 'Hicksian' *IS–LM* analysis with a macroeconomic neoclassical production function.

The *IS–LM* scheme was severely criticised by Keynes' former pupils R. F. Kahn and Joan Robinson. Thus, in *The Making of Keynes' General Theory*, Kahn (1984, p. 249) voiced the belief that 'the *IS–LM* scheme has very seriously confused the development of economic thought' and Joan Robinson crystalised her contempt for the neoclassical synthesis by repeatedly referring to its proponents as 'Bastard Keynesians'.

There is a grain of truth in criticism of the *IS–LM* scheme insofar as the *LM* part of the scheme clearly is unKeynesian in leaving out the changes in money demand generated by changes in income associated with movements along the *IS*-curve when the rate of interest changes. But this fault can be remedied by replacing the *LM*-curve analysis through a LIS-curve analysis, as we argued in the reconstruction of the Keynes effect in sect. 16.1 on p. 200 above.

In the strictest sense the *IS–LM* scheme thus may indeed be considered as being 'wrong' as far as authenticity is concerned. But Warren Young's (1987) study documented that the historical origin of the *IS–LM* scheme might be

258

seen to lie not only with the later Walrasian neo-classicist J. R. Hicks (1937) but maybe at least as much with Roy Harrod (1937a) and James Meade (1937), who themselves were intimately associated with the development of the *General Theory*. Young (1987, p. 173) even claims that in the light of the evidence supplied by him 'only one conclusion can be drawn about the originators of the *IS–LM* approach: the *IS–LM* interpretation of Keynes's *General Theory* should be termed Harrod–Hicks–Meade *IS–LM*.'

But if important members of the 'inner circle' of Keynes' pupils themselves were so strongly involved in the development of this analytical tool, then an *IS–LM* oriented line of critique against established orthodox Keynesianism – although not without some justification – cannot be considered as being so devastating for orthodox Keynesianism as some of the Cambridge Keynesians seemed to believe.[2]

In order to put into better relief the specific points of our conclusion, it might be helpful to discuss it with reference to a remark made by Luigi Pasinetti (1983, p. 207) – a stoutly Cambridge post-Keynesian participant in the Cambridge controversies in the theory of capital – who stated that 'on a purely theoretical level, Keynes started a process which was nipped in the bud. His work was not continued.' In a sense, this is exactly the lesson we believe to be the one to be drawn from inspecting the Keynes–Pigou debate of 1937/38 and from the discouragement and detachment which may be documented as far as Richard Kahn and Joan Robinson are concerned.

But this is, of course, not quite the context in which Pasinetti would like to see his statement. Thus, we must hasten to add that although we agree with Pasinetti's diagnosis, we disagree with his anamnesis when he continues by stating (*ibid.* p. 208) that:

> the direct pupils of Keynes here [in Cambridge, England] have always ... determinately insisted on Keynes's irreconcilability with traditional economics; but they have not been listened to.

We stated already – and in part IV we will enlarge on this point – that it was Joan Robinson's (1937a) intention to transpose Keynes' short-period analysis into a long-period context in order to 'generalise' the *General Theory*. Joan Robinson (1973e) herself wanted to see these endeavours in the context of Marxian models of simple and expanded reproduction and from that intended perception one might deduce an anti-'traditional' intention. To this commentator her research programme seems to stand more in the tradition of A. C. Pigou and his ideas about a stationary or a quasi-stationary state.

Thus, in this regard, Joan Robinson's research programme – and she was one of Keynes' most prominent direct pupils who implicated Richard Kahn, Roy Harrod and at least in a programmatic sense also Piero Sraffa – does not quite fit Pasinetti's recollection.

Furthermore, we saw already that the synthesis between Keynes and Pigou as proposed by Kaldor (1937) resulted in a reconciliation of Keynesian results with Pigovian economics in a way which was welcomed by Pigou but not so much by Keynes. And we documented that Kahn not only did not second Keynes' claim that Keynesian short-period analysis was irreconcilable with Pigovian 'frozen land' economics, he even persuaded Keynes 'to concentrate on what is important' and to leave the issue whether there is a fundamental difference in the short-period conceptions between Keynes and Pigou. Thus there clearly were areas where the Cambridge Keynesians were not quite that adamant about the irreconcilability of Keynes' and orthodox analysis as one might believe at first on the basis of the last quote.

But there is an additional sense in which we would like to take exception to Pasinetti's claim concerning 'Keynes' irreconcilability with traditional economics'. There were areas – though different from the stationary-state ones just mentioned – where Keynes himself by no means considered his own economics to be totally 'irreconcilable' with the classical one. The crucial point on which he insisted was that the latter is a special case of the former – and this is quite a different matter. Thus, one of the few criticisms which Keynes (JMK, XIV, pp. 85f.) did articulate against the version of *IS–LM* analysis proposed by Harrod (1937a) was *not* that it was too close to orthodox economic thinking, but that it failed to show how it linked up with it: 'You do not show how in conditions of full employment ... my theory merges in the orthodox theory.' Why did Keynes insist on such a seemingly strange agenda, namely that his readers should keep in mind how close the *General Theory* is to 'orthodox theory'? Because only if it is shown that the 'orthodox theory' is *contained*, is included, in his theory can it be claimed to be truly *general* one.

We conclude from this and similar statements that in his own view, classical economics was indeed reconcilable with Keynes' economics – albeit only in a limited sense devoid of much practical relevance, or, as Keynes (1936, p. 378) put it in the 'Concluding Notes' of the *General Theory*:

> Our criticism of the accepted classical theory of economics has consisted not so much of finding logical flaws in its analysis as in pointing out that its tacit assumptions are seldom or never satisfied, with the consequence that it cannot solve the economic problems of the actual world.

Nevertheless, in spite of his rebuke of the classical approach, it is part of the criticism of the Classics implied by Keynes that he intended to explicate the peculiarity of the assumptions which would make his own analysis collapse into a classical one.

In our view it therefore means to deprive Keynes of his specific method if one had the programme of 'always determinately insisting' that his analysis is irreconcilable with the traditional one.

What has just been said was made operational in the above discussion by going through the analytical motions of stating the Keynesian consumption function in time preference theoretic terms in such a way that under special conditions Pigou's time-preference theory of interest was seen to be indeed a special case of Keynes' analysis. Thereby we supplied the analytical background for the exchange between Keynes and Kahn in which the latter thought that Pigou committed a 'gross error' by utilising the time-preference theory of interest while Keynes thought that Pigou was quite correct given his 'frozen-land assumptions'.

But Keynes limited his borderline affinity to the Classics not only to the realm of theoretical considerations. In the concluding notes from which we just quoted he even went so far as to praise the merits of the nineteenth–century 'Manchester System' of individualistic free enterprise – once 'our central controls succeeded in establishing an aggregate volume of output corresponding to full employment as nearly as practicable' (*General Theory*, p. 378).

As George Feiwel (1989a, p. 44) observed, these passages provoked Joan Robinson (1979b, pp. 127–8) to complain about such an 'ill-considered remark' and to remark herself that: 'Here is the bastard Keynesian theory in its purest form.' But if indeed the purest form of bastard Keynesianism may be found in Keynes himself, then it is at least doubtful whether a supposedly illegitimate brainchild 'neoclassical synthesis' could not really put a legitimate claim to part of Keynes' analytical legacy.

We consider it noteworthy that it was in the context of a review of Joan Robinson's life work that Feiwel (1989a, p. 43) noted that 'the germ of the synthesis' may indeed be found in Keynes, continuing in a footnote (*ibid.*, p. 109, n. 29):

Had Keynes actually worked out such a synthesis it naturally would have been one of Marshall–Pigou–Keynes rather than the Walras–Hicks –Samuelson–Keynes variety that eventually emerged.

It is debatable whether a significant difference between these varieties of neoclassical theory does exist.[3] If we accept such a difference for the time being as a working hypothesis, then we may infer from this observation that the actual 'neoclassical synthesis' indeed might be regarded as being illegitimate Keynesianism on its neoclassical side. But this does not mean that any neoclassical synthesis must be so regarded. And we see our opinion confirmed that if an economic theoretical synthesis managed to link up Keynes analytically with his fellow Cantabridgians Marshall and Pigou, showing in which sense their analyses are special cases of the one of Keynes, then the resulting exercises might be considered as the 'natural' neoclassical consequence of Keynes' analytical programme. In fact, we documented that this type of approach, i.e. one which explicitly shows how Keynes' analysis merges with the classical one under conditions of full employment, was the one towards which Keynes tried to direct his 'pupil' Harrod.

In actual fact, the Cambridge Keynesians did not follow that type of programme at all. According to a programmatic statement made by Joan Robinson (1978, reprint, p. 213), she considered the task of the post-Keynesians to do the very thing which Keynes was *not* interested in:

> Sraffa had shown a draft [of *Production of Commodities by Means of Commodities*, GMA] to Keynes in 1928. Keynes evidently did not make much of it and Sraffa, in turn, never made much of the *General Theory*. It is the task of the post-Keynesians to reconcile the two.

Under the criterion of authenticity this programme certainly cannot be considered as being a convincing agenda: if *neither* Keynes *nor* Sraffa was interested in each other's work, both knowing what the respective work *was*, why on earth should it be the task of either a Keynesian or a Sraffian to 'reconcile' the two? The reason Joan Robinson (1978, reprint, p. 214) gives – if it really is a *reasoned* argument – is:

> The post-Keynesians must make use of Sraffa to build up a type of long-period analysis which will prevent neoclassical equilibrium from oozing back into the General Theory.

But why must one be so wary about 'neoclassical' analysis? Keynes was not in the least against neoclassical theory as such – be it the theory of production or the theory of time preference. Indeed he was quite convinced that in long-period equilibrium of the Pigou (1937) type, his own theory logically – but unrealistically – merged with that of Pigou. It was Keynes' very programme and his desire that it is shown that 'my theory merges in the orthodox theory' as was just quoted on p. 260. If Joan Robinson's programme was to *prevent* showing this by 'reconciling' Keynes with Sraffa, then this cannot possibly claim to have Keynes' authentic blessing. If, as Pasinetti was quoted as saying on p. 259 above, the Cambridge Keynesians 'always ... determinately insisted on Keynes's irreconcilability with traditional economics' then it was they who 'nipped in the bud' a theoretical intention which was important to Keynes.

An additional objection against Joan Robinson's programme can be articulated, namely, that the *intended* anti-orthodox impetus which a Sraffa-oriented approach to Keynes was supposed to have, turned out to be no alternative at all. It has repeatedly been pointed out by leading neoclassicists that Sraffa did not really offer an alternative to established economic theory. Thus, being asked by Feiwel whether he thought that Sraffian economics was a new paradigm, Arrow (1989, p. 163) declared that Sraffa did discover an interesting but 'a perfectly good neoclassical theorem', namely that under certain conditions there exists a 'wage-profit rate frontier' which is a straight line. And Arrow continues:

> What he [Sraffa] uses it for is to say, 'well, you have this frontier, and therefore the point on it is undetermined'. Of course, all he has done is to drop an equation. And this story comes back to the discount rate again.

Here, we have again the theme, once set out by Keynes in ch. 19 of the *General Theory*, of an analysis being enabled only because the system under discussion is not debated to its logical end of stating the 'missing equation'.

But there is a third criticism against a Sraffa (1960)-oriented reception of Keynes. It comes from Joan Robinson (1979c, p. 135) herself. Its essence is that whatever can be said in the context of that argumentation, it can not possibly have any direct relevance with regard to evidence:

> [Sraffa's] *Production of Commodities by Means of Commodities* (1960) is set up in terms of long-period relationships in the sense that inputs are correctly adjusted to outputs and a stock of means of production is being operated by a given labour force at its designed level of utilisation. A long-period model cannot be directly confronted with evidence because any actual situation is affected by short-period influences, such as the state of effective demand and the distribution of money income, which occupy the forefront of the picture.
>
> (Looking back now, I see that in the tumultuous years when Keynes' *General Theory* was being written, Piero [Sraffa] never really quite knew what it was that we were going on about.)

Actually, this quote contains *two* arguments which Joan Robinson directs against Sraffa. In the upper part, it substantiates the methodological argument that his 1960 model is immune against evidence. This argument in turn could now be developed further into a positivistic critique based on its lack of *falsifiability*. In addition, it could be the basis for stressing a *lack of policy relevance* of such a model and this is probably more the direction intended by Joan Robinson.

But the really astonishing (fourth) argument against Sraffa which is contained in this quote is a biographical one. The last remarks (set aside in parentheses by Joan Robinson) show a surprising *personal* disassociation with Sraffa. He is characterised here as having been 'really quite' ignorant of the goings on among a group not detailed in its composition, but from Joan Robinson's 'we' one may infer that it is the 'legendary' (Patinkin, 1977, p. 6) Cambridge 'circus' which stood at the beginning of Keynes' transition from the *Treatise* to the *General Theory*. Its main members were

Richard Kahn, James Meade, Piero Sraffa, Joan Robinson, Austin Robinson 'and others on occasion' (Patinkin, 1977, p. 6). Thus, as a prominent member of the Cambridge 'circus', Sraffa had a privileged position to understand better than most other economists of his time the issues associated with the formulation of the *General Theory*. Indeed, as Moggridge (1973, p. 341) put it:

> in the winter and spring of 1931 the 'Circus' had in its hands most of the important ingredients of the system which was ultimately to appear in the *General Theory*.

Thus, what Joan Robinson seems to be stating in that sentence is that Sraffa sat regularly in the hottest seminar debates which led to the *General Theory* and nevertheless he was essentially ignorant of what was going on.

One may have doubts about the supposed 'birth date' of the *General Theory*. Patinkin (1977, p. 15) believed that it was not until the end of 1933 that Keynes had a full grasp of his novel concept of effective demand and that *that* is the 'true' date of the transition from the *Treatise* to the *General Theory*.

But this alternative dating makes Joan Robinson's comment on Sraffa even more devastating from the Keynesian point of view than it would have been if it referred only to Sraffa's ignorance in the Cambridge 'circus'. We will argue below that there is a good reason for Don Patinkin's dating, because in the final form the *General Theory* is shaped to a considerable extent by Keynes' reaction to Pigou (1933). That could take place only after publication of that book after April 1933 (the date of its preface). Now, from the preface of that book we know that Pigou (1933, p. vii) acknowledged that 'Mr. Sraffa' had read 'Parts I and Parts II' of that book as a 'service' for the author. But we know already from the above discussion of the Pigovian model of his 'Part II' that this model was really the basis of Keynes' critique of Pigou as representative of Classical analysis. Thus, Sraffa seems to have been the only person who not only had a privileged position in the Cambridge 'circus' of the Young Keynesians but he also knew the – from Keynes' point of view – strategic parts of Pigou (1933) from the manuscript. In addition, according to the recollection of Austin Robinson (1977, p. 29):

> He [Piero Sraffa] was in one sense always in the thick of the work going on around Keynes. As a member of King's College (he was not yet in those days a Fellow of Trinity) he saw more of Keynes than most of us did.

If that person got an 'F' from Joan Robinson in 1979 for his failing to understand what was 'going on' among the Young Keynesians 'in the tumultuous years when Keynes' *General Theory* was being written', then this is a rather saddening comment on Keynesian discipleship at Cambridge.

In any case Joan Robinson's disassociation with Sraffa, published in 1979, leaves this reader wondering whether it links up with or whether it contradicts the Robinsonian programme, just quoted on p. 000, that it is the 'task' of post-Keynesians to reconcile Keynes as author of the *General Theory* on the one hand and Sraffa who had shown him a draft of Sraffa (1960) on the other. If because of its very logical structure Sraffa's approach cannot be confronted 'directly' with phenomena like 'effective demand', how then should the post-Keynesian agenda be enacted, if the concept of 'effective demand' is one of Keynes' main concerns?

Any ambiguity in this regard must be the more disturbing as the stated ignorance which dawned on Joan Robinson only when looking back 'now' – in 1979 – extends to the very time of the writing of the *General Theory*, that is to the years of 1931–5. The above passage leaves the reader with the disturbing impression that – at least in Joan Robinson's judgement – the post-Keynesians agenda might have been drawn up lacking a realisation which appeared only long after the decisive theoretical battles had been fought – and which was lost in the view of some post-Keynesians. It is therefore of considerable interest to see in more detail what Joan Robinson herself was 'going on about' in the theoretical territory between Keynes, the 'Classics' and Sraffa at the time of the writing of the *General Theory*.

In part IV we will see that there are interesting similarities between Sraffa (1960)-type analysis on the one hand and Joan Robinson's (1936) first attempts to 'generalise' Keynes in a long-period – as it turns out to be – Pigovian setting. We therefore propose to postpone a fuller assessment of the merits and demerits of Joan Robinson's 'Cambridge-Keynesian' approach until we have reconstructed her basic employment theoretical model.

Part IV

A Post-Keynesian Dilemma: Keynesian Employment and Pigovian Equilibrium in Joan Robinson's 'Keynesian Extension'

20
Problems and Methods

In the following chapters of part IV we intend to shift the focus from Keynes to the 'post-Keynesian' Joan Robinson.[1] We will investigate her attempt at 'generalising' the *General Theory* in an essay of 1937 on 'The Long-Period Theory of Employment'. In the closing passages of part III we had a brief preview of our motivation for such an extension of our analytical perspective. Let us briefly recollect some of the observations which have bearing on our present subject.

In the above discussion it emerged that prominent disciples of Keynes were remarkably silent when it came to defending his newer ideas in controversies with his 'classical' adversary A. C. Pigou. It is ironic and should not go unnoticed that posterity traditionally associated these very disciples with the development and defence of the arguments of the *General Theory*. We named Roy Harrod, Richard Kahn and Joan Robinson. But not only were they silent on matters which Keynes considered to be very important as far as his own approach was concerned. We supplied quotes from Richard Kahn and Joan Robinson documenting that in some of these questions they tried to silence even Keynes himself in trying to discourage him from reacting to Pigou. Were such attempts motivated just by consideration for Keynes' frail health?

In the following chapters of part IV it is our intention to find a few pointers for analytical reasons why some of Keynes' followers behaved in this way. This means that we will try to construct differences – even incompatibilities – in the respective paradigms of Keynes and his supposed followers.

Let us stress here, however, that it is *not* our intention to deny that Keynes' disciples did have an important influence on the development of his arguments while he wrote the *General Theory*. There are many passages bearing witness that they did: in the *General Theory* R. F. Kahn is given due credit for having developed the idea of the 'multiplier'. Roy Harrod is named as author of Keynes' savings-investment diagram on p. 180 of the *General Theory*. Joan Robinson is gratefully mentioned by Keynes in the preface to that book. Even Piero Sraffa, whom Joan Robinson remembered as having been rather unsympathetic about the *General Theory*, is quoted there (p. 223), namely as calculator of a 'wheat-rate of interest'.

But in post-*General Theory* communications between Keynes and his disciples there are signs of estrangement. This estrangement went beyond their merely refraining from seconding Keynes in his exchanges with Pigou. Sometimes it was articulated in vague complaints by Keynes about 'the young ones who have not been properly brought up'.[2]

Sometimes Keynes' disassociation from 'the young ones' was more outspoken than this, as in particular in a comment about Harrod's (1939) 'An Essay in Dynamic Theory':

As regards Harrod's article ... I do not think there has ever been an article about which I have corresponded with the author at such enormous length in the effort to make him clear up doubtful and obscure points ...

In the final result, I do not find myself in agreement.[3]

Maybe it was this estrangement which led Keynes' disciples to claim later that occasionally they had difficulties in telling Keynes what *his* revolution 'really' was (see above p. 14). But Keynes must have felt quite similarly towards them: that in spite of their long discussions with him, they were unable to grasp the significance of his concept of 'effective demand' and of his disassociation from the 'frozen-land' economics of long-period equilibrium.

It is somewhat ironic that Joan Robinson later repeatedly claimed that one of the more important inspirations for her post-Keynesian endeavours came from the very article of Harrod's from which Keynes expressly disassociated himself in the quote just given.[4] This is ironic not only because it makes a piece of analysis renounced by Keynes appear to be the vehicle for the supposed propagation of Keynesian ideas. Such remarks are also somewhat ironic in that they attribute to Harrod (1939) an inspiration which – in the 'Simple Reproduction' variant – Joan Robinson had herself, or whoever inspired her at that time[5] – long before the publication of Harrod's article.

In subsequent years there seems to have emerged an increasing awareness among economists, however, that the prime source of the type of post-Keynesianism which Joan Robinson stood for was not so much Harrod's 1939 article, as Joan Robinson sometimes seemed to claim. It was rather her own 'The Long-Period Theory of Employment' (1936), published immediately after the publication of the *General Theory* and one year later presented as one of her *Essays in the Theory of Employment* (1937a). Amadeo (1989, p. 7) considered this essay to contain one of the alternative 'three major interpretive approaches' to the *General Theory* which emerged during the first two years of its publication.[6] Frank Hahn (1989, p. 909) was convinced: 'Her *Essays in the Theory of Employment* was an important book in its time.'

Similarly, Jan Kregel (1983, p. 344) made the assessment:

The successes and failures of this initial formulation were thus to dominate investigation in growth and capital theory for nearly fifty years and lead to the development of the post-Keynesian approach.

If this is indeed the case, it is clear that this essay must be an important candidate for scrutiny if the object is to investigate critically the reception of Keynesian economics.[7]

But this essay is of major importance not only from the standpoint of tracing back key ideas of present post-Keynesianism to their first historic roots. In the context of the Keynes–Pigou debate it is also very important to come to grips with Joan Robinson (1937a) because – as we noted above – Pigou was reported by Kahn to have directed the 'simplified model' which we discussed in part III predominantly against Joan Robinson and not so much against Keynes. If Kahn's statement is correct, it means that an essential argumentative context after the publication of the *General Theory* did not cover directly what was written by Keynes, but rather the subject matter of Robinson (1936, 1937a). Thus, for a proper understanding of this part of the classical argumentation, too, it might be of some interest to find out in which way Joan Robinson's post-Keynesian approach and Pigou's classical one link up with each other.

A further motivation for a detailed investigation of this model comes from the noted peculiarity of the style of discussion cultivated by Keynes' entourage and from the fact that they left it to Keynes and – grudgingly – to the 'outsider' Nicholas Kaldor to reply to the Pigovian rejoinders to Keynes.

The method to be used in the following will be basically the same as the one we used when discussing Keynes' 'internal critique' of Pigou: just as we first established there the analytical basis of the model and then the workings of the reconstructed Pigovian model, so will we proceed here.

The following chapter 21 will see an enquiry into the basic structure of Joan Robinson's basic 'long-period' model. This involves first of all reproducing its categories of accounting in nominal terms and then to transpose the Robinsonian accounting equations into ones which are more Keynesian than the ones originally used by Joan Robinson in that they are in terms of wage units. All this must be considered as being permissible and authentic manipulations, covered either by relevant statements made by Joan Robinson herself in the immediate context of the essays here under consideration or made later by her concerning the neutrality of wage unit accounting with regard to the functioning of the models she is concerned with.[8] A simple two-sector model results from these considerations as depicted graphically in fig. 21.1 on p. 285 below. It represents conditions of *given* employment in a stationary state. The relevant algebra and the figure itself are *not* authentic. They are our personal interpretation which shows what could have been done with wage unit analysis in the authentic (post-) Keynesian discussion – but which was not done, as is well known, by Joan Robinson herself or by any other post-Keynesians in quite this formal way. Thus this chapter not only restates the authentic structure of the Robinsonian extension of the *General Theory*, it also gives a small glimpse at some of the 'unclaimed heritage' after Keynes.[9]

The subsequent chapter 22 deals with the microeconomic underpinnings of the structural equations of the macroeconomic model of chapter 21. Two topics suggest themselves in this context. Firstly, the atemporal approach which is often used in neoclassical production models. It was by and large also accepted by Keynes, Pigou, Joan Robinson and other Cambridge economists of that time. As in many other treatises dealing with costs of production – a particular *à propos* in this context is, of course, Joan Robinson's *Theory of Imperfect Competition* – this type of atemporal theory is treated as the appropriate one for deriving and discussing cost structures such as the ones which entered the basic model of chapter 21.

The second topic for a discussion of structural equations is treated in sect. 22.3, dealing with intertemporal allocation. This topic is necessarily associated with Keynes-based models which incorporate consumption and savings. Since quite a bit was written about this topic in the excursus on time preference (see sect. 15. 4, p. 179 above), the discussion can now be rather brief. In addition to time preference in consumption, brief mentioning will be made of intertemporal aspects of production.

In chapter 21 employment was exogenously given. But the object of Joan Robinson's post-*General Theory* essays was a theory determining employment as *endogenous* magnitude. Do the arguments as set out in her essays and in surrounding arguments supply such a theory? This question sets the stage for the topic of chapter 23, dealing with the 'workings' of the Robinsonian model as hitherto discussed.

Part IV will conclude with chapter 24, dealing with a summary assessment of the critical potential of the Robinsonian ground covered here.

We are aware that the programme just outlined collides with some perceptions of the essence of Joan Robinson's analysis. Joan Robinson (1956) made her mark on economic theory not least for her capital-theoretic critique in the framework of models based on linear-limitational 'discrete' technology. In view of Joan Robinson's later notoriety as a critic of (neo)classical analysis, in particular as a critic of the neoclassical production function, the reader might feel some reservation when noting that the following presentation is centred on exactly that type of approach and on straightforward neoclassical production functions. But let us emphasise: we deal here with Joan Robinson as a contemporary and young colleague of Keynes and Pigou. In this regard, we may note with Feiwel (1989a, p. 3):

> Perhaps the most important clues to the economics of Joan Robinson can be found in the influences exerted on her by her antecedents and contemporaries. In her formative years Marshall and Pigou stand out as the most conspicuous influences.

And Feiwel (*ibid.* p. 5) reiterates[10]:

> One clue to the economics of Joan Robinson is that she was a great Marshallian while she fought tooth and nail to escape from Marshall, particularly in his Pigovian incarnation.

Feiwel (*ibid.*, p. 7) then proceeds to link Joan Robinson's analysis predominantly to the influence exerted by Pigou in noting that:

> Actually Joan Robinson was a 'second-hand' Marshallian. It was Pigou and Shove who explained Marshall to her. It is the 'Pigovian orthodoxy' she fought.

There can be little 'reasonable doubt' that Joan Robinson was indeed strongly involved with Marshallian resp. Pigovian economics. It is this aspect which we stress in reconstructing the model which Joan Robinson (1937a) once propagated. In view of her intellectual surrounding of that time, it can hardly be considered to be an over-extension of her theoretical horizon if we associate important parts of her erstwhile model with what is now considered as standard neoclassical theory of quite a different orientation than the one Joan Robinson had in later years.

The analytical picture which emerges in the following is meant to be relevant only for the time here under consideration, i.e. for the years surrounding the publication of the *General Theory* up until the year 1938 (with a few isolated exceptions). But in some respects it does not contradict very much the one which was sketched by a number of prominent economists when they were questioned by Feiwel (1989a, b) about Joan Robinson's lifetime scientific achievements. Thus, if we turn to Solow (1989, p. 540), one of her opponents in the 'Cambridge Controversy' in the theory of capital, we find the assessment:

> My picture of Joan Robinson is someone using the standard apparatus, but commenting on it cynically from the outside ... But her departures from orthodoxy were mainly in the nature of iconoclastic remarks about the silliness or impracticability of the neoclassical intellectual program. So, there is this image of Joan as a cynical mainstream economist. I rather liked that in her.

Even with regard to Piero Sraffa, Joan Robinson's mentor in criticising orthodox economics, doubts were raised that his contributions were particularly appropriate for a fundamental criticism of conventional economics. Commentators repeatedly claimed that he really stayed within the framework of neoclassical marginal analysis. Thus Arrow (1989, p. 163) proclaims:

> I must admit that I do not really have a high respect for what is regarded as Sraffa's great contribution. Sraffa's [*sic*] did discover a very nice and interesting theorem – a perfectly good neoclassical theorem.

Similarly we have a verdict from Solow (1989, p. 543):

> The only non-orthodox, non-neoclassical thing in Sraffa [1960, GMA] is an erroneous claim.

But it is none of our business in this book to pass a judgement about Sraffa (1960). Our main concern is the question of how Keynes was received by those who count as his immediate disciples. Sraffa never made the claim to be one of them, but it might be an interesting question – to be pursued in a different enquiry – to ask why that was so.

21
The Structure of the Robinsonian Model

21.1 Basic analysis

The long-period extension of the *General Theory* proposed by Joan Robinson (1937a) takes as analytical reference the following characterisation of an economy:

> Consider a closed community, living under a capitalist system, with population stable ... and with given tastes and technical knowledge ...
>
> Let us first suppose that a certain rate of interest has been established and is maintained at an unvarying level.
>
> In this situation, provided that the given conditions have endured a sufficient time, net investment will have ceased. (*op. cit.*, p. 75)

It is clear from these few lines that Joan Robinson's 'closed community' is situated in the same analytical world as the one which generated Pigou's 'frozen land' economy. Here as there we have all sorts of constancy conditions which are assumed to have 'endured for sufficient' time – maybe for an eternity.

There is one important difference, however: although capital accumulation is assumed to have ceased so that net investment may be stated to be zero, Joan Robinson does *not* assume capital to be infinitely long-lived. The maintenance of its efficiency requires certain patterns of outlay and these generate analytical peculiarities which turn her model into a type of 'classical model' which rarely was discussed in other contributions. This will become apparent in the following chapters in which we intend to trace out these analytical peculiarities.

The patterns of outlay required for the maintenance of capital may differ considerably between alternative capital goods. Joan Robinson (1937) discusses this question at considerable length in an essay on 'Disinvestment'. The simplest assumption in this context is that of a constant depreciation allowance expressed as a percentage of the value of capital (*op. cit.*, p. 113).

Depreciation at a constant percentage of capital seems also to be the central assumption on which Robinson's long-period extension of the *General Theory* is based because concerning her assumptions about capital, Robinson (1937a, p. 76, n. 2) elaborates:

> In the static conditions that we are considering, equipment is conceived to be wearing out at a constant rate, each capital instrument, in equilibrium, is renewed as it wears out, production proceeds in a continuous flow, and to-day is merely a repetition of yesterday. In such conditions the logical difficulty inherent in the notion of constant capital does not arise.

The model emerging from these descriptions may be described as a 'halfway house' between, on the one hand, the Pigovian model of the 'real demand for labour' of 1933 as discussed in part II above and, on the other hand, Pigou's 'simplified model' of 1937.

In a similar way to Pigou's model of 1933, the present model has two sectors of production, namely, one for consumption goods and one for investment goods – although the latter goods are just for replacement purposes as just described. But in a similar way as the later Pigovian model it has just one single output which may be regarded as 'net national product', namely consumption goods.

Robinson (1937a, p. 75, n. 1) stresses the Marshallian roots of her model when she declares:

> The conception of equilibrium employed in this essay is the Marshallian conception of a position of rest towards which the system is tending at any moment.

Thus she herself supplies a confirmation of those views discussed in the preceding chapter which point out the importance of the Marshallian roots of her analysis.

It is important to remember the analytical predisposition of Joan Robinson because, unfortunately, she is not always particularly clear about details of the structure of her model. She seems to have presupposed the common analytical disposition of herself and her reader which would make it redundant to spell out analytical details. But nowadays when there seems to be less than perfect clarity about the analytical background before which some of her remarks were made, understanding the peculiarities of her economic theorising might require a more pedestrian approach which does not shy away from the more tedious reconstruction of analytical details of some of her rather brief propositions.

We may close this section about the basic analytical structure of the model by giving an example for the occasional lack of clarity just referred to: on pp. 84ff. of her essay, Joan Robinson discusses relations between changes in 'total output', on the one hand, and changes in 'the' amount of employment on the other hand. In this context she defines total output as a magnitude 'O' as if she had a single macroeconomic production function in the back of her mind. Although verbally she states that 'a complexity of factors' is involved in this context, her ensuing algebra does little to elucidate this complexity. But having discussed the complexities of Pigou's classical two-sector model in part II and having insisted on the importance and scrutiny which Keynes gave to this model, we think it would be interesting to trace out, at least in a very simplified framework, exactly what this sort of 'complexity' might be.

We will now proceed to investigate some of the 'complexities' of macroeconomic argumentation involved in Joan Robinson's brief exposition of her static two-sector model. First we look briefly at the accounting structure underlying her model (section 21.2) and subsequently at a Keynesian interpretation of this structure in a simple analysis in terms of Keynes' 'wage units' (section 21.3). The ensuing discussion of this model (section 21.4) will lead to a more detailed presentation of distributional aspects (section 21.5).

The implicit theory of distribution of this early Robinsonian macroeconomic model might well be considered as the most interesting aspect of the discussion of this chapter. It reveals an astonishing continuity in post-Keynesian economics and thus it supports those views discussed in the last chapter which attribute paramount paradigmatic importance to this model.

21.2 The macroeconomic accounting structure of the model

21.2.1 The accounting equations in nominal terms

In Joan Robinson's model, income payments out of current production are clearly assumed to go to workers and to capitalists. Discerning now two sectors of production along the lines just stated in the last section, we arrive at a model containing a consumption goods sector (index 1) and a reinvestment goods sector (index 2). The basic structure of the present model economy may then be represented by the sectoral turnover and cost equations

$$p_1 Q_1 = w N_1 + (v + h) p_2 K_1 \tag{21.1}$$

$$p_2 Q_2 = w N_2 + (v + h) p_2 K_2 \tag{21.2}$$

where

p_i = price		K_i = sectoral capital input	
Q_i = quantity		v = rentals rate of capital	
w = wage rate		h = rate of depreciation	
N_i = sectoral employment		$i = 1, 2$	

Adding now the sectoral turnovers as given by the two equations 21.1 and 21.2, we obtain the value of gross production Y^g as

$$Y^g = wN + (v + h)p_2K = Y + hp_2K \qquad (21.3)$$

where, in the right-hand equation, Y is net national product and hp_2K is the nominal value of total depreciation and where

$$N = N_1 + N_2 \text{ is total employment and} \qquad (21.4)$$

$$K = K_1 + K_2 \text{ is total capital stock with } \frac{K_1}{K} \equiv u. \qquad (21.5)$$

Since in this model net investment is zero by assumption, the entire production of capital must necessarily go into reinvestment so that

$$hp_2K = p_2Q_2 \qquad (21.6)$$

holds. But since rearranging 21.3 shows that net national product is given by

$$Y = Y^g - hp_2K \qquad (21.7)$$

and since gross production is given by

$$Y^g = p_1Q_1 + p_2Q_2 \ , \qquad (21.8)$$

substituting hp_2K in 21.7 via equation 21.6 will show that in the Robinsonian model total net national product is given by the value of the production of consumption goods, i.e. by

$$Y = p_1Q_1 \qquad (21.9)$$

as Joan Robinson (1937, p. 78) herself pointed out verbally, stating:

> With zero investment, output, consumption and income, for the community as a whole, are synonymous.

Since we thus arrived at a result which was also stressed by Joan Robinson, we believe that this little exercise in accounting is faithful to her analytical intentions.

Summarising the argumentation followed in this section so far, we note that it gave the basic accounting structure of the Robinsonian model economy. It is characterised by stationary and homogeneous inputs of the factors of production labour N and capital K with the uniform remuneration rates resp. cost rates w, v, h. This is why net national product in this model is identical to the value of the current production of consumers' goods.

A quote showed the authenticity of this reconstruction.

21.2.2 The accounting equations in wage units

Staying briefly with questions of accounting, we note that the formulation of this model can be given a more Keynesian bent by changing the units of accounting. So far, values were given in nominal terms. It does not change anything of analytical substance to transpose these values into 'real' values in terms of Keynes' wage units. By dividing through with the wage rate w we obtain from 21.1 to 21.9 the expressions:

$$V_1 = \frac{p_1 Q_1}{w} = N_1 + (v + h) \frac{p_2}{w} Ku \tag{21.10}$$

$$V_2 = \frac{p_2 Q_2}{w} = N_2 + (v + h) \frac{p_2}{w} K(1 - u) \tag{21.11}$$

$$V = V_1 + V_2 = N + (v + h) \frac{p_2}{w} K \tag{21.12}$$

$$Y_w = V - h \frac{p_2}{w} K = N + v \frac{p_2}{w} K \tag{21.13}$$

$$V_1 = Y_w \tag{21.14}$$

$$V_2 = h \frac{p_2}{w} K \tag{21.15}$$

In 21.10 to 21.15 the V_i-terms express the sectoral gross values of production in terms of wage units and V represents their sum, i.e. *GNP* in terms of wage units. Equation 21.14 represents *NNP* and states that in this model net national product is identical to the value of consumption.

All of these equations are, of course, logically trivial reformulations of the previous ones given by 21.1 to 21.9. Nevertheless, they are not redundant. It will be seen presently that in the version in terms of wage units the accounting equations link up with our interpretation of Keynes' original aggregate supply (and employment) functions and thus it is in this latter form that they will guide us in the discussion of long-period employment.

21.3 A Keynesian cost structure interpretation of the model

21.3.1 Price equations and cost structure equations

The relations between national product, effective demand and employment were discussed in ch. 11 above in terms of a synthesis of Pigou's and Keynes' analysis. It was seen that, in principle, there need not be any fundamental analytical antagonism between the two authors in that context and thus there could hardly be a basis for an analytical dilemma for Joan Robinson in this particular context.

The main reason why we recall this aspect of our previous analysis just now is for 'technical' reasons of proceeding from our present accounting equations to the construction of a simple Keynesian or post-Keynesian model. It was seen in part II that in a simple representation of a Keynesian approach a crucial role was played by structural parameters describing the share of wages in the total value of the relevant production. That share was seen, of course, to depend on technological and competitive conditions. In addition, we saw that a considerable part of the associated theorising by Pigou and by Keynes was in accordance with assumptions of perfect competition and of constant elasticities of production.

Modern post-Keynesians – especially those who sympathise with the work of Sidney Weintraub – might also be seen to link up with the classical idea of marginal productivity when it comes to referring back to Keynes' idea of cost-determined prices.[1] One possible formulation of that idea is contained in the price equation

$$p_i = \frac{1}{\alpha_i A_i^n} w \quad \text{where} \quad A_i^n \equiv \frac{Q_i}{N_i}. \tag{21.16}$$

If now α_i in this expression is again interpreted – as it was done in ch. 11 – as representing labour's elasticity of production, then the denominator in 21.16 will be seen to reduce to the marginal product of labour.[2] This means that in Keynesian interpretation the marginal productivity theory is predominantly a theory of the mark-up factor relating wage cost w to the price level p_i.

This expression contains Keynes' idea that for given employment levels the Classics should have argued that in their framework nominal wage changes result foremost in price changes. But this does not mean that either Keynes' argumentation or, for that matter, later post-Keynesian argumentation presupposes an abandonment of marginal productivity analysis just because unit costs like wages w or average productivities as expressed in 21.16 by A_i^n were referred to in that context.

From Keynes' standpoint it is therefore not of fundamental importance whether the discussion is in terms of marginal productivities *à la* Pigou, in terms of effective demand *à la* Keynes or in terms of pricing equations *à la* Sidney Weintraub. They all may be seen to be just different aspects of the self-same analysis.

But if this is so, we consider ourselves as being authorised to revert to any of these formalisms in order to represent the self-same analytical presuppositions. Although in her essay Joan Robinson (1937a) does not go into such discussions, they supply a simple link between sectoral turnover and sectoral employment. It may easily be verified that by multiplying 21.16 with Q_i/w it is possible to generate an expression

$$V_i = \frac{p_i Q_i}{w} = \frac{1}{\alpha_i} N_i, \quad i = 1,2 \tag{21.17}$$

which is very similar to the aggregate (sectoral) supply functions of ch. 11, except that with the V_i we now have gross values in terms of wage units (including depreciation) whereas there the values like Z_{wr} did not include depreciation.

The 'depreciation inclusive sectoral aggregate supply functions' like 21.17 may be rearranged to give sectoral employment functions

$$N_i = \alpha_i V_i \tag{21.18}$$

These equations may alternatively be interpreted as 'cost structure equations' since the left-hand side measures the cost of labour in terms of wage units – which, of course, is nothing but employment – while the right-hand side of 21.18 measures sectoral turnover V, relating the two magnitudes via a structural parameter ai.

21.3.2 'Semi-reduced forms' in the Robinsonian model

The concepts and parameters formulated so far permit us now to represent the key relationships of the Robinsonian model in an analogous way as was done in ch. 11 when we reformulated the Keynesian model on the basis of a reconstruction of the Pigovian model.

The relationship between total employment N and sectoral values of supply which was given in ch. 11 by equ. (11.20) has an analogue in the present context which follows immediately from the present accounting equations after replacing N_1 and N_2 in 21.4 via 21.18. This step generates a macroeconomic employment function

$$N = \alpha_1 V_1 + \alpha_2 V_2. \tag{21.19}$$

Next, we may use the analytical tool of 21.17 in order to express the 'value output' of net national product $Y_w = V_1$ as being based on sectoral 'value inputs' as is done in

$$V_1 = \alpha_1 V_1 + (v + h)V_2 \frac{u}{h}. \tag{21.20}$$

We find this expression by fixing our attention at equ. (21.10), replacing sectoral employment N_1 via expression 21.18 and replacing the second term in 21.10 which contains the value of capital via 21.15.

Turning next to equ. (21.11), it may be verified that a similar procedure, i.e. replacing the sectoral value of capital in terms of wage units by its associated depreciation cost via 21.15 and then rearranging, gives

$$\frac{1 - \alpha_2}{1 - u} = \frac{v + h}{h} \tag{21.21}$$

since V cancels out in this case.

The new equs. (21.19 to 21.21) give three semi-reduced equations of a system of structural equations describing Joan Robinson's model economy. What are its characteristic features?

In order to give a preliminary characterisation of Joan Robinson's model we may state that in this framework, for given employment N and given capital cost rates as expressed by v and h, we may find three endogenous variables. These are: the sectoral real values of production V_1 and V_2, and the capital allocation ratio u. Since V_2 is related to the real value of capital as was seen in equ. (21.15), the endogeneity of V_2 also means endogeneity of the value of capital.

In this model we are thus solidly established in a Pigovian world of long-period equilibrium where net investment is assumed to be nil and capital is assumed to be variable.

21.3.3 Some characteristics of the rudimentary model

The main characteristics of the rudimentary model outlined so far may now be sketched as follows: suppose that capital cost rates v and h are given with specific values. Then the sectoral allocation of capital as expressed by u in equ. (21.21) follows directly from that expression. But with v, h, and u given, equs. (21.19) and (21.20) determine V_1 and V_2 if N is given exogenously as $\bar{N}$. Since, however, the value of V_1, thus determined, is nothing but the value of the net national product in terms of the wage unit Y_w, this magnitude is also determined, and the share of wages, defined as

$$\lambda^r \equiv \frac{N}{Y_w} = \frac{N}{V_1} \qquad (21.22)$$

is given as well. What this model has to say about labour's share in income is now of particular interest. Cambridge critics of neoclassical economics repeatedly stressed that they disagree in particular with the neoclassical theory of distribution. Whereas the neoclassics regard functional distribution as being determined by technological conditions when the degree of competition is given, it will be remembered that one of the major tenets of post-Keynesian economics is that distribution depends on the rate of interest. It is now interesting to note that this result comes forth in the present 'rudimentary' Robinsonian model if the rentals rate for capital is equated to the rate of interest – a result to which we will now give some further consideration.

In the present model, the interest dependency of the share of wages as expressed by λ^r might be considered as immediately plausible, once it is realised that this model is a long-run one in the Marshallian sense – i.e. one in which capital is *not* considered as being exogenously given. Thus, if the rate of interest increases, economising on the cost of capital means that in long-run equilibrium there will be less capital and hence there will be less depreciation. Since in this case there will be comparatively little V_2-production, the given amount of labour may now produce more of a real value of V_1. But in this case it follows immediately from equ. (21.22) that λ^r is comparatively low since the denominator V_1 is relatively high. Since V_1 is identical with consumption goods, this means that the share of wages is low because the real value of the volume of consumption goods produced is high.

We may emphasise that in this 'rudimentary' model we find already at this comparatively informal level of discussion analytical support for one of the supposedly major tenets of post-Keynesian economics, namely for the doctrine that labour's share is low when the rate of interest is high. In view of the importance which has been attributed to this conclusion in the past, we proceed to a more formal derivation of this result in the following section.

21.4 The structural model in algebraic and graphic discussion

When we attempted to give an intuitive rendering of the idea of an interest-dependent λ^r the crucial step was to claim that the real value of depreciation V_2 was interest-dependent. This step of our previous argumentation may be stated algebraically in the following way.

Turning first to equ. (21.20) we rearrange it to give

$$V_1 = u(v+h)\frac{V_2}{h(1-\alpha_1)} = (v + \alpha h)\frac{V_2}{h(1-\alpha_1)} \qquad (21.23)$$

where the replacement of $u(v + h)$ in the last term follows from rewriting 21.21 as

$$u(v+h) = v + \alpha_2 h \ . \qquad (21.24)$$

We may now state algebraically how V_2 depends on the rate of remuneration of capital v: first, eliminate V_1 in the employment function 21.19 via 21.23 and then rearrange the ensuing expression. This gives

$$V_2 = h\frac{1-\alpha_1}{\alpha_1 v + \alpha_2 h} N \quad \text{with} \quad \frac{\partial V_2}{\partial v} < 0 \ . \qquad (21.25)$$

The sign value of the derivative stands for the inverse relationship between the value of depreciation V_2 and the rate of capital cost v which was employed in the plausibility argument of the last section.

Similarly, taking the employment function 21.19 and substituting there the value for V_2 via 21.25 gives the value for V_1 as

$$V_1 = \frac{v + \alpha_2 h}{\alpha_1 v + \alpha_2 h} N \quad \text{with, incidentally} \quad \frac{\partial V_1}{\partial h} < 0 \qquad (21.26)$$

so that increased requirements for depreciation (plausibly) lead to decreased real income. Using the definition of labour's share as given in 21.22, simple division and rearrangement of 21.26 will then give the algebraic expression for labour's share in the Robinsonian model as

$$\lambda^r = \frac{N}{V_1} = \frac{\alpha_1 v + \alpha_2 h}{v + \alpha_2 h} \tag{21.27}$$

with $\lambda^r = 1$ *for* $v = 0$ *and* $\lambda^r \to \alpha_1$ *for* $v \to \infty$.

Thus, the share of wages in this model is established algebraically as reaching its maximum feasible value of unity if capital were not rewarded at all ($v = 0$). It asymptotically tends towards its lowest value α_1 if the rate of remuneration for capital went towards infinity.

The total differential of λ^r is given by

$$d\lambda^r = \underbrace{\frac{\partial \lambda^r}{\partial v}}_{-} dv + \underbrace{\frac{\partial \lambda^r}{\partial \alpha_1}}_{+} d\alpha_1 + \underbrace{\frac{\partial \lambda^r}{\partial \alpha_2}}_{+} d\alpha_2 + \underbrace{\frac{\partial \lambda^r}{\partial h}}_{+} dh \tag{21.28}$$

where the sign values under the respective partial derivatives follow from the following expressions:

$$\frac{\partial \lambda^r}{\partial v} = \frac{-(1-\alpha_1)\alpha_2 h}{(v+\alpha_2 h)^2} < 0 \qquad \frac{\partial^2 \lambda^r}{\partial v^2} = \frac{2(1-\alpha_1)\alpha_2 h}{(v+\alpha_2 h)^3} > 0$$

$$\frac{\partial \lambda^r}{\partial \alpha_1} = \frac{v}{(v+\alpha_2 h)} > 0 \qquad \frac{\partial \lambda^r}{\partial \alpha_2} = \frac{(1-\alpha_1)hv}{(v+\alpha_2 h)^2} > 0 \tag{21.29}$$

$$\frac{\partial \lambda^r}{\partial h} = \frac{(1-\alpha_1)\alpha_2 v}{(v+\alpha_2 h)^2} > 0$$

The features of the rudimentary Robinsonian model discussed so far may be represented graphically. In fig. 21.1, the north-east quadrant depicts the 'employment function' of equ. (21.19). For a given $N = \bar{N}$, there exists a well-defined 'value possibility space', shaded grey. Point $\bar{V}$ is on the border of that space. The eastern quadrants depict the interest-dependent V_2-demand as given by equ. (21.25) which here is represented by the curve going through point $\bar{V}_2$. For alternative capital cost rates v the curve going through $\bar{\lambda}^r$ in the south-west quadrant is then generated as the *locus* in the λ^r and v plane which may be constructed via the two curves just described and via the hyperbola depicting a fixed labour supply of $\bar{N}$ in the north-west quadrant.

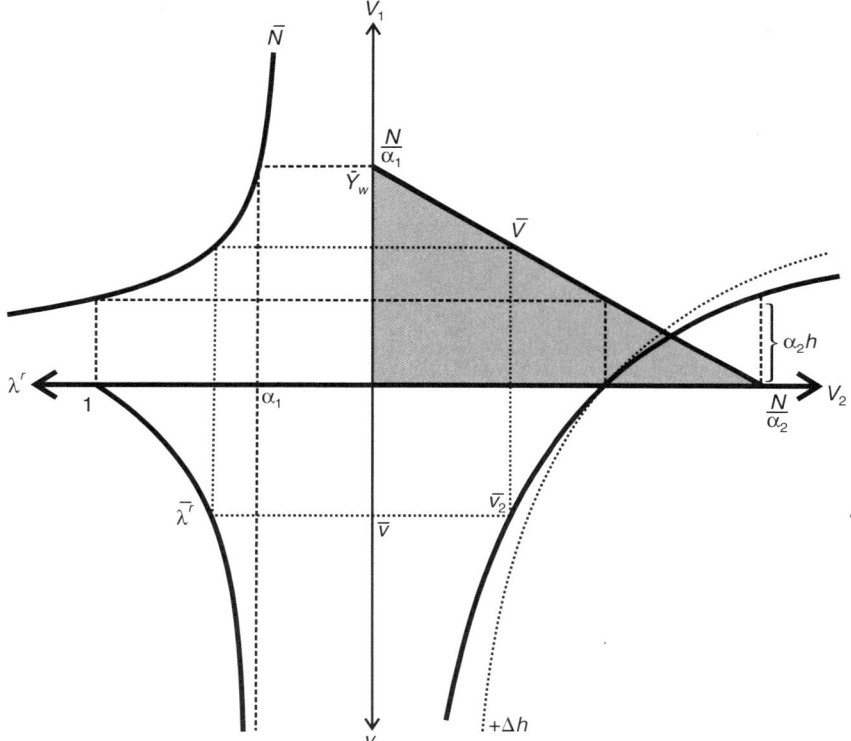

Figure 21.1 Income and distribution in the Robinsonian model

21.5 Distributional peculiarities of the structural model

We finish the discussion of the rudimentary Robinsonian model by briefly commenting on some peculiar aspects of its implicit theory of distribution.

If we compare the present expression for the share of wages as given by 21.27 with the one which was derived in the context of Pigou's 'simplified model' in ch. 16, then we have to compare our present formulation of labour's share as λ^r with its Pigovian counterpart of equ. (16.13) (see p. 213):

$$\lambda^p = \frac{\alpha}{1+r} \quad \text{with} \quad \lambda^p = 1 \quad \text{for} \quad r = \alpha - 1 < 0 \quad \text{and} \quad \lambda^p = \alpha \quad \text{for} \quad r = 0$$

$$(21.30)$$

A certain family resemblance between the Pigovian and the post-Keynesian conception of distribution was noted in ch. 16 already: in both cases there is an inverse relation between labour's share and the rate of interest resp. the rate of cost of capital. It was noted there that in the two cases a similar role played by depreciation may be taken as being responsible for this similarity.

But the Robinsonian version of interest-dependent distribution has the advantage of being based on a disaggregated view of the economy whereas Pigou's 'simplified model' relied on the idea of a single macroeconomic production function. In addition, Joan Robinson's distributional implications might easily appear to be the more plausible ones. Thus, inspecting the expression for λ^p for its characteristics, shows that for λ^p to become unity, the rate of interest would have to be negative whereas in the Robinsonian case of equ. (21.27) a unit value of λ^r required v to be zero. Another important result of the models is that in the 'rudimentary Robinsonian' case the floor for labour's share is given by α_1, i.e. by labour's elasticity of production in producing net national product V_1 and thus her model links up with modern neoclassical ideas about functional distribution. In the Pigovian case the lower limit for λ^p is zero.

The question of economic plausibility is a diffuse one, however. For many economists it is only to be debated satisfactorily in the context of evaluating microeconomic foundations of macroeconomic theories. This problem will concern us in the following chapters.

22
Microfoundations of the Robinsonian Model

22.1 Methodological considerations

In contemplating the microfoundations of the Robinsonian model we are again confronted by the methodological ambiguities which characterised the Keynes–Pigou debate.

It will be remembered that in the above we already pointed out that, in the *General Theory*, Keynes did not have particular qualms about accepting the conventional Pigovian neoclassical theory of production. This aspect of Keynes' theory was atemporal in the sense that the length of the production period, the vintage of the factors of production, and even the durability of capital, all seemed to be of no major analytical interest.

The production theoretic aspects of the *General Theory* thus seem to comply to what Hicks (1939, p. 15) in his *Value and Capital*, was later to call 'Economic Statics':

> I call Economic Statics those parts of economic theory where we do not trouble about dating; ... For example, in economic statics we think of an entrepreneur employing such-and-such quantities of factors and producing by their aid such-and-such quantities of products; but we do not ask when the factors are employed and when the products come to be ready.

On the other hand, we have Keynes' particular theory of demand where 'dating the variables' in question is of pre-eminent importance, where we have a distinction of long-term and short-term expectations relating to investment and to consumption, where we have intertemporal carrying costs, etc.

These different ways of proceeding in a microfoundation of structural relationships in an economic model might seem immaterial in the present context: we noted already that Joan Robinson's essay on long-period employment was solidly based on Pigovian equilibrium concepts – and 'equilibrium' in that sense means that we are in the realm of atemporal analysis where the distinction just made is immaterial.

But if the Pigovian conditions of equilibrium are supposed to hold, then the time-preference theory of interest was also seen to hold – as a limiting case of the type of intertemporal analysis which led to the formulation of Keynes' consumption function, as Keynes conceded to Pigou. Was Joan Robinson aware of this analytical position of Keynes'? Did she give hints how in her long-period conception one could avoid the 'classical' results which Keynes was willing to accept in a Pigovian long-period set-up? In order to be in a position to contemplate this type of question it seems indispensable to enter into a discussion of intertemporal analysis of economic decisions.

We therefore propose to cover in separate sections atemporal and intertemporal microfoundations in a discussion of Joan Robinson's long-period extension of the *General Theory*. The following section will deal with those aspects of Robinson's model which seem to have been acceptable in Keynes' own eyes to be treated in an atemporal manner.

22.2   Atemporal approaches

22.2.1   The microfoundations of the Keynesian cost structure assumptions in the Robinsonian model

In the construction of the 'rudimentary Robinsonian model' of the last chapter we ventured to assume constant labour cost ratios in the two sectors under discussion. The justification for such an assumption could be based on several alternative arguments – on empirical findings, on the quest for discussing implications of certain production-theoretic and competition-theoretic assumptions, on assumptions of satisficing firm behaviour, etc.[1]

In view of our intention to reconstruct the main features of the authentic debates, we have to concentrate in our interpretational efforts on the conventional framework of a two-factor world with perfect competition and constant returns to scale, however, since Joan Robinson (1937a, p. 81) characterised her model along the following lines:

> in effect there are only two factors to consider – labour and capital, and we will suppose that constant physical returns prevail ... Further, it is convenient to make the traditional assumption of perfect competition.

With this assumption of perfect competition and constant returns to scale we are led back to the type of model which we discussed above in Part II when we reconstructed Pigou's argumentation in his *Theory of Unemployment*. And it was demonstrated in that context already in which

way we may then proceed from that Pigovian analytical basis to a
Keynesian theory of effective demand.

The same production-theoretic assumptions now having been invoked in
principle by Joan Robinson, in the present discussion of microfoundations
we might simply refer back to that earlier discussion – if it were not for the
new aspect of depreciation which enters into Joan Robinson's discussion
and which was absent in the formal model of Pigou's elasticity of the real
demand for labour.

Indeed, with regard to labour demand there does not seem to be a need
for a formal reconsideration at all. For any firm in Joan Robinson's long-
period model there obviously exists in each sector a marginal product of
labour ($\frac{\partial N_i}{\partial Q_i}$) which is assumed to be equal to the real wage ($\frac{w}{p_i}$). Thus, we
have here the same old profit-maximising conditions of conventional clas-
sical analysis. But from such an equation we obtain immediately our
Keynesian 'cost structure magnitude' α_i if we simply multiply with the associated inverse of the productivity of labour ($\frac{N_i}{Q_i}$):

$$\frac{\partial Q_i}{\partial N_i} \frac{N_i}{Q_i} \equiv \alpha_i \equiv \frac{w}{p_i} \frac{N_i}{Q_i} \ . \tag{22.1}$$

Whether this magnitude is constant or not is, of course, a debatable matter.
In the last chapter we gave reasons why we believe that *all* the participants
of the Keynes–Classics debate did assume at some stage or other that α-s
were constant for practical purposes of analysis. But whether they are constant or not, simple manipulation of the microeconomic condition (22.1)
shows that it follows from the conventional marginal analytic assumptions
employed by Joan Robinson, that

$$(21.18') \quad N_i = \alpha_i V_i \quad \text{where} \quad V_i \equiv \tfrac{p_i Q_i}{w}$$

must hold. Thus we get here the same type of microfoundations of structural relationships concerning wage cost that were discussed earlier in
part II.

If there are only two factors of production to be considered and labour is
remunerated by its marginal product, the residual value of turnover has to
be imputed to the other factor, 'capital'. If capital depreciates at the constant and uniform rate h and fetches a uniform rate of remuneration v, the
accounting equations of the last chapter give

$$1 - \alpha_i = (v + h) \frac{p_2 K_i}{p_i Q_i} \tag{22.2}$$

when labour cost in equs. (21.1) resp. (21.2) is subtracted from the respective sectoral turnover and the resulting expression is then divided by the

absolute value of turnover p_iQ_i. We thus arrive at a 'cost structure parameter' for capital in analogy to the one just given for labour.

It is a matter of course that if a model is built such that there are just two income receiving factors of production, their total share in output must be unity. So far it might be considered as redundant to make an explicit statement of the share of capital cost as done with equ. (22.2). It is clear that in this type of model it cannot be anything else but $1 - \alpha_i$. It is also clear that in this set-up linear homogeneity of the production functions must hold.

But although Joan Robinson's model is utterly 'classical' in this regard, too, her construction offers again some peculiarities which we want to point out. Let us first note that the implicit linear homogeneity of her model gives the expression

$$1 = \frac{\partial Q_i}{\partial N_i}\frac{N_i}{Q_i} + \frac{\partial Q_i}{\partial K_i}\frac{K_i}{Q_i} \qquad (22.3)$$

where the first right-hand term is equal to α_i as defined by 22.1. Subtracting this term as α_i from both sides of 22.3 and rearranging then gives an expression for the marginal productivity of capital in the Robinsonian model, namely

$$\frac{\partial Q_i}{\partial K_i} = (1 - \alpha_i)\frac{Q_i}{K_i} = (v + h)\frac{p_2}{p_i} \qquad (22.4)$$

With this little exercise we have stated a marginal productivity of capital condition which exists in this model alongside the marginal productivity of labour condition. This statement suggests two comments:

- In view of Joan Robinson's later scruples about the concept of a definable marginal physical product of capital it might not be altogether trivial to point out that this concept is an integral part of her long-period extension of the *General Theory*.[2] We will later give some more evidence for this claim.
- In the present version of the conventional 'classical' marginal cost condition which we claim to be contained in Joan Robinson's model, there is an important modification in comparison to the customary rendering: due to depreciation cost as expressed by h, the marginal cost of capital is here not just equal to the real value of the rentals rate v, but it must also include the real value of depreciation. Because of this additional element in the Robinsonian model there will be no equality between gross production and gross factor income, as was pointed out in the previous chapter.

22.2.2 Production theoretic assumptions of the Robinsonian model

The remarks concerning the homogeneity of the production functions in the Robinsonian model lead us to go into some more detail concerning its underlying theory of production.

An important parameter describing production functions is the 'elasticity of substitution'. It is interesting that one of the major criticisms against the essay here under discussion was its lack of clarity concerning this very concept. As Harrod (1937a, p. 328) put it when reviewing this essay:

> Elasticity of substitution is introduced at a point where its propriety is not apparent and the conditions at the margin to which it is supposed to relate are not sufficiently clearly explained.

It is somewhat astonishing that a major weakness in Joan Robinson's argumentation should have been detected in connection with the concept of the elasticity of substitution. After all, in the preface of her *The Economics of Imperfect Competition*, Joan Robinson (1933, p. vii) considered herself to have been – together with Hicks – one of the inventors of this concept and she considered it as being very important in a discussion of long-period aspects of the *General Theory*.

Limiting ourselves to the production theoretic aspects of the topic of 'elasticity of substitution' in taking up Harrod's remark concerning doubts about the 'propriety' of the concept of the elasticity of substitution, we point out that this concept is, of course, obviously of considerable importance in the discussion of the elasticity of production as given by our α_i. And these magnitudes in turn are of considerable significance for the exact workings of the Robinsonian model. It was seen above that the size of the $\alpha - s$ is essential for a discussion of total and sectoral employment (see equ. (21.18) and for a discussion of labour's share in income see equ. (21.27) above).

But whether the α_i are constant – as was assumed above – or whether they are variable depends on the exact specification of the productive conditions and hence on value of the elasticity of substitution.

More specifically, it can be shown that[3]

$$E_{N_i}^{\alpha_i} = -\frac{1-\sigma_i}{\sigma_i}(1-\alpha_i) \lessgtr 0 \quad \text{as} \quad \sigma_i \lessgtr 1 \qquad (22.5)$$

holds where 'E' is the elasticity operator and σ_i is the sectoral elasticity of substitution. If σ_i were exactly equal to unity, it follows from (22.5) that the elasticity of α_i is zero, i.e. that the α_i are unchanging. But this is the case which we assumed over most of this book.

It follows from these brief considerations that the discussion of the Robinsonian model might indeed be strongly affected by assumptions concerning the characteristics of the elasticity of substitution.

It is now interesting to note that Joan Robinson (1937a, p. 86) seems to have been inclined to assign a unit value to the elasticity of substitution. She quotes D. G. Champernowne (1935, p. 225) as having stated that 'the most plausible estimate of the elasticity of substitution is unity'. In a footnote she invokes findings by P. H. Douglas and John Hicks concerning 'the apparent constancy (over long periods) of the share of labour in total income' adding, however, 'But, of course, there is a wide gap between conclusions drawn from our static community and conclusions applicable to nations of the real world.'[4]

In a certain sense it is quite remarkable, however, that Joan Robinson should have been prepared to invoke these findings with reference to the connection between the elasticity of substitution and labour's share in total income. It was seen above already when discussing equ. (21.27) that the share of wages in her model depends not only on technological conditions proper but also on the remuneration of capital as given by θ and on the rate of depreciation as given by h.

Nevertheless, it is quite convenient to have Joan Robinson invoke the authority of D. G. Champernowne concerning the plausibility of a unit value of the elasticity of substitution. This permits us to treat the α_i as constant, as was just seen in discussing equ. (22.5).

Furthermore, it is well known that for a unit elasticity of substitution the associated production function takes on the Cobb–Douglas form

$$Q_i = A_i N_i^{\alpha_i} K_i^{1-\alpha_i} \tag{22.6}$$

where A_i is a (positive) efficiency parameter. This type of production functions generates the type of expressions of marginal productivities discussed in the last section.

We may now take this particularly simple production function to be in accordance with some of the relevant discussions to be found in Joan Robinson's essay on long-period employment.

22.2.3 Atemporal determination of demand in the Robinsonian model

Questions of demand were not considered explicitly by us in the Robinsonian context so far, and they might seem to be immaterial in the present context since in the stationary economy here under consideration it is one of the basic assumptions of the model that total net national product is used for consumption. To that extent there seems to be little to be decided about consumption in this model – in particular since there is just one single type of consumption good.

But as was seen above in discussing the Pigovian 'simplified model', the assumption of stationariness does not make obsolete a discussion of demand parameters. It was seen in that context that one of these parameters, namely time preference, took on a central role in determining the model economy, since this particular magnitude was instrumental in determining the rate of interest under conditions of stationariness.

But to refer to the discussion of time-preference in the present context is not quite appropriate since time-preference is, strictly speaking, an intertemporal concept whereas in this chapter we intended to attend to atemporal questions of analysis.

It is now not without interest to note that a 'proper' atemporal approach to the relation between demand and employment did exist at the time of Joan Robinson's writing the essay here under discussion. This approach is probably best exemplified by the article by D. G. Champernowne (1935) just mentioned. It relates the well-known atemporal conception of elasticity of substitution to an equally atemporally conceived price elasticity of product demand in the attempt to make statements about the interdependence between product demand and labour demand.

This latter type of atemporal analysis of demand might be of some interest for two reasons in the present context. On the one hand, Joan Robinson herself briefly alluded to aspects of Champernowne's (1935) analysis as was just seen and therefore it seems plausible to give it heightened attention. On the other hand – but maybe for related reasons – Jan Kregel (1983, pp. 348f.), a recent reader of Joan Robinson's essay on long-period employment, advocated reconsidering the microfoundation of her essay with the help of this very type of approach.

The exact context of Jan Kregel's plea to return to the 'elasticity of demand *cum* elasticity of substitution' approach to employment was given by Joan Robinson's concept of a macroeconomic relation between the rate of interest on the one hand and her 'total output O' on the other hand. But if we do investigate this relationship more closely – for the characterisation of which, incidentally, Joan Robinson (1937a, p. 85) coined a special elasticity 'θ' – then we will see that it does not really warrant the type of approach advocated by Kregel. Joan Robinson's discussion of 'θ' is not really concerned with the price elasticity of demand. It is rather concerned with the interest elasticity of savings and the ensuing change in the stock of capital and with the further technological repercussions which such changes in the stock of capital might have for employment.

In short, Joan Robinson does seem to make a clear break with earlier pre-*General Theory* approaches to the relationship between demand and employment. In this sense her claim is indeed plausible that she intended an extension of the argumentation found in the *General Theory*. But this observation leads us now back to Keynes' conception of consumption demand – and thus it leads us to an intertemporal analysis of this phenomenon as was argued above in ch. 15 and its excursus on pp. 179ff.

22.3 Intertemporal approaches

22.3.1 Keynesian consumption and the Robinsonian extension

22.3.1.1 Time-preference theoretic microfoundation of Keynesian consumption

When economists contemplate Joan Robinson's long-period extension of the *General Theory* they do not give much treatment to associated consumption theoretic aspects. In that type of literature there seems to be an undebated understanding that in her argumentative context it is unproblematic to assume the validity of the same structural equations as in Keynes' original (short-period) context.

Consider, for example, Jan Kregel's (1983) reinspection of Joan Robinson's essay and its microfoundations. One will note that in spite of the intended microeconomic orientation of that essay this author does not supply a discussion of the microfoundation of the relevant consumption- resp. savings-function. He seems to be convinced without further consideration that these functions survive in the Robinsonian setting in a form which is not substantially altered in comparison to the standard Keynesian case.

Or take the treatment by Amadeo (1989) which covers in part a similar ground in that the author devotes a section of his book on *Keynes's principle of effective demand* to analytical problems involved in the 'extension' of the theory of employment from Keynes' short-period analysis to Joan Robinson's long-period one (Amadeo, 1989, pp. 135ff.). In that context he poses

[t]he question ... whether we lose anything by looking at the principle of effective demand from a long-period perspective. (*op. cit.* p. 139)

But consequently this question is not really discussed but dismissed, the author declaring

The role played by ... the multiplier is not altered by the extension of the notion of equilibrium to the long period.

Such a view is *not* in accordance with what Keynes himself stated in his discussion of Pigou's long-period analysis, as was seen above, and as we must remind the reader in this context again (see above p. 178).

Let us briefly recapitulate: in ch. 15 above and in its excursus we argued in some detail that Keynes was quite outspoken in that he considered the propensity to consume – and hence the magnitude of the multiplier – to be 'an aspect' of time-preference. We then reconstructed on a time-preference theoretic basis the essential characteristics of the consumption function which Keynes described in detail in the *General Theory*. It was seen that an important feature of that function is the distinction between the present and the future level of income. This distinction disappears, however, in a Pigou–Robinson type of long-period discussion. Such a discussion therefore suppresses an essential element of Keynes' analysis.

In discussing Keynes' consumption function it is essential to realise that in his argumentation the marginal propensity to consume – and hence the size of the multiplier – relates to *changes in the present level of income* while the expectation of the future levels of income is *constant*. This distinction becomes meaningless, of course, if income levels including the present one *are all constant by assumption*. But this is exactly what happens in Joan Robinson's long-period context.

It is this consideration which compels us to insist that in situations of long-period equilibrium the concept of a consumption function itself becomes meaningless: for any level of income, national consumption is always equal to national income (see above, equ. (21.9), p. 278, and equ. (21.14)). Hence the 'marginal propensity to consume' in a long-period context necessarily must be equal to unity. This analytical step is not just one of many interpretations of Keynes' utterances. It is *essential* for his claim to have a *General Theory* which contains the classical one as a special case.

In this context we also must remind the reader that it emerged from Keynes' exchange with R. F. Kahn over Pigou (1937) that Keynes was convinced that 'in equilibrium' – i.e. in a Pigou–Robinson long-period equilibrium – the rate of interest is equal to the rate of time-preference. Kahn and Robinson were seen to consider this idea as a 'gross error' but it never emerged why this should be so.

Keynes himself could live quite comfortably with the idea that Pigou assumed the rate of interest to be determined by time-preference. Since the type of long-period equilibrium assumed by Pigou was such a special case, this showed just how special a theory the classical theory was. And to show in some detail that this special case was one which could be generated by appropriate manipulations of the Keynesian consumption function was even more in accordance with Keynes' position since it confirmed his idea that he had supplied a *General Theory* which contained the classical one in an encompassing way and as a special case.

Before the background of the analysis of part III above it must now appear as a misconception if authors like Amadeo (1989, pp. 139f) – *nota bene* in a discussion of Keynes' principle of effective demand as expressed by the title of his book – utter the opinion that

> looking at the principle of effective demand from a long-period perspective ... does not make the analysis less general; on the contrary, it makes it more general.

Such a view certainly is in contrast to the one of Keynes.[5] Keynes was in little doubt that in accordance with the time-preference theoretic basis of his consumption function, extending the concept of time preference to situations of long-period equilibrium of the Pigovian type – and we may now write: of the Pigou–Robinson type – meant that the consumption function collapsed to the special case of the classical theory of time-preference determined interest rates. For Keynes the existence of a Pigou–Robinson type of equilibrium meant that one could not be fussy any more about $r = \rho$ determining the rate of interest. That is indeed how interest rates are determined in what he called the 'frozen land' of a stationary economy.

22.3.1.2　*Keynesian consumption and Robinsonian equilibrium*

Joan Robinson obviously did not go along with Keynes in this analysis and the question at hand is: what analytical reasons could she have had or which analytical escape routes could be opened in order to proceed with her intended type of employment theoretic discussion?

In her essay on long-period employment, Joan Robinson (1937a, p. 77) definitely is of the opinion that the Keynesian short-period analysis of employment 'can readily be adapted to describe the forces which determine employment in our static community'. She (*ibid.*) believes in particular that there is an analogue to a Keynesian savings function such that

> to each level of output there corresponds a certain rate of saving, which must be imagined to occur if that level of output is imagined to obtain. It is possible to draw up a schedule relating each level of output with the amount of saving (in real terms) which would take place if that output were attained under long-period conditions.

In that context she goes on to state that the schedule described in the quote depends on the individual propensities to save and on the distribution of income.

After all that has been said about Keynes and Pigou above, it is perhaps difficult to overcome qualms about assuming 'long-period conditions' on the one hand – which imply zero savings – and, on the other hand, to assume non-zero savings in connection with a long-period savings function. For argument's sake we will abstract for the moment from this conceptual difficulty, however, and we will now try to relate this Robinsonian long-period savings function to the short-period consumption function derived in the excursus to ch. 15 above, bringing in the particular problems posed by the concept of long-period equilibrium at a later stage of our discussion.

Let us remember that on p. 184 the Keynesian consumption function was seen to be given by the expression

$$(15.16') \qquad C_0 = a + bY_0 \quad \text{where}$$

$$a = \frac{\gamma_0}{\gamma_0 + \Sigma \gamma_f \tau_f} \Sigma (\frac{1}{1+r})^f Y_f \quad and \quad b = \frac{\gamma_0}{\gamma_0 + \Sigma \gamma_f \tau_f} \quad f =_{1,2,\ldots,n}$$

This expression was a short-period one in the sense that the Y_f were assumed to be given whereas the present income Y_0 was assumed to be variable.

It was noted above that it is reasonable to assume that the atemporal elasticities of utility γ and the intertemporal elasticities of utility τ are positive and that then it follows immediately that Keynes' marginal propensity to consume b is in the range between zero and unity. Since the multiplier is given by $\frac{1}{1-b}$, it is *this* condition which assures that Keynes' multiplier is typically larger than unity.

The question at hand is now: how is this Keynesian expression affected by assuming long-period conditions to prevail? As we just saw in the quote at the top of p. 276 in Joan Robinson's conception of long-period analysis 'to-day is merely a repetition of yesterday' – and this is supposed to be the case for a very long sequence of periods. Expectations are static and thus expression (15.16´) may be reduced to

$$C = (1 + \frac{1}{r})(\frac{1}{1 + \Sigma \tau_f})Y \qquad (22.7)$$

when in (15.16') the long-period condition means $n \to \infty$n and when the atemporal preferences as expressed by the $\gamma -$ s are identical in each time period.

Since we know from ch. 15, however, that in long-period conditions the series of intertemporal preferences as expressed by the $\tau -$ s must converge, we have

$$\rho = \frac{1}{\Sigma \tau_f}$$

(see equ. (15.12), p. 183). We also know that equ. (22.7) may be further transformed to give

$$C = \frac{1 + \frac{1}{r}}{1 + \frac{1}{\rho}} Y. \qquad (22.8)$$

This expression is just a further way of stating that in long-period equilibrium conditions, when $C = Y$, it is necessarily true that $r = \rho$ must hold, as was already seen in ch. 15. In the long-period equilibrium case the double fraction in 22.8 is unity, i.e. the marginal propensity to consume is unity and the marginal propensity to save is zero.

We may put this result differently by taking (22.8) and forming an explicit savings function

$$S^r = Y^r - C^r = \frac{r-\rho}{r(1+\rho)}Y^\tau. \tag{22.9}$$

for savings under long-period conditions where index ^{r} denotes real variables which might be obtained by deflating the entire savings equation by an appropriate deflator.

From inspecting equ. (22.9) it becomes immediately apparent that in long-period equilibrium proper, when $r = \rho$ holds, the numerator in this expression is zero. The savings-income schedule postulated by Joan Robinson in the above quote then cannot exist on an individual level – unless, perhaps, if we introduce special assumptions about ρ which are not discussed by her, however.[6]

We might assume, however, that Joan Robinson did *not* accept the $r = \rho$-condition even in long-period equilibrium. After all, she and R. F. Kahn were seen to believe that in making this assumption Pigou committed a 'gross error'. But when $r \neq \rho$ holds, then the savings-income schedule of equ. (22.9) shows that the zero savings condition can only be met if income, too, is zero. This follows immediately from the strict proportionality between savings and income under such conditions.

This result has serious consequences for the evaluation of Joan Robinson's discussion of her model as will be seen in the following chapter when we discuss the workings of her model in more detail. We may note here that on the basis of our consideration of the time-preference theoretic microfoundation of Keynes' consumption function we find it impossible to subscribe to a statement such as the following remark made by Jan Kregel (1983, p. 347):

'The long-period equilibrium analysis characterised by zero net saving thus reproduces Keynes's negative short-period effect of saving on output'

Contrary to this statement we must emphasise that the Robinsonian long-period equilibrium analysis cannot reproduce Keynes' analysis of the relationship between savings and output. This is so because the Keynesian consumption function evaporates under the Pigovian long-period equilibrium conditions implicitly assumed by Joan Robinson (1937a). What does survive in the stationary economy is the time preference theory of interest, as Keynes knew very well – and conceded.

22.3.1.3 The distribution of income and macroeconomic consumption

The last section's discussion of the consumption function resp. savings function in Joan Robinson's long-period context is incomplete as long as we have not dealt with questions of income distribution. Joan Robinson (1937a, p. 77) based her analysis on the belief that:

> The rate of saving corresponding to a given total output depends, if the propensities of individuals to save are given, upon the distribution of total income between classes.

In the light of such an observation it seems essential to consider how distributional questions affect the argument of the last section.

In a simple macroeconomic context it is customary to discern between workers and capitalists as separate income-receiving classes and to attribute different propensities to consume resp. to save to each class. This distinction will also be the basis for the following remarks.

(a) The case of 'Kalecki savings'. Among several authors from Cambridge, it was particularly popular to assume that workers always consume their entire wages income whereas capitalists use part of their income for savings. This distributional set-up is known as the case of 'Kalecki savings'. It played an important part in post-Keynesian discussion. As stated by Kaldor (1955–6), this case generated the provocative result that 'capitalists get what they spend' in the sense that any increase in their propensity to consume will raise their share in total income. Put differently, it means that any increase in their rate of time-preference will lower labour's share in income.

According to this doctrine, savings consist necessarily of savings by non-workers. These savings may be denoted as S^m. The Robinsonian long-period savings function for this group is then

$$S^m = \frac{r - \rho'}{r(1 + \rho')} P^r = \frac{r - \rho'}{r(1 + \rho')}(1 - \lambda^s)Y^r \qquad (22.10)$$

where ρ' is the rate of time-preference of non-workers whose real income is denoted as P_r. Labour's share in national income is represented here by λ^s. Since λ^s appears in 22.10, it might now seem that labour's share plays an important role in determining the volume of savings S^m. But we must again remind the reader that insofar as we compare alternative long-period equilibria, we have to do exclusively with cases where $r = \rho'$ holds. From inspecting (22.10) it will then be immediately apparent that in these cases the distribution of income is irrelevant for the relation of (zero) savings to income because the proportionality factor between income shares and savings as given by the fraction in (22.10) then becomes zero.

Thus, in the Robinsonian equilibrium the Kaldorian theory of distribution becomes irrelevant in the context of 'Kalecki savings'.

(b) A 'generalised' case. The case of Kalecki savings might be 'generalised' by attributing to workers, too, a specific value of time-preference, denoting it e.g. by ρ''. This specific rate of time preference must be rather high, however, if it is to be in accordance with the established view that workers are inclined to spend whatever they can get. Indeed, if there is a uniform rate of interest r, it must be assumed that

$$\rho' < r < \rho'' \qquad (22.11)$$

holds. In this case non-wage earners' savings S^m as given by equ. (22.10) will be positive whereas wage earners' savings as given by

$$S^{rw} = \frac{r - \rho''}{r(1 + \rho'')} \lambda^s Y^r \qquad (22.12)$$

will be negative. Long-period zero savings equilibrium then requires

$$S^m + S^{rw} = 0 \qquad (22.13)$$

to hold. Replacing S^m and S^{rw} by equ. (22.10) resp. equ. (22.12) and solving for λ^s then gives

$$\lambda^s = \frac{r - \rho'}{\rho'' - \rho'} \cdot \frac{1 + \rho''}{1 + r} > 0 \qquad (22.14)$$

with

$$\lambda^s = 0 \quad \text{for} \quad r = \rho' \quad \text{and} \quad \lambda^s = 1 \quad \text{for} \quad r = \rho'' \qquad (22.15)$$

In this case we have now the share of wages λ^s depend on the time-preferences of the income classes of the economy as given by ρ' and ρ''. The total differential of λ^s reads:

$$d\lambda^s = \underbrace{\frac{\partial \lambda^s}{\partial r}}_{+} dr + \underbrace{\frac{\partial \lambda^s}{\partial \rho'}}_{-} d\rho' + \underbrace{\frac{\partial \lambda^s}{\partial \rho''}}_{-} dp'' \qquad (22.16)$$

where the sign values of the partial derivatives follow from

$$\frac{\partial \lambda^s}{\partial r} = \frac{(1 + \rho')}{(\rho'' - \rho')} \frac{(1 + \rho'')}{(1 + r)^2} > 0 \qquad \frac{\partial^2 \lambda^s}{\partial r^2} = -2 \frac{(1 + \rho')}{(\rho'' - \rho')} \frac{(1 + \rho'')}{(1 + r)^3} < 0$$

$$\qquad (22.17)$$

$$\frac{\partial \lambda^s}{\partial \rho'} = \frac{(r - \rho'')}{(\rho'' - \rho')^2} \frac{(1 + \rho'')}{(1 + r)} < 0 \qquad \frac{\partial \lambda^s}{\partial \rho''} = \frac{(\rho' - r)}{(\rho'' - \rho')^2} \frac{(1 + \rho')}{(1 + r)} < 0$$

There seems to be a *formal* symmetry in these results: raising time preference – the ρ-s – *in general* lowers labour's share. But *in substance* this result is an paradoxical and socially 'offensive' as the results of the later Kaldorian theory of distribution: if ρ'' rises, this means that workers want to consume more out of any given income. They 'pay' for their 'lust' by having a lower share in income. Now, formally, the same algebraic result follows for increases in ρ'. But in substance that means that if non-workers become 'greedier' for present consumption, that also lowers labour's share – and thereby *raises* the share of non-workers. Workers get punished for increasing their time preference, non-workers get *rewarded* for increasing their time preference. Thus, if we could accept the idea to have long-period equilibrium with differential rates of time-preference in the way discussed in this section, it could be seen that it is to the benefit of non-workers' share in income to have a rise in their time preference whereas it is to the detriment of workers' share in income to have a rise in their group's rate of time preference. We are thus able to reproduce in this set-up an asymmetry between workers and non-workers which accords well with the later Cambridge theory of distribution where similar results were generated – albeit in a totally different analytical set-up.

It might be doubted whether the case presently under consideration may truly be considered as a 'general' one, however. After all, in this set-up it must be assumed that workers will constantly dissave and that non-workers will constantly save – *nota bene* in a stationary economy.

This is not a very plausible set-up. But the question of the plausibility cannot be the concern of the present discussion. The assumption of 'zero savings' of the 'average household' is propagated and accepted in a widely used textbook such as Barro (1990). The idea that workers are more spendthrift than non-workers is a generally accepted one. Both assumptions together lead to the type of model we have here presented.

No doubt, for real economies the macroeconomic steady-state and zero-savings assumptions are not very plausible either. The present set-up permits us to speculate about certain structural relations which were assumed to exist in Joan Robinson's (1937) essay on long-period employment and thus it might claim some justification in spite of its very limited plausibility.

(c) The case of income-dependent time-preference. For completeness' sake we want to deal with one further aspect of time-preference analysis, namely with the assumption made by Kaldor (1937), that time-preference is income-dependent so that

$$r = \rho(Y^\tau) \quad \text{with} \quad \frac{d\rho}{dY^r} < 0 \tag{22.18}$$

may be assumed to hold. Does this assumption significantly affect the validity of the Robinsonian savings function 22.9?

To put it briefly: assumption 22.18 is not capable of validating Joan Robinson long-period savings function analysis if it is assumed that under alternative long-period conditions there is a functional relationship between real income Y^r and real savings S^r. Since under long-period equilibrium conditions $r = \rho$ holds irrespective of the functional form of ρ, it is clear that the numerator in the 'long-period savings equation' 22.9, p. 298 still must be regarded as having a value of zero under these conditions.

We therefore conclude: the fact that in comparative-static discussions we might have to take account of income induced changes in ρ as expressed in equ. (22.18) does not alter significantly the discussion of the Robinsonian savings function. We must remember that from that equation it also follows that now with every change in ρ we have a corresponding change in r. If we take this aspect into account it will be seen that the 'Kaldor assumption' will not change the former result, namely that under conditions of long-period equilibrium savings and income are unrelated.

22.3.2 Microfoundations of the marginal productivity theory of the rate of interest

22.3.2.1 The marginal productivity of capital in Joan Robinson's long-period theory of employment

For many years one of the main targets of criticism of the Cambridge Keynesians was the neoclassical doctrine that capital is remunerated by its marginal product. Joan Robinson's (1937) extension of the *General Theory* predates that capital-theoretic discussion, however. We have had occasion already to point out that at that time she was still prepared to accept the traditional concepts of well-behaved production functions and of measurable quantities of capital.

In her employment-theoretical essay Joan Robinson (1937a, p. 82) even went so far towards classical analysis as to relate decreased interest rates to decreased marginal productivity of capital, declaring:

> A fall in the rate of interest will increase capital per head, so that a given output is produced by fewer workers using more 'roundabout' methods. The marginal physical productivity of capital will be reduced.

It is particularly remarkable that Joan Robinson, although intending to supply an extension of the *General Theory*, employed the traditional concept of 'marginal *physical* productivity of capital' and not Keynes' alternative concept of 'marginal *efficiency* of capital'.

In the following we will attempt a closer inspection of the relation between these two concepts and their respective microfoundations in an intertemporal context.

22.3.2.2 *The rate of interest and entrepreneurial production decisions*

(a) The time structure of entrepreneurial input–output decisions. As is well known, the distinction between short-period and long-period analysis in Marshallian economics is based on the variability of capital. Under short-period conditions capital is regarded as fixed. But with fixed capital, entrepreneurial decisions cannot always be regarded as an expression of a marginal calculus referring to capital input in current production. If labour were the only factor the input of which is variable in the short period, then the current production decisions can be oriented only towards the marginal product of labour.

There are thus in principle two sets of conceptually different decision problems in classical equilibrium analysis referring to the demand for labour resp. the demand for the stock of capital. Labour demand is derived from considerations *within* the short-period time span of production defined by the lack of variability of capital stock whereas the demand for capital stock must necessarily be derived from considerations *without* the period so defined.

This distinction accords well with Keynes' conception of 'The essential properties of interest and money' as set out in chapter 17 of the *General Theory*. There (on p. 222) he 'reminds' the reader that the rate of interest results from a simultaneous spot contract and a futures contract concerning the delivery of money between creditor and debtor. It is this intertemporal system of contracts which must be related to the production decision when deriving the marginal productivity theory of the rate of interest. Therefore, in a Keynesian approach, production should be conceived of in a similar way as the system of contracts associated with the concept of interest on money, i.e. production must in this context be modelled as an intertemporal process.

As far as capital inputs are concerned, a clear distinction seems to be called for between the atemporal 'cost structure' model of section 22.2.1 (p. 288) and the present intertemporal approach. In the former case, capital usage was treated as a problem of 'leasing' an object which supplied services to be contractually remunerated by a fixed rentals rate v. Implicitly it is assumed that one can sensible disassociate the 'leasing' decision associated with v from the decision to supply and produce capital as carrier of the flow of services which then subsequently are leased.

In an intertemporal context there must be some reflection about the gestation period of capital, the timing of its input and outputs in the production process etc. In view of the juxtaposition of short-run constancy of capital *vs.* the long-run variability through investment, capital input and investment decisions should require at least *two* time periods as depicted in Table 22.1.

This is, of course, a very rudimentary construction of an intertemporal setup but this structure should just suffice to catch the essence of the just

Investment decision period

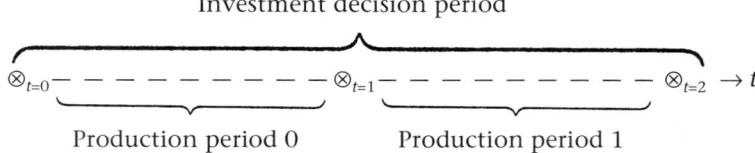

Production period 0   Production period 1

Table 22.1 Investment decision period

mentioned juxtaposition. It also gives a minimalist framework into which one may fit Keynes' occasional reference to 'short-term' expectations and to 'long-term expectations'.[7] This distinction has no significance in a stationary economy, of course. But just because of that, it is important to put a focus on it in order to assess the potential over-simplification implicit in the stationary economy approach.

(b) Marginal productivity of capital and interest in a two-period model.

1. Profits in a two-period model. For a preliminary consideration of the relation between intertemporal production and interest rates, a particular two-period model of production may first be discussed in order to clarify the accounting basis of the fundamental decision problem.

In this model a planned purchase of capital is financed by credit. The utilisation of capital is subject to depreciation at a constant rate h. Since capital has a gestation period of unit length, it can be put to productive use only in the future time period, denoted in the following by an upper index[1]. Future profits Π_{ik}^1 of a particular entrepreneur with index k who operates in an industry with index i are defined in this two-period model by

$$\Pi_{ik}^1 = P_{ik}^1 + p_2^1 K_{ik} - (1+r)D_{ik} \qquad (22.19)$$

where the right-hand symbols have the following meaning: the first term on the right-hand side of equ. (22.19), P_{ik}^1, represents that part of future profits which arises from productive activity in the future period of production. These profits may be seen as arising from a certain turnover R_{ik}^1, generated by selling the produce of period 1, i.e. the quantity Q_{ik}^1 at price P_i^1. For positive profits on this account, turnover has to cover the value of the associated factor cost. For the latter we will use symbol G_{ik}^1. It contains payments for labour and for capital in period 1. Thus, for that part of future profits which were given in equ. (22.19) by P_{ik}^1, we really have in fuller notation

$$P_{ik}^1 = R_{ik}^1 - G_{ik}^1 \qquad (22.20)$$

with $R_{ik}^1 \equiv p_i^1 Q_{ik}^1$ and $G_{ik}^1 \equiv w^1 N_{ik}^1 + hp_2^1 K_{ik}$

i.e., P^1_{ik} in equ. (22.19) stands for the difference between future turnover R and future production cost proper G as defined in equ. (22.20).

The second term on the right-hand side of equ. (22.19) represents a different component of profits. It embodies the returns which are to be expected from selling in the future at a price P^1_2 those amounts of capital K_{ik} which were bought in the present time period at a price for capital P^0_{2k}.

The third element in equ. (22.19) represents the financing cost incurred 'now' and which must be covered in the future period. It arises from the repayment of the debt incurred for the present purchase of capital plus the payment of interest at a rate r. Since debt is used exclusively for the purchase of capital we have

$$D_{ik} = p_2 K_{ik} \qquad (22.21)$$

2. Profit maximisation under perfect competition at constant prices. With this formulation of profits in mind, maximisation of future profit requires that the extreme value condition

$$\frac{\partial \Pi^1_{ik}}{\partial K_{ik}} = 0 \qquad (22.22)$$

must be fulfilled. Substituting equ. (22.21) into equ. (22.19) and differentiating, will show that in this case

$$\frac{\partial P^1_{ik}}{\partial K_{ik}} = rp_2 \qquad (22.23)$$

must hold where P must be regarded as decomposing along the lines discussed in connection with equ. (22.20).

Assuming that production may be represented by a Cobb–Douglas function of the type discussed above, we note that in the present two-period case one has to formulate *two* input–output relations, namely

$$Q^1_{ik} = N^{1\alpha_{ik}}_{ik} K^{(1-\alpha_{ik})}_{ik} \qquad (22.24)$$

for future production and

$$Q^0_{ik} = N^{0\alpha_{ik}}_{ik} \overline{K}^{(1-\alpha_{ik})}_{ik} \qquad (22.25)$$

for present production, where $\overline{K}_{ik}$ denotes the amount of capital inherited from the entrepreneurial decisions of the previous period, i.e. from the time period with index -1.

Our present concern is with the marginal product of capital. This implies variability of capital. So we have to fix our attention on the new demand for capital and thus on equ. (22.24). Standard procedure of analysing equilibrium demand by profit-maximising firms leads us to introduce equ. (22.24) into equ. (22.19) and then differentiating with respect to capital. After minor manipulations we find that the profit-maximising condition may now be written as

$$\frac{\partial Q_{ik}^1}{\partial K_{ik}} = (1 - \alpha_{ik}) \frac{Q_{ik}^1}{K_{ik}} = (r + h) \frac{p_2}{p_i^1}. \tag{22.26}$$

We thus arrive at an expression for an *intertemporal* marginal product – in contrast to the atemporal marginal product formulated in equ. (22.4) on page 290.

3. Reflections on zero-profits capitalism. Comparing the intertemporal and the atemporal versions of the marginal product of capital, we note that the main difference seems to be that in the present expression we have the rate of interest r, being the price for using *financial* capital for one period, entering the marginal calculus concerning allocation of capital goods in production whereas in a former expression on p. 290 we had v, the rentals rate for *real* capital for the analogous problem there. If we now claim that in long-period equilibrium any usage of capital should bring the same reward, we are at the statement

$$r^* = v^* \tag{22.27}$$

where the stars stand for the equilibrium assumption.

This assumption is in keeping with virtually all long-period theory. But from the little example of equ. (22.26) it follows immediately that under intertemporal conditions of equilibrium

$$(r + h) p_2 K_{ik} = (1 - \alpha_{ik}) p_i^1 Q_{ik}^1 \tag{22.28}$$

should hold. Spelled out in words, this means: the total cost for capital usage due to payments for interest and depreciation during the future time period is equal to the entire share in production which can be imputed to capital. In other words: not only *marginal* profits turn out to be zero as formulated in equ. (22.22), but *absolute* profits on productive account are zero as well. This follows in more general terms from the product exhaustion doctrine under perfect competition.

Certainly this cannot be a satisfactory paradigm for a *realistic* modelling of intertemporal behaviour of entrepreneurs. If the maximal profit out of acquiring capital for production purposes has the value of zero, there is the question why entrepreneurs embark on such an activity in the first place. This result is consistent with the long-period stationarity condition, but it is remote from any realistic scenario.

In an intertemporal context, Marshallian economics interprets models where factor payments exhaust total output as the final outcome of a lengthy process in which competition for initially positive quasi-rents motivates entrepreneurs to employ ever larger capacities until market price, marginal cost of output, and average cost of output are all equal and eventually the product exhaustion condition for factor payments is fulfilled.

But in the present set-up such quasi-rents do not occur in the first place if expectations are correct. Since we have long-period equilibrium, expectations cannot be otherwise than correct. Thus, if the atemporal marginal conditions for capital are reflected in an intertemporal setting, the whole paradigm of atemporal analysis of capital becomes questionable because it lacks plausibility as far as the underlying assumptions concerning entrepreneurial decisions are concerned.

The conceptual problems just outlined were the reason why Keynes, in the *General Theory* abandoned the whole idea of the marginal productivity of capital and replaced it by the concept of a marginal efficiency of capital (*GT*, ch. 11, pp. 135ff.). But as far as Joan Robinson in her 'extension' of the *General Theory* is concerned, we are back at the old classical idea of the existence and allocative relevance of a 'marginal physical product' of capital. Although later in her scientific life she herself became very critical of this classical concept, it seems that in her attempts to 'generalise the *General Theory*' she was not really able to follow Keynes in this matter, let alone to surpass him.

22.4 Assessing the microfoundations

In this chapter we made the attempt to probe into the microfoundations for Joan Robinson's (1937a) 'extension' of the *General Theory* in her *Essays in the Theory of Employment*. The wider context of this endeavour is to establish what was debatable and what was indeed debated in Keynes' supposedly paradigmatic exchange with Pigou.

In this context, the particular significance of these *Essays* is that they venture into the very domain of that contest of paradigms: they took Keynes' strategic concepts and transposed them into Pigou's *Stationary State*. One can well understand that at that time this must have been a fascinating programme for the young Cambridge economists Joan Robinson and R. F. Kahn. This intellectual territory had been just charted simultaneously by Keynes (1936) for the short period and by Pigou (1935) for the long period, and they – at least Kahn – having followed this process in *both* cases from the manuscript phase on, they could well have felt in a particular way the intellectual call to bridge the gap between these two authors.

As far as Keynes himself was concerned, he was convinced that this intellectual voyage can only lead into a 'frozen land' devoid of any realistic
characteristics.[8] This issue had to come up in the present context again, of
course. It must be faced that for *microeconomic* reasons the Keynesian consumption function just does not make sense in a stationary economy
where income is constant and net savings are – by definition – zero: the
assumptions of the model are set in such a way that no household would
be interested to make any intertemporal provisions. Keynes spelled this out
in some detail in a letter to R. F. Kahn (25 October 1937, JMK, XIV,
pp. 260–2) and we discussed this above in sect. 15.3, p. 177 as far as this
correspondence and its significance was concerned.[9] In this chapter we
recalled some of our earlier microanalytic results to this extent. In view of
Kregel's (1983) above quoted claim to the contrary, let us reword this
finding: in the stationary state the rate of interest is 'reserved' for the assur-
ance to make the absolute amount of savings equal to zero.

The rate of interest cannot subsequently be 'used' (analytically) again for
the 'Keynesian' job of determining the level of investment. It need not do
so, anyhow, since net investment *must* also be zero by assumption and this
in turn is assured by the classical equality of the rentals rate of capital and
the rate of interest, as was pointed out above. This leaves capital as endogenous to the model – and this in such an extreme form that it is the old
marginal *physical* productivity of capital which must adjust in Joan
Robinson's parlance.[10] In this world there is no motivation for capitalistic
accumulation, however, as pointed out above. That is, of course, consistent
with the stationary state here assumed, but for a Keynesian theory in which
the volatility of investment decisions is the *movens* of the ups and downs of
total income this is again a very unrealistic setup.

We make no claim to originality in mentioning these findings. We are
aware that it might become tedious to go on thrashing out the problematic
motivational assumptions implicit in the stationary context. But one
should add at this point that not only the efficiency of capital but also the
liquidity of money and the microeconomic preference for liquidity disappear as well in Joan Robinson's stationary setting. This happens in the
Keynesian context for the very simple reason that the element of uncertainty about the future which can make liquidity so attractive in a realistic
context does not survive in the stationary state. As Jan Kregel (1985) once
observed, the paucity of monetary underpinnings makes subsequent
Cambridge economics appear somewhat like 'Hamlet without the prince'.

In view of quite a long list of problematic elements in Joan Robinson's
'extension' of the *General Theory* into the Pigovian stationary state it is
astonishing that Keynes only occasionally burst out in outright rejection. It
can hardly have been solid agreement with her position. Otherwise Joan
Robinson would not have had the conviction that Keynes would rather not
be mentioned in the preface of her *Essays*.[11] The academic opinion is still

strongly divided about the significance of Joan Robinson's Keynesian 'extension'. While Pasinetti (2001, p. 389) is convinced that 'Keynes's remarkable analytical framework' still needs to be 'widely extended', namely into the 'long run', such calls for a continuation of the old Robinsonian programme meet the sceptical reply of Paul Davidson (2001, p. 408):

> What Keynes's general case theory of effective demand demonstrates is that the unemployment problem is nested in three words 'liquidity, liquidity, liquidity'!

These words are missing in a long-period extension of the *General Theory* for plausible microeconomic reasons. The solid analytical reason is to show that in this context the rate of interest is indeed 'blocked' by time preference. This was seen by Pigou *and* by Keynes. It was the main point of some of our previous microeconomic exercises to demonstrate that conclusion.[12] Nevertheless, it might be interesting to have a further look at the workings of the 'extension' in the analytical context chosen by Joan Robinson at that time.

23
The Workings of the Robinsonian Model

23.1 An outline

In the discussion of the Robinsonian model we first established its putative significance (ch. 20), then its 'bare bones', its structure as it appears on the basis of a close reading of the original text (ch. 21). Together with some rudimentary assumptions taken from Keynes-type modelling, in particular using the concept of sectoral supply functions in the sense of Keynes, the basic model of fig. 21.1 (on p. 285) emerged.

At that stage of the argumentation the Robinsonian model was seen as having a number of structural equations the economic logic of which was considered to need some more detailed inspection. Two basic approaches were followed in this endeavour: in ch. 22 an atemporal approach was taken, in ch. 22.3 time-preference and intertemporal analysis were resorted to in an attempt to position Joan Robinson between Keynes and Pigou. It emerged that there are *two* relationships explaining labour's share: one expressed by equ. (21.27), p. 284, related cost of capital and labour's share *negatively* with each other. The other relationship explaining labour's share, expressed by equ. (22.16), p. 300, gave a *positive* relationship. This complex will now be under closer scrutiny.

The general procedure adopted in this Part IV is – by and large – similar to the one we employed in working on Pigou (1933) in part II above. There, too, we progressed from the textual basis to an analytic reduction of the text to basic principles and then from there to a reconstruction of the model in question, exposing it in this last step to confrontations with variants of the same model, depicting some of the logic of the original construction which was not apparent at the time of its being written. Thus, in this part, too, we go way beyond what Joan Robinson had written and in particular beyond what she later would have liked to have written. But when the inner logic of economic models presented by an author is at stake, then the same standard should apply for Pigou as well as for Joan Robinson.

23.2 The rate of interest and the determination of the distribution of income

As was just noted, the Robinsonian model generated two distinct equations for labour's share in national income. The one was given by λ^r, relating it to the rate of remuneration of capital v and to the rate of depreciation h as given by equ. (21.27) above. For simple reference we reproduce below its essential comparative static characteristics as discussed above in relation with equ. (21.28) on p. 284.

$$\lambda^r = \lambda^r(v; \alpha_1, \alpha_2, h) \atop {\quad} - \ + \ + \ + \qquad\qquad\qquad (23.1)$$

This is the expression generating a *negative* relationship between labour's share on the one hand and the remuneration of capital v on the other.

The consumption theoretic expression from which labour's share λ^s emerged – under the specified conditions – as being *positively* related to the rate of interest was given by equ. (22.16) on p. 300 which is here reproduced as

$$\lambda^s = \lambda^s(r; \rho', \rho''). \qquad\qquad\qquad (23.2)$$

Obviously, it is not possible that two *different* values for the share of wages can coexist simultaneously. We must interpret the two relationships as expressing a technological condition and an intertemporal allocation condition which *must be met simultaneously*. Thus, the model is determined by $\lambda^s \overset{!}{=} \lambda^r$.

Since the discussion of the long-period conditions established the condition $^1r = v$, we get now an equilibrium condition for this model stating:

$$\lambda^s \overset{!}{=} \lambda^r = \lambda^R \quad \text{for} \quad r = v. \qquad\qquad\qquad (23.3)$$

The two expressions determining a common value λ^R together determine the rate of interest and the *equilibrium* share of wages of this model. The characteristics of this determination are depicted in fig. 23.1.

As indicated in fig. 23.1 by the negative sign values, an increase in the rate of time preference will shift the λ^s-curve in such a way that labour's share is lowered for any given rate of interest. With a given λ^r-curve the equilibrium values of the rate of interest will be raised and of that of labour's share will be lowered. Alternatively, with a given λ^s-curve, a rise in the cost share of labour α_1 or α_2 or a rise in the rate of depreciation h will shift the λ^r-curve upwards and will therefore raise the equilibrium values of both, the rate of interest and labour's share in income.

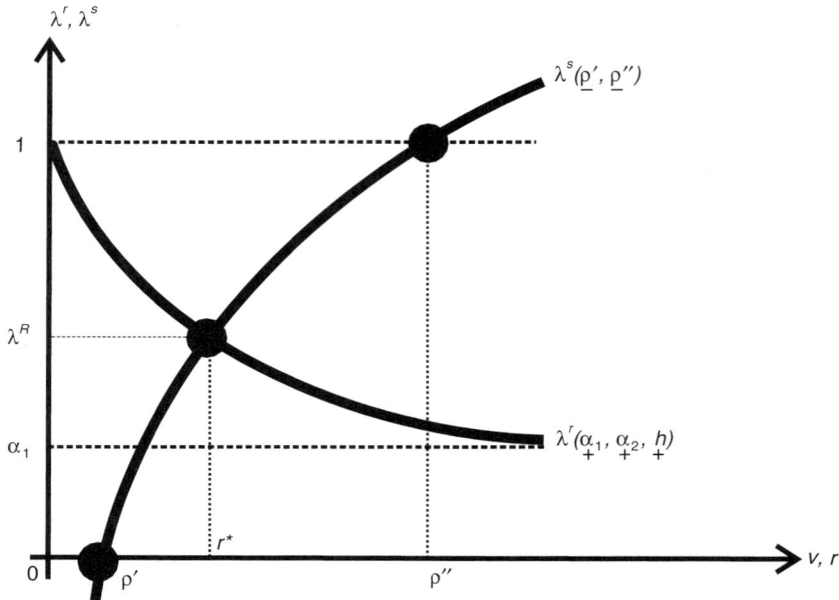

Figure 23.1 The determination of interest and distribution in the Robinsonian model

We thus arrive at the relationships concerning the rate of interest and distribution expressed by Table 23.1. From Table 23. 1 it emerges that an increase in the rate of interest does not necessarily mean that labour's share diminishes.[2] It could well *increase* if the change in the rate of interest is caused by technological conditions as expressed by the α-s and by h.

Although this result follows from a model which is very close to Joan Robinson's original argumentation – especially as far as technological conditions are concerned – it nevertheless contradicts in this latter aspect a tenet which was very dear to her. She stressed that it was a particularly note-worthy result of Sraffa (1960), that he made the 'dichotomy between

Table 23.1 The long period theory of interest and distribution

Endogenous	Exogenous variables				
	ρ'	ρ''	α_1	α_2	h
λ^R	−	−	+	+	+
r	+	+	+	+	+

technology and distribution absolute'.[3] This 'absolute' juxtaposition does not survive in this presentation. Here, the lowest feasible value of labour's share will always be set by α_1 and thus by technology. But in exchange for giving up the dichotomy praised by Joan Robinson, we gain a synthesis of 'neoclassical' and 'post Keynesian' theories of interest and distribution.

The synthesis proposed here has some ironic elements. We saw before that Richard Kahn and Joan Robinson wanted to have little to do with time preference (although Kaldor (1937) mastered and used this concept quite elegantly). But now we see that this concept can generate exactly those distributional tenets which commonly are associated with the Cambridge post-Keynesians: an increase in time preference – in particular in the time preference of the entrepreneurs ρ' – will lower the share of wages so that income distribution might appear as 'circular flow' determined in the sense of Kaldor's widow's cruse theory of profits. On the other hand, in our model a rise in the cost of labour parameters α_1 and α_2 also raises labour's share. This reminds us of the fact that there are also technological aspects to income and distribution. This latter variant is the doctrine of the 'neoclassical' theory of distribution. These two – supposedly alternative – approaches to the theory of distribution are here combined in one single model in which each approach is represented by one aspect of the model. But only the two of them *together* determine a specific distribution of income, given by λ^R.

23.3 The determination of long-period employment

In order to determine the level of employment in this model economy, definite statements are needed concerning technology including the size of capital stock. But the stock of capital requires a corresponding production of capital in order to replace depreciation. This production, in turn, requires particular inputs depending on the exact specification of the production function. Assuming a Cobb–Douglas production function of the type of equ. (22.6), p. 292, gives the relationships

$$hK = Q_2 = A_2 N_2^{\alpha_2} K_2^{1-\alpha_2}, \ K_2 \equiv (1-u)K \tag{23.4}$$

From equ. (21.21), p. 281 we know, however, that

$$\frac{1-\alpha_2}{1-u} = \frac{v+h}{h} \tag{23.5}$$

holds. Introducing (23.5) into (23.4) in order to replace $K_2 = (1 - u)K$ and rearranging then gives

$$hK = A_2^{\frac{1}{\alpha_2}} N_2 \left(\frac{1-\alpha_2}{v+h} \right)^{\frac{1-\alpha_2}{\alpha_2}}. \tag{23.6}$$

But because of the sectoral employment functions as given by equ. (21.18), p. 281, the sectoral employment N_2 may be replaced by

$$N_2 = \alpha_2 V_2 = \alpha_2 h \frac{1-\alpha_1}{\alpha_1 v + \alpha_2 h} N \qquad (23.7)$$

if we replace V_2 according to equ. (21.25), p. 283. Introducing equ. (23.7) now into equ. (23.6) and rearranging (h cancels, both sides are divided by N) then gives the capital intensity k as

$$k \equiv \frac{K}{N} = \alpha_2 A_2^{\frac{1}{\alpha_2}} \frac{1-\alpha_1}{\alpha_1 v + \alpha_2 h} \left(\frac{1-\alpha_2}{v+h} \right)^{\frac{1-\alpha_2}{\alpha_2}} \qquad (23.8)$$

and we arrive at the comparative static relationship

$$\hat{k} \equiv \hat{K} - \hat{N} = -\left(\frac{\alpha_1}{\alpha_1 v + \alpha_2 h} + \frac{1-\alpha_2}{\alpha_2 (v+h)} \right) v\hat{v} = E_v^k \hat{v} < 0 \qquad (23.9)$$

as represented in the north-eastern quadrant one of fig. 23.2

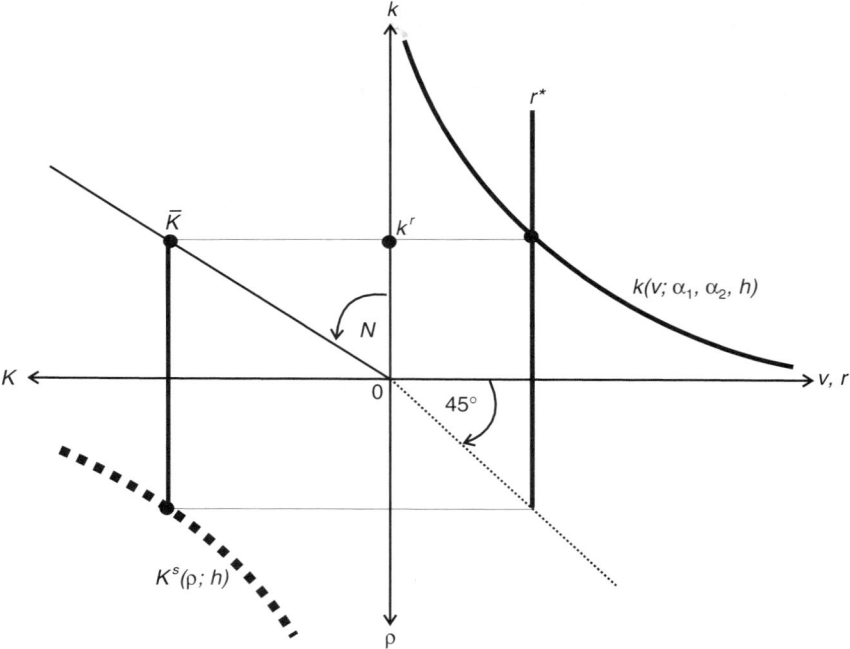

Figure 23.2 Determining capital intensity and employment in the Robinsonian model

If $v = r$ is determined as r^* in the context of the sub-model as represented above by fig. 23.1 on p. 312, the capital intensity with which entrepreneurs are prepared to engage in production is given by equ. (23.8) and by the corresponding curve in fig. 23.2. With a given capital stock K the corresponding employment is then shown to be tan $\angle N$ in the north-western quadrant of fig. 23.2. With unchanged capital stock, employment could be increased by having a higher rate of interest, therefore a lower capital intensity k^r and thus a higher level of employment as represented by a new value of tan $\angle N$ in the north-western quadrant of fig. 23.2.

Conversely, lower interest rates must mean *ceteris paribus* lower employment of labour.

Our discussion thus reaches a conclusion very similar to that of Joan Robinson (1937a, p. 86):

If it is true that 'the most plausible estimate of the elasticity of substitution is unity',[4] it appears by no means fantastic to suppose that a fall in the rate of interest may reduce the equilibrium level of employment.

Algebraically, this result follows immediately from equ. (23.9) by setting $\hat{K} = 0$ so that the relative change in employment is seen to be

$$\hat{N} = -E_r^k \hat{v} > 0 \quad \text{where} \quad \hat{v} = \hat{r} \tag{23.10}$$

in conditions when the rate of interest r is equal to the rentals rate of capital v, as already postulated in equ. (23.3), p. 311.

We have thus reached – quite in accordance with Joan Robinson – a very un-Keynesian result concerning long-period employment. Keynes would have argued that low interest rates generate a high effective demand and thus lead to a high level of employment. But the long-period analysis states: low interest rates permit an economy to operate at a high capital intensity. With a given amount of capital working at full capacity, a high capital intensity means that the given amount of capital stands in relation to relatively little labour input. Therefore *low* interest rates must mean *low* employment – and conversely, high interest rates mean *high* employment. We thus have given some formal underpinnings to results of the Robinsonian model which previously seemed to lack clear analytical foundations.[5]

With this conclusion we have moved way out of Keynes' original framework, however. The quote just given from Joan Robinson (1937a, p. 86) shows that she was fully aware of this result. It is a rather precarious and unclear result, though. It left open what *caused* the change of interest rates postulated as triggering the change in employment. If it were changes in the technological conditions listed in Table 23.1 (p. 312) which affected the rate of interest, then fig. 23.2 shows that they also affect the position of the $k(\ldots)$-curve. The net outcome might be one which is different from the result just stated. If the change in the rate of interest goes together with a different rate of time preference, then one may well ask whether the accumulated stock of capital really should be treated as being the same as before. After all, the model in question is a long-period one. A different rate of time preference cannot mean that the associated changes in the economy evolve after the change is assumed to occur. Ramsey (1928, p. 556) was quoted above already (p. 210) as remarking: in such a case 'there will be not equilibrium, but saving' – or dissaving, depending on the change. But equilibrium *is* assumed to exist. Thus, we have to assume an alternative economy which operated 'sufficiently' long *already* under these alternative conditions. But then the past accumulation is most likely to have been quite different. Therefore the capital stock is most unlikely to be 'unchanged'. Some aspects of this type of problems will be dealt with in the next section.

23.4 Capital supply and employment

The assumption of a constant stock of capital which has been made so far might appear as highly unsatisfactory. When there are changes in the rate of interest we might assume, according to Joan Robinson (1937a, p. 84):

> A fall in the rate of interest will necessarily increase the equilibrium stock of capital, provided that the direct effect upon the desire to save is not highly positive.

The south-western quadrant of fig. 23.2 tries to capture the view just expressed. It shows that lower interest rates will mean lower time preference and lower time preference will then mean higher capital stock K^s, because people might be assumed to be more prepared to forgo present consumption for the sake of capital accumulation. Again, a number of provisos are called for. Thus, capital accumulation might be also affected by the intensity of depreciation as expressed by h in the K^s-curve in fig. 23.2, but in the present context this complication will not be entered into.

There are some more fundamental concerns about this type of statement, however, which should be considered in view of later criticism. It should be particularly remembered that the present analysis pertains to stationary equilibria. But in such an analytical case no net investment could be forthcoming and therefore no increase in the stock of capital would be possible. In making the above statement, Joan Robinson must have assumed a case when long-period equilibrium is (or was) *violated*, because according to her assumption of a stationary state, capital accumulation and long-period equilibrium mutually exclude each other.

Whereas in long-period equilibrium $Y_w = C_w$ always holds, capital accumulation requires

$$I_w = S_w = Y_w - C_w > 0 \tag{23.11}$$

An increase in the long-period rate of interest must mean that $r = \rho$ increased, assuming the case of homogeneous time preference and assuming that long-period equilibrium is realised. The discussed change in the rate of interest must therefore be based on inspecting changes between alternative stationary economies with different rates of time preference.

In this rather artificial way investment and hence capital stock might be seen as depending negatively on the long-run rate of interest. We depicted such a negative relationship in quadrant III of fig. 23.2 (p. 314) The analysis of long-period capital supply should be carried much further, of course. Thus, the volume of capital stock might affect the level of income and thus it might influence the absolute level of saving positively. Also, in the process of accumulation relative and absolute prices might change and thus there might be further complications to be analysed in a realistic rendering of the process of accumulation. Delving deeper into these problems seems not appropriate in the present context, however, because Joan Robinson (1937a) does not give sufficient suggestions for the factors to be considered in the analysis of the negative dependence of the long-period equilibrium stock of capital on the rate of interest.

Refraining from further speculations concerning a possible microfoundation of Joan Robinson's postulate concerning the equilibrium stock of capital, we will accept the negative dependence on the rate of interest as plausible. In this case the employment equ. (23.10) has to be modified in order to include the interest elasticity of capital supply, thereby arriving now at an expression with indeterminate sign value

$$\hat{N} = \left(\underbrace{-E_r^k}_{\substack{>0 \\ |\hat{K}=0}} + \underbrace{E_r^{K^s}}_{<0} \right) \hat{r} \gtrless 0. \tag{23.12}$$

where the second elasticity in the brackets expresses the negative relationship between capital supply K^s and the rate of interest resp. the rate of time preference just discussed and expressed graphically in the south-western quadrant of fig. 23.2.

One could describe these considerations with the help of the terms 'capital deepening' and 'capital widening': the former means that more capital per labour is employed, or, when capital is assumed to be constant, as is here the case, that less labour per capital is used if 'deepening' occurs. A rise in the rate of interest means according to the first elasticity in equ. (23.12) that capital becomes dearer, production becomes less capital intensive, and – with given capital – this means more employment. The second term in equ. (23.12) means that with higher interest rates capital is not as abundant as with lower ones. In order to reach the lower capital intensity, the expansion of employment is not required if there is negative 'widening' due to higher interest rates. Now it turns out that alternative interest rates must be associated with opposing effects on deepening and widening of capital. Therefore no clear-cut statements are possible concerning the reaction of employment to changed interest rates.

With this result we have again reached a conclusion very similar to one stated by Joan Robinson (1937a, p. 124) who also stresses that 'a fall in the rate of interest may either increase or decrease the equilibrium amount of employment.'

But the microfoundations of this result are quite different in her case, in the case of Jan Kregel's (1983) essay and in ours. Joan Robinson explains her result with reference to changes in the scarcity of non-labour factors of production. Jan Kregel (1983, p. 350) supplies microfoundations of Joan Robinson's employment theoretic results which consider the relation between changes in the elasticity of substitution, on the one hand, and in the Marshallian elasticity of demand on the other. Our rationalisation, however, assumed the elasticity of substitution as fixed and concentrated on the employment effects of the interplay of capital widening and capital deepening which may be associated with alternative levels of the rate of interest.

24
The Robinsonian Model as a Basis for the Critique of Traditional Economics

24.1 Sraffian themes in the Robinsonian 'extension'

Having reconsidered the structure, the microfoundations, and the workings of the Robinsonian extension of the Keynesian model, we are now in a position to evaluate in our own terms Jan Kregel's (1983) attribution of strategic importance of this model for modern economic debates. Let us remember that Kregel started his essay from the remark that:

> The initial challenge to the marginalist theory of capital arose from Joan Robinson's 'generalisation of *The General Theory*' to long-period conditions. The question she raised was subsequently settled within the context of Sraffa's rehabilitation of the classical conception of prices of production.

This judgment was indeed suggested by Joan Robinson (1979d, p. xx) herself, when she remarked that her first attempt to generalise the *General Theory* 'was undertaken before we had the benefit of Piero Sraffa's re-interpretation of Ricardo'.

'A more serious defect' of her early analysis was in her opinion (*ibid.*), 'great vagueness about the meaning of the capital value of an operational stock of means of production', a problem which was noted by Harrod (1937a) already. In the production theoretic framework of her early employment theoretic essays this problem could be overcome by evaluating capital in terms of Keynes' wage units, as long as a capital good has an associated marginal productivity of *labour*. The latter's reciprocal value gives then immediately the corresponding measure of value of the capital good produced. It was recognised by Robinson (1979d, p. xx) that 'the Keynesian wage unit serves just as well' as Sraffa's *numeraire* for measures of value. Our reconstruction of her model in terms of the Keynesian wage unit should therefore have met important aspects of evaluation problems which could be seen in the context of her early extension of the Keynesian model.

The main point of the Sraffian exercise of laying the basis for a critique of 'marginal productivity' was that the 'technical specifications do not determine distribution between wages and profits' (*ibid.*).

Against the background of neoclassical teaching a particularly startling result of Sraffa's model is that in order 'to find the rate of profit on capital we must know the technical conditions of production and the share of wages in net output' (*op. cit.*, p. xxi). It should be pointed out that both these results which were considered as very important in Joan Robinson's reception of the Sraffian model were contained in her original extension of the Keynesian model as interpreted in the present paper: the first point follows immediately from equ (21.27) which shows that labour's share λ^r is by no means determined by the technological conditions alone as given by the elasticities of production in that expression. The rate of depreciation h and the rate of capital cost v are also important for distribution. The neoclassical doctrine can contradict this view by postulating the assumption of capital being eternal in the sense of $h = 0$. Joan Robinson's assumption of production for capital replacement is thus seen to be an important step away from the established neoclassical thinking in the direction of later Sraffian results. It is a simple corollary of this analysis that fixing the share of wages at a particular value means to fix the rentals rate and hence the rate of profit on capital as will be seen from inspecting the south-western quadrant of fig. 21.1 (p. 285).[1] Thus the present rendering of the Robinsonian model contains two main results of Sraffa's later construction.

We conclude that if seen in the light of the present interpretation, Joan Robinson's long-period extension of the *General Theory* will appear as heralding indeed important results of Sraffa's later and very different construction.

24.2 The Keynesian problem of employment determination in the Robinsonian extension

The main point of Keynes' critique of the Classics is quite different from that of Sraffa. It consists in a denial of a real wage mechanism in determining the level of employment. In Keynes' original formulation this determination is done by the level of effective demand. In a different guise the Robinsonian model takes up this point by also representing the level of employment as being determined without supply and demand considerations on the labour market, namely by the rate of interest.

It is true that in Robinsonian long-period equilibrium there is no room for liquidity preference so that the resulting theory of interest must be un-Keynesian in the sense of showing interest to be time-preference determined: it might then be argued that time preference refers not only to consumption but also to an intertemporal labour–leisure choice. Carrying such argument further it could finally perhaps be claimed that employment is, after all, determined by individual willingness to work. In this context we have now a new significance of the assumption of Kalecki savings discussed above. Although this assumption was seen to be unable to save the Keynesian theory of the consumption function from becoming a time preference theory of interest under conditions of long-period equilibrium, under the assumption of Kalecki savings workers' time preferences can be treated as immaterial for the determination of the rate of interest. Hence their intertemporal labour–leisure choice can be claimed not to be represented by the rate of interest, since it is only the time preference of the non-workers which determines it. The long-period model must therefore admit the possibility of involuntary unemployment although its equilibrium concept is identical with the classical one.

If Joan Robinson (1937a) can be interpreted as having successfully made the point about the existence of Keynesian unemployment even in the un-Keynesian context of Pigovian equilibrium, why then did she not proceed to a solid elaboration of her rather sketchy early essay? In answering this question Pigou's (1943) reformulation of the classical stationary state could have considerable significance.

As already mentioned in section 18.2 on p. 256 above, Pigou's (1943) article is mostly famous for its presentation of the 'Pigou effect' of the real value of 'outside money' holdings on consumption. But there is a further novel element in this restatement of the classical paradigm. As an analogue to the zero-savings condition generating the time preference theory of interest, Pigou (1943) introduced an additional zero investment equation with the capital stock as *endogenous* to the classical model. But if capital could be treated in such a way that, alongside with the real value of outside money, it adjusted in such a way that full employment was always secured, then, of course, the conclusion of the Robinsonian model concerning persistent involuntary unemployment is invalidated.

The most convenient counter-attack against Pigou's (1943) renewed defence of the classical model could have been to point out – now at last – its entirely unrealistic concept of *equilibrium*. But this line of argument could not easily be pursued by Joan Robinson since she herself was prepared to accept the Pigovian concept of equilibrium. Instead, she eventually turned to the critique of the concept of *capital* as such – but she maintained for a considerable time the un-Keynesian modelling of long-period economics. A case in point is her republication of her largely Pigovian *Essays in the Theory of Employment* declaring (Robinson, 1947, p. v):

There have been considerable developments since these essays were written, both in theory and in experience . . . At the same time I believe that they are not without relevance to the dominant problems of the present day.

She seems to have still been totally unaware of Keynes' gibe about this type of 'frozen land' – economics 'remote in its characteristics from all experience' (see above, p. 170).

24.3　The capital-theoretic critique and 'historical time'

In pursuing her capital-theoretic critique, Joan Robinson gave up the assumption of differentiable production functions and thus abandoned the production theoretic basis of her early Keynesian extension. But eventually she also dismissed a prominent element of the capital-theoretic critique itself, namely the 'reswitching debate' which originally she herself had initiated. Since Keynes himself had no problem with sectoral production functions and with corresponding conceptions of decreasing marginal productivities, it seems appropriate in the present context not to close the discussion of Joan Robinson's 'Keynesian extension' without briefly commenting on this later development.

Joan Robinson's capital-theoretic critique involved the transition from an analysis of stationary states to one of quasi-stationary 'golden ages'.[2] But such a shift of perspective does not in itself imply a change in the principle of classical long-period analysis. Such quasi-stationary states were contemplated and dismissed by none other than Pigou (1935, p. 5) who commented that the conception of such states 'stands but little nearer to reality ... than that of a stationary state proper'. To elaborate an analysis of such states means to return to an analytical framework which is generally acknowledged to be almost as remote from reality as that of Pigou (1935). It did not yet signify a return to Keynes' perspective of longer-run analysis as outlined above.

The continuity of her analytical approach was stressed by Joan Robinson (1956, p. vi) herself when she expressly related her *magnum opus* on the accumulation of capital to her early Keynesian extension and to the interpretation of Ricardo by Sraffa:

> The problem presented itself to me as the generalisation of the *General Theory*, that is, an extension of Keynes's short-period analysis to long-run development. But I was very much illuminated by Piero Sraffa's Introduction to Ricardo's *Principles*.

When Sraffa (1960) published a systematic 'neo-Ricardian' model, there developed a sizeable school in which it was believed that Keynesian long-period model building would most appropriately be done along Sraffian lines. It was then not surprising that eventually the question arose whether

> Sraffa type models 'may provide better support than was provided by Keynes himself for establishing the principle of effective demand in long-period analysis'. (Garegnani, 1979, p. 181)

Thus Joan Robinson's attempt to *extend* the *General Theory* eventually suggested *abandoning* it.

This development seems not to have been intended by Joan Robinson herself. She again shifted her analytical focus. In some of her last publications she came to question not so much the classical concept and measurement of *capital* but the classical treatment of *time*. She thus returned to important aspects of Keynes' critique of classical analysis as quoted above on p. 170.

Garegnani (1979, p. 183) pointed out, however, that what Joan Robinson herself had to offer analytically in this context was mainly in terms of 'analyses of steady growth which she would freely admit have little to do with accumulation in "historical time" '. The Robinsonian model here under discussion is a particularly poignant illustration of this characterisation since the implicit rate of accumulation is assumed to be zero so that it is set solidly in what Keynes considered to be the classical 'frozen land' economics.

We may now assess the second part of Jan Kregel's (1983: p. 344) observation that it was the 'successes and failures' of this initial formulation which came to dominate important aspects of economic theorising for several decades afterwards. From the standpoint of Keynes' original longer-run perspective as developed in the seventeenth chapter of the *General Theory*, the failure of this approach was indeed its lack of 'historical time' in the sense that it ignored the problem of alternative grades of liquidity of assets and alternative rates of appreciation. From the standpoint of Joan Robinson's later capital-theoretic intentions there is the problem of a remarkable lack of critical 'bite' of her 1937 model. In order to appreciate this fully, one will have to look back at this model under the perspective of that capital-theoretic debate. This would lead too far in the present context but it will appear that, depending an the valuation scheme, the important classical capital intensity postulates survive comfortably in the Robinsonian extension of the *General Theory* (see Ambrosi 1985). After Joan Robinson (1975) came to declare the 'unimportance' of the capital-theoretic reswitching debate which was set in 'logical time' and not in 'historical time', the most important failure of her 1937 model must be seen in its ahistorical long-period equilibrium concept. In this regard, the Robinsonian extension of the *General Theory* did not supply a fruitful line of research, although it did preserve important Keynesian points and foreshadowed essential results of Sraffa's reconstruction of Richardian analysis.

24.4 Assessing Joan Robinson's model in view of the Keynes-and-Pigou debate

The present chapter set out from the hypothesis that the reluctance of the young Keynesians to enter into a critical debate of Pigou's 'simplified model' of the classical view stemmed from a dilemma facing them. The dilemma in question was analysed with reference to the 'Keynesian extension' proposed by Joan Robinson (1937a). It might appear that in concentrating on this piece of analysis we chose an unrepresentative utterance from the camp of Keynes' contemporary disciples. Anticipating such an impression we documented that we were not alone in attributing great importance to this piece of analysis. Jan Kregel (1983) placed its 'successes and failures' at the centre of the development of post-Keynesian economics.

Put briefly, the dilemma manifesting itself in Joan Robinson's publication was the attempt to develop an analysis of Keynesian unemployment in the analytical context of Pigovian economics. This approach was understood by Joan Robinson as a 'generalisation' of the *General Theory*. She does not seem to have been aware at that time that 'extending' Keynes to conditions of classical long-period analysis meant submitting him to an analytical situation in which little survived of those concepts which were important for Keynes, for example:

- Keynes' consumption function;
- the concept of intertemporal appreciation of asset prices;
- the idea of differences in liquidity among different assets;
- the difference between the rate of interest and the marginal physical product of capital;

to name just those elements of Keynesian analysis which we were able to contrast to Joan Robinson's application of classical concepts in the present context. Nevertheless, we concede that Joan Robinson's model (1936, 1937a) contains important aspects of Keynesian and post-Keynesian economics. Concerning the former it was seen that it depicted employment determination admitting the possibility of involuntary unemployment. Concerning post-Keynesian elements it was demonstrated that this model anticipated the Sraffian trade-off between labour's share of income and the rate of interest. It is doubtful, however, whether these elements of Joan Robinson's model can be considered as particularly successful as a *critique* of 'classical' *anti*-Keynesian economics. The interest rate and wage share aspect was found to be implicit in Pigou (1937) as well, as was seen above when discussing λ^P on p. 213. So it cannot be considered as being central for an anti-classical and pro-Keynesian position in our view. Indeed, this particular analytical interconnection was an element of Pigou's intended debate with 'recent writers', this term explicitly addressing Joan Robinson.[3] Unfortunately, this debate was not taken up in a form which Keynes tried to encourage, namely by having published comments on Pigou (1937, 1938) from his Cambridge confidants.

As far as the modelling of unemployment in long-period equilibrium is concerned, this was only a passing success over Pigou's (1935) early formulation of the classical stationary state. When Pigou (1937) was prepared to include money wages into the classical scheme and when Pigou (1943) finally introduced the 'Pigou effect' and endogenous capital into the formulation of the classical full-employment model, the 'Keynesian extension' along the lines of Joan Robinson (1937a) was outdated.

Faced with this development, Joan Robinson (1956) tried to defend her earlier research programme by questioning the classical concept of capital which played an important role in Pigou's (1943) formulation of the classical stationary state already. This new approach led to an abandonment of that theory of production which formerly was cultivated by Joan Robinson herself and which was expressly accepted by Keynes in the *General Theory*. This abandonment eventually led Keynesian long-period analysis into a close vicinity with Sraffa (1960) – so much so that eventually the question arose whether, in this context, Keynesian economics should not be replaced outright by the Sraffian approach.[4]

At that stage of the debate Joan Robinson finally abandoned the research programme which had placed her in the dilemma which we analysed in the above. She now emphasised the difference between 'logical time' – which really is an abolition of time – in the classical long-period analysis on the one hand and 'historical time' in Keynesian economics. This juxtaposition led her to the declaration of the unimportance of 'reswitching' and thus of the unimportance of important aspects of the capital-theoretic controversy initiated by none other than herself. In Joan Robinson's later judgement her first 'post-Keynesian' model must be considered as a failure. But her views changed concerning its *strategic* mistake.[5] Her model of 1936 and its extensions published in the following year accepted a number of classical tenets, in particular:

* the classical concept of long-period equilibrium at perennially constant prices;
* the marginal productivity of capital theory of interest;
* the neoclassical production function.

At the time of her capital-theoretic debates Joan Robinson obviously considered the last two concepts as particularly unsatisfactory and she reworked them in an ingenious way in the course of that critique. But after she declared the capital-theoretic reswitching debate as 'unimportant', the strategic failure of the 'Classics' must be sought somewhere else. In our view it is the concept of classical long-period equilibrium. Keynes himself wanted to refer to these type of models as representing 'frozen land' economies – a characterisation which Richard Kahn rebuked at that time in the name of Pigou. The later Joan Robinson endorsed it when, in her later critique of the 'capital theoretic critique', she called for focusing on 'historical time'. Nevertheless, as far as her more or less explicit *modelling* of the working of the economy is concerned, we feel entitled to conclude with Geoff Harcourt's (1996, p. 317) observation:

> But when we look at the *substance* of her analysis ... we find her Marshallian, even Pigovian, background tending to break through. (emphasis in the original, GMA)

It is a pity, however, that this analytical family resemblance was occasionally denied and that for outsiders it is sometimes rather laborious to establish before the background of anti-classical polemics.

This assessment suggests the further conclusion that if one should endeavour to rework the Keynesian long-run economics in view of the past Keynes-and-Pigou debate, the main effort should go into avoiding the classical concept of long-period equilibrium in terms of stationary and quasi-stationary states, and not so much the classical concept of differentiable production functions.

Part V
Paradigms and Perspectives

25
Paradigms of a Re-authenticated Keynes–Classics Debate

25.1 Re-authenticating the Keynes–Classics debate

Mark Blaug (1990, p. 36) once insisted 'that economic knowledge is historically determined' and in that context he also proclaimed: 'Without Pigou:
no Keynes'. The present book is a variation on this seemingly simple
theme. It argues more specifically that without Pigou's *Theory of
Unemployment* (1933) there would be no *General Theory of Employment* as
Keynes apostrophised his last book. Complications surrounding this theme
are not necessarily inherent in its substance but rather the result of a
cacophony of secondary literature. Nowadays one must work out that
theme before the background of claims that it is wrong,[1] slanted,[2] regret-
table,[3] analytically inconsequential,[4] 'bastard Keynesian',[5] to list but a few
substantiation of discordant voices. In view of widely differing claims about
the issues relevant in this context, we made the attempt to 're-authenticate'
the original debate around the *General Theory* as far as Keynes and Pigou
were concerned. This often meant going through the relevant arguments
verbatim as they were addressed from Keynes against Pigou and *vice versa*
and then to prop up those quotes with model-building scaffolding in such
a way that it would support a wide variation of the original theme. In this
way – so it is hoped – it might be better appreciated that there were indeed
unifying themes in this *debate*. A case in point was our application of the
'*LIS* apparatus' (see fig. 16.1, p. 204) for graphically confronting the 'Keynes
effect' (see fig. 16.2, p. 206) on the one hand, with the corresponding structure of Pigou's 'simplified model' on the other hand (see fig. 16.3, p. 218),
but also admitting an analogous presentation of the 'Kaldorian synthesis'
(see fig. 17.1, p. 230).

The example just given illustrates not only the topic 'theme and variations'. It illustrates also the fact that the self-same theme can be associated
with quite different 'composers' so that it might subsequently have quite a
different significance in spite of its seemingly clear identity. But at least
since Kuhn (1970) and his analysis of paradigm changes in science it is well

known that identical bits of knowledge can be embedded in methodologically quite different systems of argumentation. Such difference in spite of all the well-known similarities was stated by Pigou (1936, p. 122) when he accused Keynes of muddling the 'stationary' state with a 'moving' one on the one hand,[6] and by Keynes on the other hand when he formulated the 'frozen land' analogy for the 'stationary state', negating any relevance of it in the world we actually live in.

We are now in the final part V of this book in which we will have to summarise and round off the above arguments. In this connection we will also attempt to point out interconnections and extensions which previously might not have fitted into the stream of argumentation. In the present chapter we will dwell in particular on the topic of 're-authentication'. In this context we address also the rather complex question of differences in paradigms, just mentioned in the preceding paragraph. In this context it might be remembered that some commentators saw an almost plagiaristic relation in Keynes' dealings with Pigou. Our assessment in this chapter therefore also includes a more detailed analysis of the indeed remarkable instances of a concordance between the *General Theory* and Pigou (1933).

In the next chapter we will then ask in more detail for the analytical aspects of our attempted reauthentication. Issues which are traditionally much discussed in connection with the Keynes–Classics debate are questions of 'microfoundations' and of general equilibrium analysis. They also find a considerable place in that assessment.

In the final chapter we propose to look beyond the confines of the issues just discussed and to open the perspective on the wider views which the *General Theory* can imply.

25.2 Basic issues – an overview

25.2.1 The futile quest for novelty in an over-aged debate

The program of re-authenticating the historical *interaction* in economics which took place at the time of the appearance of Keynes' *General Theory* was presented above in part I. The motive for such a programme was the strange state of debate in academic economics during the past decades. Over and over again the names of Keynes and of his more or less constructed adversary, the Classics, were each associated with dramatic and violent sounding programmatic statements using terms like 'revolution' or 'counter-revolution', of 'death' and 'oblivion'.

The once agitated academic community eventually discovered that the supposedly annihilated adversary position was by no means done with but soon claimed lasting victory, with the antagonistic name-giving going into further and further rounds. Thus economics, in contrast to some other branches of science, does not seem to offer a *development* of paradigms. It offers rather a little respected truce of alternative schools of thought, met with increasing doubt about substantial progress. This directionless movement not only calls into question the idea of scientific progress, it is also disorienting for the grand questions of present-day economic policy. Part I above developed this diagnosis and presented the plan of the book, namely to return to the authentic Keynes-and-Pigou debate which lies behind these recurring revolutions.

In some cases the loss of direction stemmed from the very authors who wanted to help their colleagues to find one. There are several interpreters of Keynes' putative will who proclaimed with great conviction that they – at long last – had found the strategic issue of the Keynes–Classics debate. But when they later renounced the relevance of their finding, they left a vacuum which they then could not fill themselves. The most famous case in point is Joan Robinson (1975) proclaiming the unimportance of reswitching, after having spent some of her most creative years in arguing its importance for a critique of 'classical' economics. A second case in point may be found with Axel Leijonhufvud (1974, p. 169) who denied the importance of a revolution in adjustment speeds for Keynes, after having previously emphatically proclaimed that herein lay the very essence of the Keynesian revolution (see above, p. 6). In pointing out the recantations which were done in these debates, we do not want to belittle the important work by economists who were inspired by previous interpretational proclamations. But the recantations having been made, it is of considerable interest to find a new orientation for research programmes for those economists who do consider this kind of debate to be of relevance. The unabated persistence of Keynes–Classics debates indicates that the community of researchers interested in these matters cannot be considered to be negligible.

We just mentioned cases of interpretational recantations which left their respective readers at a loss about the solutions to the puzzles of economic literature which were posed to begin with. There are other cases where one is forced to resort more to one's own critical reasoning in order to get into that state when contemplating the fate of the Keynes–Classics debate. Cases in point are comments of this debate which present Keynes' contributions as bordering on the fraudulent (see below p. 389), on the banal (see above, p. 25), or on plagiarism (see above, p. 26). Although some of these positions were seen to have been endorsed by such a high authority in these matters as David Laidler (1999) (see above p. 168), they do appear as being of rather limited plausibility as soon as one does go to the relevant sources. Again we hasten to say that this is not to deny a certain justification for the quoted positions. But exactly because and insofar as we are interested in these judgments we should consider ourselves free – or rather obliged – to make up our own minds on these much discussed issues in the development of economic paradigms.

As stated earlier, our approach is not motivated by the desire to linger on any of the isolated historical positions in the old Keynes–Classics debate. Thus, the question of the 'authenticity' of Hicks' (1937) *IS–LM* interpretation did not come up here because it is a more or less isolated *interpretation* of debatable points and not an element of the debate itself.[7] Ours was rather a new attempt at reinspecting the debate as it was conducted *between* the respective positions, i.e. predominantly between Keynes and Pigou. But silence is also an interesting point in a debate and this meant that occasionally we had to explicate in some detail positions which were present only 'silently'. This was particularly the case with Joan Robinson's (1936) model and its classical implications. The particular relevance of this model stemmed not least from the fact that Pigou claimed that his anti-Keynesian 'simplified model' (1937) was predominantly addressed at *her* model. It is in this sense that we make a claim for a re-authentication of the Keynes–Classics debate, namely in re-establishing the argumentative *context*. The perhaps most interesting argumentative entanglement which emerged in this approach was described above when Keynes was shown to defend Kaldor's synthesis with Pigou, Keynes thereby defending time preference determined interest rates against criticism from R. F. Kahn. But it was not the entanglement as such which was of interest here, it was the inner logic which intellectually motivated this argumentative constellation. This wider context then suggested intellectual connections between Cambridge Young Keynesians (R. F. Kahn and Joan Robinson) on the one hand, and A. C. Pigou on the other hand which are not expected if one cultivates a purely confrontational perspective between Keynesians and Classics like Pigou.

We readily admit, however, that this 're-authentication' must in fact be a reconstruction on the basis of published works, of snippets of published communications and reports. These elements cannot but be pieces of puzzles, the final shape of which being never-signed canvasses of the old master himself–the more so, as there are several masters to such a debate. The picture emerging is, in the last resort, the responsibility of the author who does the reconstruction.

25.2.2 Pivotal points of the debate

It appeared in subsequent parts of this book that the interaction between Keynes and Pigou was mediated and influenced in a particularly interesting way by three young economists generally subsumed as Cambridge Keynesians, namely by Richard Kahn and Joan Robinson, and by Nicholas Kaldor, the latter being really a Cambridge outsider at that time. We stress, of course, that with this observation we do not claim to offer the reader a new finding. What *is* new in this book is a specific reconstruction of a debate or of a specific instance in the Keynes-and-Pigou debate in which it was proclaimed to abstain from pursuing particular points. If matters did *not* come to a head in that debate, it appears to have been because of a seemingly insignificant episode of editorial advice.

One is tempted to resort to the language of drama in this connection: the plot of Orson Welles' much praised masterpiece, the film *Citizen Kane* (1941), evolves around one single word, 'Rosebud' – and the posthumous search for its significance. It is a claim of the present book that in a similarly evolved but fascinating way the plot of the post-Keynesian drama might be seen to hinge on one single expression: 'frozen land'. The scenes in which that expression is stated and then rescinded are maybe the most dramatic and controversial ones for posterity's understanding of the Keynes-and-Pigou debate. The theme of 'frozen land' economics meanders in our view from Robinson (1936) to Pigou (1937) and eventually to Barro (1990) and the beliefs of 'New Classical Economics'. It stands behind Joan Robinson's (1973a) flashback to the 'infinite pains' taken by Richard Kahn after 1930 to explain Keynesian thought in the context of a reinvented scheme of Marxian simple reproduction.[8] It mars Joan Robinson's look back at her brainchild, the 'reswitching debate' which she eventually disowns as being 'unimportant'–because it is set in the frozen land of timelessness. This expression stands in a way behind an empty promise given by Richard Kahn to Keynes in 1937. It is a token for illusions which misled revolutionary fervour into barren land. This expression is contained in one single paragraph which was never published by Keynes. Subsequently this expression was never again discussed by the main actors of the former debate–neither by Keynes nor by Pigou, his authentic Classic.

But this does not diminish its significance. Analysing the interaction around these suppressed words reopens the authentic debate in which Keynes himself hoped to bring about the essential clarification. But – seemingly strangely – this very debate was stopped by and among his disciples although Keynes expressly asked for its continuation. Nevertheless, its aborted beginnings are of utmost interest because they bring together not only Keynes and Pigou in direct interaction about matters central for an understanding of the *General Theory*; they also involve Nicholas Kaldor (1937) as author of the only other comment on Pigou (1937) and as author of a 'Kaldorian (pseudo-) synthesis'. This episode involves Richard Kahn as the person who successfully stopped this debate from becoming one about economic paradigms, claiming that it was just about a 'most stupid mistake' and nothing else. He was the one who got Keynes to cut out that passage – against Keynes' own conviction, Kahn claiming to know Pigou's counter-arguments. In this role he manifests himself as confidant of Pigou – a role for which he was expressly acknowledged by Pigou (1935) himself. But in this context we also see Kahn in his expressly formulated attempt to suppress Kaldor's publication, thereby foreshadowing a parallel episode concerning Keynes himself.[9]

Keynes' time-preference theoretic defence of Kaldor's contribution guides us back to his previous discussions of time preference which were documented in Ramsey (1928) – thereby reminding us not only of the high standard of debate of these matters in Cambridge at the time of Ramsey's contribution, but also of the fact that this article was later referred to by Pigou (1941, p. 111) (see above p. 210), Ramsey's article thereby forming an analytical meeting ground between Keynes and Pigou also from the latter's side. Had these two words 'frozen land' been fully discussed at the time coined by Keynes, who knows whether Joan Robinson would not then have already fully understood the classical implications of stationary and quasi-stationary states and thus have been spared of her later nihilism about her own attempts in these analytical realms? In this sense these words, if fully discussed when they were written by Keynes in 1937, might have reshaped not only Joan Robinson's academic life, but decades of economic debates. But such biographical speculations can be offered here only as an 'artist's impression', not as an economic analysis. The present book is, however, very much about economic analysis.

Arguing the above case in detailed economic analysis gives the general structure of the present argument: part II sets the stage of Pigou's (1933) classical model. This model was the expressly proclaimed point of orientation for the final composition of the *General Theory* and as such really should be the standard analytical entrance for any dealings with Keynes' arguments – whether they are recreated antagonistically or not. First the model is seen in its original context as set out by Pigou himself. Then, in the light of recent debates about Keynes' alleged misrepresentation of this model, we inspect in some detail the manipulations and extensions Keynes did in fact present in the *General Theory* concerning this very model. There emerges – or rather, there is in this part II the confirmation of – a neoclassical two-sector model with sectoral production functions and with two classes of preferences. What is interesting about this model is by no means its substance itself. That is well known and the subject of countless textbooks on real models of foreign trade, on two-sectoral growth theory etc. The interesting thing is how this model emerges in the Keynes – Pigou debate as a well-determined general equilibrium model. Since it is *Keynes* who brings this aspect out, this observation gives us the opportunity to reflect once more on the much debated question of the role of general equilibrium analysis in the context of receiving Keynes' economics. In the following chapter 26 we will elaborate this point, but then not so much from the historical perspective but from an analytical one.

Whatever the outcome of the reflection about the role and the type of general equilibrium analysis to be associated nowadays with Keynesian economics, we think that in the light of our part II it is warranted to conclude: if one specific model is to be named which is the *nucleus* of the Keynes–Classics debate, it is the one debated here. There are many pages surviving in which

Keynes discusses this model either with fellow economists in letters, or with his students in lectures or with his readers in the *General Theory*. When he put the finishing touches on the manuscript of the book, he wrote to Richard Kahn (JMK, XIII, p. 525, letter of 26 March 1935):

> I have now finished a full-dress critique of the Prof. to go in as an appendix ... It will need your very close eye to make sure I have not anywhere misunderstood him or misrepresented him. The stuff he writes seems to me the most extraordinary in some ways in the history of the subject. But it has a dreadful fascination for me, and I cannot leave it alone.

In fact, there is no other algebraic model of an economy which Keynes discussed at any length in the context of the *General Theory*. Keynes worked intermittently on this model at least from 5 September 1933 when he wrote a letter to Dennis Robertson discussing this model (JMK, XIII, p. 310) until at least the date of the letter just quoted. He corresponded over this model with some of the sharpest minds in his surroundings (Robertson, Shove, Harrod, Kahn, later Hawtrey) and on 16 and 23 October 1933 Keynes lectured on Pigou (1933) according to Rymes (1989, pp. 85–90).

The words Keynes chooses in the quote just given after more than one and a half years of discussing and scrutinising this model are remarkable and might require more explanation than we gave hitherto: why, in particular, and in which sense did Keynes consider Pigou (1933) to be 'most extraordinary in some ways in the history of the subject'?[10]

In view of these observations we can state that Cambridge Keynesian economics is in essential ways also Pigovian economics:

(i)   Pigou (1933) supplied the centerpiece of Keynes' authentic critique of Classical economics.
(ii) Pigou (1937) and its 'simplified model' had a pivotal role for defending the 'classical' view in an authentic and documentable debate between Pigou, Keynes and post-Keynesians, and finally
(iii) the long-period extension of Keynesian analysis suggested by Joan Robinson (1937a) may be seen along – what we considered to be – essentially Pigovian lines.

In part II we looked at the implications of item (i); part III had as its central model the one of item (ii); and part IV was mainly concerned with the model of item (iii). Thus, in the above we had a predominantly model-oriented approach. The advantage of such an approach is that it gives a plain structure of the arguments which are put forth and thus it should facilitate a critical evaluation. The disadvantage of such an approach is that in some respects it is too confined and it conveys too little of the motives and of the paradigms of the participants of the debate.

This is a serious limitation in an enquiry like the present one. Occasionally we were able to step beyond those limitations. But further down we must make some further attempts by addressing in a more discursive manner some of the remaining questions which arise from our central themes, i.e. the question of the significance of a personal and of an analytic Pigovian context for the economics of Keynes and for Cambridge 'Keynesians'. We use quotation marks here to foreshadow that in the end the theoretical allegiance shifted more towards Kalecki but that still remains to be argued. Before embarking on that line of argumentation we want to draw attention to what was argued so far in the more model-oriented approach.

25.2.3 Analytical results of the present re-authentication

25.2.3.1 Keynes' critique of Pigou: marginalist analysis in a short-period setting

In the analysis of Keynes' critique of Pigou (1933) it was seen that Keynes takes Pigou's model to be one of the short-period determination of employment in a two-sectorally disaggregated closed economy. The central concept of the Pigovian model was seen to be the real demand function for labour. This function was reconstructed from the microfoundations of the Pigovian two-sector model. The interdependence of supply and demand aspects in the construction of this curve was exposed and they were related to standard marginalist economic concepts.

Building on the microfoundations of the Pigovian model it was then shown that in his criticism of the Classics, Keynes extended this model in several ways. First he formulated conventional labour supply considerations for the particular context of the Pigovian model, interpreting it as one of general equilibrium. The Marshallian aspect of this view of Keynes' was investigated in detail. It was shown that one aspect of Keynes' critical discussion of the classical theory of employment – his immanent critique – was based on this extension, or rather this explication, of the Pigovian model.

But there is a further strand in Keynes' critique of the Classics which appears to be quite different from the analysis of Pigou. Nevertheless Keynes does not reject the analytical foundations of the Pigovian model as such. He rather uses a further extension of his model in order to show that it is overdetermined in the case of involuntary unemployment. The main aim of this particular strand of Keynes' critique is to show that Pigou (1933), in discussing changes in the real demand function of labour, discusses changes in the sectoral structure of labour demand. What Keynes wanted to establish as being of central importance for employment is, however, the level of demand. In arguing Keynes' case concerning the level of effective demand, Pigou's original two-sector model may be easily aggregated to give the Keynesian presentation of an economy. This correspondence between Keynes and Pigou was shown graphically in fig. 11.1

on p. 131. Chapter 12 then discussed the wider significance of this recon-struction, giving particular attention to problems of dimensionality and of aggregation.

25.2.3.2 Pigou's classical response: employment in a long-period setting

Pigou's (1937) response to the Keynesian challenge was conducted in the context of a 'simplified model'. This model is little known in the Keynes–Classics debate and its significance was discussed above in some detail. The particular significance of this stage of the Keynes–Classics debate lies in the clarification which it supplies concerning the classical theory of interest rate determination and of the classical concept of equilib-rium. In Pigou's (1937) view the rate of interest is determined by time pref-erence. Keynes' disciples Joan Robinson and R. F. Kahn saw herein a grave argumentative flaw. Astonishingly, Keynes himself saw the matter differ-ently and accepted Pigou's time preference the time preference analysis as a common ground between Keynes and the Classics as represented by Pigou. It was demonstrated that Keynes' acceptance of the Pigovian theory of interest under conditions of classical stationary equilibrium is consistent with his claim that his theory is a more general one than the classical theory. This claim was substantiated by demonstrating in some detail that, in Pigovian equilibrium, Keynes' consumption function collapses into the time preference theory of interest. There are two somewhat confusing ques-tions associated with Pigou's 'simplified model', namely:

(a) against whom did he intend to argue?
(b) what was the analytical time period involved?

Concerning (a), we established that it was indeed the workings of the 'Keynes effect' against which Pigou's critique was directed. R. F. Kahn's claim – supposedly relating Pigou's authentic position – that Pigou (1937) wanted to argue not against Keynes but against Joan Robinson could not cover the entire front of the Pigovian attack. At least it did not deter Keynes from reacting. But there is an interesting relationship to Joan Robinson, especially via the answer to (b).

Concerning question (b), it emerged that his model was a long-period one. Claims to the contrary were discussed. The presentation of Pigou's simplified model generated the following results:

(i)   It is a macroeconomic one-sector model which abstracts from much of the production theoretic refinement of Pigou's (1933) earlier work which was discussed in the previous chapter.
(ii)   The Pigovian 'cost unit' for marginal employment is not just the wage rate but it includes the rate of interest as well. This construction is similar to Samuelson's (1978) 'canonical classical model'.[11]

(iii)   The share of wages in national income is not given by technology alone but by the rate of interest as well.

(iv)   The quantity of money is not exogenous but depends positively on the rate of interest.

The essence of Pigou's classical theory of the wage-rate and interest rate nexus then is: due to item (ii) in the above list, *either* money wages *or* the rate of interest may be lowered in order to lower marginal cost and hence the price level. For a constant money income this means, in both cases, that the level of employment must increase (given constant technology in the standard sense). But since a decrease in the rate of interest will decrease the supply of money due to item (iv) above, decreasing the rate of interest might well decrease money income and possibly it might also decrease employment. This conclusion could then contradict the economics of the Keynes effect which suggests that only if the rate of interest is decreased may one count an employment expansion induced by money wage cuts.

We noted that although Keynes solicited comments an this type of analysis, none of his supposed analytical allies did in fact collaborate in a constructive way in this respect. It was just Kaldor (1937), an outsider of the Keynesian circle at that time, who, in an unsolicited comment on Pigou (1937), defended the Keynesian position. His approach was to:

(i)   accept the time preference theory of interest, thereby being in accordance with Keynes in this context;

(ii)   make time preference a decreasing function of real income;[12]

(iii)   introduce the 'Keynes effect' into the Hicksian *IS–LM* scheme;

(iv)   reinterpret Pigou's money supply doctrine in such a way as to be able to postulate a novel liquidity trap, namely a money supply trap.

The significance of this approach was: item (ii) assures that increases in employment can occur only at decreasing interest rates as was originally postulated by Keynes and item (iv) demonstrates the potential breakdown of an employment policy based an a wage-cutting mechanism which does not rely an Keynes' original money demand considerations. Item (iii) suggested a synthesis of the Keynesian, the Hicksian and the Pigovian approaches which was represented graphically in fig. 17.1 on p. 230.

The problem with the 'Keynesian synthesis', as offered by Kaldor (1937), was that it enabled Pigou (1938) to claim that it admittedly gives a plausible construction of an economic model, but that it showed, according to Pigou, that the Keynesian theory is just a special *alternative* to the classical one, and not a more general scheme of analysis. Keynes foresaw this argument and cautiously disassociated himself from Kaldor's 'Keynesian synthesis'.

The chapter finishes with discussing briefly the continuing reluctance of Keynes' disciples Joan Robinson and R. F. Kahn to enter into a serious discussion of Pigou's simplified model. It was the latter in particular, who was once described as Keynes' 'Messenger Angel' (see James Meade in JMK, XIII, p. 339), who actively tried to reduce the extent of controversy going on. He intervened unsuccessfully in order to stop Keynes from publishing Kaldor's (1937) note and he encouraged Keynes successfully to omit important comments an Pigou's muddled concept of equilibrium.

These observations prepared the ground for the next chapter in which the attempt was made to substantiate the hypothesis that some of Keynes' disciples were caught on the horns of a dilemma because they tried to be loyal to concepts of, both, Pigovian equilibrium and Keynesian unemployment.

25.2.3.3 *Joan Robinson's 'extension' and the post-Keynesian dilemma*

Part IV dealt in more detail with the uneasy position of some post-Keynesians in the tension between the analytical approaches of Keynes and Pigou.

It elaborated the dilemma just described for the case of Joan Robinson's research programme. We agreed with previous views (Kregel, 1983) that the nucleus for much of this programme is given by her essays on the theory of (long-run) employment (Joan Robinson 1937a). This part of the book supplies a new microfoundation of the Robinsonian theory of Keynesian unemployment in a long-period equilibrium context. Since Joan Robinson's original approach accepted the marginalist theory of production, we were able to continue employing further some of the results developed already in part II, namely our 'Keynesian sectoral value supply functions'.

Referring back also to our Pigou (1937)-oriented part III, it was demonstrated that the Robinsonian model must employ the time preference theory of interest – in accordance with Keynes' own view as it emerged from his discussion of Pigou's 'simplified model'. A microfoundation was now supplied for the downward sloping time-preference function already discussed in the context of Kaldor's (1937) comment on Pigou (1937). In this context a Sraffa-type trade-off between interest rates and the share of wages in national product was generated, but here on the basis of a conventional marginalist theory of production. Special attention was given to the relation between the marginal productivity of capital theory of interest, accepted by Joan Robinson in these essays, on the one hand, and Keynesian asset demand concepts on the other hand. The 'frozen-land' implications of the former were stressed. As far as results of discussing the workings of the model were concerned, it was seen that for a given capital supply it generates the un-Keynesian result that 'a fall in the rate of interest may reduce the equilibrium level of employment' (Joan Robinson 1937a,

p. 86). For endogenous capital supply, this result may be reversed. It is on this latter aspect of the model that its claim may rest for a potentially 'Keynesian' nature. The chapter finishes with a critical evaluation of this model with regard to its potential as a basis for the critique of traditional economics.

The deficiencies of this aspect of the model were fairly obvious. It is also quite obvious that Joan Robinson's own views concerning the strategic failure of this type of models changed dramatically during the subsequent years. After Joan Robinson (1975) had proclaimed the 'unimportance of reswitching' because of the concept of long-period equilibrium implied in this debate, she solved the dilemma she faced when trying to marry Pigovian equilibrium and Keynesian unemployment by now divorcing the two again and siding only with the latter. But this meant the writing off of decades of research endeavours. As Kregel (1991, p. 108) put it in evaluating Joan Robinson's (1975, 1979a) rejection of the problem of reswitching:

> The problem that had plagued analysis of the long period throughout her career was thus classified as a wild-goose chase that had only been introduced to make sense of traditional theory.

We conclude that in her own eyes the strategic failure of her type of long-period unemployment model must be seen in its utilisation of an un-Keynesian concept of Pigovian long-period equilibrium.

25.2.3.4 *Keynes' claim for generality and the re-authentication of the Keynes–Classics debate*

The theme of questioning the generality of Keynes' *General Theory* appears in many contributions to the post Keynesian Keynes–Classics debate. It is to be found in Hicks' (1937) interpretation which apostrophised Keynes' theory as pertaining to that special case in which $|L'_2| \to \infty$ where where L_2 is the speculative demand for money. It reappears implicitly in Joan Robinson's repeated attempts at 'generalising the *General Theory*' – a programme which in itself insinuates that Keynes' own theory falls short of completely fulfilling the claim which is made in the title of his book. A further variation on this theme was given by Pigou (1938) when he claimed that the derivative of the time preference function $\rho(x)$ (resp. $\rho(n)$) admits any sign value in principle but that Kaldor (1937) demonstrated that Keynesian theory allows only for a negative value of $\rho'(\cdot)$ This proves that Keynes' theory is not a 'General Theory' because in that case it would have admitted $\rho'(\cdot) \gtrless 0$. These views found a critical reception in the present enquiry.

The Hicksian interpretation was seen to suffer from the failure to incorporate Keynes' wage function $w(N)$ where N was employment, standing for Keynes' original term 'activity' as quoted above (see p. 236). It may be seen that a perpendicular branch of the *LM* curve which Hicks used to characterise 'classical' economics could not only be generated by Hicks' assumption of $L'_2 = 0$ but, alternatively, by the assumption of $w' \to \infty$. Hicks' original scheme does not permit the discussion of these alternatives. Kaldor's (1937) discussion of the Hicksian set-up was superior in this regard in that it explicitly included changes of the wage rate. The present view was that the latter alternative is the relevant one in order to characterise Keynes' perception of classical full employment when recourse is taken to an *IS–LM* scheme. The Keynesian theory is then the more general one in admitting a wider range of possible money wage changes.

The Robinsonian attempt at 'extending' the *General Theory* to conditions of a stationary state was seen to be defective in that it employed exactly that state of economics which Keynes rejected as completely unsatisfactory for a description of realistic economic conditions. Ironically, the stationary state is exactly that special case for which none other but Keynes himself admitted that it is not liquidity preference but time preference which determines the rate of interest. Joan Robinson seems to have been aware eventually that such an ahistorical state of an economic model cannot cover Keynes' theory. But she seems not to have been aware that Keynes' theory was in fact perceived by him to be so general as to contain the classical case of time preference determined interest rates as a special one. An appropriate microfoundation of Keynes' original consumption function appeared to be the crucial step in this context. This step was not taken by the Cambridge young Keynesians, however.

Finally, Pigou's (1938) negative comment about the generality of Keynesian economics was dealt with by rejecting Kaldor's 'Keynesian synthesis' as a piece of proper Keynesianism. The basic question in this context was how to appropriately generate the negative slope of the Keynesian *IS*-curve. In the generally valid case where investment is positive and/or future income is not completely determined by present income the Keynesian characteristics of this curve follow immediately from the microfoundations of the consumption function as was demonstrated above. It is only under the special conditions of stationary equilibrium where $I = S = 0$ and where income is eternally constant that Kaldor's particular $\rho(n)$-curve becomes a necessary instrument for the derivation of Keynesian results. We conclude that in the light of the present discussion one can indeed agree with Kohn's (1986, p. 1202) statement that

'classical economics' (real analysis) [is] valid only for the special case of a repetitive flow (from which all problems of time, money, and coordination have been excluded by assumption). It is precisely in this sense that Keynes considered his theory to be a *general* theory.

Agreeing with this judgement in substance we disagree with the speculation which Kohn combines with this insight, namely 'that the *General
Theory* would have been less confusing a book had Keynes ignored Pigou's
work on unemployment entirely' (see above, p. 24). The present study suggests the opposite view: predominantly by comparing Keynesian and
Pigovian analysis in a common analytical framework is it possible to state
whether the latter is a special case of the former.

25.2.4   Towards a reconsideration of macroeconomic modelling

In the course of this investigation we considered the models of Pigou
(1937) and of Joan Robinson (1937a) as *both* being based an a paradigm of
long-period equilibrium which was not in accordance with Keynes' analytical intentions. It might come somewhat as a surprise when we now
proceed to claiming that maybe these very models might give some worthwhile suggestions for a reconsideration of customary macroeconomic
modelling.

Pigou's model is one of the first in modern macroeconomic debate to
include the rate of interest in the price equation. This suggests a look at the
relevance of the rate of interest in calculating marginal cost which is rather
different from the conventional one. That suggests monetary contraction
and higher interest rates when there is the danger of inflation. But if there
is indeed a positive relation between the rate of interest and the price level,
then it must seem futile to engage in a policy of raising the rate of interest
in order to lower the rate of inflation. The main consequence of higher
interest rates might be *higher* prices and not lower ones.

Conventional neoclassical analysis as exemplified by the 'neoclassical
synthesis' relates the price of output to the marginal unit cost as expressed
by the marginal labour cost. Similarly, much of post-Keynesian analysis
relates unit labour cost to price via a mark-up factor (see p. 453, n. 1).
Interest costs do not enter directly into these calculations. The Pigovian
'simplified model' is different in that regard in taking account of the interest cost on wages. Thus it manifests a significant difference from conventional modelling practice. It can be shown that when the production
period and the associated unit cost of financing of marginal output is modelled explicitly, macroeconomic modelling could generate a number of new
results and could explain phenomena like 'stagflation' which seemed to be
inexplainable under orthodox Keynesianism (Ambrosi, 1982). These results
need not to be debated in the present context at great length. But it may be
pointed out that Pigou's (1937) simplified model could supply an additional justification for such constructions – apart from the considerations
of the economic practitioners just mentioned.[13]

Joan Robinson's model is quite similar to that of Pigou in some respects.
One might see a peculiarity, however, in that it focuses more explicitly on
the inclusion of depreciation in the construction of macroeconomic

models which, as was seen, were then based an conventional production theoretic concepts.

Although both Pigou's (1937) and Joan Robinson's (1937a) models are unsatisfactory in that they exclude *net* investment, this fault could be easily remedied by following Keynes' original suggestions in this context. But one problem with which he dealt unsuccessfully was the systematic inclusion of depreciation cost in a macroeconomic model.[14] One of the interesting features of the Robinsonian model investigated in the preceding chapters was exactly the inclusion of this depreciation cost element in a conventional production theoretic setting. We therefore conclude that a short-period version of her model should find further application in contemporary macroeconomic modelling.

25.3 Keynes' paradigm change and the Pigovian context

25.3.1 Keynes' historical involvement with Pigou (1933)

There is no prominent economist from whom we have more published communication about Pigou (1933) than from Keynes. Soon after the book appeared in 1933, we find some correspondence between Keynes and Dennis Robertson about it, Robertson supposedly being a particularly knowledgeable person with regard to this book, since he had read the entire manuscript, according to the preface of Pigou (1933).[15] On 5 September 1933 Keynes draws Robertson into a very detailed discussion, asking him whether he had read 'the Prof's book carefully' and going through various equations and algebraic expressions (JMK, XIII, p. 310). At the same time he addresses Gerald Shove about the same subject.[16] Shove may also be considered as an 'expert' with relevant knowledge, since he had reviewed very thoroughly Hicks' *Theory of Wages* (1932) for the *Economic Journal* (Shove, 1933). In the autumn of 1933 Keynes, after a thorough discussion of the book with the two 'experts' just named, gives a lecture on the *Theory of Unemployment* (see JMK, XIII, p. 420), his written lecture notes having been sent to Shove before (JMK, XIII, p. 326, n. 1).

Two years after the first letters about this subject, Keynes writes a letter to Dennis Robertson on 10 October 1935 in which he refers to previous comments from Robertson to the extent that Keynes had based his criticism of Marshall and Pigou on 'their writings on value rather than their writings on fluctuations'. He explains that he did this on purpose 'simply through an inability to discover anything relevant'. Keynes (JMK, XIII, pp. 523f.) continues:

> I have now made the omission good in the case of Pigou's *Theory of Unemployment* by devoting a lengthy appendix to this work in detail.

That detailed criticism, incorporating about two years of correspondence, writing, discussing and lecturing about this subject, was then indeed printed as appendix to chapter 19 of the *General Theory*. There, Keynes allotted eight pages of fine print to Pigou (1933) in a book which he drew up with much care and after much discussion about previous drafts and after considerable efforts concerning its composition, demonstrable by referring to the many preparatory drafts which have been published in volumes XIII, XIV and XXIX of Keynes' collected writings. But not only this appendix: a number of other passages also refer to Pigou (1933) in the final version of the *General Theory*, in particular in chapter 2 (p. 7) where Keynes mentions the *Theory of Unemployment* as being 'the only detailed account of the classical theory of employment which exists'.

Whether this assertion is right or wrong might be debatable. But what is clear from this quote and from other passages in the *General Theory* is: Keynes gave very much detailed thought to Pigou (1933) and he personally thought that this book was immensely important as a point of orientation for his own theory.

As an aside, one may note that *after* the publication of the *General Theory* the discussion of Pigou (1933) continues with Hawtrey and with Pigou himself, as was seen above. Indeed, one of the complaints which Keynes has against Pigou is that he does *not* enter into a detailed discussion of that ominous appendix devoted entirely to Pigou (1933).

In view of the very substantial attention which Keynes did give to this particular piece, Pigou (1933) must be awarded a prominent place if one wants to trace the development of Keynes' own thought towards the *General Theory*. Yet, if we look at the various essays which address this question, hardly any mentioning is made of this intellectual influence on Keynes, apart sometimes from rather cursory – and largely unsubstantiated – statements about the lack of Keynes' originality in comparison to Pigou (1933). For example Patinkin (1977), in a contribution which addresses 'The Process of Writing *The General Theory*', fails totally to mention Keynes' wrestling with Pigou (1933) while writing the *General Theory*. This is quite surprising in view of the fact that the process of this 'wrestling' and its outcome are both very well documented. Moggridge (1977), in a contribution about 'Cambridge Discussion and Criticism Surrounding the Writing of *The General Theory*: a Chronicler's View' likewise is silent about this 'episode' – if it is a mere episode – in the writing of the *General Theory*. This is particularly astonishing as Moggridge (1977, p. 70) expressly refers to Patinkin (1977) without correcting him on his dim view of Keynes' reception of Pigou (1933) in the writing of the *General Theory*. He concludes:

> Thus I would certainly go along with many of Don Patinkin's suggestions as to the difference between the *Treatise* and the *General Theory* ...

However, I think we might both get a bit further on with more knowledge of the personalities involved and more appreciation of the quality of their interaction.

The last statement in this quote might be true about many other aspects of the said transition. But Donald Moggridge, as editor of all the correspondence and papers just mentioned, must have known how very well personalities and contributions are documented concerning Keynes' reaction to Pigou (1933). As Skidelsky (1992, p. 441) remarked:

> There are the 'pooled memories' of the so-called Cambridge Circus. There is the evidence of early drafts of the new book and other of Keynes's writings, as well as fragments of lectures, and complete sets of the lecture notes of some of his students, which run from 1932 to 1935. The historian and biographer is therefore well placed to piece together the stages in the intellectual construction of the *General Theory*.

If economists' views of this whole matter still are not felt to be settled satisfactorily, the basic problem might well be not a lack of knowledge but an unsuccessful search for a proper perspective.

Some misconceptions about the interaction between Keynes and Pigou might stem from a well-meaning defence of the latter. Thus, in a book which – somewhat ironically – had the title *The Shadow of Keynes – Understanding Keynes, Cambridge and Keynesian Economics*, H. G. Johnson (1978c, p. 179) had a contribution on A. C. Pigou, claiming: 'His *The Theory of Unemployment* (1933) was one of the main objects of Keynes's derision in the *General Theory*.' But surely Keynes' treatment of Pigou (1933) had little to do with derision but far more with academic challenge and interaction. What Keynes (*GT*, p. 260) *did* write was: 'Professor Pigou's *Theory of Unemployment* seems to me to get out of the classical theory all that can be got out of it.' This is a *compliment* as far as Pigou (1933) is concerned and not a derision.[17] Keynes derides in some places the analytical potential of the classical *theory* but not the person A. C. Pigou. If we were looking for elements of derision in the context of the *General Theory* and the *Theory of Unemployment*, then we will find probably more in Pigou's preface than in Keynes' text as was argued above in ch. 5.

Some views about the topic of the interactions between Keynes and Pigou which are a bit more differentiated than the one just quoted might be found in Collard (1981, p. 125). Although that author also believes that Keynes misinterpreted Pigou (*ibid.*) (in criticising his muddled concept of 'unemployment'), he gives an interesting detail concerning the interaction between Keynes and Pigou during the time of the transition from the *Treatise* to the *General Theory* (Collard, 1981, p. 124):

Shove writes that Pigou's book [(1933)] is 'the worst book on economics that I had read for a long time – a good deal worse than Hicks' [1932][18] ... At this stage Pigou and Keynes seem to have been on reasonably good terms, as they were to be later in the thirties. Their exchanges over the *Treatise* are unfortunately almost all lost but led to no major differences once Keynes had translated his own language into Pigou's.

The remarkable bit in this characterisation – for this reader at least – is that Collard seems to be well aware that at about the same time at which Keynes attempted to come to grips with Pigou (1933), Keynes also 'translated his own language into Pigou's'. It comes therefore somewhat as a surprise when Collard (1981, p. 125) – only a few lines further down – states:

Keynes's critique of Pigou also shows him to be rather imprisoned in his own framework of analysis.

All the indications are, however, that, quite to the contrary, Keynes made a *double* movement towards Pigou: on the basis of his just finished *Treatise* he translated his own 'language' into Pigou's and in writing the *General Theory* he engrossed himself in the algebra and other argumentative details of Pigou (1933).

That the latter is true was shown in detail above in this book. It seems quite implausible that Keynes could write about the 'dreadful fascination' which Pigou (1933) exerted on him (see above, p. 335), that he could work for more than one and a half years on its model and subsequently remain 'imprisoned in his own framework of analysis'. That Keynes tried to move towards Pigou after he finished his *Treatise* is not only testified by Collard in the passage just mentioned. A similar situation is also described by Moggridge (1992): as chairman of the Committee of Economists in 1930, Keynes had the task to report on 'the present economic condition of Great Britain' and 'to indicate the conditions of recovery' (Moggridge, 1992, p. 497). His committee members were Sir Josiah Stamp, Hubert Henderson, Lionel Robbins and A. C. Pigou.

As their chairman it is natural that Keynes would have liked to rally his colleagues around some common view, and it is clear that he had a certain responsibility and a strong motivation to establish a common analytical position, as is described in some detail by Moggridge (1992, pp. 495–507). Although the *Treatise* was not published until October 1930,[19] it was due for publication at least one year before that date and much of its substance was already settled in Keynes' mind before the final publication date. The first meeting of the Committee of Economists was on 10 September 1930. Four days later Keynes sent the *Treatise* to the printer.[20]

The new situation most certainly caused him to rethink his former argumentation and to try to find one one which 'his' committee could subscribe to.

Working with Lionel Robbins was quite frustrating, however, as it also was with Hubert Henderson.[21] In the end, it was not possible to come to a satisfactory common position and this might have been a reason for Keynes to abandon the hope to find a consensual presentation of the unemployment problem and rather to bring the whole issue to a head in the *General Theory*.[22] With Pigou the co-operation did not seem to be that troublesome. Keynes discussed the draft of his final report with him in particular in October 1930.[23] It must have been in this type of situation that Keynes might have thought that he communicated fairly successfully at least with A. C. Pigou as just described above with reference to Collard's account.

The public rebuke concerning his committee work which Keynes then did experience in the preface of Pigou (1933) must have been quite a shock and even more of a challenge to come to grips with Pigou than just Pigou's bad modelling in that new book. If nowadays commentators want to discuss bad taste and lack of fairness in these controversies they definitely should first of all comment on Pigou's (1933) pompous proclamations about the duty of THE economist. They amounted to a self-applause for extensive equation mongering and to a published denigration of the type of public work done by Keynes in the previous years as was argued above in ch. 5.

All in all, it is rather implausible that Keynes should have stayed 'imprisoned' in his own analytical framework. A frequent criticism was rather that Keynes became too much involved with Pigou (1933) as was documented in the introductory chapters of this book. It is hoped that in the subsequent chapters we have been able to convince the reader that contrary to such judgements it can be quite rewarding to look at the *General Theory* through analytical eyes sharpened by the 'Pigovian provocation'.

25.3.2 The Pigovian nucleus of effective demand

The sources of the *General Theory* is a much debated topic of 'Keynesiology'. Was it the frustration experienced while acting as chairman of the Committee of Economists in 1930 as suggested by Moggridge (1992)? Was it the wish to have another bestseller and to do some Pigou-bashing for that purpose, as suggested by Leeson (1998b)? Was it the clever critique of the *Treatise* by the youngsters in the 'Cambridge circus' in 1931 as many others would like to argue? Or was the right track followed when Samuelson (1977, p. 81) asked: 'But what is there in the thesis that Keynes is God's midwife for Richard Kahn?'[24] Or was it, as we suggested in the above that Pigou's (1933) pompous and tasteless self-adulation was a driving force behind the *General Theory*? Maybe the answer lies 'somewhere in the middle' of these and other positions, not related by us. But somewhere in that middle there is definitely a good deal of Pigovian *analysis*.

If one wants to be more precise than that, an interesting starting point for the enquiry might still be the debate as documented in Patinkin and Leith (1977) and in particular the 'survey' of Patinkin (1977). Unfortunately, that survey left in the dark the pivotal role of Pigou's (1933) analysis for Keynes' transition to the *General Theory*. Nevertheless this contribution is illuminating in the sense of our hypothesis, namely in demonstrating that the *General Theory* was by no means conceived by the youngsters' 'circus' in 1931 but by Keynes himself in 1933:

> the Cambridge 'Circus' could not have included the theory of effective demand. For the 'Circus' as such functioned only during 1930–31, whereas ... the theory of effective demand was developed [by Keynes, GMA] only during 1933. (Patinkin, 1977, p. 17)

As Patinkin (1977) shows – and the subsequent discussions with the until then surviving disciples and students Austin Robinson, Lorie Tarshis, Robert Bryce and other sources as documented in Patinkin and Leith (1977) and in Rymes (1989) support this – there is no substance in the claim for almost 'co-authorship' of Richard Kahn in writing the *General Theory*.

For our purposes it is interesting to note that in Keynes' communication concerning the discussion of the 'circus' we have a letter dated 20 September 1931 and addressed to R. F. Kahn (JMK, III, pp. 373f.) which deals with 'aggregate output'. Without going into detail, let us remark that output appears here as O, and savings S are decomposed via two functions $f_1(\cdot)$ and $f_2(\cdot)$ with the arguments E/P and Q/P, the latter being real profits, the former the rest of real income. The important thing here is that the discussants – Keynes as well as Kahn – obviously do not think in terms of sectoral disaggregation along the line of sectoral production functions. This has changed dramatically by the end of the year 1933. Patinkin (1977, p. 16) quotes some lecture notes which Robert Bryce took on 4 December 1933, i.e. after Keynes' lecture on Pigou's *Theory of Unemployment*. It is those lectures the notes of which Keynes seems to have given to Shove as mentioned in the last section.[25] Patinkin (1977, p. 16) gathers from the notes taken by Bryce:

> So it is clear that by that time [4 December 1933] Keynes had achieved a full understanding of the theory of effective demand.

The details of Patinkin's argumentation are not of great interest in the present context because he concentrates much on the issue of 'saving and investment'. What might be far more interesting is, however, the new sectoral treatment which emerges from the notes which state (*ibid.*):

> Suppose N total number of men employed
> N_1 producing for consumption

N_2 producing for investment
$N = N_1 + N_2$
Assume propensity to spend and to consume given.
Then $N_1 = f_1(N)$ $N_2 = f_2(\rho)$ (r[ate]. of i[nterest].)
$N = f_1(N) + f_2(\rho)$.   [*note*: here $r \equiv \rho$, GMA][26]

We see from this that whereas in the correspondence with Kahn in 1931 from which we just quoted, Keynes had rather nebulous ideas how to divide up total demand, he now has a clear *production*-oriented foundation of his model, mentioning expressly *sectoral* production. Not only this. He also manages to derive(?) or at least to postulate a relationship between sectoral and total employment, namely via his new f_1-function '$N_1 = f_1(N)$'. This is – conceptually at least – a close relative of the $\phi(x)$ function in Pigou (1933) which also linked sectoral to total employment. In fact, as a mere functional relation and assuming that the variables correspond to each other, the respective functions in Keynes' December 1933 lecture and in Pigou (1933) are just the inverse of each other.

The little lecture note ends in the last equation with what Keynes later called the 'employment function' relating sectoral demand and employment to total employment N. Keynes will later devote an entire chapter (ch. 20) of the *General Theory* to this concept. Thus, what we have here in a nutshell is indeed the entire plan for the *General Theory* in its non-monetary aspects, namely from the principle of effective demand of ch. 3 right up to the employment function of ch. 20.

Where does this sectoral production oriented model flash up from? It certainly cannot possibly be derived from a direct interaction with R. F. Kahn as far as it was documented. But it can very well be inferred from Pigou (1933) as was seen above in part II. We know that in 1933 Keynes spent many hours reading, writing, corresponding and lecturing about this model. Could the nucleus of the *General Theory* not have sprung from this effort?

25.3.3 A table of concordance

In ch. 5 above we referred to the Pigovian 'provocation' of questioning Keynes' status as a 'true' economist and as an economist who is conceptually able to deal with problems of unemployment since he was one of those economists who excessively used monetary analysis in this context. We saw that Clarke (1988) explained Keynes' choice of Pigou (1933) as his classical adversary with such utterances coming from this very source.

We are now in a position to look in more detail into the question whether the *General Theory* may indeed be seen as an answer to that type of Pigovian 'provocation'. If that is so, there must be a number of points which indicate that Keynes reacted to Pigou (1933) in some documentable way. In Table 25.1 we list seven such points which are candidates for such a view.

Table 25.1 Concordance between Pigou (1933) and Keynes (1936)

	Topic	Pigou (1933)	Keynes (1936)
(1)	target group	p. v: This book is addressed to students of economics. Its aim is to clarify thought, not to advocate policy	p. xxi: This book is chiefly addressed to my fellow economists ... its main purpose is to deal with difficult questions of theory
(2)	place of money in book	p. v: I have chosen to write my book from the real end, and to bring in the monetary factor only at a fairly late stage.	p. 173: We have now introduced money into our causal nexus for the first time [halfway through the book, GMA]
(3)	two sectors	p. 90: ... write $(x + y) = \phi(x)$ [where x, y sectoral employment, $(x + y)$ total employment (see above p. 49, GMA]	p. 29: $D_1 + D_2 = D = \phi(N)$, where ϕ is the aggregate supply function [D_1, D_2 sectoral demand, D effective demand]
(4)	real wage	p. 89: the general rate of wage is $F'(x)$ [it falls with $+ \Delta x$ because $F''(x) < 0$, GMA]	p. 17: the real wage ... has a unique (inverse) correlation with the volume of employment
(5)	wage-price nexus	p. 101: a one per cent cut in money wages *accompanied by no change in the quantity of employment*, must involve a cut of one per cent alike in prices ...	p. 12: if money-wages change, one would have expected the classical school to argue that prices would change in almost the same direction
(6)	money economy	p. 102: What the value of E_m actually is in relation to E_r cannot be determined without reference to the nature of the monetary system	p. 246–7: ultimate independent variables ... (3) the quantity of money as determined by the action of the central bank
(7)	units	[$\phi(x)$-function: total labour $x + y$ depends on sectoral labour x, thus pure labour-labour analysis]	p. 41: only two fundamental units ... quantities of money-value and quantities of employment

Points (1) and (2) are straightforward. According to (1), Keynes aims – or at least states that he aims – at the same type of readership as Pigou. That both books are developed from the 'real end' is quite obvious (point 2). But it should be listed as a noteworthy correspondence between the two, nevertheless, because originally Keynes did not seem to have had at all the intention to hold monetary matters to the back. From his first outline of the new book which was later to become the *General Theory*, it emerges that Keynes planned to start with 'Chapter 1: The Nature and Significance of the Theory of a Monetary Economy' (JMK, XXIX, p. 62). From a 'summary of the argument' (JMK, XXIX, pp. 62–3) it appears that he wanted to stress right at the beginning that firms 'must have enough command over money to pay the wages' etc.[27] It seems that later Keynes made a conscientious effort to match the structure of the argument found in Pigou (1933) – a topic we will look into in more detail below.

With regard to (3) we saw already that the reorientation of Keynes' argumentation from two-sectoral *demand* in the *Treatise* (1930) to two-sectoral *supply* (Dec. 1933) went together with the first clear formulation of the principle of effective demand. We dared already to speculate that this particular transition might have something to do with the particular way in which the *General Theory* finally was written. Tracing the exact correspondence between Keynes and Pigou is a rather involved matter as was seen above in the discussion of fig. 11.1 on p. 131. If we do not bother to go into details of the production theoretic foundation, the two-sectoral *General Theory* may be stated in just seven lines of lecture notes, however, as we gathered from discussing Bryce's lecture notes of 1933 on pp. 348f. above. This seems to be *the* portal to the real part of the *General Theory*. It came to Keynes – so it seems – only after he embarked on studying Pigou (1933).

Point (4): Keynes embraced the neoclassical production model in much the same way as it was done by Pigou and he did it all the way, right up to the doctrine of falling marginal productivity[28] and right to marginal productivity determined real wages (*modulo* cases of not perfect competition). He could become rather emphatic about this and any denial by followers of this aspect of Keynes' theorising seems to be entirely beyond authenticity.

Point (5) is quite 'dialectical' in the sense that it contains several conflicting aspects. The wage-price nexus is the basis of the Keynes effect, as we saw above. It became a particular bone of contention between Keynes and Pigou. But the basic argument in this context was stated clearly by Pigou, as the quote shows.[29] Nevertheless, it was rejected by him, and consciously so.[30] This makes it difficult to award Pigou superior economic insight in this context. Because if he rejected the wage-price nexus out of general equilibrium considerations, as Laidler (1999) argued quite convincingly, then he also invites a further application of the standards of evaluation of macroeconomic models under this perspective and then Keynes is right that a full general equilibrium model is by definition a full employment model. If Pigou thinks that nominal wage changes necessarily have employment effects which make him step out of the general equilibrium model, then he should state those mechanisms clearly. They must result in an *overdetermination* of the basic general equilibrium model. But such considerations, although fundamental for the direct criticism levied by Keynes against Pigou, lead beyond this simple comparison.

Point (6), too, should be seen more from the structural point of view rather than under the perspective of fully-fledged substantive detail which can be discussed in this connection. The important thing here is that Pigou made an attempt at linking money supply *and* demand with the real economy. Even if we grant all the criticism which can be brought against Pigou's very selective analysis of hypothetical monetary systems – there remains his contribution of bringing together real and monetary analysis. In this, Keynes is a *follower* of Pigou as far as the *structure* of the argumentation is concerned even if Keynes is quite emancipated with regard to the details of filling that structure.

Point (7) seems to have gone largely unnoticed in the Keynes and Pigou literature so far: in the final resolve, both authors define their models over the same units. They both have a pure labour–labour analysis. There are differences. Pigou has a physical labour-physical labour analysis, building a function between non-wage goods sector employment and total employment. Keynes' labour–labour analysis differs from this by relating Pigovian 'physical labour' to 'computational labour', the latter being defined in 'labour-units' as real values on the non-physical labour end of the model. This might sound rather involved and has often been misrepresented in the exegetical literature. The issues implied by this particular context therefore merit a more extensive treatment. We can only touch upon them in the following section. But what seems to be quite plain to see after even a cursory reading of the original Keynes-and-Pigou debate is that Keynes, before he got into the supposedly complex wage-unit analysis of the *General Theory*, engaged in the self-same formulation as did Pigou, albeit with different notation, as we just noted in commenting on Bryce's lecture notes quoted above.

All of these aspects of concordance, taken individually, may appear as insignificant coincidences. But if viewed together, they give a pattern. If we also bring in the flashing up of the vision of the structure of the *General Theory* towards the end of 1933, then we easily get the impression that there must have been very strong methodical influence from Pigou on Keynes in these particular cases which, however, amount to shaping much of the structure of the *General Theory*. Maybe it was a – hitherto unarticulated – feeling that there must have been more to the interactions between Keynes and Pigou than we find in the traditional accounts. Perhaps this led to unsubstantiated growlings about quasi-plagiarism on the side of Keynes.

We hope that with the view expounded here we have established a more fruitful basis for assessing the nexus between Keynes and Pigou.

25.3.4 Pigou's (1933) employment and Keynes' wage units

In view of point (7) of table 25.1 it might be helpful to return to the question of sectoral labour, total labour and wage units. In the discussion of the Pigou model we saw that his $\phi(x)$-function, linking x-sector employment with total employment, was obviously defined in a labour–labour plane. If we complete that model along the lines suggested by Keynes, namely by bringing into focus the labour supply as depicted by Keynes via the $\chi(x)$-function, then total and sectoral employment are definitely *determined* in that labour–labour plane. This is not without analytical appeal, because if we consider the simple general equilibrium models, where the equilibrium is determined in the labour-input and goods-output plane (or space), then we have variables of different dimensionality along the axes, namely pieces of goods per time unit *vs* hours of work per year. Keynes, who worked on index number problems since before World War One should have been appreciative of the Pigovian approach.[31] In any case, he emulated it, as was just seen in the last section, in formulating his $N_1 = f_1(N)$-function.

But from a different perspective, we must face it that Pigou's real demand curve for labour is a rather clumsy concept, involving many analytical steps, as was seen above in chapter 9, in particular in discussing this curve algebraically (see, e.g. equ. (9.14), p. 64). This must have posed some headaches for Keynes. His solution was to move to the labour–labour plane (or space) similarly as done by Pigou, but on a different route, namely by constructing real values in terms of labour. All of this was discussed above in connection with fig. 11.1 (p. 131). Nevertheless, we may return briefly to these points because they obviously caused some problems to past exegetes. Thus, Patinkin (1977) seems to have entirely overlooked the labour analysis aspect in Keynes' formulation of effective demand. He returned to this question, among others, on the occasion of his *New Palgrave* contribution, where Patinkin (1987, p. 30) writes:

> the exposition of the theory of effective demand in Book I is carried out, not in terms of national income . . . but in terms of the level of employment. In part, this was undoubtedly due to the fact that the level of employment was indeed his major concern. But I also feel that this provides an instructive instance in our discipline of a basic characteristic of the physical science.

In this context he then muses about the then existing statistic measures of employment and the non-existing 'current official estimates of British national income'.

But Patinkin (1987) again does not get to the strategic point: that Keynes' effective demand doctrine stands in immediate context with Pigou (1933) – and *that* model had also a labour–labour analysis. There might indeed be good *practical* reasons for a labour measure of economic activity, as Patinkin suggests. But whatever those are, they apply to both, to Keynes' *General Theory of Employment* as well as to Pigou's *Theory of Unemployment*. Insofar as there were practical reasons for thinking in terms of labour, these reasons were not first perceived by Keynes nor are they specific for him. The theoretical model to which he reacted was *also* in terms of employment.

What really *should* be discussed in this context is: which analytical elements were there *before* Keynes and what was *specific* to his analysis? Such a discussion would then lead to a deeper understanding of his wage units analysis. There is no space here for that discussion. A possibly representative post-Keynesian position was recently formulated by Bradford and Harcourt (1997, p. 119) who argue that Keynes is plainly deficient in this regard:

> On balance, it appears that for all the ingenuity and subtlety of Keynes's reasoning on the question of [wage] units, he ultimately failed to apply it consistently in *The General Theory*. Given the importance attached to these concerns in Chapter 4 [*GT*, GMA], this is a serious defect (although it does not necessarily invalidate the major theoretical insights therein) and may shed further light an the failure of later Keynesians to employ his approach to units.

This seems to us to be an unsatisfactory assessment. All we can do here, however, is to retrace Keynes' application of the wage units analysis as it appears during the gestation of the *General Theory*. It will appear then that via that route we receive indeed a *dimensionally consistent* theory of income determination which links up with Pigou (1933) and thereby opens a venue for discussing differences in respective paradigms. Let us therefore return once more to the little model jotted down by Bryce, and quoted above on pp.348ff. For the 'propensity to spend and to consume' mentioned there we assume the simplest case of a 'classical consumption function'. In wage units it reads

$$\chi^{cl}(N) = C_w = N \quad i.e. \quad p_1 Q_1 = wN \quad \text{hence} \quad \frac{p_1 Q_1}{w} = N \quad (25.1)$$

In this case, any given employment $\bar{N}$ will bring forth a consumption demand (in terms of wage units) of $\bar{C}_w$. From the Pigovian model we know that there is a function $C_w = F_1(N_1)/F'_1(N_1)$ relating sectoral production in wage units to sectoral employment as depicted in the south-western quad-

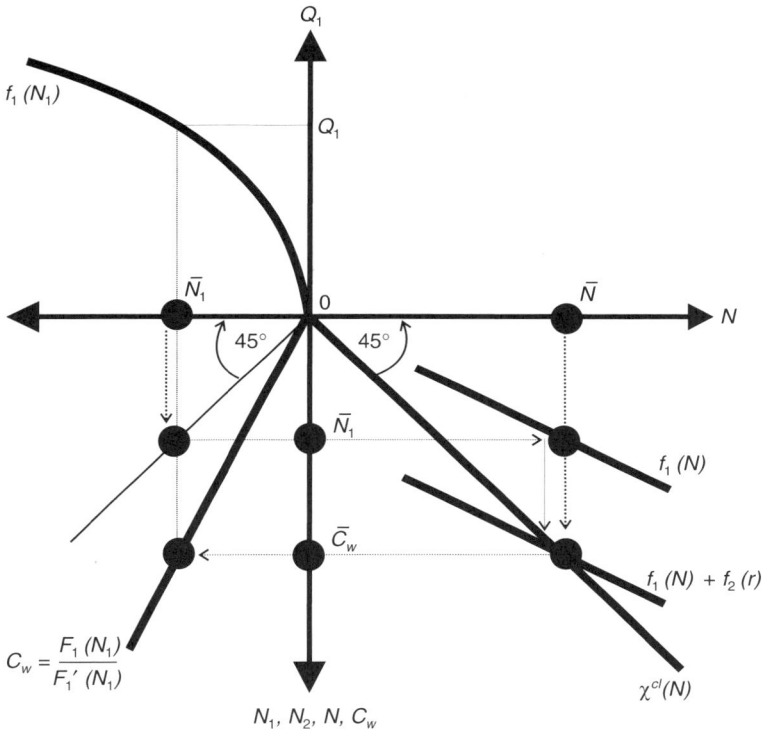

Figure 25.1 The 1933 model of the *General Theory*

rant of fig. 25.1. Hence sectoral employment is given as $\bar{N}_1$. We may further conclude that on this basis there is a functional relation between sectoral employment N_1 and total employment N as depicted in the south-eastern quadrant as $f_1(N)$-curve. This is the counterpart to the Pigovian $\phi(x)$-curve but derived in quite a different analytical context, albeit based on the same model of production. There follows now the last step of the lecture note just quoted: for total employment to be shown to be determined as $\bar{N}$, we need additional demand for goods – and hence for labour – to come up via a $f_2(\cdot)$-function so that employment can indeed be maintained at the specified level. If this additional demand is interest dependent, then for employment to be 'right', the rate of interest must be 'right'. Although that was not said in words according to those notes, it was written out in the algebra, namely through the rate of interest as argument in the $f_2(\cdot)$-function on p. 349.

It is along this or similar lines of argument that one may now say that the *General Theory* in all its essential aspects – and in its specificity as compared to Pigou's *Theory of Unemployment – was indeed contained in that lecture* note of December 1933.[32] What then followed until the publication of the *General Theory* seems to have been only refinement on the basis of an already firmly established new paradigm.

25.4 Pigovian paradigms and Robinsonian themes

What we just called Keynes' 'new paradigm' was and is strangely absent in the Keynes–Classics debate. The analytical elements just discussed, in particular questions of 'dimensional consistency' or of macroeconomic 'labour-labour' analysis à la Keynes and à la Pigou, are just not discussed – neither in New Classical camps nor in 'Post-Keynesian' or 'post-Keynesian' camps. Keynes' wage units analysis – if dealt with at all – is treated as seriously deficient and as being probably the root cause for the 'failure of later Keynesians to employ his approach to units' (see above, p. 354). In any case, none of the Cambridge Keynesians saw here a paradigm which could inspire further research. This is not the place to speculate about the reasons for this further development. It comes immediately to mind, however, that it was an old issue of Ricardo's criticism of Adam Smith that the latter's 'labour command' values should be abandoned in favour of 'labour embodied' values. Since Keynes' approach is a variant of Adam Smith's (see Ambrosi 1988) and since Joan Robinson intended to marry Keynes analytically with David Ricardo (see, e.g., above, p. 322), it is clear that there is an inconsistency of analytical perspective which obviously was not conducive for creative further developments along Keynes' original line.

Did this abandoning of Keynes' original analytical scheme liberate those who once were the confidants of his writing the *General Theory* for paradigmatic breakthroughs of their own? If we turn now to Joan Robinson in the light of this question, the answer is negative, at least in her own assessment. We will enlarge on this point in a separate subsection.[33] This is particularly noteworthy when remembering what was stated in part IV (pp. 269f.) about the Marshallian and Pigovian roots of Joan Robinson's economics. In a way they are obvious and merit hardly any elaboration: that *was* the education she received in economics and that *was* the school where she had to succeed as an academically accepted economist. But what *is* noteworthy and what asks for some comment and explanation is that she should appear in that light after she had spent decades of battling that very school under the aegis of a 'post-Keynesian' programme.[34]

One explanation for the fact that an impression of lacking impact was left by Joan Robinson's economics might be sought in the unwillingness of the 'orthodox' commentators to admit that she did effect a deep change in economics. But that cannot be the only explanation. Geoffrey Harcourt's (1996, p. 317) above quoted dictum about her *even Pigovian* background (see above p. 326) was made from the vantage point of her 'very last years'.

This was, of course, the view cultivated also in this book. The fact must be addressed that one of the major sources of Joan Robinson's uneasiness about her own role as an economist was the realisation that she was far from having eradicated the received 'neoclassical' roots in economic thinking.

This lack of impact had two aspects: one concerned the impact on the outside world. There was a strong feeling in Joan Robinson and her circle that the 'pupils of Keynes' in Cambridge 'have not been listened to', as Pasinetti (1983, p. 208) was quoted as saying above (p. 259). But why should they have been listened to?

This brings us to the second aspect of failing to break away from 'traditional economics'. It concerns the own analytical approach of the anti-orthodox school. It was an often repeated stance that the Cambridge Keynesians were not wrong but right – but they were right in the context of established economics.

It certainly was not a lesson which was learnt easily by Solow, Samuelson and their intellectual allies centred around 'the other Cambridge' in Massachusetts. But this lesson was accepted, albeit with a sigh, when Samuelson (1966, p. 245) summed up the debate with the words:

> If all this causes headaches for those nostalgic for the old time parables of neo-classical writing, we must remind ourselves that scholars are not born to live an easy existence.

Henceforth the Robinsonian problems in the theory of capital were received in the literature as problems *within* the conventional theory, not ones which challenged it from the outside. The issue became one of 'exotic themes' but not one of 'alternative paradigms'.

This development had indeed frustrating elements to it – it led to a banal anti-climax after tremendous mental and polemical exertions by Joan Robinson, her allies and her adversaries in the capital theoretic debates. But it was not a result which was specific for the participating persons of that debate. It was a result which was already contained in Joan Robinson's *Essays* of 1936/7. In spelling out the Robinsonian reasoning of that time in terms of the downright neoclassical categories which she was then still prepared to use, we showed in part IV above that one could indeed foreshadow a number of post-Keynesian results while remaining in a quite orthodox framework.

25.4.1 The Pigovian paradigm of a long-period perspective

If we do focus on the Pigovian 'background' while looking closely at Joan Robinson's theory, then we are able to discover such Pigovian elements even in her supposedly anti-'classical' endeavours to reconstruct the theory of distribution. If it was one of her intentions to liberate the theory of distribution from the strictly production theoretic shackles, then it could well be the 'simplified model' of Pigou (1937) which is an appropriate backdrop. We saw that his model generates a 'λ^P and r' relationship according to which labour's share in NNP is a falling function of the rate of interest.[35] When deriving this relationship we noted in that context already that it is virtually the same as the analogous one implicit in Joan Robinson (1936, 1937a). This is not surprising, because Pigou (1937) was *meant* by him to be more a reply to Robinson (1936) than to Keynes according to the information of R. F. Kahn.[36] This is highly significant because according to the judgement of later post-Keynesians like Jan Kregel and others Joan Robinson's *Essays* (1937a) which were based on that very contribution set the agenda for much of her later life's work. Thus it is this piece in particular which should be seen in a dialogical position before a 'Pigovian background'.

The dialogical counterpart to the Pigovian 'λ^P and r' relationship is the Robinsonian 'λ^r and v' relationship (see above, equ. (21.27), p. 284). But in the case of Pigou the final determination of labour's share happened through time preference or through Kaldor's 'r and $\rho(n)$' relation (see above, equ. (17.1), p. 228). Likewise, if one thinks Joan Robinson's model through to its Pigovian long-period end, one will detect at its 'Kaleckian' best a 'λ^s and r' relationship (see above, equ. (23.2), p. 311).

The significance of this is that under the rest of long-period assumptions which were also made in the Robinsonian approach (in particular: $v = r$) we then have a determinate share of income λ^R and not one which is open to class struggle or other external political mechanisms of determination. It is only if one bluntly negates the conclusion just stated, i.e. if one does *not* argue the case to its systematic end, only then can one have any further discussion about the model – but in this case it can be only a 'meta-discussion' which at an arbitrary point steps out of the hitherto accepted system of reference. To negate a conclusion without systematic methodological basis can hardly be considered as a generally convincing paradigm shift. To admit that the northern hemisphere is round but then to claim that the southern one is flat is not a scientific revolution but an inconsistency.

Let us stress again in this context that Joan Robinson herself had a totally 'blind spot' with regard to Pigou (1937). To Keynes she declared that Pigou was 'so far gone' that she had some difficulty to 'find a coherent error'.[37] In fact, she never published a coherent critical evaluation of it. In a way this is not surprising if the model under discussion was indeed *her* model. In that case a critique of Pigou (1937) was in danger of becoming a criticism of Robinson (1936). A negation of the basic paradigm of Pigou (1937) could have meant the death blow to the central research programme of what later became known as (a branch of) post-Keynesianism.

It follows from these considerations that if one wanted to protect Joan Robinson's (then) recent academic work, one had to avoid 'too much' academic debate of Pigou (1937) – in any case a debate which was conducted from a paradigmatic angle. It therefore had a certain inner logic to it when Richard Kahn gave out the order (letter to J. M. Keynes, dated 22 October 1937, JMK, XIV, p. 260):

> It is of the *highest* importance to make it abundantly clear, so that the casual reader will recognise, that as far as Pigou [1937] is concerned the issue is not one of schools of thought but of the most *crashing* and *stupid* errors of statement and of reasoning, such as nobody would deny once his eyes were opened. (emphasis in the original)

But although understandable from the standpoint of the academic biography of Joan Robinson, for the development of Keynesian economics this marching order was fatal.

If there ever was the chance to work at the paradigms separating Keynes and Pigou, it was in this very historic situation. At long last economics seemed to have the substantial exchange Keynes was waiting and pressing for. In this situation the Keynesian camp – if indeed it was one – received the order: for heaven's sake do not debate paradigms now. It is of utmost importance to say it is all just about a 'stupid mistake'. But what was that mistake? Time preference determined interest rates!

> It is clear that D.H.R[obertson], Kaldor, and Pigou still all fail to see the fundamental fallacy – which is the determination of the rate of interest by the rate of discount of the future (Piero [Sraffa] agrees about this). I am not so sure whether your reply [Keynes (1937b)] brings out the grossness of this error sufficiently forcibly for the ordinary reader to take in that it has been perpetrated. (Same letter as above, JMK, XIV, p. 260)

That answer did not convince Keynes as we saw above and it was not able to convince the rest of the world: not a single person from the Keynesian camp could face Pigou (1937, 1938) critically on the basis of Kahn's proclamation of Pigou's supposedly 'fundamental fallacy'. Kaldor's comment was based on the *acceptance* of time preference determined interest rates – and this was endorsed by Keynes. It was the underlying paradigm of the 'frozen land' which Keynes saw as the bottom line of the controversy and it is an additional mishap in the defence of the Keynesian position that Kaldor also refused to recognise the paradigmatic importance of this – and of his *Pigovian* analysis, a point which we come back to below (p. 368).

25.4.2 Richard Kahn's role in Robinsonian economics

Immediately after the appearance of Keynes' *General Theory of Employment*, Joan Robinson (1936) published a lengthy article on 'The Long-period Theory of Employment'. This is a remarkable feat of celerity and reorientation, covering the same ground as Keynes' *magnum opus* but, as the title says, with a time perspective different from that of Keynes. The analysis of that article was endorsed by her in the following year by republishing and extending that article in book form as *Essays in the Theory of Employment*. Again it was endorsed in 1953 when it was republished under the same title. Similar endeavours are Robinson (1954b), republished as Robinson (1979e). Thus we have here a theme which is central for much what Joan Robinson believed to be important in economics. What are the sources and what is the substance of this line of research? It is most implausible that the source of all this could be just the *General Theory*. In fact, we know from the above that Keynes derided stationary state economics of the Pigou (1937) type as useless 'frozen land' economics. How then could Joan Robinson be convinced that her just mentioned essays and books did not fall under this verdict?

A possible answer to this question could be: she was of a different opinion to Keynes. This is at least what was documented above with regard to R. F. Kahn who urged Keynes to suppress this particular comment on Pigou. Kahn framed his entreaties to Keynes with supposed denials from Pigou. But if Kahn himself had thought that Pigou's prospective denials were unfounded, then he could have tried to work out the proper argumentation together with Keynes. The fact that Kahn did not do this seems significant – he not only was unable to produce anything against Pigou, he even tried to suppress publication of what had been written against Pigou (1937) by Kaldor (1937).

But what significance does this have for Joan Robinson's writings on the *General Theory*? In order to answer this question we must go a bit into the characterisation of R. F. Kahn himself and of his interaction with Joan Robinson.

According to Skidelsky (1992, p. 448) one may say:

> Kahn was someone who liked to work behind the scenes, and advance his ideas through others. He also published very little. So his own ideas tended to be invisible. He was almost certainly the creative force behind *The Theory of Imperfect Competition* by Joan Robinson, with whom he started an affair during or soon after the end of the Circus [1932].

This is significant in the present context, because the person who had the most reason to combine mentally Keynes and Pigou was none other than R. F. Kahn. It is well known that he features prominently in the preface of the *General Theory* (p. xxiii). Schumpeter (1954, p. 1172) inferred almost co-authorship from this acknowledgement (see pp. 456f., n. 24 below). It may be less well known that Kahn also features prominently in the preface of *The Economics of Stationary States* (1935) where Pigou thanks him for his critical review of the entire manuscript. Thus, Kahn seems to have been the only person who saw in manuscript and had a potential influence on the major works of Keynes *and* Pigou – but not only this. Since the formative year for both books must have been 1934, he had this experience virtually *simultaneously*. This must have been a mind-boggling experience for R. F. Kahn in several respects.

One potential reaction to simultaneously having to work through Keynes (1936) and through Pigou (1935) could easily have been the desire to make sense of *both* approaches on an equal footing. Such a reaction would have been based on important presuppositions, however, namely that both books stood on their own and that they needed some completion. But was this not a plausible assumption? Plausibility is something which must be in the mind of the judge. One might see Keynes' novel contribution before the background of Kahn's (1929) stress on short-period analysis and of his multiplier analysis (Kahn, 1931). If R. F. Kahn was the judge, this perspective on Keynes could well have had some plausibility. From the same perspective, Pigou's (1935) new book with its explicit and well worked-out long-period stationary state offered a view on quite a different and also a novel world. Pigou's analytical world could not have been quite satisfactory for Richard Kahn, however, because it failed to receive Kahn's multiplier analysis. That Keynes was able to make good analytical use of the multiplier must have been something which made Keynes fascinating for Kahn. But Keynes lacked on the other hand on Pigou's long-period analysis. Thus, would it not be a nice programme, worthy of two great Cambridge minds, to amalgamate Keynes and Pigou in some unified presentation, in particular by 'extending' the *General Theory* into a 'stationary state'?

The argumentation of the last paragraph seems to be a speculation remote from published works of R. F. Kahn. Does this observation mean that our speculation about mental influences went astray? Not necessarily, if we accept Skidelsky's just quoted characterisation of the working of Kahn's mind and about his influence on Joan Robinson. If the pattern described there was typical, then it could well have been Kahn's 'natural' response not to write himself the 'extension' of the *General Theory* into the long-period stationary state but again to be 'the creative force' behind his intellectual and emotional partner Joan Robinson. It has been noted by other commentators, too, that great intellectual influence extended from Richard Kahn to Joan Robinson.[38] She herself praised him in most general terms for his 'enabling' and pioneering influence (Robinson, 1956, p. vi): 'As so often, it was R. F. Kahn who saw the point that we were groping for and enabled us to get it into a comprehensible form.' Thus, the most important midwife of Kahn's thoughts in economics might have been none other than Joan Robinson.

This reconstruction of events could explain to a certain extent the new long-period orientation and the extraordinary speed of output of Joan Robinson (1936). But why do we argue this case in such a roundabout way?

The person who could give the most illuminating information on this matter was, of course Kahn himself. Indeed, Kahn (1984) wrote an entire monograph about *The Making of Keynes' General Theory*. In that context he could well have given some background information about the simultaneous contacts which he had with Pigou. None of our speculations appears there, however. But it has been commented by the co-editor of Keynes' *Collected Writings*, Donald Moggridge (1994, pp. 111–12) that Kahn's contributions to the history of economics in this particular regard are astonishingly uninformative:

> Thus the reader gets no elucidation on such matters as to why Keynes devoted so much time to developing a monetary theory of production – or why he abandoned it . . . One would have thought that Kahn might have had something to say on such an issue, as well as on others such as the radical transformation of the formulations of *The General Theory* that occurred from late 1933. But Kahn, the most intimate participant in the process, left us none the wiser. His unwillingness to let documents jog his memory is unfortunate.

Were there blockages of memory or hindrances of another nature which kept Kahn from being more informative about his contacts with Keynes – and also with Pigou? Kahn was the one who could confidently write to Keynes about Pigou's (1937) intention (see p. 443, n. 3). Kahn was the one who could write to Keynes that he knew that Pigou had read Keynes' manuscript and had 'seized on' and allegedly triumphed over Keynes' frozen-land-paragraph (see above, p. 176). These certainly are signs of a continuing and very privileged intimacy with Pigou's state of mind. Does such intimacy not often imply some feeling of loyalty? Could it not imply also some sympathy for the workings of the mind one is permitted to work with?

These questions should call forth more research in the history of economic thought. Here we can only propose for discussion the following speculation: one aspect of the complexity of Kahn's situation as confidant of the authoring of *both* Keynes' *General Theory* and Pigou's *The Economics of Stationary States* could well have been that he felt to be in a situation of mixed and conflicting loyalty. This in turn could have been part of the otherwise difficult explanation as to why Kahn and his entourage stayed silent when it came to publishing something against Pigou (1937) or even against Pigou (1938). There must probably be some element of reasoning in this context which goes beyond pure academic discourse when it comes to their dealings with Pigou's 'frozen land' economics of long-period analysis. It is not only the empty promises by Kahn, noted above on p. 164, to contribute to this debate. It is also the long line of second thoughts which we have from Joan Robinson and her eventual nihilism diagnosed by authors as close to her thinking as Bradford and Harcourt (1997).[39]

There is a certain tragedy associated with Cambridge economics – or so it appears at least to the present author – stemming from its intention to cover a middle – or supposedly superior – position between Keynes (1936) on the one side and Pigou (1935) on the other side. But as far as Keynes was concerned, Pigou's vision was a *fata morgana* and unfit for economically realistic positioning. Keynes *did* speculate about potential 'conditions of a quasi-stationary community' (*GT*, ch. 16, p. 220). But the prerequisite for him is 'that State action enters in as a balancing factor' (*ibid.*). Thus he keeps the reader in mind that this condition cannot be the outcome of merely *postulating* its existence.

In a verbal way Joan Robinson seems to have realised the justification for Keynes' 'frozen land' criticism late in her life. As far as inspiration for further thinking in the tradition of Keynes was concerned, her earlier programme of generalising the *General Theory* into the long period seems now to have been a detour. If Keynes' position had been thought to its long-period end, the long-period situation would have been on the fringe of its special conclusions, not in the centre of a research programme in his tradition.

25.4.3 Joan Robinson and Pigou on the theory of production

A remarkable field of interaction between Joan Robinson and Pigou is the theory of production. In view of her later invectives against 'neoclassical marginalism' it is ironical that she herself was at the forefront of developing the groundwork of that analysis. In the 1930s she cultivated the concept and the measure of the 'elasticity of substitution' – a central concept for the neoclassical theory of production and for the production theoretic basis of the marginalistic theory of distribution. Pigou (1934) expressly mentioned her contribution in this field. He tried his best to catch up with this new development in the theory of production. But his recreation of this concept resulted in complications of exposition which almost amounted to a *reductio ad absurdum*. In the end, Pigou (1934) professed his predilection for simple production functions where the elasticity of substitution played no explicit role but implicitly was set to unity as in the case of Cobb–Douglas production functions. In fact, Joan Robinson (1937a) herself returned to this type of simple neoclassical production function in referring to Cobb–Douglas type of production functions as being a realistic and plausible analytical instrument.

It is true that she rejected the marginalistic production theoretic approach in the context of her capital-theoretic critique. But, as Samuelson pointed out, her 'book of blueprints' of alternative technologies can quite well be interpreted in such a way as again to generate a neoclassical production function. Her later disassociation from her youthful 'misdirected' efforts in this field did not invalidate them for economics in general. Her contributions to marginalist analysis survived as disowned intellectual off-spring. This is a pity in view of the important contributions which she did supply for marginalist analysis and which she once herself was proud in.[40]

In the end, Joan Robinson renounced virtually all the intellectual turns and efforts of her past.[41] But such nihilism cannot be the recipe for the further development of economics as a scientific discipline. We must find a new and independent assessment of the analytical way ahead in economics but not on the basis of failed 'iconoclasm' but rather on the basis of a critical reflection of past debates.

What can be learned from Joan Robinson's criticism and self-criticism? Our conclusion is that the particular way of modelling production appears to be immaterial for those parts of economic theory which Joan Robinson most urgently seems to have wanted to criticise, namely the theory of distribution. To put it more generally, it is the analytical context in which such production theoretic models are placed. In the last resort, the fundamental error of Pigovian analysis is, as far as Keynes' basic position is concerned, that it relies on the cultivation of a sterile steady (or, equivalently, quasisteady) state perspective. It is in this respect that Joan Robinson was inflicted by a Pigovian malady of ahistorical and therefore apolitical model building which contributed to the nihilism one may attribute to her later life. A more general pathological condition following from Joan Robinson's unnecessary negation of the significance of her youthful contributions might be seen in an analytical schizophrenia afflicting post-Keynesianism, exemplified by the continuing debates about the 'proper' analytical setting of effective demand analysis.[42]

25.4.4 The inconsequential critique of 'waiting'

It has often been observed that in spite of claims to the contrary the analytical context of Joan Robinson's economic programme is basically Pigovian. One aspect of that orientation is its being directed at the economics of a (quasi) stationary state. Nevertheless, she aspired to build up an alternative, economic politically non-sterile, world. One of the main characteristics of that new economic political world was meant to be that its distribution of income was not determined by the principles of neoclassical (Marshallian/Pigovian) economics. How was it to be freed from the old neoclassical determinism implied by the (quasi) stationary state?

One avenue through which Joan Robinson and her intellectual associates thought to be able to escape from Pigovian conclusions – although operating in the lion's den of the Pigovian analytical realm – was to negate the time preference theory inherited from Pigou and his intellectual ancestors.

Let us remind the reader that this issue is of utmost importance not only for assessing Pigou, but also for assessing the entire Keynes–Classics issue. It was seen above that the concept of time preference has two extreme analytical manifestations: Keynes' consumption function on the one hand, and the Pigovian time preference theory of interest on the other. Keynes' correspondence with Richard Kahn concerning Kaldor (1937) revealed that Keynes himself was well aware that in the Pigovian analytical realm it is logically consistent to adhere to the time preference theory of interest. For him, the issue was expressly *not* time preference – which Keynes accepted as a concept without reservation – but the 'frozen land' assumptions which generated Pigou's conclusions. It was also documented (see above, p. 177) that as far as Richard Kahn was concerned, he thought that there was a 'fundamental fallacy' involved, the 'grossness' of which Keynes supposedly failed to reveal. But since he did not react himself either to Pigou (1937) or to Pigou (1938), Kahn also failed to reveal his proof of the alleged error. It was left to Joan Robinson to argue in more detail against Pigou's theory of time preference. We quoted her basic reasoning above already (p. 251). Its essence is the claim that pure time preference might yield negative interest rates, thus conflicting with the reality of positive interest rates. In her major work Joan Robinson (1956, p. 395) relates this point in the following way:

> It is impossible to say what price would rule if there were a market for present *versus* future purchasing power, unaffected by any other influence except the desires of individuals about the time-pattern of their consumption. It might well be that such a market would normally yield a negative rate of discount – the savers predominating over the dissavers, and being willing to sacrifice (if need be) more consumption now for less in the future.

As is well known, this type of critique of the neoclassical theory of value did not prevail in the academic community and we argued above already (see n. 14, p. 451) that this might be for the benefit of Keynes' doctrine of the consumption function – and thus for the benefit of his belief that there is a positive multiplier for income.

In a more informal way than above in part IV one might repeat the essence of our previous anticritique thus: the context of the time-preference – 'waiting' – theory of interest is, of course, not the real world but the artificial one of a 'stationary state' in which everything is reduced to one single aspect: the *desired* intertemporal time-pattern of consumption. In order to make it transparent, the desired pattern is confronted with a postulated one, namely that of the stationary state. The price system has then the function to peg the model economy's agents to this state. This analysis breaks down, of course, if the 'stationary state' does not prevail. Keynes' criticism of Pigou (1937) was intended to point this out. But that intention met Richard Kahn's vehement opposition.

It is significant that exactly *this* avenue of critique was *not* taken by the Cambridge Young Keynesians. According to Joan Robinson's testimony, since Richard Kahn's attempts in the early 1930s at reinventing Marx's model of simple reproduction they were in a stationary, later quasi-stationary, mould themselves. In the quote just given, Joan Robinson is expressly prepared to have the situation boiled down to the question of intertemporal preference pure and simple. This involves identical qualities and quantities of goods consumed intertemporally – otherwise one would have additional effects on marginal utility and these are expressly assumed away. But in her thought experiment economic agents are prepared to *pay* interest after present savings in order to have *less* consumption in the future. With time-preference motivated negative interest rates future consumption can then obtain the characteristics of being not a 'good' but a 'bad'. This, however would contradict all experience. Joan Robinson (1956, p. 395) herself writes in this context that she, too, believes that 'most people have enough sense to want to be able to exercise consuming power as long as fate permit'. In that context (*ibid.*) she stresses that for an economic agent

> it is true that a comparison between his subjective discount rate and the rate of interest obtainable may be said . . . to influence his saving habits.

But if we do take these suggestions seriously and if we do feed negative rates of time preference into an appropriately formulated consumption function, then the marginal propensity to consume (parameter b in equ. (15.16) and equ. (15.17), p. 184) might well become *larger* than unity and not less as is required by Keynes.

In that case the multiplier $1/(1 - b)$ would turn *negative* and the Keynesian argumentation would be turned on its head: one must *cut* demand in this case in order to have an increase in income and employment and not expand demand as was, of course, Keynes' well-known message.

We do not claim that this was Joan Robinson's intended result. But it is a possible implication of her claim that the rate of time-preference in the sense of discounting future consumption might be negative. This claim does not seem to have been thought by her to its logical end. There just is no proof for Pigou's supposedly gross error if one leaves unquestioned the conception of a stationary state. It is small wonder that this part of Cambridge Keynesians' criticism of Pigovian economics remained inconsequential.

25.4.5 The theme and the desideratum of depreciation economics

One interesting analytical point of classical economics is its treatment of depreciation. The Pigovian 'simplified model' (Pigou, 1937), in keeping with the 'canonical classical' one (Samuelson, 1978, see n. 11 p. 456) expressly isolates depreciation and production for depreciation replacement. In the same manner Joan Robinson (1937a) expressly address this magnitude in her extension of the *General Theory* to the stationary state.

This is significant because one of the admittedly weak points of the *General Theory* is exactly its treatment of depreciations. There is the revealing exchange between Keynes and Townshend in which Keynes admits that his treatment of user cost (which corresponds to depreciation cost) is unsatisfactory.[43] He claims that that was so because he followed the Classics too narrowly in their analysis. But this is not quite correct, as the above remarks illustrate. Thus the classical models, in so far as they address the problem of depreciation, are indeed a challenge to the procedure of the *General Theory*.

Much of what Joan Robinson wanted to convey concerning the variability of labour's share can be shown with the help of a neoclassical model of a stationary economy as was shown in the respective chapter above. This observation does not invalidate what has been said above about the sterility of assuming stationary states in income determination analysis. But it shows an avenue for extending the *General Theory* into one realm which it indeed failed to cover sufficiently, namely depreciation analysis.

25.5 Nicholas Kaldor's Pigovian conceptions

25.5.1 The significance of the Kaldorian synthesis

Kaldor (1937) seemed to be able to synthesise the analytical positions of Keynes and Pigou along the lines which we detailed above in ch. 17, pp. 226ff. On the one hand he thereby had an important function of re-establishing some seeming harmony between Keynes and Pigou as Kaldor's economic biographer Anthony Thirlwall (1987, p. 61) writes:

> Indeed, he [Kaldor, GMA] did more to convert Pigou to Keynesian ways of thinking than any other economist. It is clear from Keynes' correspondence that Pigou understood what Kaldor was saying more easily than he did Keynes.

The details of this interaction were presented above and in a sense they are in accordance with the quoted assessment. But on the other hand – let us remind the reader – the seeming 'synthesis' had at least two problematic aspects:

1. Kaldor's synthesis was defined not for Keynes' analytical case, but for the Pigovian one, as Keynes insisted.[44] This follows from the $r = \rho$-assumption which Kaldor accepted as did Pigou. Then it is small wonder that Pigou quite liked what Kaldor wrote. But for general analytical reasons such results pertain to 'frozen land' economies, not to more realistic ones to which Keynes wanted to relate. That does not make the respec-

tive models logically wrong as Keynes insisted against a contrary claim by R. F. Kahn. But it made such models factually irrelevant.[45] This is then a 'Keynesian synthesis' without Keynes and one cannot say that on this basis Pigou was really 'converted' to accept Keynesian ways of thinking.[46] What happened was that he found a *modus vivendi*, conceding to Keynes that he allegedly had special conclusions while Pigou continued to live in his old paradigm.

2. One of the rather comical aspects of Pigou's acceptance of the Kaldorian synthesis was his embracing the 'Keynes effect' as a Kaldorian invention. For Keynes this was comical because it was all spelled out in the *General Theory* before. For the defendants of the idea of Pigou's analytical primogeniture (Niehans, Laidler, Leeson, etc.) this is comical because one could *almost* argue that 'it was all' in (a – dismissed – half-sentence) in Pigou (1933, p. 101) as we pointed out above in item (5) of table 25.1 on p. 350. But Pigou was obviously so unaware of the significance of his own analytical fragment that he did not recognise a money-wage to price level to employment mechanism in his own thinking neither when reading or reviewing Keynes' *General Theory* nor when reading Kaldor (1937). Pigou's reaction to Kaldor should lay to rest any further claim that Keynes' money wage effect was foreshadowed in the *Theory of Unemployment*.[47]

In the end, the consequence of the Kaldorian synthesis – for all its brilliant manoeuvering between Keynes and Pigou – was rather destructive for the analytically correct reception of the *General Theory*: it should have been plain that the $r = \rho$-condition and hence the entire "synthesis" is a special case of the *General Theory*. Keynes was totally right in making this claim in his communication with Pigou.[48] What in fact did happen was that it gave Pigou the opportunity to present Keynes' results as special cases of his own, as was restated in the last sentence of item 1 above.

Unfortunately, Keynes himself was the last one to make this point. The Keynes–Classics debate stalled because Keynes' point was not taken up in further debate with Pigou – neither by Joan Robinson nor by R. F. Kahn nor by Nicholas Kaldor. As far as Kaldor was concerned, his reason was that he thought that there just was no point in questioning the results he worked out. He was convinced that no matter what the analytical framework – i.e. no matter whether in Keynes' short period or in Pigou's stationary state – the model is equally applicable for real life conditions.

25.5.2 The question of economic political relevance

Keynes' insistence concerning the 'special assumptions' character of the Kaldorian synthesis might appear to be rather petty and pedantic. Its significance becomes clearer when one contemplates the economic political implications of Kaldor's approach. According to Keynes' characterisation this model pertains entirely to Pigou's special case, and thus it is devoid of any practical relevance. It is limited to the case of time preference determined interest rates and hence to the condition $I = S = 0$.

Kaldor himself does not see a particular problem herein. Although Kaldor (1937, p. 747) clearly recognises that in his synthesis he operates under this condition, he nevertheless claims that it 'is not significant' (*ibid.*, n. 2):

> propositions obtained under the assumption of zero-investment can be applied to cases where investment is assumed to be constant and positive, and vice versa.

This claim is quite extraordinary. It is maintained in the face of full realisation that as soon as there are non-zero savings (and corresponding values of investment) the rate of interest is not equal any more to the rate of time preference. Kaldor (1937, p. 747) expressly quotes Ramsey (1928) in this context – the author whom we quoted above already (see p. 210) as saying that when there is saving (and investment) there is *not* equilibrium and there might even be no return to equilibrium in the time preference theoretic sense at all. Nevertheless, Kaldor stood steadfast by his belief that he was on a common ground with Pigou *and* Keynes.[49]

We have not much more to commend Kaldor's position than his profession of belief in the irrelevance of the zero-investment condition because it 'is not easy to show' as he wrote (see above, p. 233). His belief clearly stands against Keynes' contrary proclamation. No attempt is made by Kaldor to argue his case. Even Robertson – who was the confidant of Pigou in much of this debate and certainly was not particularly sympathetic to Keynes' cause in this context – took offence against Kaldor's belief in the essential similarity of Keynesian and Pigovian analytical situations.[50] Kaldor's position is in this regard, of course, very near to the position later explicated by Pigou (1941, p. 43) and which we commented upon above (p. 254).

It seems that Keynes subsumed these remarks just under the heading 'Pigou's special assumptions'. He did not comment on this aspect of Kaldor's synthesis. But one can easily see in these particular passages one further indication that Keynes' seeming disciples were – most probably inadvertently in this case – in important methodological respects closer to his paradigmatic adversary than to himself.

25.5.3 Nicholas Kaldor's position as a Cambridge Keynesian

A recent essay about the relationship between Nicholas Kaldor and his Cambridge Keynesian colleagues, in particular Joan Robinson and R. F. Kahn, ends with the statement:

> no new school of economics, from Austria to Chicago, has ever been established by leaders who fought each other more vigorously than their intellectual opponents. (King, 1998, p. 430)

Are the Cambridge Keynesians a case in point or an exception? The article has the heading ' "Your position is thoroughly orthodox and entirely wrong": Nicholas Kaldor and Joan Robinson, 1933–1983', the quote being from a letter of Nicholas Kaldor to Joan Robinson dated 22 April 1960 (King, 1998, p. 425). It refers to her alleged 'thorough-going neoclassicism', in particular concerning 'the rate of profit, the choice of techniques and the amount of capital per head' (*ibid.*).[51] These are not the only invectives and James King's article makes colourful reading documenting considerable in-fighting in the supposedly homogeneous group of Keynes' supposed disciples at Cambridge.

We cannot here retrace in detail the personal interactions related in that article. But we want to point out our own reconstruction of the situation (not covered in that article) in 1937 when Kahn wanted Keynes not to publish Kaldor (1937). It conveyed that even at that early time there was a considerable sense of rivalry between Kahn and Kaldor. That episode involved Kaldor's comment on Pigou (1937) which was published by Keynes against Kahn's advice. There were two aspects to Kahn's advice: (*i*) a personal one and (*ii*) an economic theoretical one. Concerning (*i*) it will be remembered that Kahn expressly protested against the 'favour' that Keynes should publish Kaldor's article.[52] Concerning (*ii*) the issue was, of course, the (unfelicitous, as it turned out to be for Joan Robinson) idea that one could have Pigovian equilibrium without Pigovian time preference determined interest rates. This belief was indeed shattered by the Kaldorian synthesis as we saw above. We also saw that for understandable reasons Pigou quite liked Kaldor's style to argue in this context. Nevertheless, it was R. F. Kahn – under instigation from Joan Robinson – who managed to arrange a fellowship at King's College for Kaldor in 1949[53] after an earlier attempt by Keynes to secure a fellowship with Jesus College[54] failed. There were happy times of togetherness and co-operation as King (1998) also relates. But eventually it was accusations of rivalry for priority that poisoned the friendly atmosphere. The substantive difference was there from the beginning. It has often been noted that Kaldor (1937) readily accepted Hicks' (1937) *IS–LM* scheme. He openly challenged his Cambridge colleagues R. F. Kahn and Joan Robinson on this issue.[55]

All of the Cambridge Young Keynesians of that time had leftish and anti-neoclassical inclinations. But it was mainly Kaldor who managed to do something practical with his political orientation and to enter political consultancy. Joan Robinson stayed a pure academic during most of her Cambridge life. In this regard we have a constellation of personalities similar to the one at King's College in the 1930s when Pigou, the pure academic, clashed with Keynes, the man of committee work and of political consultancy. As Pigou denied Keynes academic credentials, so did Joan Robinson.[56]

In the end, the Cambridge Keynesians indeed failed to establish a successful School. But that was not so much because Keynes' disciples bitterly fought each other – which they indeed did, in part about rather petty issues like priority of publication, orthodoxy of position etc. The basic problem seems to have been that they were *united*, namely in believing that their supposed master had 'seen the light' considerably later[57] than others and not quite in the appropriate colour. Put differently: they all were unappreciative of Keynes' *contextual* programme, namely to unveil the Pigovian 'stationary state' as an economic politically sterile 'frozen land'.[58]

25.6 Defence and disintegration in Cambridge economics

25.6.1 Keynes and Pigou *vs.* the Young Keynesians

It is most remarkable that of all the paladins of the 'real Keynes', none entered on the side of Keynes' paradigm in a systematic debate in this controversy. Their 'Messenger Angel' Richard Kahn[59] made emphatic offers to Keynes on behalf of 'all of us'. In spite of this promise which was explicitly accepted by Keynes, nothing came forth. Keynes stayed convinced that this point was fundamental for the difference between him and Pigou. It is most ironic that Kahn – who, according to Samuelson's (1977) question, might be considered as being virtually a co-author of the *General Theory* – convinced Keynes himself to 'shut up' about this issue, against Keynes' express conviction. Meanwhile Joan Robinson busily poured out essay after essay on a 'long-period theory of employment' based on the Pigovian concept of the stationary state, modified only in that sense that it was amputated of its time-preference implication. Keynes, weakened by heart disease and trusting in the power of academic discourse, offered only weak resistance to her, although he could have had reason to protest, as we will reiterate in the following section. It is only after decades that she herself saw the point and virtually rescinded most of her analytical endeavours after the *General Theory*.

Keynes offered more resistance to Harrod (1939) – to not much avail, as he wrote, maybe not so surprisingly, to none other than Pigou (see above, p. 270).

The complaint about the 'young savages' seems then to have occasionally become a unifying element for the two senior Cambridge economists. In June 1940 Pigou wrote to Keynes:[60]

> The chief bad thing [about the Tripos results] we [Sraffa and Pigou were examiners] found was that a very large number of people had been stuffed like sausages with bits of your stuff in such a way that (1) they were quite incapable of applying their own intelligence to it, and (2) they perpetually dragged it in regardless of its relevance to the question … My own guess … is that the parrot-like treatment of your stuff is due to the lectures and supervision of the beautiful Mrs [Joan] Robinson – a magpie breeding innumerable parrots. I gather that she puts in the

Truth, with an enormous T, with such Prussian efficiency, that the wretched men become identical sausages without minds of their own.

Although Keynes (letter of 18 June 1940) replied defiantly 'if there can be a few of reasonable merit at the top, I do not so much mind what happens at the bottom',[61] it becomes clear from the exchanges between him and Joan Robinson to be seen in the next sub-section that he himself was opposed to too dogmatical an interpretation of his approach.

Keynes had good reason to complain about the young savages, as Joan Robinson would have later admitted herself after she had become an old savant.

At the time of Keynes' writing and publishing the *General Theory* she thought quite differently, as we may recall from her year-long attempts to 'generalise' the *General Theory*. In this endeavour, she felt utterly misunderstood in some of her immediate surrounding, as we may gather from a passage of a letter to Michal Kalecki published by Feiwel (1989c, p. 9) and written a few weeks before she published her *Essays in the Theory of Employment* (1937a). Who exactly was or were the imbecile (s) she complained about when she wrote to Kalecki on 16 September 1936:

> I cannot delay to tell you what a pleasure it is for me to be arguing with someone who is making *an advance over Keynes instead of endlessly disputing with people who have not understood the elementary points*. I am now working on a book ... with a number of essays making application of the General Theory to various problems (including international trade).' (emphasis added, GMA)

Although she left open the identity of the object of her complaint, the quote makes it quite clear that she was looking to Kalecki for 'an advance over Keynes'. We know from from JMK, XIV, pp. 134–48 that at least from the beginning of September 1936 she had long disputes over her intended book with Keynes. We know (see note 3, p. 434) that she spread Gerald Shove's alleged remark that Keynes did not spend the 'twenty minutes necessary to understand the theory of value' and we know that she complained about the difficulties 'we' had in 1936/7 to make Keynes see the true nature of his own point (see above p. 14 and p. 178). Reading some of her correspondence with Keynes of that time, one can well imagine that, subjectively, she had reason to feel that she was not too well understood by Keynes. In part Keynes wrote that himself in those very words.[62] In part she must have just felt little appreciated, although once in a while Keynes did not spare with praise. The most emphatic rebuff is contained in a letter concerning the open-economy extension of the *General Theory*. In this regard Keynes wrote on 9 November 1936 (JMK, XIV, p. 146):

Dear Joan,
I beg you not to publish. For your argument as it stands is most certainly nonsense.

After some changes she could write to Keynes 'I am most delighted to have your approval in general for the book [Robinson (1937a), GMA]' (JMK, XIV, p. 148). The reader does not know whether that was in spite of or because Joan Robinson wrote to Keynes one day before: 'I haven't mentioned in the preface that you read the proofs as I thought you would prefer not' (*ibid.*).
　Whether Keynes' wish not to be implicated by this book was the only motive for not having him in the preface may be open to speculation after Joan Robinson's complaint about the lack of understanding which she met in her surroundings at that time. In any case, she confidently continued the letter to Michal Kalecki of 16 September: 'I think you are one of the ten people in Europe who will understand what I am trying to do' (Feiwel, 1989c, p. 9). Certainly Keynes did not appear as such a person in that letter, nor did he in the correspondence of the following weeks.
　In the meanwhile, while waiting for the page proofs for her (1937a) essays, Joan Robinson had sought Keynes' approval for the next 'amelioration' of the *General Theory*, this time for a 'told-to-the-children book' of her version of Keynesian economics (18 November 1936, JMK, XXIX, p. 184) for which she detected a 'strong demand' (6 March 1937, JMK, XIV, pp. 148–9).
　The surviving correspondence conveys a bit of the wiggling and manoeuvring Keynes employed in order to avoid tactfully the publication of yet another book supposedly in his name. First there must have been some harsh words, which, in a letter dated 2 December 1936 (JMK, XXIX, pp. 185–6) Keynes tried to mellow with a kind letter stating:

My dear Joan,
Do not let what I said on Monday evening weigh with you unduly. You are altogether free to follow your own judgement.
　But as you asked me, I had to try to express my own feeling ... So I am against hurry and in favour of gestation. Yours ever J.M.K.

The context makes it clear that the plea 'against hurry' was addressed not at Keynes himself but at the addressee of the letter.
　But the appeal for gestation time went unheeded. When the new manuscript came, Keynes wrote (25 March 1937, JMK, XIV, p. 149) cautiously that he did not find it that simple – normally a damning judgement for a 'taught-to-the-children book': 'At a first reading, it strikes me as a little difficult, but if people in fact like it, that is sufficient answer.' The course of publication obviously could not be stopped. A further letter in this context is dated 20 April 1937. It is in a similar vein: 'not the least objection in the

world to your preparing something on the lines you have' etc. but as far as he himself is concerned, Keynes writes that he is in the middle of 'half-baked changes' which he does 'not want to be expounded to the world' (all JMK, XIV, p. 150). Keynes closes by writing that all of this has 'no bearing worth mentioning on your draft'. But he does mention 'this' and one is left to wonder whether Keynes is here just garrulous, scribbling little 'nothings' or whether with these passages he was appealing to some non-enforceable tact in Joan Robinson's dealings with his intellectual property. If there was such an appeal, it was not understood; in any case it was not followed.

We must leave the final judgement open concerning the intended thrust of these letters. Some readers might be inclined to read Keynes' cautioning remarks as being directed just against the *General Theory* and against Keynes' own thinking. But it must be remembered that they were written in the context of some harsh criticism against Joan Robinson. A contextual reading might also suggest, therefore, that they were directed against Joan Robinson's meddling with the message of the *General Theory*. A ruder reading of Keynes' letters to Joan Robinson might well be: 'Would you please stop telling people how to proceed on the basis of the *General Theory*? I am working at that myself and I do not want you to mess up what I intend to bring across, once I am finished.' But it would be a rather unre-warding and not necessarily convincing exercise to rewrite Keynes' letters today.

What Keynes did convey quite clearly in the context just discussed is that in his judgement Joan Robinson seemed to have been left behind his intended rethinking – and that he wanted to be left alone with his 'half-baked changes', in any case he wanted them not to be 'expounded to the world'. But as far as the *General Theory* as already published book was con-cerned, it was now history and it was now there for the grabs of anyone.

For Joan Robinson, on the other hand, Keynes by this time seems to have become stale – at least in comparison to Michal Kalecki. Among Cambridge Keynesians it became fashionable to say that it was Michal Kalecki who was the 'true' Keynes or similar *bon mots* of that kind.[63]

25.6.2 The double secession of the Cambridge *past* Keynesians

The letters exchanged between Keynes and Joan Robinson as inspected in the last section could well be read as documenting episodes without deeper significance – instances of arguments temporarily out of step. Did time heal their little verbal and psychological blemishes? Signs are that these and similar episodes were not passing clouds but heralds of a new age. Its 'true' messengers were Sraffa and Kalecki, its beacons were Ricardo's *Principles* and Marx's *Capital*. Its promise was an epoch-making revolution. Its vision was long-term, far more general than Keynes' limited short-termism.

A Ricardo-oriented research programme could perhaps claim merit in general in view of the important influence which Ricardo did have on

Heinrich von Thünen, on Alfred Marshall and, not least on Karl Marx. In the years prior to writing the *General Theory*, Keynes himself was by no means violently opposed to Ricardo. Indeed, he was quite appreciative of his anticipation of what Gustav Cassel was later to name the 'purchasing power parity' theory of exchange rate development.[64] But once Keynes embarked on the issue of 'effective demand', his programme became one of fostering a Malthusian analytical approach because it was in Malthus' writings that this issue was particularly clearly articulated. Since the contemporary opposing position against Thomas Malthus was most prominently taken by David Ricardo, that meant that Keynes' own position became one in an anti-Ricardian camp.

As far as Marx was concerned, the other intellectual lighthouse of the new generation of Cambridge economists, it is well known that Keynes conscientiously disassociated himself from any of his ideas.[65] In groping his way towards the *General Theory* he did try to use some of Marx's figures of analysis, in particular his 'pregnant observation' (*sic* in: JMK, XXIX, p. 81) of a $C - M - C'$ circuit of commodity–money–commodity exchanges. But in the end, i.e. in the published version of the *General Theory*, Keynes eradicated any trace of this approach.[66] Keynes mostly had only derision for Marxian economics and especially for the application of Marxism in the Communist movement. To interpret the *General Theory* with a Ricardo–Marx-oriented movement in mind clearly should have appeared as anathema for what Keynes himself wanted to stand for.

Young Cambridge economics thus moved to an orientation which Keynes certainly would not have approved of in the context of his *own* programme. It is therefore quite consistent that they increasingly understood themselves not as Keynesians but as *past* Keynesians who had *surpassed* their putative master. They were off to new world, leaving the old gibberish behind them. Did not even Keynes himself have difficulties in understanding his own stuff had it not been for them who explained to him 'what the point of his revolution really was', as Joan Robinson once put it (see above, p. 14). Intellectually these *post*-Keynesians, as they later were to be named,[67] considered themselves, of course, as not being just *after* Keynes, but *beyond* him. Joan Robinson's correspondence with Michal Kalecki immediately after the publication of the General Theory conveys some of this mood of eon-shattering insights, of defiant geniality.

One cannot really say, however, that these 'revolutionists' embraced Marxism in a *paradigmatic* sense. For that they were far too little interested in the fundamental philosophical issues behind Marxism. Its philosophical root is dialectical materialism. One can quite well debate whether this paradigm was developed on the *basis* of the philosophy of G. W. F. Hegel or whether it was already present in a fully developed form in Hegel's *Logic*.[68] But in any case Marxism – and also Leninism which was similarly based on an intensive study of Hegel's philosophy and in particular of his *Logic* –

cannot be received as paradigm unless one is at least rudimentarily acquainted with Hegel's philosophy. Joan Robinson abhorred 'Hegelese'[69] and Hegel. In 'An open letter from a Keynesian to a Marxist' her main message in this regard was: 'Do not for heaven's sake bring Hegel into it' (Robinson, 1973a, p. 268). That seems to have been the motto for the other Keynesians in her surroundings as well. In any case, none of them is known for any systematic study of Hegelian concepts. Their reception of Marxism was thus far removed from any methodologically founded criticism of 'bourgeois' thinking.[70]

But although there was hardly any methodologically well-founded Marxism present in this circle, it is probably not without substance when Johnson (1978b, p. 158) described the situation at Cambridge after World War Two in the following way:

> The most important key to the transmogrification of Keynesian economics into something intellectually quite different in the hands (and writings, teachings, and preachings) of Joan Robinson, however, is the understanding that the dominant influence on Joan Robinson's Keynesianism was not Keynes, but the Polish economist Michal Kalecki, who had developed a Marxist version of Keynes's theory earlier in time than, and in some respects theoretically superior to, Keynes's *General Theory*, but was unfortunate enough to publish in Polish, his native language.

It would be unfair, however, to raise this charge just against Joan Robinson. Nicholas Kaldor was also very willing to give priority to Kalecki–especially over Keynes (see p. 458, n.63).

The reception of Kalecki seemed to have been somewhat deficient at Cambridge according to Harry Johnson, however, who continues (*ibid.*, p. 159, n):

> had Kalecki been kept in Cambridge, he would have developed an economics far more relevant to, and capable of handling Britain's postwar economic difficulties than 'Keynesian economics' as it developed at Cambridge.

The reasons which Johnson gave for this assessment was that Kalecki was the better and more relevant empiricist than the Cambridge Keynesians and that he foreshadowed later quantity theoretic work. One alternative reason could be seen in the fact that Kalecki probably was the better Marxist. But this is not the issue to be pursued here.

The present question is rather: what happened to the Cambridge economic tradition itself in the mindset of this group? According to our diagnosis that tradition had been abandoned in a *double* direction. Keynes' acknowledged merit was that he had an air of relevance for economic policy and national well-being but his short-period approach was not seen as a *paradigm* but as an 'anomaly'[71] which had to be cured and overcome.[72] At the same time Marshall was declared as being outmoded, in particular in his Pigovian long-period guise. Yet, the lack of long-period orientation was considered to be the very root cause of 'Keynes' anomaly'. Thus, Marshall/Pigou were right to show how very limited Keynes' analysis was, but they were declared to be wrong in almost everything else, be it now the theory of production, the theory of distribution, the theory of capital, and, of course and seemingly self-evidently, they committed the 'fundamental fallacy' (see above p. 359) of accepting the time-preference theory of interest in a stationary long-period setting. Therefore the new Cambridge revolutionists were needed to bring together the good of both analytical worlds.

The young/post-Keynesians' analysis was in fact not that different from the classical long-period one, however, as we saw in the above. This posed a dilemma: since they were en route to a new revolution, their self-conception was that they were breaking away from the old modes of thought. But thinking about new ages seemed to be plainly a long-period exercise. Thinking Pigovian long-period economics to its logical end means, however, that one is trapped in the old long-period results. The programmatic solution to this dilemma was that the tradition was just not to be looked at any more. In particular, the Pigovian conception of time-preference was proclaimed to be just plain 'wrong'. Full stop – no debate. Once R. F. Kahn gave out this order against Pigou (1937), he never published a reasoned argument about it, although Keynes expressly invited him to do so as was seen above.

The Young Keynesians did not follow Keynes in seeing the Pigovian time preference theory of interest as the logically *correct* deduction from a paradigmatically *wrong* model. Instead, Richard Kahn *proclaimed* the opposite view: that Pigou's time-preference analysis was a 'gross mistake' in a correct model which should not be damaged by any paradigmatic discussion of the *model* itself which was, after all, the one which was used by Joan Robinson (1936). Kaldor took a technically brilliant but methodologically muddled middle way: Pigou (1937) had the *logically* right results in an – assumption-wise – *correctable* model, the correct version being delivered by Kaldor (1937). All of them, including Joan Robinson, patently missed Keynes' paradigmatic point in this debate.

The seeming gain from the Kahn=Robinson strategy appeared to be that an essentially Pigovian conception of a stationary state (later: of a quasi-stationary 'golden age' economy) was thought to be maintainable while denying its implications for the determination of the rate of interest. This strategy in economic theorising seemed to give new 'revolutionary' freedom. The eventual outcome was that *neither* could Pigovian long-period analysis be claimed as paradigmatic backdrop, *nor* could Keynes' short-period paradigm of income determination be reclaimed by the Cambridge *past* Keynesians. Pigou was 'out' for two reasons: (*i*) he was 'gaga' in accordance with Kahn's proclamation of 1937; (*ii*) he was 'out' on a second account once 'logical time' was seen as economic politically sterile. But with 'point (*ii*)'-type reasoning most of Joan Robinson's modelling was equally 'out' as Garegnani (1979) was seen to have argued.

As far as Keynes is concerned, large parts of his work were left – under invectives – to the 'bastard Keynesians', he himself having been considered as being one of them. Since his approach needed 'generalisation' through the efforts of the *past* Keynesians, his writings were no satisfactory paradigmatic 'hunting ground' anyhow.

Having left paradigmatically scorched earth behind them in both the Pigovian and the Keynesian terrains, the Cambridge 'past' Keynesians could find no intellectual refuge in a theoretically well founded 'left' paradigm either, since dialectical materialism was beyond their 'language skills'.

Maybe this sketch of our vision of the intellectual landscape of the Cambridge 'past' Keynesians' habitat is a bit too pessimistic. But it might well be that a perception of this type – of a paradigmatic no-man's-land at the triple border of the realms of Keynes, Pigou and Marx – was the reason why in her later years Joan Robinson uttered some rather pessimistic opinions about the outcome of her own life's work.

26
Economic Consequences of a Re-authenticated Keynes–Classics Debate

26.1 The scope of *Economic Consequences*

Keynes' debut as a bestseller in economics was with *The Economic Consequences of the Peace* (1919). He repeated his publicity-stirring pamphleteering in 1925 with *The Economic Consequences of Mr Churchill*. The title of this chapter paraphrases these earlier pieces without any ambition to pamphleteer, however. The issue to be inspected in the following is rather: how far do the reconsiderations of the old debates with which we have occupied ourselves in the above have consequences for an outlook on currently debated issues in economics. Part of this subject matter was covered already in the last chapter when we pulled together the earlier arguments under the heading of 'analytical aspects'. The issues to be dealt with here go now beyond the scope cultivated there in touching somewhat 'grander' topics, namely (a) 'microeconomic foundations' and their relation to conceptions of general equilibrium, (b) the general nature of Keynes' intertemporal analysis, and (c) our view of the relation of Keynes' analysis to the doctrine of rational expectations.

In a final section we want to offer a synoptic presentation of Keynes' conception of economic modelling in a way that we are not aware can be found in quite the same way in the literature. Two aspects of this synopsis might be stressed here in a preliminary introduction. The question of 45° analysis has roused much debate among interpreters of Keynes. We point out below that there are two aspects to such constructions. One aspect is faced when we have an identity or equality as in the case of Keynes' understanding of Say's Law or when trying to show that current net production is identical to current net income. The other aspect of a 45° construction is given when such a line is not the final relationship itself but when alternative such lines describe a geometric *locus* which is *not* a 45° line. This is the case with the aggregate supply curve in fig. 26. 2. This double nature of 45° constructions might not have found sufficient attention in past interpretations of Keynes' theory. A second point is made with reference to that synopsis. It derives from the fact that 'value' has two meanings in economics. This term can stand for a 'scalar' magnitude like 'the value of aggregate supply'. But value can also be a vector with potentially many single elements, namely the system of $n - 1$ relative prices of an n-good economy. This imprecise delimitation of terms is part of the terminological inheritance of our science and it is not the responsibility of any particular interpreter of Keynesian or Classical ideas. Nevertheless, one may muse whether this lack of precision might not have caused difficulties when trying to locate Keynesian economics in the system of economics as an academic discipline.

We do not attach to the exercises of this chapter any aspiration to 'revolutionise' economics or to overthrow alternative approaches. We rather hope that the present reconsiderations might settle once controversial matters in such a way that economics can draw some 'peace dividends' and henceforth can turn to new pursuits. If taken up in Keynes' tradition, such pursuits might well go beyond the boundaries of economics as it was cultivated during much of the last century. But this is a matter for a subsequent chapter of this book.

26.2 Generalised microeconomic foundations

26.2.1 The individual perspective

David Laidler (1999, p. 339) ends his critical investigation of the Keynesian Revolution with brief section on 'Microeconomic Foundations' in which he refers to

> the scepticism, noted earlier in this book, of Cambridge economists in general, and *Keynes in particular*, regarding the wisdom of taking too seriously postulates about the scope for conscientiously maximizing behaviour, and the capacity of markets to coordinate it. (emphasis added, GMA)

Since the time when Aristotle praised the 'golden middle' we all know, of course, that a claim that there is wisdom in overdoing things should be met with scepticism. Thus far there is nothing startling said in this context. But it seems that a bit more is meant here. Since Laidler (*ibid.*) makes this remark after referring to Milton Friedman's work on the consumption function and on the demand-for-money function, stating that Friedman 'brought another element into the picture, namely, the application of explicit maximizing microeconomic models', the impression might arise that such explicit maximising models were absent in Keynes' approach and in the Cambridge tradition which Keynes represented.[1]

Some sections of post-Keynesian economists might appear to be prone to endorse such attempts at viewing Keynes quite apart from traditional microeconomic analysis on the grounds that what is really needed is the *macroeconomic* foundations of microeconomics, as Sardoni (2002, p. 11) recently pointed out. But, on reflection, Sardoni (2002, p. 11) insisted:

> It cannot be ignored that aggregate outcomes derive, though in a non-simplistic way, from individual decisions and actions.

To put it differently: although it is quite plausible to assume that macro-economic outcomes do have important influences on microeconomic behaviour, the relevant method of economic analysis might nevertheless be one which reflects the microeconomic reaction to the macroeconomic setting. The Keynesian consumption function is a case in point: although for any individuum with index *i* its income Y_i is determined through the working of the economy, nevertheless, given the income, the person will have individual economic dispositions and these might very well be analysed under a microeconomic perspective. Generalisations from this type of analysis might then be the basis for deriving important structural relations – as, for example, the consumption function.

There is little reason to believe that Keynes was particularly sceptical against this type of approach. It seems that today's post-Keynesians – at least those who follow the quoted Sardoni (2002, p. 11)-type of argumenta-tion – likewise have no fundamental problem with it. Not even with hind-sight can Keynes be disassociated from this type of reasoning. We mention this here expressly because Laidler's above quoted passages might convey a different message.

As far as maximising behaviour with regard to the consumption function is concerned, we demonstrated above in ch. 15 that this is an important area of theorising where Keynes' claim for having a more *general* theory than the 'Classics' can be well substantiated, if by 'Classics' we mean those economists who would like to think of time preference determined interest rates. Cases in point were Pigou (1937) and Barro (1990). Let us therefore restate: the difference between Keynes and the other authors just named is not the negation of the economic calculus of constrained maximisation in the case of Keynes, but the negation of the zero-savings assumption of the latter authors.

There are several ways of formulating that condition, as we saw above: one can assume that the 'income effect' of interest rate changes must be zero (Barro); or one may assume the analytical condition of a 'stationary state' (Pigou). In any case, this brand of neoclassical theorising is based – more or less explicitly, as we have seen – on a number of macroeconomic conditions which go together with stationarity: apart from zero savings there is, of course, zero net investment as well as repetitive 'equilibrium' economic outcomes. Thus, in this regard, it is the 'Classics' whose micro-economics is based on specific macroeconomic assumptions and preconditions. Keynes' own analysis, because it treats income and savings as magnitudes to be determined only through the interaction of the total economic model, presupposes *less* macrofoundations of microeconomics than the Classics. Indeed, if we start out from a Keynesian consumption function and introduce specific macroeconomic 'givens' which are *not* part of the ones which Keynes did assume, namely the above mentioned constancy of incomes, the repetitiveness of economic outcomes through time, the zero savings-assumption, then we can *generate* classical results from the microfoundations of Keynes' concept of a consumption function. In several passages of this book we strained the patience of the reader in going through the motions of the latter case but we believe that this is the input needed in order to liberate received perceptions of Keynesian analysis from long-established modes of thought.

For those who comment on the title of Keynes' *General Theory* as representing an overblown claim to generality, it might be instructive to see how the 'classical' time-preference oriented case can be *generated* from Keynes' consumption function. Keynes himself was aware of this transition as appeared from his exchange with R. F. Kahn in 1937 concerning Pigou (1937). It is true that R. F. Kahn and Joan Robinson refused to follow Keynes in this conclusion and it is indeed a most unfortunate development in Cambridge Keynesianism that a rupture was seen and cultivated by the Young Keynesians where in fact there was continuity and generalisation as far as Keynes himself was concerned.

In this context one could indeed regret a kind of 'Year Zero mentality' which Leeson (1998a, p. 126) associates with the Keynesian 'macroeconomic creation myth', adding:

> This mentality was propagated, in large part, by those around Keynes, especially Joan Robinson and Richard Kahn.

It would be quite wrong to believe that Keynes himself 'in particular' considered the maximising models of economic behaviour as inappropriate for economic analysis. Since the general acceptance of Alfred Marshall's *Principles*, first published in 1872, they were integral part of Cambridge economic thinking. Keynes was strongly embedded in that tradition as he himself was prone to point out in all sorts of contexts, e.g. when he insisted that he accepted without reservation the 'first classical postulate' as an 'important point of agreement' (*GT*, p. 17).

That Keynes' agreement with classical *methods* of economic analysis went far further than this particular agreement, let us re-emphasise, was demonstrated extensively above for the nexus of time preference and the consumption function. Indeed the Cambridge 'scene' around 1928 went even so far as to develop optimal models of consumption using variational models of optimisation as is demonstrated by Ramsey (1928) who expressly acknowledges Keynes' contribution to this type of model building. It is somewhat ironic that Nicholas Kaldor (1937) – a Cambridge outsider at that time – was nearer to Keynes' analytical method than was R. F. Kahn in his comments about him.[2] It therefore comes not as a surprise if Kaldor (1983b, p. 47) insisted:

> The real author of the so-called 'neo-classical synthesis' was not Paul Samuelson, it was Keynes himself.[3]

Thus it is not the interpretation of Keynes which brought in the 'neoclassical' elements, they were there from the start, put there by Keynes himself.[4]

As far as one other particular 'microfoundations' topic mentioned by Laidler (1999) is concerned, namely money demand, we did not have much opportunity to go into this – very important – aspect of Keynes' theorising because we followed the Pigovian trail of arguing from the 'real end' of constructing the model economy by modelling production and consumption. But it is an ahistorical view to negate the important influence which emanated from the Cambridge Marshallian school on this very topic. Long before Keynes formulated his doctrine of interest-rate dependent 'liquidity preference', we have Lavington's (1921) formulation (pp. 33–4) that:

> the individual's demand for money is expressed and satisfied in just the same way as his demand for ordinary commodities; he distributes his resources in such a way as to satisfy each need down to the same level of urgency.

Thus it is from an equimarginal calculus – which particularly in the case of Lavington has to be considered to be 'unconditionally Marshallian' (Schumpeter, 1954, p. 1084) – that members of the Cambridge School contemplated money demand long before Milton Friedman could have thought about its microfoundations.

The explicit continuation of this tradition we see in Keynes' chapter 17 and in the equal (marginal) interest rate rule which he discusses there at great length.

There *are* Keynes' statements about non-calculable risks which might suggest that he negated an economic calculus in this context. But the context of such an argument is economic *analysis*. Thus these phenomena have the character of an *economic* constraint in the sense of a fact of life like sun-spot activity or technological knowledge. Liquidity preference is economically sensible exactly because there are incalculable risks which require to have parts of one's wealth in an unspecific form. But saying that does not mean that wealth and opportunity costs become immaterial. The problems of risk, insecurity and liquidity do not limit the scope of economic analysis – they extend it.

26.2.2 A Walrasian 'dis'equilibrium perspective

Let us also state in this context that it is not only a single-unit maximising perspective which was cultivated here but also a general (dis-)equilibrium one. There is some contradiction in Laidler's presentation of the issue of general equilibrium, because on the one hand he insists on Keynes' superior grasp of this point in comparison to Pigou, but on the other hand – on the final pages of his book – Laidler (1999) suggests that the general equilibrium perspective was a *post*-Keynesian development. We tried to convince the reader above in sect. 10.1 (p. 73), however, that ever since Alfred Marshall the general equilibrium perspective was deeply entrenched in Cambridge economics. Maybe it was not rigorously applied by Pigou (1933), as Laidler (1999, p. 167) himself had argued. But this very fact was part of Keynes' criticism of Pigou, as we demonstrated in sect. 10.2 (p. 75) above. This line of argumentation thus should be seen as an integral part of Keynes' approach and we should keep it in mind in trying to receive his theory.

There can be little doubt that Keynes' criticism of Pigou was based on a general equilibrium standpoint. Indeed, *involuntary* unemployment can only be understood if the (not attained) general equilibrium is formulated as point of analytical orientation. Let us recapitulate therefore Keynes' critical procedure:

1. In the commonly accepted Marshallian tradition, the traded volume of every economic good – including labour services – is determined by demand and supply. As a good Marshallian, Pigou must match his $\phi(x)$-labour demand curve with a $\chi(x)$-labour supply curve. The intersection gives one determinate value for *full* – general equilibrium – employment.
2. *Unemployment* must obviously be of a different nature if it is characterised by an excess supply of labour. It must be due to some constraint which keeps the economic system in that state. This constraint is 'effective demand' according to Keynes.
3. In the view of Keynes, Pigou (1933) is thus strictly speaking short of not one but *two* equations, namely
   (a) a $\chi(x)$-curve which he receives so to speak 'gratuitously' from the Marshallian tradition;
   (b) an unemployment-generating equation which changes his employment determination model into an *unemployment* determination model. This equation is missing in Pigou (1933) and thus the title of his *Theory of Unemployment* is a 'misnomer'.

Put positively, one may say that Keynes' view of a macroeconomic model of unemployment is that it is an overdetermined general equilibrium model.

Keynes' famous question for the 'missing equation' is then the question for the mechanism which should be modelled as causing the problematic

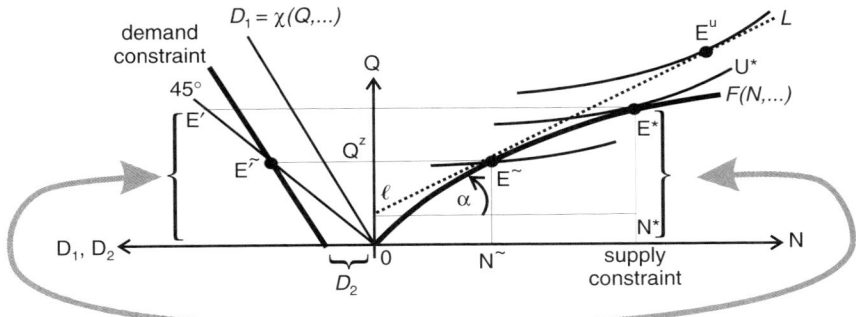

Figure 26.1 Income and effective demand: a Walrasian interpretation

overdetermination. The 'classical' answer to this question is: there is unemployment because the price system does not work – or rather: trade unions and other actors of society don't let the price system work – 'properly'. Keynes' answer is: involuntary unemployment in the 'strict' sense exists because of a deficiency of effective demand. These two positions are depicted in fig. 26.1.

Figure 26.1 depicts in the right-hand quadrant the full employment situation at point E^* with a real production $\overline{N^*E^*}$. This situation would be a general equilibrium situation similar to the one already depicted by the Koopmans-diagram of fig. 10.4 (p. 102). Any output, if it were indeed produced, accrues as income to households.[5] The identity between production and income is depicted through the grey arrow connecting the right-hand and the left-hand quadrants. But any output can be maintained only if it were also *demanded* at its respective height. This means that total income must always be equal to total demand, as is expressed by the 45° line in the left-hand quadrant. If now total demand $D_1 + D_2$ along that 45° line is smaller than the required height, i.e. reaching not E' but $E^\wedge$, then total demand is a new constraint on the economy leading to a level of employment N^- lower than the full employment one, with production and income of $\overline{N^- E^-}$.

There are now a number of argumentative paradigms imaginable in this expository framework:

1. If point E^- is the outcome of a free market society, then this outcome is what the society desires and does not require any economic political action.
2. In point E^- the real wage $\tan \angle \alpha = w/p$ is obviously 'too high'. Therefore the real wage must drop. This requires higher prices and / or lower wages. If society does not want to work on these variables, it must endure the consequences of its 'rigidities'.

3. Keynes' position is: if, given E^- resp. $E^\wedge$, total demand as depicted in the left-hand quadrant were increased, it would maintain higher production and employment. Therefore the determinants of 'effective demand' as depicted in that quadrant are the strategic variables for economic analysis and for economic policy for reaching the full employment position E^* resp. E'.

In this framework one can thus cover and evaluate a wide spectrum of arguments including a brief outline of Keynes' 'effective demand' theory. This framework is based on the 'Koopmans diagram' of general equilibrium and thus it links up with conventional relative price theory. It covers unemployment and in that sense it is a disequilibrium representation. But the demand constrained situation is one of constrained *maximisation*. In that sense the disequilibrium cannot be taken quite literally. This is the reason why the heading of the present sub-section is partly set in single quotes.

26.2.3 Effective demand and relative prices

We proposed to link Keynes' doctrine of effective demand with the Koopmans (1957) diagram of general equilibrium and we claimed that this gives a fruitful framework for further debate while not isolating Keynes from mainstream economic analysis. Exactly this claim – related to Tobin (1992) who also sees a specificity of Keynes' in his effective demand analysis – was rejected by Davidson (1998, p. 16):

> This dichotomization between a Keynes demand-oriented regime and a classical supply-constrained regime is part of mainstream folklore. It is however, in direct conflict with Keynes's argument that the principle of effective demand is a general theory applicable to *all* economic regimes, while the classical case was not applicable to any real world economy. (emphasis in the original, GMA)

There are, however, at least two different conceptions of classical economics – the 'frozen land' conception and the 'borderline' conception, as was seen above in discussing Table 15.1 on p. 172. It is only the former case to which Davidson (1998) refers later in this article, insisting that in his version of the Classics $D_2 = 0$ must hold (*ibid.*, p. 29, equ. 7). There we have indeed the unbridgeable dichotomy between Keynes and the Classics. But we also have the judgement of Keynes himself that one could quite well see the world of his involuntary equilibrium and that of classical economics in one analytical continuum set out by his *General Theory*. Otherwise it would not make much sense if he criticised Harrod (1937b) with the following remark (JMK, XIV, pp. 85–6):

You do not show how in conditions of full employment . . . my theory merges in the orthodox theory.

Thus, Keynes' analytical programme was an inclusive one, not an exclusive one as far as (neo)classical economics was concerned. He quite clearly believed that his theory does have areas of congruence with that theory and our presentation was conceived to make this congruence visible.

Let us now briefly point out the advantages of our analytical perspective. First of all, the present approach gives a choice theoretic basis for rejecting the type of 'Panglossian' argument just listed above under item 1, p. 385. A case of not-attainment of point E^* shows that the full potential of a society has not been used. Comparing the welfare levels as represented by the indifference curve going through point E^- with the one in E^* gives a choice-theoretic argument *not* to abstain from economic political intervention. Comparing the marginal rate of substitution along the indifference curve in point E^- with the prevailing real wage given by tan $\angle\alpha = w/p$ shows that the subjective valuation of goods and leisure does not coincide with the market valuation and in this sense makes it clear that the situation is one of *disequilibrium*.

This then brings us to the second argument of the above list: should 'rigidities' – in particular of nominal wages – be treated as main culprits in economic policy advice? It is true that the unemployment real wage tan $\angle\alpha = w/p$ is 'too high'. But it is so not because the real wage is 'rigid' but because demand is deficient. If workers would agree to lower wages w, competitive employers would pass on that cost advantage to prices, hoping to attract more real demand. This would lead to increased non-wage income as measured by $\overline{O\ell}$ along the Q-axis. But unless this action has an expansionary effect on D_2 as measured by the corresponding horizontal bracket in the left-hand quadrant, real demand will remain unchanged, and price competition will lead to the old and thus unchanged real wage.

Let us remember in this context that Clower (1965) had a visualisation of Keynesian unemployment quite similar to the one in our right-hand quadrant. Clower called the households' demand in point E^u their 'notional demand' which cannot articulate itself because only N^- workers do get employed in a case like this. Only they can develop 'effective demand'. Thus effective demand in this sense is that demand which meets actually produced supply. This seems to be quite an authentic usage of the term, in particular since in point E^- marginal productivity determines the real wage and this is what Keynes always accepted (*modulo* a given degree of imperfect competition).

Unfortunately, modern usage, in particular in the case of Clower, does not always follow this – in our view authentic – rendering of Keynes' unemployment. Thus, Trevithick (1992, fig. 8.4, p. 186) calls this very type of disequilibrium a case of 'Classical unemployment'. Trevithick (1992, p. 187) elaborates:

The level of excess demand [between our E^- and our E^u, GMA] is the magnitude which is relevant to Walras's Law, but it is of no operational significance either for firms or for households. As Clower pointed out, it takes a strange contortion of language to characterise the 1930s [with their very high level of unemployment, GMA] as a period in which the basic problem was that of an excess demand for goods.

But the problem which this author sees is not very convincing. If there does exist involuntary unemployment in a specific situation, then it would be quite absurd to surmise that those workers who do not find work just want to dispense with their services as labourers without getting any payment for buying goods. Against such a view which Trevithick can hardly have wanted to convey we must insist: it is indeed so that any involuntary unemployment means an involuntary underconsumption. That is true in principle and that was true in the 1930s.

There is a misconception of naming 'classical' the type of unemployment which Keynes presented as 'involuntary unemployment' in the strict sense. The confusion which results from this is then the proclamation that effective demand cannot be the reason for this case because the unemployment is 'classical' and effective demand is the domain of Keynes. One then must profess ignorance about its economic political causes and consequences. At the same time one is at a loss about the nature of Keynes' type of unemployment. Thus, Trevithick (1992, p. 188) declares:

> In brief, the mechanisms through which policy makers might bring about a reduction in classical unemployment [in the sense just critically discussed, GMA] have not been systematically worked through in most models of temporary equilibrium. Both the origins of classical unemployment and the nature of the remedy for it remain stubbornly obscure.

Let us therefore insist: this type of unemployment is the very case presented in the *General Theory*. Its origin is deficient effective demand. Its remedy is increase in effective demand. The nexus between demand and employment can be easily depicted by means of our fig. 26.1 on p. 385.

Thus we differ in this context with regard to the explanation why such an unemployment situation endures. The reason Clower gave in that context was a fix-price one which later was taken up by Leijonhufvud (1968) and then gave rise to the 'fix-price' Keynesianism renounced again by some of its spiritual fathers. Their renunciation is indeed correct in our view. The fixation of Keynes' unemployment system results not from dynamics (or lack of it) but from the problem of effective demand as outlined with reference to what goes on in the left quadrant of fig. 26.1.

To argue only with reference to real wage movements in the context of discussing macroeconomic employment means to negate the 'left-quadrant analysis'. Implicitly this assumes that there is nothing to contemplate and that can only mean that whatever happens in the economy, the $D_1 + D_2$-analysis is irrelevant for the economic outcome. This is the essence of Say's Law in the sense of Keynes.

26.2.4 Say, Marshall and Walras

26.2.4.1 Say's Law and the irrelevance of overproduction

There is still – or rather, again – much vitriolic debate about the topic of 'Keynes and Say's Law'. Thus, Ahiakpor (1998b, p. 4) is convinced that 'Keynes's rendition of Say's Law is a gross misrepresentation, bordering on the fraudulent', while Cottrell (1998) tried to argue just the opposite, that Keynes was right concerning Say's Law. But that author is now convinced that Keynes misjudged the validity of Robert Malthus' criticism against David Ricardo in this context.

We cannot cover this extensive ground here anew, however. It has been well covered in the past and it seems that Walker (1986, p. 15) gave a fair assessment when he concluded:

> [Keynes] was correct to assert that the nineteenth-century orthodox economists believed that Say's law and its implications hold true during recessions.

But the details of this assertion are not the main concern in the present context. The question in this chapter on perspectives of an authentic Keynesianism is rather: which analytical perspective did Keynes attempt to convey in this particular context and is it one which is still meaningful?

There seems to be persistent misunderstanding concerning Keynes' analytical intentions in this context. Kates (1998) is an author who, similar in spirit to the quote just given from Ahiakpor (1998b, p. 4), writes an appendix so that:

> It will be shown that every one of the statements made by Keynes on Say's Law is untrue. (*ibid.* p. 19)

He explains Keynes' intentions in writing about Say's Law in the following way (Kates, 1998, p. 218):

> Keynes's polemical skills were never better shown than in his attack an Say's Law. In creating a straw man version of the law of markets, he changed the terms of the argument just enough to ensure that he did not clearly reveal what the issues at stake were. Keynes had to discredit the law of markets which denied the possibility of *over-production* and

general gluts, but he had to do so in a way which would not alert his contemporaries to the full nature of what he was trying to do. He thus could not argue in a straightforward way that he had realised that overproduction was a problem and a general glut could occur. These words do not appear anywhere in the *General Theory*. He instead focused an the form of the classic demonstration rather than an the conclusion to which it led. (emphasis in the original, GMA)

This is a gross misconception of what Keynes wanted to convey in discussing Say's Law. He did not slyly *conceal* his belief that 'overproduction' is a relevant problem. He just did not believe that this *is* a problem in the context under discussion. Quite to the contrary, unemployment is *under*employment and therefore it is, of course, a problem of *under*production. The problem of involuntary unemployment in the 'strict sense' occurs because effective demand *restrains* production such that it is below its full employment level. Therefore it is small wonder and no sly concealment, if Keynes never mentions overproduction in the *General Theory*. In the last section we just spent considerable space clarifying the fact that the corollary to involuntary unemployment is indeed excess demand for goods. This is consistent with Keynes according to our reading of the issue and it is *not* a case of overproduction.

The problem of overproduction Keynes *did* address, namely in 1926 in the context of discussing raw material production. He did state that commodity markets might not be able to do what is expected of them, stating, e.g., that:

it is not sufficiently realised that the commodity markets of the world are almost never able to carry any material surplus of stocks at a price anywhere near the estimated normal. (Keynes, 1926, p. 549)

This type of overproduction can indeed have depressive consequences on prices and employment in the sector affected.[6] Keynes returned to related problems in 1942 when he proposed his 'Buffer Stock Plan' which subsequently saw several revisions and detailed elaborations.[7] But this is clearly by no means a paradigmatic problem of the *General Theory* – and rightfully so. It would be quite beside the point to take problems of raw material production as paradigmatically identical with those of modern deficient effective demand problems. It is therefore quite correct – in terms of relevance and in terms of intellectual honesty – that Keynes does not linger on the topic of *over*production.

The important point in this context is that any relative price theory which claims that 'it is "right relative prices" which generate general equilibrium allocation – and that is it', any such economic theory needs a corollary to this statement, namely a safeguarding clause which by *assumption* excludes the macroeconomic relevance of a potential demand constraint. This is what Keynes stressed by invoking Say's Law, and this we tried to visualise by fig. 26.1 (p. 385). The interconnection of the two quadrants depicted there should by itself make clear that any comparative static debate of preferences, technology, price rigidities etc. with sole reference to the right-hand quadrant analysis is (a) either deficient or (b) implying a reasoned disregard of the left-hand type analysis. The outcome of the latter reasoning must be that there cannot be any mechanism which exerts a constraint coming from the left-hand quadrant on the general equilibrium system as it is to be depicted in the right-hand quadrant. But this means that there is no determinate point along the 45° line. Since along this line $D \equiv Q$, i.e. total demand is always equal to total supply, fig. 26.1 depicts, as just stated, Say's Law in the sense of Keynes and as expressed above on pp. 139f. If, however, contrary to this logical interconnection of right-quadrant and left-quadrant analysis in fig. 26.1 somebody like Pigou referred to real wage movements as *explaining* or *determining* movements in the level of employment, then the least deprecatory interpretation of such a statement would be that its author implicitly assumes the said identity of supply and demand. Such a statement is not a quasi-fraudulent intellectual sleight of hand but a saving device attributing to relative price theorists consciousness for the necessary condition for their comparative static exercises to make any sense.

Say's Law is, however, only a *necessary*, not a sufficient condition for general equilibrium and full employment under disregard of effective demand problems. Postulating Say's Law does not exclude the statement that if prices were *wrong*, such wrong prices could be the causes for employment being less than full. This is, of course what many authors did say before and after Keynes. Keynes did not negate that.[8] It would in itself be a gross misrepresentation of Keynes to claim that by attributing to his Classics the assumption of Say's Law, he deprived them of any Say's Law-compatible theory of business cycles or of unemployment.

We summarise the argument of this section by noting: in receiving Keynes' economics it is indeed justified to stress the potential inapplicability of his 'Say's Law', signifying the potential significance of effective demand constraints. But although we deny with Keynes the general relevance of Say's Law, we propose to *accept* another important neoclassical tenet, namely Walras' Law in the general form that the *sum* of values of excess demand is zero.

26.2.4.2 *Walras' Law and Marshall's 'note XXI'*

This opens a further front of controversy, because there are many commentators on Keynesian economics who see a fundamental difference between Keynes and Walras. One prominent voice we may quote is Kaldor (1983b,

p. 47) who continues the quote given above on p. 383 concerning Keynes' neoclassical, Marshall-based analytical approach with the words:

> Marshall was a neo-classical economist but very different in many ways from Walras. Walras explored the logical implications of a competitive market to the point of absurdity in a way Marshall never did.

This statement presents two issues: (a) the (potential) analytical differences between Marshall and Walras and (b) the role of the assumption of competitive markets. In this section we will address topic (a).

It is, of course, true that Marshall put far more stress on the details of economic decision-makers and on the functioning of particular markets than Walras did. But in *one* point there is no fundamental difference: we saw already on p. 73 that Schumpeter (1954, p. 920, n. 1) was convinced that 'the core of Marshall's theoretical analysis . . . [is, GMA] a system of general equilibrium'. There is little ground to question this judgement. But this means that Marshall, too, had to contemplate formal consistency of his general equilibrium model and indeed that was the main concern of the famous 'note XXI' to which the quoted passage refers. There, the question was whether an economy based on (choice theoretically derived) supply and demand equations can be considered to be formally consistent. Marshall declared that he was convinced that that was indeed the case. But in that case he himself *must* have come across something like Walras' Law. In the simplest case of the 'Robinson Crusoe' economy of the Koopmans diagram we get for Robinson the profit maximizing producer and for Robinson the utility maximizing household the two equations:

$$\Pi = pQ^s - wN^d \qquad (26.1)$$

$$wN^s + \Pi = pQ^d \qquad (26.2)$$

Subtracting the lower from the upper expression then gives

$$w(N^d - N^s) = p(Q^s - Q^d). \qquad (26.3)$$

In other words: the value of any excess supply of labour must be necessarily equal to the value of the excess demand for goods. This is, of course, nothing else but Walras' Law. But that law is not an invention of Walras'. This 'Law' is a consequence of the requirement of consistent bookkeeping, not a behavioural generalisation. Despite its name, its *substance* therefore cannot be associated just with Walras under the exclusion of Alfred Marshall. Equ. (26.3) follows from the fact that equ. (26.1) and equ. (26.2) have one self-same value in common, namely the entrepreneurial profits Π which then may be eliminated, joining the supply- and demand-parts of the system so that we have an interconnected system of the entire economy. This must be an element of *any* consistent model of the economy. In the writings of Marshall the consistency condition takes on a somewhat different form. It is embodied in his construction of national 'offer curves' which identify real exchange of export and imports. But the basis of such curves is again a consistency condition of the type just discussed. On a national level such a consistency condition follows from the mere fact that profits *have* to go to households since they are the only agents to whom income can logically accrue.

There is some debate about the nature of the prices which enter the Marshallian general equilibrium system, most notably in Clower (1989). But any single transaction can occur only at one agreed-upon price and insofar a distinction between demand-price and supply-price is not meaningful for the formulation of effective demand as a concept which signifies realised or realisable production. In any case, this was not a controversial issue at the time of Keynes' original debate and thus should not occupy us in the present context.

On the basis of these considerations we may return to Kaldor (1983a, p. 13) where we find the present issues put in the following way:

> the voluminous literature concerning the reconciliation of Keynesian analysis with Walrasian general equilibrium – in terms of 'disequilibrium' economics . . . etc. – is beside the point. The two kinds of theory cannot be reconciled, simply because one concerns a purely artificial world of perfect competition, etc., whilst the other attempts to generalise about the real world. Keynes himself was by no means fully conscious of the contrast.

We have just established, however, that as far as Walras' Law is concerned, there is no need to disassociate Keynes or Alfred Marshall from this piece of general equilibrium analysis because that does not depend on any specific assumption concerning the degree of competition or other behavioural assumptions. It is based on the postulate of consistent accounting in total-economy modelling. There is no indication whatsoever that Keynes ever denied such an idea. Quite the contrary: in ch. 6 of the *General Theory* Keynes gives consistent macroeconomic accounting considerable space. We therefore conclude that in this particular context there is no need to cultivate a Keynesian peculiarity. There remains the question of 'perfect competition' which, in the quote just given, Kaldor considers to be crucial for the proper understanding of Keynesian economics.

26.2.4.3 The irrelevance of imperfect competition

Richard Kahn and Nicholas Kaldor both had strong – albeit differing – convictions about Keynes' failure to see clearly what his theory was all about. In the former case it was the denial of time preference. We saw above that

Keynes did accept its relevance, both for his own conception of a consumption function and for Kaldor's (1937) Pigovian synthesis. Similarly, there are several indications that Keynes was not just not fully conscious of the importance of imperfect competition for his theory. He consciously denied its relevance beyond the point that the degree of competition must be *given*.

The formal concept of this degree was stressed and reformulated by none other than Kaldor (1983a, p. 17) who named it the ' "Pigou amendment" ... because of its original appearance in Pigou's *Theory of Unemployment'*. This amendment consists of adding a term into the marginal productivity or marginal cost relations of the model, named η^K by Kaldor (1983a, p. 17),[9] which may be taken to represent the reciprocal of the elasticity of demand facing the individual producer according to Kaldor or which may be taken as being a short-hand notation for a whole conglomerate of parameters describing market conditions, as was seen and discussed above already in connection with equ. (11.7) on p. 126.

Having taken account of market conditions in this way – by describing them with the help of a 'given' parameter very much along the line of 'classical' economists like Pigou (1933) – Keynes was convinced that he did not need to discuss them any further in the context of his causative nexus. He conscientiously defended this position against Bertyl Ohlin's (1937, p. 196) remark about the *General Theory*:

> Keynes does not seem to me to have been radical enough in freeing himself from the conventional assumptions. When reading his book one sometimes wonders whether he never discussed imperfect competition with Mrs Robinson.

To these passages Keynes (JMK, XIV, p. 190) replied:

> The reference to imperfect competition is very perplexing. I cannot see how on earth it comes in. Mrs Robinson, I may mention, read my proofs without discovering any connection.

Certainly standard price theory may easily show that with a given sectoral demand function and increasing marginal cost, a monopolistic firm would supply the market with less output and offer less employment than the sum of a host of atomistic firms operating under conditions of perfect competition would do, if each were facing comparable production technology on the firm level and the community of these firms were facing the same total market demand. But again we can only take note that this is not what Keynes intended to show. The doctrine of effective demand constrained employment is valid for *any* degree of competition as long as that degree is given. Thus, it does not seem to be a rewarding approach to see an important rupture between Keynes' analysis and the classical analysis in this particular context of imperfect competition.

26.2.4.4 Demand constraint on the microeconomic level

There is, however, indeed a grave problem with regard to conventional neoclassical models of perfect competition. They assume that every individual firm considers market price as given and that at that price market demand facing that firm would be virtually infinite. Thus the firm is supposed to believe in a horizontal demand curve. Only technology – or rather, increasing marginal cost at the individual firm level – determines output.

Such a model is not very convincing if it is to be used for explaining effective demand constrained firm behaviour. Kaldor (1983b, p. 47) relates that the model just mentioned is indeed quite un-Marshallian:

> 'Marshall *always* assumed a downward sloping demand curve, never a horizontal curve'.[10] At the same time Marshall believed in competition . . . individual firms . . . were confined by the market.

But this does not really mean a negation of neoclassical marginal analysis. It just means its extension in such a way that not only technological constraints are identified but market constraints as well. Thus, whereas the conventional constrained maximising approach for the i-th firm might be given by the Lagrangian L_i^W as expressed by equ. (26.4), the Marshallian case might be represented by the Lagrangian L_i^M as expressed by equ. (26.5):

$$L_i^W = pQ_i - wN_i - \mu^W(Q_i - F_i(N_i)) \tag{26.4}$$

$$L_i^W = pQ_i - wN_i - \mu^{MP}(Q_i - F_i(N_i)) - \mu^{MM}(p - p(Q(Q_i); Y^e)) \tag{26.5}$$

where p is market price, w is market wage rate, Q_i is the i-th firm's goods supply, N_i its corresponding labour demand, μ^W is the Lagrangian multiplier for the conventional case which knows only the technological constraint as given by the production function. In the Marshallian case – which we might better call the Marshall–Keynesian case – there are two such multipliers, one, μ^{MP}, relating to the technological constraint as before, the other, μ^{MM} relating to the market constraint. The latter goes with a nested function with the elasticities

$$\text{(a) } E_Q^p < 0 \quad \text{and} \quad \text{(b) } 0 < E_{Q_i}^Q \equiv \frac{\partial Q}{\partial Q_i} \frac{Q_i}{Q} \lessgtr 1 \tag{26.6}$$

The first of these expresses the 'law of demand' for product Q, the second measures the impact which Q_i firm i's supply, will have on total market supply Q and hence on market price p as expressed by the the previous elasticity.

In the case of a monopoly the value of equ. (26.6 b) will be unity since total supply is equal to individual supply and hence the derivative $(\partial Q/\partial Q_i)$ as well as the market share (Q_i/Q) will both be unity. In the case of oligopoly this elasticity may have a value either larger or smaller than unity. The latter value will be relevant if rival competitors do not react when firm i moves. In this case the partial derivative as just given will be unity. But since the market share in this case is only a fraction of total supply, the total value of the elasticity will be smaller than unity. If, however, the competitors start vying for market shares, it might well be that an increase of supply by the i-th firm will push up total supply my a number of other firms as well. The partial derivative $(\partial Q/\partial Q_i)$ is then much larger than unity. If it is larger than the individual market share, the elasticity (26.6(b)) will be larger than unity.

But these details need not concern us here since we cannot do more in this context than discuss the relevant paradigm. Let us therefore just briefly mention that the Lagrangian as expressed by our equ. (26.5) corresponds to much that has been associated with specifically Marshallian microfoundations in the last years:

1. Marshall–Keynesian market demand in this formulation is a 'nested' function – a point which Colander (1996b) stressed as typical for the Marshallian general equilibrium approach. We show now what this might mean in terms of textbook type analysis of microeconomic behaviour.[11]
2. Our Marshall–Keynesian market demand has the shift parameter Y^e, expected income of consumers. Thus it has an element of macrofoundation to it. Thus it incorporates a further desideratum of recent post-Keynesian – or rather, post-Walrasian – economics.[12]
3. As in the conventional model of the firm mentioned above, expected reactions of the market price will tend to be zero under conditions of atomistic competition but for quite different reasons. Here, in such a case we have

$$\frac{Q_i}{Q} \to 0 \qquad (26.7)$$

and hence the elasticity of equ. (26.6(b)) will also tend to zero. Then the individual impact on total supply is negligible and it might *appear* as if the demand curve facing an individual firm might be horizontal. But the modelled firm here is totally aware of true market demand, even if it operates under conditions of atomistic competition. The firm just is also aware that its market share is minute. If it started supplying near infinite amounts, that, of course, would change and, as modelled here, firm behaviour would also change.

All in all, this setup of assumptions seems indeed to produce a more realistic model of the firm than the conventional model criticised by Kaldor and some others.[13]

Unfortunately, there does not seem to exist any detailed textbook type formulation of this model which would make it comparable to the myriad of textbook renderings of the conventional model.[14]

All of this does not invalidate what Keynes said in connection with the *General Theory* concerning the unimportance of imperfect competition: once the degree of imperfection is taken as given – be this now Kaldor's 'Pigou amendment' or be it the parameters of the functions and the elasticities of equ. (26.6) – then all these considerations enter Keynes' employment theories as 'givens' and give way to Keynes' *really* strategic paradigm of determining theoretically and manipulating economic politically the ultimate magnitude: effective demand.

26.3 Keynes' 'anticipated *ex post*' approach

26.3.1 The charge of 'retrograde' analysis

Reflecting on the method underlying his multiplier approach, Keynes (1936, p. 122) notes that in economic discussions there is:

> some confusion between the logical theory of the multiplier, which holds good continuously, without time-lag, at all moments of time, and the consequences of an expansion in the capital-goods industries which take gradual effect, subject to time-lag and only after an interval.

He subsequently (*ibid.* p. 124) declares that the latter aspect of the workings of the multiplier is not without interest and that it was used by himself in the *Treatise*:

> But it does not in any way affect the significance of the theory of the multiplier as set forth in this [10th] chapter; nor render it inapplicable as an indicator of the total benefit to employment.

Thus Keynes stresses that *his* analysis of the multiplier in the *General Theory* is based on the former aspect, on the 'logical theory of the multiplier'.

Referring to these passages, Shackle (1958, p. 76) declares:

> This instance [of the *General Theory*, p. 122, GMA] is, I think, likely to do more harm than good. Compared with professor Kahn's original formu-

lation it is something of a retrograde step, tending to obscure rather than to clarify. For when we look upon the Multiplier as an instantaneous functional relation between a realised upward step of the level of investment seen ex post, on the one hand, and the associated upward step of output-as-a-whole, also seen ex post, on the other, we are merely using the word Multiplier to stand for an alternative way of looking at the marginal propensity to consume. The Multiplier becomes a mere identity, and in insisting on its timeless, continual, ever-perfect operation lord Keynes was giving way to his Marshallian habits of thought and allowing the mathematician in him to opt for the concise elegance of an essentially static method.

Here we have again a Keynesian commentator who would have liked Keynes to have written something less 'retrograde'. But with due respect for alternative analytical ambitions, when trying to establish the approach offered by the *General Theory* we should take note that this was indeed the express decision made by Keynes. Before regretting the 'harm' done by his approach, let us first try to establish the advantages which one might be able to detect behind his double *ex post* analysis.

26.3.2 The problem of non-existent markets

This is now the occasion to refer back to our excursus on 'Alternative conceptions of general equilibrium' (p. 102) and to the distinction of 'collapsing' (p. 104), 'expanding' (p. 105) and 'momentous' (p. 106) conceptions of general equilibrium.

The first of these is the Arrow–Debreu (Debreu, 1959) variant which postulates total coverage of markets in time and space. Although this is the 'modern' conception of a total economy, glorified through several Nobel Prizes for their authors, its merits are of a predominantly scholastic nature. These types of model are irrelevant for a depiction of the workings of real economies in that they *postulate* the existence of markets which are just not there. This problem was stressed even by the namesake of this type of models, Kenneth Arrow. He dramatised this problem when, in a presidential address to the American Economic Association (AEA), Arrow (1974, pp. 5–6) considered this issue to be an 'obvious target' for fundamental criticism. Referring to market socialists' preoccupation with problems of allocative efficiency he declared on that occasion:

> Even as a graduate student . . . the nonexistence of markets for future goods under capitalism seemed to me a much more obvious target.
> However that may be, the nonexistence of these markets must be faced.

The relevance of such an observation for general equilibrium theorising is that it just does not address it – neither in its 'collapsing' nor in its 'expanding' variants. Or, as as Arrow (1974, p. 8) went on to point out:

Although we are not usually explicit about it, we really postulate that when a market could be created, it will be.

We thus have here a high authority, a 'high priest' of general equilibrium theory, who backs the claim that what goes on in conventional economics is to a considerable extent 'postulational' theorising.

It is clear that on this level of debate one can not fruitfully *argue* from equal to equal. One can make the counter-claim that the postulated markets just do not really exist and that consequently an important premiss of the conventional theory on which many of its conclusions depend just is not warranted. If this observation is rejected as being irrelevant, one could appeal to facts saying, e.g.: 'but look, there just *is* no futures market for shoelaces although there *will* be demand and supply for shoelaces in the future'. If the argumentative counterpart insists on the contrary assumption or on other hypothetical constructions like the existence of 'contingent markets', that really is the end of a common basis for looking at a real-life economy. It is a classic case of 'paradigm against paradigm'.

This was already the basic difference between the economic paradigms of Keynes and Pigou: should one start out from a *postulated* economic situation like, in the case of Pigou, a stationary state, and then to proceed to economic political analysis as minor deviation from that type of situation? Or should one, following Keynes, start from a snapshot of economic reality – in particular from really existing savings and net investment – and *then* to use more or less the same type of abstract economic analysis in order to derive arguments as to how to influence such an economic situation through economic political means? The Keynes-and-Pigou debate inspected here should have demonstrated extensively the analytical differences resulting from these different paradigms. The problem for economics as a science is that these paradigmatic differences have persisted for an overextended time as being of equal scientific status, albeit continuously contested within the discipline.

But let us come nearer to present debates and ask: what follows from the impasse just discussed with reference to Arrow's (1974, p. 8) observation about the postulational treatment of the existence of markets? In that type of argumentation economic research could try further to drive home the fact that many of the market situations postulated by general equilibrium theories are not there by giving 'good', i.e. choice theoretically based, economic reasons for their non-existence. If that reasoning is accepted as being up to the professional standards one could perhaps bring mainstream economics into the paradigmatic contradiction: on the one hand the non-existence of many futures markets is treated as irrelevant, on the other hand their non-existence is accepted as a relevant result of the method-ologically accepted body of economics. This tension could eventually bring new rounds of debates about a sensible paradigmatic set-up of the science. This is one perspective opened by Arrow's (1974, p. 8) subsequent program-matic proclamation:

Thus, the failure of markets for future goods must be regarded as an ana-lytical problem as well as a presupposition.

With the hindsight of more than twenty-five years having passed since this AEA presidential proclamation one may say: if there was indeed any hope for a fruitful debate about economic paradigms based on the contradictory treatment of the problematic existence of futures markets such a hope was not fulfilled by the past decades of 're-re-revolutions' in economics as dis-cussed in part I of this book.

26.3.3 The *ex post* view of market equilibria

The resigning remark just made refers only to the first part of Arrow's proclamation. The second part of the quote proposes a 'presupposition' and thereby an approach which might have a more positive perspective – in several senses. It suggests starting out from the positive acceptance – from the affirmation – of the non-existence of some markets otherwise treated as existent. This presupposition has two aspects: one is to show how individu-als deal with such non-existence of markets. This brings us back to Keynes (1937a) and his plea for analysing the allocative importance of liquidity preference. This was not a topic of paramount importance *in the present context* of the Keynes-and-Pigou debate because here the theme was set by Pigou's agenda of tackling the problem of unemployment from the 'real end'. Liquidity preference is on the agenda of *monetary* analysis. Although the two analyses must be interconnected as we saw above even in the dis-cussion of Pigou's 'simplified model', when it comes to dealing with their paradigmatic bases they must be treated as respective topics on their own.

But there is a second aspect to Arrow's 'presupposition'. It is to take the non-existence of many futures markets as a fact of life. Whether we can rationalise the non-existence of those futures markets which are postulated to exist in the said branches of general equilibrium analysis or not is imma-terial when it comes to dealing positively with an existing economy. When it does exist, an economy does have its determined realisations. All of them have their more or less specific market aspects. In any case, realised market outcomes have their accounting of realised prices, quantities and values which goes with them. There does not exist an unsolved *problem* of non-existence in an *ex post* view. One could, of course, dream – or scientifically muse – about questions like 'what would be different in outcomes if we had those ominous missing futures markets?' One could alternatively contemplate the question: 'what would be different in realised outcomes if the value of demand for certain goods were higher?' For a Keynesian it should be clear that the latter question is the more fertile one. But there need not be a problem as far as the basic analytical method is concerned. It could well be the established method of 'neoclassical economics' – but with a non-postulational orientation of dealing with positive situations and predictable and positive changes.

Here now the third variant of general equilibrium theory comes in. In its 'momentous' interpretation (see above, p. 106) it is liberated not to deal with non-existent markets in time and space. It just has an interpretational and *positive* role to play, i.e. to give choice theoretic underpinnings to what *is* there without being forced to claim the existence of that which is *not* there and without only dealing with explanations us to *why* that which does not exist does not exist.

Let us be quite clear that this does *not* mean the denial of general equilibrium analysis as an economic method. It just means that its starting point should be the realm of economic accounting and stock-taking of actual situations *inclusive* of the consistency constraints which the double-entry accounting places on the modelling of any economic system. This approach has far-reaching consequences for the conception of general equilibrium, because it acknowledges the factual non-existence of a multitude of conceivable markets. If there is no market for shoelaces ten years hence although it is well conceivable that shoelaces will be needed then, this is not necessarily a concern of the approach here proposed. In this sense the market system does 'break down' in Keynesian analysis but it is just the scholastic *postulated* market system of atemporal general equilibrium theory which is not dealt with. Otherwise, the 'momentous' *ex post* approach does not lead to a denial of optimising behaviour as basis for interpreting what is going on in an economy. It just stops us from making *counterfactual* assumptions about the existence of markets, without denying the existence of markets as such. It enables us to proceed from 'postulational economics' to a meaningful 'interpretational economics'.

26.3.4 Keynesian analysis as 'anticipated *ex post*' approach

These considerations might be helpful in finding a new answer to the question whether Keynes' 'double *ex post* analysis' was really so 'retrograde' as it appeared to be above (see p. 398). In this context one should stress that 'regression' is, in a sense, a *relative* concept. Shackle (1958) saw Keynes' multiplier analysis in relation to that of Richard Kahn (1931). But we know from Joan Robinson (1973e, pp. 252f.) that at that time Kahn 'reinvented Marx's schema for Simple Reproduction in an endeavour to explain what Keynes was doing' (see above, p. 248). We know now from Joan Robinson's own later assessments, from hindsight and from our own considerations that that approach was not really so fertile as it seemed to some Keynesians at first. One problem of such an approach is that it plants dynamics on a 'frozen land' – as Keynes wanted to express the matter (see above p. 170) – since the analytical starting point of that approach is quite akin to Pigou's stationary state. In the context of a new evaluation of that debate Keynes' 'anticipated *ex post*' approach seems nowadays maybe not so retrograde any more.

But in this section we proposed to evaluate Keynes' approach also and especially in relation to 'modern' general equilibrium analysis and in that context it does seem to have a number of advantages.

First of all, the approach here proposed enables Keynes-oriented economists to reclaim the heritage of established methods of economic analysis. The old neoclassical approach cannot monopolise economic thinking any more with postulated scholastic problems and their unhelpful solutions. Economics is brought back from the Pigovian 'frozen land remote in its characteristics from all experience' to the green – but sometimes languishing – pastures of economic reality but without being lost in intractable speculations about dynamical lags and leads.

Secondly, if we start out from an *ex post* approach, one of the analytical tasks for economists is to ask: how could that realisation be changed through economic policy in favour of a more preferred outcome? The aim of such a question is to find measures which, when applied today, will have future *ex post* outcomes which are in some sense better than the *ex post* outcomes without the economists' proposals. Thus the method of this type of economic thinking – which we claim to be the Keynesian one emerging from the above considerations – is to anticipate a future *ex post* situation and to evaluate and shape it under an economic political perspective. The viewpoint of 'momentous' general equilibrium is not in the least a hindrance for such a perspective. Quite the contrary. Economic policy could well justify its action exactly when it can show that it can do away with unwanted economic constraints in such a way that future 'momentous' *ex post* results are preferred to the past *ex post* results. General equilibrium analysis could play an important role in that type of argumentation as our interpretation of the Keynes-and-Pigou debate should have shown.

Thirdly, it should be stressed that viewing Keynes' theory essentially as an 'anticipated *ex post*' approach has important consequences for the placing of Keynes' theory in the context of economic dynamics. There has been much – and inconsequential – musing going on about Keynes' production period, about *ex ante* analysis in relation to Keynes' effective demand analysis etc. But all the sequential dynamical models face the problem that in a macroeconomic model there is the double-entry accounting constraint which must be met at any moment of economic realisation. From the standpoint of economic policy, there is not much point in modelling outcome-inconsistent *ex ante* plans unless one has also the model for the incidence of the frustrations in the case of inconsistencies and about the economic behaviour following out of these frustrations. There can be interesting models about the economic revision behaviour in the case of inconsistencies but that still is not the entire economic story needed in this context because we must also know everything about the incidence of the frustration of plans – and of windfalls – if we want to base our modelling on such behaviour in an *ex post* consistent way.

There are a number of statements in which Keynes expressly disassociates himself from *ex ante* analysis. We interpret his position as amounting to the proposal that divergent *ex ante* views are realisation-inconsistent. Since, however, we do have economic realisations going on at any moment of time, we must also embroider a frustrations oriented theory with a revision-economics theory for any moment of time. This might be feasible but so complex that such a theory would be of little help for practical use. One should apply Occam's Razor if a simpler theory were available. Such a simpler theory is indeed available if, following Keynes' above quoted passages about the 'logical multiplier', we conceive economic policy oriented macroeconomics as being based on 'anticipated *ex post* analysis'.

26.4 Rationalised expectations and Keynesian economics

26.4.1 *Ex post* and *ex ante* as expectational scenarios

The difference between momentous *ex post* analysis and dynamical *ex ante* analysis is most pronounced with regard to the treatment of expectations. Whereas the essence of the former approach is consistent accounting, the essence of dynamical *ex ante* analysis is the divergence of expectations and the adjustments necessitated by such divergence.

As a body of consistent accounting, *ex post* analysis has, strictly speaking, nothing to do with expectations. But if we want to treat the time period accounted for as a manifestation of a momentous general equilibrium, then this implies also a statement about plans. If plans must be computationally consistent, because that is the accounting framework in which they are considered, then they must also be choice theoretically consistent. This consistency requires consistent expectations concerning certain strategic variables. In our simple Walrasian model of the equations (26.1) to (26.3) this strategic variable was the profit Π (see above p. 392).

It should be noted that the 'momentous general equilibrium' modelling does not preclude the existence of 'involuntary unemployment' in the strict sense as was seen in the beginning of this chapter. Although it is a consistent and 'general' equilibrium model with regard to expectations of profits generated in production on the one hand and as profits accruing as household incomes in the period under consideration on the other hand, it is an equilibrium *under given constraints* – of technologies, preferences and, of course, of intertemporal demand as manifested by savings and investment decisions. That was the reason why this type of unemployment situations may be characterised as *quasi* equilibria, because the consistency requirement of Walras' Law being fulfilled, the model does not preclude the 'dis' equilibrium of involuntary unemployment in the strict sense, as was discussed at length above.

When we turn our analytical focus away from *ex post* analysis and its interpretation and contemplate *ex ante* analysis instead, then the expectational set-up becomes freer but also more intractable. As already stated, *ex ante* dynamical analysis is in essence one which faces *divergent* expectations. If we now take again the example of profits expectations, it might be indeed imaginable that firms and households have divergent plans based on divergent expectations. But when it comes to having to deal with predictions of a realised economic system, only *one* value can go to the accounts as being realised. Which value and whose expectation will be the one which the economic adviser can report to the economic politician as being the most likely to be realised? If the value in question is indeed 'known' in the sense of being theoretically clear and predictable, why does the *ex ante* analysis not state that result right away? The answer might be that that is the task of the model's dynamics and the dynamical processes to first make their rounds. One would give away the essence of the dynamical approach if one stated the result before the dynamics of the model had its sway. But if the dynamics were open to unclear results, what relevance does this type of theory have for economic policy-making for a specific time period? If, however, the dynamical results are quite clear, what then would be wrong with representing them by a comparative static *ex post* analysis? That is, as expectations might be treated as having their 'certainty equivalents', so dynamics might be treated as having its comparative-statics equivalent for a specified point in the future.

Economic politically relevant predictions must show up in the national accounts. The essence of economic policy is predominantly to change these accounts. But national accounting then puts the same constraints on the *prospective* view of well-argued economic political advice as it does on a purely computational variant of *ex post* analysis. Thus there is an anti-symmetry in this type of discourse: if we want to interpret the past economic accounts in the framework of economic equilibria, then, contemplating policy measures in order to change these equilibria for a future time period, the outcome of such future-oriented thought experiment must equally meet the accounting constraints as does the look into the past.

It seems to have been this type of consideration which convinced Keynes to abandon the *ex ante* approach – after having previously given it much thought in his groping towards the arguments as later presented in the *General Theory*.[15] In his 1937 lectures notes Keynes (JMK, XIV, pp. 179–183) describes this transition and explains his eventual position (p. 183):

I'm more classical than the Swedes [who insisted on the distinction between *ex post* and *ex ante*, GMA], for I am still discussing the conditions of short-period equilibrium. Let us suppose identity of *ex post* and *ex ante*, my theory remains . . .
The method of trial and error is always bringing *ex post* and *ex ante* together. Let us begin by assuming *ex post* and *ex ante* coincide.

But if they do coincide, there are correct predictions and in that sense there are economy consistent predictions.
It is because of Keynes' refusal – in the context of his *General Theory* – to give much importance to the divergence between *ex post* realisations and *ex ante* expectations that we just propagated above the characterisation of his approach as being one of an 'anticipated *ex post* analysis'.

26.4.2 Claims and scope of the rational expectations doctrine

The contemplations of the last section are reminiscent of some problems which are also addressed by the 'rational expectations' approach to macroeconomic modelling. Although it is not our task and intention here to discuss extensively developments in macroeconomics which have no direct bearing on the Keynes-and-Pigou debate here under scrutiny, a few remarks about this topic do seem in order since that might help to put the Keynesian argumentation into a better perspective.

It is now commonplace that prominent propagators of that approach argue for economic political abstinence, in particular on the monetary side, because unanticipated active policy causes frustrated plans and thereby raises the level of variance of economic variables.[16] The basis for this approach is the assumption of *model* consistent expectations. Again, as in the case of neoclassical general equilibrium theory discussed before, there is – from the Keynesian standpoint – a quite reasonable basis for this type of theory building and a quite unreasonable one.

If it is true that the eventual method of the *General Theory* came to Keynes after intensive consideration of *ex ante* analysis, it is perhaps noteworthy that this analysis is also present in the first statements of 'rational expectations' theories. In his seminal presentation of this concept, Muth (1961, p. 315) started expressly from considerations concerning *ex ante* analysis. Some aspects of his comments are similar to the ones which – we claimed – might have led Keynes to abandon this approach after having had much interest in it. The relevant passage reads:

The 'ex ante' analysis of the Stockholm School . . . has undoubtedly been a major motivation for studies of business expectations and intention data.

As a systematic theory of fluctuations in markets or in the economy, the approach is limited, however, because it does not include an explanation of the way expectations are formed.

Muth (1961, p. 316) then proceeds to propose 'rational' expectations as those which are 'essentially the same as the relevant economic theory', adding, however, that this does not claim that 'the scratch work of entrepreneurs' has much to do with the proposed model equations. Although rational expectations theory has developed considerably beyond these beginnings, we may stop here to consider the basic problem and paradigm of this approach.

The basic problem is similar to the one just discussed in the previous subsection: economic predictions deal with future realisations and those have to be economy-consistent. To take an illustrative example: it might be that in an economy ten people believe themselves able to crack the jackpot of the national lottery. Each expects additional income of one million. Expected demand from these individuals might be thought to be calculable on the basis of additional ten millions. Since, however, the lottery just redistributes the contributions, there is no additional income. With constant propensities to consume out of given income, the additional expected demand in the economy should be calculated on the expected value of an addition of zero out of these gamblers' dreams. Thus, in order to make reasonable predictions, one has to *abandon* a realistic modelling of individual expectations.

Insofar as this example goes, it is quite reasonable to stress consistency as external constraint on prediction making. The question is, however, how far this constraint should go in substance and in time. Should it embrace specific and contestable economic hypotheses – such as the quantity theory of inflation – or should it be limited to pure accountancy requirements as previously described? The present answer is that only the latter requirement is warranted – and that is the case insofar as the aim of the theory is an anticipated *ex post* account. But as far as *theory consistency* is concerned which has no formal justification in accounting requirements, there is no justification for attributing a specific contestable theory, say, of inflation, to the aggregate of the decision-makers of the economy. Thus, although one may easily subscribe to *economy-constrained expectations*, there is little reason to accept *model-constrained expectations* in a sense which goes beyond computational consistency.

A particularly problematic aspect of model endogenous expectations relates to the scope in time of such expectations. Since realisations today depend on expectations of tomorrow, the attempt to offer an explanation of the working of the economy on the basis of predicted expectations means that one must have endogenous expectations in view of 'tomorrow's' realisations. But these in turn depend on expectations of the then relevant future. Thus the theorising about expectations is driven from one future period to the next and there is no reasonable breaking-off point for such extensions which keeps them from going into ever more distant future time periods. Thus, the task of predicting economic events in a specific time period – say, next year – becomes an act of embracing eternity. This certainly is not a reasonable programme for practical economic policy advice.

26.4.3 'Rationalised expectations' and the Keynesian approach

There is a long tradition of viewing the Keynesian approach as being at variance with the rational expectations one. Sheffrin (1983, p. 67) quotes passages from Tobin (1977, p. 461) in which he describes the rational expectations models as ones where, among other characteristics like full usage of available information, 'excess supplies and demands are eliminated'. That means that in those models involuntary unemployment in the strict sense of an excess supply of labour is eliminated. Although that characterisation may be true for the models which Tobin wanted to describe, we should be clear that market clearing is by no means a corollary to accountancy consistent modelling. Walras' Law *is* an accountancy consistent modelling device but it does not preclude excess demands and supplies as was seen above.

Tobin (*ibid.*) stressed that the models he described are such as if Keynes had not written and Sheffrin (1983, p. 67) comments:

> Rather than denying this, some rational expectation theorists, for example Robert Lucas and Thomas Sargent, call themselves modern classical economists.

We mentioned this controversy in part I above and we saw there that its consequences for modern macroeconomic theorising are by no means clear one way or the other. Here we may now stop briefly in order to reflect on its significance in the light of what has been said about the outcome of the authentic Keynes–Classics debate.

In this type of discussion, one should discern between the doctrine of model consistent expectations on the one hand and the particular model used for that type of approach on the other. Thus, the idea of model consistent theorising could apply for Keynesian models of cost-induced price level changes as well as for monetarist theories of money supply-induced price hikes. In general, many of the 'classical' elements in the rational expectations approaches are to a large extent additions in model building which are not necessitated by requirements of consistent modelling. A case in point was discussed above with reference to Barro's (1990) assumption of 'zero wealth effects' on savings. This does *not* follow out of intertemporal choice itself but out of implicitly assuming a stationary state, as we saw there.

A further tendency towards classical paradigms is opened by the infinite progress of expectations into the future due to interdependence of outcomes as just outlined. This again leads to collapsing the entire timespan from the present until eternity into one single act of modelling. This leads in essence to an atemporal conception of the economy as already criticised in the context of discussing the variants of general equilibrium modelling.

In the context of general equilibrium theories it was said above that they may have a sensible function in interpreting past and future realisations if the appropriate constraints are respected. Similarly, one may say after the above considerations that there are also some aspects of 'rational expectations' theories which can have a useful place in Keynesian methodology.

It might be helpful in this context to discern between 'rational expectations' in the very wide sense known from the traditional literature and described in the sub-section above on the one hand, and a more restricted sense on the other hand, in which the term 'rational' just refers to consistent accounting. As stressed above, the rules of accounting *must* be met for falsifiable macroeconomic predictions because accounting is the way of checking macroeconomic results. If we want to discuss economic plans in such a context, they also must be required to meet the needs for consistent accounting. Thus, falsifiable predictions in macroeconomics do necessarily contain an element of *imposed* computational rationality. One might therefore speak of '*rationalised* expectations' in this comparatively narrow sense of meeting the constraints imposed by consistent accounting.

It is clear that Keynesian economics as 'anticipated *ex post* analysis' must supply accountancy consistent prediction and thus far it clearly contains an element of 'rationalisation'. In this sense rational expectations are indeed not totally anathema for Keynes' economics. But the rationalisation is limited in scope. It is also limited in time since the Keynesian predictions are short-period ones. In the end, we can agree with the answer which Axel Leijonhufvud (1983, pp. 220–1) gave to the question whether Keynes would have accepted rational expectations:

> [Leijonhufvud] tended to think that Keynes would have had no big objection to making short-run nominal expectations endogenous but he would have objected to the very attempt to make long-run real expectations about real profits endogenous.

But the similarity between this passage and our conclusion is somewhat superficial. Our position is: Keynes would by no means have accepted rational expectations in the sense of a postulated compliance of the beliefs of an entire economy with the beliefs of the builder of an economic model no matter whether the modelled timespan lasted until eternity or just for a limited time in the case of Leijonhufvud. Instead, Keynes did accept a rationalisation of predictions in order to make them internally consistent so that they can meet the requirements of consistent accounting. We infer this from the fact that he wanted to have economic politically relevant model predictions and *any* macroeconomic theory, be it now Keynesian or not, must meet this minimal requirement of rationality.

26.5 The *General Theory* revisited – a tripartite view

It might be helpful to have a synopsis in which we have a combined view of the different aspects of the paradigms proposed. Figure 26.2 uses three

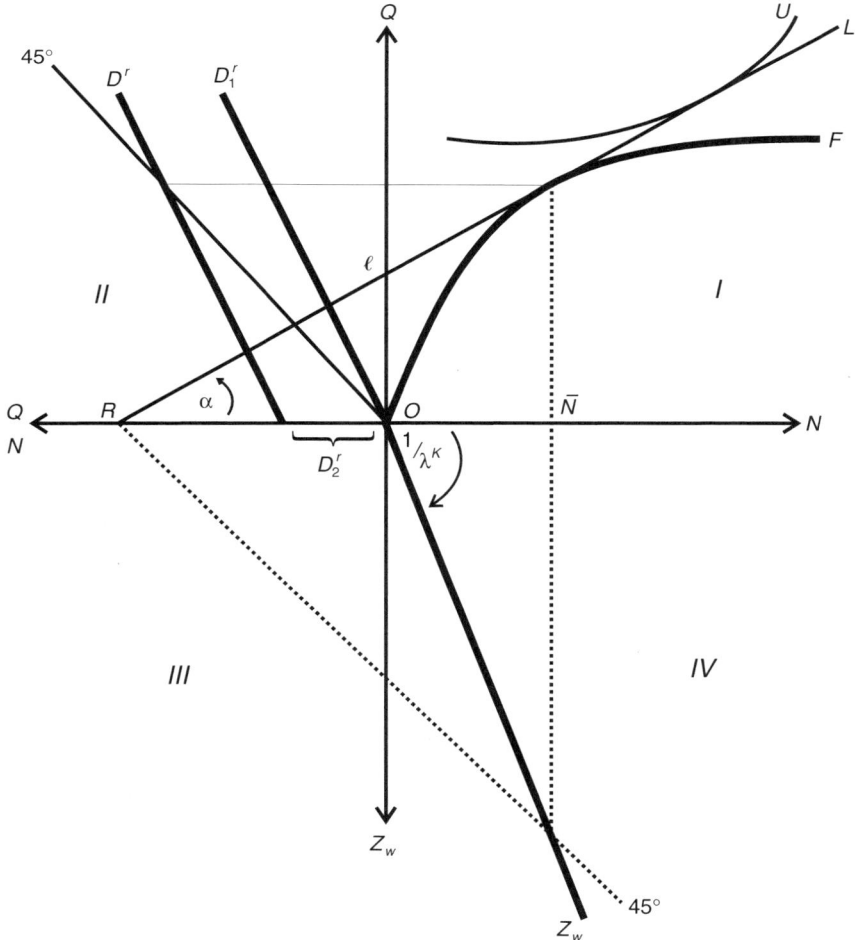

Figure 26.2 Keynes' economics: a tripartite view

quadrants in order to show: (i) the 'basic' (neoclassical) approach to Keynes (quadrant *I*) in terms of the Koopmans diagram of general equilibrium; (ii) a 'metaphorical' approach to Keynes (quadrant *II*) in terms of quantitative 'real' output in terms of products; and (iii) the 'authentic' approach to the *General Theory* in terms of wage units (quadrant *IV*) with the just discussed merits of this approach. All these elements have been discussed before. They are combined here for easy reference and synoptical discussion.

Quadrant *I* restates the Clower diagram already mentioned. It is a variant of the Koopmans diagram of general equilibrium (see fig. 10.4, p. 102). The price line *ℓL* – or, to stay in Koopmans' parlance referred to on the occasion of discussing that figure, the dividing hyperplane between the production set and a preference ordered set – is in this specific case such that more people want to work (see the tangent point on the indifference curve *U*) than can be employed under perfect competition (see the tangent point on the boundary of the production set *OF*). What keeps the economy in this state of affairs so that such a picture can be taken as representing an essential economic problem? Is it that the real wage tan ∠α is 'too high'? In an abstract sense it is indeed too high, because it goes with an excess supply of labour. But what is the reason for such a situation? It is *not* relative price and quantity dynamics, and it is not (relative) price, nominal wage or real wage rigidity 'as such' which causes the situation to be as it is shown here. Such 'dynamical' explanations of unemployment were suggested by Clower (1965), Leijonhufvud (1968) and others who for some time believed that Keynes changed the ranking of adjustment speeds of prices and quantities in relation to the 'Classics'. These explanations for Keynesian unemployment were subsequently rejected by most of the original proponents of such dynamical interpretations of the *General Theory*. The 'appropriate' view of Keynesian unemployment is still controversial.[17]

The outcome of the present discussion is that, in accordance with many other interpretations of the specificity of the *General Theory*, the reason for involuntary unemployment in the strict sense must be seen in deficient 'effective demand'. Our specific variant of this view is represented *metaphorically* in quadrant *II*. We insist on this expression because quadrant *II* is based on the single-sector argumentation of quadrant *I* and such argumentation was shunned by Pigou. This disassociation from single-sector argumentation was inherited by Keynes in adopting the Pigovian model as his economic theoretical vantage point. But if there are at least two products contained in net output, one has the much discussed index problems for the aggregate value of output. In quadrant *II* such problems are *assumed* away by postulating that real output is equal to *Q* – no further discussion being permitted about this point. For the sake of simplified argumentation, we accept this position in the framework of quadrant *II*. The 45° line in this quadrant represents Keynes' expressly stated belief that net income is identical with net production. Net income in real terms is divided between D^r_1-

consumption (in real terms) and savings, which, because of the $I \equiv S$-condition, are identical with (real) investment demand D^r_2. Together D^r_1 and D^r_2 define total effective demand D^r and thus total income. Because of the income–output identity they define output and employment as depicted in the basic model of quadrant I.

Quadrant II depicts all the basic elements of income-expenditure Keynesianism: the 45° line, the consumption function resp. the corresponding $\overline{OD^r_1}$-curve, investment (D_2r) and the multiplier for the case of a change in D_2r. But in spite of this stoutly Keynesian orientation, the 'quadrant-II analysis' may well be related to the long-established neoclassical theories of production and of consumption and to Walras' Law as we argued above in discussing fig. 26.1 (p. 385). Here we remind the readers of those interconnections by now just referring them back to quadrant I where we have neoclassically determined supply and demand for labour and products. But it must be stressed that figure 26.2 contains *both* the neoclassical and the Keynesian argumentation in one interlinked framework.

It might appear as paradoxical that because of this very *combination*, the Keynesian theory of income and output determination is *not* identical with neoclassical relative price theory – and neoclassical analysis is not the same as without this combination. The reason for this statement is that the paradigm of quadrant II has an additional co-ordination mechanism going beyond conventional neoclassicism in that not only relative price in the sense of tan α must be 'right' for full employment. In addition $Q = D^r_1 + D^r_2$ must hold in a non-trivial way for the full employment level. A trivial way would be given by $D^r = D^r_1 + D^r_2$ being postulated as describing a 45° line as well. But then Say's Law in the sense of Keynes would hold. At this point we are now confronted with the accusation that Keynes was bordering on the 'fraudulent' in this particular respect (see above, p. 389).

This is not the place to delve into Say's writings in detail. It may be readily conceded that it would be a blatant lie to claim that Say actually had ever drawn such a 45° line as we did here in the name of Keynes. But this is not the essential analytic point. The point is rather that anybody who, in the context of a frictionless neoclassical model, said that the only problem for full employment is that the relative price system is 'wrong' and that market forces must be freed again in order to generate full employment, such an author implicitly assumes the Say's Law-condition $Q \equiv D^r$ for any relevant level of relative prices. It is not deriding such a theorist when attributing Say's Law in this sense to him. It just means that one counts on such a person to be aware that any 'pure' relative price theory requires Say's Law so that aggregate demand and supply problems do not interfere with the working of the relative price determination mechanisms. Quite the contrary of being derogatory, inferring such an implicit statement is tantamount to attributing to that person so much analytical good sense as to know on which *implicit* arguments the pure relative price theory hinges.

We come now to quadrant *IV*. The Z_w-curve there measures the value of aggregate supply on the vertical axis and employment on the horizontal axis. Output valuation is based on Keynes' wage units. Thus no aggregation problem is involved as far as dimensionality of input and output variables is concerned. Therefore the analytical situation in quadrant *IV* is quite different from that of quadrant *I* where the inputs (labour services per period) were of quite a different dimensionality than the outputs e.g. tons of corn per period).

The situation in quadrant *IV* is also analytically different from the one in quadrant *II* where we had the index problem of aggregating factually heterogeneous outputs to *one* macroeconomic magnitude. The problem is that measuring in terms of goods always means that as soon as more than one sector exists, sectoral results and their prices in one sector have to be related to another sectoral result and its price in order to achieve the total valuation of 'real' aggregate output. The problem was 'solved' in quadrant *II* by negating the existence of more than one sector. Such an unrealistic assumption is not necessary in connection with Keynes' wage units analysis. Since labour services are not the output of a particular sector, they do not pose that type of problem when used as a standard of value.

In quadrant *IV* employment is identical to wage income in wage units. The associated residual income is $\overline{O\ell}$— in the basic neoclassical model. Its projection on the employment axis gives $\overline{OR}$, residual income in wage units. Total income is $\overline{RN}$. Since the value of total income is identical to the value of total production, as already pointed out above, therefore there must again be a 45° line relating total income to total output. Since this equality holds good for total income and output, it also must hold good at the margin of the last unit produced by labour. It is in *this* sense that Keynes (GT, p. 55, n. 2) writes:

since the proceeds of the marginal product is equal to the marginal factor-cost at every point on the aggregate supply curve, we have

$$\Delta N = \ldots = \Delta Z_w = \Delta \phi(N),$$

that is to say $\phi'(N) = 1$

(my ellipsis in the equation, GMA). This means that the Z_w-curve is a *locus* of points for which Keynes' condition $\Delta N = \Delta Z_w$ holds in any point of the Z_w-curve as the reader may easily check by reconstructing that curve himself along the line just discussed: the Z_w-curve is that curve which is generated by combining alternative levels of employment N with the level of total income in terms of wage units. This is done geometrically via a 45° line by projecting alternative levels of total income in wage units (here $\overline{RN}$) onto the perpendicular in the respective point N. The alternative intersection points thus derived with the help of the 45° lines describe the Z_w-curve.

This does not mean that because any point *on* the OZ_w-locus has that 45° characteristic, that the curve thereby described has the same characteristic as the individual points. If that curve relates N and $Z_w \equiv (\Sigma p_i Q_i)/w$, to take a simple case where there is a unique wage rate, then obviously the average along this curve measures $(\Sigma p_i Q_i)/wN \equiv 1/\lambda^K$, where λ^K is the share of wages in this Keynesian context.

If sufficient simplifying assumptions are made, it may be assumed that the share of wages is constant – a statement which seemed to go well with empirical results frequently referred to at that time. The consequence of this statement is that the OZ_w-locus 'is linear with a slope given by the reciprocal of the money [*sic*]-wage', as Keynes wrote at the end of the footnote already quoted from (GT, p. 56), thereby creating much confusion, as Victoria Chick (1983, p. 80, n. 9) observed. Did he switch from the 'real' aggregate supply Z_w of the quote just given to nominal aggregate supply Z in the middle of his footnote? An alternative interpretation is that Keynes, in the last quote, meant 'wages' in the Ricardian sense of 'labour's share'. If that was meant, then its inverse can indeed be taken as giving the slope of a simple aggregate supply curve, as quadrant *IV* of fig. 26.2 shows. In any case: there is clearly the difference between the characteristics of each point on the OZ_w-locus on the one hand and the characteristics of that *locus* itself on the other, as the figure shows.

In the context of this quadrant, employment is again determined through effective demand, as already discussed graphically in connection with the metaphorical model of quadrant *II*. Since we already went through a simple model of employment determination using employment and values in wage units when discussing fig. 25.1, p. 355, we do not go through the analogous motions in this context again.

As already mentioned, the main difference of quadrant *IV* to the presentation given in quadrant *II* is that here we have two axes with the same dimensionality, namely employment and value in wage units. It is true that homogeneous employment is a construction and an abstraction from considerable differences which in fact do exist with regard to alternative labour services. But the abstraction employed in this context is less adventurous than the one employed when goods like the notorious 'guns' and 'butter' are aggregated to a homogeneous single good as is necessary in the context of the single-good argumentation. Therefore aggregation and functional relations do not meet the same conceptual problems here as in the 'metaphorical' one-good argumentation just discussed.

This figure illustrates some of the important 'neoclassical' real analytic aspects of the *General Theory* which were discussed here extensively under the perspective of their Pigovian connections. We think that it is important to see Keynesian and (neo)classical analysis in some such *connection* as was offered by these three quadrants. The present synthesis of Walras' Law (quadrant *I*) on the one hand with effective demand analysis in an income-expenditure context (quadrant *II*) on the other hand with its implicit depiction (and negation) of Say's Law as a 45° line, seems to follow quite naturally out of the present discussion. But only the further synthesis of Walras' Law and the negated Say's Law as already mentioned with Keynes' wage unit analysis (quadrant *IV*) gives a sufficiently rich and complex representation of Keynes analytical intentions in the realm of 'real' analysis.

We may paraphrase our analytical tour as being one involving the transition from the confirmed Walras' Law via the negation of Say's Law to an affirmation of Keynes' Units. In a certain sense this transition is not a *tour de force* at all, as we hope to have shown with this graphical device. But it involves a strange semantic ambiguity: in the context of the picture of Walras' Law in quadrant *I* 'value' means relative price as depicted by tan α. A fully developed theory of value in this context means an enquiry into the existence of a *vector of relative prices* satisfying Walras' Law in a more or less general sense.[18] When it comes to Keynes' Units, 'value' takes on quite a different meaning and involves the values of national income, aggregate consumption demand etc. in wage units. The 'values' in question are, of course, not vectors but scalars. Similar to the 'Walrasian values' in the sense of relative prices, the 'Keynesian values' in wage units also involve a normalisation, i.e. a normalisation with a price resp. with a wage rate. But there the similarity ends.

Maybe this semantic difference – more odd than essential at first sight – has more to it than meets the scientific eye. Unreflected in academic discourse, it could be an unconscious source of a sense of antagonism between Keynesians and Classics. That the concept of 'value' stands for a vector in the context of the Classics but a scalar in the context of the Keynesians might give an analytic uneasiness between the two camps amounting to a permanent challenge. It might be the feeling in each camp that the divergent semantics of the other puts into question their own analytic justification. Once this difference is clearly articulated, a synoptical discussion of the issues involved as it is attempted here might contribute to a more fruitful debate in economics than the one which was to be witnessed in many decades after the publication of the *General Theory*.

27
Perspectives from the *General Theory*: Liquidity and Philosophy

27.1 The Keynes–Classics debate and paradigmatic perspectives

In setting out the arguments of this book, occasionally we had to go into considerable expository and algebraic detail. Our basic intention was a more general one, however, namely to trace differences in paradigms. In the forefront were differences between Keynes and Pigou. It was our aim not just to postulate such differences but to develop them in the context of a common analytical basis. We hope to have given due consideration to both, contest as well as communion. Keynes, at least, was seen to be able and willing to see the time-preference analytic points which Pigou wanted to make in the context of his 'frozen land' paradigm whereas others could not sustain such an extension of the analytical perspective.

Paradigms are like genes – full of promises of the most amazing forms of (intellectual) life. But they are not that life themselves and what becomes of them is open to some caprices of fate. On the one hand, fostered in the laboratories of narrow ideologies, paradigms can develop to mindless monstrosities. On the other hand, deprived of means of survival, paradigms can wither away, at best waiting for their time to come. Life is strife – this maxim holds also for the intellectual life of economic paradigms. But strife is not just antagonism; it is also support and communication and fortification. No economist was more aware of these aspects of novel, potentially paradigmatic, ideas than Keynes. For the further development of his novel ideas he called for the collaboration of minds. In particular he called for a continued academic interchange with A. C. Pigou and expressly asked Richard Kahn and his circle to carry on that debate once Keynes himself got it going after the publication of the *General Theory*. None of the those thus addressed did in fact respond to Keynes' invitation.

Keynes' own strife with Pigou was a dialogue-oriented and communicative one – not only in the sense of polemics but also and predominantly so in the sense of substantive debate. We traced this out in several fields: in debating the (common!) choice theoretic basis for the concept of involuntary unemployment, in pointing out Keynes' acceptance of Pigovian time preference analysis in the context of Pigou's frozen land economics, in literally recounting Keynes' account of the details of Pigou's model building, to name but a few of our attempts at showing the substantive interconnection between Keynes and Pigou. It is a sad commentary on his adversary that over and over 'The Professor' claimed that from a scientific point of reading he could not understand the writings of Keynes, the 'valued contributor to the *Daily Mail*'.[1] It is perhaps sadder that such slanderous asides were echoed by Joan Robinson claiming that Keynes never understood the theory of value.[2] But surely the saddest episode in this account was when Keynes was implicitly denied custody for his own brainchild with the claim that he was responsible for 'bastard Keynesian theory in its purest form'.[3] One could perhaps see all of this from a more comical rather than regretting side. But in any case such recollections witness a lamentable lack of perception for Keynes' own paradigmatic proposals.

What is the point of rehashing this mixture of misunderstanding, misrepresentations and belittlement? One desirable outcome is a release of intellectual energies. Human curiosity is such that it does want to know causation, history and intellectual interrelation in the development of economics. Whole libraries about the Keynes–Classics debate bear witness for this claim.[4] As long as there is no satisfactory and intellectually unbiased account of the development of modern macroeconomics, the puzzles of the Keynes–Classics debate will haunt the profession and sap intellectual energy from more future-oriented activities. But it is not only brooding over the past that saps those energies. The repetitive 're-re-revolutions' of the last decades do likewise. Too often they come up with claims for revolutionary novelties which really are no such thing. The awareness of past achievements could save the profession much commotion which sooner or later will appear as repetitive. If there can be a settlement of the paradigmatic disputes festering since the inception of the Keynes–Classics debate, economic science would gain in respectability and societal impact.

In the context of our paradigmatic considerations we have supplied new expositions for a number of different variants of macroeconomics, be it now the 'tripartite view' of the *General Theory*, the model of Pigou's *Theory of Unemployment*, the representation of his 'simplified model' of the Keynes–Classics debate, a new rendering of Kaldor's synthesis of Keynes and Pigou, and also a new representation of Joan Robinson's 'Keynesian extension'. These were expository devices developed in the attempt to bring together groups of models which did play an important role in the past debates. In so doing we hope to have shown the framework for an analytical *modus vivendi* for rather diverse variants of macroeconomics. Hopefully we have thereby substantiated our claim that it is a worthwhile aim to find an integrative settlement of past Keynes–Classics debates.

What is to be done with the new energies hopefully set free for further research on the basis of Keynesian paradigms? One topic high on any agenda following from a thorough reconsideration of Keynesian economics is monetary theory and the attempt to give it back the fascination it had for Keynes himself and for some of his appreciative readers. A further point which might be of future interest in a Keynesian context is a new perspective on the philosophical orientation which goes together with the *General Theory*. We will deal with these two topics in the following closing sections. They point well beyond the scope of the main orientation of the present enquiry. But they may convey the breadth of vision and analysis offered by a new consideration of one of the now most commented-upon books in economics.

27.2 Liquidity preference in an epochal context

It is well known that Keynes originally intended to write the sequel to his *Treatise on Money* (1930) not as a paraphrase of Pigou's *Theory of Unemployment*, but as a *Monetary Theory of Production*. This was the title of his early drafts for the planned new book. Monetary theory and politics was Keynes' lifelong speciality ever since he won acclaim for his treatment of *Indian Currency and Finance*.[5] The monetary sphere was the one from which the apocalypse of the Great Depression had befallen the world since 1929/30. How much more topical must it have appeared at such a time to write about 'Interest and Money' rather than about Pigou's intractable '$\chi(x)$'-function and Keynes' equally intractable '$\varphi(x)$'-completion of the Pigovian model. We saw above that even decades after the publication of the *General Theory* commentators regretted that Keynes let himself be drawn out to such seemingly disproportionate preoccupation with Pigou (1933). And did his basically monetary orientation not linger on in the title of his *magnum opus*? It is true that Keynes (1937a), in his reply to his critics, did refer to it as the *General Theory of Employment* thus juxtaposing his work to Pigou's allegedly *[Special] Theory of [Un]employment*. But in substance Keynes had long surpassed his *agent provocateur* to whose personally demeaning and scientifically posturing comments on other economists Keynes had good reason to react. Keynes *had* to meet Pigou (1933) and he had to meet him from the 'real end'. But once this issue was settled, his urge was to return to the basic monetary issues involved.

Thus, in spite of its title, in *substance*, Keynes' (1937a) rejoinder was about liquidity preference, as were a number of other pieces written as a sequel to his *General Theory*. Actually, Keynes' (1936) full title could well have been abbreviated to *General Theory of . . . Interest and Money*. It is therefore small wonder that some of his readers saw the topical centre of Keynes' new book in its chapter 17 on 'The Essential Properties of Interest and Money'. One of them – Hugh Townshend, a most remarkable[6] but little-known follower of Keynes' – saw in *this* chapter 'the most general theory' as he put it in private correspondence with Keynes (JMK, XXIX, p. 258):

parts of the *General Theory* should be read as indicating stages of your thought in which you are approaching the most general theory of Chapter 17.

In his view, the strategic breach between Keynes and the Classics is the 'classical idea of determinacy (at the margin of production)', referring with this remark to the 'theory of value of durable physical assets' (*ibid. passim*). Townshend (1937, p. 160) elaborates this idea to some extent. His starting point is the observation that

as usually stated, the marginal theory of value does not seem to distinguish clearly between exchange of existing assets (at the margin of exchange) and production of new assets (at the margin of production).

Since the former depend on asset dispositions in general and these in turn on liquidity preference and expectations, there is therefore no basis for objective determinacy. Apart from the more philosophical implications of such observations which call into question any conception of determinate price systems, there is the more practical question of determining the level of investment in such a world. It would lead too far to elaborate this point here but Paul Davidson's (1994, p. 69) case of low-price 'contango' with zero investment is a relevant reference in this connection.

Few later authors seem to have followed Townshend in *his* generalisation of the *General Theory*. Joan Robinson (1961, p. 138) commented on the same 'Chapter 17':

When Keynes was writing that chapter, he admitted that he was groping for ideas that were new to him, and I do not think that he ever quite succeeded in seizing them.

This is quite a remarkable comment for a scholar who herself had the ambition to 'generalise' the *General Theory*. Was this then not an important field for further research if the master could not complete an important task? The implicit answer seems to have been that this field was not so interesting as Keynes wanted to make it appear.

Kaldor's (1960b) ambitions to elucidate Keynes' 'Chapter 17' ended also with sceptical comments about the correctness of Keynes' views on liquidity. Kaldor (1960b, p. 73) criticised Keynes because he attributed to land in former times a similar position with regard to liquidity preference as the one which gold and money held or holds in modern times.[7] Kaldor (1960b, p. 73) was aware that he parallelled Abba P. Lerner's (1952) earlier treatment of Keynes' 'chapter 17' in some respects. Lerner (1952, p. 376) considered Keynes' passages about the liquidity preference for land as being 'perhaps the most challenging and memorable part of the chapter'. But he then claims (*ibid.* p. 377) that Keynes' 'intriguing speculation . . . fall[s] to the ground' for reasons similar to Kaldor's just mentioned ones.

Although the tenor of Kaldor's assessment of 'Chapter 17' was similarly sceptical to the one just quoted from Joan Robinson, she reacted to his specific criticism concerning the liquidity preference for land with the counter-argument that in such an economy the credit market could be such that land holders were at an advantage. This, however, was not well received by Kaldor. According to King (1988, p. 426), he considered Joan Robinson's paper to be trespassing on his territory and in a six-page letter dated 2.21.61 he reacted in a 'strongly negative' manner. In the end, Cambridge Keynesians found no common stand in this matter and contributed little to lift the veil from this 'mysterious chapter' (Robinson 1961, p. 132) – unless one considers Joan Robinson's just quoted comments as an appropriate 'de-mystification'. Later, Samuelson (1979, p. 175) took up this debate and tried to vindicate 'the germ of putative truth' in Keynes' views on land in this context but he also had a guarded scepticism about their relevance for the future. Clearly, neither in Cambridge, UK nor in Cambridge, Mass. did Townshend-type fascination with the most general parts of the *General Theory* find much repetition.

It is to be hoped that future Keynesians do not let the reception of 'Chapter 17' remain in the state it was left by the economists from the famous 'two Cambridges'. There might well be more to this 'mysterious' chapter than we are told by the master-interpreters until now. *One* remarkable aspect of that chapter is that it opens a truly 'epochal' perspective on human society in looking at changing means of satisfying liquidity preference. If we turn to those passages which triggered the debates just mentioned, we should note that Keynes (*GT*, p. 241) did indeed speculate about a 'liquidity premium' attributed to land:

It may be that in certain historic environments the possession of land has been characterised by a high liquidity-premium in the minds of owners of wealth.

But the context in which he put this remark is not just the working of the capital or labour market as we know it today. The next paragraph already deals with 'the world after several millennia' and one may well wonder about the timespan which Keynes considers not only in this sentence but in the preceding paragraph as well. *This* reader sees in these passages a perspective extending from antiquity over past feudalism and present *latifundia* to the human condition in general. Keynes' glimpses at history are held together in this view by one human desire: liquidity preference. In *this* context Keynes (*GT*, p. 242) then attacks Marshall's *Principles of Economics* and his sweeping statement (p. 581) about 'the great mass of humanity' and 'their unwillingness to "wait" '. His criticism of this application of the concept of 'waiting' is, of course, not a denial of the time preference analysis as such. As was seen above, he wholeheartedly accepts the economic soundness of the concept of time preference. It is rather a denial of its explicative power when it comes to explaining the human condition. It is also not the Marxian 'means of production' which shaped historic societies but Keynes' 'liquidity preference'. Under this perspective, Keynes' often-quoted letter to G. B. Shaw about his future book knocking off the bottom for old Ricardian and Marxian analysis obtains a quite new quality.

The above is, in a sense, a glimpse at the (past) future of Keynes' monetary ideas – a speculation as to what he might have said had he had the opportunity to elaborate on the passages just quoted.[8] It is not the place here to speculate whether Keynes' sketches of history can become a research programme for somebody not having quite the same vision and drive as Keynes had himself. But it probably could give us new insights about past events if we saw them once in a while under Keynes' perspective on liquidity premium – by asking what constituted 'liquidity' in the respective circumstances and how desirable liquidity was in this wider conceptualisation of 'assets' in alternative situations. What did it mean for a feudal chief to be 'liquid'? What was the 'liquidity premium' of conquered territories? Keynes did supply some hints about his peculiar 'liquidity-oriented' views of history in his defence of mercantilism. But would he not – if he had had the opportunity to do so – have taken his liquidity analysis to further historical realms? Could not *here* lie a task for future Keynesians, namely to extend his liquidity analysis into new perspectives on history and humanity?

27.3 Keynes' contextual dialectics

As there are authors claiming that the Keynesian revolution has not yet been made and still needs to come, so there is at least one recent scholar of Keynes' philosophy who claims:

> In all likelihood, no one writing today has discovered the true connection between Keynes's work in philosophy and his work in economics. (Bateman 1991, p. 318)

In the closing pages of this book it is not the place to evaluate in full the justification for such a judgement. But on the other hand, one should take note here, too, that for Keynes economics was not just a box of 'pretty tools' for scholastic exercises. It was a device for taking scholarly responsibility in our society. Such a conviction cannot be maintained without having at least some set of ideas about the mental foundations of societal interaction. Where did these ideas come from in the case of Keynes and where could they lead if his tradition were taken as an endowment for posterity? These are questions of such obvious relevance for an understanding of Keynes that biographers ever since Harrod (1951) have given considerable space to them. As Skidelsky (1983, p. 133) remarked: 'Philosophy provided the foundation of Keynes's life. It came before economics.'

But if so much attention was paid to this complex in the past, why are we nowadays not further in understanding Keynes' philosophical set-up? The ignorance attested in the above quote to present-day scholars writing about his philosophy is disturbing and challenging.

In taking up the challenge posed by reconstructing the interconnection between economy and philosophy in Keynes' thought, one might resort to Clarke's (1988) historical approach. We saw above that in the attempt at understanding better the Keynes-and-Pigou debate it might be fruitful to follow Clarke's suggestion to enter into academic Cambridge's 'parochialism'. We understand this suggestion as meaning the inspection in some detail of potentially important but ephemeral *obiter dicta*, the significance of which reveal themselves only when seen in the context of the local interactions and preoccupations. As far as our enquiry into the Keynes-and-Pigou debate was concerned, the case in point – suggested already by Clarke (1988) – was Pigou's (1933) preface. In the case of Keynes' philosophy we suggest having a look at his communication about the genesis of ideas when he presented the *General Theory* to his students in November 1933.

It is a seeming oddity that Keynes, about a month before he entered into presenting the essence of the final shape of the *General Theory* in his Michaelmas lecture of 4 December 1933 had a session on 'fluffy gray thoughts'.[9] The starting question of the lecture of 6 November was: 'What degree of precision is advisable in economics?'[10] but the subsequent discourse was more general than that:

> Even mathematical thinking is not in terms of *precise* concepts but 'fluffy gray lumps'.[11]

According to the notes of Robert Bryce, the subject matter of the lecture was 'Terminology' but the substance related is the same as just stated, involving some complimentary comments on Marshall's method. According to Marvin Fallgatter's account, Keynes said:

> there is some question as to the utility and propriety of the scholastic exercise in trying to define terms with great precision in a subject like economics. Marshall, for example, does not make any effort to use his terms precisely, but you always get his meaning from the richness of his context.

This is much better than that specious precision which some writers effect, because you are not misled by supposing the terms to be precise, and you must supply the precision from the richness of his context.

These passages are remarkable for a number of reasons in the present context. They articulate warnings against scholasticism in economics – a theme which Keynes spun further on other occasions during those years, e.g. in a letter to Robert Bryce in 1935 (JMK, XXIX, pp. 150–1), criticising the 'appalling state of scholasticism into which the minds of so many economists have got'. A further point to be noted is that we find here an express appreciation of Marshall's argumentative method. A third point to note is that this passage contains a disassociation from the 'specious precision' of 'some writers'. Whom might Keynes have had in mind when he saw an element of deception in precision?

The most interesting hints for answering such questions may be found in Keynes' paper on 'My Early Beliefs' of September 1938 (JMK, X, pp. 433–50), 'a key document for understanding his life's work' as Robert Skidelsky (1983, p. 133) wrote. He goes on to explain that the heart of this paper is Keynes' 'account of G. E. Moore's *Principia Ethica*, and the effect it had on him' (*ibid.*). That effect was enormous, as Skidelsky explains. It followed from a veritable 'Conversion' in 1906.[12]

What was so special about this philosopher? 'The secret of Moore's power as a philosopher was his literalness of mind', according to Skidelsky (1983, p. 137). As far as the questions here under discussion are concerned, the extraordinary trait of this mind was *precision*, as Harrod (1951, p. 76) relates:

> Maynard once told me that he thought that Moore had carried the use of ordinary speech as far as it would ever be possible to carry it, in conveying clear meaning. For still greater precision one would have to proceed by mathematical symbols.[13]

Looking back in 1938 at the time of his mature student days, Keynes seems to have had second thoughts about the merits of precise language, however (JMK, X, p. 440):

> It was all under the influence of Moore's method, according to which you could hope to make essentially vague notions clear by using precise language about them and asking exact questions . . .
> It was a stringent education in dialectic; but in practice it was a kind of combat in which strength of character was really much more valuable than subtlety of mind.

Keynes seems to make here a distinction between relatively mindless but rationalistic questioning for precision on the one hand and sensible exchange and appreciation of arguments on the other. The 'dialectic' he describes in this passage seems to be a 'mindless' one for him, at least one which does not get to the 'subtlety of mind' which was of relatively little value in that context, as he stresses – and implicitly criticises. A few pages later Keynes (JMK, X, p. 442), referring to his experience in that Moore-oriented circle of 'My Early Beliefs', remarked:

> Thus we were brought up . . . with a scholasticism which outdid St Thomas.

Whatever St Thomas' scholasticism might mean for economics in that context, one thing seems to be quite clear from these passages: the mental framework which Keynes describes in 'My Early Beliefs' is quite an *anti-monde* to the one he cultivated at the time of writing and defending the *General Theory*. He wanted to make his students aware of 'specious precision' and of inappropriate scholasticism. In his above mentioned lecture of 6 November 1933 he spoke to his students about thoughts as being 'wooly monsters' and to Bryce, in 1935, he deplored the 'appalling state of scholasticism' in economics.

Keynes did not polish these particular thoughts, and since many of them survived only as students' lecture notes, there is, of course, the intractable question of their correct rendering. If we may trust the texts, some passages from that context suggest that Keynes was thinking in terms of a phenomenology of thought – of how thought appears and takes shape, one of the lecture notes stating (Rymes 1989, p. 102):

> The precise use of language comes at a late stage in the development of one's thought. You can think accurately and effectively long before you can, so to speak, photograph your thought. A not quite perfect epitome of this would be to say that when you adopt perfectly precise language, you are trying to express yourself for the benefit of those who are incapable of thought.

Thus we have here again a distinction between what seems to amount to *mindless* thought of somebody requiring precise predigestion on the part of the thinker on the one hand, and some other context of thinking in which the addressee is able to grasp the spirit of the argument without the help of the rationalistic 'crutches'. It is not an outright denial of precision which Keynes advocates. It is mindful, sensible, dynamical thought which he seems to be striving at. In any case, at some time in those years Keynes seems to have had a new mental conversion away from his 'Early Beliefs'. But what was he converted to and in which respect was he converted? Put differently: what is the mindset which is most congenial to receiving and appreciating the *General Theory* if it is obviously not the one of 'My Early Beliefs' any more?

Skidelsky (1983, p. 160) closes his review of Keynes' early beliefs and of his philosophical disposition with the remark:

Philosophy, McTaggart always said, was valuable for the comfort it gave. Through philosophy Keynes reconciled himself to his own nature, and to the world.

It is a nice idea that philosophy should have had the function for Keynes, following McTaggart, to mediate between his self and the world in a 'comforting', maybe consoling, way. But where does McTaggart now come in and why should he have had any significance for Keynes? It emerges from Harrod (1951, p. 61) that Keynes was in contact with John McTaggart Ellis McTaggart from his first student days at Cambridge, probably knowing of his eminence from his father. McTaggart was a leading Hegelian at Cambridge and wrote several books on Hegel's philosophy, among them a commentary on Hegel's *Logic*.

In his first terms of study at Cambridge Keynes was quite receptive of this influence. He visited McTaggart's lectures and attended some of his social evenings. Keynes soon wrote a paper on 'Time' in the spirit of that influence, acknowledging that influence in the following way:

When I have attended Dr McTaggart's lectures, I have felt the plunge from ordinary life into metaphysics a very violent one; it usually takes me an appreciable time to gather my wits for a sustained dialectical outlook upon the Universe, despite the lecturer's efforts to relieve the tension by the introduction of so unmetaphysical a thing as laughter. (quoted after Moggridge 1992, p. 70)

One may gather from this introductory passage of the paper that via McTaggart, Keynes had quite an intensive exposure to some sort of Hegelian concepts of dialectics and to this specific way of looking at 'the Universe'. His reference to the 'unmetaphysical' aspects of that exposure seems to show that he was quite appreciative of the more mundane and real-life aspects of that philosophical exercise. Finally, the fact that he wrote that paper at all indicates that he acquired sufficient confidence and will to move in that type of mental world. Indeed, metaphysics appeared to become so important for him that Fitzgibbons (1991, p. 129) could write:[14]

Keynes began from a metaphysical outlook which constituted the foundation of his thought.

As far as the substance of Keynes' paper on 'Time' was concerned, Harrod (1951, p. 61) described it in the following way:

It was an astonishingly mature work for a freshman. Time was essentially relative.

In that context Harrod went on to point out that this was before the era of 'Relativity', meaning probably that it was written before Albert Einstein published his theories of special relativity in 1905 and of general relativity in 1915. This remark suggests that in the eyes of Harrod, Keynes, as freshman and under the influence of McTaggart,[15] wrote something which one might relate – at least parenthetically – to the general orientation of Albert Einstein's Theory of Relativity. This is, of course, quite a fascinating biographical suggestion for several reasons. One may well ask whether Harrod's remark was grounded in some wider-known Cambridge tradition about this aspect of Keynes' philosophical attempts. That would add an interesting and ironically appreciative tinge to Pigou's (1936, p. 115) gibe that

Einstein actually did for Physics what Mr. Keynes believes himself to have done for Economics.

Did Keynes or some of his Cambridge associates claim on the basis of his paper on 'Time' that Keynes, as a freshman, had done in Philosophy what Einstein had done later in Physics?

No matter how relevant such speculations are which one could spin on the basis of Harrod's remark, Keynes' paper on 'Time' seems to have been a success. Looking back with the hindsight of the experience of and comment on the relatively mindless 'dialectics' of rationalistic precision referred to above, this episode might well have had a more positive association for the later Keynes than meets a superficial reader's eye.

It could well have been under McTaggart's influence that Keynes was introduced to concepts of contextual meaning and about the formation of ideas and concepts only in interaction and relative to context – themes which we may detect in his later statements about the phenomenology of thought as just described above. It is true that McTaggart's influence on Keynes was soon swamped by that of Moore.[16] But having been quite intensively exposed to a variant of Hegelian philosophy in his early studies, Keynes was reminded of this potential mental influence on economics through Alfred Marshall. In his essay on him (*Essays in Biography*, JMK, X, pp. 161–231) Keynes (p. 172) points out that Marshall was 'greatly influenced' by Hegel's *Philosophy of History*. He reiterates this point in a footnote (*ibid.* p. 172, n. 2) by relating that:

In a conversation I had with him a few weeks before his death he [Marshall] dwelt especially on Hegel's *Philosophy of History*.

In a third place in that essay (p. 175) he quotes the account of Mrs Marshall according to which her husband, during his 'Wanderjahre' in the Alps, would habitually sit down out in nature 'sometimes on a glacier, and have a long pull at some book', mentioning Hegel in particular. We just saw that Keynes compared Marshall favourably to those writers who engaged in 'specious precision'. If one wanted to detect a Hegelian connection in this, it certainly would not be a totally fictitious one.[17]

In any case, with this background, Keynes was in a comparatively good position to understand the 'Hegelese' which Joan Robinson loathed and vehemently refused to be confronted with.[18] He was aware of the interest which Alfred Marshall had in this direction. Some of Keynes' mature disassociation from rational precision which undervalues 'subtlety of mind'[19] on the one hand, and the conceptual development of the fluffy grey thought-monsters he amused his audience with in 1933 on the other hand, might well have been more than just wise-cracks. They might have something to do with Keynes' 'well-documented' (Chick and Dow 2001, p. 711) organicism. But at Cambridge one of the remarkable experts in the field of 'organic unity' was none other than the just mentioned Hegelian Ellis McTaggart according to David Gordon (1996):

On organic unity in Hegel's philosophy, one of the best treatments is by J.M.E. McTaggart, a philosopher of outstanding merit in his own right.

Thus we are here again at the Hegelian philosophical influences which Keynes so intensively imbibed as a Freshman at Cambridge before he entered the mental world of 'My Early Beliefs'. But why should Keynes return to that mental world in November 1933? After all, the essay on his 'Early Beliefs' was not written until 1938. A full answer cannot be attempted here. But it should be noted that it was in October 1933 that Keynes (1933b) published an article about Albert Einstein, beginning by quoting (in German) the opening sentences of the latter's 'Essay on the Special and General Theory of Relativity'. We saw above that Keynes' biographer Roy Harrod mentioned 'Relativity' in connection with Keynes' 'McTaggart-ian' essay on the relativity of time. Is it then not plausible that Keynes himself could well be led back to his youthful thinking by having looked again at the essay which in some sense might be thought to be akin in spirit to his earliest philosophical endeavours as a Freshman?[20] One might well regard Keynes' warning against 'specious precision' in his lecture on 6 November 1933 in connection with his having published a quote from Einstein's 'General Theory of Relativity' about a fortnight before. But contrary to those readers who would like to see an act of clever salesmanship in this connection, we argue that Keynes' reference to Einstein's 'General Theory of Relativity' must be read in connection with Keynes' intellectual biography and in particular in connection with the relativity of time which he seems to have proclaimed for philosophical reasons even before Einstein did so for the purpose of physical explanation.

It seems to be quite clear from the above that not only in 1938 but already at the time of writing the *General Theory* Keynes had outgrown much of 'My Early Beliefs'. A number of his more mature thoughts could quite plausibly have a Hegelian family resemblance. Thus, if so far we have not detected the 'true' connection between Keynes' work in philosophy and his work in economics this might have something to do with a rather dim view of posterity concerning the Hegelian influence on Keynes.

If it is true that 'through philosophy Keynes reconciled himself to his own nature, and to the world' (see above), then it is most unlikely that Keynes' world of the 1930s could have been reconciled with his mature nature by the same philosophy as the one he embraced before World War one when he lived in the world of 'My Early Beliefs'. The most appropriate mindset of his bellicose years of creating and defending the *General Theory* might well have been that of a pragmatic dialectic shaped by a youthful understanding of some Cambridge variant of Hegelian philosophy.[21]

If the topic of the possibility of a Hegelian influence on Keynes is to be addressed, an interesting new front of research and interpretation might be opened. That is not to say that the topic of such a connection is totally new. As Francis Fukuyama (1989), known as a prominent American Hegelian, once observed:

> For Hegel, all human behavior in the material world, and hence all human history, is rooted in a prior state of consciousness – an idea similar to the one expressed by John Maynard Keynes when he said that the views of men of affairs were usually derived from defunct economists and academic scribblers of earlier generations.

An amalgamation of Keynes and Hegel along the lines of this quote seems not to be on a very systematic argumentative basis, however. But to argue this point would need more space than is available here.

In order just to fathom the scope of potential debate opened by the topic of 'Keynes and Hegel' we should also note briefly one further quote, namely from a Reverend Linleigh J. Roberts (1998) who, in an electronic publication named 'Christian Fellowship Church Online' recently declared:

> The impact of Hegel's philosophy can scarcely be exaggerated. Every area of life has been influenced – truth has undergone a dramatic change.
> * Charles Darwin applied Hegel's synthesis to biology and gave the world biological evolution.
> * Karl Marx applied Hegel's synthesis to sociology and gave the world communism.

- John Maynard Keynes applied Hegel's synthesis to economics and gave the world deficit spending, and the notion that government is God.

This lineage of Keynes as intellectual descendant from Hegel associates him with impressive intellectual company. But since he allegedly subscribes to the blasphemous proposition that 'government is God' he appears as being at the pinnacle of deviant behaviour.

Again we must refrain from any substantive comment. But we may note that this last judgement once more focuses on the extraordinary evil which Keynes supposedly spread. We thus are reminded in particular of the view quoted at the beginning of this book when we noted that David Frum – the ghostwriter of the 'axis of evil' in George W. Bush's presidential State-of-the-Union address of 2002 – saw Keynes' influence as 'almost entirely bad'.[22]

Thus we may return from our brief excursion into the fields of philosophy with the conclusion: viewing Keynesian economics in the new surroundings of Hegelian thinking is not necessarily prone to end in hagiography – it might also give new ammunition for all those who see great evil at work in Keynes' – maybe unfortunately – masterful mind.

28
Concluding Remarks

Quoting from Ortega *y* Gasset's *Revolt of the Masses*, Ana Palacio (2003), Spanish minister of foreign affairs, declared:

> The mission of the so-called intellectuals is, in a manner of speaking, the opposite of that of the politicians. A work of intellect aspires – often in vain – to clarify matters a little, whereas the job of politicians usually involves muddling things even more.

In macroeconomic debate the roles of politicians and academic intellectuals seem to be reversed, however. When politicians have to deal with macroeconomic issues, they must try to come to a viable decision. For practical reasons, the scope for such decisions mostly will be rather narrow, no matter which economic political school the actor emerged from. In contrast to that, academic economists relish in postulating their own hypothetical worlds. If it pleases them for their academic discourse, they create their theoretically preferred 'frozen land remote in its characteristics from all experience' (Keynes, see above, p. 170). They thereby *muddle* practical clarity instead of contributing to it. But when it comes to practical advice, even such academic economists may reach economic politically sensible and in that sense 'clear' proposals – which, however, their own economic theoretical edifices cannot possibly have harboured before, as Keynes once observed referring to some of his Cambridge colleagues (see p. 435, n. 3). The outcome of this type of debate is that much economic political practice nowadays must still be conducted with little economic theoretical clarification.

The Keynes–Classics debate is a particularly relevant case in point. It still goes on with much 're-re-revolutionary' ado – from 'Keynesian revolution' to 'neoclassical counter-revolution', 'Classical revolution' and 'rational expectations revolution' back to a 'new Keynesian revolution' and so on, while some 'post-Keynesians' of several denominations live an antagonistic life of their own. But few issues of practical economic advice were definitely

settled in that process. Thus the practical relevance of such debate is doubtful and its guidance for economic political advice is fickle. Part I above substantiated this characterisation. It was argued above that in order to
overcome this rather unsatisfactory state of modern macroeconomic
debate, an attempt must be made at leaving the pseudo-revolutionary posturing behind. For that purpose there should be a thorough reconsideration
of the very beginning of the Keynes–Classics debate. By now, it is encrusted
not only with – in this particular context rather comical – terms of violence
and annihilation ('revolution', 'counter-revolution', 'death') but also with
expressions of moral debasement ('the effective demand fraud', the 'whipping boy' road to bestsellerdom, concealment of issues, misrepresentation
almost bordering on plagiarism). Few serious historians have contributed to
these types of commentary. A serious proposal in this context was formulated by Clarke (1988, p. 273), however, who pointed out that the seeming
strangeness of the initial debate will disappear once it is seen 'in its own
parochial setting'. Much of this book is based on that observation. Our
endeavour was not directed at re-establishing 'the' authentic Keynes or
'the' authentic Pigou in this context, however, but rather to re-authenticate
the original roots and contexts of the Keynes-and-Pigou *debate* and its
setting among the younger economic colleagues who participated in – or
later commented on – that debate. Putting it briefly, it can be said that a
picture emerged which is quite different from the views cultivated hitherto
in the traditional Keynes–Classics debate. One important aspect of this
reconsideration was the central role attributed to Pigou (1933) in this
debate. Posterity never made it quite clear that Keynes spent not only
many pages of the *General Theory* on discussing his model but also much
time and correspondence at elucidating its essential analytical aspects. It *is*
the 'node' of the Keynes-and-Pigou debate, as the title our part II states. But
that book has that central function not just for formal reasons of model
building. It is also the 'parochial' manifestation of Pigou's proclaimed intellectual supremacy as Clarke (1988, p. 273) remarked earlier. Pigou's hardly
veiled personal challenge to Keynes is the source of many further aspects of
the *General Theory* which should be understood as a response to that challenge, as we highlighted in discussing the 'table of concordance' (p. 350).
Such concordance has nothing to do with 'quasi-plagiarism' allegedly committed by Keynes. It is rather a manifestation of the intensive dialogue
intended by Keynes. It is one of the misfortunes of the subsequent
Keynes–Classics debate – and thus also of the development of economics –
that that debate did not materialise in the intensity intended by Keynes.

The reader might demand now 'in a nutshell' the message of this book.
But a nutshell cannot replace the fully branched-out tree of developed
arguments. It is really the latter which is needed in order to stand against
the thicket of past Keynes–Classics polemics. Perhaps the simile of a 'fault
line' is more appropriate here – a disturbance seemingly minute in dimen-

sion, but eventually opening up into a divide unbridgeable by further communication. Such a fault line separating Keynes from much of 'the rest' of his physical and intellectual surroundings is given, in a rather literal sense, above in table 15.1, p. 172. It is the line separating Keynes from the 'frozen land' economics of the Pigovian stationary state and the Pigovian analysis from Keynes' starting point of short-period income determination. As it turned out in this book, the Young Keynesians participating in this debate were analytically nearer to Pigou than to Keynes in this particular, but essential, regard. It seems that Joan Robinson realised this late in her life – but that is not our main concern here, since those later re-considerations about the (un-)importance of reswitching and about the capital theoretic debates did not really shape much of the Keynes–Classics debate. If we want to search for the exact point where that debate was derailed, we should retrace the strange issue of stationary and 'moving' states which Keynes intended to discuss but eventually was left alone with. In any case, it is important to realise that the eventually dramatic fault line was *not* the issue of time preference or 'waiting' and its relation to interest rates, as R. F. Kahn originally believed. It is the analytical acceptance of the stationary state as point of orientation and it is strange that it might well have been R. F. Kahn who put Keynesian discipleship on the track of eventual derailment when he tried to relate Keynesian economics to a reinvented system of Simple Reproduction.

It is hoped that our reconsideration and re-authentication of the Keynes–Classics debate as Keynes-*and*-Pigou debate will re-establish fruitful argumentative cohesion in economic debate. But the perspective offered in this book is meant to go beyond mere historical reconstruction and reinterpretation. Keynes' own message was not limited to the technical and 'parochial' issues which came up at some time in this book. Indeed, they played a rather limited role in his argumentation. He did aspire to technical consistency. There are a number of documents in which he is shown to be eager to be technically correct in his own writings and in his criticism of others. But his perspective went beyond the petty victories to be had in logical disputes and in agitated arguments. In the end, Keynes appears to be indeed steeped in a 'metaphysical outlook', an attitude which he imbibed in his very first student days. But it was a worldly metaphysic he cultivated in his mature years, one which abstracted from much of his 'parochial' surroundings and which focused on cultivating 'good common sense' in an enlightened society.

Perhaps this is the most interesting legacy Keynes left to economics: the task of giving a solid mental home to his fluffy thought monsters – creatures eager for responsible economic political action in a *mindful* rational world.

Notes

Preface

1 See Keynes (1936). For alternative ways of referring to the *General Theory*, see the remark at the begining of the Bibliography.
2 Ambrosi (1979a, 1980a) in German with English summaries.
3 Ambrosi (1979b) in English, Ambrosi (1980b) in German with English summary.
4 See bottom of p. 163 for Kahn's suggestion not to publish Kaldor (1937).
5 See p. 176.
6 Cf. Fusfeld (1985, p. 385, n. 1), Blaug (1991a, p. 175), Clower (1989, p. 146, and n. 17), Guthrie (1997, p. 318, n. 2 and n. 8)

1. The Volatility in Macroeconomic Paradigms

1 See Niehans (1990) for a rejection of the concept of 'scientific revolution' (as coined by Thomas Kuhn (1970) for the natural sciences) in the context of the history of economic thought. See Coats (1969) for an affirmative position.
2 See the journalist Thomas Frank (2002) concerning the current 'outrage' in the wider public about the hype associated with the 'revolutionary' New Economy: 'Right up to the end, Enron [the multi-billion company that went bankrupt among accusations of criminal misdeeds of management and involvement in large-scale political party financing, GMA] was described in the exalted realms of management theory and business journalism with virtually unmodulated adoration ... Superguru Gary Hamel, who devoted a section *Leading the Revolution* to the company, waxed enthusiastic about Enron's "genius for innovation" and its "capacity for revolution" ... The Enron story ... [is] a perfect ideological reversal, a narrative that was supposed to prove the goodness of the New Economic Order and that has instead discredited it in every respect. Thanks to the vast chasm between the populist promise of the New Economy and what it has actually delivered, a corporation is today the target of a species of outrage usually reserved for enemy dictators or mass murderers.'
3 Interestingly, this writer later was one of the speech-writers of US president George W. Bush and, according to Noah (2002) and other sources, he was in this function responsible for the term 'axis of evil' appearing in the 2002 State-of-the-Union Address.
4 Cf. the judgement of Hahn (1989, p. 906), a fellow Nobel Laureate of Arrow, in a similar interview: 'That whole subject [of "new classical macroeconomics", GMA] is dead now.'
5 Italics of the first sentence omitted, GMA. For alternative ways of referring to the *General Theory*, see the remark at the beginning of the Bibliography.
6 See Davidson (1998, pp. 24–6) for an extended critical assessment of the topic of 'differing speeds'.
7 This sentence is debatable from philosophical and empirical standpoints. Ever since Plato, philosophers ponder the idea whether ideas really need the rest of the world or whether they have a life of their own. As far as empirical questions

are concerned, it may be noted that Russel (2001) finishes his review of Skidelsky (2000) by remarking: 'Keynes' legacy is therefore different from the qualified one put forward by Skidelsky. Keynes made economists relevant and useful and in the process strengthened democracy around the world.' But this is not really the crucial issue here. It is rather to show how undecided economics still is with regard to its paradigms. The undecided assessment of Keynes by his biographer is really an enforcement of our point.

2. The Problem of Authenticity in Keynesian Economics

1   Quoted in the following as JMK followed by the volume number in Roman numerals.
2   Rymes (1989).
3   Harrod (1951), Hession (1984), Moggridge (1992), Skidelsky (1983, 1992, 2000).
4   Emphasis added, GMA. Joan Robinson refers here to Keynes (1937a) where he particularly defends his liquidity preference theory. Ironically, the absence of this very theory from post-Keynesian macroeconomics as cultivated among Keynes' followers at Cambridge came under heavy attack in a contribution by Jan Kregel (1985).
5   It is not quite clear who these colleagues were, however. Piero Sraffa certainly cannot have been among them because he 'never really quite knew what it was that we were going on about', as Joan Robinson (1979c, p. 135) was later to write about his role in these debates. For the wider context of this statement see below, p. 263.
6   For the relevant quote from Joan Robinson, see p.261.
7   Even Coddington (1983, p. 77) himself, in spite of his vow to abstain from dealing with 'what Keynes actually said' or 'really meant', cannot avoid the temptation to talk knowingly about 'Keynes's *instinct* about the functioning of interest rates in a depression' (my emphasis, GMA). A post mortem trying to detect 'instinct' seems to this reader at least as forbidding as one trying to find 'meaning'. There must be some strong curiosity involved if the endeavour is made nevertheless.

3. The Problem of Authenticity in 'Classical' Economics

1   For a critical discussion of this particular charge see Skott and Dutt (1996).
2   Paragraphing added, GMA.
3   See also Leeson (1998b, pp. 125–6) for the accusation that Keynes ripped quotes 'all bloody from their context'.
4   See Baumol (1997, p. 229, n. 1) concerning the problem of counting Say's laws.
5   Aslanbeigui (1998, p. 96) correctly states that 'fully to understand the transformation of economics at Cambridge during the inter-war period, a study of Pigou's work is essential'. Unfortunately, in her footnote 3, the author (*op-cit.*, p. 86) substantiates claims concerning Pigou's theory of unemployment *before* the *General Theory* – this is the express title of the relevant section – with a lengthy quote from Pigou (1941, p. 51–2, 2nd ed.), a book which appeared well *after* the *General Theory*. This is a clear misrepresentation of that type of theory the *General Theory* argued against, namely the theory of Pigou (1933).

4. Reconsidering Pigou as Keynes' Authentic Classic

1   Actually, this charge is not really very new. Leijonhufvud (1968, p. 91, n. 18) already remarked: 'Keynes did rely to a great extent on the most authoritative

account in existence at the time – Pigou's *Theory of Unemployment* – and he has often been criticised for doing so.'

2   This misprint is a bit amusing in the light of Keynes' (*General Theory*, p. 275) comment that Pigou's title *Theory of Unemployment* is 'something of a misnomer. His book is not really concerned with this subject. It is a discussion of how much employment there will be, given the supply function of labour.' This is the central point of Keynes' 'internal critique' of Pigou (see below, ch. 10, in particular the discussion of fig. 10.3 p. 100).

3   In view of our later argumentation it is of some interest to note that Joan Robinson (1962a, p. 79) was not innocent in fostering this belief which in our view resulted in the severing of the argumentative links between Keynes and Pigou. There she claims that 'Gerald Shove used to say that Maynard had never spent the twenty minutes necessary to understand the theory of value.' But as Leijonhufvud (1968, p. 33) pointed out, she thereby just 'perpetuates an old canard'. For further substantiation see also the following footnote.

4   Cf. Samuelson (1946, p. 316), 'Indeed, until the appearance of the mathematical models of Meade, Lange, Hicks, and Harrod, there is reason to believe that Keynes himself did not truly understand his own analysis.'

5   For a characterisation of postwar macroeconomics along this line see Joan Robinson (1973d, p. 5): 'After the war, Keynes' theory was accepted as a new orthodoxy without the old one being rethought.' Nevertheless (*ibid.*): 'All the old slogans are repeated unchanged.' In this context it should be mentioned, however, that the parentage of these 'old slogans' had changed: the Marshallian and Pigovian tradition of the English School – even in Anglo-American contexts as exemplified by the writings of Hicks and Samuelson – was abandoned in favour of a Walrasian orientation. It would carry us too far to elaborate on this side issue. Some of this development is covered in Leeson (1998a), however.

6   In a similar vein, Blinder (1988, p. 286) remarked that 'the 1970s did not witness a revival of Pigou ... It saw, instead, a movement towards the high-tech economic theory of Lucas and the high-tech econometrics of Sargent.'

7   Solow's agenda for a fresh look at old theories of employment went somewhat further than the present one and included also 'the parallel evolution of the institutions of the labor market' (*ibid.*). Giving priority to theoretical questions involved in the Keynes–Classics debate, we will refrain here from a discussion of institutional developments, however.

8   See Hawtrey (1934, p. 155) and also below, n. 5 to Chapter 5.

5. The Question of Fairness in the Keynes–Pigou Debate

1   Letter of R. F. Kahn to J. M. Keynes of 18 October 1937 (JMK, XIV, p. 259). Keynes was indeed suffering from the aftermath of a heart attack at that time. But Keynes thought Pigou's professed motive for not entering a substantive discussion with him not very convincing. See below, note 8 to Chapter 15.

2   See Laidler (1999, pp. 308–9, n. 6): 'In light of his Hicks [(1937)] *failure* to remark upon the demonstrable unfairness of Keynes's treatment of it ... one wonders how carefully Hicks had actually read Pigou's book' (my emphasis, GMA).

3   For a brief further discussion of this quote see p. 425.

4   The quote is from Pigou (1933, p. v). For the context of this quote see below, table 25.1 on p. 350 where we list a number of further instances of 'Concordance between Pigou (1933) and Keynes (1936)'.

5   Hawtrey (1934, p. 155), in his review of Pigou (1933), claims that his 'real-end' approach to unemployment 'vitiate[s] all the reasoning based on that assumption [of constant real wages] in its practical application to a monetary economy'. He questions Pigou's claim that the monetary and the real approach 'must necessarily come to the same thing'.

6   See Ian Herbert (1981), p. 145 where – under the entry Coulouris, George – we read that that actor played *Yank* in the 1928/29 season as member of the company of the Cambridge Festival Theatre. (I thank Donald Moggridge for suggesting to me to supply this information.) I do not know, however, whether Pigou did himself attend that play. But it is clear that for Cambridge intellectuals a preposterous engine driver at that time was described in the lines from scene I of the *The Hairy Ape* quoted above on pp. 30–1.

7   For a few further details of this episode see below, pp. 346f. There is evidence that Pigou discussed the final report with Keynes in a private session in October 1930 (see below, p. 456, n. 23).

8   This is Pigou' original footnote: 'This poisoned dart is discharged – the skeleton must face the light – by one who himself on one occasion yielded to the blandishments of the *Sunday Express!*'

9   It is of particularly 'good taste' that Pigou 'explained' this footnote in a letter to Keynes remarking that it 'might look offensive to outsiders' if he had *not* published it – because then Pigou (1938) would have been only a reaction to Kaldor (1937). (Pigou's letter published in JMK, XIV, p. 268.)

6. An Abstract of the Arguments

1   Keynes' original formulation (see JMK, XIV, p. 238) was that it was 'remote in its characteristics from all experience'. He could have referred in this context to Alfred Marshall's (1925, pp. 305f.) marginal notes: 'In a stationary state the doctrine of value would be simple. But in the real world a simple doctrine of value is worse than none.'

7. Questions and Methods

1   This result was already stated by Solow (1980). He already pointed out that he considered this to be a perfectly plausible assumption. But the model he used was not quite to the standard which Pigou (1933) wanted to see maintained. For a discussion of this matter see section 9.3.3. on p. 69 above.

2   For the exchange between Keynes and Hawtrey concerning 'disutility' see in particular p. 77.

3   Cf. a letter of Keynes to R. F. Kahn, 20 October 1937: 'As in the case of Dennis [Robertson], when it comes to practice, there is really extremely little between us [Keynes and Pigou]. Why do they [Robertson and Pigou] insist on maintaining theories from which their own practical conclusions cannot possibly follow?'

4   Fortunately, it is Pigou (1937) himself who relieves us of some potential doubts concerning our claim that his earlier money wage theory is deficient. This question will be dealt with in more detail in part III which is expressly concerned with the Keynesian and the classical money wage doctrines.

5   Cottrell (1994) does discuss Keynes' critique of Pigou as it is to be found in the appendix to ch. 19 of the *General Theory*. But Keynes' *positive reconstruction* of the Pigovian model has so far not been evaluated in a comparable way.

6   There is a fairly recent and formally interesting reconstruction of a model of
     Pigovian unemployment by Klaiusinger (1998). With due respect for the formal
     qualities of that contribution, we must note here the fact that the author comes
     to the conclusion that 'Pigou's analysis seems to anticipate just that kind of
     "Keynesian" macroeconomics as reconstructed by the so-called neoclassical syn-
     thesis' (*ibid.*, p. 67). Such a conclusion is a far cry from the factual historical
     context of Pigou (1933), however. It is also unrelated to Pigou's subsequent argu-
     mentative development, as will emerge further below. Methodologically,
     Klausinger's reconstruction belongs to the class of 'rational reconstructions'
     mentioned at the beginning of this chapter (see above, p. 41) and against which
     Blaug (2001, p. 152) advised as quoted above. The crucial ahistorical element in
     this reconstruction is Klausinger's $h(q)$-function of 'demand for investment h'
     which is 'determined by its expected yield q.' This is not a reconstruction but an
     addendum which just does not have any textual or argumentative basis in Pigou
     (see also below, p. 174). Such an addendum is unfortunately misleading in the
     present context in that it detracts both from Pigou's stationary state assumption
     and also from Keynes' criticism in the appendix of chapter 19 of the *General
     Theory*. The textual-minded historians of economic thought should take note
     that there (p. 279) Keynes observed 'that Professor Pigou has altogether omitted
     from his analysis ... the scale of investment'. Keynes' criticism was – rightfully –
     not that Pigou (1933) had a $h(q)$-function. The reason is clear: neither for Keynes
     nor for Pigou was there such a function. An interpretation based on such a func-
     tion does not do justice to the authentic Keynes–Classics debate.

8. Pigou's 'Real Demand for Labour'

1   The most concise presentation of such a discussion is maybe to be found in
     Champernowne (1935) who demonstrates the interplay of the elasticity of sub-
     stitution of inputs on the one hand and the price elasticity of product demand
     on the other hand in determining the comparative statics of labour demand on
     the industry level.
2   The 'simplified model' in this context is a real wage model. Pigou (1937) later
     realised that he also needed a corresponding money wage model. Under the
     proper name 'simplified model' we will later refer only to the latter model.
3   Itemisation and Roman numbers added, GMA.
4   See Krugman and Obstfeld (2000, p. 42, figure 3–3).
5   See [i] and [ii] of the list of Pigou's basic assumptions.
6   See Pigou (1933, p 88): 'As throughout this book, the whole problem is treated as
     a short-period one, in the sense that slow-working reactions from changes in
     fixed capital equipment are left out of account.'
7   In particular, labour's partial elasticity of production α is well defined and lies in
     the range $0 < \alpha < 1$. See also equ. (9.15) below.
8   See [iii] in the preceding section. This assumption appears in the *General Theory*
     on p. 5 as the 'first classical postulate'.
9   This is just a slight reformulation of Jevons' labour supply analysis which was
     not in terms of a choice between alternative utilities but was based on the
     concept of 'disutility of labour' (for a detailed discussion of this concept of
     Jevons see Blaug (1968, pp. 313f). The pervasiveness of this theory of labour
     supply was stressed by none other than Keynes: 'The theory of Pigou and of
     Marshall and of all modern economists is that different quantities of labour are

on offer according to the amount of wage goods offered in return for a unit of labour' (JMK, XIV, p. 25). A detailed analysis along these lines was later supplied by Pigou (1935), particularly pp. 292ff.

10 In the *General Theory*, ch.2, Keynes refers to this assumption as the 'second classical postulate'.

11 This proposition follows from assumption [v] of the above list when the 'trading surplus' mentioned there is assumed to be positive.

12 For the central role attributed to this rule in the theory of demand of the English School see, e.g., Marshall (1920, p. 99).

13 Early representatives of this strand of the Keynesian literature are Sidney Weintraub (1957) and, building upon his contributions, Davidson and Smolensky (1964). A two-sectoral microfoundation for Keynes was supplied by Chakrabarti (1979).

14 For a concise review of the two-sector growth model literature see Burmeister and Dobell (1970, ch. 4).

9. The Workings of the Basic Pigovian Model

1 Cf. Robert Gordon (1989, p. 178) who complained: 'that new-classical macroeconomics consisted of a priori theorising in the analytically convenient setting of "representative agent models", where one could move back and forth between the individual agent and the aggregate economy simply by adding or removing the "i" subscripts ...' In our discussion of Pigou's theory of employment we demonstrate that this is not the analytical standard set by his 'old-classical' *Theory of Unemployment*.

2 See, sect. 9.3.4 on page 70.

3 See, sect. 9.3.3 on page 69.

4 For some discussion of these functions see below, equ. (9.23), p. 69.

5 See p. 71.

6 See p. 49, position [v].

7 Compare Solow (1980, p. 8) who is well aware of many of Pigou's sophistications but nevertheless reaches the conclusion that 'the *Theory of Unemployment* ... is all based on the presumption that the only possible starting point is the elasticity of the marginal-product-of-labor curve.' Actually, we tried to demonstrate that Pigou's 'basic assumptions' go considerably beyond Solow's statement.

8 In this connection see also table 15.1, p. 172 and the associated discussion of the treatment of investment in some Pigovian models.

9 Pigou as editor of Marshall (1925) was probably well aware that contemporary readers must have understood this reference as being to none other than Alfred Marshall (1925, p. 412), himself, who, in a letter to J. B. Clark dated 2 July 1900, wrote: 'I rejected the wage-doctrine in [Mill's, GMA] Book II, which has a wage-fund flavour'.

10 A different picture emerges from Skidelsky (1992, p. 533) who notes that Roy Harrod and James Meade 'were the chief Keynesians at Oxford. This had not stopped Harrod [(1934)] from calling Pigou's *Theory of Unemployment* a "supreme intellectual achievement".' But Harrod's compliments must be appreciated in the light of his just quoted extremely ironical 'praise'. Similarly, Collard (1981, p. 124) quotes Harrod praising Pigou (1933) for 'the great beauty, the exquisite workmanship, the painstaking lucidity', apparently without sensing in the least the irony which such a eulogy must have coming from somebody who congrat-

ulates Pigou for his use of 'firmly founded tautology'. But anybody who tried to trace in Pigou (1933) the relationship between $F'(x)$ on, e.g. his p. 41, and on, e.g. his p. 103 will know more clearly how Harrod's praise of 'lucidity' is meant: ironically. See also note 20 to Chapter 10 below for an example of confusing choice of symbols in Pigou (1933).

11 Pigou considered Harrod (1939) to be 'hopelessly muddled' and that Keynes should not have published him in the *Economic Jounal* (see JMK, XIV, p. 320 n.1). In essence, Keynes concurred with that judgement (see our quote on p. 270). Young (1989, pp. 42–8) gives an assessment of Harrod (1934) quite different from ours, believing that the review exemplified 'Harrod's economic *weltanschauung*' (*ibid.* p. 42) and that the praise for tautology should be taken at face value in that context. This makes it even more significant that Keynes *and* Pigou disassociate from Harrod, a phenomenon to be inspected in more detail in Part IV of this book.

10. Keynes' Internal Critique of Pigou and the Classics

1 This observation does not invalidate Keynes' invocation of the Marshall–Jevons tradition of labour supply analysis, however, since in that tradition it is well known that labour supply might either increase or decrease with real wages. The employment political consequence of the stated Pigovian assumption is that out of the four classical means for increasing employment to be discussed in sect. 10.5.1, p. 107 below, there remain only positions (a) and (b). Pigou's discussion of E_r then becomes pointless, as Keynes (JMK, XIV, pp. 38f.) pointed out.

2 This way of stating the relevant household choice was already used by Joan Robinson (1937a, pp. 120–1): 'the choice between an increase in leisure and an increase in earnings is likely gradually to turn more and more in favour of leisure, in spite of the extra inducement to work represented by a higher rate of reward.'

3 For an interesting survey under the perspective of the modern canonical model see Derobert (2001) who does not take account, however, of the labour-leisure calculus used by Joan Robinson (1937a, pp. 120–1) in the just quoted context.

4 As is customary in this type of debate, questions of aggregation will not be dealt with here. There are, of course, many open questions concerning units of analysis, functional forms, etc. The reader is requested to assume them solved in accordance with customary practice in this type of analysis.

5 Pigou (1933, p. 6) writes in a similar vein, but for *rising* real wages about 'the tendency of a *rise* in the rate of wage, by enabling the husband to support his family, without his wife working, to cause a certain number of women to *withdraw* from the labour market' (emphasis added, GMA).

6 The absence in Pigou's curve of our 'nose' described by $E'\,E-'$ could be interpreted in such a way that the 'exhaustion level' of employment is already reached for normal labour supply. This then would identify the N^s-curve as a *locus* of corner solutions and the scope for choices would be limited accordingly. Since Pigou gave no indication that he did base his curve on such a case, we refrain from giving it further consideration. But the denial of the relevance of household choice in labour supply analysis could be interpreted as meaning that there is no choice to be modelled: workers live between exhaustion (vertical branch of L) and starvation (horizontal branch of the – inverse – L).

7   Cf. also Joan Robinson's (1933, pp. 303–4) horizontal labour supply curve for men in the analysis of labour market discrimination against women 'when the men are organised in a trade union which enforces a minimum wage, and the women are not. Then the supply of men is perfectly elastic, and the supply of women is less than perfectly elastic.' In her analysis, relatively less men than women are employed, albeit at higher wages. The question of preference and 'hardship of unemployment' is not entered into but rather the equimarginal principle is stated as seen from the employer's side.

8   See Pigou's wage subsidies model just mentioned. Although he rejects subsidies as an employment political instrument, he does recommend them for social policy reasons as just stated in the text. But as far as employment was concerned, Pigou (1927, p. 366) believed in the self-healing capacity of the British economy in the face of 13% unemployment and persistently high (!) savings: 'As even in the present depressed state of our industries the annual amount of new savings appears to be in the neighborhood of 450 millions a year, the demand for labour will almost certainly continue to rise relative to the supply. Before very long, therefore, the country should be able to provide the present rate of real wages for its working population without suffering from an abnormal amount of unemployment.'

9   We do not deal here at any length with those economists who deny that there is anything like involuntary unemployment since that position clearly is irrelevant for the Keynes-and-Pigou debate.

10 For recent attempts see Corry (1997) and De Vroey (1997).

11 For the exact quote see below, note 15 to Chapter 11.

12 This claim is surprising in view of the outright rejection by his critics of the general applicability of this definition.

13 For a dissenting view see De Vroey (1997).

14 See above, p. 24.

15 See above, p. 76.

16 Note concerning the sign value of dQ_x/dn: we treat here labour, i.e. 'effort', as positive quantity. The figure treats it as negative since it is an input. The arrow along the n-axes shows, however, that we regard the *absolute* value, not the sign values of these magnitudes.

17 We went into this point in the discussion of fig. 10.1 on p. 82 when we said that point E^- in that framework was one of involuntary unemployment in the sense of Keynes. We claimed that in that point subjective valuation and market valuation of goods and effort are at variance and so the second classical postulate is invalid at that point.

18 Cf. also Pigou (1933, p. 252), 'such unemployment as exists [in stable conditions] at any time is due wholly to the fact that changes in demand conditions are continually taking place and that frictional resistances prevent the appropriate wage adjustments from being made instantaneously'.

19 See, e.g. Pigou (1935, p 44): 'Let us begin by supposing that Robinson [Crusoe] is producing only a single sort of commodity, and consider the consequences of ... a fall in his aversion from work ... It is evident ... that [such] sorts of change must lead to his both doing more work and obtaining more of the commodity.'

20 Cf. Pigou (1933, p. 114): 'the type that increases aggregate output and marginal output, over the relevant range of employment, *in equal proportions* ... I shall speak of in later chapters as the normal type of improvement.' In a footnote Pigou (1933, p. 114 n.) then proceeds to an algebraic statement of his

condition for 'normal' improvement. The reader should be warned that, as usual, Pigou does not stick to his former choice of symbols and now denotes by *F* not a sectoral production function but a demand function, his production function now being given as *phi*. His index 1 used there then stands for pre-improvement conditions, his index 2 used there denoting the post-improvement functions.

21 Actually, Pigou (1933, p. 60) himself discusses normal improvement in the wage goods sector – thus increases in parameter A_x in the present choice of symbols – pointing out its positive effect on total employment.

11. Keynes' External Critique of Pigou and the Classics

1 For the *definition* of this concept and its microeconomic formulation see above, sect. 10.3.5, p. 88 on 'Keynes' "involuntary unemployment in the strict sense" '.

2 For criticism of this preoccupation see n. 1 to Chapter 4 and the text on p. 24 to which it refers.

3 Letter to R. F. Kahn, 13 April 1934 (JMK, XIII, p. 423).

4 Letter to R. F. Harrod, 30 August 1936 (JMK, XIV, pp. 85f.).

5 One could perhaps conceive of a particular theory of employment as part of a general equilibrium oriented Economics of Welfare. But Keynes (1936, p. 5, n. 1) pointed out that Pigou, in a book under this title, declared that 'the fact that some resources are generally *unemployed* against the will of their owners is *ignored*' (italics added, GMA).

6 It is along these lines that Keynes (1936, p. 128) justifies the merits of seemingly 'wasteful' loan expenditure, starting from the observation: 'When involuntary unemployment exists, the marginal disutility of labour is necessarily less than the utility of the marginal product.'

7 Keynes (1936, p. 29) expressly accepted the idea of labour supply as analysed in the conventional 'disutility' approach being a constraint in principle in his model, too. In the context of his presentation of 'the essence of the *General Theory of Employment*' he therefore declared: 'The amount of labour *N* ... cannot exceed the value which reduces the real wage to equality with the marginal disutility of labour' (italics in the original). The significance of his observation is later elaborated by Keynes (1936, p. 284) in stating that '*it will be possible to increase employment* by increasing expenditure in terms of money *until real wages have fallen to equality with the marginal disutility of labour*, at which point there will, by definition, be full employment' (italics added, GMA).

8 Keynes (1936, p. 273) himself was fully aware of this, relating his own theory repeatedly to that of Pigou, e.g. when stating: 'Pigou's function φ is (subject to the identification of wage-goods with consumption-goods) a function of what I have called above the employment multiplier *k'*.'

9 Such a reader's impression was articulated by Ohlin (1937, p. 195) stating: 'One somewhat surprising trait in Keynes' theory of employment is that he fails to use the marginal analysis of the demand for labour ... [T]he demand for labour is explained, or rather briefly stated, by means of aggregate supply and demand functions, without any explanation of what this means in marginal terms. (See pp. 24–5 [*General Theory*].)'

10 See editors' Appendix 1 to the *General Theory* as reprinted in JMK, VII, p. 385. The quoted statement refers to p. 29 of the *General Theory*.

11 In order to distinguish the Pigovian functions from the Keynesian ones, we deviate slightly from Keynes' original choice of symbols by using only capital Greek letters for his functions.

12 Again we have a problem in consistent connotation if we want to keep Pigovian and Keynesian symbolism apart. Our $\mathcal{F}$ here stands for Keynes' original symbol F for an employment function.

13 If there are any doubts in this last regard, p. 90 of the *General Theory* should be consulted where Keynes states that his $C_w = \chi(Y_w)$ is equivalent to the expression $C = W\chi(Y_w)$. It follows from this that $C_w \equiv C/W$ where W the money wage rate which we found more convenient to denote by the lower case letter w.

14 This formulation corresponds to the one given by Keynes (1936, p. 44) as $Z_r = \varphi_r(N_r)$. The difference in notation stems from the fact that Keynes' version is in terms of nominal values and from us having reserved the lower case symbol φ for the Pigovian $\varphi(x)$-function. Therefore we take the upper case letter 'phi' as replacement.

15 In case there is any doubt concerning the authenticity of this statement, the reader should consult JMK, XIV, p. 190 (Keynes' letter to B. Ohlin, 29 April 1937): 'I have always regarded decreasing physical returns in the short period as one of the very few incontrovertible propositions of our miserable subject!'

16 Letter to R. G. Hawtrey, 8 November 1935, JMK, XIII, p. 602. Next quote *ibid.*, p. 603.

17 See JMK, XIV, p. 196. Keynes' reply is quoted from *ibid.*, p. 190.

18 Emphasis and numbering added, GMA.

19 Item [5] of this list is contained in the formulation of parameter ε of equ. (11.7) below, item [6] is contained there in parameter ξ. It is, of course, debatable whether nominal wage costs are prone to change in response to increases in employment as long as there is involuntary unemployment. But this is a question of an appropriate choice of parameters, and not one of the principal consequences of imperfect competition.

20 Under various connotations, such elasticities are to be found in Pigou (1935), Appendix XII and XIII and in Pigou (1941) where the η-s of the present formulation are given some prominence. The above order condition for η_r may be found, *mutatis mutandis*, in Pigou (1941, p. 68).

21 Compare Kaldor (1983a, p. 17), however, who attributes the 'Pigou amendment' of modifying marginal productivity according to market conditions to passages in the *Theory of Unemployment*; see p. 394.

22 See, in this context, his correspondence with H. Townshend, as published in JMK, XXIX, pp. 239–47.

23 In this formulation it is assumed that the wage unit is constant. Otherwise future values in terms of future wage units would have to be weighted by a rate of appreciation of wages, defined by $1 + a_w \equiv w^f/w$.

24 The Keynesian model underlying this supposition will be discussed further in the excursus to ch. 14 below. We will modify the notation there slightly, however, by decomposing the present elasticities ι into separate utility components γ and τ. We will also discuss the question of the authenticity of such an approach in that later context.

25 An alternative development of this expression could start from the observation that the α_r denote labour's share in the value of output Z_{wr}. Non-labour income in each sector is then $(1 - \alpha_r)Z_{wr}$ and the sum of these expression over the sectors gives total non-wage income Y_{wk} as stated in equ. (11.32).

26 For the Keynesian version of this line see equ. (11.35).

27 Keynes (1936, p. 20), italics added, GMA.

28 Algebraically, the quote just given means that when N are wage payments in terms of the wage unit and when Y_{wk} is the non-wage income in terms of the wage unit, then total income in a two-sector economy must be given by

$$Y_w = Y_{wk} + N = Z_{w1} + Z_{w2}$$

which is just a different arrangement of equ. (11.32) above.

12. Assessing the Classical Reconstruction

1 Actually, this employment-theoretical case is also implicitly dealt with by the Cambridge supply-employment equation as given by equ. (11.20) above: if total effective demand were constant and given as $\bar{Z}_w$, then reformulating that equation gives the following exressions:

$$N = \alpha_1(\bar{Z}_w - Z_{w2}) + \alpha_2 Z_{w2} \quad \text{with} \quad \bar{Z}_w \equiv Z_{w1} + Z_{w2} \quad \text{and} \quad \frac{\partial N}{\partial Z_{w2}} \lessgtr 0 \quad \text{as} \quad \alpha_2 \lessgtr \alpha_1$$

Thus a relative decrease in the output of sector 2 as measured by Z_{w2} will lead to decreased employment N under the condition that the labour intensity of that sector as measured by α_2 is comparatively large.

Such a case was expressly mentioned by Keynes (1936, p. 286) when stressing that 'employment may fall off without there having been any change in aggregate demand, if the direction of demand is changed in favour of products having a relatively low elasticity of employment.'

But since the pre-Keynesian classics had no occasion to contemplate constant total effective demand when relative product demand is changing, it is clear that this type of argument would not be found in their writings.

2 The most detailed investigation of this problem seems to be the one by Streißler (1959). See also Green (1964).

3 The dimensions involved in this example are:

$$\frac{Z}{w} \equiv p\left[\frac{\text{money}}{\text{units of goods}}\right] \times Q\left[\frac{\text{units of goods}}{\text{time period}}\right] / w\left[\frac{\text{money}}{\text{units of labor}}\right] = Z_w\left[\frac{\text{units of labour}}{\text{time period}}\right].$$

But since employment N is nothing else but a measure of labour per time period of production, it follows from this consideration that Z_w and N are of the same dimensions.

4 It should be noted that similar to Keynes' relating employment N to effective demand $Z_w = Z/w$, Pigou (1933, pp. 21ff.) set up a relationship $E = F/w$ where E is his employment variable in that context and F is a 'flow of wage-good units', his w being the real wage. It is true that Pigou treats these relationships as mere 'arithmetic of employment'. Nevertheless, we find here a further correspondence between the Keynesian wage-units analysis and the Pigovian theory of employment in that sense that it was really Pigou who set the precedent of normalising a value of output by the wage rate.

5 These expressions follow from the standard comparative static manipulations of (12.7), $|D|$ being the value of the determinant of the matrix of coefficients on the left-hand side of (12.7). In particular, in (12.8) we have, e.g.

$$|D| = (1-\theta)\frac{\mu_2}{\mu_1}(1-\frac{\mu_1}{\alpha_1}) < 0 \; ; \; D_{12} = -\frac{\mu_1\mu_2}{\alpha_1\alpha_2} = D_{22} < 0 \text{ etc.}$$

It will be seen below that the ratios D_{11}/D_{31} and D_{21}/D_{31} will be of particular interest (see equs. (12.9) and (12.10)).

6 It seems that again the Cambridge Keynesians themselves might have played a certain role in cultivating such views. We learn from the recent inquiry by Young (1987, pp. 28f.) that: 'in Keynes's *General Theory* system ... according to Kahn and Robinson ... investment is determined independently ... given investment, income and consumption are determined accordingly.' The author thus is led to believe that interpretations such as the early ones by Harrod and Hicks, which were 'characterised by interdependencies and simultaneous relations' are 'diametrically opposed to Keynes'.

7 See the discussion in ch. 9 above, in particular the one of the formulations of equs. (9.11) and (9.22) where the underlying structural relationships of the $\varphi(x)$-function were presented in considerable detail.

8 For an alternative reconstruction of the 'Marshallian core' of Keynesian economics see Parrinello (1989).

14. The Problematic Unfolding of the Keynes–Pigou Debate

1 In his review, Pigou (1936, pp. 127f.) does have a section on 'Money and Real Wage Rates' in which he deals with the main part of ch. 19, *General Theory*. But he finds himself in agreement with Keynes' 'conclusion, as distinct from his analysis'. Concerning the latter he does not go into details but he stresses the role of banking policy which Keynes is accused of not having taken account of. In this context Pigou seems to be unawares of Keynes' (1936, p. 266) statement that '[i]f the quantity of money is itself a function of the wage- and price-level, there is indeed, nothing to hope in this direction', namely an increase in employment due to a reduction in the general level of money wages. In fact, banking policy is given great importance in that context. It is Keynes' (1936, p. 267) main conclusion concerning a policy of flexible money wages that with such a policy 'we should, in effect, have a monetary management by the trade unions ... instead of by the banking system'.

2 Letter of Keynes to Pigou, 3 January 1938, JMK, XIV, p. 267.

3 Cf. a letter of R. F. Kahn to J. M. Keynes, 19 December 1937 (JMK, XIV, p. 266): Pigou's (1937) 'article was not intended as an attack an you ... "Recent writers" ... means Joan [Robinson (1936, 1937a)]'. But Joan Robinson herself did not quite know what to make of Pigou (1937), commenting privately to Keynes: 'He is so far gone ... that you have to rationalise him to some extent to find a coherent error' (JMK, XIV, pp. 239f.).

4 This nickname was given to Kahn by James Meade describing his role in 1930–1 as middleman between Keynes and the 'circus': 'Kahn was the Messenger Angel who brought messages and problems from Keynes to the "Circus" and who went back to Heaven with the results of our deliberations' (JMK, XIII, p. 339).

15. Basic Issues and Pigou's Rejoinders

1 Since the reader of Pigou (1933) can get easily entangled in the quagmire of its constantly changing definitions, we refer back to the definition of E_r as given by

Pigou (1933, p. 90, equ. ii) and which was discussed above in the context of equ. (9.4) on p. 59. If now E_m were defined correspondingly, we would have

(*i*) $E_r \equiv E_x^{\phi(x)} : E_x^{F'(x)}$; (*ii*) $E_m \equiv E_x^{\phi(x)} : E_x^w$ resp. (*iii*) $E_m \equiv E_r(E_x^{F'(x)} : E_x^w)$

where the not slanted 'E' is, as before, the elasticity operator and where w in the elasticities explaining E_m is the money wage rate. It is just the analogue to the real wage rate in E_r as represented here in equ. (*i*) by $F'(x)$. Note that (*iii*) is a reformulation of (*ii*) which follows after $E_{(x)}^{\varphi x}$ in (*ii*) is substituted by the expression which follows from (*i*) after solving that expression for this elasticity.

  This second version of E_m is given here in this form because Pigou (1933, p. 103) engages in similar reformulations of E_m in terms of E_r and x. But although he refers back to his former definition of E_r which was in terms of *sectoral* employment and *sectoral* production, he now defines x and $F(x)$ as *total* employment and *total* production and treats these symbols as being replaceable by the former expression – which, of course, they are not. We must leave it to the 'interested reader', however, to sort out the resulting muddle, since for reasons discussed in the text we refrain from giving here the same intensive discussion of Pigou's E_m as the one we gave to his E_r in part II above.

2 Again we have the problem of Pigovian notation discussed in the previous foot-note: in the original function, Pigou (1933, p. 102) gives the argument as x, but now x is not what it was supposed to be a few pages before, namely sectoral employment but it is now total employment in the sense of n of part II above. We therefore tacitly modified the notation accordingly.

3 See the quote from Pigou (1933, p. 101) on p. 166.

4 Laidler (1999, pp. 165f) identifies 'two extremes' of monetary analysis in Pigou (1933, pt. II, ch. x). One is a closed economy in which monetary policy assured a constant money income at times of falling wages Pigou, 1933, p. 104, §6). Thus $w \downarrow \rightarrow p \downarrow$ and $\bar{Y} = (p \downarrow) (Q \uparrow) \rightarrow N \uparrow$. Interest sensitive reactions to money demand were given 'but fleeting attention' (Laidler, 1999, p. 166). In the – according to Pigou (1933, pp. 104–5) – most likely variant net money market result would be that, E_m may *cet. par.* 'be substantially larger' in this case than 'on the hypothesis of §6', just discussed. The other extreme is a small open country on the gold standard in a gold standard world. Due to a constant price level, money wage cuts would imply real wage cuts with obviously beneficial consequences for employment. Similar results would also follow for a large open economy like Britain.

5 Pigou here seems to be aware of the existence of an *LM*-curve of later standard Keynesian models. But he fails to relate the changes in the real rate of interest to effective demand, i.e. he seems not to realise that in such a context he must also contemplate the shape and the position of a corresponding *IS*-curve before anything definite could be said about the real rate of interest and employment.

6 Cf. Pigou (1936, p. 128): 'Contrary to Mr. Keynes' view, the improved employ-ment seems likely to be associated, ultimately at all events, if not at the begin-ning, with an increased, rather than with a reduced, money rate of interest.'

7 Thus Pigou wrote to Keynes (see JMK, XIV, p. 257) that he rewrote the original manuscript of his 1937 article, cutting out much what he had to say about the rate of interest 'because it touched on your stuff and, while you were ill, I didn't want to write anything that might seduce you out of the cow-life which you ought to be ... leading'. And in the same vein he wrote again (JMK, XIV, p. 266)

after Keynes (1937b) published his note on Pigou (1937): 'I have said nothing about your note because, to tell the truth, I don't understand it and also I'm sure that you ought not be dragged into economic discussions while you're unfit' (emphasis added, GMA).

8   In reply to the latter remark quoted in the last note, Keynes teasingly claimed that in fact Pigou (1938) accepted all of Keynes' contentions, 'And to be told that would have done my health no harm' (JMK, XIV, p. 267). Concerning the other communication quoted in the preceding footnote, Keynes did not accept the offer to regard Pigou's (1937) article as not touching on Keynes' 'stuff' and to refrain from publishing a note of his own in reply: 'So far as health goes, it is for me certainly much better that I should get my short note off my chest' (JMK, XIV, p. 257).

9   The famous 'Cambridge Controversies' in the theory of capital of the 1960s have no relevance in this context because they were not conducted with reference to an economic analysis of 'historical time'. But such an analysis was really a major intention of Keynes' as Joan Robinson was to observe late in her life.

10   See JMK, XIV, p. 99, n. 2 for Robertson's quote of this criticism of Pigou's.

11   For a fuller quote of Joan Robinson's account of Richard Kahn's role in these debates see the middle of p. 248.

12   See the quote from Joan Robinson at the top of p. 248.

13   See n. 3 above.

14   See note 2 to Chapter 18 and the associated quote in the text on p. 244.

15   For a relevant quote see below, p. 270.

16   For detailed accounts see the articles by Harcourt (1994) and Marcuzzo (2002). The latter author sees 'an apparently paradoxical "inversion" of roles: it was the pupil [Kahn] who intervened to correct'. It is true that Keynes did listen to Kahn, as documented by the next two quotes in the text. But as the episode here under discussion shows, Kahn is *not* correct in denying the relevance of time-preference in Pigou's set-up – and Keynes is aware of this. In general, it is strange that if Kahn really did play a substantial role in shaping Keynes' ideas that he never assisted him openly in the Keynes-and-Pigou debate.

17   See Marcuzzo (1996) for details.

18   For an assessment of some 'Saturnalian jokes' made by Keynes to this extent see below note 6 to Chapter 18

19   Indeed, there seems to be no other published statement from Keynes' entourage which is so outspoken about Keynes' supposed 'failure' to see the point of his revolution. If the argument of the following excursus is correct, this appears as a rather gross misunderstanding on the Young Keynesians' part. Since Kahn's position is part of their *modus vivendi* with Pigovian long-period analysis this would be a misunderstanding of grave analytical consequences for the post-Keynesian Cambridge research agenda.

20   See, e.g. Grossman (1972, p. 28): 'Keynes' specification of the consumption function was simply *ad hoc*, and no passage in the *General Theory* explicitly avers otherwise.' The following quote on the bottom of the current page of the text (p. 179) states clearly, however, that in Keynes' view the determination of consumption in the context of the *General Theory* is derived from individual decisions determined by preferences under the assumption of given income, wealth, and prices. If this analysis is 'ad hoc' in the judgement of Grossman (1972), then any microeconomics textbook analysis which derives a demand function from individual preferences and from given income and prices is likewise 'ad hoc'. One may define 'ad hoc' in several ways, of course, but if one *defines* Keynes' argumentation as being 'ad hoc', then any microeconomic textbook analysis

referring to 'givens', to preferences, and constraints is likewise 'ad hoc'. This is a view which the present author cannot share.

21 That depends, of course, on the exegetical standard of the critic. Grossman (1972, *ibid.*), for example, concludes that just *because* of his *ad hoc*-ery, Keynes would not have 'disavowed attempts to fit his analysis into the general market-clearing framework of the classical paradigm'. But this is a *non sequitur*. Time preference analysis in Keynes' express understanding is an important tool for *criticising* the 'classical paradigm', as will be seen below: the time preference theoretic explication of the consumption function shows that the 'classical paradigm' of time preference determined interest rates is a highly special and unrealistic sub-case of the Keynesian consumption function (see pp. 198f). Therefore Keynes would *not* have been prepared to let his theory be 'fit' into the classical paradigm. It is just the other way round: classical theory fits into Keynes' theory – under very unrealistic conditions. But Keynes was aware of this and this might well have been a good reason why he called his theory the *General Theory*.

22 Keynes' further discussion of this matter may be summarised in more modern parlance as follows: he stresses that the resulting relationships of the individual thought experiments can give only structural equations, the independent variables of which – in particular current income – prove to be really endogenous to the model when it is discussed on the macroeconomic resolution level.

23 A similar type of formulation of intertemporal utility may be found in the textbook of Barro (1990, p. 81) where labour time is used as an additional argument.

24 See Henderson and Quandt (1958, p. 235) for such a definition of 'rates of time preference'.

25 Expression (15.12) might appear to be counterintuitive: why should a *higher* value of the sum of 'time elasticities of utility of consumption' lead to a *lower* rate of discounting the future? If this question should pose a problem, resort to the definition of ρ in terms of relative marginal utilities given in the text and note that in the present case we have

$$U_0' = \gamma(U / Q_{c0}) \quad ; \quad U_1' = \gamma\tau_1(U / Q_{c1}) \quad ; etc. \text{ with } Q_{c0} = Q_{c1} \quad etc.$$

for a stationary state. Therefore, if *e.g.* τ_1 *increased*, then $1 + \rho \equiv U_0'/U_1' = 1/\tau_1$ necessarily *decreased*. Thus, the impatience to consume 'now' rather than 'later' has declined in this case – and this is expressed by lowering ρ.

26 The budget equations (15.1) and (15.2) are brought into this form when they are solved for S and then rearranged accordingly.

27 For an elementary algebraic formulation of household equilibrium see below, equs. (15.19) and (15.20) to (15.22).

28 The following list is adapted from a former publication of the author (see Ambrosi, 1979b).

29 In his distinction between 'indirect' and 'direct' effects of interest rate changes, Keynes makes a distinction between a 'wealth effect' and another type of effect which we will investigate in more detail in the next section of this excursus. In the context mentioned under (iv) of our list it is then said that the 'wealth effect' of higher interest rates on present consumption is negative, whereas under point (v) it is said that the residual effect is negligible. Equation (15.16) as originally formulated reproduces the former result. The introduction into that formulation of M as a form of wealth which does not vary in its present value then reproduces the latter result.

30 A number of the following arguments may be found in somewhat different expositions in earlier publications of the author; see Ambrosi (1979b, 1980b).
31 Cf. Henderson and Quandt (1958), p. 25, equ. (2–32) and p. 29, equ. (2–36).
32 This result is reached by substituting $\lambda/(1 + r)$ via the first-order condition (15.21) and by substituting D by evaluating this cofactor of the Jacobian given in (15.23).
33 Make a monotonous transformation of utility U to $\tilde{U} = 1nU$. Since monotonous transformations of utility do not affect household equilibria, we now consider $\tilde{U}$ as supplying the extreme value conditions. But $\tilde{U}$ may be expressed by equation (15.6) on p. 181 so that its derivatives are given by:

(i) $\tilde{U}'_1 = \gamma_1 \tau_1/Q_{c1}$
(ii) $\tilde{U}''_1 = \gamma_1 \tau_1/Q_{c1}^2$.

Dividing (i) by Q_{c1} then shows that in this case we have $\tilde{U}'/Q_{c1} = -\tilde{U}''_1$. But from (15.30) we know that then the cross-price effect must always be zero.
34 We will justify the use of this term at the end of this section.
35 That D_{31}/D in (15.32) may be replaced by $-(\partial Q_{c0}/\partial W)$ follows from solving (15.23) for the latter expression which is then seen to be equal to the former one.
36 We return to this point in Chapter 16. See also note 12 to Chapter 17.
37 It is astonishing how little such passages of Keynes' are taken account of – to this day. Thus, Laidler (1999, p. 287) relates that Viner (1936) 'did not also accept Keynes's view that other variables [than current income, GMA] were essentially irrelevant to the determination of consumption'. The passages just quoted from the *General Theory* and the underlying analysis show that this is a misrepresentation of what Keynes actually wrote. From our standpoint we must regret that Laidler did not correct such a misrepresentation.

16. Pigou's 'Simplified Model' as a Rejoinder to the Model of the 'Keynes Effect'

1 Strictly speaking, c_a must be treated as a function of the rate of interest, since in a fuller representation of c_a it follows from (15.16), p. 184 to be given by

$$\frac{a}{w} \equiv \frac{\gamma_0}{\gamma_0 + \Sigma \gamma_f \tau_f} \Sigma \left((\frac{1}{1+r})^f \frac{Y_f}{w} \right)$$

This expression may be treated as constant only under the assumption of a given rate of interest and *given* future incomes Y_f. But whereas the latter assumption is covered by Keynes' assumption of given long-term expectations, the rate of interest must be treated as a variable to be determined in the present period. Hence $c_a = c_a(r)$ with $c'_a < 0$ which is in accordance with Keynes' 'indirect' interest effect on consumption as discussed in the previous chapter.
2 It should be noted that for the central result of a falling *IS*-curve the question whether $c'_a(r)$ is zero or negative is not of major importance.
3 We might notice here that occasionally the view of the Keynesian model emerging from such observations was one of a strictly hierarchical structure. Or, as Young (1987, p. 28) recently put it:

In Keynes's *General Theory* system, ... according to Kahn and Robinson, interest is determined independently ...; given interest, investment is determined independently ...; given investment, income and consumption are determined accordingly.

But it should be realised that in fact the money market equation is not independent of investment, income, and employment. Since it depends on total liquidity preference and since liquidity preference in turn incorporates transactions demand for money, it must be clear that any change in income necessarily must feed back to the money market – and hence to the rate of interest. Thus Keynes' *authentic* structure is not hierarchical but interdependent.

4   We do not claim any originality for the construction of the *LIS*-curve in that figure. Long ago, a graphical representation along the lines of equ. (16.5) was proposed in the Keynesian literature by Lerner (1951, p. 265). But his proposal subsequently fell into oblivion – maybe in part because of an unappreciative reception by Alvin Hansen (1953, p. 149) in what later became a canonisation of the orthodox *IS–LM* approach.

5   Pointing this out seems not trivial in view of contrary statements by Kahn (see n. 3 to Chapter 14) and in view of Pigou's own contention that out of consideration for Keynes's ill health he cut out things which touched on Keynes' 'stuff' (see n. 8 to Chapter 15).

6   Pigou (1937) uses the symbol x in this context. But since, following Pigou (1933), x was used for sectoral employment in part II above, we use the same symbol for total employment as before.

7   Keynes himself anticipated such a transition from the wage unit to a more general 'cost unit' in the *General Theory* (p. 302). He proposed that such a generalised wage unit may be regarded as 'the essential standard of value'.

8   It could be also argued, however, that in fact the *IS*-curve expresses primarily the co-ordination on the bonds market. Since savings are really an abstention from specific demand for goods and since the interest-dependent investment decisions are a manifestation of demand for finance and again not a demand for specific goods, there is indeed some plausibility in such a view. It would carry us too far, however, to attempt to clarify this issue in the present context.

9   The monetary aspect of this representation will be enlarged upon in the final section of this chapter.

17. The Kaldorian Synthesis of Keynes and Pigou

1   Cf. Collard (1981, p. 129): 'By far the most useful and constructive contribution during this whole interchange, both in correspondence and in print, was Kaldor's.'

2   There is some indirect evidence that doubts concerning Pigou's analytical approach must have been put to Kaldor. At least, he may be documented to negate such doubts, stating that 'I don't think there can be any doubt as to what his [Pigou's] assumptions were' (letter of Kaldor to D. H. Robertson, 23 October 1937, as quoted by Young (1987, p. 111).

3   Kaldor is aware that his 'supply trap' is only a sufficient condition for a breakdown of the Pigovian argumentation. Employment would also be unresponsive to money wage changes if $-\rho'(n) \to \infty$. But in this case there is no determinate rate of time preference and 'Professor Pigou's demonstration formally breaks down' (Kaldor, 1937, p. 750).

4   This passage is also significant for the debate whether Keynes would have rejected the idea of an *IS*-curve altogether on the grounds that there is no such stable relationship between the rate of interest and real income which this curve suggests to exist. The following passage suggests that Keynes firmly believed in the existence of such a relationship. There is, however, the question on which analytical basis such a curve should be put.

5   Documented is a letter of Robertson to Keynes of 17 October 1937 in which Robertson declares: 'Kaldor, in my view, underestimates (p. 8 [probably Kaldor (1937, p. 746, n. 2), GMA]) the difference made to the situation by the removal of the [Pigovian] assumption of nil investment.' See JMK, XIV, p. 254.

6   It is astonishing that even in a monograph about the history of *IS–LM*, Kaldor does not get credit for this. We read in Young (1987, p. 6) that 'Real income appears on the horizontal axis [of the *IS–LM* diagram] only after Lange (1938), Timlin (1942) and Modigliani (1944).' Contrary to this statement, Kaldor (1937, p. 752, n. 2) draws this diagram and declares that in his application 'the curve *IS*- ... shows the various levels of real output at which savings are equal to investment, at different rates of interest'. Since real output is equal to real income, Kaldor clearly should be first in the list of those who modified the nominal scheme of Hicks to a real one.

7   It is quite ironic that Joan Robinson (1954b, p. 73, reprint, p. 7), when mentioning Keynes' money wage theory, refers the reader for elaborations of it to Hicks (1937) and to Pigou (1937) and never mentions Kaldor (1937). But from our discussion of this topic it should be clear by now that Hicks' original scheme was analytically incapable of producing the 'Keynes effect' and that Pigou's advocacy of money wage changes in a stationary economy relied on a classical alternative to Keynes – and not on an elaboration of Keynes' analysis.

8   In a later part of his book Young (1987, p. 107) does acknowledge, however, that in his critical assessment of Pigou (1937), Kaldor (1937) 'was among the earliest, if not the first, to apply the *IS–LM* approach'.

9   We include this consideration here because this touches upon the most problematic aspect of Young's (1987, pp. 8f.) treatment of the *General Theory*: he (correctly) notes that the rate of interest is determined there by the interplay of liquidity preference with the quantity of money. But he incorrectly infers from this that the rate of interest is determined *independently* in this context, not noting that changes in output, cost units and prices occurring outside the money market proper necessarily have a repercussion on liquidity preference. Consequently his view of 'causally structured relations' cannot be the essential difference between Keynes, Harrod and Hicks etc.

10 In this context we refer the reader back to equ. (15.38) (p. 199) where this condition was derived as a limiting case of Keynes' consumption function. It will be remembered that on p. 178 Keynes *defended* Kaldor's and Pigou's articles against Kahn on this very ground that if they explicitly base their analysis on this special case, they cannot be criticised for the logical implications of this very case. Indeed it would be unsound reasoning *not* to work with the implication of time preference determined interest rates.

11 But this classical case is a limiting case of Keynes' consumption function as was seen in the context quoted in the preceding footnote.

12 It should be remembered that Barro (1990) is quite clear that he has to *assume* by postulate that the wealth effects of interest changes are zero. This means that he assumes savings to be zero, as was shown above, p. 191. This in turn means that Barro is a true 'Classic' in the just quoted sense of Keynes. For Pigou's own endorsement of the zero-savings condition, see our quote above, p. 210, where

Pigou refers the reader to Ramsey (1928) – an article which expressly acknowledges Keynes' co-operation in this type of analysis and thus draws Keynes also into the circle of well-initiated time-preference analysts.

18. The Unresolved Conflict

1 See the quote from Richard Kahn in note 3 to Chapter 14 in which Kahn communicated to Keynes that Pigou stated that his original article was not intended to be an attack on Keynes but rather one on Joan Robinson (1937a). Although Kahn continues in that context that Pigou probably had not read her book, he does not state disbelief in the statement.
2 Letter to J. M. Keynes from R. F. Kahn, 22 October 1937, JMK, XIV, p. 260.
3 See a letter to this extent from Pigou to Keynes of 23 December 1937 (JMK, XIV, p. 266). See also Pigou's (1938, p. 134, n. 1) published rejoinder where he declares: 'I have not been able to follow the reasoning of Mr. Keynes' [(1937b)] short note.'
4 For a fuller quote see above, p. 176.
5 For a relevant juxtaposition see above, table 15.1 on p. 172.
6 Keynes' Saturnalian jokes with and about his disciples to the extent that it was not *him* discussing *his* economic agenda with them but *they* – in particular his 'favourite pupil' Richard Kahn – who 'supervised' *him* were sometimes taken at face value by later readers. For a case in point and for relevant quotes see the interesting article by Maria Marcuzzo (2002) who unfortunately, however, does not consider the material discussed in the present context. What is said here is, of course, not meant to imply that Kahn was *not* 'a marvellous critic and suggester and improver' as Keynes (JMK, XIII, p. 422) wrote and Marcuzzo (2002, p. 442) quotes. But how much Keynes was left alone with his agenda becomes clear when one inspects the vain promise from R. F. Kahn here under discussion.
7 See ch. 14 above for elaborations of this, in particular pp. 163f.
8 See above, p. 170 and table 15.1, p. 172. From that table it appears immediately that Keynes' set-up was an *anomaly*, indeed, while Joan Robinson's (1936, 1937a) essays were 'normal' with regard to the stationary state approach.
9 Keynes' complaint to Harrod about 'the young ones who have not been properly brought up' (JMK, XIV, p. 85, see also below note 2 to Chapter 20) referred to economic thinking and not to himself having been at Eton or Pigou having been at Harrow.
10 One could argue that Keynes should have reacted in the same way to Pigou (1936) already but that review of the *General Theory* was so ill-humoured and superficial that it was later considered as ill-conceived even by Pigou himself. Maybe to some observers that initial non-reaction seemed to be an act of 'snobbery' committed by Keynes but it certainly was not done because Pigou did not go to a 'good school'.
11 See Kahn's letter to Keynes, above, p. 176: 'I am still opposed to your printing ...'
12 Cf. Joan Robinson (1969, p. 124) for another of several articulations of this supposed deficiency:

> Keynes' theory was deliberately confined to the short-period situation, here and now. (He used to say: the long period is a subject for undergraduates.) But when the mechanisms of the short-period was understood ... long-period

theory had to be discussed. The question was opened up by Harrod. Harrod projected Keynes theory into the long period.

Thus, Harrod as another of Keynes' disciples is also implicated in this programme. But the first attempt at a long-period extension of Keynes clearly was by Joan Robinson (1936, 1937a) herself. See also the preceding sub-section in this context.

13 Joan Robinson (1951, p. viii) herself occasionally articulated her one-time Pigovian orientation:

> Professor Pigou had ... worked the hard core of Marshall's analysis into a logical system of static theory ... Instead of abandoning the static analysis ... I followed Pigou and worked out the *Economics of Imperfect Competition* on static assumptions.

Joan Robinson's (1937a) extension of Keynesian ideas into a Pigovian stationary state context suggests that Pigou's influence on her lasted longer than she states in this quote.

14 For an algebraic rendering of this argument turn to the excursus in ch. 15. From equ. (15.12), p. 183, it emerges that for the rate of discounting the future (satisfaction) to be negative, $\Sigma\tau_f$ must be negative. But when the τ-s are sufficiently negative, it follows from the Keynesian consumption function (15.16) that the marginal propensity to consume as given by $b = \gamma_0/(\gamma_0 + \Sigma\gamma_f\tau_f)$ will be *larger* than unity since the denominator becomes smaller than the numerator. Thus, Joan Robinson's critique of Pigou is based on a *reductio ad absurdum* of none other than *Keynes*. (See also the alternative discussion of this point on p. 365.)

15 Cf. the observation made by Frank Hahn (1989, p. 898) that Joan Robinson's (1956) *magnum opus* on The Accumulation of Capital 'is about golden ages. The dynamics these people had, from Harrod onwards, are pseudo stationary states.'

16 Cf. Robinson (1956, p. 404), 'Our analysis of accumulation in the long run is largely an elaboration of R. F. Harrod's model, yet we have never come across his central ['knife-edge'] problem.'

17 See Harcourt (1972).

18 This is noteworthy also when searching for alternatives to the explanations for the lack of discussions of the Young Keynesians with Pigou given in the last section. One such alternative explanation could point to the bad health suffered not only by Keynes, but by Pigou as well in 1937. But as already noted, Keynes himself did not think much of such arguments as far as discussions with him were concerned. With regard to Pigou and in view of his many returns to this debate one may observe: it certainly should have been possible for eager commentators to find time for commenting on him in a period in which he was sufficiently fit.

19 Cf. Samuelson (1946, p. 188, n. 2): 'For a striking example of the effect of the Keynesian analysis upon a great classical thinker, compare the fructiferous recent writings of Professor Pigou with his earlier *Theory of Unemployment*.'

20 See the relevant section in Leijonhufvud (1968, pp. 315ff.) on the subject of 'The "Keynes effect" and the "Pigou effect" '. His presentation is maybe coloured by Leijonhufvud (1968, p. 342, n. 15) having a preoccupation with the erroneous 'predominance of the one-commodity model in this area'. But Leijonhufvud's treatment seems to be indeed indicative for a general trend in the literature: Patinkin (1965, p. 51n.) already admitted that in previous discussions of Pigou-type real balance effects he had forgotten about a distinction of short-run and long-run equilibria.

21 See Collard (1981, p. 137, n. 75), where the authenticity of the anecdote is said to have been confirmed by Kahn.
22 Cf. Schumpeter (1954, p. 966) who, referring to 'Marshall, who spoke of the "famous fiction of the 'Stationary state' " ', continued in a footnote: 'The crowning achievement in this line of analysis is, of course, Professor Pigou's *The Economics of Stationary States* (1935)'. It should be clear that the works of Pigou here discussed are variants in this self-same paradigmatic set-up.

19. The Evaporation of Keynes' Analytical Aspiration

1 In this context the reader is reminded of Kaldor's dictum that 'Pigou admitted that he was wrong and Keynes was right' after Kaldor's 1937 paper. For the fuller relevant quote from Young (1987, p. 109) see above, p. 226.
2 Cf. Young (1987, p. 115): 'Kaldor was asked [in the middle of the 1980s] whether he agreed with Kahn's attack on *IS–LM* in the making of Keynes' *General Theory* (1984), i.e. that *IS–LM* had done more harm than good and had confused the development of economic thought. Kaldor replied "Why? Does he explain it ... No. I would not agree that it has done more harm than good." '
3 Being asked by Feiwel whether he saw a difference between the 'short run' in the modern Walrasian sense and the usual Marshallian textbook-type concept, Arrow (1989, pp. 151f.) declared:

> I would say not that there is a contradiction between the Marshallian and Walrasian point of view, but that the Walrasian is essentially a little clearer and a more carefully worked out statement of the Marshallian position ... I believe it is correct to say that looking at the Walrasian equilibrium as of a moment of time, then it is in effect like a short-run equilibrium in the Marshallian sense.

The crucial question is, however, not so much whether there is a difference between the Marshallian and the Walrasian short run, but whether there is one between Keynes and Pigou concerning the conception of short-period analysis.

20. Problems and Methods

1 Cf. Robinson (1978, repr. p. 210): 'To me, the expression *post-Keynesian* has a definite meaning: it applies to an economic theory or method of analysis which takes account of the difference between the future and the past.' She believed in that context that there was a significant difference in this regard between (Piero Sraffa-oriented) Ricardian and Pigovian analysis: 'Keynes was right in showing that Ricardo was blind to the nature of effective demand but it was not right to throw him into the same box as Pigou in timeless equilibrium' (Robinson, 1978, repr. p. 213). This latter judgement is contestable. She herself had 'second thoughts' about Sraffa, her 'interpreter' in Ricardian matters as was seen above, p. 263. But the following refers to a time when the Sraffian reception of Ricardo was not yet an issue.
2 Letter to R. F. Harrod, 30 August 1936, JMK, XIV, p. 85. It certainly would be a gross misunderstanding of context and intention if one was to conclude from such a passage: 'If you had not been to a good school he [Keynes] cut you' – a

claim made by Joan Robinson (1973e) in the context of her account of the Keynes–Classics debate (see above, p. 248).

3 Letter to A. C. Pigou, 15 June 1939, JMK, XIV, p. 320.

4 Cf. Robinson (1973e, p. 253): 'When you turn the General Theory in the long period you have to start with Marx's schema for expanded reproduction ... Mr. Harrod [1939] ... set out the model under a weird and wonderful name, "the warranted rate of growth on national income".'

5 See in this connection, p. 361, for a quote concerning R. F. Kahn's intellectual influence on Joan Robinson. See above, p. 248 for Joan Robinson's testimony that it was Richard Kahn who, since the early 1930s, tried to translate Keynesian ideas into a model of 'Simple Reproduction'.

6 The other two in his list were: (*i*) the review of the *General Theory* by Hicks (1936) in so far as it foreshadowed the 'temporary equilibrium approach' later contained in *Value and Capital* (Hicks, 1939) and (*ii*) *Expectations, Investment, and Income* by Shackle (1938).

7 It is quite astonishing that Laidler (1999) never refers to Joan Robinson's *Essays in the Theory of Employment* (1937a). Laidler (1999, p. 306) does quote her, namely Robinson (1937b) and utters his conviction 'that her 1937 account was also cast in essentially IS–LM terms'. But this conviction is in no way substantiated. In the foreword, Joan Robinson (1937b, p. xvii, 2nd ed.) expressly mentions that this 'simplified account' is *not* meant 'to address my colleagues'. It can therefore hardly be taken to represent academic debate. She never mentions any of the authors who can be considered as originators of the *IS–LM* apparatus. As her sources Joan Robinson (1937b, p. xvii, 2nd ed.) mentions Colin Clark (1937) and Michal Kalecki (1937) – and in particular her own *Essays in the Theory of Employment* (1937a). Therefore it is *this* book which should be of prime interest when it comes to consider the role which Joan Robinson played in *Fabricating the Keynesian Revolution* – which is, after all the title of Laidler (1999).

8 Although Joan Robinson never went into the details of wage units analysis, she repeatedly accepted it as unproblematic; e.g. Robinson (1954c, p. 38, reprint p. 84): 'All costs can be reckoned in terms of wage units.'

9 The topic of wage units merits more intensive treatment than we have space for in the present context.

10 In a similar vein, Bliss (1990, p. 239) also remarked: 'Though Joan Robinson was deeply influenced by Marshall, she did not like to be reminded of the fact ... One [of the two wings of the later Cambridge anti-Neoclassical school, GMA], inspired by Joan Robinson, fought the Marshallians, to a great extent with their own weapons.'

21. The Structure of the Robinsonian Model

1 Cf. Weintraub (1973, p. 39): 'Taking only mild liberties with Keynes, his theory of the price level can be specified in a simple formula involving a wage-cost markup (WCM) relation.' Weintraub then continues by presenting a price equation like the one given here as equ. (21.16), assuming the mark-up factor i.e. our α_i) to be constant.

2 If $\alpha_i \equiv \dfrac{\partial Q_i}{\partial N_i} \dfrac{N_i}{Q_i}$ holds, it is clear that multiplying α_i by A_i^η as defined in 21.16 leads to the result stated in the text.

22. Microfoundations of the Robinsonian Model

1 For a post-Keynesian discussion of entrepreneurial behaviour see, in particular, the book by Eichner (1976).
2 It is by no means just implicit in her model. In fact, she is occasionally very explicit about her analytical use of this concept. Cf. her discussion in this essay of the consequences of an increase in the quantity of capital (*op. cit.*, p. 82): 'The *marginal physical productivity of capital* will be reduced and of labour increased, and the rate of real wages increased' (italics added, GMA).
3 For a discussion of an expression like (22.5) see Ambrosi (1980b), in particular p. 189.
4 It seems that Joan Robinson took this quote a bit out of its original context, however. Actually, Champernowne (1935, p. 225) stated that 'In the absence of further information ... *the most plausible estimate of elasticity of substitution is unity*' (emphasis added, GMA). And his discussion referred to a single industry whereas Joan Robinson referred to the elasticity of substitution of 'the total output' O of an entire economy.
5 The author seems to consider the changeability of the stock of capital in a long-period setting to be a 'generalisation' of the analysis of the *General Theory*. It must be remembered, however, that in a long-period setting comparisons can be only between alternative equilibria, i.e. between alternative economies which have been going on along their specific conditions – including their specific outfit with capital equipment – for such a long time that adjustment processes have subsided. To be asked to consider this type of analysis as a *generalisation* of the *General Theory* appears to be rather idiosyncratic and unacceptable from Keynes' own standpoint.
6 We will see below that making ρ dependent on income will not alter the negative judgement just passed.
7 For a fuller discussion of the time structure in the *General Theory* see Chick (1983, fig. 21, pp. 18–19) and Amadeo (1989). We differ here not from the latter's taxonomy of time periods as given in his chapter 2. But we do differ from his assertions that Keynes' concepts of liquidity preference, multiplier etc. are not affected by 'the' extension to the long period (see above, p. 294).
8 For relevant quotes see above, p. 170 and for Marshall's anterior 'seconding' see note 1 for Chapter 6, on p. 435.
9 The peculiar situation of that correspondence is that the self-same assumptions which are so critical for evaluating Pigou (1937) are also the basis of Joan Robinson's (1936) essay published a year earlier. This seems to be the fundamental dilemma: either reject both articles as being based on the same nonsensical 'frozen land' assumptions or reject the logical conclusions which Keynes pointed out. Since Kahn and Joan Robinson chose the latter, that was really the end of the rational critical discourse with Pigou. This is by no means what Keynes himself intended.
10 See above, p. 302.
11 For the relevant quote see p. 373 of this book.
12 See above, the excursus on time preference, sect. 15.4, pp. 179ff.

23. The Workings of the Robinsonian Model

1 See above, equ. (22.27), p. 306.
2 Compare Joan Robinson (1937a, p. 83): 'But it is by no means necessary that a fall in the rate of interest should have a favourable effect upon the share of labour in

total income'. In this context the elasticity of substitution is of vital importance for Joan Robinson whereas we assumed it to be equal to unity throughout our analysis. Thus, for quite different reasons we reached a similarly indeterminate correlation between the interest rate and distribution.

3 See below for a fuller quote of this passage.
4 Here Joan Robinson refers to Champernowne (1935, p. 255), a reference discussed above already (see note 4 to Chapter 22).
5 Cf. King (1996, p. 173) who quotes Joan Robinson's statement (1937a, p. 91), 'there will be a limited range of values over which a rise in the rate of interest will increase employment' [etc.] and adding: 'As so often true of Robinson's insights, this cries out for formal modelling. Unfortunately, she offers only a handful of discursive footnotes.'

24. The Robinsonian Model as a Basis for the Critique of Traditional Economics

1 Joan Robinson (1979a, p. xxi) stresses that 'Sraffa makes the dichotomy between technology and distribution absolute by ... leaving the share of wages in net output ... free to be anywhere between zero and unity'. In fig. 21.1, p. 285, this would give $1 \geq \lambda' \geq 0$. Contrary to that statement we have $1 \geq \lambda' > \alpha$ with $\alpha > 0$ as the lowest value. But since in Sraffa's model the *partial* elasticity of output with respect to labour may be considered to be zero due to linear technology, his results will be seen as a special case of ours with $\alpha_1 = 0$.
2 For a textbook presentation of such a transition under a capital-theoretic perspective see Jaeger (1980).
3 For the relevant quotes see above note 3 to Chapter 14.
4 For a relevant quote from Garegnani (1979, p. 181) see above p. 323.
5 For some deeper 'reflections on Joan Robinson's changes of mind' see Harcourt (1996).

25. Paradigms of a Re-authenticated Keynes–Classics Debate

1 Some commentators claim that 'poor Pigou' was just the straw man for Keynes' invention of 'Klassical economics'. The claim of specificity for the *General Theory* is the product of a 'creation myth'. According to what might be called a 'corpse theory' it is just morsels of the 'corpse' of Pigou's writings we find in the *General Theory*, the quotes from him being 'ripped all bloody from their context', see above p. 19. Keynes could have played such wilful mischievousness on any other author of his dislike according to some voices from the school of 'Keynes–Klassics' scholars. It is ethically and analytically wrong to drag Pigou into the *General Theory* according to that type of comments.
2 The 'true' focal point of the *General Theory* is not A. C. Pigou but R. F. Kahn according to some commentators – for relevant quotes see e.g. below n. 24 to the current chapter and the associated main text which mentions what we may call the 'midwife' theory of the origin of the *General Theory*.
3 According to a 'preoccupation theory' of the genesis of the *General Theory*, Keynes' preoccupation with Pigou (1933) messed up his own substance of the *General Theory*. For this line of comments see above, n. 1 to Chapter 4. Some commentators regret the 'whipping boy' function they see in Keynes' taking recourse to Pigou – see above, p. 29.

4 This is in part implied by the 'preoccupation theory' just mentioned. Some authors see the same wage rigidity theory in Pigou and Keynes so that the latter gives just a rehash of the former.

5 For the accusation that his proximity to classical analysis made Keynes himself a 'bastard Keynesian' see above, middle of p. 170. For a less dramatic statement see middle of p. 261.

6 For the relevant quotes see Kaldor's statement on p. 383.

7 We did note, however, that Keynes thought that Hicks (1937) was 'scarcely fair to the classical view' (see above, p. 28).

8 For the relevant quote see above, p. 248.

9 Hutchison (1977, p. 23 n.1) quotes Jacob Viner's account that Keynes' disciples were startled by Keynes' last (posthumously published) article and that 'there was serious consideration of the desirability of suppressing it'.

10 We return to this question below, n. 31 of this chapter.

11 Samuelson (1978, p. 1421, equ. (4*)) presents 'classical long-run equilibrium' as being defined, among other conditions, by $F'(V^*) = \bar{w}^* + \bar{r}^*$ where $F'(\cdot)$ is the marginal product of the equilibrium 'dose' of capital and labour, $\bar{w}^*$ is the equilibrium subsistence wage rate and $\bar{r}^*$ is the equilibrium value of 'both the own rate of interest and the real rental rate of capital goods expressed in output units' (*ibid.*). Thus, in Samuelson (1978) as in Pigou (1937) the marginal product covers not just the real wage rate but the real interest rate as well.

12 In essence, Kaldor introduces into his interpretation of Pigou (1937) an argument formulated by none other than Pigou (1935, pp. 171f.) himself who stated: 'I suggest that, when incomes are very low, people's minds are of necessity so concentrated on the urgencies of the present moment that the ... rate of discounting future satisfactions is likely to be high.'

13 This issue is pursued further in Ambrosi (2001).

14 See e.g. n. 22 to Chapter 11.

15 For an interesting description of Keynes' Cambridge colleagues, in particular of Dennis Robertson ('reader' at the Faculty of Economics and Politics) and of Gerald Shove (lecturer), see Austin Robinson (1977).

16 For Shove's replies see (JMK, XIII, pp. 321–6, JMK, XXIX, p. 33).

17 Compare also Keynes' letter to Richard Kahn about Pigou (1933) quoted above on p. 335 where he calls his writings 'the most extraordinary in some ways in the history of the subject'. The above shows that this is not meant in a pejorative sense.

18 Shove (1933) had published a detailed review of Hicks (1932), so he may be considered to have been a knowledgeable judge in this matter. Collard's quote from Shove is taken from the correspondence to which we already referred above in note 16 to this chapter.

19 See Skidelsky (1992, p. 285) for these dates.

20 See Moggridge (1992, p. 498).

21 See Moggridge (1992, p. 506): 'Robbins's revolt and Henderson's declaration in favour of wage reductions meant that the Committee was ... "in some disarray" during the preparation.'

22 See Moggridge (1992, p. 506).

23 Meeting with Pigou is mentioned by Moggridge (1992, p. 505).

24 Samuelson thereby perpetuated an old Harvard legend, the written reference to which might be found in a remark by Schumpeter (1954, p. 1172): 'we must record Keynes's acknowledgement of indebtedness ... especially to Mr. R. F. Kahn, whose share in the historic achievement cannot have fallen very far short of

co-authorship.' According to such a criterion Kahn could also count as sharing responsibility for Pigou (1935) since he was also mentioned in that preface.

25   See above, p. 343.

26   The Pigovian time preference theory of interest does *not* come in here!

27   In the published version of the *General Theory*, Keynes (*GT*, p. 263) treated the nexus between money wages and money demand much later in the development of his argumentation and then only cursorily.

28   See his statement to this effect, quoted above on pp. 123f. and in n. 15 to Chapter 11.

29   It also shows that it is not correct when Joan Robinson (1962b, p. 100) writes: 'Strange as it now seems, the question: What would be the effect upon the general level of prices of an overall revision of money-wage rates? was simply never put.' No, it *was* dealt with by Pigou (1933, p. 101), as just seen. He came up with the wrong answer but in this he was in good company. Karl Marx also came up with the wrong answer according to Joan Robinson (*ibid.*).

30   For a fuller discussion of this point see above, p. 166.

31   Maybe it is this appreciation which lies behind Keynes' comment that the *Theory of Unemployment* was 'most extraordinary in some ways in the history of the subject' – see above, p. 335.

32   Skidelsky (1992, p. 496) refers to these lecture notes when writing, in general agreement with the present assessment: 'Had they been published as delivered, the world would have got a pretty clear idea of what it later received as the *General Theory of Employment, Interest, and Money*. All that remained was tidying up.'

33   See below n. 41.

34   For an explanation of her programme see n. 1 to Chapter 20.

35   See above, p. 213, equ. (16.13).

36   See above note 3, to Chapter 14.

37   See above, p. 163.

38   See Harcourt (1979, p. 5).

39   See below, n. 41.

40   See Robinson (1933) and the preface there where she points out her contribution to (neoclassical) analysis of the elasticity of substitution.

41   In their 'tentative conclusion' Bradford and Harcourt (1997, p. 126) state that, in the end, Joan Robinson felt that the economic theory of long-period equilibrium 'had come to pieces in her hand'.

42   See, e.g., Pasinetti (2001) *vs.* Davidson (2001)

43   See above, n. 22 to Chapter 11.

44   See above, p. 241.

45   This was not palpable to the long-period 'extensionists' *à la* Joan Robinson (1936) since they wanted to believe that their endeavours, too, were of great relevance for reality. We return to this point in the next sub-section.

46   It is therefore important that Thirlwall (1987, p. 68) points out that Pigou did *not* accept Keynes' liquidity preference theory in this context. This stresses the un-Keynesian character of the 'synthesis'.

47   For Niehans' claim that Keynes' money wage mechanism was in Pigou's *Theory of Unemployment* see above, p. 27.

48   See above, p. 241.

49   See above for his correspondence with Robertson to this effect.

50   For the relevant quote see above, n. 5 to Chapter 17.

51   Especially in view of such accusations, we think that the 'Pigovian reconstruction' of Robinsonian ideas in the above part IV can be quite instructive for an

assessment of Joan Robinson's contribution to this debate. There do remain quite a number of novel points – in particular the production theoretical lack of determination of the share of wages – even if 'we' are totally neoclassical, as was argued in that context.

52 See above, p. 163. This is somewhat comical in view of the fact that there never was – then or later – any competing article on Pigou (1937) which could have been set back by Keynes' 'favouring' Kaldor.

53 See Thirlwall (1987, p. 110).

54 See Thirlwall (1987, p. 80).

55 See above, n. 2 to Chapter 19.

56 Joan Robinson in a letter to R. F. Kahn dated 28 May 1974: 'you cannot take him [Kaldor] seriously as an intellectual only as a menace', unpublished, quoted from King (1998, pp. 427–8).

57 For this figure of speaking see below, n. 63.

58 Joan Robinson's belated incantations of the importance of 'historical time' were rejected by her Sraffian colleague Pierangelo Garegnani (1979) as being unsubstantiated in her own publication (see above, sect. 24.3, p. 322).

59 See above n. 4 to Chapter 14.

60 Quoted from Skidelsky (2000, p. 77). It is interesting to note that Sraffa had this position to comment on the exams and the teaching. One might want to see this information in connection with Hahn's (1989, p. 908) observation that Sraffa was the only person Joan Robinson was afraid of.

61 Quoted from Skidelsky (2000, p. 77).

62 JMK, XIV p. 138, letter from Keynes to Joan Robinson, dated 15 October 1936: 'Dear Joan, I am not at all happy about the enclosed. It may be that I have not understood it.' Similarly, on 4 November 1936: 'Dear Joan, I find much difficulty about the enclosed on Foreign Exchanges' (*ibid.* p. 141).

63 Kaldor (1983c, p. 10) later placed also Hanns-Joachim Rüstow, a German economist associated with the IFO economic research institute, above Keynes – in certain respects: 'Hanns-Joachim Rüstow, together with John Maynard Keynes and Mihail [*sic*] Kalecki, were the three "founders" of modern macro-economics … Keynes saw the light much later than Rüstow and Kalecki … in some respects Rüstow had shown the deeper insight.' Since this piece was in honour of Rüstow's 80th birthday, it had a logic of its own. Nevertheless, it demonstrates a – we claim here – typical preparedness of a Cambridge economist to view Keynes' economics not as the outgrowth of the Cambridge School but as a singular event which in certain respects can be seen to have had comparable antecedents with a better claim to priority.

64 See Keynes (1923, p. 71).

65 For details see Skidelsky (1992, p. 514): 'Keynes versus Marx'.

66 It is one of the major puzzles for commentators of Keynes' development towards the *General Theory* why Keynes did this drastic reorientation some time before the autumn of 1933. The reason why Donald Moggridge (1994) had a rather reserved judgement about R. F. Kahn as a historian of Keynes' thought was exactly this puzzle and Kahn's total silence about it, although he was *the* confidant, the 'Messenger Angel', of Keynes' during those very years. For a relevant quote see above, p. 362.

67 I disregard here the subtleties of spelling variants for the names of diverse post-Keynesian positions. For Joan Robinson's choice of spelling see above, note 1 to Chapter 20.

68 For a debate of the issue of Hegel and Marxism see, e.g. Lucio Colletti (1973).

69 Joan Robinson (1973e, p. 250) alludes to '... Hegelese, a language I have never mastered'. She obviously was rather unaware that it is not just a jargon but a way of thinking, a paradigm *par excellence.*

70 See also Rosdolsky (1969, ch. 33) who deals at length with Joan Robinson's reception of Karl Marx. Full of respect for her intellectual stature, the author sets out from quoting her disdain for 'Hegelian stuff and nonsense' and continues that on that basis she must necessarily misunderstand and misinterpret even the most elementary doctrines of Karl Marx.

71 Joan Robinson used the term 'anomaly' as emerges above in n. 8 to Chapter 18 and in the associated quote.

72 The long-period perspective in which Keynes was thus received in the group around Joan Robinson and Richard Kahn is quite ironic since according to Marcuzzo (1996) it is these very two persons who must be seen as 'The origin of short-period analysis' according to the title and the argument of her article.

26. Economic Consequences of a Re-authenticated Keynes–Classics Debate

1 Cf. Tobin (1989, p. 556), however: 'I do not think that Keynes violated the canons of rational behavior in the sense of attributing to actors in the economy irrational money illusion. That is a common misinterpretation of what he was saying.'

2 See the discussion on p. 177 above for some quotes from the exchanges between Keynes and R. F. Kahn concerning this point.

3 For a continuation of this quote see p. 392.

4 Kaldor could have pointed out that Keynes' synthesis went even further than the conventional textbook one in embracing not only marginal productivity but also time preference analysis.

5 Keynes' commitment to 'production ≡ income' was quoted and discussed above on p. 141.

6 As Pigou (1929, pp. 306–7, n. 2) noted, there is indeed some scope for controversy in this question. Keynes' (1926) position is claimed to have contradicted the one which Marshall took in the *Principles* on this issue. Marshall (1920, pp. 375ff.) addresses the issue of overproduction at considerable length, making interesting distinctions between short-period and long-period effects on a particular market. These issues are reminiscent of the ones discussed between Keynes and Pigou, but not really applicable here since they relate to partial analysis.

7 For the history and the details of these plans see Skidelsky (2000, pp. 234–9).

8 Neither did Keynes confirm the theory that a wrong real wage was the *causa causans* for unemployment as Niehans (1990, p. 354) suggested (see above, p. 27). Hopefully, the reader can discern here the Keynesian statement: 'effective demand is deficient and therefore employment and real wages do not have their full employment values' from the Classical statement: 'real wages are wrong and therefore there is unemployment'. The difference between the two statements is, in terms of fig. 26.1, p. 385: the Classical refers just to the eastern quadrant, the Keynesian one refers to both quadrants in conjunction with each other.

9 Index K is added in the expression for the Pigou amendment in order to distinguish Kaldor's usage of η from Pigou's original one.

10   Emphasis in the original. This sentence is given as a quote from an undocu-
     mented lecture by Claude Guillebaud, Alfred Marshall's nephew.
11   Cf. Colander (1996b, p. 116): 'A mathematical specification of Marshall's general
     equilibrium involves specifying all decisions as a system of multiple nested
     equations: $y = f(g(h(l(x))))$.'
12   Cf. Colander (1993, p. 57) who argues that 'a change in perspective is currently
     underway in macro and that a new Post Walrasian perspective which requires a
     "macrofoundation of micro" is emerging.'
13   For some further criticism of the conventional assumption of horizontal demand
     curves in the context of interpreting Keynes' original approach see Marcuzzo (1999,
     p. 145). In this context she critically evaluates Clower's concept of 'thin' markets.
14   For a detailed application of these 'Keynes – Marshallian' type of models of the
     firm see Ambrosi (1981b) in the context of giving microfoundations to Keynes'
     employment function. The product market conditions mentioned here are there
     extended analogously to factor markets and the 'surprising' cyclical constancy of
     real wages is explained in such a framework.
15   See Amadeo (1989) for some discussion of Keynes' conceptual transition.
16   For an overview see, e.g. Sheffrin (1983). Attfield *et al.* (1985, p. 49), in a section
     on 'The variance of aggregate demand policy', discuss the negative effect of such
     variance.
17   See above, p. 7.
18   The less general sense might be seen as being the one requiring each and every
     single excess demand to be zero, i.e. the situation of Classical general equilib-
     rium. A more general case covered by Walras' Law is used here since in this
     representation of Keynesian unemployment only the *sum* of excess demands is
     zero – the products and labour market being in disequilibrium.

27. Perspectives from the *General Theory*

1   See above, p. 32.
2   See above, note 3 to Chapter 4.
3   See above p. 261.
4   The force of this curiosity is perhaps best illustrated by those authors who abjure
    any attempt at authenticity and then go on to muse and postulate about Keynes'
    theoretical 'instincts'. See above, note 7 to Chapter 2.
5   See Harrod (1951, p. 339): 'There are still purists who give the first prize to his
    book on *Indian Currency*' – i.e. placing it before the *Treatise* and the *General
    Theory* which Harrod mentioned just before that sentence.
6   Victoria Chick (1987): 'Townshend ... show[s] a breadth of conception and
    keenness of intellect from which one wishes Economics had benefited more.' Cf.
    also Lawlor (1994, p. 76): 'Townshend's fascinating writings extend Keynes'
    views on interest and money in novel directions.'
7   In effect, Kaldor negates the relevance of the just mentioned low-price contango
    effect if land is the object of liquidity preference.
8   In essence I thus agree with Joan Robinson (1961) that these ideas were not
    worked out to the full by Keynes. But I appeal to (post) Keynesians not to leave
    matters at that. It ought not to suffice in this context just to argue that Keynes
    himself never quite 'seized' these novel ideas. This comment is not invalidated by
    the fact that Lawlor (1994, pp. 78–9) attributed to Joan Robinson an appreciation
    for the wider historic scope of Keynes' vision on liquidity preference. It remains a

desideratum for Keynesian secondary literature to supply methodologically sound instruments for expounding Keynes' admittedly speculative suggestions.

9   Quote from Lorie Tarshis' lecture notes according to Rymes (1989, p. 101).

10 See Rymes (1989, p. 101). In the following we relate his reconstruction of the notes of a 'representative student', *ibid.* p. 101–3.

11 *ibid.* p. 101. From p. 102 it emerges that Keynes was referring not to everyday mathematical proofs but to 'mathematics, *when it is a matter of original work*' (the latter emphasis added, GMA).

12 Letter of Keynes to Lytton Strachey, 17 January 1906: 'Oh! I have undergone conversion. I am with Moore absolutely and on all things', quoted from Harrod (1951, p. 13).

13 In a footnote, Harrod (1951, p. 76, n. 1) refers in this context to Keynes' *Treatise on Probability* without further comment. But the most relevant passage (JMK, VIII, p. 20, n. 1) praises Moore's *Principia Ethica* for its 'intermediate style' and claims that 'those writers, who strain after exaggerated precision ... are sometimes merely pedantic'. It seems that at that time Keynes already distanced himself from overvaluing precision of expression.

14 Astonishingly, in spite of the following sentence, Fitzgibbons never mentions Keynes' interest in McTaggart and the attendance of his lectures on metaphysics.

15 See, e.g. Ellis McTaggart (1901, p. 11) who writes that 'on Hegelian principles ... existence in time is inadequate, and relatively unreal'.

16 It should be noted, however, that even at the time of his 'early beliefs' Keynes was occasionally considered to be under the influence of McTaggart as we may read from a letter by the later philosopher Ludwig Wittgenstein dated 3 Jan. 1913 and stating: 'Dear Keynes, Thanks for your very kind letter ... I excuse your slanging Philosophy as you were just coming from McTaggart ...' (Wittgenstein, 1995, p. 22). This associating Keynes with McTaggart might be one of the reasons why in spite of considerable affinity between Keynes and Wittgenstein there is an air of disassociation between the two. This complex relationship is documented to some extent by Coates (1996).

17 A Hegelian connection can also be seen in Frank Ramsey's programme to distinguish between 'formal logic' and 'human logic' which Keynes (1933a, p. 339) endorses – expressly retracting his own more 'rational' beliefs about probability which he had earlier. Such a distinction was, of course, the basis for Hegel's *Logic*, the object of McTaggart's lengthy commentary. It would be strange if Keynes was not aware of this parallelism at some stage of his probing into this matter.

18 See above p. 376.

19 Keynes' already noted criticism of 'specious precision' links up nicely with an anecdote which Andrew Schotter (1996, p. 204) relates about the Nobel laureate physicist Niels Bohr who 'was once in a fierce argument about a point in physics. At a moment of great frustration, he turned to a colleague and said, "You're not making sense, you're just being logical." ' Schotter continues (*ibid.*): 'To my mind Bohr's statement goes a far way toward indicating what is wrong with some of economics today – we tend to be more concerned with being logical than with making sense.'

20 Compare Skidelsky's (1992, p. 487) comment concerning Keynes (1933b): 'Keynes's identification with Einstein is also too clear to miss.' In Skidelsky's interpretation this identification seems to be predominantly emotional. We believe that it may also be related to Keynes' McTaggart-inspired relativism of his paper on 'Time'.

21 Coates (1996, p. 143) believes 'that Wittgenstein exerted the strongest influence' on Keynes in his escape 'from the formative ideals of analytic philosophy'. But it seems that Wittgenstein had little appreciation for Keynes' interest in McTaggart (see above, n. 16).

22 See note 3 to Chapter 1 and the associated quote in the text on p. 4 above.

List of Symbols

α	labour's partial elasticity of production, first used equ. (9.15), p. 65. See also note 7 to Chapter 8 tan $\angle\alpha$ real wage, first used in fig. 8.1, p. 52
β	parameter determining the elasticity of substitution σ between labour/leisure on the one hand and products on the other, first used in equ. (10.9), p. 98
δ	discount factor, first used in equ. (11.27), p. 135
δ_ℓ	workers' (partial) elasticity of utility from consuming leisure, first used in equ. (10.4), p. 95
δ_x	workers' (partial) elasticity of utility from consuming wage goods, first used in equ. (10.4), p. 95
ε_r	parameter describing how marginal returns are affected through price changes when there are variations in output O_r, first used in equ. (11.7), p. 126
η	Pigou's elasticity of labour demand in the wage goods sector, first used in equ. (9.6), p. 60
η^K	Kaldor's 'Pigou amendment': the reciprocal of the elasticity of demand facing the individual producer, p. 394
γ_i	goods elasticity of utility of consumption, $i = 0$ for present time period, $i = f$ for future time period, first used in equ. (15.4), p. 181
γ_x, γ_y	elasticity of utility of wage goods resp. non-wage goods, first used in equ. (9.16), p. 65
ι	elasticity of utility of consuming in the present time period, first used in equ. (11.28), p. 135
ι^f	elasticity of utility of consuming in the future time period, first used in equ. (11.28), p. 135
λ	Lagrange multiplier, first used in equ. (15.19), p. 187
λ^K	share of wages in fig. 26.2, p. 409
λ^P	labour's share in Pigou (1937), first used in equ. (16.13), p. 213
λ^R	labour's share in Robinsonian model as determined by $\lambda^r = \lambda^s$, first used in equ. (23.3), p. 311
λ^s	labour's share as determined by 'Kalecki savings' in Robinsonian model, first used in equ. (22.10), p. 299
λ^r	Labour's share in Robinsonian model – as determined by technology and cost of capital services, first used in equ. (21.22), p. 282
μ^{MM}	Lagrangian multiplier for the market constraint under 'Marshallian' condition of price calculating suppliers, first used in equ. (26.5), p. 395
μ^{MP}	Lagrangian multiplier for the production constraint under 'Marshallian' condition of price calculating suppliers, first used in equ. (26.5), p. 395
μ^W	Lagrangian multiplier for the production constraint under 'Walrasian' condition of price taking suppliers, first used in equ. (26.5), p. 395
Ω_i	simplified notation for more involved algebraic expressions, $i = 1, 2, x, y$, first used in equ. (9.10), p. 63
$\Phi(N)$	aggregate supply function, first used in equ. (11.1), p. 121
$\phi(x)$	Pigou's function relating sectoral employment to total employment, p. 49

$\Phi_r(\cdot)$	value supply function for sector r in terms of wage units, first used in equ. (11.6), p. 124
Π	profits, first used in equ. (16.7), p. 211
Π_{ik}^1	future profits in period[1] of a particular entrepreneur with index k who operates in an industry with index i, first used in equ. (22.19), p. 304
$\Psi_r(N_r)$	production function for the r-th industry, first used in equ. (11.3), p. 122
ρ'	rate of time-preference of non-workers under the assumption of 'Kalecki savings' in Robinsonian model, first used in equ. (22.10), p. 299
ρ''	rate of time-preference of workers under conditions of 'Kalecki savings' in Robinsonian model, first used in equ. (22.11), p. 300
$\rho(n)$	Kaldor's assumption that time preference is a decreasing function of employment (as proxy for income), first used in table 15.1, p. 172 and then in fig. 17.1, p. 230
$\rho'(\chi)$	derivative of $\rho(\chi)$- function, first used in equ. (17.1), p. 228
σ	elasticity of substitution between labour/leisure on the one hand and products on the other, first used in fig. 10.1, p. 82
σ_i	elasticity of substitution between capital and labour in the i-th sector, first used in equ. (22.5), p. 291
τ_f	time elasticity of utility of consumption for future time period f, first used in equ. (15.4), p. 181
$\chi(x)$	Keynes' reconstructed Pigovian labour supply function, first used in equ. (10.1), p. 94
$\Xi(\cdot)$	consumption function, first used in equ. (11.1), p. 121
ξ_r	parameter describing how marginal labour cost in nominal terms are affected through wage changes when there are variations in labour input N_r, first used in equ. (11.7), p. 126
A_i	technological efficiency parameter for sector i, first used in equ. (10.13), n. 98
A^n	average productivity of labour in sector i, first used in equ. (21.16) p. 280
a_w	rate of appreciation of money wages, first used in note 23, p. 441
b	marginal propensity to consume, first used in equ. (15.16), p. 184
C_w	consumption in terms of wage units, p. 122
D_2	value of investment in nominal terms, first used in equ. (11.1), p. 121
D_{ij}	the cofactor of the element in the ith row and in the jth column of the Jacobian matrix, first used in equ. (15.25), p. 188
D_{ik}	debt in money terms incurred by a particular entrepreneur with index k who operates in an industry with index i, first used in equ. (22.19), p. 304
D_{w1}	the value of demand in terms of wage units for sector 1 products (consumption), first used in equ. (11.4), p. 122
D_{w2}	the value of demand in terms of wage units for sector 2 products (investment goods), p. 132
D_{wr}	amount of effective demand, measured in terms of wage units, directed to the r-th firm or industry, first used in equ. (11.2), p. 122
E	(not slanted E:) Elasticity operator; upper index: dependent variable; lower index: independent variable, first used in equ. (9.4), p. 59
E_m	Pigou's 'elasticity of demand in terms of money for labour as a whole', first used on p. 169
E_r	Pigou's 'elasticity of the real demand for labour', first used in equ. (9.1), p. 57
$F_r(D_{wr})$	sectoral employment function, first used in equ. (11.2), p. 122
$F(x)$	Pigou's symbol for the production function in the wage goods sector, p. 49
$G(y)$	production function for non-wage goods in Pigou-model, first used in equ. (8.2), p. 54

g_a	Harrod's 'actual rate of growth', first used in table 15.1, p. 172
g_n	Harrod's 'natural rate of growth', first used in table 15.1, p. 172
g_w	Harrod's 'warranted rate of growth', first used in table 15.1, p. 172
h	rate of depreciation, first used in equ. (21.1), p. 277
K_{ik}	real capital bought by a particular entrepreneur with index k who operates in an industry with index i, first used in equ. (22.19), p. 304
$L\ell$	relative price line representing the dividing hyper plane separating the production set from the preference set in the Koopmans diagram of general equilibrium, first used in fig. 10.4, p. 102
$L_1(\cdot)$	the function explaining the transactions and precautionary motive for money demand, first used in equ. (16.3), p. 202
$L_2(\cdot)$	the function explaining money demand due to the speculative motive, first used in equ. (16.3), p. 202
L_i^M	Lagrangian for 'Marshallian' demand function constraint, first used in equ. (26.5), p. 395
L_i^W	Lagrangian for 'Walrasian' production function constraint, first used in equ. (26.5), p. 395
M_1	money demand due to the transactions and precautionary motive, first used in equ. (16.3), p. 202
M_2	money demand due to the speculative motive, first used in equ. (16.3), p. 202
n	total employment in Pigou-model, first used in equ. (8.10), p. 55
O_r	output in the r-th industry, first used in equ. (11.3), p. 122
p_x	price for wage goods, first used in equ. (8.3), p. 54
p_y	price for non-wage goods, first used in equ. (8.4), p. 54
P_{ik}^1	future profits in money terms which arises from productive activity in the future period of production in period[1] obtained by a particular entrepreneur with index k who operates in an industry with index i, first used in equ. (22.19), p. 304
Q_x	output of the wage goods sector in Pigou-model, first used in equ. (8.1), p. 54
Q_y	output of non-wage sector in Pigou-model, first used in equ. (8.2), p. 54
Q_{ci}	consumption good in i-th time period, first used in equ. (15.4), p. 181
Q_{xk}	wage goods consumed by non-workers in Pigou-model, first used in equ. (8.8), p. 55
Q_{xw}	wage goods consumed by workers in Pigou-model, first used in equ. (8.6), p. 54
r	index for real values with unspecified deflator as in S^r = real savings, first used in equ. (22.9), p. 298
S^m	real savings by non-workers, first used in equ. (22.10), p. 299
S^{rw}	real savings by workers, first used in equ. (22.12), p. 300
$\bar{t}$	workers' time constraint in Pigou-model, first used in equ. (8.6), p. 54
$U^k(\cdot)$	utility function of non-workers in Pigou-model, first used in equ. (8.11), p. 55
$U^w(\cdot)$	utility function of workers in Pigou-model, first used in equ. (8.6), p. 54
U_1	alternative notation for: partial derivative of $U(x, ...)$ with respect to the first argument x where x stands for any variable, first used in equ. (8.7), p. 55
U_x	alternative notation for: partial derivative of $U(x, ...)$ with respect to x where x stands for any variable, first used in equ. (8.6), p. 54
V	value of total output in terms of wage units in Joan Robinson's 'generalisation' of the *General Theory*, first used in equ. (21.12), p. 279

υ	rentals rate for capital, first used in equ. (21.1), p. 277
V^T	income velocity of money in Pigou (1937) model, first used in equ. (16.16), p. 215
V_1	value of output of the wage goods sector in terms of wage units, first used in equ. (21.10), p. 279
V_2	value of output of the capital goods sector in terms of wage units, first used in equ. (21.11), p. 279
W	consumers' wealth, first used in equ. (15.19), p. 187
w	nominal wage rate, first used in equ. (8.3), p. 54
x	Pigou's symbol for workers in the wage-goods sector, p. 49
y	Pigou's symbol for workers in the non wage goods industries, p. 49
Y_o	income in period O, first used in equ. (15.1), p. 180
Y_f	income in future time period, first used in equ. (15.2), p. 180
Y_w	national income in terms of wage units, p. 122
Y_{wk}	non-wage income in terms of the wage-unit, first used in equ. (11.32), p. 137
$Y_{w\ell}$	labour income in terms of the wage-unit, first used in equ. (12.2), p. 148
z	cost unit in Pigou's 'simplified model', first used in equ. (16.14), p. 214
Z_{wr}	value of sectoral production in terms of wage units, first used in equ. (11.6), p. 124

Bibliography

In order to avoid to much repetition, references to Keynes are not all listed in full and sometimes in varying ways. In the text e.g. 'JMK, XX, p. 111' refers to vol. XX, p. 111 of: *The Collected Writings of John Maynard Keynes*, 30 vols, Macmillan for Royal Economic Society, London and Basingstoke, 1971–9.

'GT' or *'General Theory'* or 'Keynes (1936)' in the text refers to John Maynard Keynes, *The General Theory of Employment, Interest, and Money*, Macmillan: London, 1936, vol. VII of JMK.

Ahiakpor, James C. W. (ed.) (1998a) *Keynes and the Classics Reconsidered, Recent Economic Thought* (Boston, Dordrecht, London: Kluwer).

Ahiakpor, James C. W. (1998b) 'Editor's Introduction', in: Ahiakpor (1998a), pp. 1–13.

Amadeo, Edward J. (1989) *Keynes' Principle of Effective Demand* (Aldershot: Edward Elgar).

Ambrosi, Gerhard Michael (1979a) 'Der Nominallohn in der Keynesschen Beschäftigungstheorie: Behauptungen und Belege [The Money Wage in the Keynesian Theory of Employment: Assertions and Evidence]', in: *Konjunkturpolitik*, 25, pp. 123–35.

— (1979b) 'Intertemporal Substitutability and the Keynesian Consumption Function', in: *Bulletin of Economic Research*, 31, pp. 93–7.

— (1980a) 'Nominallohnpolitik und Technologie in Keynesschen Makromodellen', in: *Konjunkturpolitik*, 26, pp. 171–92.

— (1980b) 'Der Keynessche Vermögenseffekt und seine wahltheoretische Begründung [The Keynesian Wealth Effect and its Choice Theoretic Foundation]', in: *Jahrbücher für Nationalökonomie und Statistik*, 195(5), pp. 435–48.

— (1981a) 'Keynes and the 45° Cross', in: *Journal of Post Keynesian Economics*, 3(4) (Summer), pp. 503–9.

— (1981b) *Die Keynessche Beschäftigungsfunktion [Keynes' Employment Function]* (Berlin: Duncker & Humblot).

— (1982) 'Monetarismus, Keynesianismus und das Stagflationsdilemma', in: *Konjunkturpolitik*, 28, pp. 139–69.

— (1985) 'Die Samuelson-Umhüllende und das Kapitalwertproblem. Kritische Bemerkungen zu einer kapitaltheoretischen Debatte [The Samuelson Envelope and the Problem of Capital Value – Critical Remarks Concerning a Capital-theoretic Debate]', seminar contribution, unpublished, Institut für Wirtschaftstheorie, Free University Berlin. http://www.uni-trier.de/ambrosi/publik/Samuel/SAMUEL-2002.html

— (1988) 'Adam Smith's Labour Command Values: a Post Keynesian Interpretation', in: *Œconomia, série PE de la revue Economies et Sociétés*, 1988 (9), pp. 17–33.

— (2001) 'Angebotswirkungen von Geldpolitik – der *Föhl-Patman Effekt* und seine makroökonomische Bedeutung [Supply Effects of Monetary Policy – The *Föhl-Patman Effect* and its macroeconomic significance]', in: *Ökonomie als Grundlage politischer Entscheidungen [Economics as Basis for Political Decisions]*, edited by Jürgen Gabriel and Michael Neugart, pp. 243–70 (Leverkusen: Leske + budrich).

Arestis, Philip (ed.) (1996) *Keynes, Money, and the Open Economy: Essays in Honour of Paul Davidson* (Aldershot: Edward Elgar), 2 vols.

Arestis, Philip, Palma, Gabriel J. and Sawyer, Malcolm C. (eds) (1997) *Capital Controversy, Post Keynesianism and the History of Economic Thought: Essays in Honour of Geoff Harcourt*, vol. 1 (London and New York: Routledge).

Arestis, Philip, Desai, Meghnad and Dow, Sheila (eds) (2002) *Methodology, Microeconomics and Keynes – Essays in Honour of Victoria Chick*, vol. 2 (London and New York: Routledge).

Arrow, Kenneth J. (1974) 'Limited Knowledge and Economic Analysis', in: *The American Economic Journal*, 64(1), pp. 1–10.

— (1987) 'Oral History I: an Interview', in: Feiwel (1987), pp. 191–242.

— (1989) 'Joan Robinson and Modern Economic Theory: an Interview', in: Feiwel (1989a), pp. 147–85.

Aslanbeigui, Nahid (1992) 'Pigou's Inconsistencies or Keynes's Misconceptions?', in: *History of Political Economy*, 24(2), pp. 413–33.

— (1998) 'Unemployment Through the Eye of a Classic', in: Ahiakpor (1998a), pp. 65–99.

Attfield, Clifford L. F., Demery, David and Duck, N. W. (1985) *Rational Expectations in Macroeconomics – an Introduction to Theory and Evidence* (Oxford: Basil Blackwell).

Baker, Gerard and Crooks, Edward (2001) 'Keynes Revisited – in the US, economic policy is changing after more than a decade to a Keynesian approach', in: *The Financial Times* (6 October), (internet site gives publication date as 09 (!) October 2001). URL www.bized.ac.uk/case/case_studies/case010-fulltext.htm

Baranzini, Mauro (ed.) (1982) *Advances in Economic Theory* (New York: St. Martin's Press).

Barro, Robert J. (1990) *Macroeconomics* (New York: John Wiley & Sons), 3rd edition.

Barro, Robert J. and Grossman, Herschel I. (1971) 'A General Disequilibrium Model of Income and Employment', in: *The American Economic Review*, 61, pp. 82–93.

Bateman, Bradley W. (1991) '*Das* Maynard Keynes Problem', in: *Cambridge Journal of Economics*, 15(1), pp. 101–11, quoted from Wood 94–VIII, pp. 310–23.

Baumol, William J. (1997) 'J.-B. Say on Unemployment and Public Works', in: *Eastern Economic Journal*, 23(2), pp. 219–230, part of a symposium on Say's Law.

Blaug, Mark (1968) *Economic Theory in Retrospect* (London: Heinemann), 2nd edition.

— (1990) 'On the Historiography of Economics', in: *Journal of the History of Economic Thought*, 12(1) Spring, pp. 27–37.

— (1991a) 'Second Thoughts on the Keynesian Revolution', in: *History of Political Economy*, 23(2), pp. 171–92.

— (ed.) (1991b) *John Maynard Keynes (1883–1946) Volume II*, Pioneers in Economics, vol. 46 (Aldershot: Edward Elgar).

— (1997) 'Say's Law of Markets: What Did it Mean and Who Should Care?', in: *Eastern Economic Journal*, 23(2), pp. 231–5, part of a symposium on Say's Law.

— (2001) 'No History of Ideas, Please, We're Economists', in: *Journal of Economic Perspectives*, 15(1) (Winter), pp. 145–64.

Blinder, Alan S. (1988) 'The Fall and Rise of Keynesian Economics', in: *The Economic Record*, 64, pp. 278–94.

Bliss, Christopher (1990) 'Alfred Marshall and the Theory of Capital', in: *Centenary Essays on Alfred Marshall*, edited by John K. Whitaker, pp. 223–41 (Cambridge: Cambridge University Press).

Bradford, Wylie and Harcourt, Geoffrey Colin (1997) 'Units and Definitions', in: *A Second Edition of The General Theory vol. 1*, edited by Geoffrey C. Harcourt and Peter A. Riach, pp. 107–31 (London and New York: Routledge).

Brady, Michael Emmett (1994) 'A Note on the Keynes–Pigou Controversy', in: *History of Political Economy*, 26(4), pp. 697–705.

Burmeister, Edwin and Dobell, Rodney A. (1970) *Mathematical Theories of Economic Growth* (London: Macmillan).

Casarosa, Carlo (1982) 'Aggregate Supply and Expected Demand Analysis in Keynes' General Theory: an Essay on the Micro-Foundations', in: Baranzini (1982), pp. 67–79.

Cassel, Gustav (1903) *The Nature and Necessity of Interest*, quoted from the reprint (New York: Kelley & Millman, Inc.) 1957.

Casson, Mark (1983) *Economics of Unemployment – an Historical Perspective* (Oxford: Martin Robertson).

Cate, Thomas (ed.) (1997) *An Encyclopedia of Keynesian Economics* (Cheltenham, UK and Brook-field US: Edward Elgar), associate editors: Geoff Harcourt and David C. Colander.

Chakrabarti, Santi K. (1979) *The Two-Sector General Theory Model* (London and Basingstoke: Macmillan).

Champernowne, D. G. (1935) 'A Mathematical Note on Substitution', in: *The Economic Journal*, 45(178) (June), pp. 246–58.

Chick, Victoria (1983) *Macroeconomics After Keynes: a Reconsideration of the General Theory* (Oxford: Philip Allan).

— (1987) 'Townshend, Hugh (1890–1974)', in: *The New Palgrave: a Dictionary of Economics, vol 4, Q to Z*, edited by John Eatwell, Murray Milgate and Peter Newman, p. 662 (London and Basingstoke: Macmillan).

Chick, Victoria and Dow, Sheila C. (2001) 'Formalism, Logic and Reality: a Keynesian Analysis', in: *Cambridge Journal of Economics*, 25, pp. 705–21.

Clark, Colin (1937) *National Income and Outlay* (London: Macmillan).

Clarke, Peter (1988) *The Keynesian Revolution in the Making, 1924–1936* (Oxford: Clarendon Press).

Clower, Robert W. (1965) 'The Keynesian Counter-Revolution: a Theoretical Appraisal', in F. H. Hahn and F. Brechling (eds), *The Theory of Interest Rates: Proceedings of a Conference held by the IEA* (London: Macmilllan), pp. 103–25.

Clower, Robert W. (1975) *Reflections on the Keynesian Perplex*, Zeitschrift für Nationalökonomie, vol. 35, pp. 1–24.

— (1989) 'Keynes' *General Theory*: the Marshallian Connection', in: *Perspectives on the History of Economic Thought*, Volume 2, *Twentieth-Century Economic Thought*, edited by Donald Anthony Walker, pp. 133–47 (Aldershot: Edward Elgar for the History of Economics Society), Selected Papers from the History of Economics Society Conference, 1987.

— (1994) 'The Effective Demand Fraud', in: *Eastern Economic Journal*, 20(4), pp. 377–85.

Clower, Robert W. and Howitt, Peter (1998) 'Keynes and the Classics: an End of Century View', in Ahiakpor (1998a), pp. 163–78.

Coates, John (1996) *The Claims of Common Sense – Moore, Wittgenstein, Keynes and the Social Sciences* (Cambridge: Cambridge University Press).

Coats, Alfred William (1969) 'Is there a "Structure of Scientific Revolutions" in Economics?', in: *Kyklos*, 22, pp. 289–96.

Coddington, Alan (1983) *Keynesian Economics: the Search for First Principles* (London, Boston, Sydney: George Allen & Unwin).

Colander, David (1993) 'The Macrofoundations of Micro', in: *Eastern Economic Journal*, 19(4), reprinted as ch. 4 in Colander (1996a), p. 57–68.

— (ed.) (1996a) *Beyond Microfoundations: Post Walrasian Macroeconomics* (Cambridge, New York, Melbourne: Cambridge University Press).

— (1996b) 'Marshallian General Equilibrium Analysis', in: Colander (1996a), chapter 7, pp. 109–23.

— (1999) 'Teaching Keynes in the 21st Century', in: *Journal of Economic Education*, 30, pp. 364–72.

Collard, David (1981) 'A. C. Pigou, 1877–1959', in: *Pioneers of Modern Economics in Britain*, edited by Denis P. O'Brien and John R. Presley, pp. 105–39 (London: Macmillan).

Colletti, Lucio (1973) *Il marxismo e Hegel* (Guis. Laterza & Figli), quoted from the German translation: *Hegel und der Marxismus* (Ullstein: Frankfurt a. Main), 1976; English translation: *Marxism and Hegel*, London, 1973.

Corry, Bernard A. (1978) 'Keynes in the History of Economic Thought. Some Reflections', in: *Keynes and Laissez-Faire*, edited by Anthony P. Thirlwall, pp. 3–34 (London: Macmillan).

—— (1997) 'Keynes's Use of the Term "involuntary unemployment" – a Historical Perspective', in: Arestis *et al.* (1997), chapter 18, pp. 212–25.

Cottrell, Allin (1994) 'Keynes's Appendix to Chapter 19: a Reader's Guide', in: *History of Political Economy*, 26(4), pp. 681–95.

—— (1998) 'Keynes, Ricardo, Malthus and Say's Law', in: Ahiakpor (1998a), pp. 63–75.

Davidson, Paul (1994) *Post Keynesian Macroeconomic Theory – a Foundation for Successful Economic Policies for the Twenty-first Century* (Aldershot: Edward Elgar).

—— (1998) 'Setting the Record Straight', in: Rotheim (1998), pp. 15–38.

—— (2001) 'The Principle of Effective Demand: Another View', in: *Journal of Post Keynesian Economics*, 23(3) (Spring), pp. 391–409.

Davidson, Paul and Smolensky, Eugene (1964) *Aggregate Supply and Demand Analysis* (New York).

Davis, John B. (ed.) (1994) *The State of Interpretation of Keynes, Recent Economic Thought* (Dordrecht, the Netherlands and Norwell, Massachusetts USA: Kluwer Academic Publishers).

De Vroey, Michel (1997) 'Involuntary Unemployment: the Missing Piece in Keynes's *General Theory*', in: *The European Journal of the History of Economic Thought*, 4, pp. 258–83.

Debreu, Gérard (1959) *The Theory of Value* (New Haven: Yale University Press).

Derobert, Laurent (2001) 'On the Genesis of the Canonical Labor Supply Model', in: *Journal of the History of Economic Thought*, 23(2), pp. 197–215.

Dimand, Robert W. (2002) 'Keynes, IS-LM, and the Marshallian Tradition', paper presented to L'Association Charles Gide pour L'Étude de la Pensée Économique, UQAM, Montreal, June, URL: www.philo.uqam.ca/Keynes/docs/dimand.pdf

Eatwell, John and Milgate, Murray (eds) (1983) *Keynes's Economics and the Theory of Value and Distribution* (London: Duckworth).

Eichner, Alfred S. (1976) *The Megacorp and Oligopoly: Micro Foundations of Macro Dynamics* (Cambridge).

Ellis McTaggart, John McTaggart (1901) *Studies in Hegelian Cosmology* (Cambridge), quoted from the reprint, by Batoche Books: Kitchener, 2000.

Feiwel, George R. (ed.) (1987) *Arrow and the Ascent of Modern Economic Theory* (Basingstoke and London: Macmillan).

—— (1989a) *Joan Robinson and Modern Economic Theory* (Basingstoke and London: Macmillan).

—— (1989b) *The Economics of Imperfect Competition and Employment* (Basingstoke and London: Macmillan).

—— (1989c) 'Towards an Intergration of Macrodynamics: Kalecki, Keynes, Joan Robinson', in: Feiwel (1989b), pp. 3–145.

Fisher, Irving (1930) *The Theory of Interest* (New York: Macmillan), quoted from the reprint (New York: Augustus M. Kelly), 1967.

Fitzgibbons, Athol (1991) 'The Significance of Keynes's Idealism', in: *Keynes and Philosophy*, edited by Bradley W. Bateman and John B. Davis, chapter 8, pp. 126–32 (Aldershot, UK and Brookfield, Vermont, USA: Edward Elgar).

Frank, Thomas (2002) 'Shocked, Shocked! Enronian Myths Exposed', in: *The Nation*, Feature Story. URL www.thenation.com/doc.mhtml?i=20020408&s=frank&c=1

Friedman, Milton (1970) 'A Theoretical Framework for Monetary Analysis', in: *Journal of Political Economy*, 78, pp. 193–238.

Froyen, Richard T. (1976) 'The Aggregative Structure of Keynes' *General Theory*', in: *The Quarterly Journal of Economics*, 90, pp. 369–87.

Frum, David (1994) 'The Genius of Capitalism', in: *The New Criterion (on line)*, [Review of Skidelsky (1992)]. URL www.newcriterion.com/archive/12/apr94/frum.htm

Fukuyama, Francis (1989) 'The End of History?', in: *The National Interest*, 1989, pp. 3–18. URL http://www.cla.wayne.edu/polisci/krause/Comparative/SOURCES/fukayama.htm

Fusfeld, Daniel R. (1985) 'Keynes and the Keynesian Cross: a Note', in: *History of Political Economy*, 17, pp. 385–9.

Garegnani, Pierangelo (1979) 'Notes on Consumption, Investment and Effective Demand: a Reply to Joan Robinson', in: *Cambridge Journal of Economics*, 3, pp. 181–7.

Gerrard, Bill and Hillard, John (eds) (1992) *The Philosophy and Economics of J. M. Keynes* (Aldershot: Edward Elgar).

Gordon, David (1996) *The Philosophical Origins of Austrian Economics: Bibliographical Essay* (Auburn, Alabama: Ludwig von Mises Institute), electronic publication. URL www.mises.org/philorig/bibessay.asp

Gordon, Robert J. (1989) 'Fresh Water, Salt Water, and Other Macroeconomic Elixirs', in: *The Economic Record*, 65(189), pp. 177–84.

Green, Harold A. John (1964) *Aggregation in Economic Analysis* (Princeton: Princeton University Press).

Grossman, Herschel I. (1972) 'Was Keynes a "Keynesian"? A Review Article', in: *The Journal of Economic Literature*, 10, pp. 26–30, reprinted in Wood (1983), vol. III, Nr. 110, p. 479–85.

Guthrie, William (1997) 'Keynesian Cross', in: Cate (1997), pp. 315–19, associate editors: Geoff Harcourt and David C. Colander.

Hahn, Frank H. (1989) 'Robinson–Hahn Love–Hate Relationship: an Interview', in: Feiwel (1989a), pp. 895–910.

Hansen, Alvin H. (1941) *Fiscal Policy and Business Cycles* (London: Allen & Unwin).

— (1953) *A Guide to Keynes* (New York: McGraw-Hill).

Harcourt, Geoffrey Colin (1972) *Some Cambridge Controversies in the Theory of Capital*, quoted from the reprint 1974 (London: Cambridge University Press).

— (1979) 'Joan Robinson', in: *International Encyclopaedia of the Social Sciences. Biographical Supplement, vol. 18*, edited by David L. Sills, pp. 663–71 (New York: Free Press), quoted from the reprint in Harcourt (1993), pp. 3–20.

— (ed.) (1985) *Keynes and his Contemporaries* (London: Macmillan).

— (1993) *Post-Keynesian Essays in Biography. Portraits of Twentieth-Century Political Economists* (Basingstoke and London: Macmillan).

— (1994) 'Kahn and Keynes and the Making of *The General Theory*', in: *Cambridge Journal of Economics*, 18, pp. 11–23.

— (1996) 'Some Reflections on Joan Robinson's Changes of Mind and their Relationship to post-Keynesianism and the Economics Profession', in: Marcuzzo *et al.* (1996), chapter 26, pp. 317–29.

Harrod, Roy F. (1934) 'Professor Pigou's Theory of Unemployment – [Review Article]', in: *The Economic Journal*, 44, pp. 19–32.

— (1937a) 'Review of Joan Robinson (1937)', in: *The Economic Journal*, 47, pp. 326–30.

— (1937b) 'Mr. Keynes and Traditional Theory', in: *Econometrica*, 5(1), pp. 74–86.

— (1939) 'An Essay in Dynamic Theory', in: *The Economic Journal*, 49, pp. 14–33.

— (1951) *The Life of John Maynard Keynes*, Quoted from the Norton paperback edition (New York W. W. Norton & Co.), 1982.

Hawtrey, Ralph George (1934) ' "The Theory of Unemployment" by Professor A. C. Pigou', in: *Economica*, 1, N. S. (May), pp. 147–66.

Henderson, James M. and Quandt, Richard F. (1958) *Microeconomic Theory. a Mathematical Approach* (New York: McGraw-Hill and Kogakusha).

Herbert, Ian (ed.) (1981) *Who's Who in the Theatre*, vol 1, Biographies, 17th edn (Detroit: Gale Research Company).

Hession, Charles H. (1984) *John Maynard Keynes: a personal biography of the man who revolutionized capitalism and the way we live* (New York: Macmillan), quoted after the German translation *John Maynard Keynes* (Stuttgart: Klett-Cotta), 1986.

Hicks, John R. (1932) *The Theory of Wages* (London: Macmillan).

— (1936) 'Mr. Keynes' Theory of Employment', in: *Economic Journal*, 46 (June), pp. 238–53, reprinted in Hicks (1982), pp. 84–93.

— (1937) 'Mr. Keynes and the "Classics": a Suggested Interpretation', in: *Econometrica*, 5, pp. 147–59, quoted from the reprint in Hicks (1967), pp. 126–42.

— (1939) *Value and Capital* (Oxford: Clarendon Press), quoted from the second edition, 1946.

— (1974) *The Crisis in Keynesian Economics*, Yrjö Jahnsson Lectures (Oxford: Basil Blackwell).

— (1982) *Money, Interest and Wages: Collected Essays on Economic Theory*, volume II (Cambridge, MA: Harvard University Press).

Hoover, Kevin D. (2001) 'Review of Laidler (1999)', in: *Journal of the History of Economic Thought*, 23(4), pp. 541–4.

Howitt, Peter Antoni, Elisabetta de and Leijonhufvud, Axel (eds) (1999) *Money, Markets and Method – Essays in Honour of Robert W. Clower* (Cheltenham, UK and Northampton, MA, USA: Edward Elgar).

Hutchison, Terence Wilmot (1977) *Keynes versus the 'Keynesians' …? An Essay in the Thinking of J.M. Keynes and the Accuracy of its Interpretation by his Followers*, 2nd imp. (London: IEA).

— (1978) *On Revolutions and Progress in Economic Knowledge* (Cambridge: Cambridge University Press).

Hutt, W. H. (1939) *The Theory of Idle Ressources* (London: Jonathan Cape).

Jaeger, Klaus (1980) *Wachstumstheorie. Eine kapitaltheoretische Einführung* (Stuttgart: Kohlhammer).

Johnson, Elizabeth S. (1978a) 'Scientist or Politician?', in: Johnson and Johnson (1978), pp. 17–29.

Johnson, Elizabeth S. and Johnson, Harry Gordon (eds) (1978) *The Shadow of Keynes: Understanding Keynes, Cambridge and Keynesian Economics* (Oxford: Basil Blackwell).

Johnson, Harry G. (1978a) 'Cambridge in the 1950s', in: Johnson and Johnson (1978), pp. 127–66.

— (1978b) 'Arthus Cecil Pigou, 1877–1959: an Obituary', in: Johnson and Johnson (1978), chapter 13, pp. 173–80.

Kahn, Richard Ferdinand (1929) *The Economics of the Short Period* (Basingstoke: Macmillan), quoted from the publication in 1989.

— (1931) 'The Relation of Home Investment to Unemployment', in: *Economic Journal*, 41, pp. 173–98.

— (1984) *The Making of Keynes' General Theory* (Raffaele Mattioli Lectures), 1978 (Cambridge: Cambridge University Press).

Kaldor, Nicholas (1937) 'Prof. Pigou on Money Wages in Relation to Unemployment', in: *The Economic Journal*, 47, pp. 745–53.

— (1955–6) 'Alternative Theories of Distribution', in: *Review of Economic Studies*, 23(2), quoted from the reprint in Kaldor (1960), pp. 209–36.

— (1960a) *Essays on Value and Distribution* (London: Gerald Duckworth).

— (1960b) *Essays on Economic Stability and Growth*, chapter on 'Keynes' Theory of Own Rates of Interest', pp. 59–74 (London: Duckworth).

— (1983a) 'Keynesian Economics after Fifty Years', in: Worswick and Trevithick (1983), pp. 1–44.

— (1983b) 'Lord Kaldor replied to the comments as follows', in: Worswick and Trevithick (1983), pp. 46–8, as reported by the editors of Worswick and Trevithick (1983).

— (1983c) 'Common Features and Controversial Issues in the Theories of Keynes, Kalecki, and Rüstow', in: *IFO-Studien*, 29, pp. 1–10, article in German under the title 'Gemeinsamkeiten und Unterschiede in den Theorien von Keynes, Kalecki und Rüstow', English summary, p. 10.

Kalecki, Michal (1937) 'A Theory of the Business Cycle', in: *Review of Economic Studies*, 4(2), pp. 77–97

Kates, Steven (1997a) 'On the True Meaning of Say's Law', in: *Eastern Economic Journal*, 23(2), pp. 191–202, part of a symposium on Say's Law.

— (1997b) 'A Discussion of Say's Law: the Outcome of the Symposium', in: *Eastern Economic Journal*, 23(2), pp. 237–9, part of a symposium on Say's Law.

— (1998) *Say's Law and the Keynesian Revolution – How Macroeconomic Theory Lost its Way* (Cheltenham, UK, Northampton, MA, USA: Edward Elgar).

Keynes, John Maynard (1919) *The Economic Consequences of the Peace* (London: Macmillan), quoted from the reprint in: *The Collected Writings of John Maynard Keynes*, vol. II, Macmillan, St. Martin's Press, London and Basingstoke, 1971.

— (1923) *A Tract on Monetary Reform* (London: Macmillan), quoted from JMK, IV.

— (1926) 'The Control of Raw Materials by Governments', in: *The Nation and Athenaeum* (12 June), quoted from: JMK, XIX, part II, 1981.

— (1930) *A Treatise on Money: Volume 1: The Pure Theory of Money* (New York: Harcourt-Brace-Jovanovich), quoted from JMK, V.

— (1933a) *Essays in Biography* (London: Macmillan), quoted from the reprint in: *The Collected Writings of John Maynard Keynes*, vol. X, Macmillan, St. Martin's Press, London and Basingstoke, 1972.

— (1933b) 'Einstein', in: *The New Statesman and Nation*, quoted from the reprint in: *The Collected Writings of John Maynard Keynes*, vol. XXVIII, Macmillan, St. Martin's Press, London and Basingstoke.

— (1936) *The General Theory of Employment; Interest and Money*, quoted from JMK, Collected Writings, vol. VII, London, 1973.

— (1937a) 'The *General Theory* of Employment', in: *The Quarterly Journal of Economics*, 51 (February), pp. 209–23, quoted from JMK, XIV, 109–23.

— (1937b) 'Professor Pigou on Money Wages in Relation to Unemployment', in: *The Economic Journal*, December 1937, quoted from JMK, XIV, 262–5.

King, John E. (1996) 'The First post Keynesian: Joan Robinson's Keynesian *Essays in the Theory of Employment* (1937)', in: Arestis (1996), chapter 10, pp. 164–84.

— (1998) ' "Your Position is Thoroughly Orthodox and Entirely Wrong": Nicholas Kaldor and Joan Robinson, 1933–1983', in: *Journal of the History of Economic Thought*, 20(4), pp. 411–32.

Klausinger, Hansjörg (1998) 'Pigou on Unemployment', in Philippe Fontaine and Albert Jolink (eds), *Historical Perspectives on Macroeconomics: Sixty Years After the General Theory* (London and New York: Routledge).

Knoester, Anthonie (1988) 'Pigou and Buffer Effects in Monetary Economics', in: *Kredit und Kapital*, 21(1), pp. 92–117.

Kohn, Meir (1986) 'Monetary Analysis, the Equilibrium Method, and Keynes' "General Theory" ', in: *Journal of Political Economy*, 94(6), pp. 1191–224, reprinted in Blaug (1991b), pp. 139–72.

Koopmans, Tjalling C. (1957) *Three Essays on the State of Economic Science*, chapter I: 'Allocation of Resources and the Price System', pp. 2–126 (New York, Toronto, London: McGraw-Hill).

Krauss, Melvyn B. and Johnson, Harry G. (1974) *General Equilibrium Analysis – a Micro-Economic Text* (London: Georg Allen & Unwin).

Kregel, Jan A. (1983) 'The Microfoundations of the "Generalization of *The General Theory*", and "Bastard Keynesianism": Keynes' Theory of Employment in the Long and in the Short Period', in: *Cambridge Journal of Economics*, 7, pp. 343–61.

— (1985) 'Hamlet without the Prince: Cambridge Macroeconomics without Money', in: *American Economic Review, Papers and Proceedings*, 75, pp. 133–9.

— (1991) 'On the Generalization of the *General Theory*', in: Rima (1991), pp. 104–9.

Krugman, Paul (1999) *The Return of Depression Economics* (New York: W. W. Norton and Company).

Krugman, Paul R. and Obstfeld, Maurice (2000) *International Economics. Theory and Policy* (Reading, Mass: Addison-Wesley), 5th edn.

Kuhn, Thomas S. (1970) *The Structure of Scientific Revolutions* (Chicago: University of Chicago Press), 2nd edition.

Laidler, David (1999) *Fabricating the Keynesian Revolution: Studies of the Inter-War Literature on Money, the Cycle, and Unemployment* (Cambridge and New York: Cambridge University Press).

Lange, O. (1938) 'The Rate of Interest and the Optimum Propensity to Consume', in: *Economica (N.S.)*, 5 (Feb.).

Lavington, Frederick (1921) *The English Capital Market*, Reprints of Economic Classics (London: (Methuen & Co., Frank Cass), quoted from the reprint, New York: Augustus M. Kelley, 1968.

Lawlor, Michael Syron (1994) 'The Own-rates Framework as an Interpretation of the *General Theory*: a Suggestion for Complicating the Keynesian Theory of Money', in: Davis (1994), pp. 39–90.

Leeson, Robert (1998a) *The Economic Consequences of the Klassical Caricature*, volume 166, March of *Working Paper* (Murdoch, WA 6150: Economics Department, Murdoch University).

— (1998b) 'The Consequences of the "Klassical" Caricature for Economics', in: Ahiakpor (1998a), pp. 125–40.

Leijonhufvud, Axel (1968) *On Keynesian Economics and the Economics of Keynes: a Study in Monetary Theory* (New York: Oxford University Press).

— (1974) 'Keynes' Employment Function. Comment', in: *History of Political Economy*, 6 (2), pp. 164–70.

— (1983) 'What Would Keynes Have Thought of Rational Expectations', in: Worswick and Trevithick (1983), pp. 179–221.

Lerner, Abba P. (1951) *The Economics of Employment* (New York: McGraw-Hill).

— (1952) 'The Essential Properties of Interest and Money', in: *Quarterly Journal of Economics*, 66, pp. 172–93, quoted from the reprint in: *Essays in Economic Analysis*, Abba P. Lerner (Westport: Hyperion Press), 1953, reprinted 1979, pp. 354–85.

Malinvaud, Edmond (1977) *The Theory of Unemployment Reconsidered* (Oxford: Basil Blackwell).

Mankiw, N. Gregory (1992) 'The Reincarnation of Keynesian Economics: Keynesian Economics Today', in: *European Economic Review*, 36(36), pp. 559–65.

Marcuzzo, Maria Cristina (1996) 'Joan Robinson and Richard Kahn – the Origin of Short-period Analysis', in: Marcuzzo *et al.* (1996), chapter 1, pp. 11–28.

— (1998) 'Comment [on Aslanbeigui (1998)]', in: Ahiakpor (1998a), pp. 99–101.

— (1999) 'Thick Markets and Thin Theories: R. W. Clower and the Economics of J. M. Keynes', in: Howitt *et al.* (1999), chapter 7, pp. 140–52.

— (2002) 'The Collaboration between J. M. Keynes and R. F. Kahn from the *Treatise* to the *General Theory*', in: *History of Political Economics*, 34(2), pp. 421–47.

Marcuzzo, Maria Cristina, Pasinetti, Luigi L. and Roncaglia, Alessandro (eds) (1996) *The Economics of Joan Robinson*, Routledge Studies in the History of Economics (London and New York: Routledge).

Marshall, Alfred (1920) *Principles of Economics* (London: Macmillan), 8th edition, quoted from the ninth (variorum) edition with annotations by C. W. Guillebaud (Macmillan for the Royal Economic Society) 1961.

— (1925) *Memorials of Alfred Marshall* (New York: Kelley and Millman), edited by A. C. Pigou; quoted from the reprint, 1956.

McKibbin, Ross (2001) ' "They mean us no harm" – Review of Skidelsky (2000)', in: *London Review of Books* (8 Feb.), pp. 12–13.

Meade, James Edward (1937) 'A Simplified Model of Mr. Keynes' System', in: *Review of Economic Studies*, 4, pp. 98–107, reprinted 1983 in *John Maynard Keynes – Critical Assessments*, ed. J. C. Wood, pp. 129–40 (London: Croom Helm).

Mizen, Paul and Presley, John R. (1998) 'Keynes, Hicks, and the Cambridge School', in: *History of Political Economy*, 30, pp. 1–17.

Modigliani, Franco (1944) 'Liquidity Preference and the Theory of Interest of Money', in: *Econometrica*, 12 January).

Moggridge, Donald Edward (1973) 'The Cambridge Circus, 1930–1', in: *The General Theory and After, Part I, Preparation, JMK, XIII*, edited by Donald Moggridge, pp. 337–43 (London and Basingstoke: Macmillan), editorial note.

— (1977) 'Cambridge Discussion and Criticism Surrounding the Writing of *The General Theory*: a Chronicler's View', in: Patinkin and Leith (1977), chapter 5, pp. 64–71, Proceedings of a conference held at the University of Western Ontario, October 1975.

— (ed.) (1990) *Perspectives on the History of Economic Thought, Volume IV, Keynes, Macroeconomics and Method* (Aldershot: Edward Elgar), Selected Papers from the History of Economics Society Conference, 1988.

— (1992) *Maynard Keynes: an Economist's Biography* (London and New York: Routledge).

— (1994) 'Richard Kahn as an Historian of Economics', in: *Cambridge Journal of Economics*, 18, pp. 107–16.

Muth, John F. (1961) 'Rational Expectations and the Theory of Price Movements', in: *Econometrica*, 29(3), pp. 315–35.

Niehans, Jürg (1990) *A History of Economic Theory. Classic Contributions, 1720–1980* (Baltimore and London: Johns Hopkins University Press), ch. 27: 'John Maynard Keynes', pp. 345–55.

Noah, Timothy (2002) 'David Frum's "Axis of Evil": Authorial Vanity Strikes the Bush White House', in: *Slate*, posted Tuesday, 5, February 2002, at 3:49 pm PT at http://slate. msn.com/id/2061695.

Ohlin, Bertyl (1937) 'Addendum: Ohlin's Original Remarks', quoted from JMK, XIV, pp. 191–200.
O'Neill, Eugene (1922) *The Hairy Ape* (New York), in Feb. 2003 available under http://www.eoneill.com/texts/ha/contents.htm.
Palacio, Ana (2003) 'EU Divisions over Iraq Can Be Mended', in: *Financial Times* (30070), p. 13.
Parrinello, Sergio (1989) 'The Marshallian Core of the General Theory', in Alain Barrère (ed.) *Money, Credit and Prices in Keynesian Perspective*, proceedings of a conference held at the University of Paris I, Pantheon, Sorbonne (New York, NY: St. Martin's Press), pp. 170–81.
Pasinetti, Luigi L. (1983) 'Comment', in: Worswick and Trevithick (1983), pp. 205–11.
— (2001) 'The Principle of Effective Demand and its Relevance in the Long Run', in: *Journal of Post Keynesian Economics*, 23(3) (Spring), pp. 383–90.
Patinkin, Don (1965) *Money, Interest, and Prices* (New York: Harper & Row), 2nd edition.
— (1976) *Keynes' Monetary Thought: a Study of its Development* (Durham, N. C.: Duke University Press).
— (1977) 'The Process of Writing *The General Theory*: a Critical Survey', in: Patinkin and Leith (1977), chapter 2, pp. 3–24, Proceedings of a conference held at the University of Western Ontario, October 1975.
— (1978) 'Keynes' Aggregate Supply Function: a Plea for Common Sense', in: *History of Political Economy*, 10(4), pp. 577–96.
— (1982) *Anticipations of the General Theory? And Other Essays on Keynes* (Oxford: Basil Blackwell).
— (1987) 'Keynes, John Maynard (1883–1946)', in: *The New Palgrave: a Dictionary of Economics, vol. 3, K to P*, edited by John Eatwell, Murray Milgate and Peter Newman, pp. 19–41 (London and Basingstoke: Macmillan).
Patinkin, Don and Leith, J. Clark (eds) (1977) *Keynes, Cambridge and The General Theory: the Process of Criticism and Discussion Connected with the Development of The General Theory* (London and Basingstoke: Macmillan), Proceedings of a conference held at the University of Western Ontario, October 1975.
Phelps, Edmund S. et. al. (1970) *Microeconomic Foundations of Unemployment and Inflation Theory* (London and Basingstoke: Macmillan).
Pigou, Arthur] Cecil (1914) *Unemployment*, Home University Library of Modern Knowledge (London: Williams & Norgate), quoted from Volume 4 of A. C. Pigou, *Collected Economic Writings* (Macmillan Press, Houndmills, Basingstoke, 1999).
— (1920) *Economics of Welfare*, quoted from A. C. Pigou, *Collected Economic Writings*, vol. 3, Macmillan: Houndmills, Basingstoke, 1999.
— (1927) 'Wage Policy and Unemployment', in: *Economic Journal*, 37, pp. 355–68.
— (1929) *Industrial Fluctuations* (London: Macmillan), 2nd edition.
— (1933) *The Theory of Unemployment* (London: Macmillan), quoted from the reprint (London: Frank Cass & Co.), 1968.
— (1934) 'The Elasticity of Substitution', in: *The Economic Journal*, 44 June), pp. 232–41.
— (1935) *The Economics of Stationary States* (London: Macmillan).
— (1936) 'Mr. J. M. Keynes' *General Theory of Employment, Interest, and Money*', in: *Economica*, N.S., 3, pp. 115–32, reprinted in: Wood (1983), vol. II, nr. 40, pp. 18–31, quoted from the original.
— (1937) 'Real and Money Wage Rates in Relation to Unemployment', in: *The Economic Journal*, 47, pp. 405–22.
— (1938) 'Money Wages in Relation to Unemployment', in: *The Economic Journal*, 48, pp. 134–8, reply to Kaldor (1937).
— (1941) *Employment and Equilibrium*, quoted from the 2nd ed. (London: Macmillan).

— (1943) 'The Classical Stationary State', in: *The Economic Journal*, 53, pp. 343–51.

— (1945) *Lapses from Full Employment* (London: Macmillan).

Ramsey, Frank Plumpton (1928) 'A Mathematical Theory of Saving', in: *The Economic Journal*, 38, pp. 543–59.

Reich, Robert B. (2000) 'John Maynard Keynes – His Radical Idea that Governments Should Spend Money they Dont Have May Have Saved Capitalism', URL www.time.com/time/time100/scientist/profile/keynes03.html

Rima, Ingrid H. (ed.) (1991) *The Joan Robinson Legacy* (Armonk, New York and London: M. E. Sharpe).

Robbins, Lionel (1930) 'On the Elasticity of Demand for Income in Terms of Effort', in: *Economica*, 10, pp. 123–9.

Roberts, David L. (1978) 'Patinkin, Keynes and Aggregate Supply and Demand Analysis', in: *History of Political Economy*, 10(4).

Roberts, Linleigh J. (1998) 'Whatever Happened to Truth?', in: *The Whetting Iron – Christian Fellowship Church Online*, III(10), URL www.cfcnb.org/1998wia/oct1998b.htm

Robinson, Austin (1977) 'Keynes and his Cambridge Colleagues', in: Patinkin and Leith (1977), pp. 25–38, proceedings of a conference held at the University of Western Ontario, October 1975.

Robinson, Joan (1933) *The Economics of Imperfect Competition* (London: Macmillan).

— (1936) 'The Long-period Theory of Employment', in: *Zeitschrift für Nationalökonomie*, pp. 74–93, reprinted, with changes, in Robinson (1937a), pp. 75–100.

— (1937a) *Essays in the Theory of Employment* (Oxford: Basil Blackwell), quoted from the reprint, 1953.

— (1937b) *Introduction to the Theory of Employment* (London: Macmillan), quoted from the second edition, 1969 (London and Basingstoke: Macmillan).

— (1947) 'Foreword [to the second edition]', in: Robinson (1937a), p. v, quoted from the reprint 1953.

— (1951) *Introduction*, volume 1 of *Collected Economic Papers*, pp. vii–ix (Oxford: Basil Blackwell).

— (1953/4) 'The Production Function and the Theory of Capital', in: *Review of Economic Studies*, XXI(2) (No. 55), quoted from the modified reprint in: Joan Robinson, *Collected Economic Papers*, Vol. 2, Oxford: Basil Blackwell, 1960, pp. 114–31.

— (1954a) *The Rate of Interest and Other Essays* (London: Macmillan), quoted from the reprint (Westport, Connecticut: Hyperion Press), 1982.

— (1954b) 'The Generalisation of the General Theory', in: Robinson (1954a), pp. 68–142, reprinted in Robinson (1979e), pp. 1–76.

— (1954c) 'Notes on the Economics of Technical Progress', in: Robinson (1954a), pp. 33–65, reprinted in Robinson (1979e), pp. 79–111.

— (1956) *The Accumulation of Capital* (London: Macmillan), quoted from the 3rd edition of 1969.

— (1961) 'Own Rates of Interest', in: *The Economic Journal*, 71, pp. 596–600, quoted from Robinson (1965), pp. 132–8 (with 'Postscript').

— (1962a) *Economic Philosophy* (Chicago: Aldine).

— (1962b) 'The *General Theory* after Twenty-Five Years', in: *The Economic Journal*, quoted from the reprint in Robinson (1965), pp. 100–2.

— (1965) *Collected Economic Papers*, volume 3 (Oxford: Basil Blackwell), quoted from the second edition, 1975.

— (1969) 'Economics Today', in: Robinson (1973b), chapter 13, pp. 122–8, Lecture delivered at the University of Basel 1969, quoted from the reprint.

— (1973a) 'An Open Letter from a Keynesian to a Marxist', in: Robinson (1973b), chapter 28, pp. 264–8, originally published as one of three essays in *On Re-reading Marx*, 1953, The Students' Bookshop, Cambridge. Also published in Robinson (1980).

— (1973b) *Collected Economic Papers*, volume 4 (Oxford: Basil Blackwell).

— (ed.) (1973c) *After Keynes* (Oxford: Basil Blackwell), Papers presented to Section F (Economics) at the 1972 Annual Meeting of the British Association for the Advancement of Science.

— (1973d) 'What has Become of the Keynesian Revolution?', in: Robinson (1973c), pp. 1–11, Papers presented to Section F (Economics) at the 1972 Annual Meeting of the British Association for the Advancement of Science.

— (1973e) 'Would You Believe It?', in: Robinson (1973b), chapter 26, pp. 249–53, originally published as one of three essays in *On Re-reading Marx*, 1953, The Students' Bookshop, Cambridge.

— (1975) 'The Unimportance of Reswitching', in: *The Quarterly Journal of Economics*, 89, pp. 32–5.

— (1978) 'Keynes and Ricardo', in: *Journal of Post-Keynesian Economics*, 1(1), quoted from the reprint in Robinson (1979b), ch. 19, pp. 210–16.

— (1979a) 'Garegnani on Effective Demand', in: *Cambridge Journal of Economics*, 3(2) (June), pp. 179–80, quoted from the reprint in Eatwell and Milgate (1983), pp. 70–1.

— (1979b) *Collected Economic Papers* (Oxford: Basil Blackwell).

— (1979c) 'Misunderstandings in the Theory of Production', in: *Greek Economic Review*, 1(1), quoted from the reprint, Robinson (1980), pp. 135–40.

— (1979d) 'Introduction–1978 [to *The Generalization of the General Theory and other Essays*]', in: Robinson (1979e), pp. ix-xxviii, republication of Robinson (1954a) under a new title.

— (1979e) *The Generalization of the General Theory and Other Essays* (London and Basingstoke: Macmillan), republication of Robinson (1954a) under a new title.

— (1980) *What are the Questions? and Other Essays* (Armonk, New York: M. E. Sharpe).

Rosdolsky, Roman (1969) *Zur Enstehungsgeschichte des Marxschen >Kapital<* (Frankfurt; Wien: Europäische Verlagsanstalt; Europa Verlag), quoted from the German original. English translation appeared under the title: *The Making of Marx's Capital*, translated by Pete Burgess (London: Pluto Press), 1971, distributed in the USA by Humanities Press.

Rotheim, Roy J. (1992) 'Interdependence and the Cambridge Economic Tradition', in: Gerrard and Hillard (1992), pp. 32–58.

— (ed.) (1998) *New Keynesian Economics/Post Keynesian Alternatives* (London and New York: Routledge).

Russel, Don (2001) 'Keynes' last battle', Book review of Skidelsky (2000), www.theage.com. au/books/2001/05/07/FFXG6M14FMC.html. *The Age*, 7 May 2001.

Rymes, Thomas K. (1989) *Keynes's Lectures, 1932–35: Notes of a Representative Student. A synthesis of lecture notes taken by students at Keynes's lectures in the 1930s leading up to the publication of The General Theory* (Houndmills, Basingstoke and London: Macmillan).

Samuels, Warren J. (ed.) (1986) *Research in the History of Economic Thought and Methodology: a Research Annual* (Greenwich, Connecticut and London: JAI Press).

Samuelson, Paul A. (1941) 'Professor Pigou's Employment and Equilibrium', in: *The American Economic Review*, 31(3), pp. 545–52.

— (1946) 'Lord Keynes and the *General Theory*', in: *Econometrica*, 14, pp. 187–200.

— (1966) 'A Summing Up', in: *The Quarterly Journal of Economics*, pp. 130–245.

— (1977) 'Discussion', in: Patinkin and Leith (1977), pp. 72–89, *passim*, Proceedings of a conference held at the University of Western Ontario, October 1975.

— (1978) 'The Canonical Classical Model of Political Economy', in: *Journal of Economic* 16, pp. 1415–34.

— (1979) 'Land and the Rate of Interest', in: *Theory for Economic Efficiency: Essays in Honor of Abba P. Lerner*, edited by Harry I. Greenfield, Albert M. Levenson, William Hamovitch and Eugene Rotwein, chapter 12, pp. 167–85 (Cambridge, Mass. and London: MIT Press).

Sardoni, Claudio (2002) 'On the Microeconomic Foundation of Macroeconomics: a Keynesian Perspective', in: Arestis *et al.* (2002), chapter 2, pp. 4–14.

Schotter, Andrew (1996) ' "You're Not Making Sense, You're Just Being Logical" ', in: *Foundations of Research in Economics: How Do Economists Do Economics?*, edited by Steven G. Medema and Warren J. Samuels, chapter 17, pp. 204–15 (Cheltenham, UK and Brookfields, US: Edward Elgar).

Schumpeter, Joseph A. (1954) *History of Economic Analysis* (London: George Allen & Unwin), quoted from the sixth printing 1967.

Shackle, G. L. S. (1938) *Expectations, Investment and Income* (Oxford: Oxford University Press), quoted from the second edition, 1968.

— (1958) *Time in Economics* (North Holland), repr. Greenwood 1983.

Shapiro, Robert J. (1988) 'Look Who's Making a Comeback', in: *U. S. News & World Report* (1 Feb. 1988), pp. 43–45.

Sheffrin, Steven M. (1983) *Rational Expectations*, Cambridge Surveys of Economic Literature (Cambridge: Cambridge University Press).

Shove, Gerald F. (1933) 'Review of *The Theory of Wages*. By J. R. Hicks [(1932)]', in: *Economic Journal*, 42, pp. 460–72.

Skidelsky, Robert (1983) *John Maynard Keynes vol. 1: Hopes Betrayed 1883–1920* (London: Macmillan).

— (1992) *John Maynard Keynes vol. II: the Economist as a Savior 1920–1937* (London and New York: Macmillan and Penguin Books), quoted from the paperback edition, Penguin Books, 1995.

— (2000) *John Maynard Keynes, vol. III: Fighting for Britain 1937–46* (London, Basingstoke and Oxford: Macmillan).

— (2001) 'In the Long Run is Keynes Dead or Alive?', Manuscript prepared for a conference at the Banco Central de Venezuela, Caracas, 10–12 September, 2001, about the relevance of economic thought. For the event, see the press notice at 200.44.39.14/info/n2001/050901.htm.

Skott, Peter and Dutt, Amitava Krishna (1996) 'Clower on Effective Demand', in: *Eastern Economic Journal*, 22, pp. 89–96.

Solow, Robert M. (1980) 'On Theories of Employment', in: *The American Economic Review*, 70, pp. 1–11.

— (1989) 'Testimony I: an Interview', in: Feiwel (1989b), pp. 537–53.

Sraffa, Piero (1960) *Production of Commodities by Means of Commodities. Prelude to a Critique of Economic Theory* (Cambridge: Cambridge University Press).

Streißler, Erich (1959) 'Die volkswirtschaftliche Produktionsfunktion in dynamischer Betrachtung', in: *Zeitschrift für Nationalökonomie*, 15, pp. 86–161 [The Production Function of a National Economy under Dynamical Perspective'].

Taylor, John B. (1989) 'The Evolution of Ideas in Macroeconomics', in: *The Economic Record*, 65(189), pp. 185–9.

Thirlwall, Anthony P. (1987) *Nicholas Kaldor*, Grand Masters in Economics (Brighton: Wheatsheaf).

Timlin, Mabel Frances (1942) *Keynesian Economics* (Toronto: University of Toronto Press).

Tobin, James (1977) 'How Dead Is Keynes?', in: *Economic Inquiry*, 15, pp. 459–68, reprint, Wood (1983), Section 3, No. 128.

— (1989) 'Testimony II: an Interview', in: Feiwel (1989b), pp. 554–68.

Townshend, Hugh (1937) 'Liquidity-Premium and the Theory of Value', in: *Economic Journal*, 47, pp. 157–69.

Trevithick, James Anthony (1992) *Involutary Unemployment. Macroeconomics from a Keynesian Perspective* (Hemel Hempstead: Harvester Wheatsheaf).

Viner, Jacob (1936) 'Mr. Keynes and the Causes of Unemployment', in: *Quarterly Journal of Economics*, 51 (November), pp. 147–67.

Walker, Donald Anthony (1986) 'Keynes as a Historian of Economic Thought: the Perspectives of the *General Theory*', in: Samuels (1986), pp. 1–36.

Weintraub, Sidney (1957) 'The Micro-Foundations of Aggregate Demand and Supply', in: *The Economic Journal*, 67, pp. 455–70.

— (1973) *Keynes and the Monetarists and other Essays* (New Brunswick: Rutgers University Press).

Wittgenstein, Ludwig (1995) *Ludwig Wittgenstein, Cambridge Letters: Correspondence with Russell, Keynes, Moore, Ramsey and Sraffa* (Oxford, UK and Cambridge, Mass: Blackwell), edited by Brian McGuiness and G. H. von Wright.

Wood, John Cunningham (ed.) (1983) *John Maynard Keynes – Critical Assessments*, The Routledge Critical Assessments of Leading Economists (London: Croom Helm, Routledge), quoted from the reprint, 1990.

Worswick, David and Trevithick, James (eds) (1983) *Keynes and the Modern World Proceedings of the Keynes Centenary Conference, King's College, Cambridge* (Cambridge: Cambridge University Press).

Young, Warren (1987) *Interpreting Mr. Keynes. The IS–LM Enigma* (Cambridge: Polity Press).

— (1989) *Harrod and his Trade Cycle Group: the Origins and Development of the Growth Research Programme* (Basingstoke: Macmillan).

General Index

Index of Quotations

Remark: Editors of collections etc who are quoted only indirectly appear with their reference in the bibliography.